T0350120

Brilliant Business Models in Healthcare

Jeroen Kemperman • Jeroen Geelhoed
Jennifer op 't Hoog

Editors

Brilliant Business Models in Healthcare

Get Inspired to Cure Healthcare

Editors
Jeroen Kemperman
Zilveren Kruis, Achmea
Amsterdam, The Netherlands

Jennifer op 't Hoog
Achmea
Tilburg, The Netherlands

Jeroen Geelhoed
&samhoud
Utrecht, The Netherlands

ISBN 978-3-319-26439-4   ISBN 978-3-319-26440-0   (eBook)
DOI 10.1007/978-3-319-26440-0

Library of Congress Control Number: 2016941331

Printed on acid-free paper

This Springer imprint is published by Springer Nature
The registered company is Springer International Publishing AG Switzerland

Foreword

One of the greatest challenges in our time is to make and keep qualitatively good healthcare affordable, transparent, and accessible to as many people as possible. This issue goes further than merely selecting the best possible healthcare system. It is a global puzzle independent of the manner in which countries have organized healthcare and the financing thereof. Healthcare costs are increasingly taking a bigger portion of domestic income via taxes, insurance policies, and direct payments. And still, the percentage of countries having qualitatively good care available for all citizens does not exceed 5 %. The solutions that are currently being found to solve the problems of one stakeholder are often implemented at the expense of another stakeholder. Lower healthcare costs only seem achievable either by making cuts in the healthcare treatments which are funded or by making healthcare available to fewer people. But this takes us only further away from the ambition of good healthcare for all. More healthcare for more people at lower costs demands pioneering organizations. That brings us to the question: Do cases of brilliant business models in healthcare exist in this world? Are there companies that have already shown solutions in the fields where breakthroughs are required? Businesses that we can learn from across the border and across time? The authors of this book investigated these questions in a quest to find brilliant business models in healthcare. Their straightforward answer is: Yes, they do exist! Organizations that provide fundamentally more healthcare for the same amount of funding that is of a superior quality and/or has a greater impact on health in general. Healthcare that can be delivered by the organizations themselves, but, for instance, also by giving customers and patients a role that is structurally different in managing healthcare and health in general for themselves and others.

The current huge challenges to provide good and affordable healthcare seem to offer fertile soil for the rise of disruptive new brilliant business models which actually show how this can be done. We need these sorts of examples and landmarks to improve healthcare and health in general — not by unquestioningly adopting other systems, but rather to get new insights and gain inspiration. By studying examples that generate the confidence and courage to let go of existing interests and the business models of yesterday, we can get inspiration for the solutions of tomorrow to really improve healthcare and health in general on a sustainable basis. It is this angle that is valuable to join the authors in this book and their quest to identify and understand unique healthcare organizations — ones that have used a different approach to generate a valuable impact for themselves and their surroundings. We hope that it provides inspiration to build and renew brilliant business models which help to make and keep qualitatively good healthcare affordable and accessible to as many people as possible. Enjoy the journey!

Roelof Konterman, Vice Chairman Achmea, amongst others responsible for the divisions Health and International.

Contents

Part I   The Framework for Brilliant Business Models in Healthcare

1   What Are the Cornerstones of a Brilliant Business Model? 3
  1.1   Vision 5
  1.2   Brand Positioning... 8

2   What is a Business Model?.. 11
  2.1   Market Segments.. 12
  2.2   Customer Value.. 15
  2.3   Delivery.. 18
  2.4   Operation.. 21

3   Value Creation and Overall Framework 25
  3.1   Value Creation for All Stakeholders 26
  3.2   Conceptual Framework and Phasing... 30
  3.3   Permanent Brilliance?... 31

4   Challenges for Brilliant Business Models in Healthcare 35
  4.1   Good, Affordable, and Widely Accessible Healthcare
         Is Unique.. 35
  4.2   Cost Increases Put Accessibility, Quality,
         and Healthcare Systems at Risk... 37
  4.3   Desired Breakthroughs in Healthcare 42

**Part II   Brilliant Cases Involving Brilliant Business
           Models in Healthcare**

5   Breakthrough: Strengthening Mutual Caring and Sharing 53
  5.1   Algemeen Ziekenfonds Amsterdam (A.Z.A.).............................. 60
         5.1.1   The Cornerstone: "The Little Man and the Doctor" 63
         5.1.2   The Business Model: Solidarity-Based Exclusivity............. 66

        5.1.3   The Result: "The Little Man, the Doctor
                and the City Taken Care of"..   71
        5.1.4   The Brilliant Lessons of A.Z.A...   73
    5.2   DHAN..   74
        5.2.1   The Cornerstone: Empowering the Poor
                to Help Themselves...   76
        5.2.2   The Business Model: Self-Management...............................   80
        5.2.3   The Result: The Value of Sustainable
                Poverty Reduction...   85
        5.2.4   The Brilliant Lessons of DHAN   88
    5.3   Courtyard Houses...   89
        5.3.1   The Cornerstone: Acts of Mercy..   91
        5.3.2   The Business Model: Self-Sufficient
                Within the Own Group..   95
        5.3.3   The Result: Altruism and Self-Financing Complement
                One Another... 101
        5.3.4   The Brilliant Lessons of Courtyard Houses......................... 104
    5.4   Stiftung Liebenau.. 106
        5.4.1   The Cornerstone: Value for Every Individual 107
        5.4.2   The Business Model: Lebensräume für Jung und Alt.......... 110
        5.4.3   The Result: A Positive Spiral.. 115
        5.4.4   The Brilliant Lessons of Stiftung Liebenau......................... 118

6   **Breakthrough: Letting Prevention and Self-Management Work**....... 119
    6.1   Discovery 128
        6.1.1   The Cornerstone: Permanently Healthier............................. 129
        6.1.2   The Business Model: Prevention as Well as Insurance........ 133
        6.1.3   The Result: Healthier Participants and Lower Costs 141
        6.1.4   The Brilliant Lessons of Discovery 142
    6.2   Healthways.. 144
        6.2.1   The Cornerstone: A Healthier World,
                One Person at a Time... 147
        6.2.2   The Business Model: A Longer and Healthier Life............. 150
        6.2.3   The Result: Equal Interests Among All Stakeholders 156
        6.2.4   The Brilliant Lessons of Healthways................................... 159
    6.3   Kaiser Permanente 160
        6.3.1   The Cornerstone: Prevention Is Better Than Cure.............. 161
        6.3.2   The Business Model: From Medical Care to Healthcare..... 164
        6.3.3   The Result: A Healthier Population with Lower Costs........ 170
        6.3.4   The brilliant lessons of Kaiser Permanente 173
    6.4   PatientsLikeMe 174
        6.4.1   The Cornerstone: "Live Better Together"............................. 175
        6.4.2   The Business Model: "To Get Paid for Making
                Patients Better" 179
        6.4.3   The Result: Far-Reaching Value Creation 184
        6.4.4   The Brilliant Lessons of PatientsLikeMe............................. 187

**7 Breakthrough: Patient-Centered Organization
of Information and Everyday Care**.. 189
7.1 UCLA's Value Quotient 195
7.1.1 The Cornerstone: "Measure and Motivate, Learn
and Live".. 197
7.1.2 The Business Model: "Redefine Value
for Responsible Care"... 200
7.1.3 The Result: "A Value Program with Essential
Outcomes"... 205
7.1.4 Brilliant Lessons to be Learned from UCLA's
VQ Program.. 208
7.2 ParkinsonNet... 209
7.2.1 The Cornerstone: Putting the Parkinson's Patient
in Control 211
7.2.2 The Business Model: Self-Management in a Network........ 214
7.2.3 The Result: Self-Management Key to Alleviate Pressure
on the Healthcare System... 219
7.2.4 Brilliant Lessons to Be Learned from ParkinsonNet.......... 222
7.3 Laastari Lähiklinikka 223
7.3.1 The Cornerstone: Real Entrepreneurs Spy a Market.......... 225
7.3.2 The Business Model: Predictable Healthcare
for a Low Fixed Price... 227
7.3.3 The Result: Benefits for Customers and for Society........... 233
7.3.4 Brilliant Lessons to be Learned from Laastari.................... 236
7.4 Patrick Lund Dental Happiness 237
7.4.1 The Cornerstone: Dental Happiness 238
7.4.2 The Business Model: From Stress to Happiness................. 242
7.4.3 The Result: A Radiant Smile for All Stakeholders.............. 247
7.4.4 Brilliant Lessons to be Learned from Patrick
Lund Dental Happiness.. 250

**8 Breakthrough: Deploying Services and Instruments
to Help Customers Take Control** 251
8.1 Ryhov.. 257
8.1.1 The Cornerstone: Always the Best for You 258
8.1.2 The Business Model: From Care Receiver to Cocreator 261
8.1.3 Result: Self-Care—A Value or Condition for Good Care ... 266
8.1.4 The Brilliant Lessons of Ryhov 269
8.2 BerylHealth... 270
8.2.1 The Cornerstone: Connecting People to Healthcare............ 271
8.2.2 The Business Model: Two Target Groups
with One Stone.. 273
8.2.3 Result: It Starts with Happy Employees 278
8.2.4 The Brilliant Lessons of BerylHealth 281

8.3   M-PESA 282
      8.3.1   The Cornerstone: Simple, Efficient,
              and Customer-Oriented 283
      8.3.2   The Business Model: Secure Banking
              and Living in Safety 287
      8.3.3   Result: "Relax, You've Got M-PESA" 293
      8.3.4   The Brilliant Lessons of M-PESA 296
8.4   The Jaipur Foot of Bhagwan Mahaveer Viklang
      Sahayata Samiti (BMVSS) 296
      8.4.1   The Cornerstone: A Prosthesis at Hand 298
      8.4.2   The Business Model: Participating in Society Again 301
      8.4.3   Result: Participation in Society 306
      8.4.4   The Brilliant Lessons of Jaipur Foot 307

9   **Breakthrough: Implementing Differentiation
    in Specialized Healthcare** 311
9.1   Narayana Hrudayalaya 320
      9.1.1   The Cornerstone: Why Bigger Is Better 321
      9.1.2   The Business Model: When Bigger Is
              Better—Economies of Scale in Healthcare 325
      9.1.3   Result: The NH Cardiac Hospital: A Beating Heart
              in Cardiac Care! 332
      9.1.4   The Brilliant Lessons of Narayana Hrudayalaya
              Cardiac Hospital 335
9.2   ThedaCare 337
      9.2.1   The Cornerstone: Patient Centered Continuous
              Improvement 338
      9.2.2   The Business Model: Lean, But for People 342
      9.2.3   Result: You Get What You Measure 348
      9.2.4   The Brilliant Lessons of ThedaCare 351
9.3   Princess Margaret Cancer Centre 352
      9.3.1   The Cornerstone: "We Will Conquer Cancer
              in Our Lifetime" 353
      9.3.2   The Business Model: Top Research in Practice 356
      9.3.3   Result: What Is the Impact of Dedication Towards
              Science and the Patient? 363
      9.3.4   The Brilliant Lessons of Princess Margaret
              Cancer Centre 366
9.4   Mayo Clinic 367
      9.4.1   The Cornerstone: "The Needs of the Patient
              Come First" 368
      9.4.2   The Business Model: "Care Should Be Available
              for Everyone" 372
      9.4.3   Result: How Does Putting the Patient First, Pay Off? 377
      9.4.4   The Brilliant Lessons of Mayo Clinic 380

**10 Lessons for Creating Brilliant Business Models
in Healthcare** 381

   10.1   Phase 1: Start from a Vision and Bring the Brand
           Positioning in Line with It 383

   10.2   Phase 2: Persevere Consistently in the Conversion
           of the Vision into the Business Model 387

   10.3   Phase 3: Use Pioneering Value Creation for All Stakeholders
           to Realize the Business Model 392

   10.4   Phase 4: Retain the Core and Stimulate Progress
           in the Business Model 395

About the Editors 401

About the Case Authors 403

Acknowledgment 407

Key Terms and Definitions 409

Sources 413

Index 425

Introduction

Why, What?

"Never go to a doctor whose office plants have died."

—Erma Bombeck

Over the years we conducted a quest to identify inspiring organizations in all kinds of sectors and learn from their brilliant business models.[1] That is a quest based on our fascination with organizations that truly make a difference in their spheres of influence. These are companies that do not wonder how to compete, but rather what to compete for[2]; businesses whose *raison d'être* is to change their own environment, sector, or even the world; companies that change the rules of the game and turn entire markets upside down; organizations that sincerely know how to rise above their own self-interest to create value for their customers and society. Paradoxically, it is because of this approach that they also become very successful for employees and shareholders. Simply put, companies like these make all parties concerned happy, which in turn results in value for the business.

We are looking for and have identified companies that are characterized by pioneering, self-reinforcing value creation for all stakeholders. The non-negotiable in the selection is that the value creation had to be measurable and demonstrable. We are looking specifically for businesses that have four distinct attributes: those that are profitable, enjoy very loyal customers, have very satisfied employees, and make a contribution to society. Businesses that create value in this way are what we define as brilliant. When our selection of companies that put up awfully good numbers expanded, we posed the question as to whether these businesses have even more in common. How do these companies succeed in achieving this position? Brilliant

---

[1] The results thereof are recorded in the book *Brilliant Business Models* by Kemperman et al. (2013).

[2] Spence and Rushing (2009).

business models turn out to be unique in three aspects, each of which was rolled out in phases over time:

1. *They are vision-driven*: They started from the conviction that things really have to be different. Brilliant business models are driven from the *inside out* by their ambition to change the world. It is not good enough for them to merely meet existing market needs from the *outside in*; they themselves want to be the source of new markets and needs. Subsequently, they have brought their brand positioning in line with their vision.
2. *They persevere in the business model*: They are conspicuous by their entrepreneurship and creativity. Businesses with brilliant business models are really focused on implementing their vision. The ambitions and brand promises are embedded structurally and extremely consistently in the business operations, the organization, and the cooperation with partners. In this way it has been possible for these ambitions and promises to be fulfilled in a sustainable, distinctive, and profitable manner.
3. *They are pioneers for and by stakeholders*: Based on these first two aspects, they changed the market, the lives of stakeholders, and the rules of the game in the business sector. Brilliant business models make the impossible possible by breaking through conventions and creating surprising paradoxes. This is visible not only in what the businesses do for their stakeholders but also in what the stakeholders do in turn for the businesses.

In brief, a brilliant business model ensues from the company's vision and positioning. Subsequently, that must be consistently converted, embedded, and adhered to in the business model (not always an easy task). Then that has to result in success for and by stakeholders. That is why these are prepared in turn to give back more and to invest time, energy, money, or material in your company. This consequently results in a self-reinforcing and self-financing spiral. The organization can broaden its impact for customers and society and further itself at the same time. This is exceptional and valuable. In this way it is possible for an organization to become a platform where customers, employees, and shareholders work together in such a way that society also benefits from this. The advantage this provides is that the world becomes better in a way that organizes and finances itself. It need not be organized by the government and financed with taxpayers' money. The right type of company can make a contribution to mutually resolve substantial societal issues.

And Now Healthcare

We took the quest for brilliant business models a level deeper, this time within healthcare! And then we did so from an inverted perspective. We had observed that there are organizations that create breakthroughs to make the world a better place, while increasing value for all stakeholders simultaneously. We wondered what areas were truly in need for these sorts of organizations. So we did not look at random brilliant businesses and then investigate how they strive to change the world. On the contrary, we took the change in the world we want to see as starting point and asked ourselves which brilliant business models could help us in achieving this. Within health, this involves the huge challenge to make and keep qualitatively good healthcare affordable and accessible to as many people as possible. Additionally it is demanded that this is done while simultaneously creating value for different stakeholders. In healthcare, this concerns the widely shared ambition to realize the triple aim: How do we improve the patient experience of care and the health of populations while reducing the per capita cost of healthcare?[3] So we concluded that healthcare was definitely in need for the sort of brilliant business models we had seen in different sectors.

As our quest now originated in the ambition to improve healthcare and health in general, we first formulated which breakthroughs that requires. In the process, we focused on the necessary breakthroughs in healthcare in the West and in the world in general. We certainly included inspiring examples from developing countries, but looked not so much at the specific, non-medical breakthroughs required in these countries where it concerns, for instance, clean water, sewerage systems, and nutrition. Based on the international changes required, we looked for businesses and organizations that are accomplishing this. After all, they provide inspiring examples for actually implementing the desired breakthroughs.

In the past few years, we have had the privilege of often working together with individuals who share the ambition to improve healthcare and health in general. Like us, they are fascinated by organizations that make a contribution in a brilliant way, people who are generally employed in roles relating to the provision of healthcare, as professional in a management position or in an advisory capacity. We wondered which breakthroughs are necessary in healthcare and which organizations are accomplishing this and consequently provide an inspiring example. As such, it made sense to pose the following two questions to all of them:

- Which breakthroughs are necessary to improve healthcare and health in general?
- On the global level, what are the most inspiring organizations that accomplish these breakthroughs and therefore could serve as examples of best practice?

We posed these two questions hundreds of times. Sometimes they were an item on the agenda. More often than not, we posed them at the start or end of a discussion or rather casually during lunch or on a coffee break. That resulted in growing piles of literature, reports, and presentations on improving healthcare and health in general. In addition, the number of pieces of scrap paper, business cards, and texts with the names of potential brilliant business models grew steadily. We were also able to tempt a number of our discussion partners to not only think along with us but also put their thoughts down on paper. We challenged them to delve into an organization that inspires them, an organization that they think is truly brilliant and then to submit a case description thereof.

---

[3] Berwick et al. (2008) and Institute for healthcare improvement (2012).

The selected organizations have been described based on a fixed conceptual framework developed to describe and create brilliant business models. Online and offline co-creation was employed. Joint writers' and editors' evenings were organized, and we continued our collaborative effort on www.wikibusinessmodels.com. Ultimately, of more than 300 possible case organizations on the long list, 20 were selected for inclusion in this publication. This book and the online community are our way of bundling and sharing all the experiences in a structured manner. It is our hope that it helps readers make their own contribution to improving healthcare and health in general.

The editorial team:

Jeroen Kemperman
Jeroen Geelhoed
Jennifer op't Hoog

P.S.: Just as co-creation and inspiration never cease, so we also desire to continuously improve. We will continue compiling new cases and therefore want to invite and challenge you to share the case of your own favorite brilliant business model.

Guide for Your Reading Enjoyment

We hope that you will find reading this book as enjoyable and fascinating as we — the editors and the case authors — did researching and writing it. We recommend that readers focus their energies in particular on reading what is currently the most interesting topic to them and will consequently excite or energize them the most.[1] That is what they are the most open to and it requires the least effort. In other words, that always yields the best return on investment. In order to make that possible, we have shaped this book in such a way that it can be read sequentially and as a collage. It consists of the following parts:

- *Part I: The framework for brilliant business models in healthcare.* The discussion revolves in Part I, Chaps. 1–3, around the conceptual business framework used to analyze and describe brilliant business models. This model is used in healthcare and beyond. This ties in with broad business terms, such as customers, markets, and positioning. In compliance with the aspects of brilliant business models, we first dwell on the vision and brand positioning that form the foundation for the business model. It is on this basis that a closer look is taken at the market segments, customer value, delivery, and operation that form the building blocks of the business model itself. Then the focus turns to the value that the business model provides for customers, shareholders, employees, and society — and what is received in return. This is an important consideration, for a business model only qualifies as brilliant if it actually results in value creation. Chapter 4 subsequently ponders developments in healthcare. We conclude here that independent of the healthcare system, the same fundamental challenges are visible throughout the world. Our attention then turns to five breakthroughs that are prerequisites to keeping healthcare qualitatively good, broadly accessible, and affordable.
- *Part II: Cases of brilliant business models in healthcare.* Attention is paid in Part II, Chaps. 5–9, to the required breakthroughs and the corresponding brilliant business models. This is the focal point and highlight of this book. We repeatedly

---

[1] This is inspired by the Montessori method of education (1967).

dwell on one of the five necessary breakthroughs and the kind of organizations that demand them. Then, for each breakthrough, four cases are developed of organizations that accomplish this in an inspiring manner somewhere in the world either now or at some point in the past. These descriptions have been drawn up based on the framework for brilliant business models discussed in Part I. In other words, for each case, the vision and brand positioning, the consistent adherence to the business model, and the resultant value creation for stakeholders are explained. Chapter 10 concludes this section by pondering the lessons drawn from the 20 cases. Reflections and insights are given for building brilliant business models that have a positive impact on healthcare and health in general. We logically proceed with a step-by-step expansion of vision, from business model to value creation.

Readers may decide to start, stop, and skip subject matter at their discretion. To start with, Chaps. 1–3 can be skipped if you want to go directly to practical experiences. The cases can also be scanned by studying the infographics in them; you can always decide later whether to read the entire text or not.

For instance, if you are most curious about a certain case in Part II, you might start by scanning that section first. We then hope that you will look at the next case, focusing, for instance, on the same breakthrough (the same chapter), and then continue reading from there. If at some point you find that the need arises to take a step back and get more in-depth information, then you will need to leaf backward. If you need to gain insight into the conceptual model used in our research, go to Chaps. 1–3, or look below in the abridged reproduction as boxed text. For more insight into the challenges facing healthcare, turn to Chap. 4; for more in-depth information, go to the first section of the five chapters from Part II featuring four cases.

For those who want to proceed as quickly as possible with building a brilliant business model, we recommend selecting one inspiring case from the book that is close to your own practical situation. You can then share it with colleagues to discuss what can be learnt from it for your own organization and/or go ahead online to create your own brilliant business model.

We hope you enjoy reading this book.

Conceptual Framework for Brilliant Business Models

The conceptual framework used to analyze and describe brilliant business models is described in Part I. In short, a historic, existing, accentuated, and new brilliant business model can be described and built with the following figure:

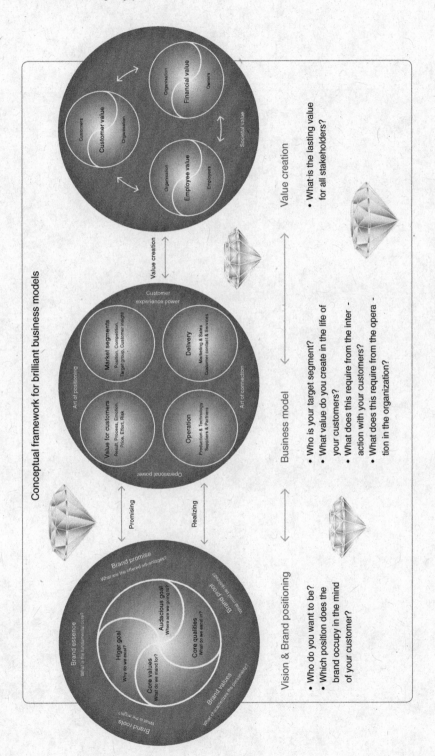

Conceptual framework for brilliant business models

Value creation
- What is the lasting value for all stakeholders?

Business model
- Who is your target segment?
- What value do you create in the life of your customers?
- What does this require from the interaction with your customers?
- What does this require from the operation in the organization?

Vision & Brand positioning
- Who do you want to be?
- Which position does the brand occupy in the mind of your customer?

Part I
The Framework for Brilliant Business Models in Healthcare

Chapter 1
What Are the Cornerstones of a Brilliant Business Model?

- *The truly brilliant business models do not arise accidently but are almost always based on a deep ambition to make a difference and to capture a unique new spot in the world. They are driven by the "why." The cornerstones of a brilliant business model are the vision and the brand positioning. A vision sets an organization in motion. It explains where the organization comes from, what the organization is and what it wants to be. In other words, an organization's vision is the most essential component underneath its business model. Everything the organization undertakes must be verifiably consistent with this touchstone. The vision of an organization can be defined by its higher goal, its audacious goal, its core values, and its core qualities.*
- *Brand positioning. The brand positioning is the position the organization wants to occupy in the minds of existing or potential customers. The positioning of a brand can be defined by its brand essence, its brand roots, its brand promise, its brand values, and its brand proof.*

The conceptual framework used in this book was developed in the field based on a number of proven and oft-used business models and insights. It has been honed in our own work at the Dutch insurer Achmea and at the consultancy firm &samhoud.[1] It is a general business framework that can be applied in different sectors. It is frequently used in for-profit and nonprofit organizations. It has also been used to describe (1) an organization's specific brand or proposition or (2) the joint activities in a network or chain of organizations. It has even been used as an aid by individuals who wanted to describe themselves relative to the rest of the world.

For a number of specific parts, other terminology is used in various sectors (which incidentally reveals a lot about the perspective of the various organizations). In this work, the choice has been made to adopt the most used umbrella term in management literature. Take, for instance, the target group or users for which/whom the organization exists. They are often described in terms of what someone does in

---

[1] Kemperman et al. (2013).

J. Kemperman et al. (eds.), *Brilliant Business Models in Healthcare*,
DOI 10.1007/978-3-319-26440-0_1

relation to the relevant provider. In that case, we usually talk about nouns derived from verbs. Examples of this include viewers, readers, guests, shoppers, or callers. Within healthcare, it concerns, for instance, patients (for healthcare practitioners), the insured (for healthcare insurers) or voters (for politicians). Keeping in line with management literature, we will use the umbrella term "customers" in this context.

The framework for brilliant business models arose as a direct result of the conclusions drawn from the analysis of a large number of organizations achieving exceptional results. These businesses realized rather good profit margins, extremely satisfied customers, very engaged employees and a better society. All these aspects made them in our eyes brilliant. We discovered that these exceptional companies have more in common that rises above the business model alone. Specifically, every one of the businesses in question is vision-driven. In addition, their brand positioning is completely in line with their vision. Further, the vision is converted into the "capillary system" of the business model. Everything ties together in the cases that we researched. In short, a brilliant business model that creates value for all stakeholders is not brilliant merely due to the business model used. This confirmed our sense that many existing business models are focused too much on one of several considerations—vision, brand positioning, business models, or value creation—instead of taking a broader look at how strongly they actually cohere with and should reinforce each other to build a truly brilliant business.

The ambition in developing the framework for brilliant business models was to integrate vision, brand positioning, the actual business model, and value creation into a conceptual model in order to develop and understand them coherently.[2] Throughout this process, the main message was that the brilliance of a business model is substantiated by balanced value creation for all parties concerned. Becoming successful always requires a good balance between both "inside out" and "outside in"—between making promises and fulfilling them.

The integration and application in one conceptual framework is innovative. The cornerstones and building blocks from this model originate in existing and proved concepts, as well as in the theory and practice of others and ourselves. This relates to theories, models, and insights regarding vision, strategy, segmentation, value chains, value creation, chain management, organizational change, marketing, positioning, and brand management. Similarities to known concepts are, in short, no accident, but rather the result of diligent study and conscious learning and copying by the authors. Thankful use has been made of existing brainwork and the prestige of giants such as Collins, Heskett, Zeithaml, and Aaker. And it makes this approach easier to work with in practice, for many companies have already gained experience with it.

If an organization or brand wants to create sustainable value, a thorough foundation is vital. In that case it concerns the vision of the organization on the one hand and the brand positioning on the other. To put it differently, the answer to the question "Who do you want to be?" (vision) must be fully coherent with the answer to the question "What position does the brand have to occupy in the minds of customers?"

---

[2] Previous books which laid the basis for the conceptual framework of brilliant business models are, in particular, Kemperman and Trampe (2012) and Geelhoed et al. (2014).

(brand positioning). It is evident that organizations with brilliant business models generally have an inspiring and authentic vision and brand positioning that is inextricably linked with their business model. It is for that reason that this chapter will first discuss vision and then brand positioning.

1.1 Vision[3]

"The beginning is the most important part of the work.".

—Plato, *as cited by Richard Branson*

A vision sets an organization in motion. It explains where the organization comes from, what the organization is and what it wants to be. In other words, an organization's vision is the essential component. Everything the organization undertakes must be verifiably consistent with this touchstone.

The vision of an organization can be defined by answering the following four questions[4]:

- *Higher goal*: Why do we exist?
- *Audacious goal*: Where are we going?
- *Core values*: What do we stand for?
- *Core qualities*: What do we excel at?

It sounds logical to assume that a brilliant business model begins with researching the market by means of customer interviews, competition analyses, and market research. Based on the identified hole in the market, a suitable offer is made. After all, it is eventually about the needs of the customer, one might think. In other words: find out what the needs of the customer are and anticipate that.

Well, that is *not* the way things work at the start with brilliant business models! On the contrary, Brilliant business models almost always seem to start from the organization's own vision of what they want to offer and change in their environment (inside out). This is nevertheless often a dream defined by looking from the outside world at the organization's future activities or desired change. The first motive is usually an insight that makes it possible to fundamentally serve customers better, that shakes up the market or that is considered beautiful and nice to create by the founders. It is only afterwards that tests are conducted (or simply attempted) as to whether customers are waiting for something like that to happen. And if it is in fact pioneering, it often concerns latent needs. No IKEA customer would have gone to the store mentioning that they want a set of shelves and a set of instructions in a box when what they really wanted was a bookcase. Whereas a business model ultimately only works if it is in line with what the organization is and what customers

---

[3] Aside from Kemperman et al. (2013), reference can be made to Collins and Porras (1994), Van der Loo et al. (2007), and Geelhoed et al. (2014).

[4] Van der Loo et al. (2007).

want, the vision has been deliberately chosen as the starting point in this theoretical foundation (and later also in the case descriptions in this book).

The ways in which organizations define their vision can vary. This also includes differences in the terminology used. For instance, elements of the visions can also be found in texts concerning mission, values, identity and strategy. This book describes an organization's vision based on its higher goal, its audacious goal, its core values, and its core qualities.[5]

The founder's vision often forms the starting point of a brilliant business model. From that moment on, however, the vision is not set in stone. Especially when success is achieved, there is an extra challenge to renew the vision with all parties concerned. The vision serves as the basic philosophy (the root) for the picture of the future (the wing) of an organization.[6] Jim Collins and Jerry Porras reveal in their research into successful visionary companies that these organizations are able to continuously find a good balance between retaining their core (ideology) and stimulating progress (ambition).[7] The higher goal and the core values are primarily associated with the roots and the identity that the organization wants to maintain. The audacious goal and the core qualities are more dynamic in nature and give substance to stimulating progress based on a common ambition for the future.

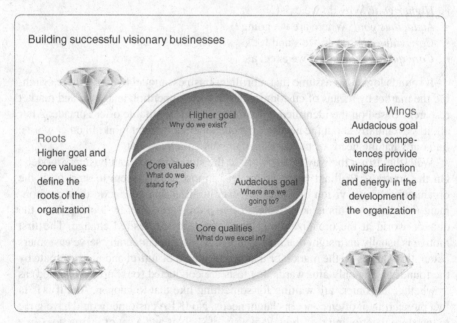

Building on your core guarantees a link to the identity and strength that traditionally form the core of the organization. In this way both knowledge and expertise,

---

[5] Idem.
[6] Vision described as such by Franzen and Van den Berg (2003).
[7] Collins and Porras (1994).

which are embedded—consciously or not—in your people and processes are utilized. A good link to the activities where the organization has always proved itself serves as a recognizable focal point, making it possible for customers and other parties concerned to understand why it is (and feels) logical that you, as an organization, are operating in the relevant market and are able to make a meaningful, distinctive, and attractive offer.[8] Whereas products or technologies can often be copied, an organization's unique approach generally cannot—and certainly not when it concerns the work of man, such as those of healthcare providers, where this aspect is deeply embedded in the organization's own employees.

The formulation of a vision for an existing organization is not an "invention" but rather a discovery or rediscovery. It is an incremental or fundamental definition or redefinition of what is already in the organization in terms of roots and potential. The discovery or rediscovery of an organization's vision is sometimes compared to the manner in which the Italian Renaissance artist Michelangelo (1475–1564) made his sculptures.[9] Michelangelo shared the conviction of Socrates that every block of stone has a statue inside it and that it is the task of the sculptor to discover it. By hewing away the rough walls, he can reveal the figure "imprisoned" in stone. Likewise, the vision is encased in the organization. It has to be taken out by removing the unusable and obscuring parts. In order to make maximum use of a vision, it is necessary for this vision not only to be visible and clear, but also that it is shared. Only then can it serve as both a fundamental, common basic principle and a guiding touchstone for everyone in the organization.

A clear and shared vision provides a common starting point and goal. An organization's vision can be defined (or jointly specified in the development of a vision) by answering the following questions[10]:

- *Higher goal: Why does the organization exist?* This reflects what the organization's *raison d'être* and essence are and what it wants its core to be. The higher goal indicates in a clear, inspiring, and concise way what an organization's ideals are and what unique contribution it provides to all stakeholders. It gives a sense of purpose. In doing so, the higher goal provides a fixed focal point and a guideline for each action. For instance, the higher goal of The Walt Disney Company is: "to always deliver, with integrity, the most exceptional entertainment experience for people of all ages."
- *Audacious goal: Where is the organization going?* This is a challenging picture of the future that nonetheless can be achieved through maximum effort. It relates to the dream(s) that an organization wants to achieve. The primary function of an audacious goal is to provide energy and an upward spiral for all involved stakeholders. The end result must be defined as specifically as possible, including the deadline by which it has to be accomplished. The archetypal example of an audacious goal is the ambition formulated in 1962 by President John F. Kennedy to committing the USA to achieve the goal "of landing a man on the moon and returning him safely to earth, before the decade is out."

---

[8] Taylor (2007).

[9] Kemperman and Trampe (2012).

[10] Van der Loo et al. (2007).

- *Core values: What does the organization stand for?* These are deep-seated convictions that reveal what an organization's members think is correct and vital. They are moral objectives that individuals strive to pursue and value, and that motivate them. Values also have emotional overtones: they reveal what individuals really like to do. The core values of IKEA, for instance, can be defined as simplicity, cost-consciousness, and common sense.[11]
- *Core qualities: What does the organization excel at?* Core qualities reflect what areas an organization is extremely good in, where it excels. These are the deep-down characteristics, gifts or strengths typical of an organization that result in superior performance.[12] The core qualities of Aravind Eye Hospital in India are, for instance: top-quality eye care, connection, and improvement.[13]

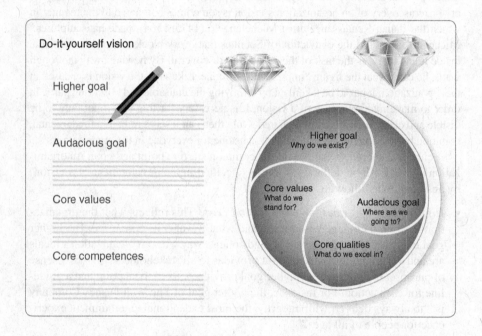

1.2 Brand Positioning[14]

The positioning or brand positioning is the position that the organization wants to have in the head of existing and potential customers in relation to other brands on the market. This choice provides the answer to the question: "Who do you want to

---

[11] Kemperman et al. (2013).

[12] Hamel and Prahalad (1994).

[13] Kemperman et al. (2013).

[14] For brand positioning, reference is also made to Ries and Trout (1981) and Aaker (1996).

be on the market for which customers?" As a result thereof, two questions are spanned: "Who do you want to be?" and "Which customers do you want to serve?" Like the organization's identity, good positioning is not an invention but rather a discovery. The formulation thereof is therefore a voyage of discovery based on the question as to how and in what aspects the organization can be (more) exclusive or special for the existing or potential customers on the market. If such a voyage ends with positioning that feels completely new, then something went wrong along the line and became artificial, whereas it should really be genuine. Not surprisingly, the same holds true for the repositioning of an existing business or brand. But even the positioning of a completely new organization must somewhere logically tie in with the latent needs and gaps at the parties concerned and in the world. Consequently, really good positioning also feels in this case more like a discovery of something that should have been there all along.

The image that you want to project to the outside world through the positioning or brand positioning must be in line and even connected with what you really are and want to be in the vision. The positioning of a brand is the position the organization wants the brand to occupy in the hearts and minds of existing or potential customers. The positioning of a brand can be defined by the following five questions:

- *Brand essence*: What is the fundamental core and heart of the brand?
- *Brand roots:* What are the brand's origins and credibility?
- *Brand promise:* What are the benefits to be offered by the brand?
- *Brand values:* What are the brand's underlying values and personality?
- *Brand proof:* What must be accomplished in a compelling and distinctive way?

In order to be embraced by customers, shareholders, and society, a brand must first be embedded in the heart of its employees. Those brands for which this condition is valid are the most powerful and sustainable. Employees go public and their brand perception must therefore be authentic and consistent. That is the difference between *having* a brand and *being* a brand.[15] In order to realize that, a brand must have been directly linked to the vision. Therefore, the elements from the four components of the vision provide input and inspiration for the positioning of the brand.

This can be defined by the following five elements[16]:

- *Brand essence in core and heart.* What essentially distinguishes us from other brands and is that distinction relevant to customers? What is the essence in a limited number of key words? As a result, what is the heart and soul of the positioning?
- *Brand roots in origin and credibility.* Where do we come from? What is our story and why do we exist? Which roots and historical bonds exist with the market? How do these origins give the organization a basis for credibly fulfilling a role on the market? What is the connection with the higher goal for which the organization stood and stands? How is this embedded in consistent and clear visual char-

---

[15] Winter and Van der Weijden (2008).

[16] Kemperman and Trampe (2012).

acteristics (color, logo) by which the organization's distinguishability is guaranteed for the long term?

- *Brand promise in benefits.* What is the promise to the customer that is part of the audacious goal and how is that formulated forcefully and succinctly. What does the organization stand for and what does it mean specifically from the customer's viewpoint? What difference does the organization promise to make in the customer's life or business operations?

- *Brand values in values and personality.* What does the brand stand for and if the brand were a person, what type of person would it be? What is the personification of the core values? Where was it born? Which friends does it have? What type of clothes does it wear? Or more fundamentally: what is it like to be this person? Are there other archetypes, such as an animal, a political party, or a car that help define this personality?

- *Brand proof in compelling and distinctive qualities.* How is the customer going to experience that the organization does not make any empty promises, but rather actually make a difference? What is the evidence that the organization is delivering or can deliver on the promised benefits based on its core qualities? What are the unique resources (such as distribution channels, technology, or buying advantage) on the basis of which it can fulfill promises to the customer daily?

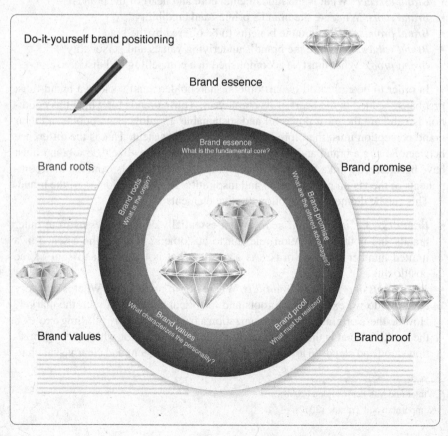

Chapter 2
What is a Business Model?

It is one thing to have a terrific, but something else for it to be effected in a manner that creates value. A business model helps to systematically define the manner in which the organization creates value and for whom. It consists of four components which each answer a number of fundamental questions:

- *Market segments: For which customers does the brand want to exist? Which market segment do we want to serve or are we serving? On the basis of relevant segmentation methods, market focus is applied to position, competition, target group, and customer insight.*
- *Customer value: Which value are we providing in the lives of customers? This is the value that current or future customers expect and experience with your product or services, expressed in terms of results and benefits divided by costs and efforts.*
- *Delivery: What does this require in the organization's interaction with customers? Via which channels will value for the customer be delivered? This describes the requirements of the organization to secure, serve, and retain customers.*
- *Operation: How are we going to realize value for our customers? This describes the requirements which the operation (which often takes place behind the scenes for the customer) must meet to actually deliver to the customer and to raise the results above the costs.*

Of course these elements do not work independently. The actual value is created by the entire model, the synergies between the elements and the alignment with the vision.

© Springer International Publishing Switzerland 2017
J. Kemperman et al. (eds.), *Brilliant Business Models in Healthcare*,
DOI 10.1007/978-3-319-26440-0_2

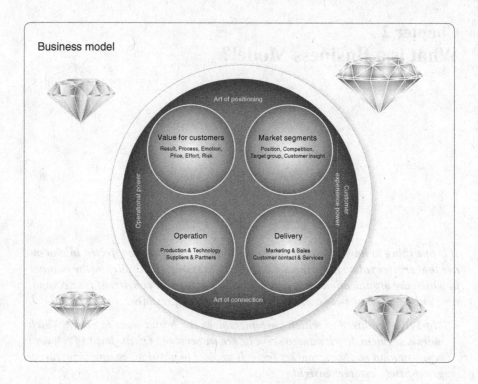

2.1   Market Segments[1]

The vision lays down who the organization is and wants to be. It can use one or more brands to serve the market. The definition of market segments identifies the market in which the organization realizes its vision and for which customers. The process starts by determining ways of segmenting the market relevant to the brand(s). Once the organization is clear about the way(s) in which the market is segmented and on which segments the organization wants to focus, these market segments can be assessed and defined by the following four questions:

- *Position*: What is the current position of the organization in these market segments?
- *Competition*: What is the competitive environment?
- *Target group*: What is the target group in terms of volumes, accessibility, and profitability?
- *Customer insight*: What is the unique customer insight by which the segments want to be served?

A vision is incredibly important. It sets the organization in motion and reflects who the organization is and what it wants to be. A beautiful dream, however, is by

---

[1] For segmenting, reference is also made to Kemperman and Trampe (2012).

far not yet a brilliant business model, as that is formed by a business together with its customers. This has to be embedded in the business operations and environment. In order to gain insight into the business model as a whole, it must be clear who the customers are, what they are being offered, and how that is organized. In sum, this must produce such a result in value creation for all parties concerned that they are (and continue to be) prepared to invest their energy and funds in the organization.

The initial question in a business model is: who is the customer? Management literature implicitly and automatically assumes that this relates to one type of customer that chooses, buys, uses, pays for, and replaces the product. That simple starting point, however, is often not borne out in practice. Many businesses operate in a chain: they deliver a component or subcomponent of a product that is then sold on by their direct customer or that customer's customer to the end customer. If they modify their component in such a way that the entire product gains in value for the end customer, this adds value to the middleman too.[2] Often, however, it is even less one-dimensional. The decision-maker, the buyer and the user are often not the same party; and then there are the different segments within each of these groups.[3] LinkedIn has consumers that partially pay for services. They earn the most by furnishing recruiters with data on these users. A professional sports club generates higher revenues if it has a larger public and more fans. It does so in part through ticket sales and merchandising, but especially via sponsorship and the media, for instance via advertisers during broadcasts of their matches. Zappos earns good money by making customers happy, but also generates good extra income by teaching other companies how they can do the same. Within healthcare there are often several "customers" as well. Whereas the focus is ultimately on the patient, the overall picture is less one-dimensional. Take, for instance, the situation in which medicine prescribed by a specialist and paid for by the insurer is first delivered to the patient via the hospital by the hospital pharmacy and then by its own in-house pharmacy. In this case, the patient can be defined as the primary customer for whom, if things are right, the other parties are all working together. If other players are very important in the business model, they can also be included as a separate customer group, partner, or service provider.

A customer group can be classified in different segments. In the process, the focus is on which way(s) of segmenting is/are relevant to the organization. It is then relevant to analyze which position the organization already occupies in these segments, against whom it is competing and how big the segments are in terms of numbers and financially. The most fundamental question then is which insight the brand offers into the needs of customers. Aside from analysis and testing, this requires creativity and fundamentally putting yourself in the customer's shoes.

More traditionally specific and factual criteria, such as geography and income, are often easier to measure and objectify. Logically, when it comes to patients in the healthcare sector, it is first and foremost about the health of individuals. A distinction is made between people who are healthy, individuals with an increased risk, those with an acute condition and patients with a chronic disorder. Further, physical

---

[2] Kemperman et al. (2000).

[3] Kemperman et al. (2013).

condition, age and educational level are important in connection with additional risks and disorders. And the situation at home must also be taken into consideration. Non-mobile individuals living on their own are more inclined to become lonely. Male pensioners whose wives have recently died run a strong risk of dying due to the fact that they do not care well for themselves (what is not the case for female pensioners).[4] Aside from this kind of traditional and easily measurable segmentation criteria, there are also more abstract segmentation criteria (such as norms and values). In this way, for instance, the extent to which someone feels like he/she is responsible for his/her own body and health and is actively doing something about that, can be looked at. The same goes for the extent to which someone complies with the recommendations of a healthcare practitioner—or not at all. Another example is the social-political perspective as regards the right to healthcare and a customer's own deductible, the religious-moral perspective regarding existential issues, and the willingness and possibility of travelling to obtain healthcare. The customer groups that the organization serves and the various segments within the customer groups can be defined based on the following questions:

- *Position*: What is the organization's current position in these market segments? This relates to the "photo" of the current customer base in numbers, turnover, and margin. It also concerns the "film" that preceded this photo. Today's customers often became customers yesterday or the day before. It is wise to realize, therefore, where the organization's customers come from, how they became customers, how long they have been a customer already, and how the customer base has developed.
- *Competition*: What is the competitive environment? This concerns the general competition on the market, but in particular also the organizations that focus on the same market segments, and their existing and historical positions in relation to these customers. In that regard, the competition can be much broader than merely the suppliers of the same product. When people feel uncertain about the economy and their future, the bank account and mortgage repayments suddenly become important competitors with a luxurious holiday or a new car.
- *Target group*: What is the target group in terms of volumes, accessibility, and profitability? This concerns the customer groups, the market segments within those groups and their characteristics. It is about numbers, as well as the extent to which (1) their communication channels are open and (2) they require a supplier, and (3) the financial margin in these market segments.
- *Customer insight*: What is the unique customer insight used to serve the segments? This relates to the most essential and fundamental needs in the market segment for which the organization is currently providing or wants to provide. It is not just about the clearly formulated desires of customers that had been clear to customers and competitors alike from the beginning. It is in particular also about the latent or underlying needs for which the organization stands head and shoulders above the competition in providing and being able to provide. In that respect, the challenge is to get to the core issue, whereby the ultimate customer

---

[4] With thanks to Jan Willem Kuenen, who pointed out this phenomenon to the authors.

insight can be rather simple. For instance: if people have lunch at 12.00 am and dinner at 7.00 pm, they will be hungry during the commute home. That is therefore an ideal time to sell a nutritious and convenient bite to eat at the railway or petrol station.

Almost equally important as the choice concerning who your customer is, is the choice concerning who your customer is *not*. A brilliant business model demands clear choices. It is almost impossible to be everything to everyone. Part II of this book highlights different examples in this regard. One of them is Patrick Lund Dental Happiness, which chooses customers for whom their teeth are really important. Another example is Healthways, which selects groups of customers whom they expect to be able to make demonstrably healthier at affordable prices. A clearer choice of target group makes it much easier to truly deliver value to customers. And it is precisely the discussion of this point that the following element of the business model turns to.

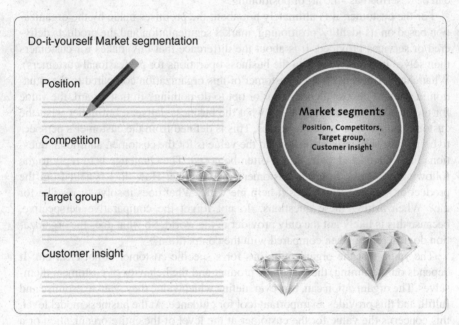

2.2 Customer Value[5]

Once it is known how the brand(s) will be positioned for which market segment, it is possible to specify the value the organization wants to deliver with the brand(s) from the customer's perspective. What do customers get? What do they have to give

---

[5] For value for the customer, reference is also made to Heskett et al. (2003) and Kemperman et al. (2000).

up in return? And what changes in their lives as a result of this exchange? The value from the customer's perspective can be defined by the following six questions:

- *Result*: What do I get?
- *Process*: How do I get it?
- *Emotion*: How will it make me feel?
- *Price*: How much will it cost?
- *Effort*: What do I have to do to get it?
- *Risk*: How much risk is involved?

The value *of* a customer is important to the organization, but the relationship starts with the question as to what the value is *for* the customer. Without customers, you have no work to do and you will not get paid. If the value for the customer cannot be clearly formulated, the organization is not in business. The connection between the selected market segments and the value delivered to these customers can be described as "the art of positioning."

For the customer, it is ultimately not about the promises made by the organization based on its identity, positioning, market segmentation and the products delivered or services provided. It is about the difference that this makes for customers themselves in their lives (or in the business operations for professional customers). What changes because I am a customer of this organization compared to the situation in which I choose a competitor or opt to do nothing? In that regard, the value for the customer does not relate to what the business delivers, but rather what the customer anticipates and experiences. This is defined from the customer's perspective. In order to clearly identify what the value is for the customer, additional questions like "what" and "why" must often be posed. The challenge is to reply to the following questions from the customer's perspective: How do I benefit from the product or service? What does it help me with? What does it solve or resolve for me? When asking these questions, do not forget the comparative perspective, because this is likely not the only provider in the world. So what does the organization do differently when compared with the competition?

The value that the organization has for a specific customer is not clear-cut. It depends on the timing, the place, the product and the behavior of customers themselves. The organization can, however, define which value they want to promise and fulfill, and this provides an important tool for guidance. At the business model level, this concerns the value for the customer at the level of the entire organization or a brand thereof. This can then be specified for different market segments, products, and services or specific customers. In that regard, the entire term of the customer relationship or series of transactions must often be reviewed. Even before a product or service is purchased, customers have to make an effort to orient themselves, to reduce uncertainty as a result thereof and to obtain a better picture of what they will receive or must give later on.

The value that the customer attributes to an organization's products and services comes about through a mix of different elements.[6] These are the elements that the

---

[6] Kemperman and Van Engelen (1999), Kemperman et al. (2000), Heskett et al. (2008), Kemperman and Trampe (2012), and Geelhoed et al. (2014).

customer expects to receive upon purchase and then experiences afterwards. They are listed below with a couple of short sample questions that customers might have if they purchase a mobile phone and a subscription.

For elements that cause the value to appreciate, the value for customers increases if they receive more of these elements (and decreases if fewer are received):

- *Result*: What type of product or service do I receive? Do the new telephone, apps, and provider perform well? Do I always have a good signal and a quick connection? Does this telephone have all the functionalities that I want? Does it have enough memory for what I want?
- *Process*: How do I get it? Am I being properly advised about which device and subscription match my needs? Am I being assisted quickly and competently if I have any questions, complaints or problems?
- *Emotion*: How will it make me feel? What kind of feeling do I get from the brand and what is it like to have and use this telephone? What do my friends think about it? Does this suit me and does it reinforce who I want to be?

For elements that cause the value to depreciate, the value for customers decreases if they receive more of these elements (and increases, of course, if fewer are received):

- *Price*: How much does it cost? Do I pay now and then not too much every month? What are the fixed and variable costs and how would they change if I were to use the device in a different way?
- *Effort*: What do I have to do to get it? Does it cost me a lot of time to figure out which device and subscription I should purchase and how these work? Does it cost me a lot of time to use or to learn how to use this device?
- *Risk*: How much risk is involved? If the device breaks down or if I switch to a new provider, do my costs double? Are all apps and interfaces available both now and in the future? Can I count on the provider not abusing my independence and privacy after I have made my choice?

It is, of course, attractive to customers to have a product or service with the biggest possible value at the lowest possible price. It is, however, mostly about the ratio—the customer value must be a good and logical deal for the customer. Determining what that value is for the customer by placing yourself in their shoes and investigating it, can help to optimize the ratio. During that process, a brand can define on the basis of which element(s) present in the total mix the company wants to use its product or service to truly distinguish itself and where it is fine with offering the same as the competition.

The value that an organization promises and that a customer expects and experiences forms the core of the "contract" between the brand and the customer. In that regard, there is always an exchange ratio. You want, of course, to deliver value to your customer, but at the same time customers must also return value to you or someone else has to do that for them. Otherwise, you might just as well put an immediate end to the relationship. The joint "contract" of what the customer receives and gives depends on a product, which is emotional or functional to a certain degree. It can be agreed implicitly or explicitly. The implicit perception of what a customer receives and gives can ultimately be just as concrete as formal legal agreements. Examples of this include what happens if customers leave, start protest campaigns, or spread negative publicity, even if they are perhaps wrong in formal legal terms. Many brilliant business models distinguish themselves because on this point they are more transparent, so that it is clear to customers not only what they receive and give, but also how that relates to the costs and the organization's revenue model.

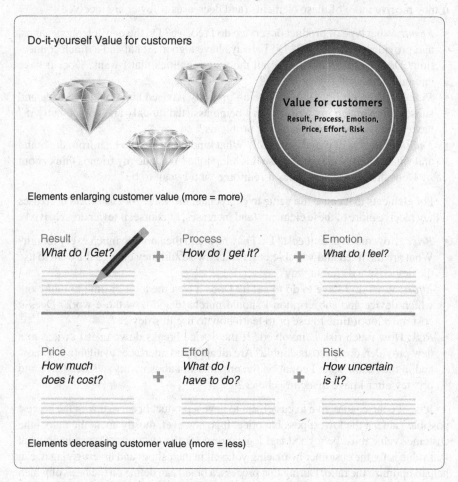

2.3   Delivery[7]

Once it is clear what value has been promised to which customers on the basis of the vision and brand positioning, this has to be implemented through delivery and operation. Delivery relates to the organization's activities where the interaction for and

---

[7] For delivery, aside from Kemperman et al. (2013) reference is made to Frei and Morriss (2012), Grönroos (2000) and Osterwalder and Pigneur (2010).

with the customer takes place. This includes the actual product transactions during the sale, as well as the relationship as a whole and the contact moments before and after the sale/service. Delivery can be defined by the following four elements:

- *Marketing*: What does brand and customer communication look like?
- *Sales*: How are activities organized to canvass and retain customers?
- *Customer contact*: Which channels are used to contact customers?
- *Services*: How are services for and with the customer arranged?

The theoretical framework for brilliant business models has a top focused on promises and a bottom aimed at the fulfillment thereof:

- *Promise*: The organization's higher and audacious goals as well as the brand's essence, roots and promise define which value the selected market segments can expect.
- *Fulfill*: Based on the organization's core values and core qualities and the brand's values and proof, the promised value for the customer must be realized in operation and delivery.

The value that the customer was promised must be realized in operation and delivery. What the organization creates for the customer in the delivery and operational processes is the organization's product. Delivery relates to the activities where the interaction between the customers and the organization takes place. The manner in which the delivery is implemented for the market segments on which the organization focuses determines the strength of the customer experience. Depending on the nature of the products, there can be years between contact moments, such as when buying a home. It can be about a series of transactions that occur in quick succession, for instance as with buying groceries. It can also be a combination of a sustainable, physical product combined with services, as is the case to an increasing extent for cars and equipment. The interaction between customer and organization can itself also be the product. Examples of this are certain services like training courses, massages or theme parks, as well as the provision of healthcare.

The identity, positioning and promises in relation to the customer generate focus for an organization. Subsequently, a clear choice must be made in delivery and operation as regards the aspects on which the organization really wants to differentiate itself and on which it wants to be at the same level as the most important competitors (or even opt to deliver somewhat less).

The design of the delivery starts with a proper analysis of the customer's contact points with the organization. To that end, the organization is analyzed from the customer's perspective and the significant brand touch points that shape the customer experience are identified. The journey that the customer makes through the organization is not a given, but rather can be designed and shaped by the organization with the aim of delivering the desired customer value to the desired market segments.

A significant part of the design of the delivery is the channel strategy. The organization uses the channel strategy to determine the channels by which it is going to deliver value to the customer. The question is simply how customers can purchase their services from the organization and use them. To what extent and at what moment is contact face-to-face, by telephone, on paper or online? The selected channels must be in line with the brand positioning, the promised value for the customer and the nature of the products delivered and services provided. If this emphasizes the personal, human relationship, voice response technology and the Internet will not suffice. If customers are promised that they will not have to make much of an effort, the delivery must be designed in such a way that they do not lose their way or have to figure out a lot on their own. If you want to keep things affordable, you can require customers to do as much as possible themselves and teach them to do it as long as it ends up being a good deal for the customer. Within healthcare, an important part of the work requires direct contact with customers. At the same time, it is desirable to have customers do a lot themselves and resolve issues among themselves where possible. In the process, though, for healthcare practitioners for instance, it is often extremely important in daily practice to work very closely together with other healthcare practitioners in a chain. At the organizational level, it might be desirable to maintain intensive professional relations with other parties, such as healthcare insurers, pharmacists, and suppliers of equipment among other things.

An organization's delivery can be defined by the following components:

- *Marketing*: What do brand and customer communication look like and how is that integrated into the product? This relates to the communication about the organization and the media used to that end. It also concerns the communication material supporting the recruitment and retention process and the services plus the role of the customers and persons directly involved themselves in communication, such as via social media, word-of-mouth advertising, and referrals.
- *Sales*: How are sales and customer retention activities organized? This relates to the channels being used and the people deployed. Is there, for instance, physical contact and/or orders via the Internet? This also concerns the design of the contact points as well as the experience and self-motivation for the customer. Recruitment and retention can relate to a specific group of customers who decide, use, and pay on their own. It can also concern various parties who co-determine, refer, pay, or recommend.
- *Customer contact*: How is the customer contact process designed and what does that contribute to the product or the service delivered to the customer by the organization? This relates to the various contact moments with existing customers and the channels used to that end. Is there, for instance, contact by telephone or online, are there service locations or door-to-door campaigns? What is the role of the employees and the customers themselves in this relationship? Where does a transfer with or between partners or suppliers occur and how does that work for the customer?
- *Services*: How are additional services for and with the customer arranged and what do these processes contribute to the product? What kinds of services are offered? What happens to the services at the practical and emotional level in the relationship and what does that demand of employees and the customer?

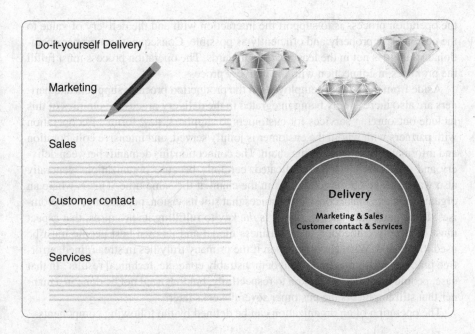

2.4 Operation[8]

Needless to say, the term "operation" here does not refer to medical treatment, but rather to the organization's activities "behind" the delivery and therefore often behind the scenes. A streamlined operation forms the heart of the organization. It serves as the backbone for the delivery and commonly provides opportunities and challenges for the realization of synergies and cost-efficiencies. The operation can be defined by the following four components:

- *Production*: How are production activities organized?
- *Technology*: What technology and knowledge are needed for production and delivery?
- *Suppliers*: What requirements and selection criteria do suppliers have to meet?
- *Partners*: What existing or other partners are required and what do they add?

In the traditional view of industrial, physical products, products were made in the operation phase before being marketed and sold in the delivery phase. As delivery is increasingly a significant part of the product,[9] this requires a more intensive coordination between delivery and production. In short, the art of establishing a solid link between operation and delivery has become more important. The challenge in

---

[8] For operation, aside from Kemperman et al. (2013) reference is made to Porter (1980), Porter (1985) and Osterwalder and Pigneur (2010).

[9] Reddy et al. (1993).

the operation process is to support the interaction with and the delivery of value to the customer as properly and efficiently as possible. Consequently, a proper operational strategy is not in the least focused inwards. The operation process must fulfill the promises in connection with the delivery process.

Aside from their "own" employees in the production process, suppliers and partners are also increasingly being integrated in the delivery process. Examples of this include outsourcing services for customers to suppliers, new forms of cooperation with partners with whom the customer is jointly served, and intensive collaboration and information exchange in the chain. The connection this demands between delivery and operation can be complicated, certainly because organizations generally also want to save on the total costs in the chain at the same time. This is where an organization can make conscious choices that suit its vision, positioning, and promises. If the personal, human contact is *the* key to fulfilling its promises, that aspect must be deeply embedded in its business model and its own best people must be used to that end. What should happen if the primacy truly lies in streamlined, error-free processes with maximum and demonstrably concrete, technical results? In that case, people must also be spoken to respectfully, but that need not be done in a manner that still impresses the customer several weeks later.

The operation of an organization can be defined by the following components:

- *Production*: How are production activities organized? What do the production processes look like if no personal customer contact exists and what are the resulting contributions to the organization's product(s)? How are employees enabled to effectively and efficiently perform their daily work?
- *Technology*: What technology and knowledge are needed for production and delivery? What does this demand of the company's own managers, specialists and employees? How is the knowledge present in individuals maximized, so that everyone does what he/she is best at? How do you organize the company so that people are not deployed above or below their level? What does this demand in terms of training and decision-support systems plus recording and transferring information? What are the requirements for supporting technology, equipment, and instruments?
- *Suppliers*: What requirements and selection criteria do suppliers have to meet? What do the production processes of suppliers look like and what do they contribute to the organization's product(s)? What is demanded, for instance, of pharmacists and suppliers of equipment, instruments, and aids in the healthcare sector?
- *Partners*: What other partners are required and what value do they add? Is there a need for joint venture partners other than suppliers in the operation or delivery? Which production processes do partners have and what type of contribution does that make to the organization's product(s)? How is, for instance, the cooperation between different healthcare providers organized in the provision of healthcare?

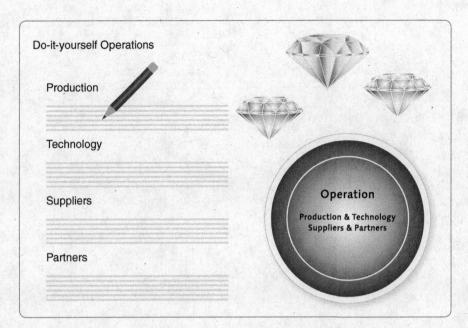

Do-it-yourself Operations

Production

Technology

Suppliers

Partners

Operation

Production & Technology
Suppliers & Partners

Chapter 3
Value Creation and Overall Framework

Business models prove their brilliance by the value they create for all stakeholders and are challenged to renew themselves for the future.

- *Value creation. A brilliant business model is the source for satisfied, more loyal and profitable customers on the one hand and the basis for value creation for shareholders and employees on the other. Together these contribute to value creation for society. The value created is the result of the business model and is therefore the ultimate test and the evidence for the brilliance thereof. The organization can set value creation targets and measure them relative to customers, shareholders, employees, and society.*
- *Phasing. The sequence from the cornerstones vision and positioning, to the business model and the resulting value creation is not random. This is also the step-by-step order in which brilliant business models can be best described. It also appears to be the sequence in terms of time and causality. Whereas the objective is value creation for all stakeholders, that result is not present from the beginning, but rather the desired outcome. To effect that, a working and consistent business model must be present. And that demands once again clarity of vision and positioning. Permanent brilliance? A company is and continues to be a social construct. Paradoxically, it is actually extra difficult for an organization that has successfully completed the steps above to maintain that success. The challenge in "phase 4" becomes sticking to the core of the business model and simultaneously renewing the organization for the future.*

© Springer International Publishing Switzerland 2017

J. Kemperman et al. (eds.), *Brilliant Business Models in Healthcare*,

DOI 10.1007/978-3-319-26440-0_3

3.1   Value Creation for All Stakeholders[1]

A brilliant business model that is completely in line with the organization's vision and positioning is the source of satisfied and more loyal and profitable customers. This, in turn, is the basis for value creation for shareholders and employees. The value created for stakeholders and the organization itself is the result of the business model as a whole and is therefore the ultimate test of its brilliance. The organization can set value creation targets and measure these targets per stakeholder:

- *Customers*: What does the value created for the customer in the business model give back to the organization?
- *Shareholders*: What value is created for shareholders and other owners, and what do they give back to the organization?
- *Employees*: What value is created for employees and what do they give back to the organization?
- *Society*: What value is created for society and what does this give back to the organization?

The importance of fulfilling and proving promises is a dominant theme not only in branding theory but also in the Value Profit Chain theory that has been built up over the past 25 years thanks to research into services marketing.[2] The key topic is the realization of sustainable financial and commercial success by not only promising as an organization to deliver relevant value to customers but also to fulfill this promise. The causal relationship behind this is that sustainable success is realized on the basis of loyal customers.[3] Customers become loyal because they are satisfied. Customers become satisfied because the expected value upon purchase of the product or service is also experienced in the use thereof.[4] Simply stated: the causal relationship exists that is outlined in the figure below.

---

[1] For value creation, reference is also made to Zeithaml et al. (1990), Reichheld (1996), Heskett et al. (2003, 2008), and Geelhoed et al. (2014).

[2] See for instance: Zeithaml et al. (1985, 1990), Reichheld (1996), and Heskett et al. (2003, 2008).

[3] See for instance: Bügel (2004).

[4] Kemperman and Van Engelen (1999).

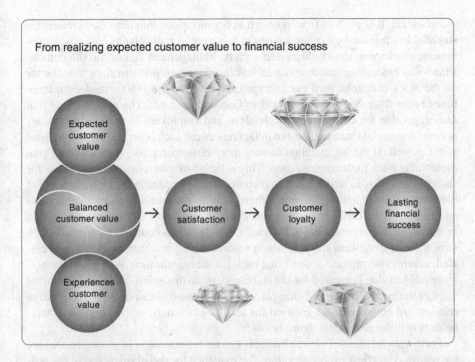

From realizing expected customer value to financial success

Expected customer value

Balanced customer value → Customer satisfaction → Customer loyalty → Lasting financial success

Experiences customer value

Where healthcare is provided, this relationship is different than for a "normal" commercial service provider. When looked at from the point of view of the patient, the objective of the cure is to ensure that the customer does *not* return! That being said, the loyalty mechanism does appear to definitely be important within healthcare. If, in terms of healthcare, patients are properly helped and are also satisfied themselves, that reinforces the reputation of the healthcare practitioner in relation to other patients, referring physicians, and insurers. These "customer groups" surrounding the patient will be more inclined to rely again on the healthcare practitioner themselves or refer others to them. As long as there is little transparency regarding results and findings, the fulfillment of expectations will only be rewarded to a limited extent. The quality of healthcare practitioners and the results and findings are not always transparent for patients. Individuals are often barely aware of the enormous differences in findings and prescribed treatments between healthcare practitioners. The extent of transparency is growing and that is being promoted by social media. With the growing insight into healthcare concerning quality, practice variety, and patient safety, the causal relationship of the value profit chain is also increasingly having more of an impact on healthcare.

There can seem to be an area of tension between satisfying customers, employees, shareholders, and society. In the short term, there might even be a discrepancy between the value for various parties. For instance, a decision can be made that the margin on products is increased at the expense of existing customers and for the benefit of shareholders. A decision can also be made to distribute part of the profit in the past year as salary or a bonus to employees and consequently less to shareholders. It is evident from research at organizations into the value created for stakeholders that the best organizations in fact excel for all persons concerned: customers, employees, shareholders *and* society. Management author Sisodia demonstrates that businesses that focus on all stakeholders even perform eight times better on the stock exchange than the average company (the S&P 500)[5] and even three times better than the legendary Good to Great companies.[6] The conclusion is that realizing value for customers, shareholders, and employees in the long term does not exclude any of these parties, but in fact reinforces each other and creates societal value as well. If the organization creates more customer value, they will also give more value back to the organization. This is the source for creating more value for shareholders who, in return, are also prepared to invest more in the organization and the further growth and development thereof. With the investments of shareholders and the positive feedback of customers, the organization can offer more to and invest in the employees, who, in exchange, also create more value for customers. In sum, there is an upward spiral in which stakeholders, for whom added value is created, in turn, also provide added value back for the organization. As a result thereof, more added value is created for the stakeholders. In this spiral the level of involvement of the people concerned changes from satisfaction to ownership.[7] The positive relationship between value creation for and by customers, employees, and shareholders is illustrated in the figure below.[8]

From a social point of view, a business can be considered to be a construct where the parties concerned exchange value. The evidence for and ultimate test of the brilliance of the business model is value creation: the extent to which (1) value is created for all stakeholders and (2) this ensures that these stakeholders give value back to the organization. If this is positive and all persons involved are satisfied, the organization has in fact a sustainable *raison d'être*. The organization can set value creation targets and measure these targets per stakeholder:

- *Customer value*: Aside from the organization's value for the customer (which has already been defined in the business model), the customer also has value for the organization. This can be measured in terms of loyalty, co-creation, referral behavior, and portfolio share. Within healthcare, this often concerns, as previously discussed, not only the patient, but also groups and influencers around them, such as the social network, referrers, insurers, and patient organizations.
- *Shareholder value*: The organization's value for the shareholders concerns yield, the organization's market value, profitability, and growth. Conversely, the shareholder has value for the organization via loyalty, investments, referrals, and portfolio share. Within healthcare, a shareholder does not always exist in the traditional sense of the word. Attracting external capital is much more difficult in

---

[5] Sisodia et al. (2007). Sisodia reviewed the return on investment of these organizations over a period of 10 years.

[6] Collins (2001).

[7] Heskett et al. (2008).

[8] Heskett et al. (2003) and Geelhoed et al. (2014).

some countries; in those cases investments must therefore be made from the company's own resources. Logically, bank loan requirements are simultaneously set for equity, collateral, and the management of business risks. Consequently, the organization's continuity is certainly as strongly associated with a sound financial result and reserves as in other sectors.

- *Employee value*: The organization's value for the employees relates to the appreciation and the pleasure derived in the form of chances and challenges, inspirational working environment, reward, appreciation and confirmation, openness, degrees of freedom, celebration moments, and work-life balance. It concerns material rewards, as well as the space for a private life in addition to training and development. Conversely, the employee has value for the organization via performance in increasing customer bonding, turnover and productivity, attracting other employees and applying and tranferring ideas, motivation, knowledge and culture.
- *Societal value*: The organization's value for society relates to the creation of employment, welfare, health, happiness and prosperity. Conversely, society has value for the organization via the acquisition of goodwill, a positive image and the confirmation and appreciation of the societal contribution made by the organization.

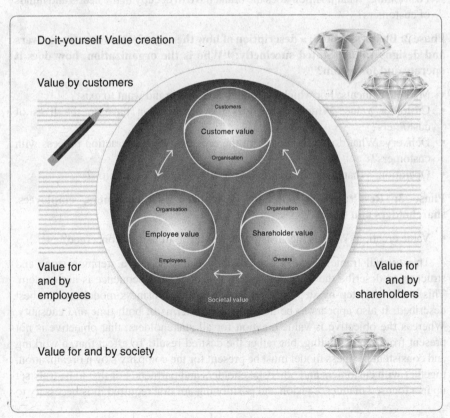

3.2   Conceptual Framework and Phasing

Now that we have looked at the different components (vision, positioning, business model and value creation), it is time to turn to summary and action. How do these different components relate to one another? And how is a brilliant business model to be defined and developed? What steps should be completed to that end?

Based on the cases we have analyzed, there is a certain sequence and connection between the fundamentals, the business model and a good performance. In the conceptual model central to this book, the theory regarding vision, positioning, business models and service marketing has consequently been integrated and placed within an overall framework. To be precise, we see three phases, in each one of which a number of vital questions are answered. This sequence of questions forms, as it were, a step-by-step plan.

Phase 1: Vision and positioning: "who do you want to be and why?"

- Vision: What is the organization's vision regarding who it wants to be and why it wants to exist?
- Positioning: What position does the brand have to occupy in the hearts and minds of customers?

Phase 2: Business model: a description of how the organization creates, delivers and designs value.[9] Stated succinctly: "Who is the organization, how does it operate and for whom?"

- Market segments: For which customers does the brand want to exist?
- Customer value: Which value does the organization have in the lives of customers?
- Delivery: What does this require in the organization's interaction process with customers?
- Operation: What does this require in the organization's operation?

Phase 3: Result: What outcome is realized for customers, employees, shareholders and society?

- Value creation: What is the sustainable result for all parties concerned?

This overall framework has consequently been used as a stepping stone and structure to describe the brilliant cases in this book. The sequence is not random. This is also the step-by-step order in which brilliant business models can be best described. It also appears to be the sequence in terms of both time and causality. Whereas the objective is value creation for all stakeholders, that objective is not present from the beginning, but rather the desired result. To effect that, a working and consistent business model must be present for the company's own organization, together with customers and other stakeholders and partners. For that to be truly set up in a focused manner, a vision and positioning are first required. It is necessary to

---

[9] Heskett et al. (2008).

consider from the start how the business model must work and how it must create value for all stakeholders. The fire for a brilliant business model starts with a spark, i.e., the vision and position that you want to occupy based on the question "why."

3.3 Permanent Brilliance?

A company is and continues to be a social construct. It ceases to exist, however, if more value is demanded of the existing stakeholders than is given to them. It is valuable to all parties concerned as long as it lasts. It need not continue into eternity. The lunar landing in 1969 is and continues to be valuable, but the highlight was also the final destination of the project. History was written, but that is not enough. If you were the National Aeronautics and Space Administration, you would not want to be some temporary construct, but rather continue to be brilliant.

Paradoxically, there are reasons why continued existence is all the more difficult for organizations that have successfully completed the first three phases of a brilliant business model.[10] The pioneering value produced for all stakeholders changes the playing field. There is more at stake for all stakeholders. This exposes the company to the risk of stagnancy, because the parties concerned are scared of losing something. At the same time, there is actually the risk of an escape forwards whereby stakeholders become opportunistic—or too much so—and always want more, as a result of which the core is forgotten. As a brilliant business model, it is, in short, best to keep calm, whilst you are being fawned upon, and to keep your feet on the ground instead of getting carried away. At the same time, success also attracts competitors who will start doing the same thing; this makes things exciting, but not necessarily any easier. In that regard, success elicits different responses from society. As long as you are the new kid on the block, you will be given a lot of slack and given the benefit of the doubt. But that changes as soon as you have outgrown that role and become a dominant player.

In short, a brilliant business does not always automatically remain brilliant. After the three phases have been completed, the challenge arises in keeping the corresponding three criteria consistently connected and continuing their development. In this fourth phase, the challenge is to not collapse under your own success. If the organization holds onto the past too much, it will be overtaken and become obsolete. If things get out of hand during the renewal phase, the connection to the roots and the core qualities will be lost—precisely the things that make the organization unique. In short, the challenge then becomes maintaining the core and specifically continuing to innovate on that basis.[11] Actually, you want to return to the future of phase 1, where the freshness and ambition of this phase is enriched by the experience gained and successes achieved. At the same time, doing so has not become any easier. The organization is less nimble. There are now many more parties depending

---

[10] Kemperman et al. (2013).
[11] Collins and Porras (1994).

on the value that the organization is creating and vice versa the organization also depends on the value that all these stakeholders give back in return.

It seems as if all the healthcare systems in the Western world are stuck in the "mud" of phase 4. That seems also applicable to many of the players involved in this phase: large enough to stay afloat, but too cumbersome to be able to really soar. Things are going too well to really have to change on the basis of urgency, but at the same time not well enough to dare to change on the basis of excitement.

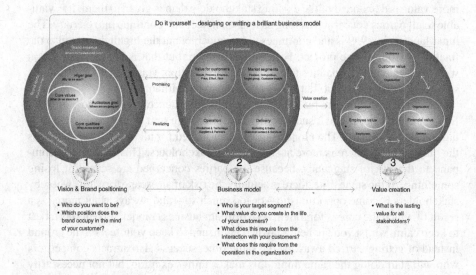

In Part II of this book, we will look at examples of companies that stand out and really make a contribution to the breakthroughs necessary to make proper health-care affordable and accessible and to keep it that way. Incorporated into this book as case studies, these organizations also need not to remain brilliant forever. They have not been selected as a prediction. Even more: some of them have been included because they were brilliant in an earlier stage, whereas the gloss has dimmed a bit since then—which is then also described as such. We do not learn what these businesses will be able to do tomorrow, but rather what they did yester-day or are doing today. They are included in this publication because they represent an inspiring and pioneering example for our consideration today (and sometimes even coming from the past). They are not in the future, but do provide an inspiration for it.

To test and reflect upon the brilliance of business models this chapter concludes with a self-assessment in 13 questions. These questions help to evaluate whether the own business model has a compelling vision which is executed without compromises and delivers such a success to stakeholders that they would jointly restart the organization if it stopped to exist.

Self assessment Brilliant Business Models

Brand essence

Question: Are our customers, employees, shareholders and society better off because we exist?

Higher goal and brand roots

Question: Do we understand why we exist and are we still loyal to this challenge?

Audacious goal and brand promise

Question: Do we have an audacious goal that goes further than merely staying alive in the present market?

Core and brand values

Question: Are we transparent and trustworthy for the future?

Core qualities and brand proof

Question: Are our promises and qualities visible in clear examples for our customers? Do they tell each other about this?

Value for customers

Question: Do customers understand what they get from us and is that relevant for them?

Market segments

Question: Do we have a stronger position than our competitors with our target group?

Operation

Question: Do we have a lean operation with the needed technology and knowledge to fulfill everyones expectations?

Delivery

Question: Do we have contact with our customers based on a human approach in which we jointly create the best solution?

Value by customers

Question: Would our customers buy from us again today and will they recommend us to potential customers?

Value for and by employees

Question: Would our employees work for us again today and will they recommend us to potential employees?

Value for and by shareholders

Question: Would our shareholders invest in us again today and will they recommend us to other shareholders?

Value for and by society

Question: Would our society support us and all our activities, if we would start out again today?

Chapter 4
Challenges for Brilliant Business Models in Healthcare

In the ideal world all medically necessary care is universally accessible and at a high quality level. In reality good care is financially and/or practically only available for a portion of the population. Healthcare costs have risen quickly all around the world. While healthcare systems differ, all countries are challenged to realize the triple aim to improve the patient experience of care and the health of populations while reducing the per capita cost of healthcare. The challenges facing healthcare can be bundled into five desired breakthroughs:

- *Breakthrough 1: Strengthening mutual caring and sharing—How can we live together with shared responsibilities, support, and risks?*
- *Breakthrough 2: Letting prevention and self-management work—How do we create incentives and reward systems for demonstrable health benefits?*
- *Breakthrough 3: Patient-centered organization of information and everyday care—How should we share treatment and diagnostic information and bring primary care closer to the patient?*
- *Breakthrough 4: Deploying services and instruments to help customers take control—How can innovation and process streamlining be used to improve the lives of patients?*
- *Breakthrough 5: Implementing differentiation in specialized healthcare—How can schedulable and academic healthcare be organized best in the second and third line?*

4.1 Good, Affordable, and Widely Accessible Healthcare Is Unique

What makes people happy? If you ask what people think is the most important thing for a happy life, "health" is always in the top three answers provided. More often than not it even tops the list. The concern for the health of individuals is worth

© Springer International Publishing Switzerland 2017
J. Kemperman et al. (eds.), *Brilliant Business Models in Healthcare*,
DOI 10.1007/978-3-319-26440-0_4

fighting for. In that regard, the rise in both the quality of care and life expectancy in the Western world is unusual and unique. People eventually become accustomed to everything and if you have spent your entire life in an affluent country or environment with good healthcare, you take it for granted. Nonetheless, it is not "common." Historically speaking, life expectancy has never been so high; in the past 100 years it has doubled worldwide to an average of approximately 70 years. People are becoming older more than ever. In many Western countries, people are now living on average 5 years longer than 30 years ago, and roughly half of this increase is considered healthy.[1] More and more of the illnesses that we used to die from have become chronic disorders that we can still become rather old with in many cases.

The international ideal as advocated by the World Health Organization (WHO) is that all medically necessary care should be universally accessible and at a high quality level. This dream is, however, a reality for only a very small percentage of the world population. Whereas relatively good care can be obtained everywhere in the world, it is often financially and/or practically only available for a portion of the national population—often only for the elite. A review of access to qualitatively good healthcare reveals that a distinction can be made between three types of healthcare systems around the world:

- *Good, universal healthcare*. Internationally, there are only a few places in the world where healthcare is basically good qualitatively and accessible to everyone. In that regard, it often concerns systems in affluent countries where healthcare and the financing thereof is provided for via the government or where market forces are subjected to strict government regulation. That is particularly the case in the swathe of countries in Europe that runs from Norway, Sweden, and Denmark via the Netherlands, Belgium, France, and Germany to Austria and Switzerland. There are a few other places on the globe, such as Singapore, Cuba, Canada, and Japan, which also fall in this category. Overall, fewer than five out of every 100 people in the world live in a country where good healthcare is universal.
- *Private healthcare with a public safety net*. In many more countries, there is no equal access to healthcare as a whole, but rather a public safety net with lesser-quality healthcare to outright poor healthcare. In that regard, it often concerns systems where basic healthcare is available via the government or regulations and where access to the best healthcare can be acquired via private insurance companies. The difference between the countries with good, universal healthcare and those with more diversity results from differences in prosperity levels as well as the ideological perspective concerning the free market and income distribution. We are referring, for instance, to rich Western countries, such as the USA and the UK, as well as emerging and still relatively affluent countries, such as Turkey, South Africa, and Russia and large parts of South America and part of Asia. Roughly half of all people in the world live in a country where this is the case.
- *Private healthcare without a public safety net*. The reality for the rest of the world is that they live in a country where truly good healthcare is only available

---

[1] To be precise, 2.3 years. Based on an analysis of figures from Statistics Netherlands.

to the elite. Alternately, they live in an area where the journey to healthcare practitioners is for all intents and practices not feasible and certainly not in the case of emergencies. They have to save hard, borrow money, and take out insurance to obtain a basic level of healthcare. For many, the biggest part of the healthcare system is in effect hermetically sealed off. In order to make an inhabitant of a (relatively) affluent country understand again what the value is of both good healthcare and the system of financing and legislation that makes that accessible, it helps to take the perspective of these countries. Examples of the involved countries are India and Kenya where they need new initiatives such as a micro-insurance to give more people access to healthcare.

The World Health Organization's (WHO) ideal of good, universal healthcare is in practice uncommon and the exception to the rule. The question then is: is the healthcare in the few countries where good healthcare for all is regulated also brilliant? The answer is: No! Diamonds are hard and practically indestructible. Whereas the number of countries with good, universal healthcare is growing, it is also vulnerable in those countries where this is already a reality. It seems as if it is no longer a rock-hard diamond, but rather a special and fragile piece of porcelain. Healthcare costs certainly rise more quickly than the Gross Domestic Product, something that is visible in all Western countries. That puts access to healthcare at risk in the long term.

4.2 Cost Increases Put Accessibility, Quality, and Healthcare Systems at Risk

Healthcare costs have risen quickly all around the world. The amount of these costs and the speed of the increase differ between countries and healthcare systems, but the same rising trend has been apparent in every country for years. The growth prognoses for the next few years vary: healthcare costs will either rise quickly or spike. That is an ominous forecast. The underlying factors for the growth in healthcare costs and the problems associated with the financing thereof are known from media and political circles:

- *Economy*. Increases in healthcare costs are often largely compensated for and financed by economic growth. What happens if the economy does not grow became, for instance, visible in many affluent countries during the economic crisis from 2008 onwards. Healthcare costs simply continued to rise in that period, whilst the economy simultaneously contracted or stagnated in many countries. Consequently, the level of affordability declined and the pressure of rising healthcare costs increased.
- *Life expectancy*. The increased life expectancy and the number of people that continue to live with a chronic disorder are evidence of the success and improvements in healthcare. Where being able to live longer is regarded as a positive goal, the ageing population also comes with negative associations. This also places more pressure on care and cure, and particularly on care. As a result, the

ageing population demands extra economic growth to compensate for rising healthcare costs. At the same time, an older population is in fact less productive. It has a burdensome effect on economic growth. The economic effect of an ageing population is visible, for instance, in Japan: labor productivity levels per worker have risen impressively, whilst increasingly fewer people work, with the end result being stagnation and deflation.

- *Technology*. Technological developments make more existing or potential disorders visible and more (often expensive) medical procedures possible. Technological breakthroughs and especially disruptive innovations generally increase productivity and result in cost-savings. In practice, however, the effect of new technology in healthcare often reinforces, extends and optimizes existing applications and treatments and drives costs up particularly in affluent countries. Since users often do not pay the bill, there is no natural brake on consumption. In countries where there are traditionally a lot of care institutions, these institutions often all want to offer the exploding number of new specializations and technologies, so that economies of scale cannot be taken advantage of. There are rises in productivity, but in affluent countries they do not compensate for the extra expenditure due to an increase in the ageing demographic, chronic disorders and more medical possibilities.

A common global challenge is to ensure that as many people as possible gain and retain access to good, affordable healthcare. All countries are challenged to realize the triple aim to improve the patient experience of care and the health of populations while reducing the per capita cost of healthcare.[2] At the same time, however, affluent countries have challenges to deal with other than those facing developing countries.

If we take a look at healthcare in affluent countries it appears that many healthcare systems and care institutions operating within them, in terms of brilliant business models have ended up in the so-called fourth phase. They face the challenge to maintain and renew themselves. In the first phase, in many countries a vision to make good healthcare affordable for and accessible to as many people as possible was the basis for working towards the creation of a healthcare system. In the second phase, the infrastructure for the provision of healthcare was erected along with the corresponding financing, technology and legislation. In the third phase, the parties concerned began to consider this normal and all players started behaving in accordance with the system that was successfully created. Now many affluent countries find themselves in the difficult, challenging fourth phase. They have to face this paradox of maintaining and renewing the healthcare system in a changing environment. The issue is how to keep good healthcare and new technological possibilities accessible to as many people as possible, whilst the percentage of these people that structurally require care and cure is increasing. It often seems as if the only solutions to be found are those where the suffering of one stakeholder or set of stakeholders can be eased by shifting the suffering onto another group. In this way, certain fees can be drawn out of the public system or collective insurance plans to increase the affordability,

---

[2] Berwick et al. (2008) and Institute for Healthcare Improvement (2012).

but then people will have to pay for it themselves. The challenge is actually ending up back in the first phase, but then in a new style. If we were to express this in terms of a board game, we have to go around the board and pass "Go" to start again. It seems that all players are now primarily hanging on to the assets they have already earned and received. In a board game, you can sometimes choose to skip your turn, but generally speaking you have to simply roll the dice when it is your turn or you will most likely lose the game. If everyone passes on the opportunity to roll the dice, it is not that nothing changes but rather the game will come to an end. Under the current circumstances in the healthcare system, passing a turn is not a way to keep and maintain everything, but rather to slowly lose it all.

Scarcity is a rich driver for innovation. When the problems are overwhelming and huge, the solution is often on its way. This is not a matter of coincidence but a matter of cause and effect. The need drives the solution, or in economic terms the demand drives the supply. It is a very hopeful thought that mankind appears to be capable to solve the true challenges it faces. On the other hand this also means that often it is not possible to avoid problems upfront since they are an integrated and needed first step in the solution. This triggers the sort of disruptive innovation which Schumpeter called creative destruction.[3] It is not always nice to be a part of it as customer or business since you can take part in the suffering and you never know if your are also part of the solution or will become obsolete in the change process. A lot of true breakthroughs require a level of change that cuts into established interests and can only be realized by getting rid of established barriers. It often involves innovations which are technically even inferior at the start but for instance make it possible to reach and help far more people by radically lowering costs.[4] These sort of breakthroughs are not comfortable and that is why they are only realized when this is the last resort. Besides scarcity there is also abundance. Available resources and technological possibilities can provide new means and creativity for innovation.[5] A true need in the market based on scarcity combined with new resources and technologies to solve the problem logically offers the most fruitful soil for breakthroughs.

Developments such as eHealth and self-management in lifestyle appear to offer a lot of innovative possibilities to improve the health of people while lowering costs. At the same time businesses from outside the traditional healthcare are still a faster and richer source for these sorts of innovation then traditional care providers. Things in established healthcare systems and organizations in many affluent countries are apparently still going too well to be really forced to transform, and too poorly to get the confidence to dare to change. Current systems with good healthcare for as many people as possible can, paradoxically, only be maintained and expanded by letting go of the existing system and improving in a pioneering manner, i.e., escaping forwards to phase one and starting to build again based on a vision. That is very scary and feels counterintuitive. It is somewhat akin to going bungee jumping or parachuting, whilst

---

[3] Schumpeter (1934).
[4] Christensen (1997, 2009).
[5] Ismail et al. (2014).

possessing a highly developed warning system in the form of vertigo. Nonetheless, sometimes that is the only and best way if you want to get to higher ground and there is a chasm or a border separating you from your destination. The authors of this book believe that the paradox that it is possible to retain the good things only by letting them go and innovating largely applies to healthcare in affluent countries. Consequently, we want to extend a heartfelt invitation to everyone to grab their parachutes and get into the airplane to help improve healthcare and health in general.

If it is so difficult to maintain access and quality in affluent countries, is it then not impossible to make good healthcare available to many more people in developing countries? Major efforts must be made not only to keep pace but also to catch up. Here, too, the population is ageing. The challenge jumps in a few years' time from malnutrition to nutritional diseases due to overconsumption. At the same time, new technological possibilities are rapidly coming onto the market and the established defense mechanisms and barriers to adoption are less developed and institutionalized. While healthcare providers in Western countries are not so much limited by the costs of an individual treatment and compete for the number of treatments here it is often the other way around. In many Southeast Asian countries, double-digit growth is required in terms of productivity increases, technological development and the number of healthcare practitioners in order to just keep pace with the growing demand for healthcare resulting from demographic development. At the same time, there are also sensational and hopeful developments on their way. Here scarcity indeed proves a rich source for disruptive innovation. The old cliché "the darkest hour is just before the dawn" seems to be not so much coincidental here but rather a natural consequence of acting as a magnet. In developing countries the challenges are so major that true transformation is clearly and urgently needed, and recent improvements in a lot of countries give confidence and inspiration for renewal. If there is no funding in the budget available for standard expensive solutions, the scarcity will in turn often give rise to unorthodox alternatives outside budgetary constraints and beyond classical barriers for a fraction of the cost. Many rapidly developing countries appear not to be stuck in phase four in terms of the phases of brilliant business models. This is where examples are visible of parties who, based on the vision in phase one, arrive at fundamentally new business models in phase two. Using the analogy of the board game, they are behind more affluent countries and still have a lot to learn in fields, such as training systems, infrastructure, and financing. Healthcare institutions in Western countries can copy little directly from healthcare providers in developing countries. The solutions in developing countries often do not meet existing safety standards and are more risky then regular procedures. If this is the case they are not considered as option in affluent countries where they compete with established, proven and available treatments. They are only an alternative if they compete with no treatment. Many of the unorthodox solutions can therefore only arise in a world where this is the only way to meet the needs, as the demand for healthcare is largely exceeding supply. At the same time, a number of healthcare providers in developing countries are about half a game board ahead of more affluent counterparts when it comes to innovative strength, creativity, and ability to surpass themselves. A part of the procedures, legislation, regulations, automatisms, and vested interests adds little and must be lanced to realize innovation. It helps to keep asking yourself if you are actually half a game board ahead or behind in this perspective.

In short, the rising costs of healthcare are creating fundamental challenges in countries with all different types of healthcare systems:

- *Good, universal healthcare is difficult to maintain.* The countries where good, universal healthcare exists, are confronted with a major challenge. Whilst healthcare costs are increasing, how do you maintain the system and distribute the costs and responsibilities in a manner that keeps it affordable and acceptable now and in the future? How do you avoid decline and create the urgency and scarcity which is needed for continuous renewal and disruptive innovation?
- *Private healthcare with a public safety net risks creating a widening gulf between the two.* In the countries where the best healthcare is available for a part of the population alongside a universal public system, the risk exists that they will end up with an ever widening gulf. How do you ensure that the costs for the best healthcare do not explode, making healthcare even more exclusive, and how do you keep the public system affordable, whilst preventing a reduction in the quality and substance thereof?
- *Private healthcare without a public safety net is akin to shooting at a moving target.* In those countries where no broad public basis exists for universal healthcare, the frustrating thing is that the target is not stationary. Whilst wanting to give more people access to elementary healthcare, people discover that this is simultaneously becoming more and more difficult due to complicating societal challenges such as an ageing population, chronic disorders, and technological developments. The inspiration in this case comes from the insight that the darkest hour itself triggers the creation of a new dawn.

A review of healthcare at an international level provides inspiration. When various systems and countries are surveyed it appears that the pole position at the start differ widely but the developments and movement go into the same direction. As the costs and demand for healthcare are rising everywhere the main features of the puzzle remain the same everywhere.[6] The discussions about increasing healthcare costs are expressions of and solutions for the same quest: what is the best (or least worst) balance between affordability, quality, and accessibility and how do we improve the patient experience and health of the population while reducing the cost to get the balance on a higher level?

The value that people place on health in general as well as the importance of access to good, affordable healthcare makes it absolutely worth the effort to fight for it. However, with the growing elderly population, chronic disorders, and technological developments, that fight is not a trivial wrestling match. If that is the case, is every attempt at improving healthcare and health in general in a pioneering fashion not futile from the outset? The answer is: No! Something will definitely have to change and not just with a single party, but with all stakeholders within healthcare. Yet with a common goal in mind and with the awareness that the issues have to be solved, it will be realized.

---

[6] World Economic Forum and McKinsey (2013a).

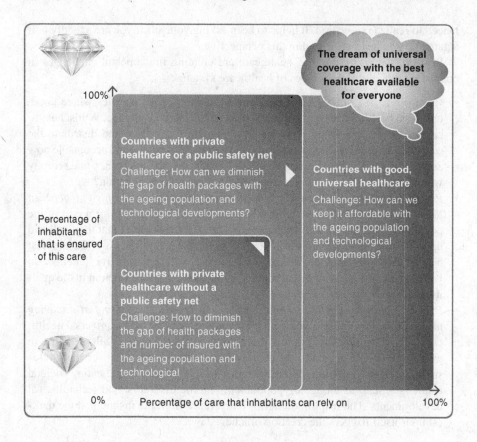

4.3 Desired Breakthroughs in Healthcare

What is the best healthcare system in the world? The search for the Holy Grail has been underway for a long time already.[7] It seems that no one system exists that solves every problem. When looking at the individual elements of systems such as remuneration structures and guiding mechanisms, it is possible to find interventions and components that truly can help to keep good healthcare affordable and accessible. In that regard, it especially helps if interests tie in with each other, functioning as common driving forces in the chain.[8] It is beneficial to study principles that help in this process and to learn from them. In addition, there are, if required, many instruments to distribute the total revenues and the healthcare services already available in the most equitable manner possible. This also includes the trade-off examples where the triple aim, of a healthier population via better treatments for lower costs, is not realized but we rather see the creation of value for one stakeholder on expense of another. Pharmaceutical companies who are praised and criticized for launching new pharmaceuticals which help for patients with a very special disease but are very

---

[7] Since 2005, for instance, the various European healthcare systems have been compared annually by the Health Consumer Powerhouse (HCP), which has its registered office in Sweden. See Björnberg (2012).

[8] Kemperman et al. (2000).

expensive. Healthcare providers who increase the perceived quality for an individual patient with additional treatments but overall health outcomes are vague and costs increase. Governments who face difficult decisions to control healthcare spending by reducing the publically available treatments or number of care providers. Insurance companies who keep healthcare premiums affordable by cutting on reimbursements or not accepting people with chronic or special diseases. These sort of trade-offs are a rich field for tension and debates between parties. It involves explicit and clear conflicts and negotiation between parties based on different interests. It also involves misunderstanding and emotions when people from their own viewpoint believe that they do the right thing and are truly surprised that they are criticized and not praised for their work. Underlying almost all of these conflicts and discussion in healthcare are the different business drivers of stakeholders based on their own objectives, professional ethics and responsibilities in healthcare. Those are fundamental issues for political circles, society and business, but they do not solve the challenges facing healthcare. What is required to that end goes deeper than new allocation formulas. There is a need for ways to realize the truly triple aim to improve the patient experience of healthcare and the health of populations for the same amount of funding or less.[9] Whereas this would still leave us with the issues about who is going to get which additional piece of the pie and who will foot which part of the smaller bill this makes matters far less complicated since there would be more healthcare and health in general to be distributed for the same amount of money.

At the global level there are many examples of organizations that fundamentally provide superior healthcare or, on the contrary, operate much more economically or enable people to become old in a much healthier manner. These are the kinds of organizations that you encounter along the way and wonder why we do not yet have them in every country. If we want to increase the pie and realize the best universal healthcare, we will need these kinds of organizations. Within healthcare, technically sound, scientific ideas and more advanced treatment methods are easily shared around the world. Extensive networks have been set up for the purpose of sharing knowledge by way of publications and conventions, as well as the international exchange of individuals. Sometimes it takes a while, but every generation of recent medical graduates and all new technologies eventually fan out. Corporate and business models of the traditional healthcare providers who feel that they are bound to a physical location tend to stay closer to home. The same also holds true to more "soft" factors and comprehensive healthcare procedures around patients extending beyond organizational boundaries. The not-invented-here syndrome is rather deeply rooted at this level. National system-specific legislation, regulations, and reimbursement systems often make the gaps even more difficult to bridge and give excuses why different solutions will not work at home. The nature of the healthcare system is also such that whereas people prefer to have those services close to home, the scope, import and export thereof is limited. Incidentally, it should be noted that people with a more complex or more severe disorder are prepared to travel further for the right treatment. Additionally eHealth crosses borders in legislation and between nations more easily. This definitely accounts for lifestyle products, interventions, and apps which are paid by people themselves and not part of the medical reimbursement and related procedures, approvals, and clinical tests. In sum, there are

---

[9] See Berwick et al. (2008) and Institute for Healthcare Improvement (2012).

several reasons why we could learn more from abroad. In other words, we can find foreign sources of inspiration yet!

In the quest for inspiring business models in healthcare now before you, examples have been selected that challenge healthcare practitioners to fundamentally reconsider their own way of organizing and approach to matters. Examples were reviewed that were able to effect a breakthrough in healthcare. It was not our ambition to achieve completeness, but rather optimum diversity in perspectives. The care institutions that can be used to learn from are partially the usual suspects: reputable quality hospitals known around the world. At the same time, the desire existed to avoid clichés and share surprising examples. Examples from various parts of the world were reviewed. Our perspective was broadened to include various kinds of care and cure and prevention. Aside from the physical provision of care, the scope of the survey included information, self-management, and financing. This did not only mean looking at the most modern organizations, but rather the review looked also at past sources of inspiration. In those instances, it is not so much about the technical innovation, but much more about the social design, societal component and solidarity. How did people in the past share resources to be able to finance healthcare? How was care for each other organized and integrated in the daily life and interaction of people in those days? How can we innovate by simply organizing things in a simpler fashion?

Many healthcare organizations are confronted with existential issues sooner or later. For instance, they have to choose between specialization or expansion: are operations being performed on patients closer to their home, supporting them as completely as possible in their process, or is an optimized procedure-based, national approach preferable? When successful examples are surveyed, it seems that a number of types of organizations arise that look strikingly alike between each other. This is also the case if they operate in different countries. The question that this raises is whether perhaps archetypes exist of business models needed in healthcare. Upon review of hundreds of examples of healthcare organizations, a picture of several different types of business models did indeed form. We did not carry out emperical research into the differences in success based on that typology. We did, however, strive to include examples of the most important different kinds of pioneering business models observed in the market that make a demonstrable contribution to the required breakthroughs in the healthcare system.

Healthcare straddles the public and private domain. In that regard, there is a surprising number of hybrids of organizations that can go bankrupt and are competing on a market but do not have any primary profit motive, stock-listing, or dividends. The truly purely public organizations seem to be less nimble in the fast-changing field that the health sector is. In that regard there are also new initiatives without a direct commercial approach. Examples of this include new forms of networks, the exploding number of home-made eHealth apps and the almost daily rise of new sympathetic prevention initiatives. In a lot of cases, these hybrids cannot be maintained in the long term. What is often missing is a clear revenue model. As long as that is missing, the initiative will continue to depend on sympathy and altruism. That often works very well in the start-up phase and the growth phase immediately afterwards. In time, however, the initiative often fails or remains small in scale. As argued by Dr.

Shetty, the founder of Narayana Hrudayalaya, the world's largest cardiac hospital in India: "Charity is not scalable." If you want to make universal healthcare affordable and accessible, you also have to ensure that your own organization continues to function independently. At the same time, a purely commercial profit motive is not always acceptable as well as insufficient for the long term. Only wanting to earn as much money as possible on the market of sick and unhealthy individuals arouses opposition in many countries. Rightly or wrongly, it is associated with self-enrichment by specialists and directors and with mismanagement and misuse.[10] The healthcare practitioner's bill is often not paid by patients themselves. This results in an opportunity for the healthcare practitioner to charge and earn more money. At the same time, this places an extra moral responsibility upon the healthcare practitioner to do the right thing and not strive for turnover maximization and to use healthcare sparingly. A payer such as an insurer exists to assume the responsibility to pay for all medically necessary costs if someone needs it and it is not acceptable and sustainable if the payer is only there for healthy people as long as things go well. Doing business in the healthcare sector altogether has an extra societal dynamic focused on doing the right thing and uniting the interests of private and public stakeholders. Consequently, it is not surprising that during our quest for brilliant business models we encountered many public entrepreneurs and commercial philanthropists.

The challenges facing healthcare are enormous. This makes it simultaneously difficult and easy for healthcare organizations wanting to protect, prove, and fulfill their *raison d'être*. Brilliant business models in healthcare must make a demonstrable contribution to solving the challenges in the sector. If they do that, the market is as large as the challenges facing healthcare and consequently there is a lot of work to be done. If they do not do so, however, instead of being part of the solution, they are part of the problem. This was used as the starting point in the quest for brilliant business models and the kinds of business models looked for. The desired breakthroughs in healthcare were reviewed and examples were looked at of organizations that truly help to realize these breakthroughs. It is evident from previous research that companies can earn money by improving the world. Now the quest has changed directions. How can the world be improved by realizing good, sustainable business models in healthcare?

When we take a step back to consider the grand visionary narratives regarding the necessary changes wrought within healthcare, there is a lot of consensus.[11] There are differences in the desired outcomes, but when the starting point and the goal are looked at, the direction is nonetheless clear. The agenda is actually rather concise. The challenges facing healthcare have been bundled in this publication into five desired breakthroughs that each require brilliant business models. It is important to retain financial and social solidarity between people. Prevention is needed that truly works to stimulate and seduce customers to assume responsibility for their own healthcare and health in general. Day-to-day care must be set up in an accessible and integrated manner and deployed nearby based on clear and shared diagnoses and

---

[10] This is substantiated, for instance, by Christensen et al. (2009).

[11] See for an illustration of the response to the (potential) misuse of collective funds in healthcare: van Wijngaarden (2012).

information. There is a need for real service to be provided as a result of which healthcare can become better streamlined and customer-friendly. Additionally, specialized healthcare must be differentiated into urgent, recurring, and academic healthcare.

The five desired breakthroughs in healthcare are summarized below. Each of these five breakthroughs is illustrated in a separate chapter in Part II of this book. The four selected brilliant business models corresponding to each breakthrough receive a short introduction and examples are given of organizations with comparable business models. The selected four cases are then discussed at length one at a time.

As the breakthroughs are discussed, you will note that the focus gradually broadens from "nearby" to "distant" and from "self" to "care." We will start off with organizing mutual care in groups of people, self-management. After that we will turn our attention more broadly to the information on the patient and the healthcare in the vicinity. We then consider the services and instruments which help people to take control over their treatments and eventually we investigate specialized healthcare. This is visualized in the figure below.

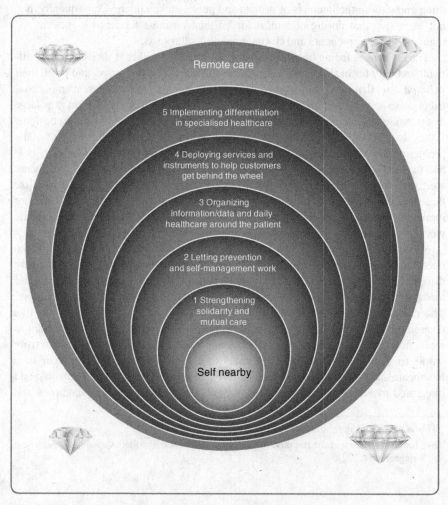

Remote care

5 Implementing differentiation
in specialised healthcare

4 Deploying services and
instruments to help customers
get behind the wheel

3 Organizing
information/data and daily
healthcare around the patient

2 Letting prevention
and self-management work

1 Strengthening
solidarity and
mutual care

Self nearby

Breakthrough 1: Strengthening mutual caring and sharing—How can we live together with shared responsibilities, support, and risks?

The starting point for making and keeping healthcare universally accessible is continuous innovation and the reinvention of mutual caring and sharing. It concerns the readiness to pay and care for each other within a group and in society, so that others will also do the same for you in the unfortunate case that this is necessary. It relates to caring and sharing the risks between people who resemble one another or, even more, not at all in terms of income, age, health, and lifestyle. It is also about the corresponding rights and obligations in terms of behavior, such as using health-care sparingly and assuming your own responsibilities involved in treatment compliance, healthy living, self-management, and informal care. The desire to provide everyone with the best healthcare seems, as described, to be universal in nature and has been laid down as such by the WHO. In practice, however, this is an exceptional situation. The manner in which the system and principles such as mutual caring and sharing in everyone's "own" country is designed often feels like a logical given, but is very much a product of its time and is restricted to a particular area. Technological developments and innovation within healthcare will partially help to keep or make it affordable. It will most certainly also produce new, expensive screening and treatment opportunities that cannot yet be financed for everyone. An increasing number of people who have chronic disorders and are becoming extremely old from a social perspective deserve more human attention than can be made available and affordable from public or collective funds. This goes beyond money and involves the need for breakthroughs in society in such a way that the system of caring and sharing evolves with the developments in healthcare and health in general.

Breakthrough 2: Letting prevention and self-management work—How do we create incentives and reward systems for demonstrable health benefits?

More and more frequently, people are being encouraged to undertake prevention and self-management measures to improve their own health. After all, by doing so, people can be prevented from needing healthcare again or for the first time. This is in contrast to a cure, which is only focused on "repairing what is broken" and "suppressing symptoms." It is in line with a perspective on health which takes the own perceived condition of someone as the important measure and not the objective medical condition as diagnosed by the doctor. This breaks with the traditional viewpoint in which someone is either a dependent patient or an independent consumer. It fits better with the current situation in affluent countries but also a lot of developing countries where the lifestyle related diseases are most dominantly present. With the exception of special cases, such as accidents, there are many disorders that develop slowly and from which the human body recovers slowly and this holds especially true for disorders related to prosperity and lifestyle. Blood and vascular diseases and chronic pulmonary conditions occur over the course of time. Heart conditions, diabetes, COPD, and part of cancer and Alzheimer diseases do not occur overnight. There are a number of stages before someone becomes sick. Prevention can occur in each stage to ensure someone does not become really ill. As well, the goal of "curing" someone cannot nearly always be realized if he/she simply has a disorder. If an illness changes into a chronic disorder after a treatment, the term "cure" is simply not applicable. In that case, the symptoms in particular have been treated and need to be kept under control in such a way that in the best-case scenario they are merely a bother, and in the worst-case scenario the patient does not die. In that regard, it can also be noted that the treatment itself and chronic care are very costly and that someone who is ill is often less productive for himself/herself, his/her family, and society in general. Knowing all this, you would expect that there are many successful prevention and reintegration programs where people are purely cured and the self-repairing resources of the body are fully used. Is that also the case? The answer is: unfortunately, no. In reality more—a lot more—is invested in care during and after a disorder instead of preventively. A reason for this is that sustainable lifestyle changes are difficult to realize. An important other cause of this has everything to do with business models and value creation. There is a lot of value in making someone feel better physically and mentally and preventing someone from becoming ill. At the same time, it is difficult both to demonstrate that prevention works and to earn back investments based on illnesses that have not taken place. While it can result in less medical expenses this does not mean that this is also a logical source for financing since it concerns relaxation, exercise, and healthy eating in daily life. In short, there is a real need for this breakthrough, but there are only a few functioning, broadly applied business models around. Still, they do exist! Given the importance and the potential of prevention to keep people healthy and productive and to prevent healthcare costs, it is relevant to thoroughly investigate this further.

Breakthrough 3: Patient-centered organization of information and everyday care—How should we share treatment and diagnostic information and bring primary care closer to the patient?

There is often a lot of discussion whether healthcare should be organized closer to the patient based on a personal approach or whether that should in fact be concentrated on the basis of process efficiency and/or knowledge. That is not an antithesis, but rather a paradox. Both sides of the argument are correct, but relate to a different type of care. For part of the care the proximity to the patient is the most important organizing principle and there is less of an advantage to be realized through scaling and bundling. This is the care described in this chapter. From this perspective, it is desirable to organize the care in a truly accessible manner around the patient. This relates to the integrated healthcare system and care in general around both chronic patients and close to or in their own home. The challenge here is in particular that there are many different persons treating the patient and other parties involved who have to find out from one another what is going on. That concerns different healthcare practitioners who work for instance with the patient in home care, at the doctor's practice, in the pharmacy or in the hospital. In the process, the patient is ideally in control himself/herself, has access to his/her own file, and updates his/her own health data. But that ideal is often not realized. Streamlined cooperation demands greater integration of the treatment and information surrounding the patient. Aside from the integration for people who need a lot of care, there is need for accessible healthcare of a daily household type. This relates to the more simple diagnoses, repeat prescriptions, and standard treatments. In that regard, opening times, the provision of service and speed are most important provided there is a good "squeaky wheel system," so that referrals can be made in the event of doubt.

Breakthrough 4: Deploying services and instruments to help customers take control—How can innovation and process streamlining be used to improve the lives of patients?

For many healthcare practitioners, there never really was a shortage of patients or resources. Labor productivity in the healthcare sector has not risen as quickly as in other sectors.[12] There was never really a big fight about customers or cost-efficiency. This is even truer when compared to service-oriented businesses with years of experience in cost-cutting, such as in recreation, telephony, logistics, and retail. Consequently, the provision of healthcare is not always superior when it comes to optimum services at minimum costs. There are currently a number of innovative developments on the go in the general service industry that are also visible within healthcare. These are developments that help to streamline those processes, to increase accessibility to healthcare by lowering the threshold in terms of effort and finances. In that regard, the social and technological developments that help customers take control can be reviewed. This is about self-service that enables people to function independently and at the same time keeps the healthcare system affordable. This relates to customer contact to make the entire logistical process of selecting a service provider and planning and making appointments simpler and better. It concerns the developments in technology by which the mobile telephone can serve as an instrument to pay for and insure care anytime anywhere, and eHealth can be used to retrieve information or to consult a doctor at a remote location. Finally, radical product simplifications can be reviewed by which resources and instruments can be made much cheaper and by extension much more accessible without any loss of quality.

Breakthrough 5: Implementing differentiation in specialized healthcare—How can schedulable and academic healthcare be organized best in the second and third line?

In most affluent countries that set up their healthcare infrastructure in the nineteenth century, many local hospitals were built. These could exist pretty close to each other without many differences between them. There was sufficient scale within their own care area, because there was only an internist and a surgeon needed as specialists. With technological development and specialization within hospitals, this model no longer works. Countries currently setting up a healthcare infrastructure and selecting new healthcare practitioners are opting for much more differentiation and focus. In Western countries and for existing healthcare practitioners, the challenge is to transform their infrastructure in this direction. Over the past few years hospitals have increasingly chosen in which areas they want to stand out and the role they want to play in the cooperation in networks to provide good healthcare paths to patients. The changes that this brings about have only just begun and many older hospitals still bear a strong resemblance to one another. The infrastructure is in flux, but a number of broad lines are already visible. Diagnosis centers and hos-

---

[12] See for instance: World Economic Forum and McKinsey (2013b).

pitals will remain in existence with a more regional function for acute care and less complex surgeries that are frequently performed. Schedulable treatments where economies of scale can be realized in terms of quality and/or price, will become increasingly concentrated. That applies to simple surgeries, such as laser eye procedures and hip and knee surgeries, but also to complex procedures, such as open-heart surgery. Many patients require integrated treatments which cannot be provided by a regional hospital, but which are not so complicated as to require true academic expertise. In that light, there seems to be a need for a limited number of broad-based hospitals that organize and coordinate processes efficiently and in a customer-oriented manner for patients with various disorders. Further, there is and always will be a need for a very select number of top academic institutes. This concerns in particular those areas that are truly knowledge-intensive. In terms of disorders, this can relate to complicated combinations of symptoms and disorders. In those situations a combination of expertise is ideal. It can also concern a very specific disorder that occurs seldom and is pretty much a stand-alone issue. In that case patients want to go to the expertise center specialized in this type of disorder.

For each of the five breakthroughs above, four examples have been chosen for this book. These 20 cases are all selected as a brilliant representative of a business model that in a related or even similar form occurs more often and in various countries around the world. The selection of cases for the above breakthroughs was not made on the basis of an excluding scientific analysis of the very best business models. We have included organizations that we ourselves, together with the case authors and discussion partners, think are brilliant and showed their resilience when tested. These are not the only brilliant business models around. Thankfully there are many more. In the introduction to each chapter, we include examples of comparable business models, but this is not exhaustive. The selection was not prepared as a prediction for the future but because we can learn from their past and present. There is no guarantee that all the organizations included in this publication will continue to be brilliant. Business models are not static but rather dynamic in nature and must continuously develop themselves—something that often turns out to be extra difficult when success has been achieved. Sometimes business models must be radically changed, for instance in times of crisis or when new technologies arrive.[13] What we find important is that in the described period the organization has put up truly brilliant "stories" and "numbers" that are a source of instruction and inspiration. This history will never disappear, and by defining the business model, we are helping to immortalizing it. At the same time, it is just like a film—a recording with a beginning and an end. In fact, the most brilliant business models often have a passion to make a difference and to break through systemic barriers. As a result thereof, they are able to grow extremely quickly, but also run all the more risk as well. This is precisely the dynamic that arises when stakeholders react to a successful business model that produces extra challenges for the continuity and the resolve of the organization. We return to this matter in Chap. 10.

---

[13] This is also described as the Baumol effect.

Part II
Brilliant Cases Involving Brilliant Business Models in Healthcare

Chapter 5
Breakthrough: Strengthening Mutual Caring and Sharing

How can we live together with shared responsibilities, support, and risks?
The starting point for making and keeping healthcare universally affordable, and accessible is mutual care and sharing. This concerns the readiness to pay and care for each other when this is necessary. It relates to sharing the risks and fulfilling the corresponding rights and obligations in terms of behavior and responsible use of shared scarce resources. This concerns financial means but also creating and maintaining a society in which people take care of other people who need attention, help and support. Four examples of brilliant business models who show the way are the following:

- *Algemeen Ziekenfonds Amsterdam: This concerns a general insurance fund which was initiated in 1846 by doctors who wanted to take good care of their patients for a fixed membership fee which provided themselves with a decent living as well.*
- *Dhan foundation: This is a mutual microfinance organization in India which facilitates and stimulates groups of people to take care of themselves and each other.*
- *Courtyard houses: Which go back to the moyen-âge and illustrate how groups of people with a shared background can live apart together in social communities after retirement.*
- *Liebenau Foundation: Which started a living concept in Germany where people from different generations share what they can offer in a community given their own age and abilities.*

Finding ways to keep proper care affordable and accessible is becoming increasingly difficult due to rising healthcare costs. This is placing pressure on mutual caring and sharing between people. The question how groups of people can provide and share care mutually is therefore of even greater importance. They can divide the cost of care or help one another in kind without payment.

You only realize what you are missing once it has gone. In countries where (practically) everyone has access to good care, a system of care provision and mutual

© Springer International Publishing Switzerland 2017
J. Kemperman et al. (eds.), *Brilliant Business Models in Healthcare*,
DOI 10.1007/978-3-319-26440-0_5

cost sharing via collective resources and/or healthcare insurance is perceived as perfectly normal. The historical perspective in the West and the current perspective in developing countries are sources of inspiration in this respect. They offer an insight into how mutual caring and sharing of costs and risks can be organized if this is not yet a given situation. Moreover, they clarify the role of enlightened self-interest, and how the motives of the various parties concerned can be aligned. We can use these insights to examine how we can create self-financing and self-reinforcing business models that keep healthcare widely accessible in a financial context. During the organization of this mutual caring and sharing, agreements must be made about which risks will or will not be shared between groups of people that differ in terms of income, age, health, and lifestyle, and about the conditions under which this will occur.

Mutual caring and sharing is not only about money, it is also about attitude and behavior. Formal and moral rules and responsibilities are required to maintain the system and keep it operational and affordable. The "sharing economy" in which people give what they have in abundance in exchange for matters which are scarce for themselves is renewed by social media and the Internet, but it is also as old as the civilization.[1] This includes topics such as the classic problem of "common fields." If grazing land is shared, how do you prevent every villager from allowing more and more cows to graze there, resulting in overgrazing and lower yields?[2] The risk of an individual allowing an unnecessary operation to be performed or swallowing medication just because it is free is not as great within healthcare—yet another reason why medicines should remain loathsome. There is less reticence in relation to aids, physiotherapy, and home care because these are often also pleasant. This imposes the moral duty on all parties involved to avoid abusing the system as a free rider and therefore treat healthcare sparingly as a shared scarce commodity. People also have a personal responsibility to ensure they do not fall ill, be self supportive in their recovery and look after themselves so that they stay as healthy as possible. Chapter 6 also takes a detailed look at ways to encourage and organize prevention and self-management.

Whereas mutual caring and sharing in healthcare relates primarily to sharing costs, daily living assistance more often revolves around caring for each other. Besides sharing financial risks in order to pay for care, mutual caring and sharing can therefore also be expressed in a nonmonetary form via informal care provided by family members, friends and neighbors. The daily living assistance that is provided can be more nursing in nature. It can also entail helping out with household chores or giving personal attention. This usually concerns people who care for children, people who are physically or mentally handicapped or elderly people in need of additional care. Housing for the elderly is an example of a major, topical theme with which this can be made concrete. Few people dream about ending up in a care home where they are dependent upon professional nurses. People often want to stay at home as long as they possibly can or, in any event, within an environment that

---

[1] Kemperman, Geelhoed en Hoog (2015).
[2] See for instance: Hardin (1968) and Axelrod (1984).

is as familiar to them as possible. From a social and societal perspective, it is ideal if you can grow very old independently in as healthy a manner possible with assistance from family members. This is increasingly becoming a great challenge. The cost of care and living assistance explodes the moment people leave their home, which also poses a major financial problem for society and the parties involved. The starting point is the situation in which people actually do not require professional care yet, but develop a need for communality and informal care provided by family and friends as a safety net. Due to the combination of an ageing population and technological progress, people are growing increasingly older and developing more and more chronic illnesses. The number of people with dementia is also on the rise, and this condition makes it difficult to live safely and independently.

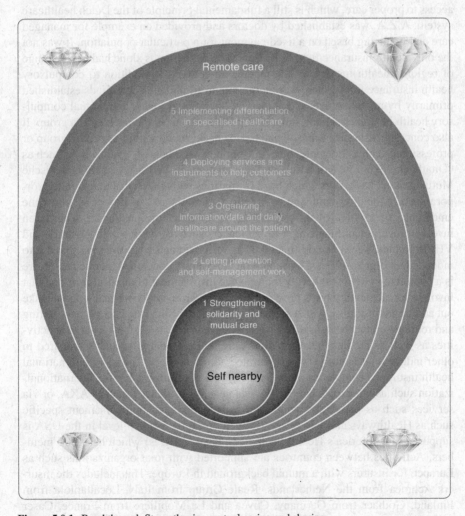

Figure 5.0.1 Breakthrough Strengthening mutual caring and sharing

Business Models Like Algemeen Ziekenfonds Amsterdam (A.Z.A.) To understand the value of mutual caring and sharing and how this can be structured, we can take a look into the past at the archetype put in place by the first healthcare insurers. This chapter examines the Algemeen Ziekenfonds Amsterdam (A.Z.A.) in the Netherlands. Via Z.A.O., Agis and Zilveren Kruis, it is a key player in the establishment of Achmea (the largest healthcare insurer in Europe and the largest general insurer in the Netherlands) as it exists today. A.Z.A. has been selected for several reasons. It was founded in 1946 and became operational in 1847 at a time when ordinary working people had no access to adequate healthcare. Consequently, it truly did make a difference in peoples' lives. A.Z.A. was the greatest example for subsequent health insurance funds that insured Dutch citizens below a fixed income threshold. The aim of these funds was to provide everyone in the Netherlands with access to proper care, which is still a fundamental principle of the Dutch healthcare system. A.Z.A. was established by doctors and provided an example for managed care and financing based on a fixed payment for a particular population. It was not the only health insurance fund of its time. The Netherlands alone had a wide range of regional health insurers in the nineteenth century. In addition to compulsory health insurance funds, there were more nonprofit philanthropic funds established primarily by notable citizens, commercial operational funds, and mutual compulsory health insurance schemes in which people organized themselves as a group. It also concerns insurance funds which have a background within a specific group or professional such as the mutualities in Belgium. Members of organizations such as "Onafhankelijke Ziekenfondsen and the Nationaal Verbond van Socialistische Mutualiteiten" have roots which have similarities with Dutch health insurance corporations. In the nineteenth and twentieth century, the rest of Europe also saw the emergence of a range of different systems for financing healthcare. This often involves government financing. Market leaders such as Medibank in Australia and VHI in Ireland were once originated by government and later on transformed into independent organizations. Depending on the country concerned, public healthcare is a complete system that hardly requires the involvement of an insurer or one that involves an elementary basis provided by the government where many people take out additional insurance with a private health insurer. Since the background, setting and reimbursement systems differ widely between countries, most insurance activities as well as the healthcare providers are still national in nature. Compared to other industries it is not very concentrated across borders. The more international health insurance companies often have found a specific strategy for internationalization such as via expats like BUPA, via general insurances such as AXA, or via services such as prevention which are less country and reimbursement specific such as Healthways and Discovery. Cooperation on a national level in the USA is supported by America's Health Insurance Plan's (AHIP's) which has 1300 members. Activities between countries are supported with joint organizations such as Eurapco for insurers with a mutual background in Europe. This includes the insurers Achmea from the Netherlands, Reale Group from Italy, Localtapiola from Finland, Gothaer from Germany, Covea and La Mobilière from France, Caser from Spain, and Länsförsäkringar from Sweden. The leading international platform for cooperation in health insurances is the International Federation of Health Plans (IFHP) with members such as AXA, Medibank, BUPA, VHI, Discovery, Helsana, Sanitas, Blue Cross & Blue Shield, Kaiser Permanente, AHIP, UPMC and Achmea. The current Dutch system like in most countries has its very own characteristics. It operates via health insurers but is also highly regulated at the same time. It uses market dynamics while controlling the downsides by mandatory enrollment, laws against selection and pooling of risks of the people with higher expected health costs via an equalization fund. It is relatively unique in an international context and the history of A.Z.A. plays a key role in this.

Business Models Like DHAN The search for ways to foster mutual caring and sharing risks is still relevant today. Microfinancing and insurance in developing countries are the contemporary version of the health insurers established in the West in the nineteenth and twentieth century. Faced with similar challenges, they offer solutions that are essentially very similar to those of the first insurers in the West. These solutions fully take into account the own culture, traditions, and problems in developing countries. Mutual health insurance is often the Holy Grail at the end of the journey: it is difficult to obtain and requires other matters to be taken care of first. This frequently involves sharing damage-related risks such as fire, flooding, and crop failure. It often only arises after people have acquired possessions to lose and protect. Money is usually spread over time in the period before people start to insure themselves: borrow now what you will repay later or save money now that you want to spend later. The cornerstone is the community, the mutual group itself. Microfinancing and insurance are often combined with collective activities, such as the joint purchasing of seeds or equipment, or sharing information about the weather, prices, or organizing community healthcare. DHAN in India is an example that we have selected here. This foundation also extends beyond (care) insurance. It is also about lending money to one another and joint activities such as water management and hospital construction. DHAN is an impressive example of an organizational model which realized a large size while keeping the human dimension in sight. It has developed into an organization with over one million members and still has only a very small central organization. The members are primarily groups that multiply organically on the basis of shared values relating to self-employment and rules pertaining to the organizational setup. The number of micro-bankers and insurers in general has increased significantly over the past few decades. The most famous initiator with a Nobel Prize-winning business model is Grameen Bank in Bangladesh. Another renowned leader from the 1980s is Bank Rakyat in Indonesia, which has become a stock exchange-listed company. Both Grameen Bank and Bank Rakyat developed into organizations with more than a million members even though they still had a manual administrative system. Examples of other micro-insurers and in particular micro bankers are Banco Solidario in Ecuador, Equity Bank in Kenya, SKS and SEWA Bank in India, BRAC in Bangladesh, and Compartamos and Fin Comun in Mexico. These successful examples have prompted other commercial financial institutions to venture into this market. They often do so out of social responsibility, but also due to a business perspective geared to creating market share and expanding it in the future. Examples include Credifé, part of Banco Pinchincha from Ecuador, Banco SOL in Bolivia, Sagebank in Haiti, ICICI Bank in India, Banco Bradesco and Banco Real in Brazil, and Banco Caja Social from Colombia. Micro-bankers and insurers have also emerged from other sectors. The starting point often is to lend money to people so that they can buy the supplied product. Banco Aztecan in Mexico does this for electronics and household equipment and CEMEX does likewise for construction material. SELCO in India lends money for the acquisition of solar panels.[3] Mobile telephony providers such as G-Cash constitute a fascinating, rapidly emerging group within financial services in developing countries. Section 8.3 takes a closer look at the M-PESA case which shows what instruments this can provide to enlarge access to healthcare.[4]

Business Models Like Courtyard Houses In the quest for new forms and formulas enabling people to live at home for as long as they can and in as healthy a manner as possible, one can look—in addition to professional care homes—at mutual solutions that have been implemented within society according to a small scale approach. As is the case with healthcare insurance, this search can be initiated by drawing inspiration from the past. Centuries ago in the Netherlands, for example, a surprisingly simple combination was conceived whereby accommodation, care and pensions were provided via courtyard houses. These were structured according to a small scale approach within the own group and established by means of a bequest. A one-off payment entitled elderly people to live in a courtyard house until their death. The additional alms they received took the form of a weekly supply of food and drink. A combination was therefore found between private altruism and personal contributions and responsibility that has continued for centuries. This case examines the establishment of these courtyard houses, of which there were hundreds. The majority of the courtyard houses were originated by private individuals and usually contain 12 to 15 small appartments. There were also larger courtyards houses. The majority of these originated from guest houses, leper houses, plague houses and lunatic asylums, which existed in most European countries from the middle ages on. If we examine the versions of courtyard houses in existence today, we can look at the very same ones. Most of them are still in use, occupied partly by senior citizens on the basis of a similar formula, but usually with a regular monthly rent. They are often inhabited by students since senior citizens desire greater comfort and privacy nowadays. Luxury residential care homes, are becoming more popular. These target wealthy senior citizens who want to swap their large, high-maintenance private homes for a flat that offers living assistance facilities and comfort. Remarkably, realizing this independently as a group of

---

[3] For more background information and examples, see for instance: Collins, Morduch, Rutherford, and Ruthven (2009), Rhyne (2009), and Preker, Lindner, Chernichovsky, and Schellekens (2013). The cases of Rakyat, SKS, Grameen and G-Cash are also included in Kemperman, Geelhoed en Hoog (2015).

[4] For more background information and examples, see for instance: Collins, Morduch, Rutherford, and Ruthven (2009), Rhyne (2009), and Preker, Lindner, Chernichovsky, and Schellekens (2013).

seniors appears to to be a difficult task and promising ideas often do not come to fruition.

Business Models Like Stiftung Liebenau We also see examples nowadays of local communities that have organized mutual care completely differently, in which living assistance is integrated perfectly naturally within the day-to-day lives of a group of people with strong ties. The German foundation Stiftung Liebenau is an inspirational, modern-day example of such an approach, in addition to the Dutch historical courtyard houses. This foundation provides residential communities where the very elderly can live together with people who have just retired as well as families with children. The concept works since these groups participate in the community in accordance with their individual abilities and needs. Liebenau is additionally unique thanks to the creation of a formula that can be reproduced quickly. The foundation approaches a municipality and asks it to assist with the acquisition of a specific plot of land intended for the establishment of the new residential community. Once the project has been completed, the building and the guaranteed rental agreements are sold to investors and the money can then be reinvested in the following residential community. This allows the capital to be reused again while investors enjoy a solid and safe return on their investment. The communities created in this manner can best be compared to a small neighborhood, a street or a large building where people have strong social ties and are ready to help each other. Unusually normal, in other words. It is therefore also similar to a wide range of social residential solutions. As a business model, it is comparable with capital providers and real estate developers who truly engage in vertical integration. They do not merely construct a building, but are also intensively involved in its purpose and utilization. This is very common in modern large infrastructural projects. This sort of social-design and programming is used less in the construction of affordable homes with living-assistance facilities for senior citizens, especially if this involves nonfinancial solutions supported via new forms of financing. This truly is a challenge as a senior if you need to take the specific situation into account. Often (some) pension money and savings and occasionally some equity in an existing house exist, but you are not sure how much time you still have left to live and the full extent of the living assistance that you will require. Additionally you can not purchase care or living assistance using the bricks of your existing home. A inspirational example with another perspective is provided by Argoz, a land developer that moved into finance in El Salvador. Argoz purchases plots of land, builds roads and facilities upon these and also constructs homes especially for low-income groups. These people can also obtain loans to finance their new homes if required. The company offers new residents a way out of the slums, an opportunity that never existed before. At the same time, it is a highly cost-effective approach for Argoz.[5] It is therefore not only valuable but also scalable for all parties concerned, just like Stiftung Liebenau.

---

[5] Rhyne (2009).

5.1   Algemeen Ziekenfonds Amsterdam (A.Z.A.)

"Doctors for the little man"

Wim Niesing & Jeroen Kemperman @: Jeroen.Kemperman@achmea.nl, Phone: 0031 651222099

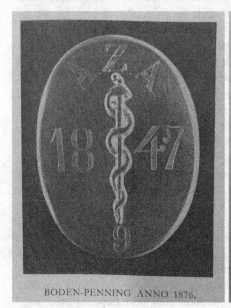

BODEN-PENNING ANNO 1876.

Prelude[6] *The Dutch Minister of Home Affairs requests in a letter from 24 August 1842 that the Provincial Committee for Medical Control and Prevention in the province of Noord-Holland notify him about "the objections raised about illness funds and to provide him with measures that could yield improvements."*[7] *The local Committee in Amsterdam subsequently publishes a report in December 1842 detailing the situation in the Netherlands concerning these small private insurance funds for illness.*

The Committee's conclusion is as follows: "We are therefore of the opinion that, if illness funds cannot be kept out altogether, their number should be decreased, as should the number of members, to the extent that not too much care be placed in the hands of a single practitioner, or to avoid the appointment of more than one practitioner from the circle of associated members; that a practitioner should not be allowed to accept a larger number of patients than he can care for properly; that

---

[6] This article is largely based on Leclerq (1947) and passages from that research have been incorporated into the article (adapted or not). A number of literal quotations have been given an endnote in the text.

[7] Leclerq (1947), p. 16.

henceforth no new illness fund may be founded before authorization has been granted following a thorough investigation by the proper authorities whereby the number of members has been established as well; and that—in order to rule out any abuse—financial management should be placed under the supervision of a notary public or another authoritative type of surveillance; and, if it were possible to achieve this, that only the representatives from what we usually call the lower classes of society are admitted to the illness fund, with the exclusion of those who can rely on their financial resources to ensure proper medical care. As a result of all of this, which is crucial, the number of illness funds members could be suitably reduced while in addition—which is equally important—the medical profession (with too many practitioners owing to the multiplication and extension of illness funds) would regain its traditional esteem and, moreover, an associated benefit would be that abuse, so rife in pharmacy, would be eliminated rather effectively as well."[8]

The report is filed and the Dutch Minister of Home Affairs leaves matters as they are. This does not suffice though for some doctors and surgeons in Amsterdam, who want to create an alternative for the small illness funds. On 24 October 1846, in the Oude Wapen van Amsterdam, a building situated on the corner of Kloveniersburgwal and Rusland, they therefore decide to establish the Algemeen Ziekenfonds van Amsterdam. These doctors introduce principles such as the welfare threshold and the freedom to choose a doctor (among the many doctors exclusively affiliated to A.Z.A.). A.Z.A. provides the cornerstone for the health-insurance system that followed later and that lies at the heart of Achmea's current health-insurance activities. Achmea is now the largest health insurer in Europe in terms of premiums and, partly thanks to its strong position within healthcare, the fifth largest insurer in Europe for non-life including health, and the market leader for insurance in the Netherlands.[9]

Introduction The French Revolution at the end of the eighteenth century gave people many things: freedom, equality and fraternity to be precise. The Netherlands was also "liberated" by the French in 1795. However, the rigid organization of professions within guilds in the Netherlands at that time is entirely contrary to the concept of "freedom" embodied by the French Revolution. If terms and conditions must be complied with before a person may exercise a particular occupation, this is not exactly indicative of freedom. The Constitution of 1798, which is the Netherlands' first, therefore also abolishes all guilds, including guild funds. Members deposited fixed sums of money into these guild-administered funds periodically. In the event of illness, they were used to offset any loss of income and cover the costs of medical assistance later on. This mutual care for one another in accordance with strict rules observed by people with a similar craft, including prohibitions and penalties, dissappeares when guilds are abolished. A replacement is not forthcoming. The working population is therefore left to its fate and has to endure poor conditions. The lower and lower middle class have no access to medical care. What happens next?

---

[8] Idem.

[9] Duffhues (ed.), Korsten and Vonk (2011), p. 67.

Entrepreneurs jump in to fill this gap and continue on a commercial basis, and new guild funds are established. People try to make arrangements amongst themselves. But it is all too small-scale to really bear the associated risks, completely dependent on a single (commercial) administrator, and riddled with mismanagement. The power wield by the administrator meant that medical care is often of insufficient quality due to the excessive burden and underpayment endured by healthcare practitioners. Doctors and pharmacists in Amsterdam can no longer bear to witness the lack of proper healthcare. What can they do about this?

On 15 March 1846, the home of Dr. M. Busch Geertsema hosts a meeting attended by doctors and surgeons with no affiliation to the sickness funds. They come together to discuss a proposal on "the creation of a general health-insurance fund from the corps of doctors themselves." The founders deem this necessary in the interest of doctors as well people in need of care in order to combat misuse, lack of care and the degradation of the medical profession. The health insurance fund will involve "participants" (the doctors) and "members" (the insured). A draft regulation and an explanatory memorandum are drawn up to attract doctors and pharmacists to this initiative. The response is very positive and over 80 doctors indicate in writing that they are willing to participate. A similar number provide a verbal commitment to this end. And so on 24 October 1846, the decision is taken to establish the *Algemeen Ziekenfonds te Amsterdam* (A.Z.A.). On 1 December, the General Board was chosen from among the participants, heralding the first time in The Netherlands that a health insurance fund is managed by doctors. It is a precursor to integrated managed care, with the insurer and healthcare practitioners working together as a single organization as is internationally visible in various countries. Doctors seize the opportunity to turn criticism into action and prove that it really can be done better. The health insurance fund becomes operational on 1 April 1847 and members are now able to register. Just a few months after its establishment, A.Z.A. is already the second largest health insurance fund in Amsterdam.

As is customary in managed care, doctors provide the treatment they deem to be medically necessary without any further limitations. This is substantially more than what existing illness funds are offering. Of course this appeals completely to people who are unhealthy and very care-dependent. That much appeal was extremely dangerous. The fledgling health insurance fund immediately suffers a substantial financial deficit and has to take drastic survival measures in its first year. To ensure A.Z.A. remains financially sound, the premium is increased, members are asked to pay an additional contribution and new participants are charged an admission fee. Measures are also taken to limit the prescription of treatments, lower medicine prices and reduce doctors' fees. Even more startling, participating doctors are asked to help tackle the deficit by making a voluntary deposit. However, a form of profit sharing for doctors is introduced so that they can also benefit when things go well in the future. The roller-coaster ride continues. All the measures implemented to deal with the deficit make A.Z.A. much less appealing to the insured, and 40 % of its members leave at the start of the second year. These drastic measures are justified, however. Financial results improve and grow steadily, along with membership, after the second year.

Table 5.1 Financial results A.Z.A. 1847–1852

Period	Balance	Members
1-4-1847 to 1-4-1848	Deficit USD 6363 (EUR 5408)	9205
01/04/1848 to 01/04/1849	Deficit USD 1451 (EUR 1233)	5712
1-4-1849 to 31-12-1849	Positive balance USD 669 (EUR 569)	6132
1850	Positive balance USD 2181 (EUR 1853)	6907
1851	Positive balance USD 3403 (EUR 2892)	8959
1852	Positive balance USD 2411 (EUR 2049)	11,644

The difficult start-up phase imediately provides doctors and "their" members with important lessons and experience. Even when losses are made, members receive the care promised to them. Doctors prove they are willing to make personal sacrifices when the situation becomes tense and require the adoption of such measures. This fosters mutual trust in the healthcare fund and shows that members' and participants' interests are equally represented by the General Board.

5.1.1 The Cornerstone: "The Little Man and the Doctor"

Let us return to the situation that existed prior to the establishment of the healthcare fund. At that moment poor relief is provided to people who have the least money. Wealthy citizens are in the position to pay for the care they desire out of their own pockets. Highly expensive specialist treatments do not exist yet. Very few arrangements are in place for the working class and if something has been organized with an illness fund, it can be nullified due to mismanagement by the administrators. "Insuring the little man (the lower and lower middle classes) with medical assistance" forms the essence of the creation of A.Z.A. It is not only about offering insurance, but also about ensuring that good medical care is provided at all times.

The higher goal of A.Z.A is to "Insure the interests of the less fortunate class in times of illness in the most effective way."[10] Members have to be able to rely on their health insurance. Doctors establish A.Z.A. to combat the misuse of the existing smaller illness funds by their administrators. Administrators want priority treatment for themselves and their dependents, and decide who is and is not entitled to join an illness fund. In addition, doctors believe that these individuals are trying to benefit financially from the illness fund. Many administrators own a pub or wine house and like organizing illness fund meetings within their own establishments, where members spent their hard-earned money on drinks. Members of A.Z.A. board do not receive any remuneration in order to avoid conflicts of the interest. In addition to the medical board, a supervisory board comprising prominent citizens of Amsterdam is

---

[10] Leclerq (1947), p. 142.

tasked with managing the fund's finances independently. During the establishment of the fund, wealthy citizens are asked to assist with the creation of a reserve fund, which they duly do. Amsterdam is therefore closely connected to A.Z.A., which inspires profound trust among all concerned.

A.Z.A. promises to "Provide medical assistance that is as comprehensive as possible to the little man for a moderate weekly contribution, and ensure that those providing this assistance are properly remunerated."[11] In addition to members, it is therefore also about the own interests of participating doctors. The interests of both groups has to be represented and remain in harmony. Both groups have to be willing to compromise when circumstances require them to do so. But upon the establishment of the health insurance fund, it is stated during the participants' meeting held on 30 June 1848, when financial deficits emerge, that "the first knocks would have to be weathered not by members but by participating doctors."[12] This also stems from the birth certificate of A.Z.A., which features an audacious goal for the new health insurance fund: "What needs to be done to vigorously combat increasing pauperism and support the needy."[13] Solidarity between doctors and members as well as within each of the groups plays a pivotal role in the establishment of A.Z.A. This means that all resources and care have to be handled frugally. There is no room for wastage, in any form whatsoever. Participants and members alike have to be able to rely on A.Z.A. all the time, and this reliability inspire the trust of both participants and members. All of this require the professionalism of participating doctors, but also provides the scope to do so. This addresses a major reason behind the establishment of A.Z.A.; participants want to provide members with professional care and avoid being exploited by the administrator(s) of an illness fund.

A.Z.A. is unique in relation to the other sickness funds in that members are free to choose the doctor they want. They can therefore personally choose the A.Z.A.-affiliated doctor they desire. These affiliated doctors can independently decide which treatment to provide and are financially independent from individual patients. As a result, the quality of care A.Z.A. offered is higher than that of other illness funds. Doctors also have more time to devote to members because the number of members per doctor is limited. A.Z.A. additionally demonstrates that it practises what it preaches since the supervisory board reduced the fees of participating doctors when the organization experienced financial deficits. The extremely rapid growth in members and participants reveal that members and participants truly view A.Z.A. as a reliable insurer that defends the interests of the little man. This is not temporary either, given that A.Z.A. is still around today. It no longer exists independently, but first became Z.A.O. via a merger and then Agis and then, via another merger, part of Achmea.

---

[11] Idem, p. 29.
[12] Idem, p. 20.
[13] Idem. 18.

Brand essence: healthcare insurance for the working class

Higher goal
- Safeguard the interests of the working class when they are ill

Brand roots
- Founded by doctors to stop abuse of the insurance via small illness funds and provide proper healthcare funding

Audacious goal
- Effectively fight increasing pauperism and support the needy efficiently with good affordable healthcare

Brand promise
- Offer the working class healthcare that is as complete as possible for a modest contribution that provides a reasonable income for doctors and pharmacists

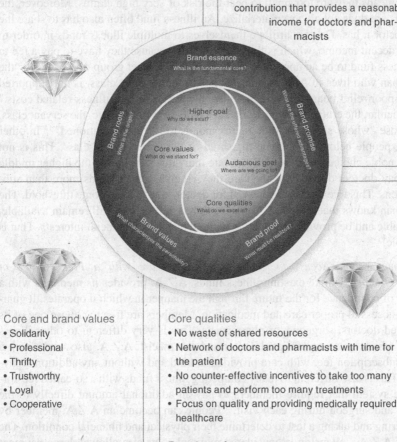

Core and brand values
- Solidarity
- Professional
- Thrifty
- Trustworthy
- Loyal
- Cooperative

Core qualities
- No waste of shared resources
- Network of doctors and pharmacists with time for the patient
- No counter-effective incentives to take too many patients and perform too many treatments
- Focus on quality and providing medically required healthcare

Brand proof
- Fees of the participating doctors and pharmacists reduced in times of budget shortages
- Contributions (temporarily) reduced for members in times that they could not pay due to crisis, strikes or unemployment

Figure 5.1.1 Vision and Positioning of A.Z.A.

5.1.2   The Business Model: Solidarity-Based Exclusivity

Market Segments: Market Leader in Amsterdam with Doctors at the Helm From its third year onwards, A.Z.A. grows rapidly and quickly becomes the largest illness fund in Amsterdam. The services offered to its members are considerably better than those of its competitors, thanks to its deeply rooted and solid position within the corps of doctors in Amsterdam, which appeal to people. This position is very different to that of the competition, which is more fragmented. In 1842, Amsterdam has 71 illness funds with 52,771 members. Medical care is entrusted to 33 doctors and surgeons. Membership of the illness funds ranges from 30 to 900 insured, which means they are too small to bear the risk of very high claims. Moreover, the agreed care does not always materialize. An illness fund often also has to share the one doctor it has. Doctors affiliate themselves to multiple illness funds in order to earn a decent income, which is limited primarily because they have to pay a fee to the illness fund to be an appointed fund doctor. The target group of A.Z.A. is: "the little man who lives in Amsterdam, belongs to the working class, is not supported by the poor relief board and does not have the means to bear illness-related costs." In particular, the craftsman who works on a daily or weekly wage, the servant class, and those "whose social condition corresponds to the aforementioned."[14] In other words, people below the income threshold of the lower middle class. This is not only a noble choice. More wealthy private individuals including the higher middle class pay doctors directly for the care they receive, which yields more than sub-scriptions. This free market is reserved for doctors due to the income threshold. The little man knows that with A.Z.A. he is assured of care that will remain available, affordable and be provided by doctors without any direct financial interests. That is valuable!

Customer Value: Access to Good, Affordable Care with a Free Choice of A.Z.A. Doctors Unlike existing illness funds, A.Z.A. provides its members with a source of confidence for the future through the manner in which it operates. It guar-antees access to proper care and medication. Members are free to choose one of its affiliated doctors, surgeons, or pharmacists. This is very different to other illness funds, which have one affiliated doctor and pharmacist. A.Z.A. also works with a fixed subscription fee, with care provided in kind and without any additional pay-ment. This is also different to many competing illness funds with a so-called fee-for-service system that require members to pay an additional amount directly to the doctor and surgeon during each visit.[15] People can become an A.Z.A. member by registering and taking a test to determine their physical and financial condition. The risk of A.Z.A. collapsing is considered minimal as its size allowed large payment peaks to be accommodated without any problems. That is reinforced via the finan-cial management of the supervisory board, which reduces fees in times of shortages. The risk that members will receive poor care quality is low since doctors are jointly

---

[14] Idem. 30.
[15] Duffhues (ed.), Korsten and Vonk (2011), p. 62.

responsible for the quality standard. For members, there is also the value of a temporary contribution reduction if they temporarily have no money to pay the full contribution.

A special added value that participants offer customers are the ex gratia payments financed from the *rijksdaalder* fund, which is fed with admission fees from participants and fines imposed on those who arrive at board meetings too late or fail to turn up. Participants' solidarity with members is far-reaching.

Delivery: "A.Z.A. Must Shine Gently Thanks to Its Virtues" A.Z.A. pursues a conservative policy in relation to its members, which can be characterized as very robust and fatherly. The organization experiences rapid and organic growth upon its establishment, but does not focus solely on expanding its membership. Positioning and branding itself has never been one of A.Z.A.'s strongest points. The board discusses the pros and cons of "propaganda" at length, but that also speaks volumes about the organization's ambivalent attitude. As advertising by doctors is considered inappropriate, advertising by a health insurance fund administrated by doctors is viewed in a similar light. However, "propaganda books" are produced regularly that focus the public's attention on the benefits offered by the organization in an "appropriate manner." In 1882, advertisements are placed in (weekly) newspapers. In 1894, a wall calendar is handed out to members (and continued to be distributed until 1942). In 1883, bills and posters are placed in gatehouses, in 1898 at public soup kitchens, public baths, coffee houses, and establishments near the population register, in 1899 at stations, in 1903 at the homes of collectors, shops, and factories, and in 1910 on steam ferries.[16] In 1910 advertisements start being printed on the back of tram tickets. Some board members think things are going too far when banknotes are also proposed: "Advertising may not degenerate into the shouting of a market seller. The purpose is not to deprive members of other funds, but rather to proclaim all the good provided by A.Z.A. It is not impossible that conferences in the trams about health insurance funds will have the opposite effect that was envisaged. A.Z.A. must shine gently thanks to its virtues and avoid imposing itself."[17]

The most important contact with members is established directly via a doctor. In addition, health insurance collectors visit members to collect their weekly contribution. A committee assess whether new members belong to the working class or were equivalent on the basis of their income, and therefore whether they fall below the income threshold. Another committee is also charged with verifying the health of new members. A.Z.A. has favorable conditions for accepting people with chronic illnesses. Those with a lingering illness can be accepted, subject to a higher contribution if necessary. Members can submit requests and objections both orally and in writing. Initially, new members have to appear before the committee in person for a physical and financial assessment. Direct consultation and contact with

---

[16] Leclerq (1947), p. 39.
[17] Idem. 39.

administrators is minimal. In addition to normal care provided by an institution, A.Z.A. offers several additional services such as prevention by offering free inoculations against infectious diseases like chickenpox.

Operation: Care in Kind with Exclusivity All doctors, surgeons and pharmacists can participate. An important restriction is that participating doctors and pharmacists can not promote the existence of other illness funds in any way. A.Z.A. itself has no direct contact with other illness funds and also demands exclusivity from its participants (the doctors). During the first few decades this concerns funds other than those to which they were already affiliated. In 1880 all cooperation with other illness funds is prohibited. Doctors can then perform their day-to-day work independently and personally decide which treatment they wish to provide. However, instructions about treatment are issued, prescribing behavior is evaluated, and everything is done to limit administrative costs. The financial remuneration of participating doctors is organized in a way that helps eliminate incorrect financial incentives but also simplifies administration. An essential element of A.Z.A. is to avoid the development of a financial relationship between participating doctors and insured members. The remuneration is independent of performance or the number of treatments. The fee for participants compromises the subscription money for each registered member. Doctors therefore have very little administration to take care of. The history of A.Z.A. states the following in this regard: "Doctors are simply not administrators, nor should they become that. Their task is to cure sick people, not to fill in forms. Every system that burdens a doctor with administrative work is based on an incorrect division of labor and therefore wrong."[18] The supervisory board detemines and revises the remuneration of each doctor, if required. The fee is in fact the closing entry of the budget. A type of profit-sharing scheme also exists: any positive result from the health insurance fund is divided among participants according to a predetermined ratio (3/9 for doctors, 2/9 for surgeons, and 3/9 for pharmacists) and the reserve fund (1/9). However, a limit is imposed on the size of the reserve fund for each member. This means that careful prescribing behavior among participants and treatments on an overarching level also offers all participants a financial advantage. Such an approach also helps ensure meticulous financial management in that all commitments to members are fulfilled first.

In addition to participating doctors who work exclusively for A.Z.A., honorary participants (professors, and doctors and pharmacists with a large private practice and an established name) are also affiliated to the organization and work for free. Up until 1915, specialists assist A.Z.A. members free of charge (in the interest of science) and are therefore also honorary members. They receive "fire and light" at no cost and a subsidy for the purchase of their instruments. After 1915, specialists also receive a fee for each member, which is to the detriment of the fees of other participants. Agreements are made with other healthcare practitioners such as male and female midwives, dentists, suppliers of trusses and leeches, and enema providers. Detailed instructions are also drawn up for them.

---

[18] Idem. 57.

Value for customers

Result *What do I get?*
- Guaranteed access to good healthcare

Process *How do I get it?*
- Delivery by all the doctors and pharmacists of A.Z.A. from whom I can choose

Emotion *What do I feel?*
- Safe, secure and certain

Price *What are the costs?*
- Pay with weekly subscription fee without additional costs for treatment

Effort *What do I have to do for it?*
- Register and pass the test on physical health and financial situation

Risk *What are the uncertainties?*
- Fewer risks than smaller insurance fund competitors and safety net via reduced fees and contributions

Market segments

Position
- The largest health insurer in Amsterdam which is the case practically ever since its launch. Position based on the network of doctors and pharmacists in Amsterdam

Competition
- In 1842 in Amsterdam there are 52,771 members of 71 commercial health insurance funds (sizes ranged from 30 to 900) serviced by 33 health practitioners. These are small funds that can not bear major risks and mostly employ doctors only on a part-time basis

Target group
- The working-class citizens of Amsterdam. This concerns the people with lower middle incomes who do not qualify to receive government assistance but do not have enough money to bear the costs of healthcare out of their own pocket

Customer insights
- It is very valuable to be assured of healthcare which is available, affordable and provided by professional doctors who do not have any financial interest in treatments

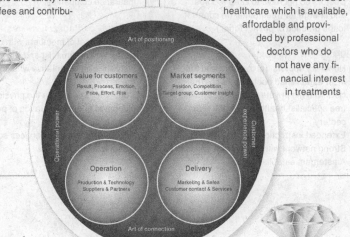

Figure 5.1.2 Value for customers and Market segments of A.Z.A.

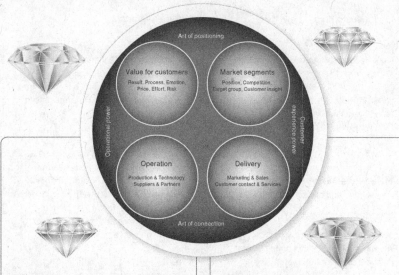

Operation

Production & Technology

- All doctors and pharmacists can participate provided they work exclusively for A.Z.A.
- Participating doctors get a fixed fee per member which they levie (subscription basis)
- Doctors do not have to keep records and charge for treatments (in contrast to the practice of private funds)

Suppliers & Partners

- Honorary doctors (professors and the most established doctors and pharmacists with big private practices) provide free specialist healthcare in the 19th century
- Extended instructions for suppliers
- Strong network with city council and in Amsterdam establishment

Delivery

Marketing & Sales

- Conservative policy towards members; more stable and paternal than focused on attracting new clients
- Ambivalent approach towards advertising. Aimed to explain what A.Z.A. did and not lure people away from other insurance companies

Customer contact & Services

- Direct contact of members with own doctor and pharmacist and with the insurance representative who collect the fees
- Committees to assess the physical condition and financial situation of potential members
- Additional preventive services such as immunizations

Figure 5.1.3 Operation and Delivery of A.Z.A.

5.1.3 The Result: "The Little Man, the Doctor and the City Taken Care of"

The confidence in the future provided to members is also paid out in the value offered by these members. It translates into faith and an increase in the number of members, and a greater loyalty towards A.Z.A.

The future with A.Z.A. is also considerably sunnier compared with existing illness funds for doctors. A reasonable existence was guaranteed, with a good fixed fee and the opportunity to share additional profits. Doctors and pharmacists affiliated to A.Z.A. can practice their profession independently and enjoy a large degree of freedom. They do not have to worry about being overloaded thanks to the maximum number of patients. Participating doctors merely have to worry about their patients' health. The fact that they are not required to keep records reinforces this and made their work even more appealing.

A.Z.A. does not have any regular shareholders. Due to the profit-sharing structure, for example, doctors themselves are actually the owners for the most part. In addition, participating doctors have a seat on the medical board while prominent citizens of Amsterdam are on the supervisory board. Both boards are not paid and the results that participants receive takes the form of respect and a contribution to society. The medical board can improve care and the medical rank in Amsterdam. The supervisory board is able to ensure care remains accessible by keeping the illness fund in good financial health.

The situation in Europe and especially in The Netherlands and Amsterdam in the first half of the in the nineteenth century in terms of wealth distribution, poverty and social issues bares many similarities with poorer developing countries nowadays. The value of A.Z.A. in such a society is encapsulated in the preceding sentence. It fulfills the need created by illness and its consequences for the large group of the working class. This group is not supported by the poor relief board and can not bear healthcare costs itself. The organization guarantees the health of the large middle group of Amsterdam's population. Besides offering regular care, it also prevents the spread of infectious diseases by administering free vaccinations. A.Z.A. also focuses specifically on providing care to people suffering from chronic illnesses who are not covered by other illness funds. In this way, it can ensure better health for a large section of Amsterdam's population.

It is not the first and only health insurance fund to be established in the mid-nineteenth century in the Netherlands. The approach and principles used by A.Z.A. serve most clearly as the example in the creation of numerous sickness funds across the Netherlands. Links exist, for example, with the establishment of the *Nutsziekenfonds* in The Hague in 1848, and with the *Afdeelings Ziekenfonds Rotterdam* founded in 1858 (which is now also part of Achmea via *Zilveren Kruis*). The government asks the A.Z.A. board for advice on several occasions. It also received frequent requests to provide information and advice throughout the Netherlands, the former colony of the Dutch East Indies and internationally.

Value by customers
- Rapid growth in the number of members in a short period of time to become the largest health insurer in Amsterdam
- Large degree of loyalty among members

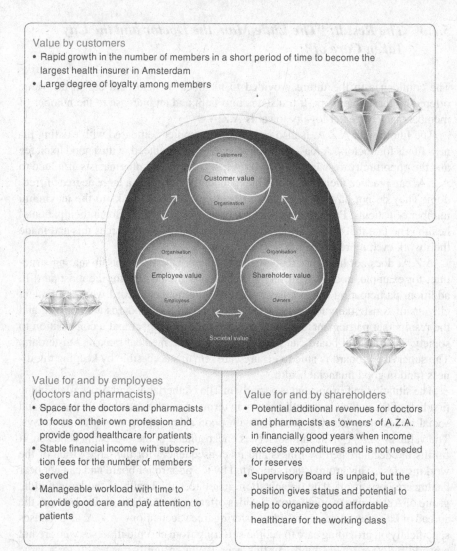

Value for and by employees
(doctors and pharmacists)
- Space for the doctors and pharmacists to focus on their own profession and provide good healthcare for patients
- Stable financial income with subscription fees for the number of members served
- Manageable workload with time to provide good care and pay attention to patients

Value for and by shareholders
- Potential additional revenues for doctors and pharmacists as 'owners' of A.Z.A. in financially good years when income exceeds expenditures and is not needed for reserves
- Supervisory Board is unpaid, but the position gives status and potential to help to organize good affordable healthcare for the working class

Value for and by society
- Meets the need for healthcare for working-class citizens with lower middle incomes who do not receive government assistance and can not pay healthcare costs out of their own pocket
- Guiding role in the Netherlands as best practices for the other healthcare funds and later the public healthcare system
- Advises governments, officials and professionals on city, national and international levels on the organization of integrated healthcare insurance systems

Figure 5.1.4 Value for and by stakeholders of A.Z.A.

5.1.4   The Brilliant Lessons of A.Z.A.

Someone has always lived in your future… What can we learn from A.Z.A. in the perspective of our era? The business model of A.Z.A. had its greatest innovative strength during the time of its establishment, the impact of which is still visible today. It brought major benefits for the development of the doctor and pharmacist ranks and the health of Amsterdam's population. The example it provided was followed elsewhere in the Netherlands and laid the cornerstone for the subsequent health insurance system untill 2006. Its principal elements are still apparent in the current basic health insurance system that everyone in the Netherlands can rely on nowadays to receive the best available care.

The level of care provided in 1846 was inadequate or unaffordable for most of the population, which in turn had a negative impact on society. It was everyone for himself. An initiative such as A.Z.A. succeeded in realigning the interests of citizens, patients, and caregivers on the basis of mutual caring and sharing. Principles, responsibilities, and remuneration mechanisms were used, and clear to everyone concerned. The challenge to ensure more shared interests is topical again at this moment. This is the case in developing countries, where it is currently being set up for the twenty-first century. However, this also applies to prosperous countries where existing systems must renew and innovate themselves again. That is where we must halt the spiral of rising healthcare costs, increasing contributions, restrictions on health insurance cover where there is a medical need and dwindling confidence in whether the agreed care can be provided. Assuming joint responsibility for care and healthcare costs is the only way to achieve this. If this fails to happen, only the wealthy will have access to high-quality care, and the "little man" will be back to where he started.

Important inspirational lessons provided by A.Z.A. include:

- A common higher goal to overcome social "injustice" for the insured and health-care providers at the same time can be a powerful source of inspiration and an incentive to break through an existing system. The challenge is to recognize everyone's own interests without opposing them, and bring these into line.
- Constructions such as fixed population payments and separation of the direct relationship between decisions taken by doctors regarding treatment and financial remuneration may result in cost-efficient measures, proper patient care, intrinsic professional motivation for the healthcare practitioner, and reduced administrative costs.
- A shared responsibility and objective of a group of healthcare practitioners with an insurer to offer good, affordable, and accessible care to a group of people can help realize this.
- Instruments that reinforce mutual caring and sharing in good and bad times, such as reductions in subscription fees during periods of economic adversity and profit sharing during periods of prosperity will help the system to be more flexible and robust when setbacks occur, and boost mutual loyalty and confidence between everyone concerned.

- It is useful to have a good knowledge of the source and original context in order to understand and reuse principles. The income threshold in the Netherlands was introduced, as in most countries, when wealthy people could still pay all medical treatments in cash. It also served to protect this lucrative market for doctors. The concept of "free choice of doctor" is now often used as a counterpart to "managed care," but it actually originates partly from the Netherlands. Back then, it entailed choosing a doctor who had affiliated himself exclusively to an integrated care system, with all accompanying rights and obligations.

5.2   DHAN[19]

"Be the change you wish to see in the world"

Tom Buijtendorp & Jeroen Kemperman[20] @: Jeroen.Kemperman@achmea.nl, Phone: 0031 651222099

Prelude *Sitting in the sweltering heat in a circle with women dressed in colorful robes, primary case author Tom Buijtendorp seems very far removed from his day-to-day life in Europe. As a visitor, a dot is also painted on his forehead—the eye of Shiva. A priest is busy performing incomprehensible rituals. Nothing here reminds*

---

[19] This case is described based on the personal experiences and contacts of Tom Buijtendorp, supplemented by the experience of Annette Houtekamer. Generic public information can be found on the website and in the Annual Report (DHAN Foundation 2013A, 2013B).

[20] As in all cases in this book, this brilliant business model was defined by the case authors, including a member of the book's editorial team. The primary case author, Tom, has a large personal involvement in DHAN. It is worth noting here that he is the mental owner of this case, with Jeroen providing a contribution.

you of Europe. Nevertheless, this self-help group of 15 people has managed to make their care costs affordable to the poorest people, and has demonstrated that the poor can save. They are realizing a dream with the local development organization DHAN. A dream that is now being lived by over four million people, a number that is increasing rapidly. After the ritual has finished, a visit is paid to a restored temple with a water basin. This would appear to be a pointless tourist trip for the friend visiting from the West who knows more about insurance, But delve deeper into the case and you will discover the essence of DHAN's philosophy. It is the key to the sustainable development realized here in a remarkable manner. DHAN has received numerous awards, including one for the best development organization in India, a country that is home to nearly a fifth of the world's population.

As a Western outsider, Tom had the privilege of putting the vision and strategy down on paper together with the management team of DHAN and helping them come up with ideas about their following step. During the annual Foundation Day it was an exceptional experience to see and feel how so many from the "bottom of the pyramid" assume responsibility for their own future. It was unique to witness that the essence of mutual sharing and caring is experienced here, on the basis of enlightened self-interest. The actual purpose of the visit was to convey knowledge, but it became increasingly clear that the opposite would occur here: a wealth of essential insights could be acquired.

Introduction The social challenge facing India is enormous, including within the domain of health and care. The economy is developing rapidly, especially in knowledge-intensive sectors. At the same time India is a very poor country. According to estimates, some 500 million people in India suffer from malnutrition while 300 million live on less than one dollar a day. This translates into more than a quarter of the poorest people in the world. India lags in healthcare way behind surrounding countries in Southeast Asia and the world. The government is unable to provide care at a socially acceptable minimum level.[21] The care system is mostly private and does not provide any safety net for the majority of the population.

DHAN initiates and encourages communities to engage in self-help activities, such as micro-insurance, micro-credit, and small-scale irrigation. It therefore ensures, for example, that groups of people share risks, can lend small amounts from each other and jointly manage water used for agriculture. The organization helps people care for one another, something which begins right from the bottom. By tackling poverty, DHAN ensures that people remain healthy or healthier and can protect themselves against loss of income should they fall ill nevertheless. Steps are also being taken now to build hospitals and provide healthcare insurance. This sequence is common: within micro-insurance, medical expenses are often seen as the most difficult and important piece of the puzzle.

The first projects started in 1990 and laid the foundation for DHAN, which was established on 2 October 1997. An important source of inspiration was Mahatma Gandhi (1869–1948), the man who achieved what appeared impossible with his

---

[21] Hsiao, Medina, Ly and Dukhan (2013).

peaceful revolution: he drove the seemingly invincible British Empire from his country without an army. "Be the change you wish to see in the world," Gandhi said. And he heeded his own advice. When a mother asked him to tell her son to stop eating so much sugar, he refused. Gandhi asked her to come back 2 weeks later, even though she had made a long journey to see him. Two weeks later he gave her some advice, prompting the mother to ask him why she had needed to wait so long. "Two weeks ago I myself was still eating too much sugar, madam," was his reply. He could only give advice about what he personally did and was prepared to adapt his lifestyle in order to help a single boy. He understood the power of example, the essence of its impact.

DHAN's approach is characterized by a similar, far-reaching consistency that emanates from within. Inspired by Gandhi's patience and unrelenting efforts, DHAN wants to expel poverty from India, and even throughout the world. Its dream, as a mental leader, is to serve as an example itself and ensure it is emulated elsewhere in India, and preferably also outside the country given that poverty does not stop at borders. Over one million families are now members of DHAN, with an average of four to five members per family. The organization is throwing a pebble into the pond of poverty in the hope that the ripples will spread out and reach other poor people. Around 4.5 million people appear to be nothing but a drop in an ocean of 500 million undernourished people. But a ripple can make a great deal possible. This vision gives DHAN the calm to work with great consistency amidst overwhelming poverty on its own organization, which is now active in twelve different states.

In the spirit of Gandhi, DHAN is also fighting against the caste system and the extreme differences that exist between social classes in India. The organization works for the benefit of all poor people without making any distinction. Staff at all levels of the organization use only their first names because their surname would betray their own caste. This helps build religious bridges. While most staff and customers are Hindu a poem penned by the Catholic Mother Teresa (1910–1997) is sung with great conviction during the morning ceremony held on the rooftop terrace of DHAN's headquarters in Madurai. Staff do so simply because its message appeals to them, just as Gandhi was partly inspired by Jesus' Sermon on the Mount. This is consistent with a devoted organization.

Although India is already an old democracy, the central government of this vast country is geographically far away from its poor population. In the spirit of Gandhi once again, DHAN advocates the reinforcement of local democracy through local governments that have already existed for centuries. It is a crucial element in the dream of empowering the poor to help them escape poverty. The empowerment of women is playing a pivotal role in this. Coercion is being rejected: freedom of choice is a high priority for DHAN.

5.2.1 The Cornerstone: Empowering the Poor to Help Themselves

Many brilliant business models build with a consistent focus inspired by the past applied to the present and developed into the future. This also applies to DHAN to a large degree. It translates this focus to local communities and the people within them.

The forces needed to attain DHAN's higher goal are therefore released: empower the poor to help themselves grow out of poverty through cooperation and mutual caring and sharing.

Respect for local history and the connection with contemporary culture is one of the distinctive elements of such an approach. This helps prevent the not-invented-here syndrome that corrodes the sustainability of much development work. As the word says, the traditional development being on a 'mission' from the West focused more on sending than receiving. The moment traditional aid stops, the attained result often vanishes and the community relapses back into its former state of poverty. DHAN, on the contrary, succeeds in making participating self-help groups self-sufficient and self-financing within 5 to 15 years. They then remain a member of the "family" to which they can turn in times of need, but they save themselves. In line with the higher goal, self-help is the brand essence of DHAN: becoming a member of the DHAN organization entails an important step towards self-help. For many, this is a crucial step in life.

The past is a powerful source of inspiration. Many centuries ago, the management of water reservoirs occurred via local cooperation. This system is still applicable to almost two-thirds of small farmers in India. During short, intense rainy seasons, increasingly scarce water is stored in collective reservoirs, some of which are located at temples. This old Vayalagam approach comprises a system of local cooperation, which is cherished as an early seed of local participatory democracy. Many water reservoirs fell into disuse during the British occupation and local cooperation made way for large overarching structures. DHAN encourages local communities to use old reservoirs again and rekindle the accompanying cooperation. The same applies to traditional saving systems. An example is the Kalanjiam system used in a particular region, involving the storage of rice in a traditional pot. DHAN has introduced a savings program and used the old name of Kalanjiam deliberately. Anyone visiting the communities will still find a Kalanjiam pot, which symbolizes the anchoring in the past. It is reminiscent of the first automobiles at the end of the 19th century that deliberately resembled horse-drawn carriages so that people would recognize them as means of transport and not be afraid to use them.

Building on old traditions and local cultural practices is essential. Doing so helps avoid the not-invented-here syndrome where possible and an aversion to innovation. New programs quickly feel "familiar" as a result. They can therefore also be maintained during the phase when local communities need to continue on their own. This is also deliberately linked to reinforcement of the local community as the basis for the required cooperation and mutual caring and sharing. By restoring old temples with reservoirs, for example, DHAN is consciously helping foster local pride and self-confidence. Traditional festivals are also supported. In DHAN's vision, development partially involves rediscovering what already existed and building upon this. The past and the local culture are important roots for DHAN because they contribute significantly to credibility. DHAN also attaches importance to strengthening the local community with a view to the future. When one looks at the West and prosperous city dwellers in India, the belief arises that greater prosperity will increase the tendency towards individualism. This could eventually undermine the solidarity that has been fostered.

The higher goal is to fight poverty, on the basis of self-help, throughout India and even the rest of the world. The audacious goal focuses on fighting poverty on the basis of self-help for members of the own local level. It is the belief that the maximum limit comprises approximately 395 federations compared with the 300 or so at the moment. Each federation consists of different clusters that in turn contain various self-help groups to which families belong. A federation unites some 15,000 family members on average. That means that the approximately 4.5 million people at present could possible reach a maximum of 7.5 million in the future. By the time such a number is attained, DHAN wants to have developed itself into a widely respected model that others copy on a large scale (with the foundation's support where needed). The brand promise focuses primarily on this potential group, with the prospect of members developing and escaping poverty on their own within a maximum of 15 years. And they will do so while retaining their self-respect and in close cooperation with their immediate surroundings.

DHAN's values have been formulated from a social perspective. Unlike the values that exist within numerous organizations, here it is truly about moral objectives: deep-rooted convictions that indicate what members expect of the ideal society, and what they themselves would therefore like to be in order to contribute to this. In line with the inspiration provided by Gandhi, DHAN therefore wants to be the change it considers necessary, and create this within society. It is about a fair community focused on these values. The core values mentioned in the annual report include: "poverty-free with self-respect", "gender equality", "respect for diversity", "participatory democracy", "freedom of choice", and a "mutually supportive society". These guiding values are deeply embedded within the organization and confirmed annually during the Foundation Day in October, for example. Those permitted to participate on stage can experience the passion of members.

DHAN has to realize a series of core qualities in order to demonstrate brand proof. These core qualities are: the ability to empathize with local tradition and culture, the ability to be self-sufficient (instead of offering help), and the ability to cooperate well with multiple stakeholders.

Brand essence: DHAN feels like a family that helps people to escape poverty together through caring and sharing

Higher goal
- Empowerment of the poor so that they can help themselves and escape poverty in a sustainable manner through cooperation based on mutual caring and sharing

Brand roots
- Track record since the 1990s to stimulate the poor to help themselves building upon the local culture and history
- Gandhi is an important source of inspiration

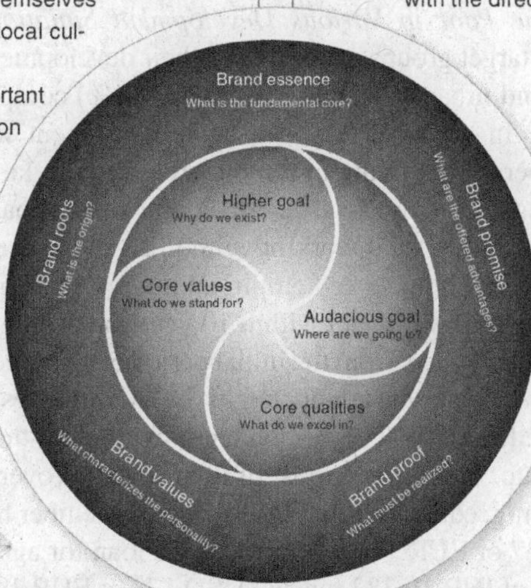

Audacious goal
- Expand the current 4.5 million members via their own families to 7.5 million organized in 500 federations

Brand promise
- Members can sustainably escape poverty in 5 to 15 years while keeping self-respect and in close cooperation with the direct environment

Core and brand values
- Escape poverty with self-respect
- Equality between the sexes
- Respect for diversity
- Participative democracy
- Freedom of choice
- A society based on mutual caring and sharing

Core qualities
- Empathy in members and communities
- Make people self-reliant
- Cooperation with all involved stakeholders

Brand proof
- Acting close to the people with a family feeling and as guardian of shared values

Figure 5.2.1 Vision and Positioning of DHAN

5.2.2   The Business Model: Self-Management

DHAN is focusing on self-management and empowering the poor to help themselves grow out of poverty permanently through cooperation and mutual caring and sharing. This is being achieved in three ways, namely:

(a) By stimulating scalable cost efficiency and sustainable innovations such as micro-insurance, micro-credits, and small-scale irrigation;
(b) By developing support institutions required for that purpose, such as consultative structures and hospitals;
(c) By training thousands of development staff using its own educational institute, namely the TATA-DHAN Academy, for example.

Market Segments: The Poor in Various Development Situations DHAN distinguishes between four target groups according to their development potential: countryside, tribal, coast and urban.[22] The largest group (76%) comprises poor farmers from the countryside. In practice, they can be self-sufficient within 10 years on average. Tribal members (8%) living in remote areas require far longer in practice than farmers in order to become self-sufficient. People on the coast (7%) are mostly fishermen. DHAN has only started working with this group recently following the tsunami in 2004 and does not have any empirical figures yet. Poor city dwellers in the slums (9%) become self-sufficient within 10 years on average.

A hundred thousand members from the initial period can now consider themselves independent. A large-scale survey conducted by DHAN to investigate the needs of new members revealed that 90% of respondents live below the poverty line and almost half are illiterate. They spend most of their income (over half) on food and almost a fifth on clothing, education, and healthcare. A member has an average loan of INR 8521 (USD 137 or EUR 116). A third have a loan for agricultural purposes, with an average value of INR 10,783 rupees (USD 173 or EUR 147). Around a third take out housing loans while approximately one in ten do so to develop their own business. Money is also loaned to pay education and repay old debts. Healthcare can cause a substantial financial deficit and has a double-pronged effect since this often goes hand in hand with a loss of income. A crucial customer insight was "*poor people can save*": the realization that the poor want to and can help themselves, and will take advantage of temporary assistance if this is linked to their own traditions and culture.

Customer Value: Lasting Prosperity The result for customers is the opportunity to escape poverty permanently as part of a strong social community. The retention of self-esteem plays an important, emotional role in this. The process occurs largely within the own community and under its own steam where possible, with ample

---

[22] DHAN Foundation (2013A).

scope for the human dimension. The organization is based on simplicity and low costs. Thanks to the system of social control and small-scale practice, the cost for members in the form of interest and insurance premiums is as low as possible. Members must make an effort though. The risk is limited and can be covered by insurances such as a credit insurance. All in all, DHAN fulfills a huge need as the farming population has very few opportunities to take out loans or insurance (and lacks knowledge in areas such as water management).

A series of products has been developed over the years. Apart from physical ones, such as water reservoirs and water pumps for water management, services such as the provision of credit and insurance also exist. Savings are made and then lent to other members under the motto "the poor can save." Thanks to the resulting buffer, three times as much money can be lent compared to the amount that is saved. The interest rate is also less than half of what commercial providers ask. To ensure that the money is paid back later, strict social controls on the expenditure of the loaned money are enforced within the self-help group. Preferably, this money is used productively to boost agricultural production by purchasing better-quality seeds or a storage barn so that the borrower can produce more and repay the loan from the proceeds. There is therefore a collective interest in ensuring that the money is spent wisely. This is important. The global credit crisis which started in 2008 has been attributed to the fact that this relationship between lenders and borrowers had disappeared completely and along with it the means to curb reckless spending.

As prosperity increases, so too does the need to insure the acquired prosperity. That is the reason why mutual insurances have been introduced to cover the risk of death and also insure livestock, crops and income. It usually begins with simple products to familiarize members with insurance and frequently culminates in relatively complex products such as health insurances. The challenge is to ensure available care: where necessary, DHAN builds hospitals together with the community to this end, such as in Madurai and Theni. Prevention programs focusing on better sanitation and drinking water are also implemented. Specific programs have been launched after it transpired that many members of the target group suffer from an iron deficiency. Insurances are covered by paid contributions and backed up by reinsurance for larger claims.

Delivery: In the Own Circle The most striking aspect of DHAN's operation is that everything is organized in a highly decentralized way. The organization is not led by a large central holding company. The umbrella federation is small and barely automated. From a Western perspective, it seems a miracle that this functions effectively. Shared values and ideals and intelligent organizational principles containing considerable wealth and wisdom are used as primarily management mechanisms. The self-help groups comprising between 15 and 25 families form the base or "foundation of the organization." These families are members and themselves constitute the operation of DHAN. The term "self-help" dovetails with the cooperative principle upon which the model is based. In the century-old brilliant business model the German cooperative bank Raiffeisen, the guiding motto was "helping people help themselves" and there was also an awareness that the groups should not become too large in order to ensure they could continue to steer and correct themselves.[23] In India, the same principle forms the core of self-help groups that work on the basis of consensus. The human dimension is important. Based on experience, a group size ranging between 15 to 25 families is ideal for self-management. Anything above that will make the group too large and prevent members from getting to know one another and meeting up.

Operation: Simplicity Whereby Members Are the Organization Members themselves lie at the heart of the operation. Broader partnerships that focus on organizing education, sharing knowledge and spreading greater risks also exist. The next level comprises regional clusters of around 20–30 self-help groups that collectively form a kind of large family with 150 and 500 members. The level thereafter consists of federations in which 100–200 self-help groups work together, totaling around 3000–4000 families on average.

The basic principle of the model is that self-help groups manage themselves where possible. DHAN assists in their establishment and development, and provides the values and setup principles. The self-help groups take many decisions themselves, preferably on a consensus basis. On this level there is a strong awareness that resources are scarce. Although self-help groups can provide a warm family feeling, participation is based on enlightened self-interest. You help the other in order to be helped yourself later on, if required. Savings are regarded as a joint possession. The same goes for collected contributions. The self-help group system is evidently perfectly capable of keeping payments under control with very limited resources. Considerable focus is placed on accident prevention since this is in everyone's interest, and an assessment is made to see how damage, once inflicted, can be limited where possible.

Simplicity, self-motivation and cost management play a pivotal operational role in the ability to offer scalable, cost-effective and sustainable innovations. In view of the limited resources, as little as possible must be lost to complex administrative processes. In the countryside especially, mobile technology is used extensively to transmit data to coordination centers. Additional coordination is kept to a minimum because much of the work and control is organized within the self-help groups. DHAN goes beyond the primary process and the products. As already indicated, the foundation also assists by creating supporting bodies such as consultative structures and by building the required infrastructure. It also disseminates its knowledge by training thousands of development staff via its own educational institute, the DHAN Academy. The bargaining power of over four million members is used in relation to suppliers to make attractive agreements for these members. Furthermore, DHAN works together with universities, financial institutions, governments, professional networks and donors.

---

[23] Case description: Geelhoed and Geelhoed: "Raiffeissen: Hilfe zur Selbsthilfe," in: Kemperman, Geelhoed, and Op 't Hoog (2013).

Value for customers

Result *What do I get?*
- Support to escape poverty using own strengths

Process *How do I get it?*
- Primarily offered nearby via self-help group with DHAN organization as back-up

Emotion *What do I feel?*
- Strong sense of own culture, roots and responsibility as part of DHAN family

---

Price *What are the costs?*
- Interest and premiums kept low thanks to efficient approach, self-service and self-control

Effort *What do I have to do for it?*
- Providing self-support and taking responsibility within own direct environment

Risk *What are the uncertainties?*
- Risks are reduced because it is shared with acquaintances and the danger of a return to poverty is reduced via insurance

Market segments

Position
- Organizing 1 million families with 4 to 5 family members, totaling 4.5 million people spread out over 12 Indian states, 66 districts and 12,404 villages

Competition
- Local providers of single offerings, such as usurers for loans who demand extremely high interest rates, and limited solutions with own group, such as lending directly from each other

Target group
- All the poor, no matter what caste or religion. Spread over 4 groups: primarily rural (74%), tribes, on the coast and in the cities

Customer insights
- The poor are capable of saving money and escaping poverty in other ways. Building upon tradition and culture prevents the not-invented-here syndrome and helps to make the impact sustainable

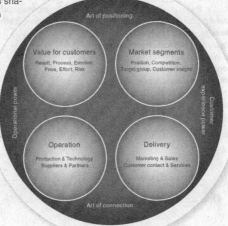

Figure 5.2.2 Value for customers and Market segments of DHAN

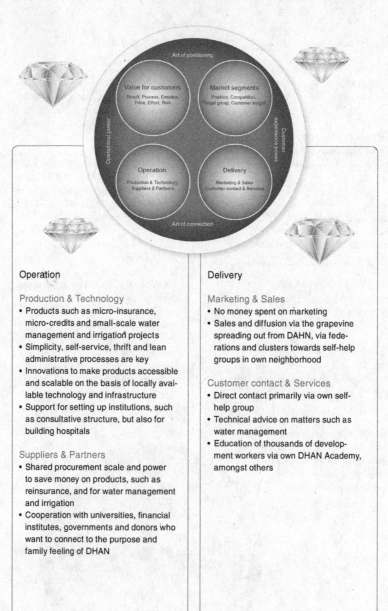

Operation

Production & Technology

- Products such as micro-insurance, micro-credits and small-scale water management and irrigation projects
- Simplicity, self-service, thrift and lean administrative processes are key
- Innovations to make products accessible and scalable on the basis of locally available technology and infrastructure
- Support for setting up institutions, such as consultative structure, but also for building hospitals

Suppliers & Partners

- Shared procurement scale and power to save money on products, such as reinsurance, and for water management and irrigation
- Cooperation with universities, financial institutes, governments and donors who want to connect to the purpose and family feeling of DHAN

Delivery

Marketing & Sales

- No money spent on marketing
- Sales and diffusion via the grapevine spreading out from DAHN, via federations and clusters towards self-help groups in own neighborhood

Customer contact & Services

- Direct contact primarily via own self-help group
- Technical advice on matters such as water management
- Education of thousands of development workers via own DHAN Academy, amongst others

Figure 5.2.3 Operation and Delivery of DHAN

5.2.3   The Result: The Value of Sustainable Poverty Reduction

The emphasis placed on self-management and self-help means that the customer is not sitting idly by in the passenger seat, but is actually at the helm of the operation. In other words, customers are also active suppliers and create value for themselves and other customers. This attracts new (groups of) customers in turn. The table below outlines the organization's growth in terms of the number of federations, clusters, self-help groups, and families:

Talk to a DHAN staff member and you will immediately notice the immense passion and satisfaction on all levels. It is abundantly clear that an awareness of doing meaningful work for society is motivating, but the intrinsic motivation of staff is also significant. The contact with members—mostly direct—makes the work very gratifying. Staff receive only a third of the salary they could earn elsewhere in India. Although the financial rewards are deliberately lower than average, staff are nevertheless attracted to the foundation by other benefits. They opt for DHAN because of the immense satisfaction derived from helping people help themselves. The moral relationship for staff is stronger than the financial relationship with the organization. Considerable importance is attached to nurturing this relationship. That is why you can meet someone at DHAN who used to earn a handsome salary as a marketing manager of a large group, but now finds much more enjoyment in fighting poverty. DHAN refers to such members of staff as "social entrepreneurs".

The Kothur community and its 2500 members are a typical example of the positive impact of DHAN. Both agricultural productivity and area of used ground increased. For each family, this translated into an average income increase of USD 57 (EUR 45) in relation to a minimum of USD 353 (EUR 300) annually. Food safety improved for almost two-thirds of participants. Some 100,000 members crossed over the poverty line on a sustainable basis. Almost one million insurance policies have been taken out. This includes a health insurance system linked to own hospitals which provides cover to over 120,000 poor families.

Table 5.2 Growth of DHAN in federations, clusters, self-help groups, and families

DHAN	2010	2011	2012	2015
Federations	260	283	303	395
Clusters	1648	1432	1728	2090
Self-help groups	33,039	37,071	45,525	55,000
Families	810,185	923,865	1,047,924	1,353,500

Table 5.3 Number of staff in 2012

DHAN in figures	2012	2015
Professionals	331	312
Program staff	430	415
"People functionaries"	2261	2140

DHAN's work in India has been acknowledged with a series of social awards. These include the Best NGO Award for 2008–2009 and the India NGO Award in the category Large NGOs in 2010. The 2011 Jindal Award was awarded to the foundation in February 2012 for its substantial contribution to the reduction of poverty in the countryside, along with the international AGMUND Award for pioneering projects that help ensure food security for the poor. And in spring 2013, the Times of India Social Impact Award 2012 was given in the NGOs category. The awards represent an important public recognition of DHAN's work in India. The model can be of social relevance outside India as well, providing it can be applied there successfully and in accordance with local culture. The establishment of DHAN International marked the first step towards this objective.

DHAN faces challenges at the same time. The examples of other brilliant business models reveal that success over time can also prove to be a pitfall. If people overestimate their abilities, there is a risk that too many new activities are undertaken even though the original task has not been completed yet. Although the tale of DHAN has been very inspirational for others up until now, the challenge ahead is still considerable. Nevertheless, what it has achieved so far can be an important source of inspiration, including for breakthroughs in healthcare within more prosperous countries.

Value by customers
- The key to DHAN is that customers receive the self-created value and are co-suppliers in realizing sustainable wealth for themselves and their own groups
- The number of families surpassed the 1-million-member mark in 2012
- 100,000 members currently live sustainably above the poverty line. The average income in Kothur, for example, has grown 15%. It was USD 341 (EUR 300) and is now USD 391 (EUR 345) per year

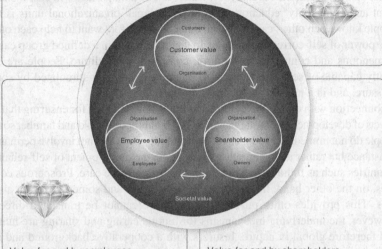

Value for and by employees
- Lower salary but a lot of fulfillment and sense of purpose in work
- Approximately 3000 employees of whom one quarter works fulltime. Via shared values and self-support, each fulltime employee can service 13,000 families (more then 50,000 people)

Value for and by shareholders
- The initiators and providers of funding contribute to sustainable welfare improvement which becomes self-reinforcing via people who help themselves

Value for and by society
- Sustainable reduction of poverty and reinforcement of the self-reliance of people reduces the need for public and private assistance and strenghtens the economy.
- Range of prizes and awards such as: Best NGO Award (2008-2009), India NGO Award (2010), Jindal prize (2011), AGMUND prize (2011) and Times of India Social Impact Award (2012-2013)

Figure 5.2.4 Value for and by stakeholders of DHAN

5.2.4 The Brilliant Lessons of DHAN

Some key insights that may also be relevant for healthcare in prosperous and still-developing countries are listed below:

- The local scale is and remains crucial in healthcare, particularly in the provision of living assistance and non-specialized care. Shared values and intelligent setup principles can help limit the bureaucracy, which can be a major factor in cost management and complexity reduction. The power of small organizational units is that people know each other, can trust each other and therefore want to help each other.
- The power of self-correction and self-management within a defined group can be tremendous and contribute to the joint control of expenditure. People are evidently capable of self-management to a large extent when stimulated by social pressure, and in a manner that feels "familiar."
- A connection with one's own culture and traditions is crucial for ensuring that the effects of development are sustainable. DHAN builds upon the old and familiar so that people do not immediately adopt a reticent attitude. This does not involve permanent assistance but rather a collaboration focusing on the development of self-reliance.
- Countries such as India have a huge shortage in available care. Prosperous countries, on the other hand, have an extensive selection and sometimes even a surplus. This provides other puzzles and therefore cannot be translated directly. However, the underlying mechanisms for mutual caring and sharing are human and therefore global in nature. Insurers with a cooperative background and any other interest groups can develop a profound bargaining power on the behalf of members, for example. And since everything comes together in one place, new technologies such as the Internet can clarify the overall cost of care for someone, which helps restore the transparancy and trust. An own-risk element with a certain maximum can increase cost awareness, without posing a great risk to the customer.
- An inspirational exemplary role such as that of Gandhi for DAHN allows a relatively small activity to be scaled up to a large activity with much greater effect. Anyone with sufficient patience to free a country as large as India from a superpower can successfully motivate poor people to attain prosperity and possibly also inspire solutions for healthcare issues in other countries.

5.3 Courtyard Houses[24]

Security and good care assured
for the rest of your life as a pensioner

Jeroen Kemperman & Ida Kemperman-Wilke @: Jeroen.Kemperman@achmea.
nl, Phone: 0031 651222099

Prelude[25] *Christoffel van Brants passes away on 5 November 1732 in his home at Keizersgracht 317 in Amsterdam. He can look back on an impressive life. He has helped Russia to learn from the Netherlands (and vice versa). Christoffel is in close contact with Tsar Peter the Great for much of his life. During his visit to the Netherlands to learn how to turn Russia into a comparably modern country, the Tsar resides in Christoffel's home on the Keizersgracht and in his countryside home on the Amstel river. Christoffel assists him by recruiting specialists in the Netherlands and dispatching them to Russia. As one of the key traders between these two countries, he also plays a pivotal role in the war the Tsar is waging against Sweden over the passage through the Sound. Peter the Great also does a great deal for Christoffel.*

---

[24] Jeroen Kemperman wants to thank Wouter Schouten for his support by reviewing this case about courtyard houses. Wouter was Alliance Manager at Zilveren Kruis Achmea and is currently working at the insurer CZ. During his MBA studies, he became inspired by new business models and value propositions. In that regard he has a special interest in segments relating to domestic care and seniors.

[25] An extensive description of the life of Christoffel van Brants and the Brants Rus courtyard house is found in Donga (2008).

The highlight comes in 1717 when Christoffel becomes a noble and is appointed a member of the Russian Royal Council and resident minister and ambassador to the Tsar in Amsterdam. Trade with Russia turns Christoffel into an immensely wealthy man. Before his death, he chooses an office where the executor of his will spends a year and a half making an inventory of his possessions and arranging the inheritance. At the time of his death he has no direct heirs other than two distant nieces. On 29 October, a week before he passes away, he amends his will once again. The nieces receive around USD 106,000 (EUR 90,000), a pittance when one considers the millions he leaves behind. Christoffel is seemingly more concerned with ensuring that his name lives on. Two small boys called Christoffel receive part of the inheritance on the condition that they adopt the surname "Van Brants." But Christoffel's greatest and most enduring claim to fame is the Van Brants-Rus courtyard house, which is founded thanks to his bequest. Compared with other Amsterdam courtyard houses, this one is spaciously designed. The Van Brants-Rus courtyard house is intended to accommodate 48 women over the age of 50 and of the Lutheran faith for the remainder of their lives. The plans includes 21 double rooms and 6 single rooms. Christoffel does his utmost to organize all of this in detail before he passes away. He finds a site at Nieuwe Keizersgracht 28–44 and construction work commences. Regulations are drawn up for the governors (recruited from the ruling class of merchants), the "house father" and "house mother"; and residents. The part of the inheritance that Christoffel sets aside for his nieces' bequest is used as an additional reserve for his courtyard house. His legacy is therefore assured for eternity, and so too is his courtyard house! The Van Brants-Rus courtyard house still exists to this very day.

Introduction Members of the baby-boomer generation that emerged after the Second World War in many Western countries are gradually reaching an age that necessitates a degree of rest and care. For a long time society was expected to take care of this on their behalf, but the ageing population is complicating this task. At the same time, baby-boomers are one of the first generations to have mostly generated capital thanks to their own home and a pension. The financial crisis that started in 2008 has had some effect, but this has often not been profound in nature. The puzzle—and brain teaser—now is how to ensure this baby-boomer generation can enjoy a good retirement in a fine home that provides care and nursing where required. While many senior citizens have plans to start a large home-care villa, they often fail in realizing them. How can you implement appealing initiatives in practice while simultaneously retaining the human dimension? Will society pay for the desired living assistance? Is it possible to finance this entirely or partially from the equity of elderly people or family members? In that case, how will their personal income suffice up until the end of their lives? Although these questions are topical and urgent in nature, they are not at all new. The past returns in a different form. What can we learn from this?

Since the Middle Ages, North-Western European countries such as Sweden, Norway, Denmark, Germany, and the Netherlands provide a small yet interesting experiment in social welfare and mutual care and living assistance. The elderly and the poor in the Netherlands enjoy better benefits than in most other Western countries in the aforementioned period. Judging from the "tweets" they post in their diaries, tourists like the Swede Bengt Ferrner and the Englishman Harry Peckham are amazed when they visited the country in 1759 and 1772, respectively.[26] The affordability/non-affordability and sustainability/non-sustainability of social welfare provisions in the Netherlands often feature on the Dutch agenda since the country's "Golden Age" in the seventeenth century. City administrators have devoted themselves to assisting poor and elderly people unable to care for themselves. In doing this, the focus in that and our own time is often placed on economies of scale, ambitious plans for new buildings and stricter government control over care.[27] The idea that these measures will resolve problems and make care affordable do not always materialize. Do other solutions exist?

Let us look at a small-scale, private alternative for elderly healthcare that emerged in the Netherlands from the fifteenth century onwards, namely "*courtyard houses.*" The name relates to the fact that these houses are built around courtyards. They are established thanks to an inheritance. Elderly people go there and continue living there until they pass away. New residents are required to pay a one-off sum upon arrival. In exchange for this, they receive fixed supplies of food and drink in addition of accommodation. The amount due depends on the assets of the courtyard house. People can pay less if these assets are still sizeable, which means it is at least partly a type of charity. If the reserves are depleted, the establishment has to cover its costs. Market competition thus plays a distinct role. The courtyard houses formula is multiplied extensively during the five centuries that follow up until the second half of the twenteeth century. The buildings still exist today, but are to a large extend no longer used as houses for seniors. They do not always comply with modern Dutch requirements for facilities (such as own toilet and shower facilities) and the number of square meters for living space. Students are often housed there nowadays and one-off purchases are no longer common. Housing concepts such as courtyard houses seem to be solutions and at least offer inspiration for resolutions to the social problems of today. Can this type of housing teach us something? Where does it conflict with the automatisms and value judgments of our time? Do courtyard houses, free of the dust of centuries, offer a fresh perspective on the current issues with housing, care and pension arrangements for senior citizens?

5.3.1 The Cornerstone: Acts of Mercy

A courtyard house essentially is originated to provide people with a place where they will receive shelter and care during old age. The higher goal is linked to Biblical acts of mercy.[28] The real roots of and inspiration for courtyard houses lie in the

---

[26] Kernkamp (1910) and Peckham (1772).

[27] Medema (2010).

[28] Matthew (first century A.D.).

Christian ethics of Europe. These do not always serve as the source of connection, but the requirement that the weak must be cared for does really help. That is why guest houses are established throughout Europe during the Middle Ages. They emerge in countries such as Britain, Germany, France, Spain, and Italy, along permanent travel and trade routes in cities as well as monasteries. As the name suggests, "guest houses" are meant to temporarily accommodate passers-by such as travelers and vagrants as guests. Over time this also extends to poor and sick people. Greater focus was therefore placed on the local population and guest houses also become almshouses for example houses where lepers receive care. When guest houses run out of funds and/or people who have some form of income wanted to live there, these institutions also start taking in people who pay a deposit.[29] In exchange they receive their own room or home along with a guarantee that they can remain there until they pass away. They also receive a periodic gift in the form of a payment in cash and/or in kind.[30] Several guest houses and almshouses specialize later on. This trend is also visible across Europe. The guesthouses turn into homes for elderly men and women, hospitals or orphanages, but sometimes also into houses where people can live until their death after paying a one-off purchase sum. This is, for example, how the leper houses in Schiedam and Amsterdam, transformed during the seventeenth century.[31]

In the Netherlands the system of a one-off purchase sum for life-time living inspires the development of courtyard houses. These are established from the fifteenth century onwards by private persons. This is usually executed for and by the own religious community. These establishments often change accordingly when the prevailing religion makes way for another during the Reformation. Some Catholic establishments became Protestant, for example.[32] This embedding within the own ecclesiastical group is in keeping with Dutch tradition. While significant consideration and tolerance is given to different beliefs, each group looks after itself in particular. This solidarity within the own circle is an important way to live alongside one another, organize effective social welfare facilities and keep them affordable at the same time. This phenomenon is reflected hundreds of years later in the Netherlands through the Poor Law of 1854, which assumes that the State will only be deployed once all other safety nets have been missed. Mutual caring and sharing within the group is still firmly embedded within the Netherlands in the civil society organizations of pension funds, housing organizations, purchasing corporations such as banks and insurers, and sales corporations in the agricultural sector. This is also visible in other countries with a "Rhineland" tradition such as Germany, Belgium, and France. But that is a different story. What about the Dutch courtyard houses?

---

[29] Kam (1998).

[30] Spaans (2002).

[31] Van Essen (2012).

[32] Driessen (1948).

Going back in time the Dutch courtyard houses make a simple and fundamental promise to residents to provide them with protection and care for the rest of their lives. A moment occurs when an individual resident passes away and makes way for a new resident. But since people do not die simultaneously, the courtyard house has to continue existing in order to keep that promise to all residents. An individual courtyard house is also not focused on expanding, but on still existing tomorrow, the day after tomorrow and the following day, etc. It aims to be there for eternity. This is also appealing to founders since a courtyard house allows wealthy people to continue helping others after their own death. It also offers them a unique opportunity to live on after their death because the establishment can be named after them. Although individual courtyard houses do not have any growth-related ambitions, the concept is multiplied extensively and hundreds of similar courtyard houses appear.

The values of courtyard houses can be summed up as compassion, mutual caring and sharing, and security. Biblical charity is organized on the basis of solidarity, which applies to the establishment of courtyard houses but also to the subsequent form of habitation whereby residents assist one another. A feeling of mutual caring and sharing exists between residents because they put their personal money into a collective pot. This provides residents with mental and physical security.

The courtyard house has to excel in several core qualities in order to give substance to the promises and values. They are organized according to the human dimension in a small scale with usually 10 to 20 appartments. They form communities of people who live together until their death. This requires a sound balance between taking other people into account and reinforcing mutual assistance, but also respecting each other's privacy.[33] Moreover, the courtyard house would outlive its residents. They have to treat the courtyard house as good stewards and bequeath it to following generations. The governors and administrators also have to handle assets prudently. The resident house fathers and/or mothers have to look after the courtyard house carefully and keep the calm. Residents are expected to conform to the establishment and not vice versa. They remain guests, after all. In exchange, the courtyard house has to fulfill the promises weekly by means of gifts. The right to exist in the long term stems from always being there for new residents year in year out, and century after century.

---

[33] Leene (1997).

Brand essence: Security and good care assured for the rest of your life as a pensioner

Higher goal
• Be a place where biblical works of mercy are performed: feed the hungry, refresh the thirsty, care for and house the sick and the widows

Brand roots
• Based upon Christian ethics: built upon the legacy of the guesthouses and alms-houses from the Middle Ages
• Rooted in private initiative and the help of a benefactor in own religious community

Audacious goal
• Build and sustain a place which is self-financing and where the poor and retired can be assured of housing, care and provision for their old age

Brand promise
• Be assured of a sheltered and secure old age for the rest of your life

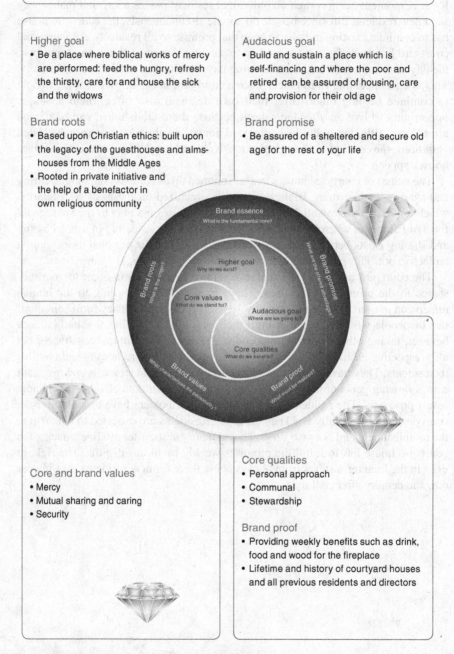

Core and brand values
• Mercy
• Mutual sharing and caring
• Security

Core qualities
• Personal approach
• Communal
• Stewardship

Brand proof
• Providing weekly benefits such as drink, food and wood for the fireplace
• Lifetime and history of courtyard houses and all previous residents and directors

Figure 5.3.1 Vision and Positioning of Courtyard houses

5.3.2 The Business Model: Self-Sufficient Within the Own Group

Market Segments: Focused on the Middle Class Within the Community What position do the courtyard houses occupy? Let us go back in time. They are always deeply rooted in the specific local religious community and often affiliated to a church via a foundation. These establishments are found primarily in several Dutch cities, the majority of which were in Amsterdam, but also in Leiden, Groningen, Haarlem, and Utrecht. It is a supply market: over the centuries almost all of them have a greater demand from people wishing to live there than the supply of available rooms or homes. Minimal competition is required to attract residents. The main alternative for potential residents is to remain at home and live independently. That is what the very wealthy do: allow themselves to be served and cared for within their own homes. The somewhat romantic notion today that elderly people are often taken in by their children is something that never occurs that much in the Netherlands at in that time. It is certainly not common in cities. When no other option exist, a place might be available in an almshouse or in an old men's and women's house, but these are much larger and offers less privacy and inferior food and drink. This is the last alternative for the poor. Courtyard houses are intended for middle-class groups such as craftsmen and domestic servants.[34] They can pay the deposit for such an establishment from their savings or via a contribution from a grateful employer. They also comply with the requirement that gifts be supplemented with own income and means of support where necessary. The target group for each establishment is specified in statutes. Apart from the religious community, there is often also a provision that priority would be given to family members or acquaintances of the founder if they will face difficulty. Many of these courtyard house are intended exclusively for women. They live longer than men, after all, especially at a time when the mortality rate among military personnel and seafarers is exceptionally high.[35] Women also have the benefit of being more inclined to live together in harmony and less susceptible to drunkenness. From the sixteenth until the nineteenth century, people have to learn how to live together in close proximity without engaging in public fights, parties and/or sexual encounters. Back then, that is more often a challenge outside in cities and factories than is the case today where people are more accustomed to living and working in close proximity to each other.[36] Fighting and drunkenness are also reasons for being evicted from courtyard houses, something that most certainly did occur.[37] Establishments in which couples could live also exist, but these face a specific problem. As spouses do not die at the same time, a courtyard house eventually

---

[34] There are, of course, exceptions. For instance, the "Grand Dame" Henriette Amelie van Haren de Nerha from 1804 to 1818 in the Deutsenhofe at Prinsengracht, Amsterdam. See Van Eeghen (1967).

[35] The mortality risks of soldiers and seamen in the Dutch East India Company (VOC) are listed, for instance, in the similarly named case in Kemperman, Geelhoed, and Op 't Hoog (2013).

[36] Mastenbroek (1993).

[37] Donga (2008).

houses couples as well as single people. The establishments usually have a minimum age of around 50–60 to ensure that residents no longer have children still living with them, which potentially could result in insufficient accommodation space.

The reason why people want to live in courtyard houses is very simple. You have no inkling of what will happen in the future or what age you will reach. That underlines the importance of having the certainty and security that you will receive care and shelter during your old age, preferably in a separate physical and social world where you feel at home and protected.

Customer Value: "I Entrust Myself to the Good Care and Community of the Courtyard House" In concrete terms, the gifts entail an own home and vital necessities. Residents live together with other group members who can help each other when necessary. Gifts and house rules are provided and arranged by the resident house father and/or mother in the interest of compassion, mutual caring and sharing, and security. In principle, a one-off purchase sum has to be paid in order to live in a courtyard house. As noted the amount depends on the own assets of the relevant courtyard house at that moment. Future residents do not all pay the same amount. Some courtyard houses have start-up capital from their founder and initially require no payment whatsoever while others offer free places for poor people. Prospective residents are often also required to bequeath all or part of their possessions to the courtyard house upon their death. The proceeds were then used to renovate the home for the next occupant. Prospective residents are placed on a waiting list, have to observe the house rules and also help residents as much as they can. They are usually expected to look after themselves and also take care of their own cooking and cleaning. From a social perspective, they also run the risk that fellow residents will dislike them. However, the likelihood of this is mitigated given that they generally belong to the same group in terms of class and religion. From a financial perspective, they may only benefited from the investment for a short period if they pass away soon, but can also profit more if they reach a ripe old age. From a modern-day perspective and in line with twenty-first-century morals, the loss of independence is a striking aspect of a courtyard house: the resident is a passer-by and subject to the establishment's rules, and therefore has to adapt. It is an agreement based on acquiescence and trust.

Delivery: Recruitment Within the Own Network, Living Together Independently Within the Courtyard House Larger elderly houses where people can buy a life time place for a one-off purchase sum, occasionally place advertisements to attract potential residents. For smaller, private courtyard houses, however, it is primarily a supply-side market. The amount of capital of each establishment varies, but each one starts in principle with a private "subsidy" in the form of immovable property. If a landlord wants to launch a chain of courtyard houses to earn money, he will have to request a larger contribution. That can also explain why the demand is always greater than the supply. Prospective residents are tipped off through word-of-mouth advertising and proposed and selected on the basis of references and favors. The initiative lies with prospective residents, but also within their environment. An example of this is when someone has to find a good place for an elderly member of staff or a family member who no longer has anyone else to lean on. The size of the courtyard house and the life expectancy of existing residents constitutes the physical limits. The real limitation lies in the shortage of space. A place on the waiting list after a ballot is not yet enough to guarantee the availability of a home before your death.

The governors of the courtyard house are mostly prominent representatives of the involved church community. They are actively involved in the selection of new residents but then have little contact with existing residents thereafter. Day-to-day care is taken care of mostly by the resident house father or mother who report to these governors. The amount of contact outside the establishment differs from resident to resident and also depends on residents themselves. There is of course also mutual contact. The manner in which this occurs depends logically on the group dynamic and therefore varies from establishment to establishment and over the course of time. Evidently, most establishments do not intend to forge a single, very tightly knit community. They are not communal living groups like those from the 1970s in the US and Europe. Instead, they focus more on treating one another with decency and friendliness while maintaining a certain distance. With people living in such close proximity to one another, this appears to be the right recipe for maintaining privacy and avoiding explosive and complex group processes.[38]

Operation: the Organization of Psychological, Financial and Physical Security The heart of the courtyard house is its physical location and the building. Remarkably, the design itself is a direct reflection of the calm, protection and security that the establishment provides. What aspects do the various designs share? Just like a monastery, the courtyard house is litterally oriented inwards. Front doors and many windows do not face the street but the courtyard instead, as the name already indicates. The human dimension is retained in the social design but also in the size of the physical design. Private courtyard houses usually comprise around 10–20 cottages or rooms. They often have 12 homes with a single occupant or a couple, which is an easily manageable number of people. The number 12 is also a number of significance in the Bible and is also often referred to when describing the number of rooms.

The organization and much of the work in the establishment is carried out by house fathers and/or mothers who also live there. They fulfill the role of intermediaries to the governors, gatekeepers of the establishment, guardians of house rules and coordinators of maintenance and service facilities. Practical tasks such as domestic work for the communal area, chores and gardening also fall under their responsibility. The assistance provided by the house father and/or mother and the mutual aid between residents involves primarily informal care. Residents have to personally call in and pay for medical and personal care that is really intensive. Bear in mind that medical care up until the twentieth century is much more limited, with considerably fewer people in need of intensive care as a chronic patient.

The governor's primary task, in addition to the selection of new residents, is to ensure continuity and financial solidity in particular. The contribution paid by new residents has to be calculated properly. If everyone grows much older than antici-

---

[38] Leene (1997).

pated, available funds will be used up quicker (the "long-life risk"). And if everyone dies earlier than anticipated, the requested contribution will have been too great (the short-life risk). The excess contribution of people who die younger has to cover the additional costs of people who grow older. Maintaining financial equilibrium is essential, in other words.[39] This is fairly precise and requires high-level calculations. The Dutch leading politician Johan de Witt writes about this in 1671 in a book about The Worth of Life Annuities Compared to Redemption Bonds.[40] Besides a leading politician, he is therefore also a "leading actuary" and his book is still considered one of the milestones in modern pension and life insurances. Due to the uncertainty at the moment of death, the courtyard house requires equity capital as a "solvent" buffer. This equity has to be invested, managed and protected with care. Excess equity provides additional scope for greater charity. The contribution requested from residents decreases and gifts can be increased. When the available equity is too little, the establishment will not be able to fulfill the obligations undertaken in relation to residents and can go into liquidation, in the worst case scenario. In a nutshell and on an elementary level, these are the same issues that still occur today in the proper and orderly management of pensions and life insurance. The phenomenon of life annuities described by Johan de Witt which forms the basis for courtyard houses is still a wonderful, old-school life insurance construction. "Immediate annuities": a one-off sum of money is invested in return for a sum of money that you receive in monthly installments until your death. It is also not very different to the issues prevalent within healthcare and non-life insurance since here it is not clear either beforehand how much will have to be reimbursed. Reserves are intended as a solvent buffer for getting by in times when the outflow of money exceeds the inflow, and also when it is the other way round. Sailing too close to the wind with equity and solvency and returning everything immediately and in full to the customer is tempting in the short term and makes you popular. In the long term, it inevitably leads to a financial crisis in bad times.

Besides suppliers of the day-to-day needs of the courtyard house and its residents, suppliers and partners of a more strategic nature also exist. As indicated, the church community plays a key role. Furthermore this includes, of course, the builders and architects who help construct, maintain and renovate the establishment. Finally, there are the politicians and civil servants, who have a considerably less active role in day-to-day care because it is based on a private initiative. They can be either a help or a hindrance. That is also evident during the twenty-first century within courtyard houses that still exist today in the form of residential communities. This does not appear to dovetail with current regulations and permits. Over the past few decades many such establishments have had to comply with Dutch regulations pertaining to individual residential units for each room, all of which prove to be somewhat puzzling. It sometimes even results in changing the focus to housing students in one household as the only way to comply with regulations.[41]

---

[39] Schmitz (1965).

[40] For the real scientist in this field, it is interesting to know further that the first scientific mortality tables were compiled in 1693 by the Englishman Edmond Halley. See Halley (1693).

[41] Donga (2008).

Value for customers

Result *What do I get?*
- A home providing the basic necessities of life

Process *How do I get it?*
- Independent but communal living with familiar people and a live-in landlord

Emotion *What do I feel?*
- Social and physical feeling of shelter, protection and security

Price *What are the costs?*
- A non-recurring contribution and part or all of my possessions revert to courtyard house when I die

Effort *What do I have to do for it?*
- I have to wait to enter, hope that a place will become available and adjust to the courtyard house rules.

Risk *What are the uncertainties?*
- I have certainty no matter how long I live, but I cannot go back on my decision easily plus my possessions are also gone if I die earlier than expected

Market segments

Position
- Part of the local religious communities and the directors and networks
- Primary located in cities, especially in Amsterdam, Haarlem, Leiden, Groningen and Utrecht

Competition
- Primary option for people is to stay living in their own home
- Soft competition among different courtyard houses due to scarcity
- Alternatives include large organized communities for the elderly, the sick and the poor such as almshouses and retirement houses

Target group
- Own religious circle in the neighborhood starting with the founder
- Specifically single elderly females and to a lesser extent also elderly couples and men
- The middle class or lower middle class including those who perform duties such as serving, cooking, and public/private teaching

Customer insights
- It is very valuable to know that you are assured of a protected old age in a sheltered physical environment in a familiar social circle

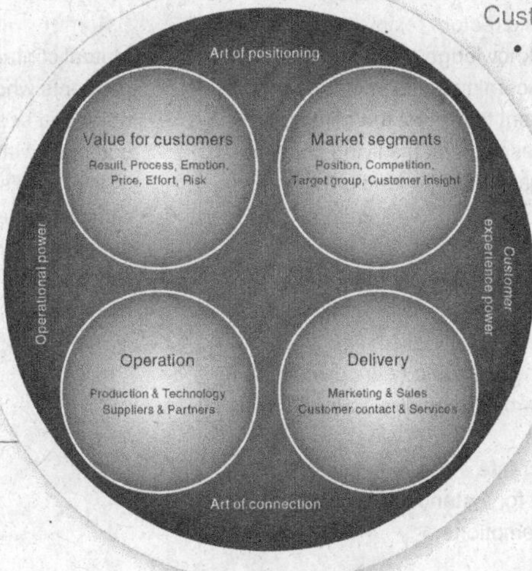

Figure 5.3.2 Value for customers and Market segments of Courtyard houses

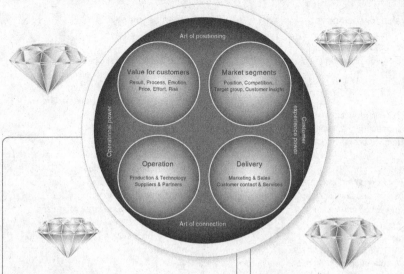

Figure 5.3.3 Operation and Delivery of Courtyard houses

Operation

Production & Technology

- Physical materialization of shelter and safety in architecture of courtyard built around a garden with frontdoors towards enclosed inner space and not out onto open street
- Personal approach of 10 to 20 homes (often 12 or 13) among a courtyard
- Daily coordination of supplies, maintenance and abiding by the rules of the live-in landlord with the courtyard house directors residing off-site
- Expertise with and knowledge of actuarial mortality tables concerning life expectancy and solvency management to protect the continuity and pay expenditures such as the living supplies, maintenance and wages for the landlord

Suppliers & Partners

- Primary suppliers to build and maintain the courtyard house such as architects, constructors and craftsman
- Partners such as churches and religious communities that often also provide the directors and own the courtyard house
- Governments that create a context, limits building permits but for instance also give tax advantages and exemptions

Delivery

Marketing & Sales

- New residents are recruited via the grapevine in own network.
- It is a privilege if you are allowed to enter through own network or initiator's circle of surviving relatives of courtyard directors

Customer contact & Services

- Mutual contacts between residents who can help each other and keep each other company within the boundaries of everyone's privacy
- Support, care and basic living supplies via live-in landlord (housemother, housefather or housecouple)

5.3.3 The Result: Altruism and Self-Financing Complement One Another

Courtyard houses often start with substantial capital but the returns are not sufficient to remain self-financing. Nevertheless, they often manage to operate for centuries. Although they no longer function as courtyard houses nowadays, there are still some 200 establishments in the Netherlands where people live together. Of the 51 courtyard houses founded in Amsterdam over the centuries, only seven have disappeared completely. Particularly striking is the number of centuries during which they function as a courtyard house. The social design and revenue model evidently succeeds in striking a balance between value creation for and by stakeholders that works effectively and is resistant. How is that achieved?

Let us travel back in time to find out. The contribution which new residents pay, the gifts they receive and the degree of self-motivation among residents differ among courtyard houses. This provides scope to make adjustments over time during financially difficult periods and to do something extra if people have little money or unexpectedly reach a very old age. People are keen to live in one of these establishments, as evidenced by the long waiting lists. When the requested contribution or self-motivation is somewhat higher, or the gifts lightly less, vacancies hardly rise. At the same time, governors do not abuse this system. From a purely commercial perspective, places could have been auctioned off or sold to people on the waiting list for the highest bid. But that is not the case. Such an approach does not correspond to the original goals of compassion and would not have been tolerated within the own circle to which administrators and residents belonged.

The founder's name is immortalized in exchange for his or her inheritance. Governors acting on behalf of the church or foundation usually receive no financial compensation, although they are able to enjoy fine dinners. It revolves primarily around social status. In addition, favors can be granted within the own immediate surroundings or religious community.

Staff does not enjoy the comprehensive conditions of employment and working hours we are accustomed to in many North-Western European countries nowadays. In this respect, it is more akin to developing countries and countries with a more flexible labor market, such as the USA. Supervisors at the courtyard house do not head off to work and return home at the end of the day. Instead, it is more like working from home. The name "house father" or "house mother" is therefore more appropriate than "staff member." As the head of the "family," these individuals have a relatively large degree of freedom and responsibility to manage day-to-day affairs in the establishment. They receive a small salary in return, but the reward is mainly nonmonetary in nature because they live in the courtyard house alongside residents and receive gifts in the form of food and drinks. This give them certainty as well as the feeling they are doing something beneficial that matter to others.

The courtyard houses are based on private initiative and governance within the own social circuit. From a public perspective, this is beneficial in that they do not depend on common collective facilities. Over the centuries, this sort of approaches makes it possible to finance and implement the high-quality social system in the Netherlands. This offers additional calm and stability in society.

And today? Can we learn something from courtyard houses with regard to living and caring for ageing people in the twenty-first century?

Value by customers
- The one-off contributions and assets of residents make it self-financing. They are set at and used to keep the funds on a level which is sufficient to pay for the day-to-day expenses such as living supplies, maintenance and wages.
- Residents have duties to help each other and participate in the overall tasks within the courtyard house, so that they contribute in kind to the community within their own physical capabilities

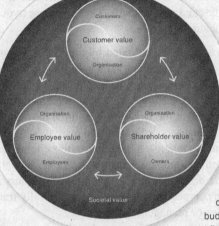

Value for and by employees
- Live-in landlords primarily receive non-monetary compensation, since they can also live and use living supplies in the courtyard house.
- Landlords are offered long-term certainty in that the necessities of life are provided for and residents can play a valuable and respected role within their own group

Value for and by shareholders
- Founder provides the initial starting capital and potential donors create surplus budgets. Their merciful contribution results in respect, ensures that their name will live on after their death and contributes to their salvation
- Directors receive respect, strengthen their reputation and have a position in which they can grant people the privilege to be allowed to live in the courtyard house.
- The official owner (often the church and/or a foundation within own network) gets an additional instrument to do good works and strengthen their own group

Value for and by society
- Solutions within the own group limit the demands on public funding and over the centuries have been an important instrument in the provision of communal arrangements with high standards for good care for those who truly need it
- Good solutions for living, care and old age strengthen and maintain social peace and stability
- Still offers an inspiring example of a self-financing social solution with a personal approach to communal living and access to care and provisions for seniors

Figure 5.3.4 Value for and by stakeholders of Courtyard houses

5.3.4 The Brilliant Lessons of Courtyard Houses

It is becoming increasingly clear that care and human attention for all senior citizens in countries cannot be fully provided collectively in countries with a significantly large ageing population. Types of housing are being sought in which people can continue living at home longer and look after themselves and each other more. The old system of living in courtyard houses offers several surprising and inspiring elements in this day and age. It also seems to conflict with a number of points relating to Western standards, values and automatisms. That gives rise to questions and puzzles that can serve an educational purpose:

- Elderly people can live together facilitated by a house father/mother. How can they do this and what is the appropriate human dimension to this end? As indicated, many old courtyard houses only had 12 rooms or cottages and therefore rarely 25 residents. This size ensured everything remained transparent for both the residents and the organization. Does this constitute the human dimension that healthcare is seeking? Primary coordination and everyday matters at these establishments were entrusted to a house father and/or house mother. These individuals also lived on the premises and always acted as a point of contact for residents. This was a formula that demanded flexibility in terms of hours and tasks. When viewed from a modern perspective, however, it was a totally transparent system: no handovers, schedules or management layers.
- Common background creates community. Another aspect was the common background with respect to the environment and religion, which ensured that the environment felt familiar to residents. This is a philosophy that is still embraced today and valued within different forms of care, but it is sometimes also critized since it conflicts with the ideal to treat everyone equal.
- A good balance between privacy and communality. Many people are not accustomed to living in close proximity to one another. It results in too much intrusiveness among residents and gives rise to complex social processes. On the other hand, too much privacy can lead to loneliness. The courtyard house appears to be a type of accommodation that can ensure privacy and communality due to the social as well as the physical design. The question this also gives rise to is how democratic and how proactive you make the residential community. New, more luxurious residential concepts are often created by people including active senior citizens who are still in the prime of their lives. Often they also assume that older senior citizens are highly active and wish to remain in control. This is a wonderful perspective but perhaps not suitable for everyone, and neither until the end of someone's life. Courtyard houses are based more on the concept of a protected environment that provides shelter and care for you and not on fulfilling all different needs for proactive individual consumers.[42]

---

[42] Differentiation in target groups and a comparison between communes and courtyard houses are elaborated on in Leene (1997) and by Veltman (1995).

- The one-off purchase sum. Can we learn something from the simple and elegant revenue model used by courtyard houses? Are they an example when it comes to contributing one's own assets in exchange for a guarantee of care if this is required? Even after several years of economic crisis, equity in homes and the pensions of many senior citizens in western countries evidently provide an adequate source for the payment of care if it cannot be financed through collective resources. Macroeconomists also see that very clearly, but how to translate that into everyday reality on a micro level still poses a conundrum. Part of the problem is that you cannot exactly take your home along brick by brick in order to pay for care if needed. You also have no idea how long it will take before "you'll eventually have eaten up your home." The old principle of the one-off purchase sum with fixed gifts or annuities until you die seems a logical part of the solution.
- Continuity is ensured because the institution is larger and outlives individual residents. Many people nowadays consider selling their home and starting a private home-care villa with a group of acquaintances. This has not yet resulted in a large number of establishments as they often come up against problem of practical organization, legal snags and pitfalls, and the entry-exit strategy. What happens, for example to the home care villa you share when people leave, or die? How do you find and select a new resident? How do you jointly divide and/or purchase care and domestic help? What is the best mix for housing senior citizens who are old and those who are not as old? In short: the organization of such a type of housing is already so complex that it often only remains in the planning stage. If you are not careful, collective aspirations lead to conflict before even a single brick has been laid or purchased. The advantage of courtyard houses is that the organizational aspect is taken care of and the applicable rules are not open to debate.
- Self-contributing. What can people do for themselves and for each other? The courtyard houses have a tiered system. Residents are, in principle, self-sufficient, self-motivated, and self-contributing. In addition, mutual neighborly assistance is provided within the court courtyard house community. If residents differ in terms of age and dependency, they can organize much of the normal human care and attention amongst themselves. House fathers and/or house mothers do lend a helping hand, but are not total healthcare practitioners.

The courtyard house model which originated from the sixteenth century is somewhat rusty five centuries later. But below the surface lies a wonderful, refreshing and inspiring concept for the issues we face today. It is high time to discuss the business model of courtyard houses 3.0!

5.4   Stiftung Liebenau

Lebensräume für Jung und Alt

Rick Kasper, Tim Widdershoven, Sanne Boevé & Jeroen Geelhoed @: J.
Geelhoed@samhoud.com, Phone: 0031 622408791

Stiftung Liebenau

Prelude *It is around 10 o'clock on a Thursday morning and we are driving on the
premises of Stiftung Liebenau. We immediately notice the hustle and bustle around us;
mothers are pushing prams, elderly men are strolling along the street with the aid of
their walking sticks, and a young woman wearing tracksuit bottoms is pushing an
elderly lady around in a wheelchair. The moment we enter the reception area, with
charming children's paintings adorning the walls, we notice the informal nature of the
establishment. The receptionist, who looks incredibly relaxed, shows us the way and
we soon arrive at Wohnanlage Meckenbeuren, a residential community where young
and elderly people alike live together in the same apartment complex. The foyer is
filled with photos of elderly people pushing prams, children playing, elderly people
cooking to an accompanying recipe and cheerful children's drawings. Convivial,
almost cozy, are the words that spring to our mind. A large board on the wall is covered with photos of elderly and young people, colored prints of large and small hands
and the text "Wir Stärken uns Gegenseitig" (together we strengthen one another).
"Yes!" exclaims an elderly lady enthusiastically when asked if she really does feel
more fit and vital because she is surrounded by so many young people. And that is
precisely what Stiftung Liebenau wishes to achieve with its Lebensräume projects.*

Introduction Let us return to the nineteenth century to obtain a better picture of the
foundation. Adolf Aich was a vicar in the chapel of St. John in Tettnang. He decided
to establish a hospital that could provide care for the "incurable" since almost no-
one was interested in assisting handicapped and chronically ill people. In 1866, he
therefore founded the "St.-Johann-Verein" together with a socially engaged citizen
in Tettnag. The aim of this association was to create an independent hospital using
voluntary contributions. He visited twenty dioceses and regions to collect donations.
In 1870, Aich purchased Schlösschen Liebenau himself and established a nursing
home for disabled and poor people. He called it the *Pfleg- und Bewahranstalt*

Liebenau (Liebenau Hospital and Custodial Institution), and his establishment soon garnered an excellent reputation in the region. In 1873, the association was officially founded Stiftung Liebenau. In 1893, the foundation purchased Schlösschen Liebenau from Aich and by the end of the nineteenth century it housed up to 400 people.

Adolf Aich could probably never have imagined where all of this would ultimately lead to. Today Stiftung Liebenau and its subsidiaries have more than 6400 employees. The foundation is active in over 100 locations spread across five different countries, namely Germany, Austria, Italy, Switzerland, and Bulgaria. All of them account for an annual turnover of USD 294 million (EUR 250 million). The foundation no longer focuses solely on people with a disability but also trains and educates children and young people with learning difficulties. It also provides assistance and support to parents of children with a chronic illness or disability. The foundation also runs several businesses that offer employment to people with disabilities. Finally, elderly care is also provided now in various ways. The most striking are the Lebensräume (Living area) projects, which make elderly people part of close-knit community. Fellow residents assist the elderly with activities they themselves can no longer carry out. Professional care is only provided when assistance from the community is no longer sufficient. The Lebensräume projects are remarkable and brilliant due to the collaborative structure between the municipality, the foundation, healthcare practitioners and property developers, but this will be discussed later in greater detail. We will first take a closer look at Stiftung Liebenau as a whole in order to obtain a good overall impression. A notable aspect of the foundation's activities is that it gives people opportunities to participate fully in society. Often, however, people need to take action themselves. They have to be active if they wish to benefit from the foundation.

5.4.1   The Cornerstone: Value for Every Individual

The idea that everyone should be able to participate in society and play an active role is reflected in the foundation's brand essence: "Creating conditions for a dignified life." The foundation helps people to help themselves. A fine example of this is the help offered to disabled people. The foundation creates the conditions that enable people to participate in society as fully as they personally wish to and can. The foundation offers educational and employment opportunities so that these people can live independently later on. They must, however, seize these opportunities.

The organization's higher goal can be described as: striving to allow every individual to lead a dignified life from birth until death. It focuses on value for the individual as well as society. His or her gender, nationality or religion play no role in this. It is also irrelevant whether the individual has physical, mental or emotional limitations. This conviction originates from the organization's Christian roots. All its activities revolve around giving a dignified life to people who would otherwise not be able to participate or fully participate in society. Ever since the foundation's very first day, it has endeavored to offer a dignified life to the disabled, chronically ill, and poor.

The foundation's audacious goal is twofold. Firstly, to make people believe that God is present in our world through the work of the organization. Secondly, to create an inclusive society where people think less about themselves and take better care of one another. The audacious goal is expressed in the brand promise to offer every individual a dignified life and help every human being to participate in society as fully as possible. Finally, the facilities of Liebenau provide safe and dignified shelter to those in need of long-term support.

Everything is done according to the Christian conviction that people must look after each other. That is why care is one of the foundation's core values. It permeates throughout all of the foundation's activities, ranging from providing education to children and young people with learning difficulties to offering employment to people with disabilities. The other core values of brotherly love and solidarity are also clearly evident in the organization's numerous activities. These values are reflected in the huge number of volunteers active within the organization. This is also apparent from the success of the Lebensräume projects, which appeal to brotherly love and solidarity among residents. The fourth core value, independence, can be derived directly from the brand essence. Independence plays a major role in the organization. Within a Lebensraum project, for example, professionals will only mediate and assist if people in the community cannot resolve something themselves.

The core values of care, brotherly love, solidarity, and independence are also the brand values used to realize the brand promise. These values are expressed externally and reflected in the foundation's activities. The foundation's social workplaces exemplify this, and also serve as brand proof. These workplaces employ disabled people to give them a useful purpose in society. The manner in which care for the elderly is provided in community projects, which permit older people to retain their dignity, also proves how the foundation has kept its promises since the outset. An event from the Second World War is indicative of the foundation's fight to fulfill its promises regardless of peoples' origins. The Nazi regime systematically murdered people with a disability during the war. Some 1500 Stiftung Liebenau residents perished in the gas chambers of the Grafeneck Euthanasia Centre during this atrocious period. Liebenau managed to save 150 people from this horror.

The foundation can fulfill promises because of its community-focused approach. It therefore knows how to create the right preconditions that almost automatically give rise to self-help and neighborly assistance. Residents are also allowed to assume responsibility within projects. Other core qualities of the foundation include its independence from the state and the degree of autonomy stemming from this. The organization is therefore free of any political influence. This independence is achieved because the financing of day-to-day operations originates primarily from entitlements to statutory subsidies and payments from private insurance funds. These are neither political- nor government-dependent. Donations and occasionally proceeds from wills are used to finance new projects. Ultimately, the evidence is provided by the success of the foundation and its projects. The number of projects has grown significantly and hence the number of employees and turnover too.

Brand essence: Creating the prerequisites for a dignified life

Higher goal
- We want to offer people a dignified life: dignified for both the individual and society

Brand roots
- Founded in 1870 by a group headed by Adolf Aich, with the aim of helping handicapped and chronically ill people
- Originated based on Christian love of one's neighbor

Audacious goal
- Creating an inclusive society
- Demonstrating the presence of God in our world

Brand promise
- A dignified life for everyone connected to the Foundation
- Having people participate in society to the fullest extent possible
  - Offer shelter to the underprivileged

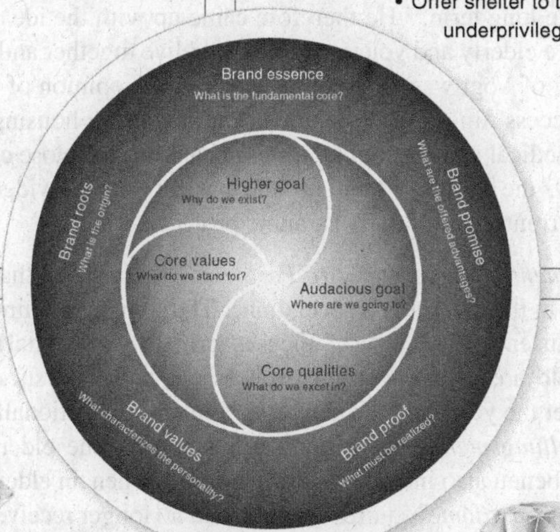

Brand essence
What is the fundamental core?

Higher goal
Why do we exist?

Brand roots
What is the origin?

Core values
What do we stand for?

Brand promise
What are the offered advantages?

Audacious goal
Where are we going to?

Core qualities
What do we excel in?

Brand values
What characterises the personality?

Brand proof
What must be realized?

Core and brand values
- Care
- Self-reliance
- Love of one's neighbor
- Mutual sharing & caring

Core qualities
- Independent
- Community-focused
- Customer insight
- Responsibility

Brand proof
- Social workplaces
- Community-focused projects
- Rescue of patients during the Holocaust

Figure 5.4.1 Vision and Positioning of Stiftung Liebenau

5.4.2   The Business Model: Lebensräume für Jung und Alt

Stiftung Liebenau has numerous subsidiaries and participating interests. This business case focuses on the *Lebensräume für Jung und Alt* (Living Area for Young and Old), in other words projects set up and run by two daughter foundations called Liebenau Leben im Alter and St. Anna Hilfe. The development of these projects commenced around 20 years ago. In the early 1990s, the first residential community based on the *Lebensräume für Jung und Alt* concept started operating in the municipality of Vogt.

Gerhard Schiele, the director of *St. Anna Hilfe für ältere Menschen*,[43] believes that if you want to ensure that elderly people remain active, you must not offer them care they do not require. In view of the increasingly ageing population, he believed that the various age generations could help each other to continue supporting the elderly in the long term.[44] He therefore came up with the idea to initiate a housing project where elderly and young people could live together and help each other. The municipality of Vogt was very enthusiastic. In the opinion of Gerhard Schiele, the project's success hinged on a central location for the housing community nearby shops and medical and cultural facilities. Thanks to the close collaboration with the municipality, the building land for the project was provided for free. Southern Germany currently has 26 Lebensräume projects.

Market Segment: Competitors Are Partners The position that Lebensräume projects occupy in the market is a special one. The foundation aims to offer residents a dignified existence. The project focuses primarily on (vital) elderly people, but young people are also important even essential for its success. The know-how acquired over the years and the networks create an exceptionally unique position, or an *Alleinstellungsmerkmal* (unique selling point). The elderly care provided by Stiftung Liebenau also includes nursing homes. When an elderly person residing in one of the *Lebensräume* requires care and can no longer receive it in their home, this individual is entitled to stay at a stationary care facility in a nearby nursing home.

As its name suggests, the point of these communities is to allow young and old(er) people to live under the same roof. These can be elderly people in need of assistance, active and energetic senior citizens, old or young couples, single parents or young families. The aim is to create an age mix where children and young adults make up a third of residents and middle-aged or older people account for two-thirds. Residents must be able to identify with the social model and want to be part of a *Lebensräume* community. The *Gemeinwesenarbeiter* (GWA) or community worker and the residents' council verify this during the selection procedure for new residents. In line with the foundation's vision, they do not make any distinction between religion and income.

In the future, professionals will no longer be able to fully meet the growing demand for care. Director Gerhard Schiele is pursuing the idea that much of the demand for professional care can be avoided by optimizing the use of the community.

---

[43] See also http://www.stiftung-liebenau.de and http://www.st.anna-hilfe.de.

[44] http://www.zorgwelzijn.nl/Welzijnswerk/Nieuws/2007/5/Lebensraume-fur-Jung-und-Alt-Burenhulp-als-uitkomst-voor-de-vergrijzing-ZWZ011433W/.

People will remain more vital and independent if they help themselves and others. This will enable people to live without or with less professional help. At the same time, residential areas are made accessible to young people who would otherwise have difficulty finding a home. In return, these young help assist the elderly.

Customer Value: Self-Esteem, Satisfaction, and Vitality   Although every *Lebensräume* project is different, the higher goal of Stiftung Liebenau is always the focal point. It will therefore always revolve around creating a valuable life for residents themselves and for society. Residents organize a wide range of activities in the Meckenbeuren and Amtzell establishments, for example. These include joint activities such as festivities, eating breakfast together, cooking together, and participating in courses.

The age structure ensures that young people and active senior citizens can always assist the elderly. Should an elderly resident require professional help, this is communicated and organized. If possible, this will take the form of extramural care so that elderly residents can continue living at home. This approach gives them a feeling of self-esteem, independence, and vitality. Residents feel like they belong to a community, but can also lead their own lives and retain their own identity. This is different to residential communes from the 1970s where people did everything together and their own identity was weakened.

The projects are not only interesting for elderly people in need of assistance, but also for young people and active senior citizens. First of all, they can live in a pleasant, central location. These projects also give them a feeling of satisfaction and responsibility thanks to the voluntary community care they provide to fellow residents. It is also wonderful for active senior citizens to live in a community with young people and children, and not only with other elderly people. This keeps them more in touch with the youth and ensures in turn that they remain more youthful. It is also interesting for young people—young families with children—because they can benefit too from a helpful community, such as babysitting for their children.

The costs for residents are limited to the purchase or rental price of the home and the normal cost of living. The purchase or rental price is just below the price of similar homes in the vicinity. Residents of Lebensräume projects can register if they are willing to offer basic support and assistance to neighbors and fellow residents. This help is voluntary.

Delivery: Together We Are Strong   The building has shared rooms in which activities are organized. Residents can rent the rooms for a small fee to celebrate their birthday with family members, for example. The rooms and corridors in the building radiate communality and conviviality thanks to photos of residents and children's activities and works. One community worker (GWA) is employed to ensure that everything runs smoothly within the community. This individual often works part-time and is employed by the foundation, but never personally lives in the residential community. He or she acts as the first point of contact for residents, brings residents into contact with each other and encourages self-help and neighborly assistance. Residents do not provide actual care, such as physical nursing. Neighborly assistance can be offered in various ways, such as walking a fellow resident's dog, tending the garden or doing the laundry. Activities within the community that residents organize themselves for free include childcare, grocery-shopping services, courses, morning gymnastics, group lunches, cooking together or book clubs. Everyone can contribute. In this way, elderly residents can keep an eye on their fellow senior citizens. A unique example is the roll-down shutter check. If desired, residents can ask their neighbors to knock on their door if their roll-down shutters are not opened by a specific time. In the event of an emergency, a spare key to the home is on hand so that the neighbor can enter the property and "save" the resident. Professional help is sought in situations where neighborly assistance no longer suffices. Cooperation with local healthcare practitioners plays a pivotal role in this respect. If possible, professional help is provided at the resident's home to allow him or her to continue living within the community. If the requisite care can no longer be provided in the resident's own home, he or she is entitled (with priority) to receive care in a Stiftung Liebenau home.

Operation: Working Together Municipalities usually approach Stiftung Liebenau to construct and run a residential community. In most cases they do so out of a desire to delay the demographic change somewhat or to alter the demographic structure.

Homes are sold to homeowners and investors during the construction phase. All of them are normally sold before construction work has been completed. Homeowners do not always personally occupy their home but view it as a capital investment. Stiftung Liebenau takes care of the rental process and guarantees rent returns. Investors enjoy a high degree of certainty and can therefore be assured of a safe investment. To finance the community project, Liebenau and the municipalities involved at the time set up a *Sozialfonds* (social fund). Proceeds from the sale of homes, contributions from resources paid by the municipalities concerned and gifts and donations flow in and out of this fund. A treaty of principles determines that resources from this fund are assigned directly and exclusively to residents from the relevant municipality. In the event of a deficit, which is realistic given the low(er) housing returns and interest on contributed resources nowadays, the municipality will step in. A community worker is the focal point of the Lebensräume concept. This is usually a professional woman with a background in social education, such as a social worker or a social pedagogue, who works part-time. Her salary is covered by the social fund.

A round-table meeting is held in the *Lebensräume* twice a year, during which residents are given the opportunity to express themselves and identify problems. The residents' council then addresses these problems in consultation with the community worker. The projects' success depends largely on the residents of the residential group, which is why the selection of new residents is so important. The residents' council, in cooperation with the community worker, looks at age first since the age structure must be maintained. This council also verifies whether the family or person in question has relatives of friends in the area, with a view to family reunions later on.

The most important partner in a *Lebensräume* project is the municipality. Municipalities are often the first to approach Stiftung Liebenau and they are responsible for the provision of public utilities and public services within the care area of their citizens. The involvement of the municipality and the community in a Lebensräume project is therefore considerable and also crucial to a project's success.

Value for customers

Result *What do I get?*
- I remain a part of society and I live a dignified life. I remain more active and with a higher vitality*
- A central location to live and an involved community with helpful co-residents**

Process *How do I get it?*
- I am selected to live here. I receive help from my neighbors and other co-residents when I ask for it

Emotion *What do I feel?*
- I feel responsible, more self-reliant, younger and safer*
- It is a good feeling to be part of a social community**

Price *What are the costs?*
- Accommodation in a community such as this one is slightly less expensive than the average rental prices

Effort *What do I have to do for it?*
- As part of the community, I am expected to make a contribution according to my ability

Risk *What are the uncertainties?*
- Residents should show involvement and actually offer to help out

Market segments

Position
- Stiftung Liebenau has occupied a special position in the market with its 'Lebensräume' (Living Space) concept

Competition
- Traditional nursing homes are considered partners rather than competition. The elderly can divert to living in such homes when living in the community is really no longer possible
- Home care organizations are not seen as competition either. In the end, the people should be the priority

Target group
- All people that wish to live in a Lebensraum-community and that wish to contribute to it are seen as the target group. The aim is to create a mixed-age group. The selection is based on age, local contacts, urgency and the belief in the philosophy

Customer insights
- In the future, increasing demands for care can no longer be put on just the professionals' plate. Therefore, people should rely on mutual care to a much larger extent

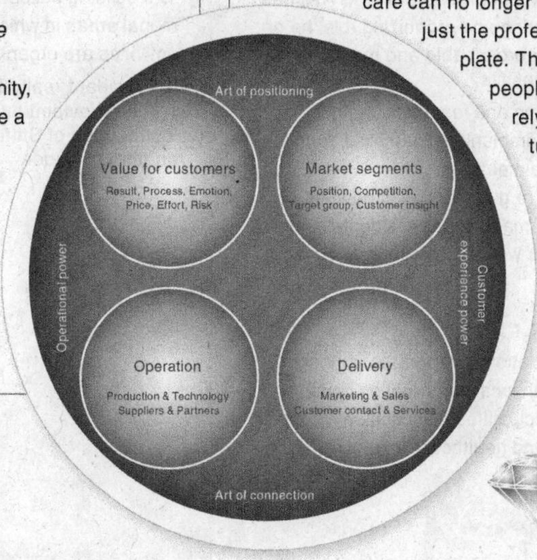

*Specifically elderly   **Specifically young

Figure 5.4.2 Value for customers and Market segments of Stiftung Liebenau

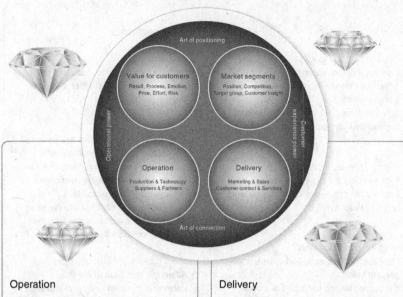

Operation

Production & Technology
- The community in the municipality takes the initiative to submit a plan to the Foundation and is responsible both for financing and building the residential unit. The Foundation takes a steering role in this (organizational philosophy).
- The Community Worker ('Gemeinwesenarbeiter(in)' or GWA) has a coordinating and organizing role, he or she is is approachable and mediates in case of conflicts
- Consultation and feedback originating from the community is gathered during roundtable meetings.
- Decisions (e.g., selection of new residents) are made by the residents' council together with the Community Worker

Suppliers & Partners
- The Foundation collaborates, among others, with local construction companies, municipalities, associations, communities and healthcare institutions

Delivery

Marketing & Sales
- The Foundation engages in marketing activities, the municipality suggests potential clients and the projects are reinforced through word-of-mouth advertising

Customer contact & Services
- The building possesses several communal areas in which for instance the activities are organized.
- If a resident really needs extra care this can be provided by professional care instututions of Stiftung Liebenau or another provider.

Figure 5.4.3 Operation and Delivery of Stiftung Liebenau

5.4.3   The Result: A Positive Spiral

Stiftung Liebenau as a whole has achieved significant results. With respect to business models, this chapter focuses mainly on the *Lebensräume für Jung und Alt*. The results in this section are based on our visits to the two Lebensräume projects in Amtzell and Meckenbeuren.[45]

Customers—read: residents—are immensely satisfied, and a 76-year-old resident had the following to say about the residential community: "I adore watching children play. I love them and they love me. There are also so many activities here such as gymnastics for senior citizens, handicrafts, singing or drinking coffee. You never have to feel bored. Who would not want that?" Younger residents believe that the residential community is a fine place to raise their children. Elderly people provide additional supervision in the area and even babysit children sometimes. On the other hand, young people assist elderly residents with new technology by giving them computer lessons. The waiting lists that have developed reveal that this community is also interesting for young people. Numerically, value for the customer can be expressed in a satisfaction survey.[46] Approximately 90 % of respondents in both Amtzell and Meckenbeuren are satisfied with their state of health, their quality of life and the absence of barriers in the residential community. In addition, over 95 % of respondents are satisfied with the situation in their private life while more than 90 % are satisfied with the general situation in the residential group.

Amazingly, only one paid employee (a community worker) is active within a Lebensräume project. The number of hours this individual works during the week depends on the number of residents in the residential group. She manages the neighborly assistance and works closely with the residents' council. A community worker from one of the projects says: "I feel I can provide a useful contribution to society through this project, which really gives me a feeling of satisfaction." Community workers also have considerable freedom in how they fulfill the role. As long as they succeed in organizing and managing the project properly, the foundation is satisfied. These individuals can therefore really turn the residential community into a personal project for the relevant municipality.

In fact, a project always involves multiple partners. The first is Stiftung Liebenau, with its know-how. With the realization of each residential community, the foundation takes one step closer towards its goal of giving everyone a dignified life. The second partner is the municipality. It proposes the establishment of a Lebensräume project, looks for a location, and draws up a financing plan to this end. The municipality derives value because it fulfills the duty of care imposed upon it by the state.

---

[45] With thanks to the employees of Stiftung Liebenau and the residents of the *Lebensräume* projects that we spoke with.

[46] Befragung der "Lebensräume für Jung und Alt" zur Weiterentwicklung des Qualitätsmanagementsystems: March 2010.

The Mayor of Amtzell explains: "The project also creates a positive spiral for the municipality: quality of life is good, which keeps a working population in the municipality (something that is quite exceptional for a rural municipality). In fact, it actually attracts people. This is favorable for companies based in the municipality, and we the municipality therefore receive more revenue—and corporation tax, for example—that allows us to continue developing the rest of the municipality. In addition, the demand for professional care is decreasing thanks to the project." Homeowners and investors the final partner. They make the municipality's plan financially viable and receive a guaranteed rental income for their property.

Finally, a project also yields value for society. The professional care system is unburdened thanks to Lebensräume projects. Hospital admission is deferred because elderly people continue living on their own for a longer period of time. The projects also ensure integration between young people and elderly people within the project, but certainly also beyond. The neighborhood or town often actively cooperates with this community. Lebensräume projects are a step in the right direction, a step towards a more inclusive society.

Value by customers

Results of satisfaction surveys (N = 54) in Lebensräume projects in Meckenbeuren en Amtzell:

- 90% are satisfied with their state of health or even experience this as satisfactory or very satisfactory, 58%
- 98.5% are satisfied with their quality of life or even rates this as satisfactory or very satisfactory, 72.2%
- 94.4% are satisfied with their barrier freedom or even rates this as satisfactory or very satisfactory, 80.5%
- 98.6% are satisfied with their private life or even rates this as satisfactory or very satisfactory, 72.7%
- 95.8% are satisfied with the residential group or even rates this as satisfactory or very satisfactory, 62.5%

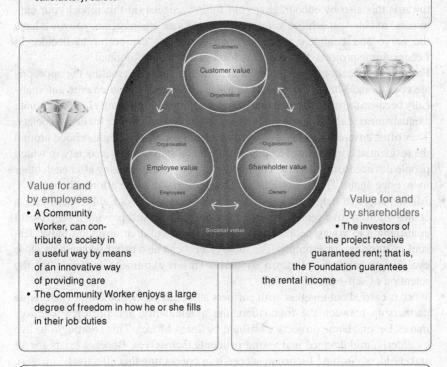

Value for and by employees

- A Community Worker, can con- tribute to society in a useful way by means of an innovative way of providing care
- The Community Worker enjoys a large degree of freedom in how he or she fills in their job duties

Value for and by shareholders

- The investors of the project receive guaranteed rent; that is, the Foundation guarantees the rental income

Value for and by society

- Unburdening the provision of professional healthcare and welfare
- Lower costs due to informal care giving and postponement of intramural admission
- A better integration of the young and the elderly along with an inclusive society
- A Lebensräume project often leads to more participation of the neighborhood or the village surrounding the project.

Figure 5.4.4   Value for and by stakeholders of Stiftung Liebandau

5.4.4   The Brilliant Lessons of Stiftung Liebenau

What lessons can we learn from the work of Stiftung Liebenau?

- Allow people to do a lot themselves. Much of the demand for care can be avoided by encouraging people to remain active and by organizing care and neighborly assistance within a social network. People continue to be more active and vital and require less care when less work is automatically taken off their hands. Simple support and assistance can be provided by neighbors or active elderly people in the neighborhood, who act on the basis of brotherly love and community spirit. A corresponding lesson is the fact that a company does not need to organize everything by itself in order to attain its higher goal. You can work towards this also by encouraging your fellow citizens (in this model your customers) to help you achieve your higher goal. As an organization, you must have the nerve and confidence then to give customers the power to decide. In Lebensräume projects, this takes the form of a residents' council.
- Facilitate connection; you can foster community spirit by creating the appropriate conditions. Mutual caring and sharing, and tolerance can emerge automatically because the inclusiveness that prevails within the community helps eliminate exclusiveness. Lebensräume projects are a step towards a more inclusive society. They often ensure a high level of involvement in the area or neighborhood around the residential community. In other words, it is a step towards a society in which people deviate from individualism and we as people start looking after each other more once again. This is a crucial step towards making care affordable.
- Allow people to help each other. Everyone, young and old alike, can make a contribution. Active senior citizens, for example, can still provide a very useful contribution to young people by babysitting their children or giving music lessons or tutoring, for example. The most elderly can also help by keeping a close eye on one another (roll-down shutters). This is extremely important for the retention of self-esteem.
- Work is carried out together with partners and each partner benefits. The unique partnership between the foundation, the municipality, and property investors makes Lebensräume projects a brilliant business Model. This is brought to live by elderly, middle-aged and young residents themselves. Benefits exists for all stakeholders. Stiftung Liebenau succeeds in connecting this effectively.

Chapter 6
Breakthrough: Letting Prevention and Self-Management Work

How Do We Create Incentives and Reward Systems for Demonstrable Health Benefits?

If we look for the ambitions in the triple-aim to make populations more healthy and improve treatments for lower costs per capita, prevention and self-management are key elements to solve the puzzle. We would like health to take over care and not the other way around! The needed medical treatments and medicine should be reduced because people live a regular healthy life. There is a lot of value in preventing someone from becoming ill. It is at the same time difficult to earn back investments based on illnesses that have not taken place and reimbursement of all healthy daily living is not the ultimate answer. There are however business models that make money by making people healthier:

- *Discovery has built a vitality company besides its insurance activities which focuses on promoting a healthy lifestyle by combining incentives, fast-moving consumer goods marketing, and superior actuarial number crunching of big data.*
- *Healthways has built a business model in which employers, insurance companies, and people themselves pay them for proven improvement of the health of populations with multiple chronical diseases.*
- *Kaiser Permanente originated from an employer who wanted to provide care and from that perspective not only originated own healthcare but also prevention to keep employees healthy and productive.*
- *PatientsLikeMe links people with rare diseases in online communities to share experiences on their medical conditions but also to exchange experiences to cope and improve daily life.*

If we end up with medical advice and reimbursement for riding the bike and eating tomatoes, the costs will rise and healthy living will not become something people enjoy and choose for themselves but an obligation which the doctor prescribes. This way of thinking is in line with a new dynamic approach to the concept of health in which this is defined as "the ability to adapt and to self-manage, in the face of social, mental and physical challenges of life." Compared to the traditional WHO

© Springer International Publishing Switzerland 2017

J. Kemperman et al. (eds.), *Brilliant Business Models in Healthcare*,
DOI 10.1007/978-3-319-26440-0_6

approach the emphasis shifts from "complete well-being" to the "individual's potential to be or become healthy, even when affected by disease, as well as the potential of personal growth and development towards fulfillment of personal aims in life."[1] What's extra interesting in this perspective is that it not only takes an holistic view on health. It also opens up the possibility to take the own perception of the person and patient on life as factual input and goal for improvement to assess the quality of healthcare and lifestyle interventions.

Ensuring that people become and remain healthy is a collective interest of the individual, the employer, the insurer, the government and society as a whole. There is a great need to feel mentally and physically healthy, to prevent illnesses and to learn how to live with chronic diseases. That raises the question why there are so few successful companies who make money by making people more healthy? Healthcare practitioners are in abundance, but a "healthy lifestyle provider" is not (yet) a professional group. An important crux of the problem is that prevention and reintegration entail significant investment costs especially for the people who need it most. At the same time, the effects of interventions are difficult to demonstrate and attribute and it is often questionable who should pay. Avoiding a (new) medical treatment requires a real change in daily patterns, such as adopting a healthy diet, quiting cigarettes and exercising more. These behavioral changes are difficult to achieve and have more to do with daily life then with medicine. Those who focus least on leading a healthy life logically have the greatest health risks and challenges. The required change is most profound among this group of people and they appear difficult to reach and motivate. That is why altering people's behavior to ensure they lead healthier lives entails considerable and (continuous) hard work. It is also a very costly matter if it is paid according to the number of hours worked by health providers. Actually most of the work should be done for free by people themselves supported and jointly with their own social networks. An additional complication is that prevention often only produces a result in the long term and appears to be far vaguer and holistic than treatments that usually yield an instantaneous result. It is also difficult to demonstrate and declare outcomes if it is purely analyzed on medical terms; can a health provider prove that the incurred healthcare costs are lower compared to what they would have been without prevention? Many illnesses develop slowly, and inhibiting or even reversing them often necessitates a long-term approach. It is difficult to demonstrate who was behind the behavioral change and when, which also makes it more difficult to receive payment in return. Such causes make it difficult to find approaches and revenue models where prevention-related investments are earned back. The comment "Charity is not scalable" is applicable to a large extent here. Within the context of prevention, numerous appealing charity initiatives exist with a high degree of willingness to participate, but there are considerably fewer business models that are sustainable and successful. Yet there is light at the end of the tunnel here, and it does not appear to be an approaching train.

---

[1] See for an in-depth study and the full proposal for the new definition of health the dissertation of Huber (2014).

What developments bring about a breakthrough involving prevention and self-management? The problem is growing, which creates momentum. Meanwhile the possibilities increase as well: Information technology and big data will help, the interests of stakeholders can be united and medical knowledge is growing. From the consumer marketing perspective the good news is that a healthy lifestyle is becoming more popular as a way of living to look and feel good. An increasing number of senior citizens and people with one or more chronic illnesses are adopting and increasing self-management and prevention. At the same time, it is also clear that merely fighting and repairing symptoms is no longer sufficient to organize healthcare effectively. Not only individuals desire this. Other relevant stakeholders in the field, such as the government, healthcare practitioners, and insurers, are also encouraging this movement. Producers and service providers in foods, sports and recreation are challenged to their responsibility but also see market opportunities. Additionally, the application of information technology on big health data can clarify the effect of prevention more effectively, even if this is in the long term and involves a range of interconnecting variables. This allows a better understanding of what works and what does not, making it easier to align stakeholders with an interest in healthy employees, insured people and citizens. It also gives sources for mirror-information to stimulate and advise people with health apps. In addition to a common agenda, mutually reinforcing activities, constant communication and a joint organization, this also requires performance-related measurement.[2] This measurement in particular is a key factor behind failure or success. Data pooling and analysis is essential in order to identify those prevention-related investments that will yield cost-savings. Facts and feedback provide guidance and facilitate the better integration of prevention and self-management with health conditions, medical knowledge, and treatments. Essentially, prevention is about the interaction between one's body and potential or existing illnesses. That quickly becomes somewhat vaguer. In the past, when no proper evidence could be obtained (via randomized trials), this sometimes remained in the realm of complementary medicine. Sound, in-depth data analysis makes the effect clear and more factual. The wheat can be separated from the chaff in esoteric theories about energy channels and weak areas in the body. It demonstrates, for example, that using your immune system and your body's self-healing ability can be of real benefit. This is attractive since it results in a stable healthy condition. The life-long use of devices and medication is costly and appears to disturb the balance which creates side-effects that require additional treatments. This poses challenges for the twenty-first century, such as the extent to which illnesses that have changed from fatal to chronic also can be reversed or even cured. In Diabetes type II, for example, there is convincing scientific evidence that a lot of people in an early stage of the disease can even get better again by exercising and following a proper diet consisting of more plants with fibers and fewer carbohydrates[3]. At the same time, it also becomes clear that prevention and the self-management of

---

[2] Kania and Kramer (2011).

[3] See for instance Lindström et al. (2006), Redmon et al. (2010) and Kumar et al. (2012).

one's personal health and illness with lifestyle interventions in exercise, relaxation and food can be logically combined with regular treatment and/or cutting.

Diagnoses can be expanded with health-related advice and automated, and therefore personalized in an affordable manner with the ambition to realize precision medicine. Where this is being discussed as an individual medicine cocktail, the term *precision medication* would often be more apt as the initial target since a lot of treatments and pharmaceuticals are prescribed without having the picture on the mix as a whole, but some forms of personalization are definitely present. Where lifestyle is concerned, tailor-made advice is further away. Nutrition and exercise instructions are still very black and white in terms of what is good and bad for everyone. In addition, promoted food categories in Western diets often change. Dairy was good and is now bad, but is still advised by the government of Thailand. Eggs are now healthy, unless you suffer from high cholesterol. Carbohydrates are now bad. Fat is not always harmful or even perceived as healthy, provided you eat the right type. Such commonplaces are turning healthy eating into more of a religion than a science, and therefore into fodder for cynics, something that does not help promote healthy behavior. On the contrary it sometimes can be dangerous to exclude full segments of nutrition from the diet drastically because a body adepts to that as well. The same is also increasingly applicable to sport. Many people jog even though they dislike this physical activity. It is a matter of time before the discussion centers on whether running does not harm or age the bodies of many people too much, and whether the focus for those above the age of 50 should shift increasingly from cardio exercise to muscle strengthening. Information technology and personal advice can help people to eat and exercise in a manner that is demonstrably more healthy and not harmful. This will undoubtedly depend on personal characteristics, weaknesses and strengths, condition and age. Prominent information technology partners such as Microsoft, Google, Apple, Philips and Samsung also view health-related data and platforms as major pillars for their future strategy. It is interesting to note that this to a large extend does not concern medical and reimbursed applications and files but personal lifestyle apps and data which are integrated in consumer products such a tablets, smart-phones, sport wearables, watches, and home-equipment. In addition, more and more people are active in the movement called "quantified self" and are compiling all kinds of personal health data. They do this to understand and improve their body as some sort of machine using precision food, precision sport and an overall precision lifestyle. Prevention will be aided by the fact that people will also focus more on following a healthy life and lifestyle. The social healthy movement has already been set in motion. The aim is not always to grow older in a healthy manner, but to also simply look good and feel content with oneself. Even the number of man who want to look like Homer Simpson appears to be declining. That is also important as it helps broaden the appeal of a healthy lifestyle via popular role models from sport and entertainment and prevents adoption by only a small, well-educated elite (where intervention is probably the least needed). It supports the desirable movement in which healthy living takes over healthcare instead of the other way around in which daily living is made medical.

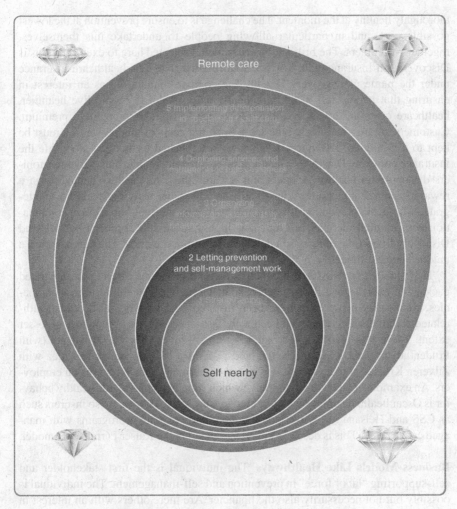

Remote care

5 Implementing differentiation
in the delivery of care

4 Deploying services and
instruments directly to patients

3 Organising
information and mutuality
between patients

2 Letting prevention
and self-management work

Self nearby

Figure 6.0.1 Breakthrough letting prevention and self management work

Business Models Like Discovery Health and Discovery Vitality Commencing with the interested party or parties is critical for feasible and scalable prevention. It is initially in the interest of people themselves and their family members to stay healthy. It starts with healthy people and those subject to additional risks but who do not yet have an illness. This does not yet involve prevention that is really part of recovering from medical treatment or learning to live with an illness. The challenge therefore lies in also making prevention fun, appealing and accessible for many people. In the healthy group without serious medical issues, the relationship between greater prevention and lower healthcare costs is more indirect. It is a long-term process. The expected healthcare costs per person are lower, and less can be saved. This applies to people with an elevated risk, but particularly to those who feel thoroughly healthy at the moment. The challenge is to ensure prevention at the lowest possible cost, and in particular allowing people to undertake this themselves, together with others. The brilliant business model selected here to exemplify this is Discovery, an insurance company in South Africa that sells healthcare insurance under the name of Discovery Health. The company naturally has an interest in ensuring that people fall ill as infrequently as possible. If people live healthier, healthcare costs are lower, enabling Discovery to offer a competitive premium. Customers are also happier. At the same time, the costs of this prevention must be kept to a minimum. Discovery Vitality was established to this end alongside the insurance company Discovery Health. It offers preventive programs, gives customers discounts on healthy products and rewards them for healthy behavior via a reward system. For customers, the vitality and insurance activities feel like an integrated whole, but prevention-related activities are financed by suppliers in combination with a small membership fee. This highly successful approach has allowed Discovery to become the largest health insurer in South Africa. The company has a unique business model.

There are many individual providers of health programs offering an integrated package of exercise in a fitness center and dietary advice. Health insurance companies, which may or may not have been inspired by Discovery, also offer health-related activities integrated with healthcare insurance policies to a greater or lesser extent. These also involve joint ventures with Discovery, such as PruHealth (with Prudential) in the UK. In the Netherlands, Achmea is a pioneer in this area with Zilveren Kruis. Another example is Central in Germany, which focuses on employers. An example of a new fresh initiative which supports and rewards healthy behavior is Oscar health insurance which started in New York. There are also insurers such as CSS and Helsana in Switzerland that combine prevention programs with managed care as well. This is described in greater detail in the Kaiser Permanente model.

Business Models Like Healthways The individual is the first stakeholder and self-supporting "labor force" in prevention and self-management. The individual is possibly but not necessarily also the financier. Are there others with an interest in making someone healthier who are willing to contribute and/or pay? There are stakeholders among employers, healthcare insurers, and society with an interest in making people healthy. If people run a greater risk or suffer from a chronic illness, the extent of the potential "damage" can be such that it justifies actual investment. It seems logical to seek business models that allow stakeholders to pay (part of) the bill. The selected example involves the American company Healthways, which has a completely pure approach: it allows itself to be paid by sharing the benefits attained by making major risk groups and chronically ill people healthier. The interests among stakeholders are aligned in this way. Healthways does this for individuals and at the request of employers, insurers and authorities. These stakeholders also have similar interests. Employers have traditionally played a crucial role in providing care and prevention for their staff and family members. This is also apparent in the stories shared by many healthcare practitioners and insurers concerning the establishment of the organizations, which often involves employers in many countries. It is visible in the number of people insured via employers or working on prevention in this manner. Employers have an interest in the health and care of their employees for various reasons. A large part of one's salary goes towards healthcare costs, which is why it is essential that this is kept affordable. Healthy employees are more productive and have a more positive effect on the atmosphere at work. Unhealthy and sick employees, on the other hand, are often responsible for additional costs. Employers have therefore also developed their own health programs and engage parties that provide assistance with reintegration. Healthcare insurers have an interest in ensuring that people stay or become healthy, given the high cost of medical treatment. It also helps if a long-term relationship exists between the insurer and the policyholder so that the common interest is greater. As discussed above in the Discovery example and below in the Kaiser Permanente example, various insurers are also actively involved in health programs to a greater or lesser extent. Finally, the social aspect has an enormous impact on the economy if people who are no longer fit for work can become productive once again. Consequently, it is often also in the government's interest to invest in prevention and a healthy lifestyle. This is also apparent, for example, in supporting and coaching vulnerable groups such as the unemployed, the homeless and vulnerable families. It is also reflected in programs aimed at increasing the quality of life in neighborhoods.

Business Models Like Kaiser Permanente "Perverse incentives" and rewards exist that would stimulate healthcare practitioners to focus more on treating instead of preventing disorders. Remuneration according to the number of interventions is seen as a major reason behind inefficiency within the care sector, incorrect treatments, treatment variation, overtreatment, and a lack of effective prevention.[4] This is not only about financial remuneration, but just as much about appreciation, attention, and professional honor. It also concerns detailed process instruction on the way a treatment should and should not be conducted, which impedes improvement and innovation. It would already solve a lot of issues if all financial and procedural barriers to give the right treatment were removed and people would be purely motivated based on their professional integrity. Healthcare practitioners should in principal have the responsibility to provide a group with the best possible care for a specified budget which is in line with the health conditions of the population. It helps if they are further focused and a little bit extra rewarded on the triple aim to increase the health of a population, improve the experience of care and reduce the cost per capita.[5] Decisions whether or not to provide treatment and the type of treatment involved must be taken in consultation with the patient. Understanding the patient perspective and goals is part of a good medical diagnosis. The best outcome can be to reflect for a while or to decide not to provide treatment at all. Additional remuneration, substantive appreciation and feedback for improvement must occur on the basis of health-related results

---

[4] For "perverse" incentives, overtreatment, personal responsibility, and self-management, see the arguments of Van der Gaag, Meerdink, Monissen, Florijn, and Rutgers in the publication *Financierbaarheid van de Zorg van Coincide*. See: Gruijters (2013).

[5] See Berwich et al. (2008) and Institute for Healthcare Improvement (2012).

for the entire population and a comparison with exchanged equivalent data on results in relation to others. As shown by analysis from BCG implementing such mechanisms can yield demonstrable improvements in the quality of care and also reduce healthcare costs by between 15 % and 20 %.[6] This is demonstrated by insurers and healthcare practitioners that implement managed care in an integrated or collaborative manner. The providers concerned render the insured care in kind. The most well-known international example of managed care is Kaiser Permanente from the USA, whose brilliant business model is also detailed here. Kaiser Permanente employs its own doctors and also owns hospitals in California, where it was founded. From an integrated care focus, it has taken the lead in health programs and the development of electronic patient records. The narrow definition of managed care relates only to truly integrated care in Health Management Organizations where insurance and the provision of care are integrated completely within a single organization. The broader definition involves intensive supply chain collaboration between the insurer and healthcare practitioners such as doctors. This with the focus, information, appreciation and/or remuneration geared towards actual and demonstrable health benefits. A distinction can be made between different types of managed care. The three most commonly used are the Health Maintenance Organization (HMO), Point Of Service (POS), and Preferred Provider Organization (PPO). With an HMO, healthcare practitioners receive a fixed amount for the patient's entire care. With a POS, customers receive a combination of an HMO with options to consult doctors outside the network. The customer has a doctor who acts as a supervisor and is employed or exclusively contracted by the insurer. Insured people can make use of the provided care at no additional cost within a hospital that is part of the insurer's network. If the insured person wishes to receive care outside the network, only part of the associated cost is reimbursed by the insurer while the remaining costs are borne by the policyholder. A PPO is the most pure form of managed care, whereby the insurer purchases care at a reduced price from hospitals that are a preferred supplier. Managed care does not always include a compulsory doctor and/or referral. The manner in which managed care is structured depends on the infrastructure existing within the country from the outset. At a regional level, there are various experiments involving managed care, such as in the Overvecht district in the Netherlands and in three municipalities in Kinzigtal in Germany. The USA has different examples of managed care, such as the Veterans Health Administration, Via Christi Health Systems in Kansas, and Intermountain Healthcare in Utah. Blue Cross/Blue Shield, just like Kaiser Permanente, has its roots in the Great Depression in the 1930s and focuses on employers and employees.[7] In Switzerland, for example, insurers have been obliged since 2004 to also offer managed care propositions, with this system now accounting for roughly 50 % of the market thanks in part to discounts. Doctors and hospitals were already here, of course. Some insured people also had existing insurance policies that excluded aspects of managed care. Managed care is then shaped firstly by regional

---

[6] Figures based on analysis by Boston Consulting Group with Zilveren Kruis Achmea of international best practises.

[7] For the examples from the USA, see Christensen et al. (2009).

group contracts with doctors and secondly by selected healthcare practitioners on the basis of telephone referrals. Examples here include the market leaders CSS and Helsana, and parties such as Sanitas, Swica, and Concordia, with a managed care proposition available to two-thirds of policyholders.[8]

Business Models Like PatientsLikeMe   When people with an illness are involved, patients themselves are still the first and most important stakeholder. If people who do not suffer from too many complications can live with their illness, they are more productive for themselves and society, and high healthcare costs can be (at least partly) avoided. If people are really ill, they have to rely increasingly on society for their livelihood, accommodation, care and healthcare. Those who do relatively more themselves and improve their health again reduce this dependency and increase the feeling of control and self-reliance. Self-management is called self-management for good reason. The patient ultimately always has a decisive role in the personal prevention program. In the end, people will have to restructure their lives themselves and play a leading role in the process to learn how to live with an illness and to become healthier again, if possible. Patients and those closest to them account for 99 % of the time spent on their illness since they have to live with this on a permanent basis. The patient is therefore the first expert and treatment provider. Thanks to programs in which people with elevated risks or chronic illnesses support one another, they know what to do and how to deal with their personal situation. These are of course more affordable than programs where most of the work is done by or with healthcare practitioners. An inspirational example is described in the business model of PatientsLikeMe (patientslikeme.com). This is an online platform where communities of people with similar illnesses can interact with each other. It is unique in that it has been established based on the insight that the Internet allows people to find fellow sufferers and stay in contact with them regarding extremely rare illnesses. The information is shared not only amongst patients themselves but also with the pharmaceutical industry, which sponsors the platform. While this involvement of a commercial player may sound somewhat strange, a sustainable form of financing has been found and the information is also used to develop more effective medicines and treatments. PatientsLikeMe is merely one example of the many online patient communities in the USA.[9] A large community for diabetics, dLife.com, has its own newsletters, recipes, TV shows, radio channel, courses and interaction resources. Crohns.org in the USA is another example. While the Internet offers unique opportunities for intensive mutual interaction from the comfort of one's home, the underlying phenomenon is not new of course. The group processes and mutual support in prevention appear very similar to the methods employed by Weight Watchers and Alcoholic Anonymous. From an even broader perspective, it entails forms of mutual caring and sharing and support within a group as described in Chap. 5, but for patients in this case.

---

[8] For the information on managed care in Switzerland, the authors thank Jan Willem Kuenen, Wouter van Leeuwen and their Swiss colleagues of Boston Consulting Group (BCG).

[9] See for instance: Christensen et al. (2009).

6.1   Discovery

It's not about winning but about playing the game

Thomas Bachet, Raheel Raisi & Jeroen Kemperman @: Jeroen.Kemperman@achmea.nl, Phone: 0031 651222099

Prelude *Lindi, a working mother in South Africa, has just turned forty and is now in a phase of her life where she is conscious about her health. She has been insured with Discovery Health for a number of years and decides to join Vitality, Discovery's health program. During the registration procedure Lindi immediately completes an online vitality check featuring questions about various topics, including her lifestyle. Her Vitality age, which indicates how rapidly her body is ageing, is apparently forty-seven years. Seven years older than her actual age! She is now even more motivated to work on her health and get back into shape. The test also identifies areas she can focus on best, namely her physical condition and cholesterol level. Fortunately, Vitality helps her improve these areas by providing a personalized pathway with intermediate goals, for example. For every goal Lindi attains, she earns points that she can then redeem for attractive rewards. Her goals and results appear in her personal profile on the Living Vitality platform.*

As Lindi desires quick results, she wants to know how she can achieve these. She takes two more Vitality tests: the fitness test and the nutrition test. These reveal that she can improve her condition to an acceptable level very quickly if she adjusts her diet slightly and participates in sport a few times a week. She enrolls at a sports school. She is entitled to a discounted subscription as a participant in the Vitality program. She also receives Vitality points each time she visits the sports school. A good outfit is also essential, of course. Her Vitality card gives her a discount on Adidas clothing and she buys herself a fine new pair of running shoes.

Some of Lindi's regular running friends are also active on the Living Vitality platform. The great thing about this platform is that it allows them to challenge each other. Her friend Susan, for example, organized a fun run recently. Lindi won by a whisker and earned 150 Vitality Points once again. She wanted to celebrate this by doing something fun with her daughter and therefore decided to use the Vitality points she had saved to go the cinema one evening with her daughter An, who is mad about movies.

Introduction Discovery Health has 2.6 million members with healthcare insurance in South Africa. With around seven million customers, it is the leader in this private market.[10] Discovery started off in 1992 as a healthcare insurer and pioneered new concepts such as Vitality. This platform—aimed at promoting health—was launched by Discovery Health in 1997. Vitality is a fully fledged subsidiary of the organization. It was deliberately set up in addition to and separate from the insurance organization from a financial and organizational perspective. Today, Discovery is a fully integrated financial service provider that operates in various markets, including non-life and life insurance. Discovery Holdings is a listed international financial service provider that also operates in the UK, China, and the USA via partnerships.

Healthcare insurance accounts for 57.4 % of Discovery's turnover and 41.7 % of its profits.[11] The company is renowned for its activities in the fields of care and health, the focal points of this case. Discovery is convinced that involving consumers in their health and encouraging them to lead a healthy life is best for them, the insurer and society. It is crucial that risks are assessed properly and reduced since Discovery personally bears all the risks of the insured person as a private insurer.

The cornerstone of insurance is providing customers with security and protection during adversity. Many insurers opt to do this by paying for the required care. Discovery goes further and helps customers avoid having to use their insurance. Prevention has a twofold effect: it is better for the patient and cheaper for the insurer. This is not rocket science. It is nevertheless difficult to identify ways in which prevention-related investments can also provide a demonstrable return on investment, or better yet: finance itself. So how does Discovery do this? The most important solution for the insurer is to create the conditions but entrust the responsibility and investment to buyers and providers of healthy products and services. To this end, Discovery offers a health program in addition to health insurance.

6.1.1 The Cornerstone: Permanently Healthier

Discovery offers the health insurance scheme Discovery Health and the health program Discovery Vitality. The latter encourages people to lead a healthy life and rewards them for doing so.[12] The Vitality programs compile a vast amount of data about the (un)healthy behavior of participants and immediately determine whether

---

[10] Floor (2012).

[11] Annual results presentation 2013.pdf Discovery.

[12] Discovery (2013a, b, c, d, e, f, g).

interventions have yielded the desired effect.[13] Adrian Gore, the founder and CEO of Discovery, started the company in 1992.[14] Remarkably, he found investors without showing them a detailed business plan or financial perspectives, but by offering them a concrete vision about how Discovery would create value by limiting risks. He knew a great deal about risks due to his actuarial background. He came up with the idea of offering a health program combined with health insurance that would help assess risks more effectively while reducing them in turn.[15] Adrian Gore's philosophy is that companies should not only focus on direct profit, but also on changing the market on a permanent basis. The organization's audacious goal is to be not only dependent upon South Africa but to become one of the best insurers in the world by shaking up markets with innovations. The concept has already proven to be highly successful in South Africa, and Discovery is focusing on expanding its business to other countries.

Within this context, being "one of the best insurers" means being a market leader which is dedicated to obtain the best for its customers. Discovery also has another goal: make people healthier and enhance and protect their lives. The company has various challenges: offering an appealing product, giving insured people access to a good network of hospitals, and compiling sufficient data to ensure risks remain manageable. Discovery has done precisely that over the past two decades and built a sustainable business that creates value for all stakeholders.

Discovery embraces two values that are deeply rooted in its vision, strategy, and business operation: integrity and honesty. These come before everything else, including financial gain. Discovery assumes that people who are treated fairly and honestly will in turn act with integrity and do the right thing. All activities within Discovery are furthermore based on the three principles of drive, perseverance and urgency. Discovery believes it can achieve great things and looks beyond (organizational) boundaries. This mentality can be characterized as a "can do" one, with the company doing its utmost to make things happen. Making it happen is equally important as promising it, which is why measurements are carried out constantly to ensure continued learning and improvement. Discovery changes the rules of the game through innovation and optimism. It can then use these rules to innovate the market and do things differently and better in particular compared to competitors. According to Discovery, at least 250 care-related innovations have been realized between 2004 and 2014, 48 of which are in the Vitality program.

The company has several core qualities that distinguish it from its competitors, such as the ability and courage to be different. Discovery has the ability to devise innovative ideas and the courage to make them happen, even against the tide. This yields new products and services, and allows Discovery to retain its distinctive character.

---

[13] Nossel (2011).

[14] Economist (2013a, b).

[15] Gore (2012).

The manner in which Discovery studies its customers closely, is unique for an insurer. It can assess behavior thanks to the Vitality program. The company also examines customer behavior, and even established a separate institute in 2013 that focuses specifically on understanding well-being and prevention.[16] Discovery does business in an intelligent and sensible way and endeavors to operate as optimally as possible so that all its ideas also dovetail with its ambition to do good business. This means it does not gamble, but calculates and manages risks properly. An organization is only as good as the people who work there. Discovery is committed to hiring, retaining and developing the best people. Positive people who are in a position to create an environment that is encouraging, fun and challenging. It is also important for people to be aware that everything is possible: trying and failing is better than not trying at all!

The strongest proof of Discovery Vitality's success is that members who actively participate in the Vitality program enjoy a lifespan demonstrably longer than that of non-active insured members. In addition to a health benefit of 8 years for the most active participants, this yields a win–win situation for Discovery, because healthcare costs decrease while customer loyalty increases. The same also applies to other product groups: active Vitality participants are involved in fewer traffic accidents thanks to Vitality Drive, and are also more loyal when it comes to repayments. The brilliant part is that the relative positive effect on healthcare costs is always applicable, regardless of age, gender, or chronic condition. This result is based on programs that demonstrably succeed in helping people to positively and permanently change complex habits such as unhealthy eating behavior and a lack of physical exercise.[17] Data from online health risk assessments reveal that participants in the Healthy Food program have a healthier eating pattern: they eat more vegetables and fruit, and consume less sugar, salt and processed foods.[18] This yields health benefits and also provides people with enjoyment. Participants give Discovery Health a score of 8.9.[19]

Discovery has grown organically to its current size without making any acquisitions. Expanding to other countries on its own turned out to be more difficult than anticipated, which is why it opted for partnering as the basis for its international expansion. It has forged partnerships with Humana (the number four in the USA), Ping An (the number two in China) and through PruHealth with Prudential (the largest insurer in the UK). It should be noted that these markets have not achieved the same success as in South Africa. Why? To be truly successful, the product, the organization and the country have to be in complete harmony. Perhaps that is more difficult with joint ventures in a less familiar market. But this does not in any way detract from the brilliance of the model in South Africa!

---

[16] Vitality Institute (2013).

[17] Polard (2008).

[18] An et al. (2013).

[19] Discovery (2012).

Brand essence: Creating value for customers by stimulating healthy behavior

Higher goal
• Improving and protecting human live

Brand roots
• Founded in 1992 by Adrian Gore without
  a business plan and financial projections, but with a clear dream to make
  people healthier and a distinctive vision
  on insurance

Audacious goal
• Become one of the best insurers in the
  world

Brand promise
• We protect you when you need it
• We help you to develop and maintain a
  lifestyle which is as healthy as possible

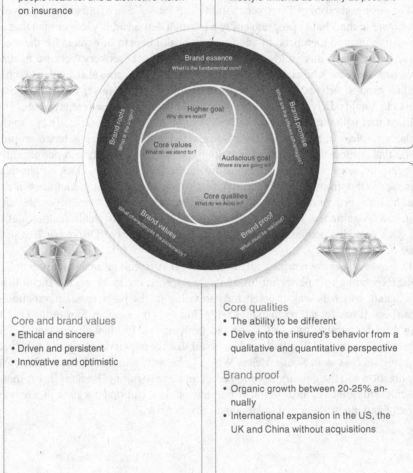

Core and brand values
• Ethical and sincere
• Driven and persistent
• Innovative and optimistic

Core qualities
• The ability to be different
• Delve into the insured's behavior from a
  qualitative and quantitative perspective

Brand proof
• Organic growth between 20-25% an-
  nually
• International expansion in the US, the
  UK and China without acquisitions

Figure 6.1.1   Vision and positioning of Discovery

6.1.2   The Business Model: Prevention as Well as Insurance

Both prevention and insurance are the cornerstones of Discovery's business model. In this case, the focus is placed on care and health, but the principle is also used in combination with other products, such as the car insurance scheme to which Vitalitydrive is affiliated.

Market Segments: Large Country, Limited Market Africa is currently the continent experiencing the fastest economic growth. While the economic development has not been very positive in the last years, South Africa has grown from a GDP of USD 115 billion in 2002 towards USD 313 billion in 2015. South Africa still leads the way with a GDP growth of 3.5 % annually.[20] The effect of this is a growing middle class.[21] The number of people with "lifestyle diseases" has grown exponentially. Many South Africans are dying because of obesity, diabetes, cardiovascular diseases, heart attacks, and lifestyle related types of cancer.[22] Leading a healthier lifestyle can help prevent a substantial number of these cases.

Discovery Health focuses on employer group contracts and private individuals. The number of group-insured members is by far the greatest: 2.3 million policyholders from over 800,000 SMEs and large companies. Some 300,000 people are privately insured. With 2.6 million insured people, Discovery Health is the largest insurer in South Africa.[23]

The success of the combination between the healthcare insurance of Discovery Health and the health program of Discovery Vitality has not escaped the attention of competitors. The health program has 1.3 million members, making it the largest in South Africa. Four other healthcare insurers currently offer a health program in the South African market, but use it primarily as a marketing and loyalty program and are considerably smaller. The insurer Multiply, with just over 100,000 members in its health program (Momentum Health), is the second largest player in this market. The following are Own Your Life (Liberty Health), Reality (Sanlam), and Zurreal 4Life (Resolution).

Context: The South African Healthcare System in a Nutshell South Africa has a broad selection of healthcare options, ranging from very basic primary care to highly specialized care. The differences between public and private care are profound. Public institutions have had to contend with poor management, insufficient funding and an obsolete infrastructure. Numerous examples exist of patients who were dependent on public care and died because hospitals could no longer care for them.[24] The private healthcare sector is run by commercial parties and often better equipped. Their customers

---

[20] World Bank (2016).

[21] Reuters (2013).

[22] South African Medical Research Council (2013).

[23] Preez (2013).

[24] World Health Organization (2013).

are middle- and higher-income people. Around 79 % of doctors work in private healthcare.[25]

The income gap among ethnic groups is huge. A black South African family has an annual income of ZAR 69,632 (around USD 6000 or EUR 5100), an Asian family ZAR 252,724 (USD 22,000 or EUR 18,600), and a white family ZAR 387,011 (USD 33,600 or EUR 28,600). The current government is busy implementing a new insurance scheme called the National Health Insurance (NHI) in the hope it will ensure greater equality in care between the different socioeconomic groups. A strong correlation still exists between the use of private or public care and ethnic background. In 2011, 81 % of black South Africans and 63 % of colored South Africans used mostly public healthcare facilities. With regard to white South Africans, 88 % use private facilities, like 64 % of Asian South Africans.

These differences are also reflected in healthcare insurance. Almost 70 % of the white population has private healthcare insurance compared to 41 % of the Asian population, 20 % of the colored population and 9 % of the black South African population.[26] The number of insured people differs from region to region. The wealthiest provinces, namely the Western Cape (25 %) and Gauteng (24 %), have significantly higher percentages of insured people compared to poor regions such as the Limpopo (7 %).[27] Your annual income determines what you do and do not pay for each treatment in the public healthcare sector. People earning more than ZAR 72,000 (USD 6200 or EUR 5300) pay the costs in full. The group that earns less receives a supplement. People who are unemployed or dependent on the state receive free care, as do children under the age of six, people with disabilities, and pregnant women. Out in the countryside, the lack of people and resources sometimes hinders the provision of good local care. Many South Africans simply cannot afford to travel to a hospital.[28] Consequently, even free care is inaccessible to many poor South Africans.[29]

Customer Value: Reward Is Better Than Cure With the addition of Discovery Vitality, the customer value that Discovery Health provides extends far beyond insurance against healthcare costs. Discovery Vitality encourages VIPs (Vitality Insured Persons) to develop and maintain a healthy lifestyle. These VIPs use test results to set themselves multiple goals, such as attaining a healthy weight, remaining physically active and undergoing annual preventive care. The aforementioned care involves screening, testing, and preventive treatment at a healthcare practitioner within the Discovery network. Special protocols exist for customers with a specific illness to

---

[25] Ataguba (2010).

[26] Statistics South Africa (2012a, b).

[27] Davis (2013).

[28] Chuma et al. (2006), Russel and Abdella (2002), and Goudge et al. (2012).

[29] Stassen (2012).

keep their health at an optimal level. VIPs are motivated by rewarding healthy activities with Vitality points that yield the widest possible range of benefits.

Discovery wishes to make insured persons aware of the important role they play in protecting their own health and reducing healthcare costs. Besides the Vitality program, Discovery does this via a personal Medical Savings Account for insured persons.[30] Discovery deposits a sum of money into this account at the beginning of the year. It is then paid off using part of the customer's monthly contribution. Day-to-day care-related costs such as a visit to a doctor and the purchase of a pair of glasses are paid from this account. The personal "control" over how money is spent on everyday care makes members more aware of costs and challenges them to make conscious choices. The money left over at the end of the year is carried over to the following one. The combination with Vitality is ingenious. Customers who lead a healthier life thanks to Vitality notice that they have more money in their Medical Savings Account at the end of the year.

Discovery: Packages and Products Discovery Health offers six different insurance packages, each of which includes an optional health program. Which private hospitals are covered depends on the package. The Keycare packages offer the least cover. The cheapest insurance costs ZAR 450 (USD 40 or EUR 34) per month. Customers must pay many day-to-day medical costs themselves. The KeyFit health program costs ZAR 33 (USD 3 or EUR 2.50) per month and offers basic tools and facilities for keeping fit.

Besides Keycare, Discovery offers five packages with increasing cover and contributions: Core, Saver, Priority, Comprehensive and Executive. The Saver packages, for example, offer an insurance with a Medical Savings Account and start from ZAR 980 (USD 87 or EUR 74) per month. The insurance also includes screenings and prevention. Daily medical costs are paid from the Savings Account. Priority, Comprehensive and Executive provide the most cover. The cheapest package costs ZAR 1778 (USD 157 or EUR 134) per month. Besides more extensive cover, a Medical Savings Account, and a larger network of hospitals you can visit, the excess is also limited. All of these packages allow you to purchase the Vitality health program, which costs ZAR 155 (USD 13 or EUR 11) per month. The additional costs for the Vitality program are perceived as a bargain. It gives customers access to a wealth of health-related tools, and they can recover these costs in no time thanks to numerous discounts that often total up to 25 %.

Delivery: Every Day, Step by Step Like most insurers, Discovery sells its products via financial advisors and directly over the telephone and the Internet. The delivery is unique if you are going to use both the Health and Vitality products which are, technically speaking, two separate products. This split is essential in the business model because preventive measures do not have to be financed from

---

[30] Discovery (2013a, b, c, d, e, f, g).

insurance money earmarked for care. In terms of perception the combination is of key importance and they are exceptionally well integrated.

Most customers belong to a collective health insurance scheme, which means they fall under a joint scheme from their employer or another party. Such a "collectivity" has its own board, website, and insurance policy.[31] All administration and services are provided by Discovery. A collective partner such as an employer has an interest in ensuring the health of employees. They value a health program and therefore often help to actively participate with own employees. Discovery Vitality is also able to identify the health benefits over a specific period. One of the initiatives to encourage companies to operate in a healthy manner is the "most healthy company list," which is drawn up using a health scan of individual employees and the company as a whole. This maps out, amongst other things, the (likelihood of) chronic illnesses in each department and the Vitality age of people in relation to their actual age.

The introduction of Discovery Health in combination with Vitality was a major social innovation and therefore highly complex too. It initially required considerable time and money to familiarize customers and intermediaries with the concept and the benefits thereof for insured persons. Discovery learned that customers were very focused on obtaining as many options as possible, but were not entirely sure how to use these. The insurer has since devoted additional energy to educating people with the help of instructional videos. It is important for Discovery that people use the Vitality program properly, otherwise they will not enhance their lifestyle and health.

Discovery Vitality motivates people through a combination of loyalty initiatives and game mechanisms. Vitality is an enticing program that complies with all rules of marketing and brand management in the fast moving consumer goods sector. At the same time, it is much more than a loyalty program. It has a scientific basis and is strongly connected to and organized with communities. Experiments with golf players, for example, have revealed that people are more strongly motivated when they stand to lose something (require more strokes than the objective) compared to when they stand to win something (require fewer strokes than the objective). Such insights play a key role in defining the program more sharply.

The personal pathway is person-dependent and starts with a comprehensive sports program, or assisting someone to quit smoking, for example. VIPs are motivated by allowing them to earn Vitality Points if they participate in activities. Participants start off as members and can become gold members if they follow the program properly and score points. A higher status offers new benefits, such as a better interest rate on your Medical Savings Account and greater discounts with partners.

Vitality gives access to a physical network of parties that can help members attain the goals on their pathway. Customers can enjoy a discount of up to 80 % at a fitness partner, for example. They also receive redeemable points each time they participate in a sport. The VitalityCard plays a key role in delivery as it gives access to benefits. Another card also entitles the bearer to various benefits. The HealthyGear Card, for example, must be presented when paying at Adidas and Totalsports partner stores. The discount is then deposited into the customer's account. The same principle applies to HealthyFood. If customers use multiple benefits, the DiscoveryCard is the

---

[31] Altron Medical Aid (2013a, b).

most convenient option because everything is included on a single card. At the same time, Discovery is physically visible in numerous places, such as in Woolworths and Pick n Pay supermarkets where all Discovery customers receive a 25 % discount on healthy (Vitality) products. The same applies if you pay the "Discovery price" for hotel reservations or flights, with the level of the discount depending on your membership status. Dual branding is also carried out with other top brands such as Nike and Adidas. All of this has a profound effect on branding and positioning of the brand. That is why Discovery is also an absolute top brand in South Africa.

An interesting mechanism is the discount percentage that can be increased by performing additional checks. New members who have not yet undergone any checks are entitled to a 10 % discount. This discount rises to 15 % once the Vitality Health Check has been carried out. In this way, Discovery ensures that people actively provide information and helps customers overcome the hurdle of starting the program.

Everyone can use the website and app of the Living Vitality platform, including nonmembers. It offers customers advice and tools to start looking after their personal health as well as an online community. It also integrates input from various health platforms and wearables such as miCoach from Adidas, your Polar heart-rate monitor, your JawBone, Garmin, or Nike+. Customers receive Vitality points for every workout they do. The platform is important because it integrates all information relating to the health program.

Operation: Big Health Data The customer experience and health programs are mostly online. Integrated information is an essential part of Discovery Health and Vitality. Apps have to be developed and blogs and experts must be available. The large-scale setup of a personal pathway for every VIP is also impossible without the help of ICT. The platforms and systems are the drivers behind Discovery. All Discovery health customers, for example, have their own electronic patient file that merges their healthcare use, medical data, and health-related data.

The combination of Discovery Health and Vitality is an important source of information for ensuring continuous improvement. A vast amount of "big health data" is compiled that relates to the health of VIPs who participate in Vitality. Discovery is a world leader in this field. Around five million people around the world are currently participating in this program.[32] Besides facilitating better risk assessment, it also yields new insights into the effects of health and care-related interventions. Working together with leading research institutes enables the stimulation and selection of more effective treatments, which in turn results in better care and lower healthcare costs. The results of studies are shared with universities and research institutes. Discovery's data is a veritable goldmine for them. Privacy naturally plays an important role here. Personalized data will never be shared. The partnerships deliver interesting results. The Vitality Age, for example, is based on a meta-analysis of more than 5000 international studies containing data on over 75 million years of peoples' lives. The annual international Discovery Vitality Summit gives people the opportunity to share their care-related knowledge.[33]

[32] Vitality Group (2013).
[33] Vitality Summit (2013).

Providers and partners play a crucial role in the Discovery Vitality concept. It is also important for Discovery to select the best partners without granting exclusivity. Partners can be divided into three categories:

- *Health and Fitness Partners*, where VIPs can use sports facilities for a reduced fee;
- *Reward Partners*, where VIPs can redeem their collected points for rewards;
- *DiscoveryCard Partners*, where VIPs can receive additional discounts and other benefits by using the VitalityCard.

To change behavior, it is important to strike a good balance between what VIPs should do and what they gain from doing so. The value of the reward for the customer and the frequency with which it is used are important aspects. Discounts on the purchase of healthy food at a supermarket, for example, have a low value, but are commonplace and used frequently. It is also healthy for everyone so all members receive the same discount. The other extreme is a ticket to a holiday destination, which has immense value but is used sporadically and differs in terms of membership status. Since VIPs can use small and frequent rewards and save for less frequent, large rewards, they are motivated to maintain their behavior. Discovery has compiled a sophisticated portfolio of rewards to help VIPs remain motivated. The types of participants and their motivation are also taken into consideration. Altruistic VIPs, for example, can redeem their points by giving these to a good cause.

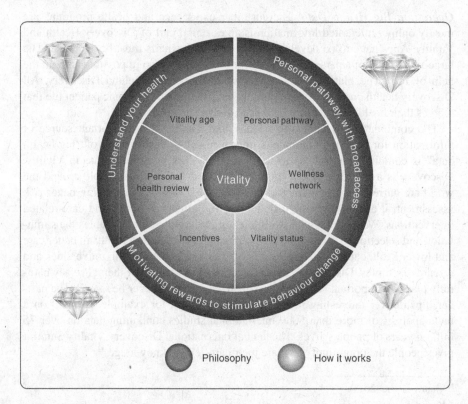

Figure 6.1.2 Vitality model

Value for customers

Result *What do I get?*
• Protection, better and healthier life

Process *How do I get it?*
• Discovery Card, Living Vitality platform and in shops

Emotion *What do I feel?*
• Feeling better about your self

Price *What are the costs?*
• Vitality costs roughly USD 13.50 (EUR 11.50) per month; insurance starts at approx. USD 44.50 (EUR 37.80) per month

Effort *What do I have to do for it?*
• Get insight into yourself, how to change behavior and how to adapt to this new lifestyle

Risk *What are the uncertainties?*
• Discovery should be entrusted with private information

Market segments

Position
• Market leader in South Africa with a market share of 38% and more then 2.6 million people insured
• 1.3 million of the insured are members of Vitality, the largest health program

Competition
• Competition in South Africa from other insurance companies that have founded their own health programs
• International competition from traditional insurance companies per country

Target group
• Healthy people
• People with chronic conditions who want to lead a healthier lifestyle

Customer insights
• People are willing and able to invest in their own health. Over half of the insured participate in the Vitality program and show a sustainable change in behavior

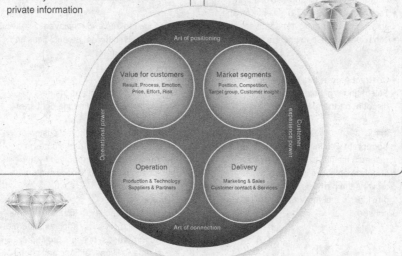

Figure 6.1.3 Value for customers and market segments of Discovery

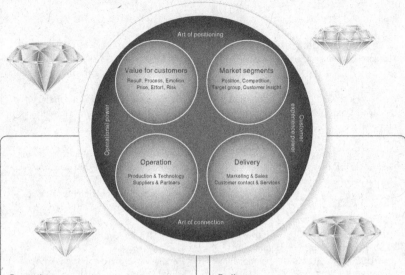

Operation

Production
- Streamlined insurance product processes
- Living Vitality platform including apps & systems to organize and register Vitality points

Technology
- IT architecture as insurance company
- Technology and skills to collect and analyze big health (improvement) data
- Behavior expertise to change lifestyles

Suppliers
- Contract regular healthcare providers
- Select and organize network of vitality discount partners

Partners
- Cooperate with international leading research institutes and universities
- Integrate activities with the most strategic health partners and technology providers out of the Vitality suppliers network

Delivery

Marketing
- Smart combination of Health (insurance) and Vitality program increases attraction of customer loyalty
- Visual presence of the 'Vitality price and products' in shops and other customer contact points of suppliers

Sales
- Sales via brokers and employers
- Cross-sell via different product lines and the Vitality program

Customer contact
- Regular contact points as insurer
- Support in helping to find the right care and cure
- Intensive 'lifestyle changing' customer interaction if the client participates in the Vitality program supported by app and locations such as fitness centers

Services
- Discounts and ability to exchange points for rewards at suppliers such as supermarkets, sport brands, telecom providers, travel organizations, airlines and shops

Figure 6.1.4 Operation and delivery of Discovery

6.1.3 The Result: Healthier Participants and Lower Costs

Vitality studies reveal that participants become healthier: that is valuable for customers as well as for Discovery. That applies to truly fit people, but couch potatoes can also earn Vitality points by carrying out tests and giving up smoking. The results for active Vitality participants are astonishing: the most active participants live 8 years longer than nonparticipants on average! The number of hospital treatments and the length of stay for each treatment are significantly lower, resulting in lower healthcare costs as well, as depicted in the table below. This table has been adjusted according to age, gender, chronic conditions, and the number of admissions to avoid bias.

Table 6.1 Results of VIP study[34]

	Not registered	Vitality participant		
		No involvement	Average involvement	High involvement
Percentage of insured persons	37.7%			
Days in hospital per patient	6.10	6.12	5.62	4.77
Costs per patient in rands (dollars/euros)	30,420 (2,641/2,165)	31,332 (2,721/2,230)	31,078 (3,698/2,212)	27,538 (2,391/1,961)
Costs per incident in rands (dollars/euros)	18,494 (1,684/1,317)	19,044 (1,653/1,356)	19,189 (1,666/1,367)	18,011 (1,564/1,283)
Number of days' stay in hospital per treatment	3.61	3.60	3.32	2.97

In addition to the impact on healthcare costs, the Vitality program also plays a pivotal role in binding and retaining customers of Discovery Health. On average, customers are rewarded with a 15.2% lower premium. A customer who has invested in all the activities required to become a bronze or silver member and receives all accompanying benefits will not go elsewhere quickly. A Discovery study involving Vitality members indicates that the number of these active and therefore more loyal customers has grown from 38% to 48% over a 5-year period.

Medical costs for highly involved insured persons are 10% lower on average than those for insured persons who do not use Vitality. While the program finances itself it meanwhile also saves healthcare costs such as in the event of hospitalization. Average daily costs per patient in a hospital amount to USD 665 (EUR 492).[35] In 2012, insured persons were hospitalized a total of 547,705 times (roughly 30% of overall claim costs). Without Vitality, hospital admissions could be estimated at over USD 1.31 billion (EUR 970 million) annually. With Vitality, this totaled USD 1.25 billion (EUR 930 million) annually. A difference of USD 58 million (EUR 40 million) annually (i.e., a saving of almost 4.1% on the entire population).

---

[34] Discovery Vitality Journal (2013).

[35] International Federation of Health Plans (2012).

Discovery's business model is very attractive to shareholders. The positioning makes Discovery more appealing to people who consider health important, the compilation of data provides input for the proper estimation and selection of risks, and healthcare costs are lower because people are made healthier. The overall result is 18.8 % lower claims per insured person.[36] The Vitality program, which is responsible for this decrease, is paid for by participants and providers and not by the insurance premium itself. The program itself is profitable to a degree, but the real benefit and significance for the organization naturally stems from the health advantages and high loyalty among its customers. The selection also attracts numerous customers, resulting in rapid organic growth. Over the past 11 years, profits rose from ZAR 122 million (over USD 10 million or EUR 8.5 million) in 2000 to ZAR 2838 million (USD 237 million or EUR 202 million) in 2011. Profits grew by 50 % over the past 5 years, mainly due to new business (40 %). Discovery's equity fund is one of the top five on the South African Stock Exchange. A dividend of 90 cents per share was paid in 2011, compared to 69 cents in 2010 and 48.5 cents in 2008.

Discovery aims to work with smart people who perform optimally and can connect with the company's vision. The company therefore pays close attention to the career prospects, motivation, encouragement, and retention of employees. During "stay interviews," for example, employees are asked why they continue working at Discovery and given the opportunity to provide feedback on how the company is doing. New employees complete a 3-month program first that familiarizes them with the company, its history, raison d'être, and core values. They are then interviewed to determine whether the company meets their expectations. This allows Discovery to use the fresh perspective of employees to ascertain whether the link between what is said and what is happening in practice actually corresponds.

The results achieved in enhancing the health of people are Discovery's most important contribution to society. Healthy people also create greater value for society because they earn money for their family and need to use collective resources less often. In addition to its primary activities in private healthcare, Discovery also helps improve public healthcare. It does so not only to unburden the public sector, but also to create capacity in the future healthcare system of South Africa. Infrastructure-related investments are made, for example, by training people and providing resources. The provision of primary care delivery is supplemented by counseling, tests, and home care for HIV/AIDS sufferers. Investments are also made in projects aimed at children and young people.

6.1.4 The Brilliant Lessons of Discovery

What can we learn from Discovery?

- Start with a clear vision, lay down a new concept and continue embracing that dream, even if it is against the tide. This approach has permitted Discovery to realize one of the few international examples of preventive care that really does

---

[36] Stassen (2012).

Value by customers
- Discovery Vitality gets a score of 8.9 out of 10 from customers who are more loyal and act as ambassador in their social networks
- On average the most active participants in the Vitality program have a proven life expectancy that is 8 years higher then the comparable non-active members

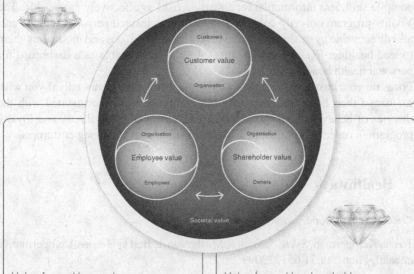

Value for and by employees
- Stay interviews are conducted to test if the values of Discovery match the experience of employees
- Employees are selected on the basis of knowledge, expertise and a positive drive. This creates a sphere of like-minded individuals

Value for and by shareholders
- Average growth of the dividend of 20% per year
- Healthy company with a A++ credit rating
- International expansion with the Vitality concept through joint ventures

Value for and by society
- Discovery creates healthier people who are more valuable and less costly for society
- Knowledge gathered via the Vitality program is shared via the Vitality Institute
- Social programs are aimed at improving the healthcare in South Africa, especially concerning HIV and AIDS

Figure 6.1.5 Value for and by stakeholders of Discovery

make people healthier, and which is self-financing and therefore scalable. The inspirational solution that this insurer has found entails organizing prevention and insurances into two separate companies that are self-reinforcing from a customer's perspective.

- Make a virtue out of necessity and let customers personally compile the information relevant to you and them. It is difficult for every insurer to obtain and compile sufficient information for assessing risks as effectively as possible. The Vitality program not only collects data relating to insured persons, but also creates direct value by raising the awareness of insured persons and motivating them to lead healthier lives by making this information available as a dashboard for personal health benefits.
- Focus on your customers and their motives sincerely and profoundly if you wish to change their behavior. Discovery has combined and experimented with the theories of behavioral change and the mechanisms of game theory and loyalty program in order to bring about actual behavioral change among customers.

6.2   Healthways

Create a healthier world, person for person

Jeroen Kemperman, Sytze de With & Mirthe van de Belt @: Jeroen.Kemperman@achmea.nl, Phone: 0031 651222099

Prelude *Jim Johnson's 80th birthday was some time ago. He has recently spent eleven days in hospital after undergoing heart surgery. His cardiologist told him he had to start exercising if he wanted to continue living for a while longer. He heeded this advice and joined Healthways' SilverSneakers program. This program, which he discovered via his health insurer, is aimed specifically at senior citizens with chronic illnesses. An exercise and nutrition program is created based on the personal data of participants. Jim now walks five miles on a treadmill every day and trains with weights. He firmly believes that he would not be alive today without this program. Besides exercising, he has also shed 46 pounds while at the same time gaining muscles. Currently he weighs 194 pounds, the same weight he had when he played football at high school! The program has made him healthier and also allowed him to get his life back on track.*[37]

Introduction The predecessor of Healthways starts in 1981 and focuses primarily on hospitals, addiction clinics and diabetes centers. In 1984, the management team sees a consolidation battle occurring within hospitals in the USA. They feel that they are at a crossroad and wonder whether they wish to continue taking over hospitals in order to grow even bigger in this rat race. They opt for a different path and start to move away from hospital-related activities. Instead of focusing on hospitals themselves, they shift their attention to disease management within hospitals. In 1989, they begin promoting good health for people with specific complaints, such as diabetes.

In 1993, American Healthcorp introduces the health program Diabetes Healthways, and in 1996, the first disease management contract is concluded. While this is a challenging new field, the shift in focus still causes sales to decline. This is logical since traditional sales focusing on healing in hospitals are being reduced, but it is also scary.[38] Overall sales consequently fell from USD 41 million to USD 30 million (EUR 44 and EUR 25 million respectively) in 1998. The strategy did however work out in the long run. The market positioning was such that profitability improved and growth could be achieved again in the long term. In 1999, 10 years after the start with the promotion of good health, American Healthcorp changes its name to American Healthways (and to just Healthways in 2006 in order to compete more effectively outside the USA).

American Healthways initiates more activities outside the domain of diabetes programs and introduces a comprehensive disease management program to tackle heart failure (Cardiac Healthways), followed by one for dealing with respiratory illnesses (Healthways Respiratory). Up until the turn of the century, Healthways sells disease management programs geared to a specific condition. They discover that this is restrictive and relatively costly. In 2000, Healthways offers disease management contracts for multiple diseases for the first time, which marks an important step forwards. Most people with a chronic illness also suffer from other disorders. Patients who participate in disease management programs often have more than one condition. It is expensive and not always effective to constantly use individual and specialized

---

[37] See Jim Johnson et al. explain this themselves in a video about Silversneakers (1 October 2013):95 http://www.silversneakers.com/TellMeEverything/WhatisSilverSneakers.aspx.

[38] http://www.fundinguniverse.com/company-histories/american-healthways-inc-history/.

nurses for illnesses who can intervene together. Preventive measures such as more exercise and a healthier diet are often similar for various disorders. Moreover, you want to know when various disorders impose conflicting requirements for interventions. This integrated approach to disease management appears to work well. During that period, Healthways is the first to publish standards that make the approach to disease management transparent: measurable and verifiable. This is ground-breaking. At the time, many programs are still being used primarily as a marketing tool or on the basis of faith, hope and love. Healthways is able to prove that its approach actually works. The patients feel healthier and happier, but the approach itself has developed into one that clearly pays for itself through savings on healthcare and/or greater labor productivity. Healthways demonstrates with this enhancement programs that its approach is not a hype, like many other cost-saving initiatives that cannot be verified. The publications and the approach enable Healthways to secure major contracts in 2001. The 10-year contract with Blue Cross Blue Shield of Minnesota is a resounding success from a commercial and reputational perspective.

Healthways proves its ability to obtain verifiable results and is a reliable partner within the medical world. This image is reinforced in an evaluation carried out by the Johns Hopkins University. Blue Cross Blue Shield and Healthways ask the university to study the effectiveness of the enhancement program, the results of which are positive. The Johns Hopkins University approves the results of the cardiac and diabetes care enhancement programs. This marks the first time that such investigations are carried out in the USA. In June 2002, Healthways is the first organization to receive the stamp of approval from the Disease Management Accreditation program, an institution managed by the National Committee for Quality Assurance (NCQA). Healthways is subsequently certified by the largest healthcare accreditation bodies in the USA, and is the first company to implement disease management programs.

These programs enable Healthways to offer demonstrably good care while saving money simultaneously. They let themselves increasingly be rewarded on a "no-cure-no-pay" basis in which they share the financial benefits they have realized with employers, insurers, and/or government. That is a unique and highly distinctive business model, but is not always the easiest way. From a business perspective, a boom period commences after 2002. The contract with Blue Cross Blue Shield of Minnesota, however, remains the key revenue generator. It is not renewed in 2008, and Blue Cross Blue Shield operates the purchased services itself from that moment onwards. The telephone services, staffed by 200 people and previously acquired from Healthways, are transferred in-house in order to expand them further.[39] Additionally, Healthways and seven other companies had participated in a large disease management experiment (the Medicare experiment), and at that time the positive results of this are challenged by Medicare.[40] These two events affect Healthways financial results and since the start of the economic crisis in 2008, the organization's growth has slowed compared to the preceding period. Nevertheless, Healthways is generally recognized as being at the forefront of proven and self-

---

[39] http://www.startribune.com/business/18787234.html.
[40] http://www.nytimes.com/2008/04/07/business/07medside.html.

financing disease management programs. At the same time, this business model also continues to be a challenging one for Healthways. What can we learn from this pioneer in the field of prevention?

The Medical Expenses System in the USA The medical expenses system in the USA is a key factor that helps with the commercial development of the disease management market. There is a large difference between healthy people who earn money and people unable to work because of their health. The best care in the USA immediately translates into the best care in the world. However, such care is unaffordable for many people. Due to the prohibitive cost of care, it is logically also worth more if you can avoid it.

Prosperity in the USA has its corresponding problems. Many people suffer from obesity- and lifestyle-related chronic illnesses such as diabetes. The average life expectancy is no longer increasing nowadays, but actually appears to be decreasing. Healthcare in the USA is provided by a myriad of organizations. Healthcare institutions are owned and operated largely by private organizations. Health insurance for workers in the public sector is provided primarily by the government. Employers contribute significantly to their employees' healthcare premiums. For them, disease management is a tool for boosting labor productivity as well as for curbing medical costs.

Insurers have contracts with certain healthcare practitioners (organized and non-organized). If insured people visit a healthcare practitioner with whom they do not have a contract, they will pay a higher percentage themselves.

Most of the population under the age of 65 is insured via their own employer or that of a family member. Some people insure themselves. A large percentage of people in the USA are not insured, namely 49 million inhabitants or 16.3 % of the population. ObamaCare has made basic healthcare more widely accessible, but this is significantly less than the broad level of care available to everyone in the strip between Scandinavia and Switzerland.

According to the World Health Organization (WHO), the USA spent the most on healthcare per capita (USD 8608/EUR 6336) and more on healthcare as a percentage of GDP (17.9 %) than any other country in 2011.

6.2.1 The Cornerstone: A Healthier World, One Person at a Time

Healthways wants to create a healthier world and does so one person at a time.[41] The well-being of people is improved through specific and resulted-oriented programs. Investments made in Healthways' programs are recouped because the care costs of

---

[41] www.healthways.com.

participants decrease while productivity increases. The approach taken by Healthways unites several aspects. Key ones include a personalized approach that focuses on behavior, prevention, and lifestyle. At the same time, the approach must be backed up with scientific proof as is customary within the medical world. These elements are also evident in Healthways' roots.

The organization is founded by five hospital administrators: Thomas G. Cigarran, James A. Deal, Henry D. Herr, Robert E. Steen, and David A. Sidlowe. The primary activities Healthways concentrates on at that moment include hospitals, addiction clinics, and diabetes centers. The combination between the medical physical side of health and the behavioral side is already present at that very beginning. The disease management approach commences within healthcare facilities. Healthways' focus on proving and demonstrating results is therefore a logical extension of its own medical background.

The introduction of the health program Diabetes Healthways in 1993 reveals the eventual cornerstone of Healthways: focus on a population's risk groups and on well-being. It launches a population-oriented approach to diabetes based on customer needs and self-management. The medical world has never seen such an approach before. Up until then, healthcare practitioners opt for a traditional approach, with hospitals playing a pivotal role in the provision of a diabetes program. The shift is now made from a hospital-based diabetes approach to a population-based diabetes approach. The focus is placed on the population instead of the illness, resulting in a different perspective on the result. It becomes far more logical to view this in an integrated manner and focus on the integrated perspective of general well-being, life, and overall healthcare costs. In addition to the approach based on the perspective of people instead of that of healthcare practitioners, a personal approach is also chosen that is still an important feature of the way Healthways operates. It is no coincidence that an American company is playing a pioneering role with such an approach. Additional labor productivity is of the greatest value here, and healthcare costs are the highest. A personalized program within a collective approach appears to be a good cultural fit, and the USA has the dubious honor of leading the way with respect to lifestyle-related diseases.

Healthways wants to take the lead in making the world healthier, one person at a time. To this end, it makes promises to different groups of customers that are both simple and revolutionary. Healthways promises people that it will increase their well-being and help them lead a longer and healthier life by making them healthier thanks to a customized approach. The organization has the self-confidence to make payments to Healthways increasingly dependent upon the realization of this promise. The organization approaches employers, governments, insurers and other collective groups with a financial interest in ensuring more productive and healthier people while lowering healthcare costs. Healthways offers to make a selected "unhealthy" part of "their" population demonstrably healthier on a no cure, no pay basis.[42]

---

[42] Healthways 2012 Annual Report (2013).

Brand essence: Make the world a healthier place, one individual at a time

Higher goal
- Improve the well-being of people with a personal approach for a healthy change and healthcare cost savings

Brand roots
- Experience, know-how and network building upon the origins as hospital
- Stimulated by social-economic and healthcare system in the US where preventing costs and increasing productivity are even more important

Audacious goal
- Play a leading role in making the world a healthier place, one individual at a time

Brand promise
- Use a personal approach to empower people to improve their well-being and happiness for a longer and healthier life

Brand essence
What is the fundamental core?

Higher goal
Why do we exist?

Core values
What do we stand for?

Audacious goal
Where are we going to?

Core qualities
What do we excel in?

Brand roots
What is the origin?

Brand promise
What are the offered advantages?

Brand values
What characterizes the personality?

Brand proof
What must be realized?

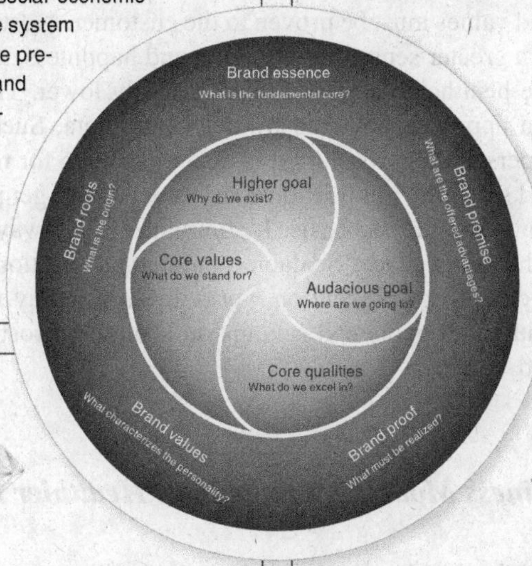

Core and brand values
- Passionate
- Goal-oriented
- Responsible
- Innovative
- Expert
- Partnership
- Progressive

Core qualities
- Scalable and commercial approach to realize and execute self-financing well-being programs
- Scientific and verifiable approach based on big health data as input for continuous improvement

Brand proof
- Measurable and tangible results in a longer and healthier life and in lower healthcare costs
- Success of approach evident from scientific proof in reports and publications and export of approach to other countries

Figure 6.2.1   Vision and Positioning of Healthways

To deliver on these promises, Healthways works according to the following values[43]:

- passionate: inspiring, optimistic, and motivated with an everything-is-possible attitude;
- deliberate: solutions correspond to the mission and yield measurable results;
- responsibility: promises are kept by a reliable partner judged on results;
- innovative: being creative, no problems exist that cannot be solved;
- expertise: 30 years of experience in the creation of workable solutions;
- partnership: be a partner in well-being and joint improvement-related initiatives;
- forward-looking: a desire to lead the quest for improvement in well-being.

The promises and values must be proven to the customer. Most important of all is that people have a greater sense of well-being and happiness, and a longer and healthier life, while healthcare costs are demonstrably lower. This is supported with a personalized approach powered by big health data. Such data not only helps to achieve a personal approach, but is also the source for recording within research reports and scientific publications, and is needed to get paid when work is conducted on a no-cure-no-pay basis. It stimulates Healthways to really help make the world a healthier place. Scalable commercial solutions arise when it becomes clear which type of prevention works in such a way that this can be financed from productivity gains and savings on healthcare costs. These can be exported and copied.

6.2.2   The Business Model: A Longer and Healthier Life

Market Segments: Unhealthy People In 2013, over 40 million people had access to the Healthways' programs through collective contracts. The focal point still lies in the USA, but contracts and activities are also prevalent in countries such as Australia, Germany, France, and Brazil. Healthways reaches the end users of its services through these "collectivities," namely the social groups in which they find themselves. This can be done through the employer, insurance company or hospital, but also via government health programs. The underlying reason for these parties to invest in Healthways' services stems from the insight that people with a higher well-being also perform better, live a longer and healthier life and require less care.[44] Healthways therefore assists in doing something good for people, but also boosts productivity and reduces costs at the same time. Within the collectivities, Healthways focuses on groups in which the greatest health gains can be attained. These are the

---

[43] Healthways Brand Guidelines V.02.2011, Healthways.
[44] Healthways 2012 Annual Report (2013).

people who truly find themselves in major risk groups or already suffer from one or more chronic illnesses. Few competitors go as far as Healthways when it comes to a personal approach judged according to measurable results. Healthways' competitors are primarily parties that help improve health or reintegration in another way. They are mostly parties with revenue streams greater and more important than disease management, such as healthcare practitioners that offer medical assistance to the chronically ill or reintegration assistance. However, they also provide services as part of an insurance program, internal corporate programs or consultancy. Competition also stems from businesses offering sports programs, fitness facilities, and nutritional advice to organizations and private individuals.[45] The greatest competitor in terms of volume and relevance falls within an entirely different category, however. The most commonly used alternative to Healthways is … no health program. The result is a shorter and unhealthier life, with less well-being and higher healthcare costs. This is of course the real reason why Healthways competes because it wants to make the world a healthier place. A significant share of the market is yet to be conquered, in other words.

Value for the Customer: A Longer, Healthier and More Productive Life The result for an individual is a longer and healthier life. The personalized services of Healthways give customers the feeling that they can work directly on their personal well-being and therefore on their happiness and social participation. The services, programs and advice it offers are based on specific health risks arising from the customer's personal profile. That increases the involvement and justifies the effort and time required to participate and transmit data.[46] Healthways embraces an integrated and holistic view on health and well-being, and also focuses on underlying mental factors. The value of Healthways for people in programs is significantly greater than that obtained from regular medical treatment. Its philosophy dovetails directly with a positive perspective on health but also with the traditional WHO's definition: "Health is a state of complete physical, mental and social well-being and not merely the absence of disease or infirmity."[47]

The investment in an individual's health is usually borne by the collectivity. The "hard" result for this organization is additional productivity and/or reduced healthcare costs. There is also the more 'soft' result, whereby it is valuable and useful to assist people with health risks and problems from an own group. This not only feels good but also projects a positive social image to other people in the group. Healthways' services may therefore also contribute to the distinctiveness to staff, patients, and/or citizens to do the right thing and care for people. Healthways partly still operates on a fee-per-participant basis, but is leaning increasingly towards a performance-linked remuneration approach, which also reduces the financial risk

---

[45] Idem.

[46] Effective Communications, Meaningful Incentives Help Customers Set New Bar For Biometric Screening Participation.

[47] http://www.who.int/about/definition/en/print.html.

for the customer. The price paid is based, in principle, on half the amount that is saved. The health benefits are shared, in other words.[48]

Delivery: Access via Collectivity and a Personal Approach in Programs Collectivities and decision-makers are the parties Healthways focuses on particularly with regard to sales and marketing. Hard evidence that the approach works helps bolster Healthways' reputation and position among these collectivities. It also provides direct contact persons with instruments to convince their colleagues. Once Healthways' services have been engaged, the collectivities "stamp" of approval helps ensure access to people, but also encourages people to actively participate in health programs. The diagnosis is the key element in the approach that is shaped person by person. This is achieved using information about present well-being, the health risks someone is facing, the medical background, and the limitations and possibilities. An analysis of this information is then used to create a tailor-made package of scientifically proven health and well-being interventions for the individual in question. In addition to the content of these services, an equally crucial element for success entails ensuring that they are offered to the end user in a manner that corresponds to the person. The philosophy that only a personal approach leads to a measurable positive result constitutes a key part of the entire process. Personal information is translated into appropriate strategies and means for communication and interaction.[49] In the end, the most important production factor for success is people themselves. These individuals will ultimately have to change their behavior to become healthier by exercising more and eating and drinking differently. Healthways assists in this regard by also offering related health services that complement the health programs. SilverSneakers, for example, is a large-scale fitness program dedicated entirely to older adults with health risks and mostly chronic illnesses.[50]

Operation: People and Data for Behavioral Change Healthways is a strong knowledge-driven service provider. People, systems and information are the main components in the operation. Staff undergo intensive training in the field of personal behavior. This approach is combined with the required technology that enables a personal approach to customers. The Healthways operation is based on making solid and accurate analyses that map an individual's health profile.[51] The Embrace Technology Platform combines the identified health and well-being risks with relevant personal characteristics in relation to behavioral change. The Healthways Well-Being Assessment combines validated questionnaires about health, work and well-being, with benchmark information from the Gallup-Healthways database. This database contains national data relating to the health and

---

[48] Healthways 2012 Annual Report (2013).

[49] http://www.healthways.com/approach/default.aspx?id=86.

[50] http://www.silversneakers.com/TellMeEverything/WhatisSilverSneakers.aspx.

[51] www.healthways.com.

well-being of reference groups within the USA. Specific health risks within a population are identified by finally complementing this information with demographic data, medical history and medical declaration information of individuals.[52] Healthways is constantly searching for the newest, scientifically substantiated and proven interventions relating to health and well-being in order to include these within its services portfolio. Healthways innovativeness in the application of information technology is demonstrated by the fact that it has been ranked among the top organizations of the InformationWeek 500 for six consecutive years. In 2013, Healthways was in thirteenth position, and was also included in the list of "20 great ideas to steal in 2013." The flexibility and innovativeness to continuously respond to the changing demands of customers is achieved in part through partnerships and acquisitions. Healthways has succeeded in binding parties to itself via a network strategy that delivers breakthrough results and insights in health management.

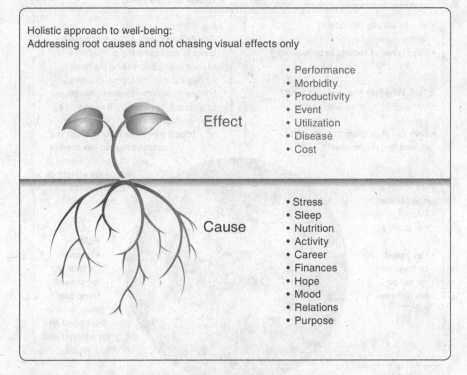

Holistic approach to well-being:
Addressing root causes and not chasing visual effects only

Effect
- Performance
- Morbidity
- Productivity
- Event
- Utilization
- Disease
- Cost

Cause
- Stress
- Sleep
- Nutrition
- Activity
- Career
- Finances
- Hope
- Mood
- Relations
- Purpose

Figure 6.2.2 Holistic approach to well-being: Addressing root causes and not chasing visual effects only

---

[52] See also the video about the Healthways Gallup index: Video Feature: A Tale of Two Cities: Raleigh and Hickory NC Well-Being Differ Significantly.

Value for customers

Result *What do I get?*
• Longer, healthier and happier life*
• Healthier and more productive people**

Process *How do I get it?*
• Personal approach*
• Tailored approach for people who are not as healthy**

Emotion *What do I feel?*
• Happiness, well-being and control of own life*
• Helping people become healthier gives sense of purpose**

Price *What are the costs?*
• Mostly reimbursed by third party*
• Prize is half of savings to be realized**

Effort *What do I have to do for it?*
• Healthier living is something you do yourself*
• Own role in program towards participants and Healthways**

Risk *What are the uncertainties?*
• Record increases probability of results*
• Pay based on no-cure-no-pay policy reduces risks**

*Individual
**Group

Market segments

Position
• More then 40 million people have access to Healthways via a group plan/contract
• Primarily active in the US, but now also in countries such as Australia, Brazil and Germany

Competition
• Commercial, governmental and internal suppliers of well-being programs such as healthcare providers, reintegration services, healthcare insurers, coaches, fitness gurus & dieticians
• No access to a 'well-being program' is actually the largest competitor both in volume and in urgency

Target group
• Groups and communities that have a stake in increasing the productivity of people and decreasing the need for healthcare: employers, insurers, integrated or non-integrated healthcare providers & governmental institutions
• Individual targets within group are people who have chronic diseases or an increased risk thereof and can be motivated to reduce the effects or even reverse their condition

Customer insights
• People with a higher well-being cost less, perform better and enjoy a longer and healthier life

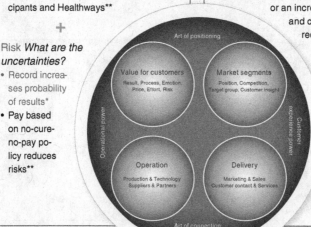

Figure 6.2.3 Value for customers and Market segments of Healthways

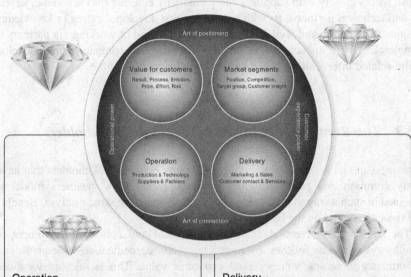

Operation

Production & Technology
- Training of employees to become experts in health and behavioral change
- Strongly driven by learning and improving from big health data
- Innovative in using IT platforms and
  applications to collect, link and analyze
  data and results and translate that into
  (new) automated and personalized
  advice

Suppliers & Partners
- Network of innovative suppliers and
  partners in science, technology and
  services
- Focused Merger & Acquisition strategy
  to build and expand on Healthways'
  leading role in well-being and health

Delivery

Marketing & Sales
- Marketing and sales focused on groups
  and decision makers. Approach to enter
  and influence on the basis of substantive
  content with results and references via
  networks
- Recruitment of individual participants
  in programs in consultation with and via
  contacts within groups

Customer contact & Services
- Strongly personalized approach in
  services and communication in strategy
  of interaction with participants and
  professionals
- Core tasks for participants themselves to
  realize own changes in behavior
- Support with services and programs
  for target groups that help people to
  become and stay healthy

Figure 6.2.4 Operation and Delivery of Healthways

It also works closely with suppliers and partners by entering into academic, strategic and technical partnerships with companies that develop services or knowledge that match its health and well-being vision. The method of working via partners is complemented by an acquisition strategy focusing on companies that develop health-related interventions based on this knowledge.

6.2.3   The Result: Equal Interests Among All Stakeholders

A business model is often about giving and taking between stakeholders that have partly common and partly different interests. Healthways' business model is designed in such a way that all parties in the chain share the same motives. Benefits and risks are shared on the basis of common goals.

The causal value creation chain for individual and collective customers of Healthways works as follows: by improving welfare, medical costs decrease and performance increases, which creates economic value. This is relevant for those directly concerned, but also for society as a whole. After all, more people can actively participate in society and the collective resources of the government are burdened less. This is depicted in the figure 6.2.5.

Healthways uses a personal approach to help people lead longer and healthier lives. They must ultimately take responsibility for their own health. The intended result is that people fall ill less frequently and are more productive in society. Healthways looks for a party for whom this is of value and that is willing, in principle, to share 50 % of this benefit in the form of a fee to Healthways.[53] Learning, adjusting and demonstrating health benefits requires open and high-quality data from individual and collective customers. When people participate in Healthways' programs, they must therefore also commit to an intensive partnership and complete openness and transparency in data and knowledge.

A study was conducted on how involvement, healthy behavior and physical health influences the performance and absenteeism of employees.[54] To this end, analyses were carried out on 20,114 employees who completed the Healthways Well-Being Assessment 2008–2010. The results corroborate the approach of Healthways. They reveal the efforts to boost employee productivity require a

[53] Healthways 2012 Annual Report (2013).

[54] Shi et. al. (2013).

[55] Healthways 2012 Annual Report (2013).

[56] http://performance.morningstar.com/stock/performance.

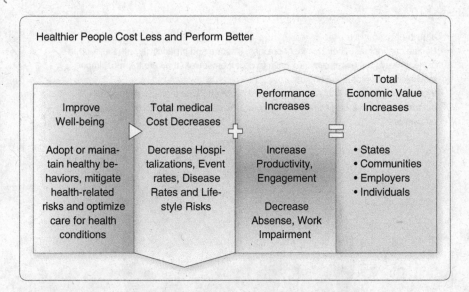

Healthier People Cost Less and Perform Better

Improve Well-being	Total medical Cost Decreases	Performance Increases	Total Economic Value Increases
Adopt or maintain healthy behaviors, mitigate health-related risks and optimize care for health conditions	Decrease Hospitalizations, Event rates, Disease Rates and Lifestyle Risks	Increase Productivity, Engagement Decrease Absense, Work Impairment	• States • Communities • Employers • Individuals

Figure 6.2.5 The chain of value creation for stakeholders and society via the improvement of well-being and health

holistic approach with strategies aimed at increasing the health and involvement of employees.

Healthways is primarily interesting as a leader that has found a revenue model where prevention benefits all parties involved. In the meantime, shareholders have not fared too badly either. Since its establishment in 1982, Healthways has developed into a company with a turnover of over USD 700 million (EUR 515 million).[55] From 1996 until 2008 in particular, Healthways grew strongly, but the last few years have been slower and growth, margins and contracts are under pressure.[56] Competition in the US home market has increased. Substantial investments have been made in technology and data, and this platform makes economies of scale possible and necessary. Healthways finds itself in a transitional phase and wants to return to the path of growth by expanding internationally.[57] It has a unique business model that makes it a leader in substantive terms, but simultaneously also requires people to simply work for the business.

---

[57] http://finance.yahoo.com/news/healthways-reiterated-neutral-220003700.html.

Value by customers
- People can increase their health, happiness, lifespan and productivity with the support of Healthways but eventually they have to do it themselves: they are the most important link in the value-creation chain
- Individuals and groups have to be open and cooperate based on mutual trust to determine, adjust and/or settle the proper actions and interventions on the basis of outcomes

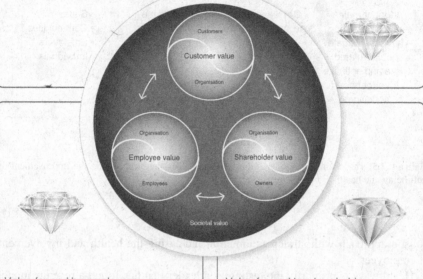

Value for and by employees
- Employees make a valuable contribution for their fellow citizens
- Employees receive and form an inspiring environment for innovation and continuous learning in the rapidly developing world of technology, data, behavior interventions and the management of health and well-being
- 'Top 100 Best companies to work for' in 2008

Value for and by shareholders
- Turnover since its launch has grown to more than USD 598 million (EUR 518 million)
- Growth in the US (especially from 1996-2008) and potential international growth on the basis of a unique business model in the 'growth market' of health management and eHealth for chronic diseases

Value for and by society
- Increasing the health and employment rate of groups of individuals and decreasing the healthcare costs together have direct economic benefits and reduce the pressure on public funding and budgets
- Inspiring contribution to the learning and thinking in society, science and healthcare on ways in which well-being and prevention in health can replace cure, medical treatments and medicine

Figure 6.2.6   Value for and by stakeholders of Healthways

Healthways has 2,400 employees. In 2008, the organization was one of the Fortune 100 Best Companies to Work For. If offers the opportunity to perform valuable work for other people, which is even more appealing because it does this by leading the way in relation to technology, science, data and interventions in order to bring about actual behavioral change. This makes Healthways attractive to the best people in fields such as IT, analysis and behavioral change.

With the focus on improving health, reducing healthcare costs and increasing labor productivity, Healthways is working directly on socially relevant objectives. In addition to the result for the organization itself, it also offers policymakers, government, opinion leaders and investors an insight into methods for attaining these objectives and therefore has an additional leverage effect.

6.2.4 The Brilliant Lessons of Healthways

Healthways has a working business model based on prevention, which is unique. "Prevention is better than cure" is always emphasized at macro level and in public discussions. At the same time, the bulk of investments made in care and health are still not earmarked for prevention, but for recovery. Prevention is frequently difficult and stubborn in practice. Initiatives in this direction often remain as good intentions only. They have limited scalability and are the first to perish when cuts need to be made. Healthways provides a number of lessons that can help overcome this and ensure successful prevention and focus on health:

- Searching for a collective party interested in the health of a group of people is a good start. This can be an employer, but also an insurer, a healthcare practitioner or a government. That is a logical party with which to conclude agreements about objectives and benefits. The most elegant option is to work where possible on a no-cure-no-pay basis and link revenue to health benefits, just as Healthways does.
- Along with the business model and medical background, Healthways focuses on research and demonstrable results. This makes the organization a source from which others can also learn. Which interventions work and which do not? How should they be used and at what moment? Which target group should be focused on and in what manner in order to ensure promising health benefits that have an impact?
- The results and approach of Healthways demonstrate that many healthcare costs and productivity losses can be avoided through solutions that reinforce well-being and happiness. The hard evidence for the benefit of soft values can inspire people to earn money by making other people happy.

6.3   Kaiser Permanente

Boosting health and lowering costs together

Koen Harms & Jennifer op't Hoog @: Jennifer.op.t.hoog@achmea.nl, Phone: 0031 651226420

KAISER PERMANENTE®

Prelude *Following a regular preventive mammogram, Lonny Catalan receives the bad news that cancer cells have been found in one of her breasts. While she is momentarily at a loss about what to do after this news, the doctors and staff of Kaiser Permanente ensure that they jointly will do anything they can to turn this bad news into a successful treatment story. Lonny praises her doctors not only because they take the time to explain the treatment process in detail, but also because she truly does feel she is undertaking this battle against cancer together with her doctors.*

Besides medical care, Lonny also receives tips that allow her to determine what she is capable of physically and mentally. Lonny decides to participate in a nutrition and exercise program for cancer patients, which also brings her into contact with fellow sufferers. The care process is supported with an online patients and insurance dossier that clarifies her medical data. This allows Lonny to read what doctors have discussed and decided in joint meetings, and to submit questions and schedule appointments online with her doctors. After a three-year battle, Lonny is told that her cancer has disappeared. She is advised to continue participating in prevention programs that can reduce the chance of recurrence. Her wholehearted response is: "Yes, I'll do that, otherwise I'll have to miss you and all the wonderful people I've got to know over the past few years."[58]

Introduction The business model of Dr. Sidney Garfield, founder of Kaiser Permanente, transformed traditional healthcare into real *health*care. To ensure care was affordable for workers, during the 1930s in the USA he combined his hospital with an insurance based on a prepaid contribution, or a premium in other words.

---

[58] Kaiser Permanente 2012 Annual Report (2013).

This combination of fixed income and integral care ensured a shift from focusing on providing care to ill people as cheaply as possible to keeping the population as healthy as possible and lowering the cost of care. Eighty years later, Kaiser Permanente has become one of the best insurers in the world, renowned for the high quality of care it offers and effective prevention programs at an affordable price. Kaiser Permanente customers purchase an integral insurance product with managed care. To put it simply, customers are insured for care provided by doctors and specialists who are mostly employed by the organization itself. Kaiser Permanente is the most famous and most frequently used example of managed care where the insurer and provided care are part of a single organization. Thanks to this care system, doctors can be rewarded for the quality and effectiveness of care, a healthy life, care and insurance can be linked via information dossiers, and the responsibility for health can be divided between the customer, doctor and insurer.

6.3.1 The Cornerstone: Prevention Is Better Than Cure

The guiding principle of Kaiser Permanente is joint responsibility as the cornerstone for affordable care. This has always been the case and is part of the very fabric of the organization. The roots of Kaiser Permanente can be traced back to the height of the Great Depression.

In the early 1930s, a recently graduated doctor called Sidney Garfield sees an opportunity to treat thousands of sick and injured workers involved in the construction of the Colorado River Aqueduct Project. He borrows money to build a small hospital in the vicinity of a little town called Desert Center. Finding structural funding for this care proves to be a difficult task, however. Insurers are late in paying bills for care that already been provided and many workers are not insured back then. Since Dr. Garfield refuses to turn away uninsured workers, he receives no financial remuneration whatsoever for some of his services. How can he solve this puzzle?

Harold Hatch, an engineer involved in the construction of the aqueduct, proposes a potential solution, namely the creation of a new financing system that will require workers to pay 5 cents a day upfront for health coverage to the healthcare practitioners. The hospital is guaranteed a steady income and assumes responsibility for the health and safety of insured workers. The business model shifts from *medical* care to *health*care. Fewer accidents and diseases mean less hospital costs and therefore less pressure on the prepaid contribution. Legend has it that Doctor Garfield is looking at that time for loose nails as these could injure a worker and require the appropriate care. Thousands of workers join the insurance scheme of Doctor Garfield and Harald Hatch, turning it into a resounding success. The aqueduct is completed a few years later and the workers leave. The hospital is no longer required. Shortly before Doctor Garfield closes it, he receives a surprising call from Henry J. Kaiser. This is an industrialist who owned various business including construction companies and shipyards. He asks Garfield to implement his healthcare model for the 6500 workers and their families at the largest construction site in history, the Grand Coulee Dam on the Columbia River in Washington State. The story continues!

The dam is completed in 1941 and it appears once again that Dr. Garfield's work had come to an end. But a few months after the dam is completed, Japan attacks Pearl Harbor. The USA's involvement in the Second World War is now a fact. Tens of thousands of workers go to the Richmond shipyards to meet the demand for new naval vessels. The shipyard's owner—the same Henry J. Kaiser—has to provide good healthcare to this inexperienced, unhealthy group of workers. Convinced by the previous partnership, Kaiser engages the help of Dr. Garfield. Kaiser even writes to President Roosevelt, asking him to relieve Garfield of his military obligation. Once Roosevelt grants his approval, Garfield leaves for California and together with Henry J. Kaiser establishes a cooperative called the Permanent Foundation, which organizes healthcare for tens of thousands of workers. The cooperative is named after the Permanent stream that flowed past the first company founded by Kaiser. The war ends in 1945 and the number of workers employed in the shipyards drops. Convinced of the power of the healthcare system, Garfield and Kaiser jointly decide to make this system accessible to all individuals. After rapid growth with the support of a number of trade unions, Kaiser Permanente develops into the company it is today.

The organization's core values and higher goal have been forged in its history. Kaiser Permanente focuses not only on facilitating medical care, but also on improving the health of individuals and the community in which insured people are active. The organization also opts for a partnership with the customer, whereby both parties assume shared responsibility for the customer's health and therefore share the same interest. Kaiser Permanente wants to do this at a price that is affordable to the greatest group possible. The organization exists in order to provide affordable, high-quality healthcare aimed at improving the health of insured people and the community in which they live. A sense of responsibility, flexibility and innovation are the core qualities used to achieve this objective. The organization and services of Kaiser Permanente are set up in such a way that everyone feels responsible for the individual care of customers, from policymakers to doctors and patients themselves of course. The provided care focuses on the patient's individual needs, with a continuous quest for innovative ways to deliver better health at the lowest possible cost. During a period when the American care system is under pressure, Kaiser Permanente is trying to demonstrate that the provision of high-quality, patient-oriented healthcare is possible and even contributes to the system's affordability.

In its pursuit of the audacious goal, Kaiser Permanente promises a complete health experience tailored to personal needs and geared towards strengthening its members. This means that the organization is not only trying to make sick members healthier, but to also keep healthy people healthy. This is done at the individual level, but also for a group of employees, a family or community members. Kaiser Permanente has always devoted considerable attention to a healthy workplace. The social environment and residential area form a key element in health. The role that Kaiser Permanente assumes in this involves helping to make such an environment safer and healthier by modifying hazardous intersections or planting trees.

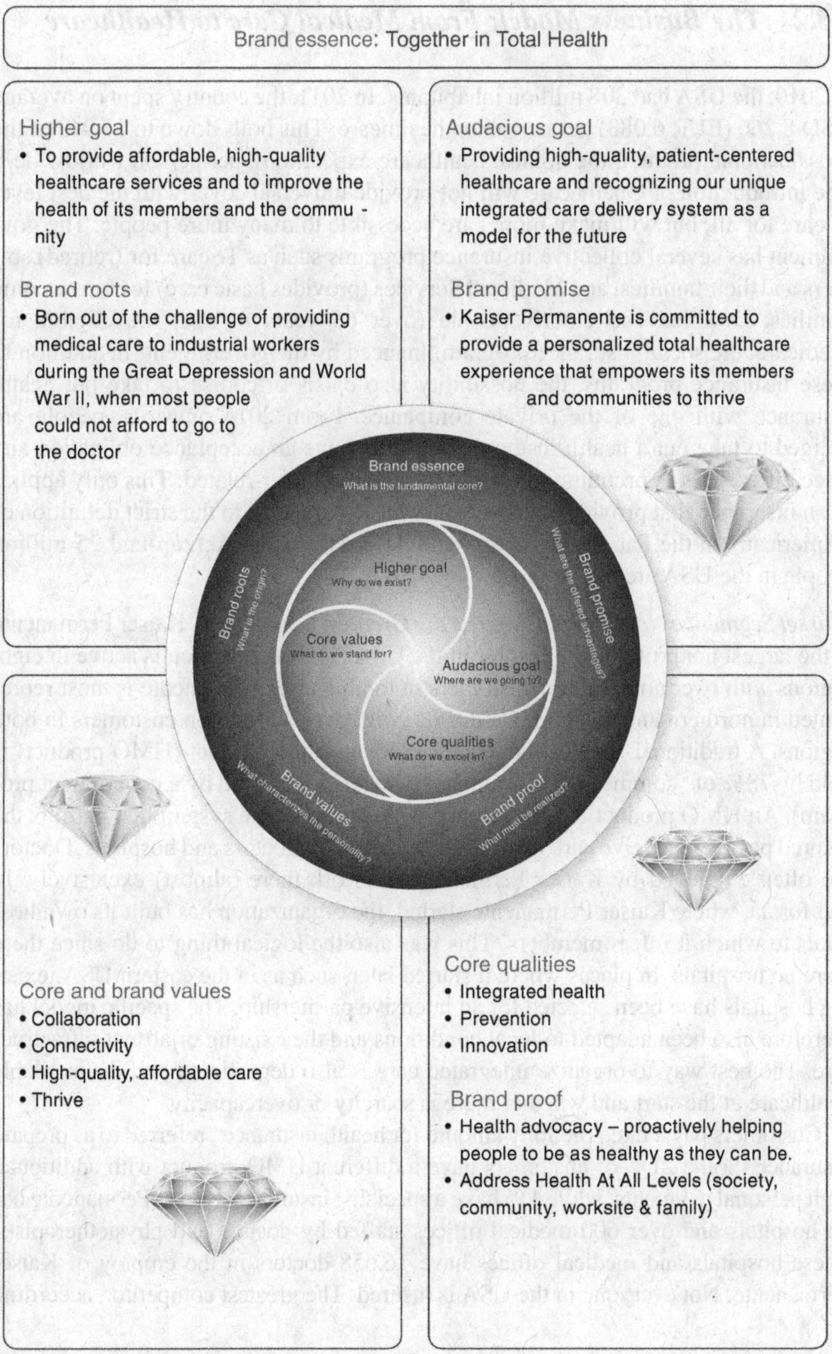

Brand essence: Together in Total Health

Higher goal
- To provide affordable, high-quality healthcare services and to improve the health of its members and the commu- nity

Brand roots
- Born out of the challenge of providing medical care to industrial workers during the Great Depression and World War II, when most people could not afford to go to the doctor

Audacious goal
- Providing high-quality, patient-centered healthcare and recognizing our unique integrated care delivery system as a model for the future

Brand promise
- Kaiser Permanente is committed to provide a personalized total healthcare experience that empowers its members and communities to thrive

Brand essence
What is the fundamental core?

Higher goal
Why do we exist?

Brand roots
What is the origin?

Brand promise
What are the offered advantages?

Core values
What do we stand for?

Audacious goal
Where are we going to?

Core qualities
What do we excel in?

Brand values
What characterizes the personality?

Brand proof
What must be realized?

Core and brand values
- Collaboration
- Connectivity
- High-quality, affordable care
- Thrive

Core qualities
- Integrated health
- Prevention
- Innovation

Brand proof
- Health advocacy – proactively helping people to be as healthy as they can be.
- Address Health At All Levels (society, community, worksite & family)

Figure 6.3.1 Vision and Positioning of Kaiser Permanente

6.3.2   The Business Model: From Medical Care to Healthcare

In 2010, the USA had 308 million inhabitants. In 2011, the country spent on average USD 8,266 (EUR 6,083) per person on healthcare. This boils down to 17.9 % of the gross national product; the highest healthcare expenditure per person worldwide.[59] The introduction of Obamacare will not provide universal cover with the best level of care for all, but will make more care accessible to many more people. The government has several collective insurance programs such as Tricare for (retired) soldiers and their families, and Medicaid Services (provides basic care) for low-income families. Disabled and elderly people (over 65 years of age) are eligible for Medicare, the social insurance program financed by the government. In addition to these insurance programs, the possibility also exists of course to take out health insurance with one of the private companies. From 2014 onwards, people are obliged to take out a health insurance, insurers have an acceptance obligation and price differences in premium may only be age- or gender-related. This only applies to an insurance that provides the necessary basic care. Due to the strict definition of "American" in the Patient Protection and Affordable Care Act, around 25 million people in the USA are not be insured in 2014.[60]

Market Segments: Not Being Insured as the Greatest Competitor Kaiser Permanente is the largest nonprofit health insurer in the USA. The organization is active in eight regions with over nine million customers in total. Kaiser Permanente is most represented in northern and southern California, with over 3.5 million customers in both regions. A traditional Health Maintenance Organization product (HMO product) is held by 78 % of "commercial" customers (who are not insured by a government program). An HMO product is an insurance with a closed care system that permits the insured person to receive care from a select number of doctors and hospitals. Doctors are often employed by Kaiser Permanente or work there (almost) exclusively. In California, where Kaiser Permanente started, the organization has built its own hospitals to which it refers members. This was also the logical thing to do since there were no hospitals. In places where it started later, such as in the eastern USA, existing hospitals have been selected for an intensive partnership. The specific model has therefore also been adapted to local conditions and the existing or absent infrastructure. The best way to organize integrated care is also dependent upon the available healthcare at the start and whether there is scarcity or overcapacity.

Customers pay a fixed monthly amount for health insurance , referred to as prepaid insurance. Some 21 % of customers have a different HMO product with additional, high personal payments, while 1 % have a specialist insurance. Kaiser Permanente has 36 hospitals and over 600 medical offices staffed by doctors and physiotherapists. These hospitals and medical offices have 16,658 doctors in the employ of Kaiser Permanente. Not everyone in the USA is insured. The greatest competitor, according

---

[59] Center for Medicare and Medicaid Services (2011).
[60] Smith & Medalia (2015).

to Kaiser Permanente, is therefore the option for people to be part of the group of uninsured Americans. Competition from insurance companies usually stems from healthcare insurance giants such as United (36 million policyholders), Anthem (33 million policyholders), and Aetna (18 million policyholders).[61] These healthcare insurers provide normal insurance products as well as insurance products with managed care. They are also active in areas covered by Kaiser Permanente.

Traditionally, Kaiser Permanente has targeted the working class. Since the system was opened to everyone (after the Second World War), this group has expanded to include employers intent on contributing to their employees' health. Since the 1950s, individuals have also been able to take out an insurance. In other words, Kaiser Permanente is there for employers, employees and individuals, and aimed at people who consider health important and are willing to assume joint responsibility for ensuring that they and their environment are as healthy as possible. However, there are regional limits for the target group. Unless it concerns emergency care policyholders can only use hospitals and healthcare facilities belonging to the organization, and people can therefore also only take out health insurance in areas where Kaiser Permanente operates.

According to the organization's philosophy, only 10 % of the demand for care originates from medical reasons, 30 % to family history, 40 % to behavior and 20 % to environmental and social factors. This reveals a completely different way of looking and thinking. A playing field is created as a result, involving the reduction of care consumption by improving behavioral and contextual factors such as the environment and social surroundings. In brief: by improving behavior and the environment, insured members remain healthy for longer healthy and make less use of care.

Customer Value: Personal, Affordable High-Quality Care and Insurance in One The healthcare insurance concept created by Garfield and Kaiser developed over the course of the twentieth century into what is referred to nowadays in the USA as a Health Maintenance Organization (HMO). Upon conclusion of the contract, the insured person chooses a doctor from the Kaiser Permanente list, who provides all basic services. If a customer requires specialist care, the doctor will refer the individual to a hospital or specialist. This role fulfilled by the doctor is common in many countries, but not in the USA. Only emergency care provided by a hospital or doctor not affiliated with Kaiser Permanente is reimbursed. This guarantees the patient-oriented treatment method of Kaiser Permanente, keeps care costs transparent and limits these as much as possible. Products are subject to standard, minimal excess fees and personal contributions so that costs are felt and borne collectively. A higher excess or personal payments result in lower monthly costs. Additional products are offered for the (non-urgent) use of doctors outside the Kaiser Permanente network.

Approximately 38 % of the American population (120 million)[62] are insured through their employer. This percentage is higher at Kaiser: 56 % of Kaiser Permanente customers were insured via an employer in 2011.[63] This corresponds to

---

[61] Henry Kaiser Foundation (2012).

[62] RAND (2012).

[63] Henry Kaiser Foundation (2012).

its roots, but is also logical because employers share the importance of keeping people healthy and productive and are therefore even more pleased with Kaiser Permanente who is a partner in doing that. In terms of remuneration, the products for businesses are not that different to products for individuals. The distinction lies in the product range that matches the risk profile of employees. The larger the organization, the more specific the prevention program, and HMO package. Doctor Garfield helped uninsured workers even though he knew his bills would not be paid. Kaiser Permanente now also supports over 560,000 Americans who are not eligible for other insurance programs [64] via charitable coverage or charitable care programs.

The price of a health insurance policy depends on the policyholder's age and gender. Healthy customers pay less than people with a greater care need, and a risk selection is carried out. Kaiser Permanente customers receive high-quality care at an affordable price. In the event customers decide to change health insurers, they can switch to another doctor and hospital. Customers are expected to focus actively on their personal health to help reduce or prevent care costs.

Delivery: Thriving The main element in Kaiser Permanente campaigns and statements is thrive, or to allow people to thrive. The campaign focuses on prevention, a healthy lifestyle and well-being in every phase of life. Slogans such as "A car runs on money and makes you fat, a bike runs on fat and saves you money," are used to encourage people to exercise. A key element is that in addition to the group approach with companies, a community approach also exists whereby local programs are initiated to promote healthier cooking or jogging. This goes further than just a lifestyle approach and may for example also entail improving the quality of life in the neighborhood. At district and local community level, programs are organized to encourage sport and healthy living. Investments are also made in safety and mobility by lending financial support to parks, and making traffic intersections and cycle routes safer for young people. Contributions are also made to ensure safer schools and workplaces.

The insurance product can be purchased individually, online, via an insurance agent or the employer. Businesses can seek the advice of a consultant. The integrated healthcare system (care facilities as well as insurance) also enables an integrated customer contact system. An online platform (My Health Manager) allows customers to communicate via secure e-mails with doctors, make appointments (including a logistical function that minimizes waiting times between visits to multiple doctors). In addition, this online environment provides an insight into medical information and insurance products, and offers the opportunity to register for workshops, programs or training aimed at prevention or treatment. If the answer cannot be found online, customers can call or visit the doctor or hospital. Kaiser Permanente offers different programs for healthy eating, sports and community involvement. Activities for secondary prevention also exist in order to prevent the deterioration of care. For example, Kaiser Permanente has programs for avoiding lower back problems, managing a chronic condition and overcoming depression. Self-sufficiency is encouraged through training and providing support to people

---

[64] Kaiser Permanente 2012 Annual Report (2013)—by the numbers.

with a chronic illness such as diabetes. This prevention focuses where possible on the assistance and care needs of the individual. Besides medical issues, family history, behavior and social aspects are also considered in the diagnoses and action plans. In this way, the patient's actual needs are addressed and unnecessary invest-ments are avoided where possible.

Operation: The Pinnacle of Efficiency Through Full Integration For the most part, Kaiser Permanente owns the care infrastructure such as hospitals, customer domains and IT infrastructure, and often employs the doctors, nurses and other care staff who work there. Each region is a separate legal entity, with each regional entity comprising Kaiser Foundation Health Plans (KFHPs) and Permanente Medical Groups. The organization's insurance branch falls under KFHPs, which take care of sales, policy-making and the administration of health plans. The KFHPs have no profit motive, but invest in the development of Kaiser Permanente hospitals and the organization's entire care infrastructure. The Medical Groups are the for-profit partnerships consisting of doctors, and they receive almost all of their income from the KFHP. Care financing occurs within a closed system, which allows funding to be organized in an optimal manner that facilitates the delivery of effective and efficient care. Besides a fixed salary, doctors are given the opportu-nity to earn some additional rewards by offering effective, high-quality care. This is significantly different to a large percentage of doctors and specialists around the world, including the USA, whose income depends in part on the volume of care they provide. This is referred to as the "perverse incentive" in which additional treatment is remunerated, leading to a risk of overtreatment. The Kaiser Permanente model also allows the organization and use of diagnostic technology to be managed more efficiently. It is possible, for example, to match the number of MRI scanners to the number of expected scans per year, centralize the location of the scan, and organize care logistics around the scan. Linking insurance and the overall provision of care helps simplify the organization of IT systems. Kaiser Permanente uses Health Connect, a single system in which doctors as well as insurers work. Doctors therefore have access to the information they require and are authorized to consult. The integrated IT system provides solid management information for making sup-ply-related choices and selecting prevention-related investments, for example. Health Connect lets customers consult their medical files on Health Manager (an electronic patient dossier), along with information about their insurance and oppor-tunities to schedule appointments with a doctor or insurance specialist.

Kaiser organizes its prevention program at different levels within society. The broadest level focuses on society by supporting health policy, research and lobbying the government for prevention and safety initiatives. In 2012, Kaiser Permanente invested USD 230.2 million (EUR 169.4 million) in clinical and policy research. Kaiser believes in measuring and financing care on the basis of the quality of results and is constantly looking for ways to measure the quality of results effectively and adapt the procedure accordingly.

Employers are an important customer since they act as a gateway to employees. They are also a natural partner for working together to ensure the health of person-nel. Government authorities with support programs are also a key partner.

Value for customers

Result *What do I get?*
- I get a (prepaid) individual or employer-sponsored integrated healthcare plan

╋

Process *How do I get it?*
- I can retrieve the individual insurance online or subscribe via my employer

╋

Emotion *What do I feel?*
- I secure, and have a counterpart that helps me to stay healthy in shared responsibility

─────────────────

Price *What are the costs?*
- Able to charge one of the lowest prices in the US

╋

Effort *What do I have to do for it?*
- Expects me to take my own responsibility in health and provides me with tools to stay healthy

╋

Risk *What are the uncertainties?*
- Shared responsibility; which results in co-payments when I get sick

Market segments

Position
- The largest non-profit integrated healthcare system in the US. Kaiser Permanente (2011) 8.9 million health plan members in 8 regions. 167,300 employees: 14,600 physicians, 37 medical centers and 611 medical offices

Competition
- Three important regional competitors are: HCA Holdings, Dignity health, Sutter Health

Target group
- The community and employer health plans. People who want to have access to total health and are concerned about health also when they are not ill and like to share responsibilities to stay healthy

Customer insights
- Insuring healthcare begins by keeping people healthy. Kaiser Permanente believes that roughly 10% of people's health is determined by medical need; 30% by genetics and more than 60% by behavior and/or environmental and social factors. As a result, it helps members to support healthy behavior and healthy societies

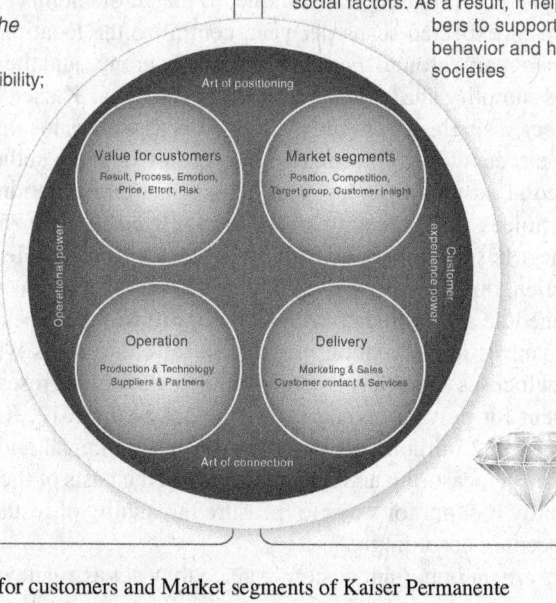

Figure 6.3.2 Value for customers and Market segments of Kaiser Permanente

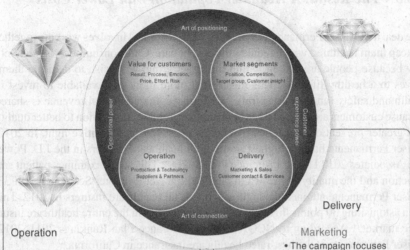

Operation

Production

• Integrated health plan: Kaiser Permanent is the insurer and care delivery company. Hospitals are owned and all physicians employed. Programs are focused on changing unhealthy behavior at all levels of society, from neighborhoods, to schools or companies, to families and the individual

Technology

• Leader in Electronic Patient files. Since the 1980s an electronic system has been developed. The patient is the owner of his/her medical file and co-decides on what care suits his/her needs

Suppliers

• All care suppliers (such as hospitals and physicians) are owned/employed by Kaiser Permanente. In this way they have built a closed system with shared responsibility for the end result

Partners

• The most important partners are the employers, teachers and community servers of their members. In cooperation programs are organized to make society, communities and people healthier

Delivery

Marketing

• The campaign focuses on (a) prevention, wellness and "thriving" at every stage in life and (b) how Kaiser Permanente differentiates itself from other healthcare providers by being a health advocate

Sales

Kaiser Permanente has a combined sales strategy. Employers and individuals can buy their insurance via the broker channel or directly online via the website

Customer contact

• With My Health Manager, a web-based personalized portal, members can make or cancel appointments; refill prescriptions (shipped to their doorstep   free of charge); email the doctor; view medical records; and understand the benefits of their plan. And customers can contact the call center or reach out to a health center or hospital for assistance

Services

• Programs such as: Healthy lifestyle programs, Total health assessment, Eat healthy, Lose weight, Manage back pain, Manage chronic conditions, Overcoming depression, Quit smoking or Reduce stress

Figure 6.3.3 Operation and Delivery of Kaiser Permanente

6.3.3   The Result: A Healthier Population with Lower Costs

The deal that Kaiser Permanente concludes with customers involves working together to keep them healthier, which reduces the cost of care. Care consumption is relatively low because people are sought within the target group who wish to dedicate themselves to a healthy lifestyle. This means that more money is available to invest in health and safety (an upward spiral). Furthermore, the additional revenue is shared because customers are offered a lower insurance premium in addition to better quality and greater prevention. Customers view this procedure in a positive light. In 2012, Kaiser Permanente had the highest score of all healthcare insurers in the J.D. Power and Associates 2012 Health Insurance Plan Study.[65] This study examines patient satisfaction and the quality of the health plan. With a Net Promoter Score (NPS) of 33, Kaiser Permanente attained the highest score of all healthcare insurers in 2012. This is an astonishing 30 points higher than the average NPS in the entire healthcare insurance market.[66] According to NCQA's Health Insurance Plan Rankings 2011–2012, Kaiser Permanente is the best-rated healthcare insurance in California.[67]

Loyalty is an additional value that the customer has for Kaiser Permanente. Since Kaiser Permanente provides integrated care, customers tend to switch less to another provider. In the event customers wish to change, they do not only have to switch healthcare insurers, but also doctors and hospitals. Moreover, their premiums may become significantly more expensive. The hospitals of Kaiser Permanente are rated positively on the quality they deliver. Eight Kaiser Permanente hospitals feature in the top hospital rankings of the U.S. News and World Report, placing them among the very best in the country. In 2011, 2012, and 2013, the clinical quality of Kaiser Permanente hospitals, according to consultant Aon Hewitt, was around 30 % higher than the average of other HMO hospitals, and even 123 % higher than that of all hospitals.[68] The Leapfrog Group rated 900 hospitals, with only 53 receiving the label of top hospital, 18 of which were Kaiser Permanente hospitals.[69] In 2011 and 2012, the organization was one of the few healthcare companies to appear in the top 50 of the InformationWeek 500, a ranking that includes the most technically innovative businesses.[70] The Harvard Business Review also praised the organization's leading position in the innovation and improvement of care.[71] The electronic patient dossier developed by the organization ranks among the top 20 innovative IT ideas that are worth stealing.

---

[65] J.D. Power and Associates Member Satisfaction Study (2012).

[66] Satmetrix Net Promoter® Benchmark Study 2012 (2012).

[67] *NCQA's Private Health Insurance Plan Rankings 2012–13,* National Committee for Quality Assurance, 2012; Kaiser Foundation Health Plan of Colorado—HMO, Kaiser Foundation.

[68] AON Hewitt Quality of HMO plans 2013.

[69] The Leapfrog Group's annual 'Top Hospital' designation 2012.

[70] InformationWeek (2012)—http://www.informationweek.com/iw500/2011/top250.

[71] Lew McCreary, 'Kaiser Permanente's Innovation on the Front Lines,' *Harvard Business Review,* September 2010.

Kaiser Permanente knows how to combine the delivery of quality with effectiveness and efficiency. For the eleventh year in a row, consulting firm Aon Hewitt has calculated the cost-effectiveness of healthcare insurances in the USA. After correction to make populations of insurers comparable, Kaiser Permanente was 17 % more cost effective than other insurers in 2012.[72] Thanks to the combination of cost effectiveness and high quality, Kaiser Permanente has managed to achieve an operational profit of USD 2 billion (EUR 1.5 billion) over the past few years. In 2012, the organization's turnover totaled USD 49.96 billion (EUR 36.77 billion) with a net profit of USD 2.57 billion (EUR 1.89 billion). Its profits are managed by a fund. In 2012, USD 1.97 billion (EUR 1.45 billion) of the USD 2.57 billion (EUR 1.89 billion) profit were invested in society and the development of Kaiser Permanente hospitals and the organization's entire healthcare infrastructure.[73]

The organization has 172,997 employees in total, including nursing staff, administrative staff and cleaners. Kaiser Permanente lives up to its own vision. In 2011, 2012 and 2013, Kaiser Permanente was proclaimed the healthiest employer in California in the San Francisco Business Times Survey.[74] The Workplace Wellness Program certainly contributed to this accolade, and was itself the recipient of a Top Honor Award from the National Business Group on Health in 2012.[75] The training program for new doctors is also greatly appreciated. With an immense training capacity and intensive supervision, Kaiser Permanente states that it is training the next generation of outstanding doctors.

The value and benefits of the integrated approach can be found on different levels within society. The first is the most prominent result of healthier and more productive people. Most revenues are invested directly in society to this end. This occurs on different levels in society (individual, community) and for various issues such as health and prevention, but also for broader themes such as mobility and safety. There are, of course, also investment and studies that foster a deeper insight into the treatment and prevention of diseases such as cancer and diabetes, and more tailored, outcome-based and demand-driven healthcare. This not only benefits own customers, but also society overall. In 2011, 22 Kaiser Permanente researchers received awards and USD 24.9 million (EUR 18.3 million) in research funds from the National Institute of Health. This money was used to support the largest-ever population study involving 500,000 participants and focusing on genes, the environment and health. In the belief

---

[72] Hewitt Health Value Initiative benchmarking study—Kaiser Foundation Health Plan, Inc., Aon Hewitt, April 3, 2013.

[73] Kaiser Permanente 2012 Annual Report (2013).

[74] Business Times Survey (2013).

[75] National Business Group on Health (2013).

Value by customers
• Medicare health plans in the California, Northwest, Hawaii and Colorado regions received an overall Medicare Star Quality Rating of five stars. No less than 18 Kaiser Permanente hospitals were named "2011 Best Hospitals" based on the results of the Leapfrog Group's national survey
• High member satisfaction. KP plans in California, Colorado, Georgia and the Mid-Atlantic States were also rated highest in member satisfaction in a J.D. Power and Associates' regional 2011 Member Health Plan Study

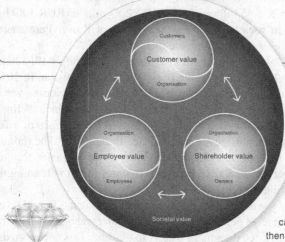

Value for and by shareholders
• Kaiser Permanente is a not-for-profit company that invests more then 80% of its net income in society to increase quality of health-care and research, strengthen society or create a safer workplace. In its most recently reported year, the non-profit Kaiser Foundation Health Plan and Kaiser Foundation Hospitals entities reported a combined USD 1.6 billion (EUR 1.35 billion) in net income on USD 47.9 billion (EUR 40.7 billion) in operating revenues. Each independent Permanente Medical Group operates as a separate for-profit partnership or professional corporation in its individual territory

Value for and by Employees
• Among commercial health plans, Kaiser Permanente ranked highest in employer satisfaction in the J.D. Power and Associates 2011 U.S. Employer Health Insurance Plan Study

Value for and by society
• In 2011, Kaiser Permanente celebrated the opening of the Kaiser Permanente Center for Total Health in Washington, D.C., a place to gather and discuss the future of health and healthcare and explore new ways to advance health through innovation and technology
• The support of total health for its patients, members, workforce and communities by providing services and promoting clinical, educational, environmental and social actions that improve the health of all people. Kaiser Permanente invested 1.8 billion of the 2.0 billion net income in the community

Figure 6.3.4 Value for and by stakeholders of Kaiser Permanente

that better data and communication contribute to improved care, Kaiser Permanente has made its self-developed software for medical terminology available to all professionals and hospitals in the USA for free. By doing so, it is endeavoring to help standardize the language and data used in medical records.

6.3.4 The brilliant lessons of Kaiser Permanente

- The focus on shared responsibility and cooperation at Kaiser Permanente ensures that a personal approach to healthcare is paramount. Care is not provided because a doctor says so, but because the patient wishes to lead a healthy and happy life. Such an approach means that ownership for improving one's health lies with the patient first.
- Kaiser Permanente has created a system of integrated care whereby all parties focus on attaining the best level of health and care. Doctors are rewarded for high-quality and effective care (and not for the number of treatments). Customers receive support to help them lead a healthy life and are partly responsible for their own healthcare costs via own contributions which remain at an affordable level. Employers and government authorities operate better and more efficiently when citizens/employees are productive and look after themselves well. The insurer earns more money if less care is needed because policyholders remain healthy.
- By integrating insurance and healthcare, Kaiser Permanente is responsible for health and not only for treatment. While hospital care can also be obtained via partnerships, employing primary healthcare practitioners yourself in particular makes a significance difference for Kaiser Permanente. This shifts the business model from *medical* care to *health*care. Every dollar that can be saved in healthcare costs is a profit, allowing the financing of prevention and resulting in high-quality care and reduced costs. The nonprofit organization reinforces this by not paying a dividend to shareholders; profits are invested in better care, research, and society.
- Thanks to shared responsibility and motives to improve care and health, the organization focuses continuously on enhancing and innovating its performance. It is also important to measure quality and results constantly in order to take the following improvement-related step. The continuous and joint compilation, enrichment, sharing and analysis of data for health records is a logical requirement and a necessary key.
- The integrated organization of care enables the development of the electronic patient dossier. Besides the fact that it is easier to link and secure IT services within the integrated healthcare system, it also helps that all stakeholders are part of the organization and agree on objectives amongst themselves. This results in a system that allows customers to view their dossier online and gives doctors access to the information they require at all times.

6.4   PatientsLikeMe

Using the Most Unutilized Resource in Healthcare

Annemijn Kuenen, Heleen Borleffs, Tim Widdershoven & Jeroen Geelhoed @:
J.Geelhoed@samhoud.com, Phone: 0031 622408791

Prelude *E-patient Dave, as he calls himself, has a story that describes precisely why PatientsLikeMe was established. Dave was diagnosed with stage IV kidney cancer and then read that the average survival period after the moment of diagnosis was only 24 weeks. Shortly thereafter, he joined a social network for cancer patients where he discovered a treatment involving Interleukin-2, a drug most kidney cancer patients had never heard of. Ultimately, this treatment even saved his life. Today, E-patient Dave is a healthy guy, but also an outspoken ambassador for many of the things PatientsLikeMe stands for. He believes that patients are "the most underused resource in healthcare" and that they need access to their own medical data. He is of the opinion that patients can only crack the code of their own health situation and treatment with complete information.[76]*

In 1998 Stephen Heywood is diagnosed with ALS. As Stephen's situation deteriorated, he and his family repeatedly try to delay his illness and treat his symptoms. They experience the time-consuming and repetitive nature of this trial-and-error approach and become convinced that a better manner has to exist. Not only Stephen and his family but also millions of people around the world who live with life-changing and chronic illnesses have the same feeling. They often have specific questions about their treatment options and what awaits them. They wonder: "Is what I'm experiencing normal?" Or: "Is there someone else just like me?"[77] PatientsLikeMe is created in 2004 by Stephen's brothers Jamie and Ben Heywood and family friend Jeff Cole, and provides answers to questions such as these.

---

[76] PatientsLikeMe (2011).

[77] http://news.patientslikeme.com/about/background.

Introduction PatientsLikeMe is an online network where patients can find answers to their questions and are connected with other patients who know what they are going through. Today members share their experiences on more than 2000 medical conditions. These include rare illnesses such as ALS, but also more prevalent ones such as depression, fibromyalgia, multiple sclerosis and psoriasis.[78] Via a patient profile, members can monitor how they are doing between doctor and hospital visits. They can document the severity of their symptoms, identify triggers, note how they are responding to new treatments and keep track of side effects. Patients also learn from their respective experiences and support one another. This helps them improve their quality of life from day to day.[79] By sharing their practical experiences, members also help the rest of the world obtain a better understanding of various medical conditions and healthcare.

PatientsLikeMe has a philosophy of openness. Information from patients is compiled and analyzed. The information and results are shared with researchers and companies from the healthcare sector, and especially the pharmaceutical world, in order to expedite research into and the development of more effective treatments. Data and results are always made anonymously to ensure personal details cannot be traced back to the individual patient.[80] The value of this open, community-driven approach to research into healthcare was demonstrated for the first time in 2011, when PatientsLikeMe unveiled the results of an operational study initiated by patients. A publication from 2008 claiming that lithium carbonate can halt the progression of ALS was refuted.[81] Ben Heywood explains: "As the family of an ALS patient, we thought we already knew everything there was to know about ALS as we were closely involved. What is fascinating about the website is how much more we learned that we did not yet know when we started the online network for ALS patients. That is the power of PatientsLikeMe; you do not know how much you do not know yet."[82]

6.4.1 The Cornerstone: "Live Better Together"

The brand essence of PatientsLikeMe is encapsulated in its motto "Live better together." It is an online network that wants to help patients with a life-changing illness to obtain a better quality of life and thereby change how they cope with their illness. At the same time, the aim is to alter the manner in which the healthcare industry carries out research. By acting as a real-time research platform that focuses on patients, treatment options can be improved according to the patient's needs.[83]

---

[78] http://www.patientslikeme.com/conditions.

[79] http://news.patientslikeme.com/about/background.

[80] http://www.patientslikeme.com/about/openness.

[81] http://news.patientslikeme.com/about/background.

[82] Williams (2008).

[83] Draft Q&A with Jamie Heywood for UK Newsletter Aug. 2013.

The higher goal the company wishes to attain is more patient-oriented care. The online network gives patients a place where they can connect to one another, learn from each other, and learn how to deal with their illnesses.[84] The key phrase "Making healthcare better for everyone through sharing, support, and research"[85] articulates this noble pursuit. This philosophy is underpinned by the life experiences of Stephen Heywood from the prelude. His brother, Jamie Heywood, starts ALS TDI in 1999 shortly after Stephan is diagnosed with ALS in 1998. ALS TDI is at that time the first organization in the world to engage in nonprofit biotechnological research in order to accelerate the development of new treatment methods.[86] PatientsLikeMe is eventually established in December 2004 with the idea to share all acquired knowledge about ALS with other patients. The website is officially launched in 2006. Initially dedicated to ALS, the focus quickly expands after the launch to encompass other life-changing and chronic illnesses such as epilepsy and MS. Today, it provides a platform for over 2000 medical conditions.

The audacious goal is strongly linked to the company's higher goal. This audacious goal is to transform healthcare into a sector that implicates patients more, so that greater patient value is created. PatientsLikeMe represents the voice of patients around the globe.[87] One of the company's goals is to ultimately create an online community for every life-changing illness.[88] To truly transform the healthcare industry, the strategy of PatientsLikeMe is to develop itself into a real-time health educational system. The aim of this educational system is to make analyses of health conditions that can be of value to patients, but that can also simultaneously align medical research with patients' needs.[89] PatientsLikeMe can then be used for treatment methods, clinical trials and insurance payments, for example.[90]

To achieve this goal, PatientsLikeMe's brand promise is to encourage its members to actively participate in the opportunities provided by the online network and to inform patients as extensively as possible about their illnesses and conditions. The website gives patients a place where they can submit status updates about their health, share experiences, find other patients with similar complaints and learn from their respective experiences.[91] The provided services and tools allow patients to manage their health more effectively,[92] or in other words: it enables personalized discovery and management of the patient's health.[93]

---

[84] Interview, Sept. 2013.

[85] http://www.patientslikeme.com/.

[86] http://www.patientslikeme.com/members/view/jamie.

[87] Interview, Sept. 2013.

[88] http://www.patientslikeme.com/help/faq/Corporate.

[89] Idem.

[90] Gupta and Riis (2012).

[91] http://www.patientslikeme.com/.

[92] http://money.cnn.com/2013/04/15/technology/patientslikeme-heywood.pr.fortune/index.html.

[93] http://www.patientslikeme.com/help/faq/Corporate & TED Video Cambridge by Ben Heywood January 2012.

The above actually clearly reflects the company's core values. These values form the basis of the business model, but also appear to explain the success of PatientsLikeMe. The first and perhaps most important core value is "patients first." The patient is the focal point of all of the organization's core activities—this is a major driving force. The trust that the patient gives must not be undermined under any circumstances. The other core values cannot be ignored, however. Every decision is taken and measured using the complete set of values. Transparency, openness and ensuring a "wow" effect[94] correspond seamlessly with the first core value and with the business philosophy and vision as a whole. Openness among patients is stimulated intensively; it is only by sharing information, experiences and results that patients can learn from and support each other, and that healthcare can improve significantly on a large scale. It is obvious that PatientsLikeMe runs thanks to patients who are members of this network and the information they share upon it. The wow effect that PatientsLikeMe endeavors to create must occur when you look on the website. It is important that patients see and feel that they are not alone; people should actually feel they are receiving social support from each other. PatientsLikeMe also offers value such as education.[95] It goes without saying that transparency should be an important core value for the company. No surprises about what PatientsLikeMe does may arise, nor about what it does with the patient-related information it shares, where the money comes from or existing partnerships.[96]

The company's core qualities are closely linked to its core values. Following on from the creation of a wow effect, one of the qualities of PatientsLikeMe involves making patients feel connected; part of a family. This results in friendships and participatory members of the website. The company does a great deal to teach about health conditions in order to meet members' needs and therefore bind them to the community. Real life and ethnographic studies also form part of the qualities therefore. The accumulation of knowledge about health conditions but also about what the company does with data relating to its members forms part of its core qualities. This data is compiled and processed into structural results, symptoms and treatments, but is also used to create a learning system that can improve the healthcare industry. The research and insights become available in a language comprehensible to patients. Results that PatientsLikeMe shares with its partners are also shared with its members.

---

[94] http://www.patientslikeme.com/help/faq/Corporate.

[95] Interview, Sept. 2013.

[96] http://www.patientslikeme.com/help/faq/Corporate.

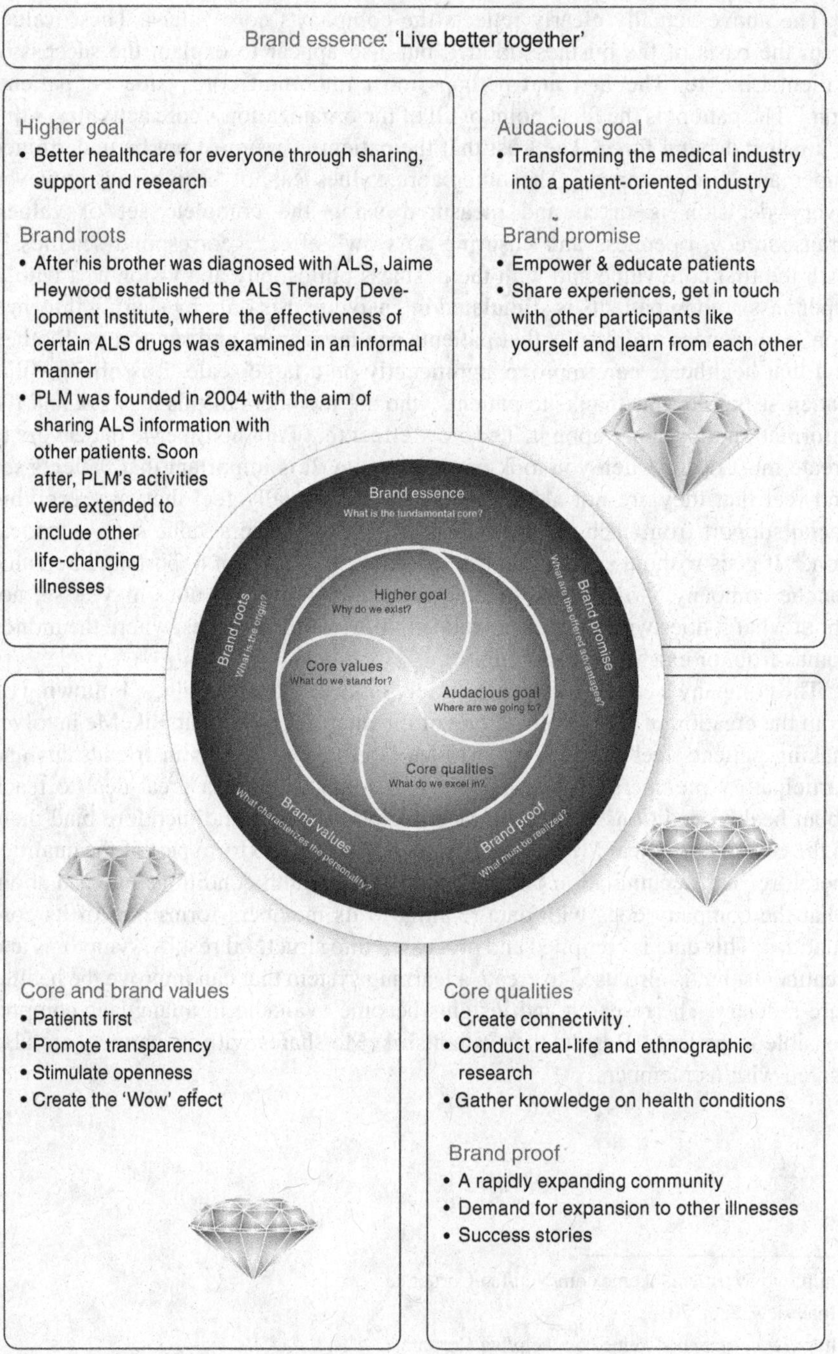

Brand essence: 'Live better together'

Higher goal
• Better healthcare for everyone through sharing, support and research

Brand roots
• After his brother was diagnosed with ALS, Jaime Heywood established the ALS Therapy Development Institute, where the effectiveness of certain ALS drugs was examined in an informal manner
• PLM was founded in 2004 with the aim of sharing ALS information with other patients. Soon after, PLM's activities were extended to include other life-changing illnesses

Audacious goal
• Transforming the medical industry into a patient-oriented industry

Brand promise
• Empower & educate patients
• Share experiences, get in touch with other participants like yourself and learn from each other

Brand essence
What is the fundamental core?

Brand roots
What is the origin?

Higher goal
Why do we exist?

Core values
What do we stand for?

Audacious goal
Where are we going to?

Brand promise
What are the offered advantages?

Core qualities
What do we excel in?

Brand values
What characterizes the personality?

Brand proof
What must be realized?

Core and brand values
• Patients first
• Promote transparency
• Stimulate openness
• Create the 'Wow' effect

Core qualities
• Create connectivity
• Conduct real-life and ethnographic research
• Gather knowledge on health conditions

Brand proof
• A rapidly expanding community
• Demand for expansion to other illnesses
• Success stories

Figure 6.4.1 Vision and Positioning of PatientsLikeMe

6.4.2 The Business Model: "To Get Paid for Making Patients Better"[97]

PatientsLikeMe reaches many patients, who can enhance their quality of life through the online network, while simultaneously assisting healthcare and the pharmaceutical industry. But what precisely makes this business model so exceptional?

Market Segment: for Patient and Company What makes PatientsLikeMe so special is its unique position in the market. The concept works from patient to patient, but also from patient to professional at the same time. The company's target group therefore involves two parties: patients, on the one hand, and healthcare industry professionals on the other. In principle, all users of the illness community are encouraged to visit the website or participate in it. These can be caregivers, patients, doctors, and clinical and visiting researchers interested in learning more about different conditions and healthcare.[98] The members of the online network come primarily from the USA, in addition to 40 other countries. PatientsLikeMe is actively working to extend its network across American borders.[99] Patients find understanding and answers to questions to which doctors have no answer. The participation of patients also creates a dataset containing highly valuable real-time information on experiences and outcomes of treatments and medication by a range of patients. The pharmaceutical industry is eager to obtain this wealth of knowledge because it can help significantly improve treatments, medication and equipment. By integrating clinical and behavioral research, PatientsLikeMe acts like a data compiler, analyzer and intermediary of information for the medical industry.[100] Although the online network can distinguish itself in different ways, some competition does exist in other online information websites and forums for health and health-related conditions. Pharmaceutical companies can also act as competitors when they provide condition-specific information and set up patient networks but this often remains more in the field of clinical trials with test groups then learning from the data of real life.[101] There is not one explicit other company that offers full competition. While PatientsLikeMe focuses on over 2000 health-related conditions, the competition often focuses on single diseases or a few related illnesses. It is precisely one of the network's strengths that it bundles together so many diseases and conditions, because information and experience are brought together in this way. Symptom treatment, treatment experiences and daily tips in particular can be applied to multiple illnesses.

---

[97] Gupta and Riis (2012).
[98] Idem.
[99] Williams (2008).
[100] http://vimeo.com/61429662.
[101] Gupta and Riis (2012).

Customer Value: Where Customers Strengthen One Another As has already been pointed out, both patients and professionals within the industry constitute the company's target group, thus allowing PatientsLikeMe to create customer value in two ways. Patients can become site members for free, learn a great deal about their condition and maintain their personal self-care model[102] online. In this way, members are connected to a community, and the severity of each condition and its impact on the patient is measured. This information should effectively help support patients' life choices, doctors' treatment choices, and researchers' knowledge about various conditions.[103] To obtain this information, pharmaceutical companies enter into partnerships with the company and pay for reports and surveys that are conducted within the online community.[104] The associated costs are borne by the professional partners of PatientsLikeMe. This can occur for a separate study, or pharmaceutical companies can take out a subscription for analyses and aggregated data from PatientsLikeMe, for which they pay an unspecified amount. "We have created a website where people can learn from each other, share experiences and at the same time contribute to knowledge about health data. We have removed traditional barriers between researchers and patients," says Michael Evers, Executive Vice President of Marketing and Patient Advocacy at PatientsLikeMe.[105] The company also develops tools such as the prediction tool, which creates a control group for individual patients with a predictable illness featuring ten others with the same illness progression. Merging the data of these patients makes it possible to predict the progression of the illness for the patient using the tool.[106] This knowledge can then be used not only by the patient but also by healthcare practitioners when taking decisions aimed at improving patient-focused care.[107] Another valuable aspect for the patient and pharmaceutical industry is that all the information is linked to the network for clinical studies. Patients who have registered are notified about clinical studies being carried out within a 40 km radius of their home for which they are eligible.[108] This enables patients to voluntarily participate in tests they are interested in and makes it easier for researchers at the same time to find enough test subjects to yield test results. An awareness of not being alone is created for members of the online network. It should be noted, however, that when personal data is shared online, there is a risk that people with malicious intentions may abuse this dossier knowledge. Although information that can allow members to be identified directly is not shared publicly, such a system is not watertight and members must be aware of this. Ben Heywood has the following to say on about this matter: "Patients understand that the value they provide by sharing information outweighs the potential privacy risks."[109] To date, PatientsLikeMe has never had to deal with any cases where

---

[102] http://vimeo.com/61429662.

[103] Idem.

[104] Gupta and Riis (2012).

[105] In Ventiv Health (2013).

[106] http://vimeo.com/61429662.

[107] Interview, Sept. 2013.

[108] Idem.

[109] Williams (2008).

medical information is misused and harms patients. Patients can also increase their anonymity by registering under a fake name and using an avatar.

Delivery: "Tell the World!" The marketing expressions focus firstly, of course, on new members and potential partners. But the company also uses other marketing approaches. One such example is the sponsorship program of PatientsLikeMe called "In Motion." Teams are sponsored to participate in local nonprofit walks and runs to raise awareness about specific illnesses. A wealth of online material (under the motto: "Tell the World!") can also be downloaded, and contains information about the initiative and results of PatientsLikeMe.[110] The "Value of Openness" blog keeps everyone abreast of the latest events, successes, experiences, and patient stories. Employees, researchers, and patients regularly post on this blog. In addition, the "PatientsLikeMeOnCall Podcast" broadcasts interviews with patients and companies about healthcare trends, patients' needs and much more.[111] Most importantly, patients who become members of the online network often act as ambassadors for the organization and its philosophy. Word-of-mouth advertising is therefore the most valuable tool in the end. PatientsLikeMe also has partnerships with nonprofit organizations, patients' associations, and other associations that can be potential members.

Operation: Customers Are the Key Player In this business model, patients are the goal and the means. They are the supplier of the organization's most important resource: real-time information about various illnesses and experiences. The primary task of PatientsLikeMe is to facilitate the online network and act as a mediator for the community. It conducts various analyses on all the information obtained through the website to ensure it can be used. One of the organization's other primary tasks is to engage in business-to-business networks so that partnerships can be concluded with authorities and companies that purchase the analyzed data. These partners include researchers and academics, nonprofit organizations and the medical industry, such as pharmaceutical companies and developers of medical equipment.[112] Customization is needed to meet these partners' changing demands. On average, contracts for community partnerships last 2–3 years, but many projects and partnerships also last around 3–9 months.[113] The Management Team is responsible for research; scientific and clinical are responsible for data analysis and generating knowledge. The Technology Team focuses on the product while Design and Engineering is responsible for implementing website functionality. The Patient Experience Team and the PatientsLikeMe Customer Service Team are responsible for moderating communities and forums. Finally, the Health & Data Integrity Team is responsible for the completeness and accuracy of data, while the Marketing and Business Development Team takes care of patient acquisition and engagement.

---

[110] http://www.patientslikeme.com/about.

[111] https://itunes.apple.com/us/podcast/patientslikeme-oncall-mp3/id364055239.

[112] http://www.patientslikeme.com/about/partners.

[113] Interview, Sept. 2013.

Value for customers

Result *What do I get?*
- Access to a community of people with the same syndrome through a personalized file*
- Empirical data**
- Patients for research**

Process *How do I get it?*
- Create a file and keep it up to date*
- Partnership**
- Buy / request data**

Emotion *What do I feel?*
- A sense of connection*
- Improved knowledge**

Price *What are the costs?*
- Free of charge*
- A one-time fee for a qualitative report**
- An annual subscription fee for outcome studies**

Effort *What do I have to do for it?*
- Create a file, keep it up to date and share it*
- Form partnerships**

Risk *What are the uncertainties?*
- Harm caused by incomplete information**
- Abuse of knowledge of files by third parties**

Market segments

Position
- A unique position in the market thanks to patient-to-patient idea plus patient-to-professional concept
- Not exclusive for just one single syndrome

Competition
- General websites with medical information
- Websites of pharmaceutical companies that provide general information and possibly also set up patient communities
- Other online communities and forums

Target group
- Patients and professionals who are either active in the healthcare industry or are interested in it

Customer insights
- Patients are assisted in feeling more in control of their own health
- Professionals can significantly improve their products and knowledge by getting in touch with patients

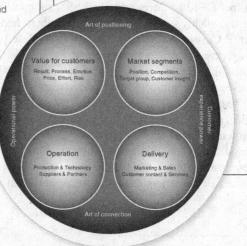

**Patients*
Professionals

Figure 6.4.2 Value for customers and market segments of PatientsLikeMe

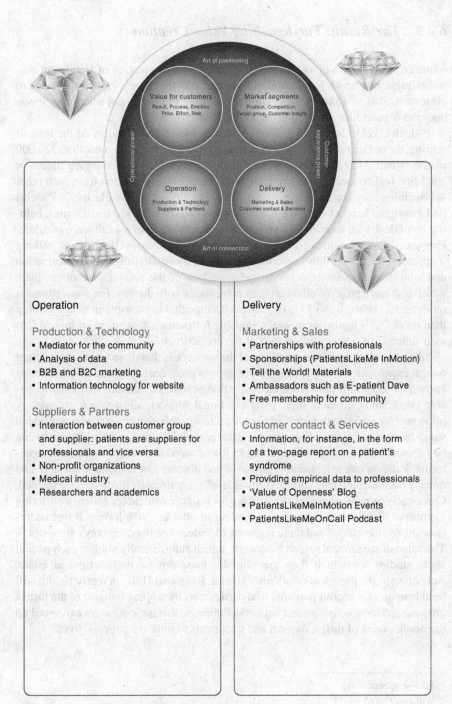

Operation

Production & Technology
- Mediator for the community
- Analysis of data
- B2B and B2C marketing
- Information technology for website

Suppliers & Partners
- Interaction between customer group and supplier: patients are suppliers for professionals and vice versa
- Non-profit organizations
- Medical industry
- Researchers and academics

Delivery

Marketing & Sales
- Partnerships with professionals
- Sponsorships (PatientsLikeMe InMotion)
- Tell the World! Materials
- Ambassadors such as E-patient Dave
- Free membership for community

Customer contact & Services
- Information, for instance, in the form of a two-page report on a patient's syndrome
- Providing empirical data to professionals
- 'Value of Openness' Blog
- PatientsLikeMeInMotion Events
- PatientsLikeMeOnCall Podcast

Figure 6.4.3 Operation and Delivery of PatientsLikeMe

6.4.3   The Result: Far-Reaching Value Creation

Value creation plays a pivotal role in this company. The creation of significant customer value is a major focal point in organizations that attach great importance to customers. PatientsLikeMe looks further than that, of course. On what other levels does the organization succeed in creating even more value?

PatientsLikeMe is able to generate considerable customer value. At the time of writing, the online network is enormous and growing rapidly with more than 220,000 members and 2000 illnesses. The fact that patients with a life-changing illness or condition feel connected and can learn about their health condition from each other is something they appreciate immensely; they can find a "patient like me." "Patients find emotional support and give each other tips on how to tackle small things, helping them deal with their illness and enabling the creation of a healthcare standard. Peer pressure also ensures greater pressure on patients amongst themselves, making it apparent that they follow prescribed treatments more carefully. Good information and education also foster a better understanding of the patient's treatment plan, which also has a positive effect on their compliance with therapy. For some illnesses on PatientsLikeMe, up to 45 % of patients become therapy compliant which is more than usual."[114] It is also immensely valuable for patients to acquire an insight into their future thanks to resources such as the prediction tool.

"An interesting aspect of members of the network is that there are many different patient expertises. Some patients simply know a great deal about the disease; others know a lot about how to best manage daily things; others in turn are very knowledgeable about studies; others offer great emotional support, all of which are equally important for our community."[115] In practical terms, this also has considerable added value for the professional help that patients receive. Doctors' and hospital visits can be far more efficient and effective thanks to enhanced knowledge and health monitoring. Patients can ask specific questions and doctors can respond accurately and quickly because their condition and any side-effects caused by medicines are tracked. Completely measurable improvements are for instance evident for epilepsy-suffering members; 59 % have a better understanding of attacks; 50 % have a better understanding of side-effects and there is even a 23 % decrease in emergency care visits.[116] The value of the clinical research network, which automatically notifies each patient about studies for which they are eligible, must not be underestimated either. According to the president of inVentiv Health, Raymond Hill: "inVentiv Health will be able to quickly recruit potential trial participants by tapping into one of the fastest growing and most active patient networks online, so that our customers can speed up the development of drugs, devices and treatments to improve patients' lives."[117]

---

[114] Interview, Sept. 2013.

[115] Williams (2008).

[116] Interview, Sept. 2013.

[117] In Ventiv Health (2013).

The fact that patients enrich the medical world with valuable knowledge is also considered very important by members. They do not only become better themselves thanks to the knowledge they acquire, but many (future) patients are also helped. PatientsLikeMe has developed into a reliable and valued source for empirical disease-related information as well as a clinical robust source that has published over 30 peer-reviewed studies.[118] The aggregated and depersonalized information members share on the website is analyzed and insights are sold to partners who develop products or sell to patients. By selling these insights and involving partners in discussions about patients' needs, PatientsLikeMe helps them better understand the actual medical value of their products so that they can improve these. Partners also receive help with expediting the development of new solutions and treatments for patients.[119] In short, value creation for professionals lies in improved knowledge and products.

PatientsLikeMe is a for-profit organization that benefits from the sale of patient information. However, it has no annual reports to consult and does not disclose turnover and profit details because it is a non-listed private company. Since professionals often have varying demands and are looking for specific information, reports, surveys and studies are customized. This makes it difficult to acquire a good insight into actual revenues stemming from PatientsLikeMe partnerships. A Harvard business case estimates potential revenues for the business if it expands its focus on market research towards insurance companies. If PatientsLikeMe can convincingly demonstrate that patients become more therapy compliant because they are engaged members of the site, a good value proposition can be created for both pharmaceutical and insurance companies.[120] Each partnership entered into with the organization must bring it closer towards its audacious goal. All partnerships must ensure that the interests of patients and the industry are more aligned. The ultimate goal is: better care and a better quality of life for the patient.[121]

The company's employees all share the same ideal; making better healthcare a reality. Contributing to this by working for PatientsLikeMe is considered the greatest added value of the job by more than 60 employees. According to an employee: "We are all dedicated to the creation of a meaningful experience for our patients and customers. It is wonderful to see that we are all happy to work on bringing about change within healthcare."[122] Greater employee value is also derived from the fact that the health and well-being of its employees is a priority for the company. PatientsLikeMe even ranks among the top 44 healthiest companies to work for.[123] It offers flexible working hours and encourages exercise by providing yoga classes and Nintendo Wii games. The company also offers major medical and dental benefits to its employees.[124]

---

[118] Idem.

[119] http://www.patientslikeme.com/help/faq/Corporate.

[120] Idem.

[121] http://www.patientslikeme.com/help/faq/Corporate.

[122] http://blog.patientslikeme.com/tag/patientslikeme-yoga-class/.

[123] http://greatist.com/health/healthiest-companies.

[124] http://www.patientslikeme.com/about/careers.

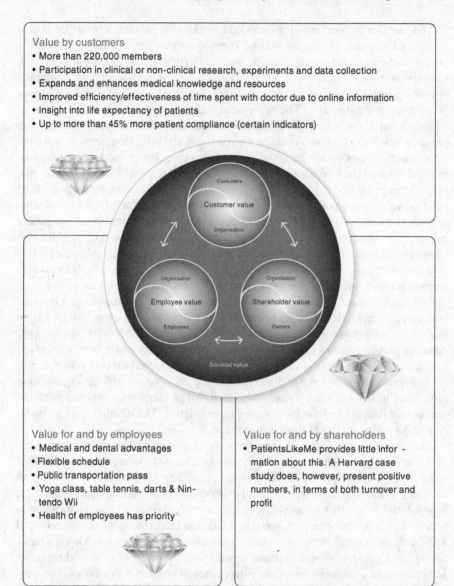

Value by customers
- More than 220,000 members
- Participation in clinical or non-clinical research, experiments and data collection
- Expands and enhances medical knowledge and resources
- Improved efficiency/effectiveness of time spent with doctor due to online information
- Insight into life expectancy of patients
- Up to more than 45% more patient compliance (certain indicators)

Value for and by employees
- Medical and dental advantages
- Flexible schedule
- Public transportation pass
- Yoga class, table tennis, darts & Nintendo Wii
- Health of employees has priority

Value for and by shareholders
- PatientsLikeMe provides little information about this. A Harvard case study does, however, present positive numbers, in terms of both turnover and profit

Value for and by society
- Sharing information and helping others serves a therapeutic and healing function
- Breakthroughs in medical research
- More patient-oriented care

Figure 6.4.4 Value creation for and by stakeholders of PatientsLikeMe

In addition to customer, shareholder and employee value, PatientsLikeMe also creates immense social value. Research breakthroughs are achieved and even greater breakthroughs are expected in the medical world because of a business model that focuses on sharing patient information. Not only members of the online network and direct partners of the company benefit from the successes that are achieved; the medical world learns and improves as a result of this.

6.4.4 The Brilliant Lessons of PatientsLikeMe

Several lessons can be learned from this special and brilliant business model. It is worth taking a more in-depth look at the following six lessons.

- Allow your one customer to benefit from the input of the other. Patients fill in all kinds of data (for free). This provides value for patients because they come into contact with similar patients. This is very valuable data and this is then analyzed, aggregated and used for another customer group. In this way, the efforts and insights of one customer group also benefit the other, while PatientsLikeMe provides the intelligent platform. Patients pay for something which is very valuable for them bij giving their data which is very valuable for the industry.
- Connect your customers to one another. One of the strongest qualities of PatientsLikeMe is that customers are connected to each other. Patients are not only connected to each other, but also to researchers and medical professionals. On the first level, a strong sense of community arises and the connection between private and professional customers ensures an interaction that permits both parties to make desired improvements. The business model therefore has a self-reinforcing effect. PatientsLikeMe has attached the following goal to this: "*To get paid for making patients better*."[125]
- Connect your customers to your business philosophy and make your goals known. When customers are aware of the business philosophy and goals you wish to attain with it, they can be of a greater value compared to when they have no knowledge of this. The philosophy of openness resonates with customers and is linked to a robust audacious goal with which customers can identify. Privacy-related risks are even considered acceptable because the goal outweighs the risks. Customers can actively share and cooperate in the attainment of the company's audacious goal.
- Make your customers ambassadors of your company. Who else can sell your company better than a satisfied customer? Ensure therefore that your customers are satisfied, but also give them all the possibilities and information to actually act as ambassadors. By being open and transparent about the way you work and conveying your philosophy to your customers with conviction, they know what you stand for and can share this with others. Word-of-mouth advertising is one

---

[125] Gupta and Riis (2012).

of the most effective marketing tools, so invest in it and also express your appreciation for ambassadorship.

- Create value on various levels. A brilliant business model provides value creation for customers, shareholders, employees, and society. The value created on each of these levels has a reinforcing effect on the next level.
- Dare to create a social impact. The audacious goal of PatientsLikeMe is not only aimed at internal performance, but also endeavors to bring about change within the healthcare sector. By extending the audacious goal to achieve a social impact, all the parties concerned are stimulated to work together in achieving this objective.

Chapter 7
Breakthrough: Patient-Centered Organization of Information and Everyday Care

How Should We Share Treatment and Diagnostic Information and Bring Primary Care Closer to the Patient?

In organizing primary care and chronic diseases proximity to the patient is the most important principle and there is less of an advantage to be realized through scaling and bundling of expertise. This relates to accessible retail solutions for care of the daily household type where service is more important than deep medical expertise. It also concerns the integrated healthcare for chronic and elderly patients who need solutions close to home. The challenge here is in particular that there are many different health practitioners treating the patient and there is a need for streamlined integration of the treatment and information surrounding the patient. There are brilliant business models in this patient-centered everyday care:

- *UCLA's Value Quotient organizes care for chronical diseases such as IBD truly around the patients perspective by a shared focus with health-practitioners and researchers on improvements in quality of life, self-control, participation, and productivity.*
- *ParkinsonNet creates networks of health practitioners in especially primary care who share experience, expertise and who cooperate in helping Parkinson patients as good as they can.*
- *Laastari has created a sort of Minute Clinic in Sweden and Finland which offers the standard and basic care of the general practitioner in a retail formula.*
- *Patrick Lund has reinvented dental care in such a way that it does no longer frighten people but make the visitors and the dentist happy.*

As we see in Chap. 9, it is useful to concentrate facilities when care involves schedulable treatment for which there may be genuine scale advantages and/or treatment and diagnoses that require highly specialized knowledge. Where that is not the case, care is more effective when organized in close proximity to patients in order to avoid complexity and overheads and keep things on a human scale. This concerns primary care, i.e., the general practitioner, the dentist, the pharmacist, the physiotherapist, and the dietician; it

© Springer International Publishing Switzerland 2017
J. Kemperman et al. (eds.), *Brilliant Business Models in Healthcare*,
DOI 10.1007/978-3-319-26440-0_7

also concerns relatively common diagnoses and treatment such as an echocardiogram in the case of heart complaints, broken bones, or pregnancy. Two notable trends in this context are integrated and streamlined care for people with chronic diseases and making the common primary care tasks more easily accessible and efficient.

It is important for patients that healthcare practitioners cooperate closely and efficiently in the chain. This is especially critical when caring for and treating the chronically ill.[1] Increasingly, the complexity of healthcare lies in making the correct diagnosis and avoiding duplicate analyses.[2] The right tests and examinations should be carried out, and information should be shared among all the relevant healthcare practitioners. This means both professional information and information about the patient, his or her illness, past and future treatment and medication. It has often been said that we need coordinators in healthcare to link all the parties to one another and organize things from the patient's perspective. The candidate mentioned most frequently for this task is the general practitioner, who already bears overall final responsibility in many healthcare systems; otherwise, there is a risk of duplication, which only makes matters more complicated rather than simpler. Of course, general practitioners do not monitor patients every single day. That being the case, it appears that the patient dossier itself (which should accompany the patient on his or her journey through the healthcare system with the patient as final owner) increasingly fulfills the vacant role of the operational "coordinator." It can become the channel with built-in intelligence through which all those involved catch up with and inform one another and which has a built-in alarm system that goes off in the event of a wrong combination or test result. Patient and treatment information can currently only be shared or transferred between parties to a limited extent in many countries, leading to many duplicate tests and errors.

Besides help with understanding their own disorder and coordinated care, patients also need to understand which treatment options are available. They need transparency about the different treatment categories and the results they can expect. That also requires them to understand the level of quality and the safety risks associated with the various places where they can receive a treatment.[3] But that is not always how things operate right now. The treatment options offered by healthcare practitioners differ quite considerably. There is also a high level of "practice variation" in quality. Specialists differ considerably in the number of surgical procedures that they carry out and in the safety of those procedures and quality of the outcomes. These are real differences, and not a mere 10 % increase in a certain type of complication or mortality. We are talking about figures of 200 %, with deviations of up to 1000 %. Knowing more about one's disorder, the treatment options, and the quality of healthcare practitioners is better for one's health. It's also more efficient because it prevents duplication and repair work.[4] It does require breakthroughs in diagnosis and information technology, as well as in the attitude and conduct of the relevant stakeholders, the openness of information sharing and in the governance to ensure that the personalized medical information is only used for the treatment and in the interest of the patient.

---

[1] Brouwer et al. (2013).

[2] Christensen et al. (2009).

[3] Wennberg (2010).

[4] For more insight into the importance and the nature of quality in healthcare, see the speeches of Berwick (2004).

Besides self-management and integrated care for the chronically ill, patients also need retail solutions for their primary care needs.[5] In this context, service and personal attention is often more important than deep medical expertise. Physical visits are possible, but teleconsultations via voice and/or screen can be equally effective, faster (and therefore cheaper) and more convenient. A doctor who is broadly trained to a very high level of skill is often somewhat overqualified for part of the work that he or she does. The healthcare practitioner does not need to be a doctor but must be properly trained for the task at hand, have a service-minded attitude and be empathetic to a high degree. A required condition is to have a good alarm system that recognizes when a genuine problem has arisen and refers the relevant case to the correct specialist or facility. Quality and safety of this kind can often be built right into the process and the treatment itself. Direct care can then often be provided by a nurse who focuses on personal care or, on the other hand, by an efficient service provider of teleconsultations with medically trained staff supported by IT.

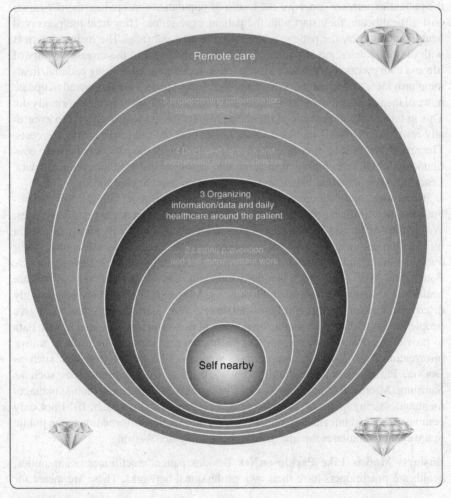

Figure 7.0.1 Breakthrough: Organizing information/data and daily healthcare around the patient

---

[5] Christensen et al. (2009).

Business Models Like UCLA's Value Quotient Alongside patient communities such as PatientsLikeMe, there are also platforms that support interaction between patients and healthcare practitioners. These encompass general patient/practitioner communities, but they also support dedicated, efficient interaction concerning a specific patient's treatment. Such platforms can replace some physical contact, but more importantly they offer additional options. For example, patients can participate more actively in updating and sharing their own health information and learn from it while also helping to cut down on the cost of paperwork. This makes it possible to ask for and share more specific information about test results, treatment outcomes and future treatment. It may still be several steps removed from precision medicine, but it is in any event much closer to precision medication and treatment because everyone knows what the others are up to! An example that we have chosen by way of illustration is UCLA's Value Quotient. This is a program that began with a specific focus on Inflammatory Bowel Diseases (IBD). Within the triple aim to improve the patient experience, improve the health of populations and reduce the per-capita cost of healthcare, they start with the patient experience. They treat the perceived health outcomes by the patient as the actual reality and facts. The main concern is with the value delivered to patients in the form of control of the disease, quality of life and own productivity. These aspects are in fact measured, uniting patients, treatment providers and researchers in a common cause. Patients are motivated to update more of the information themselves and at a higher frequency than they normally do. This in turn makes it possible to measure progress more specifically and to eventually reward on the basis of added value, health benefits and lower healthcare costs. The results are used to directly improve the treatment of the patient but also to continuously fuel the machinery of research and improvement with the combined data. Learning takes place and expertise is accrued at an unparalleled speed.

There are numerous examples like UCLA's Value Quotient in the USA of groundbreaking new online networks for sharing treatment information and outcomes. Waterfront Media and Web MD are two such networks with a vast array of patient information and insurance data. They allow patients to compare and contrast their own cases with similar patients. Other examples include the Restless Legs Syndrome Foundation (RLS.org), which is mainly a patient network but also aims to educate healthcare practitioners about this condition.[6] Insurance companies increasingly discover the richness of their claims-databases. They start to open that up to give people access to their own medical records and they depersonalize and bundle data to provide feedback to customers and healthcare providers in the form of mirror information (how do I do compared to someone like me). Companies such as Docvia, Philips, and increasingly also nonmedical information giants such as Samsung, Microsoft, Apple, and Google, offer tools for online and mobile management and sharing of one's own patient and personal health dossier. IBM not only combines medical information but also brings this medical information to the public in a way that stimulates the imagination by naming her Watson.

Business Models Like ParkinsonNet Besides patient/practitioner communities, healthcare practitioners have their own professional networks. These are meant for

---

[6] See for instance: Christensen et al. (2009).

information-sharing about individual patients in order to effectuate streamlined, integrated treatment. They are also intended to create a mutual network for referrals, with the quality of all participants being guaranteed. A further aim is knowledge-sharing in order to achieve and maintain a certain level of quality and to build and disseminate knowledge. We can illustrate this with a brilliant Dutch business model, known as ParkinsonNet. Legally speaking, this is a small, centralized network organization. For the participants and Parkinson's patients, however, it goes much further. The participants are involved in Parkinson's disease as healthcare practitioners, and the network allows them to learn from one another and upgrade their knowledge. A patient-centered network of professionals has considerable impact in the case of Parkinson's, a condition that involves a large number of different healthcare practitioners. A single network organization has been set up. For patients this provides a much higher level of treatment and that makes it easier for the various treatment providers to find one another and work together. In addition, there are numerous networks in which doctors and specialists can share information. One example is the online community SERMO. com, which has more than 70,000 participating doctors. Another is SimulConsul, a spin-off of Harvard Medical School that contains diagnoses by thousands of specialists and makes them available to doctors. It offers online diagnostic support, using symptoms to suggest possible disorders and indicating the probability of their occurrence. Another example of a diagnosis-support platform is Aetna's SmartSource. This platform features a collection of the medical profiles of insured persons linked to a medical search engine.[7] Knowledge is something we can share without ending up with less. In fact, knowledge can even multiply—something that is now taking on a new dimension. The online communities in which medical knowledge is shared create new options because they can be used internationally. That is a source of major change in developing countries, which used to have poor access to such expertise. Although surgery and surgeon's training are still local matters, knowledge transfer and remote diagnosis by means of teleconsultations have become much easier. Increasingly, they are also being used in accredited educational courses. Since the number of users does not need to be limited to the size of the classroom, the distance that needs to be travelled or the cost of an overnight stay, there are fewer barriers to training new generations of nurses and doctors around the world.

Business Models Like Laastari Some of the work carried out in primary care is relatively standard and commonplace. It mainly concerns the easily accessible, affordable and customer-driven care covering 80 % of the most common disorders, prescriptions and treatments. Examples include the flu, fungal infections, sore throats, ear infections and bladder infections, all treated by the doctor. They also include common medicines, refills at the pharmacy, regular check-ups and treatment by the dentist and oral hygienist. This type of diagnosis and treatment can often be made more patient-friendly, with a lower threshold, cheaper and more efficient. An example that we have chosen by way of illustration is Laastari, a retail formula for consulting the doctor about non-life-threatening but frequent illnesses in Finland and Sweden. Care is publicly organized and of excellent quality in these countries, but waiting lists are long and a patient may sometimes have to wait up to

---

[7] Idem.

2 months to see his or her doctor about a nonurgent matter. Laastari is a commercial formula and, unlike in the public healthcare system, patients simply pay out of pocket for it. The cost is kept low, however, because nurses carry out the consultations and check with doctors remotely. It all happens as quickly and easily as going to a normal shop.

Laastari itself was inspired by a well-known US business model, MinuteClinic. The case of Laastari also exemplifies the challenges and issues that arise when copying a business model such as MinuteClinic from a private to a public healthcare system. The USA remains the most prominent example of the primary care retail formula. There are now more than 1350 clinics being run according to this model, making it a standard business model. More than one out of six residents of the USA has been treated in a retail clinic. MinuteClinic was launched in 2000 and is now part of CVS, a major, listed pharmaceutical company. The chain grew rapidly thereafter, peaking in 2005. The number of clinics has quadrupled. Other chains also took off, including Target Clinic (part of the Target department store chain) and Takecare Clinics (which belongs to Walgreens, the USA's biggest pharmacy chain). Growth stopped when the financial crisis hit in 2008, but has started recovering slowly in recent years. Another example that resembles MinuteClinic is Rediclinic, which focuses on prevention and weight loss in addition to treatment. Examples for standard medications are MedCo, but also Walmart which sells a broad range of medicines for the standard price of USD 5 (EUR 4,50).[8]

Business Models Like Patrick Lund Dental Happiness Primary care offers more scope for patient-specific innovation based on service. In the retail sector, the point is usually to offer standardization and efficient, customer-friendly service. Another strategy is to exceed customer expectations by providing a superior service. An inspiring example is the Australian dentist Patrick Lund. He became unhappy with his work, but instead of looking for another job he looked for a way to make himself and his customers happy again. He analyzed his work and transformed his practice to eliminate all the negative connotations of visiting a dentist. For example, the patients' chair has a red button that they can press if they are in too much pain. Treatment then stops immediately. Patrick Lund does not represent an archetypal business model in dental care. His company is a surprising example of the social redesign of patient journeys to make treatment paths more customer-friendly, reduce anxiety and increase self-control. This is often seen in the schedulable care described in Chap. 9 that is provided by Aravind and Narayana in India and Shouldice in Canada. Patrick Lund also inspires us to think about making healthcare more fun. His approach is reminiscent of the way that the Ford Clinics in the USA deal with food. They have made their clinic kitchens and restaurants much healthier and customer-friendly and got the neighborhood closely involved. As a result, patients and neighbors have healthier diets and the restaurants have become a fun place to hang out. It's a little like having Disney run the clinic.[9] As the following breakthrough shows, there are many more examples in other service sectors that offer inspiration for making specialist care more accessible and community-based.

---

[8] Christensen et al. (2009).
[9] Lee (2004).

7.1 UCLA's Value Quotient

Measuring and adding value to disease management while controlling costs

Heleen Borleffs, Daniel Hommes & Jeroen Kemperman @: Jeroen.Kemperman@ achmea.nl, Phone: 0031 651222099

Prelude *"In 2006 I was diagnosed with Crohn's disease. From the time that I received the diagnosis, the disease has had a huge impact on my daily life. I've spent countless days in hospital, seen a lot of doctors and pretty much used all the drugs out there. And my illness causes me severe pain, fatigue and stress. I've never felt so alone and I'd already given up hope, until I signed up for the Inflammatory Bowel Diseases or IBD program at the University of California in Los Angeles (UCLA) in May 2012. Since I joined the IBD program, my symptoms have been reduced, my sense of well-being has improved significantly and I finally have the disease under control. What I appreciate most is how the IBD team sympathizes with me, how helpful they are and how willingly they respond to any question or concern. The communication is great and supports my feeling that I have a doctor and a team who reassure me and have a medical plan for my future. I have so much confidence in my IBD team that I'm willing to travel four hours from my home in Clovis, California to consult them. I feel blessed to be able to participate in the IBD program and would like to help in any way possible with its growth and on research into my disease."*[10]

---

[10] Statement of a patient who is participating in the IBD program of UCLA, Clovis CA, USA, 2012. In: UCLA Center for Inflammatory Bowel Diseases™ (2012), p. 64.

Introduction   More than 70 % of the costs associated with healthcare are related to chronic illnesses.[11] They are increasingly becoming the biggest challenge facing healthcare systems worldwide. Many people with a chronic disorder are not getting sufficient suitable care and feel that they are fighting the battle to control their disease alone. In the USA, about 40 % of people with a chronic disorder are not getting the care they require according to evidence-based standards.[12,13] There is growing evidence worldwide that patients with chronic disorders improve if they receive effective treatment in an integrated system of self-management support and regular follow-up.[14] As UCLA puts it: "If we want to reach affordable and sustainable success in achieving full disease control, we need to redefine and re-create actual value for individual patients and all other healthcare participants."[15] The team at UCLA's Center for IBD is doing pioneering work in IBD with its Value Quotient (VQ) program, which focuses on the concept of value-based healthcare. This program is very succesfull and extended to numerous chronical diseases but it all started with IBD so let's look at what they did in this field with the VQ program.

IBD is a group of disorders that involve chronic inflammation of the bowel. Crohn's disease and ulcerative colitis are the two most common manifestations of IBD. When the illness is active, patients may suffer diarrhea, pain and weight loss. Patients with Crohn's and ulcerative colitis seldom succeed in managing their illness in the longer term without resorting to medication. About 1.4 million Americans have IBD, with 74,000 new cases being diagnosed every year. The cost of treating IBD in Los Angeles alone is estimated between USD 1.1 billion and USD 1.4 billion annually (EUR 1 billion to 1,25 billion). Surgery and clinical care account for more than 60 % of that cost.[16] The cost of care depends mainly on the seriousness of the condition and the extent to which patients abide by their prescribed treatment. The annual cost of IBD-related paid labor in Los Angeles is approximately USD 560 million (EUR 450 million).

UCLA's VQ program is an innovative, promising and inspiring IBD initiative. It brings together all the various stakeholders, from patients to healthcare professionals and from researchers to payers. The aim of the program is to improve the results of treatment while reducing costs at the same time. The program provides a quantifiable, flexible and scalable work environment that makes use of sound decision support systems, national and international guidelines and e-health functionality to achieve continuous improvement. The VQ program goes a step further than a standard chronic disorder management program. The value quotient (VQ) is a measure that combines

---

[11] Video provided by the UCLA Center for Inflammatory Bowel Diseases, www.uclaibd.com, accessed on October 2013 via http://www.youtube.com/watch?v=da7dRLSQPEI.

[12] Epping-Jordan et al. (2004), p. 299.

[13] Smith et al. (2012), p. 1637.

[14] Epping-Jordan et al. (2004), p. 304.

[15] David Geffen School of Medicine at UCLA (2012), p. 2.

[16] Ananthakrishnan et al. (2011), pp. 267–276.

disease control, quality of life and work productivity. The program infrastructure consists of four parts that are mutually reinforcing and drive continuous improvement: care, research, education and support. The Tight Control system of coordinated care helps patients and their healthcare team actively manage the illness. It also encompasses interaction with specialists in the quest to optimize treatment. Research unites specialists in different fields to investigate new forms of IBD treatment, with the results being adapted for incorporation into healthcare programs. Education is included in the program in order to share know-how with patients, nurses and doctors so that they are better informed about IBD and the VQ program. Support consists of illness-specific data warehouses, e-learning modules for patients, nurses and doctors, biobanks and a platform for systems biology.

7.1.1 The Cornerstone: "Measure and Motivate, Learn and Live"

The VQ program offers an integrated healthcare system of consistent measurement, reliable performance, and continuous improvement following every care encounter. In short, it is an all-encompassing system with self-learning capacity. A program participant said the following: "Every time I visited, I was excited and eager to tell you how I was feeling, whether that was fine or less than 100%, because I knew that the information I gave you would be entered into the 'formula' and that you'd learn something that would benefit me. I also liked receiving weekly e-mails and forms asking me about my progress."[17]

Case coauthor Daniel Hommes has headed UCLA's new Center for IBD for the past years. He set up the VQ program with a multidisciplinary team as an evolving research solution, with new lessons being learned every day. Following the example of Accountable Care Organizations (ACOs), the team aims to create a group of healthcare practitioners that join together to deliver coordinated, first-class care to a specific population of patients. Their collective goal is to ensure that chronic illnesses are treated correctly at the right time, without unnecessary services or duplication—in other words, without wasting money. That is why, for example, healthcare practitioners involved in clinical decision-making are obliged to coordinate with one another according to evidence-based best practice protocols.[18]

The VQ program aims to improve patients' care experience, motivate them to stick to their medication and treatment regime, and permanently reduce the number of hospitalizations and costs in the long term. The program thereby works on the triple aim to improve patient experience and population health, and reduce healthcare costs, starting with the patient. IBD is an ideal springboard to new approaches,

---

[17] Patient statement in UCLA Center for Inflammatory Bowel Diseases™ (2012), p. 42.
[18] Hommes (2013), p. 1.

to improving coordination and the results of treatment for chronic diseases. "This aims to make IBD care proactive rather than reactive, and to give every patient personalized care."[19] One of the goals of UCLA's Center for IBD is to develop a flexible and scalable model for managing chronic diseases. That model should be easy to disseminate and adapt within the clinical spectrum of the UCLA Health System, the University of California and then beyond. UCLA Health set up the Care Redesign Project for that very reason. Thirty-one diseases are being modeled according to the principles of value-based care and insurance. The purpose is to build knowledge on a continuous basis, to learn, and to improve and optimize the healthcare system at the same time.[20]

As defined by the Center for IBD, a patient's Value Quotient® is expressed by three measures of his or her everyday existence:[21,22]

- 60 % disease control: physical health, disease activity, complications, medication side effects and hospitalizations;
- 20 % quality of life: mental health, well-being, and the patient's ability to enjoy social situations;
- 20 % work and/or school productivity: the ability to do daily tasks.[23]

The measures above make up the numerator of the value quotient. The denominator consists of the costs associated with delivering the health benefits of the numerator. The VQ program captures the value of the healthcare services delivered to individual patients over time and correlates this with its associated costs (both direct and indirect). All the various parts are analyzed each year to see whether the numerator (health benefits) can be increased or whether the denominator (costs) can be decreased, so that the net VQ improves. The higher "triple" aim of the Center for IBD is to add tangible value to the lives of individual patients and to improve health considerably while lowering the cost.

---

[19] David Geffen School of Medicine at UCLA (2012), p. 2.

[20] Hommes (2013), p. 3.

[21] UCLA Health System Center for Inflammatory Bowel Diseases, www.uclaibd.com, accessed on October 2013 via: http://www.uclaibd.com/care-programs.php.

[22] Inversed disease activity scores—Harvey-Bradshaw Index (Lancet 1980;8:514); Quality of life score with IBDQ—Partial Mayo Score (IBD 2008); IBDQ (Am J Gastroenterology 1996); Work productivity—WPAI (Clin Ther. 2008). In: UCLA Center for Inflammatory Bowel Diseases™ (2012), p. 55.

[23] http://www.uclaibd.com/team.php.

Brand essence: Add measurable value to the life of chronic patients starting with IBD

Higher goal
- Striving to add value to individual patients' disease management, quality of life and productivity while reducing costs

Brand roots
- Initiated with involvement and cooperation of all participants in IBD healthcare: patients, care providers, healthcare professionals, scientists, payers, industry and government
- Integration of scientific and technological insights to improve everyday patient care in IBD

Audacious goal
- Transform the management of chronic diseases (starting with IBD) into measurable, accountable and prevention-oriented "right care @ right time" – with more self-control for patients, improved health at lower costs'

Brand promise
- Together we will help you to increase control over your disease and improve your quality of life and productivity

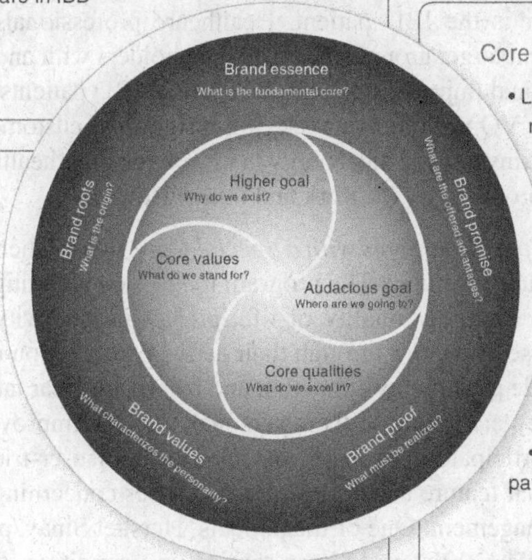

Core qualities
- Learn: gather and translate empirical data and scientific progress to improve care in treatments
- Improve: increase value for individual patients measuring disease control, quality of life and work productivity
- Interact: direct interaction between patients and healthcare professionals (Tight Control programs/home care)
- Empower: educate and support patients to enable self-management

Core and brand values
- Be excellent: offer a self-improving infrastructure for chronic disease management
- Be cooperative: offer integrated care to and with chronic patients
- Be accountable: service patients with measurable, transparent, relevant and educational programs

Brand proof
- Proven track record and experience with measurable improvements in disease control and cost reduction for IBD patients
- Increased feeling of control is shown in perceived quality of life by patients
- Growing community of IBD patients and care providers
- Method applied to other chronic conditions

Figure 7.1.1 Vision and Positioning of Value Quotient UCLA

7.1.2   The Business Model: "Redefine Value for Responsible Care"

Steps have been taken to extend the VQ program to other chronic disorders, but in the business model as it is described below, the focus is on IBD.

Market Segments: Quantifying and Qualifying the Management of Chronic Disorders   The VQ program has the advantage of being part of UCLA, which has a renowned healthcare institute uniting patients, professionals and researchers in a robust network. In turn, the pioneering work being carried out in the VQ program is enhancing UCLA's reputation as an innovative healthcare center. The program makes it possible to coordinate the interests of patients, professionals, researchers and other stakeholders (e.g., insurers, employers, and government), which all benefit from better disease management, including self-management. Its competitors consist of academic and specialist centers that also deliver integrated care to IBD patients. Other competitors are general healthcare practitioners that do not offer integrated care systems (as yet) and/or that do not specialize in IBD. Finally, there are naturally other online and offline initiatives for IBD healthcare practitioners and patients. The VQ program's direct customer is the IBD patient. Healthcare professionals and researchers are another important target group, as well as stakeholders with an interest in lowering the cost of care and improving the productivity of IBD patients such as insurers and employers. The VQ program's underlying insight into customers is that patients want to, can and do invest time and energy in improving their health, the quality of their lives and their productivity (at work and otherwise).

Value for the Customer: Participating Patients with a Special Care Team   The value for the customer has been explicitly defined. The program focuses on attaining better management of the disease, a better quality of life, greater productivity and lower costs. Patients gain a sense of control through their active participation in the program, something that is made possible by education and by setting clear targets. Despite their chronic IBD, they can increase their personal VQ and improve the quality of their lives. They participate in the program by means of user-friendly e-health homecare platforms that feature accredited questionnaires concerning disease management and self-management. One of the patients, Hershel Sinay, puts it this way: "The iPad is the perfect assistant to keep tabs on my condition, and it enables me to take part in monitoring my progress. It is interactive, and questions can be asked and responded to in quick order. It is empowering in that I have input to my medical team and can see my progress online."[24]

The utilization of e-health services allows for continuous capture of patient data, resulting in more valuable information. That information is relevant in that it supports decisions concerning direct intervention when needed. Close monitoring of this kind eliminates the need for unnecessary hospital visits and reduces the number of consultations with other doctors, tests and procedures. In addition, it makes it possible to trace "latent" disease activity (when the disorder is active but does not present any symptoms yet) and respond immediately to alarming symptoms. Patients are more likely to stick to their treatment, feel less stress, and are less likely to be depressed. If

---

[24] Patient statement www.uclaibd.com, accessed on 24 October 2013 via http://www.uclaibd.com/hershel-sinay-patient-story.php.

a patient's VQ declines owing to abnormal input or symptoms, the clinical team is alerted and the collected data provides a basis for further action. Examples include e-consulting by specialist nurses. That in turn may result in the care plan being adapted, for example a change in medication. Patients can also communicate with their own doctor and the specialist nurses in order to discuss or evaluate options. This form of home care has been shown to boost the value of patient care. If a patient's condition worsens, the treatment scenarios can be easily altered where necessary, ensuring more personalized treatment. Patients who so require can be assigned a personal care manager (a specialist IBD nurse) who offers 24/7 support. In terms of emotional support, the Tight Control program gives patients a sense of security.

The program's costs are covered largely by the insurance. Patients who adhere to 80 % of the VQ program, participate in the education segment, stick to their treatment, show up for hospital consultations and submit to laboratory tests may even qualify for a discount on the costs of the care plan. Patients take the lead in managing and inputting their own data. After an introduction, they begin entering the required datasets (clinical and laboratory results) on their tablets and/or smartphones. The data is automatically monitored based on home care indices associated with the relevant disease activity. If the disease is active, the patient is asked to enter certain values every 2 weeks for a 6-week period (the length of time for disease management/remission); if the disease is less active, the patient is asked to enter those values every 2 months. The data is shared with the network of healthcare practitioners and researchers, improving both knowledge and efficiency.

Delivery: Supporting Patients in Value Creation The VQ program is considered one of UCLA's most innovative programs. It is communicated by means of newsletters, on the web and in social media. Word-of-mouth promotion plays an important role, as does the sharing of personal experiences online and in conversations. Collective contracts are concluded for IBD patients with financing bodies such as insurers and employers. Individual patients are referred to the program by care professionals in the network, patient organizations and other patients.

A cornerstone of the strategy for raising the VQ of patients is their active participation through online education. In addition to the e-health monitoring strategy, the VQ program includes support programs that are based in part on patient needs and that add value to contacts with customers:

- My Academy: an online course that educates patients about their disease and possible treatments;
- My Work: a virtual job coach that analyses the extent to which a patient can work or go to school given his/her state of (IBD) health;
- My Coach: an integrated, holistic care program that helps patients cope emotionally with various psychological problems common among IBD sufferers, for example depression and stress.

The My Academy e-learning program empowers patients by educating them on the disease, treatments, lifestyle, home care and individual care pathways. The e-learning approach is also being used to keep IBD healthcare professionals and healthcare practitioners up to date on the latest IBD knowledge.[25]

---

[25] David Geffen School of Medicine at UCLA (2012), p. 3.

Operation: Strict Monitoring and Care, Research, Education and Support Components Care is provided according to Tight Control care scenarios or coordinated care pathways. The aim is to give patients more effective help so that they can move into a category with less serious medical symptoms, contributing to the best-case and most cost-effective VQs for individual patients. The team of healthcare practitioners work with the patient on customizing the scenarios to his or her individual needs and proven treatment protocols. The scenarios consist of standardized schedules of e-visits, laboratory work and hospital consultations, all meant to achieve the best possible quality of care at the lowest possible cost.

Higher VQ scores also result in cost-effective and valuable treatments. One positive side effect is that the data used to quantify value-based care is transparent and comprehensible for everyone. This data supports healthcare practitioners and external payers in their efforts to manage costs and improve the quality and effectiveness of IBD-related care.

At the moment, the complete care cycle is defined on an annual basis. This means that at the end of each year, the IBD team analyses the VQ of each individual patient and the associated costs over the previous twelve months. The analysis results in a list of factors that have either a positive or a negative influence on the individual VQ scores. That knowledge drives personalized improvement strategies. The treatment priority is early intervention and moving patients from a serious to an average or mild phase of IBD, and on prevention so that patients remain symptom-free for as long as possible.

Doctors are able to take on many more patients this way; one specialist IBD nurse monitors and instructs 160 patients, and one doctor instructs an average of three nurses. The total number of patients in the doctor's care is therefore about 480.

The IBD care system consists of four mutually reinforcing components:

- *Healthcare*: The VQ program creates value for individual patients because it improves the patient's health outcomes by actively managing diseases through the Tight Control programs. If a patient does not respond to treatments as anticipated, the IBD specialists can discuss alternatives, for example the patient's participation in clinical trials for experimental medicines or stem-cell therapy.
- *Research*: The Center brings together information from different fields, for example neuroscience, immunology and endocrinology, and about different conditions, for example inflammation and obesity, and develops new IBD treatment methods. Patients who do not respond to the various treatment pathways can participate in clinical trials, giving them access to new medication technologies that are awaiting FDA approval.
- *Education*: The education program trains nurses in IBD so that patients have access to more care professionals who are familiar with Crohn's disease and ulcerative colitis.
- *Support*: Biomaterial is collected from patients and stored in dedicated biobanks. This is then analyzed by the systems biology platform. The results are adapted to the Tight Control scenarios and help improve the VQ and lower costs. Quality assurance guarantees that these scenarios are updated continuously.

The key supplier of the VQ program is the patient. It is the patient who creates value along with the participating healthcare practitioners in the network. Other important partners are research institutes and the pharmaceutical industry, which is willing to invest in the VQ initiative in exchange for data and information, as is the case in the PatientsLikeMe community.

Value for customers

Result *What do I get?*
- More control of the disease, better quality of life

+

Process *How do I get it?*
- Through home care, cooperation between and with care providers and e-Health support

+

Emotion *What do I feel?*
- Feeling of security and of control since you have an active role

---

Price *What are the costs?*
- Costs of treatment for patients included in healthcare plan with potential rebate

+

Effort *What do I have to do for it?*
- Investment in time, data entry and disease management

+

Risk *How uncertain is it?*
- Information & measurements can be trusted based on scientific approach

Market segments

Position
- An innovative way for chronic disease management with UCLA: increase patient's value while driving down costs

Competition
- Academic and specialized IBD centers that offer integrated care
- Care providers that do not (yet) offer an integrated care approach for IBD (and are trusted by their patients)
- Other online and offline initiatives for IBD care providers and patients

Target group
- IBD patients via existing and potential care providers in the Value Quotient network
- Care professionals and researchers in IBD and for other chronic medical conditions
- Customer groups and representatives such as insurance companies, employers, industry and government

Customer insights
- IBD patients want to be in control of their disease and increase their quality of life
- Self-management with dedicated team improves state of condition

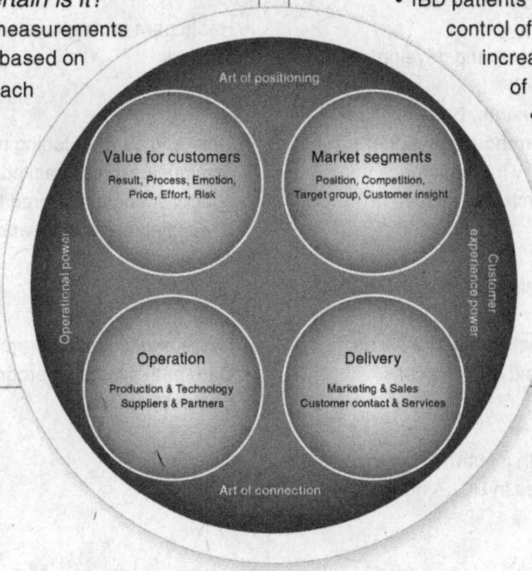

Figure 7.1.2 Value for customers and Market segments of Value Quotient UCLA

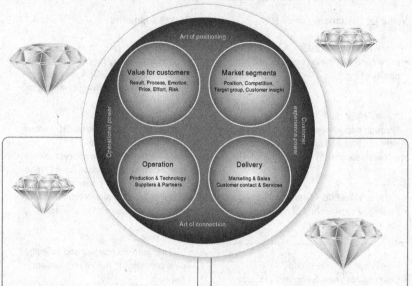

Operation

Production
- Tight control scenarios for care are extracted and constantly updated from national/international guidelines

Technology
- Care supported by information technology
- Research to reinforce and develop expertise
- E-learning components, Biobank infrastructure, data warehouse and platform for systems biology for continuous innovation in research and education

Suppliers
- Patients are suppliers in their own care process
- Health professionals are suppliers as part of the care-and-cure process

Partners
- Pharma and health insurance companies
- Research institutes in UCLA network and beyond

Delivery

Marketing
- Branded as part of UCLA's innovative programs and communication supported by PR in newspapers, media, internet and social media

Sales
- Healthcare professionals within UCLA network

Customer contact
- Care and cure, including homecare communication, is backed up by tight control scenarios offered to patients depending on severity and state of condition

Services
- Nurse educational programs
- Care path execution program
- Second Opinions

Figure 7.1.3 Operation and Delivery of Value Quotient UCLA

7.1.3 The Result: "A Value Program with Essential Outcomes"

UCLA's VQ program has been operational for the first years now. Not only is its approach interesting, but the results for patients have so far been very promising and the program itself has proven to be highly cost-effective.

In 2012 more than seven hundred IBD patients had signed on since the start of the program; 60 % of these were known to UCLA, and 40 % were new. The VQ measurement correlates closely with disease control. At 98 %, the patient satisfaction rate is high.[26] Better informed, educated and trained patients are less stressed, have more control over their illness and do not require as many tests and procedures. This form of involvement supports and stimulates patients in self-management, and they are more likely to stick to their treatment. In other words, better information equals better results.[27] The program appears to be successful at moving patients into a category of less serious, less expensive illness, with symptoms successfully being reduced in 83 % of the cases, whereby the patient moves into the maintenance scenario.[28] To put it simply: patients have fewer episodes of illness. Patient participation in e-health and self-management with home care and solid decision support for healthcare practitioners results in fewer hospital visits and less medication.

The cost of healthcare appears to be declining, which is a valuable outcome for all the stakeholders and society as a whole. Decision support tools mean that healthcare practitioners can offer integrated care more often. The necessary support is available immediately, indicating that patients make notably less use of the healthcare system. A doctor who compared preprogram and postprogram statistics found that his patients made 67 % fewer hospital visits, reduced their use of steroids by 87 %, halved their hospital admissions, had 36 % fewer endoscopic procedures and 17 % fewer radiology tests.[29]

The Tight Control scenarios are a harmonizing factor for the care offered by all the participating care practitioners. Other treatments from individual doctors are permitted. The effect becomes apparent in the rise or decline of the patient's VQ. If it does not prove to be effective, they are automatically discouraged from continuing in the next care cycle. This creates a learning and self-improvement system. More than 80 % of the preventive care consists of monitoring individual patients. Instead of doctors, coordinating nurses at the Center for IBD often carry out this task. Each nurse acts as the care manager for approximately 160 patients. One doctor instructs

---

[26] UCLA Center for Inflammatory Bowel Diseases™ (2012), p. 61.

[27] www.archimedesmodel.com.

[28] UCLA Center for Inflammatory Bowel Diseases™ (2012), p. 53.

[29] Idem, p. 63.

an average of three nurses, and is therefore medically responsible for 480 patients. Patients enter some of their own data, superfluous data is no longer collected, data traffic is entirely digital, and data capture and analysis are computerized.

The results are very promising. When patients are healthier, they become more productive and the cost of care declines. Extra savings are achieved by making patients responsible for more of the administrative and self-management activities. Growth can thus be attained on the basis of a self-financing business model. This approach makes outcome-based finance possible, eliminating the need for approvals, claims and reimbursements per treatment. Each year, a "value payment" is awarded based on a report stating the seriousness of the disease (mild, average, and serious). The payment covers all scenario activities. At the end of the year, the return on investment is distributed among the participants (including lower premiums for patients or a discount for those whose participation in home care and e-learning exceeds 80 %).

The VQ program offers UCLA opportunities to generate extra income and that is starting to work. The success of such innovative programs may enhance UCLÁ's reputation among current and potential students, healthcare practitioners, researchers and charitable sponsors and add luster to its brand image. The program and the user-friendly e-health services are such that they can be extended and their approach differentiated to suit other chronic diseases. UCLA has explored this possibility for 31 other disorders and a lot of new disease areas have been added. In addition, UCLA has spun out a company, DEAR Health, which is rolls out these programs across California with partners such as insurance companies.

The VQ program offers the employees involved a new and exciting platform for working closely with patients and colleagues who specialize in similar or other fields. Their employment at an institution that leads the way in its field gives them a fertile basis and information for research and publications. At the same time, it also offers healthcare practitioners and researchers a way to make a meaningful contribution to the well-being of patients and society.

The VQ program contributes directly to society because it not only improves patients' quality of life but also reduces the cost of healthcare and increases the participants' productivity. It creates an effective way in practice working on the triple aim of society to improve patient experience, improve population health and reduce healthcare costs at the same time.

The program has been further extended to function as a disease management solution for medical disorders such as pain, diabetes, asthma and COPD, cardiovascular disorders, rheumatoid arthritis, gout, psoriasis, cancer, depression, and multiple sclerosis. The program is offered to new partners and will involve other medical conditions. Additional e-health management solutions are also implemented, for example information on health, nutrition, weight management, fitness, behavioral therapy, meditation, acupuncture and job coaching.

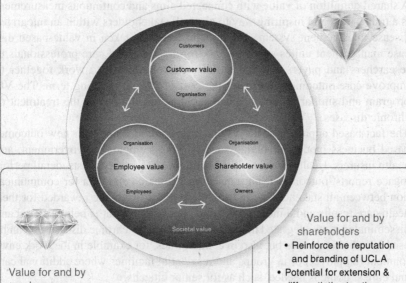

Value by customers

- The VQ program is a growing community with more than 1000 IBD patients (98% satisfaction rate)
- Increased loyalty toward medical treatments.
- Reduced health system utilization: 67% fewer clinic visits, 50% less hospitalization
- Better alignment with payers based on proven contribution to life and disease control

Value for and by employees

- A growing number of health professionals work directly in the VQ program
- Multidisciplinary teams and networks of care providers
- Support in professional development, education and fellowships including the accreditation of UCLA
- Doctors: Work on innovative treatments of chronic disease management
- Nurses: more responsibilities and support in delivering integrated care

Value for and by shareholders

- Reinforce the reputation and branding of UCLA
- Potential for extension & differentiation to other medical conditions
- Growing revenues of Value Quotient program for UCLA (40% new patients)
- More productive workforce: coordinated care paths, more patients per doctor through delegated care provided by nurses

Value for and by society

- Deliver higher quality of care, measure value added to life while reducing costs
- Scalable health solutions: the VQ program for other chronic medical conditions
- Breakthrough in care delivery and in innovative treatment of IBD
- Increased participation and self-support of (IBD) patients in society

Figure 7.1.4   Value for and by stakeholders of Value Quotient UCLA

7.1.4   Brilliant Lessons to be Learned from UCLA's VQ Program

The VQ program began only recently, but its approach and results are very promising and the field of application has already extended from IBD to numerous chronical diseases. What can we learn from this brilliant new approach?

- A shared definition of value with connected aims and continuous measurement is a transparent and inspiring way to align all stakeholders within an integrated disease management system. The holistic approach taken in value-based disease management unites stakeholders, from patients and care professionals to researchers and payers. All stakeholders make an effort to work together to improve care outcomes and lower the cost of care in the long term. The VQ program and similar approaches can serve as inspiration for the treatment of chronic diseases.
- The fact-based approach of the VQ program provides input for new outcome-based business models involving such payers as employers, government, and health insurers. Healthcare practitioners offer lower medical costs, detail performance reports, outcomes from translational research and data for communication between all stakeholders. In turn, these practitioners are rewarded for their healthcare results and a more productive population. What is being offered and disseminated is an integrated model of cost control for chronic diseases. It can be used in individual cases but also in communities, for example in the work environment (employer) or in groups and residential facilities where additional care and cure at home is needed, such as for senior citizens.
- The VQ inspires e-health innovations for patients with chronic diseases. Disease management methods such as these are becoming more mobile thanks to the growing popularity of health and lifestyle apps for smartphones, tablets, wearable technology and medical and health devices. E-Health is making healthcare more accessible to the masses. Patients now have more preventive healthcare tools at their disposal including mass-technology which is widely spread. E-Health also offers integrated platforms for managing the generated data, and new insights about illness, health, care resources and continuously improving care systems.[30] Applications such as the VQ program are beneficial for patients and healthcare practitioners, allowing them to make better use of their time and take better clinical decisions. They also offer researchers a valuable resource for investigating the effectiveness of self-management and treatments. The results include better clinical interventions and outcomes, creating value for the patient and other stakeholders.

---

[30] Hommes (2013), p. 3.

7.2 ParkinsonNet

Cooperating on patient-centered care for Parkinson's disease

Rosanne Preyde, Kerwin Hartman & Jennifer op't Hoog @: Jennifer.op.t.hoog@achmea.nl, Phone: 0031 651226420

Prelude *Teus van der Kolk (53)*[31] *feels embarrassed. When his two children ask him to play outside, he doesn't really want to go. He has been suffering from Parkinson's for the past seven years, and it has taken its toll. His muscles are rigid and painful, and he is often so tired that he has to lie down during the day. He has a typical Parkinson's gait: small steps, with arms hanging lifeless at his side. He does try to take short walks, but his leg then drags.*

But one day he decides he is fed up with being a boring father. His children are playing ball. Teus goes outside and sprints towards them. He feels a searing pain in his calves, but thinks "Hey, I can still run!" Now, three years later, he would rather run than walk. In fact, he would rather run than stand still. When at rest, his arms, legs and head sometimes twitch uncontrollably. When he runs, he regains control over his body, and he can even move his arms naturally back and forth.

Parkinson's patients have a tendency to become inactive, but more movement can actually be beneficial for them. Teus did not need research to discover this. He enumerates the positive effects. "For starters, I'm enjoying my life again—just the fact that there's something that I can do!"

What is Parkinson's disease?[32]

Parkinson's disease, also known as primary Parkinsonism, is a generative disorder of the central nervous system in which nerve cells slowly die off. It is named after an English doctor, James Parkinson (1755–1824). In atypical Parkinsonism, patients respond less clearly to medication or do not respond at all, resulting in a reduced life expectancy. It is difficult to distinguish between primary and atypical Parkinsonism and the symptoms are very similar. Many patients develop Parkinson's in middle age and have a normal life expectancy. It is an emotionally distressing and also very expensive disease.

People with Parkinson's disease have trouble with normal everyday activities such as walking, getting dressed, speaking, and/or eating. The disease takes many different

---

[31] Spijkerman (2013).

[32] http://nl.wikipedia.org/wiki/Ziekte_van_Parkinson.

forms, and there are 19 different disciplines involved in caring for Parkinson's patients, for example neurologists, physiotherapists, occupational therapists, speech therapists, and nurses. Such combined care makes it vital to work with expert, patient-centered healthcare practitioners who deliver integrated care services.

Introduction In the Netherlands, 50,000 people have Parkinson's disease or a form of atypical Parkinsonism. The number of Parkinson's patients will double by 2020 to approximately 100000. How can we give these patients the best possible care while relieving the social welfare system at the same time? At Radboud University Medical Centre in Nijmegen, neurology professor Bas Bloem, and researcher Marten Munneke came up with a solution that can justifiably be labeled brilliant: ParkinsonNet.

ParkinsonNet is a Dutch network of healthcare practitioners who specialize in treating and monitoring patients with Parkinson's and atypical Parkinsonism. Founded in 2004, it currently has more than 2700 specialized healthcare practitioners as members. The aim of ParkinsonNet is to ensure top-quality treatments by maintaining commonly defined criteria for selecting healthcare practitioners. It links healthcare practitioners and fosters specialization, interaction and knowledge-sharing. Each region is encouraged to organize disciplinary and multidisciplinary meetings at which members get to know one another personally, share their knowledge about the disease and discuss cases. In addition, ParkinsonNet offers training and refresher training, develops national guidelines for treatments, and links healthcare practitioners and patients online. It also makes the quality of treatments in each region transparent in its ParkinsonAtlas.

The online Parkinson's Care Search Engine allows patients to find the right expert closest to them. Thanks to ParkinsonNet, healthcare practitioners can treat many more Parkinson's patients than they otherwise would, allowing them to gain more experience. Ultimately, this improves the quality of treatments. Whereas before a primary healthcare practitioner, for example a physiotherapist, might treat only three Parkinson's patients a year, ParkinsonNet's method of concentration has increased that number to about ten patients per physiotherapist per year. The network also encourages neurologists to refer patients to healthcare practitioners in the regional network. The practitioners also cooperate more closely. By linking the professionals and improving patient-centered care, the network ensures more efficient personalized care. It also makes treatment more affordable. By now more than 20,000 Parkinson's patients (40 % of the total number in the Netherlands) are members of the network. The approach has received international praise and recognition, and is currently spreading to other countries such as Germany and the USA.

ParkinsonNet is notable for its enterprising approach and creativity. The quality of care has improved and treatment is more efficient. For example, there are fewer complications such as broken bones, and costs in the Netherlands have been reduced by no less than USD 86 million (EUR 77,5 million) per annum.[33] What is the underlying concept, how are the 18 permanent staff members organized, how does the network create lasting value for all the stakeholders, and why is it so successful? Let us share the remarkable and inspiring answers to these questions.

---

[33] Advertorial ParkinsonNet (2013).

7.2.1 The Cornerstone: Putting the Parkinson's Patient in Control

As a network organization of more than 2700 healthcare practitioners, ParkinsonNet is basically meant to facilitate the cooperation of Parkinson's practitioners to jointly support patients in disease self-management. When patients have more say in their own treatment and when they work with their healthcare practitioners, their health improves. Such improvement is individually defined; for some patients, it means sleeping better, for others a reduction in tremors, and for still others resolving conflicts with their partner. Patients who have more control over the care process are not only more satisfied, but also require less care, thereby reducing the cost to society.

Self-management is a much-discussed subject at the moment—but what precisely is it? The Dutch Parkinson's Association defines it as finding and monitoring the balance between how patients arrange their lives and what the disease demands of them. In other words, patients need to know what their illness entails, what consequences their decisions will have, and where they can get the right care. Specialized healthcare practitioners play a major role in this.

The aim of ParkinsonNet is to provide all patients with primary Parkinson's or atypical Parkinsonism with the best possible care. It was not set up to meet a market demand but to actually change the way care is organized based on a particular strategic approach, and to serve as a source of new markets and demands. ParkinsonNet believes that when healthcare practitioners specialize in diagnosing and treating Parkinson's and cooperate closely with one another, the best possible care becomes feasible. The organization behind ParkinsonNet coordinates the network and facilities the participating healthcare practitioners, the ultimate aim being to offer better, less expensive healthcare.

Bas Bloem's mother had MS. She was in and out of hospital. All Bloem wanted as a child was to take care of her and make her better. It motivated him to become a neurologist, to cure brain disorders. What Bloem finds most tragic in Parkinson's patients and people with chronic diseases in general is that their world becomes much smaller. Parkinson's patients are unable to move normally, have reduced cognitive function, find it difficult to speak and are no longer taken seriously. Bloem studied neurology in the Netherlands under Professor Axel Wintzen, who constantly encouraged him to really look at patients and to think for himself. Wintzen did not give him solutions to the medical problem. This same approach has been adopted in ParkinsonNet.

It is all about seeking solutions to get the most out of patients.[34] One of Bloem's studies involved getting Parkinson's patients to take more physical exercise outdoors. Although their tremors and rigidity were not reduced, the patients themselves felt fitter than before. They enjoyed the more active lifestyle and felt they had more control over their own lives. Bloem is now encouraging patients to exercise more intensively. Perhaps that will help alleviate their symptoms.

---

[34] www.parkinsonatlas.nl.

Bloem and cofounder Munneke met about 10 years ago while attending a course. Munneke trained as a physiotherapist and human movement specialist. His PhD research concerns the effect of intensive exercise on people with severe rheumatoid arthritis. During his research, he set up a network at Leiden University Medical Centre of physiotherapists specializing in rheumatism. After they met, Bloem and Munneke worked together on an assignment during the course, a research project involving physiotherapy for Parkinson's patients. Their collaboration proved so stimulating that after the course, they applied for funding for the plan they had developed. A year later, they both transferred to Radboud University Medical Centre to work on improving Parkinson's care there. Munneke used his experience setting up the physiotherapy network when founding the first ParkinsonNet at Radboud UMC.

ParkinsonNet is a network organization whose core values are patient-centered, quality-driven and community-based. Care is patient-centered. Patients and their healthcare practitioners continuously search for ways to improve the quality of their lives, to get the best out of themselves. The underlying philosophy is that the healthcare practitioner does not take the lead. At the Parkinson Centre (ParC), patients decide what they want to tackle first, whether that's insomnia, difficulty walking or nutritional problems. The drive to attain quality is expressed in the continuous effort to provide the best possible care. ParkinsonNet is also very good at facilitating a community, getting people and parties to work together, and generating support for itself among patient associations and interest groups. Support also arises within a wider context, with government and medical insurers expressing their enthusiasm. The project has received a string of awards, for example the "Most exceptional Pearl project," awarded in 2011 by the Dutch Organization for Health Research and Development (ZonMw).

When ParkinsonNet was launched, it had the audacious goal of becoming a national network. It achieved that aim in 2011. By now, it provides national coverage consisting of 66 regions[35] that are centered around one or more neurology partnerships at regional hospitals. That does not mean that ParkinsonNet can stop moving forward—on the contrary. It has set other challenging aims, for example making the quality of Parkinson's care more transparent, building its image, and drawing society's attention to Parkinson's patients. Bloem and Munneke would like ParkinsonNet to serve as a role model so that patients can access medical care based on the Parkinson's model across international borders. The best care for all—that is their goal. They make their dreams come true. ParkinsonNet is currently also going international. In 2013, it set up the first Parkinson's network in Germany, giving German patients access to multidisciplinary care. A remarkable success in 2014 is that the approach has been adopted by another brilliant business model: Kaiser Permanente (which is described in Chap. 6). Kaiser Permanente and ParkinsonNet are jointly implementing this way of working in the USA. Besides Germany and the USA, the UK, Sweden, and Australia have also taken an interest in ParkinsonNet. The Net is therefore spreading further afield.

---

[35] ParkinsonNet and Vektis (2013).

Brand essence: To facilitate self-management under Parkinson's patients and integrated management under care providers

Higher goal
- The best possible care for people with Parkinson's or atypical Parkinsonism

Brand roots
- ParkinsonNet wants to enable patients to empower themselves and to improve the quality of Parkinson-related care by improving the expertise of and connection between care providers involved

Audacious goal
- Making care quality transparent & contract care based on impact instead of paying per treatment

Brand promise
- We will support patients in managing their disease. Our network will guide you towards the best specialists

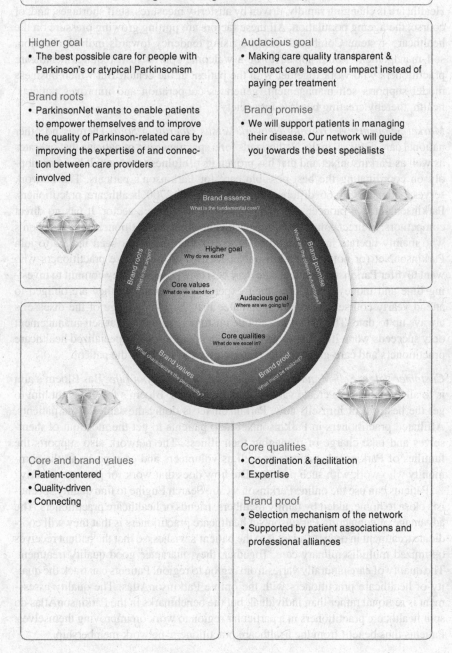

Core and brand values
- Patient-centered
- Quality-driven
- Connecting

Core qualities
- Coordination & facilitation
- Expertise

Brand proof
- Selection mechanism of the network
- Supported by patient associations and professional alliances

Figure 7.2.1 Vision and Positioning of ParkinsonNet

7.2.2   The Business Model: Self-Management in a Network

Healthcare is changing rapidly, driven by austerity measures, staff shortages, and, of course, the ageing population. All these factors are putting growing pressure on the healthcare system. Combined with the rising tendency towards individualization, self-management would appear to be a welcome approach. It requires healthcare practitioners who work together with the patient at the center. But which business model supports self-management, generates cooperation and improves patients' health, thereby creating benefits for society?

Market Segments: A Growing Network Versus Operating Solo There is no other national care network in the Netherlands for a specific group of patients that operates as well as ParkinsonNet and that has proven its usefulness as much. It has a monopoly on coordinating the best possible care for Parkinson's patients. The network serves patients,[36] in 66 different regions with its 2700 healthcare practitioners. ParkinsonNet is a pioneer and remains unique in the care sector. It has no direct competitors. Indirect competitors are existing healthcare practitioners for Parkinson's who mainly operate independently. These providers have not been invited to join ParkinsonNet (or not yet). ParkinsonNet focuses on healthcare practitioners who want to offer Parkinson's patients the very best care possible. They commit to investing time and money in building their expertise. For example, they are obliged to attend yearly courses in order to guarantee that their knowledge of the disease is always up to date. The network's unique customer insight is that self-management only succeeds when it is supported by close cooperation with specialized healthcare practitioners and care-givers in the community who focus on the patient.

Customer Value: Self-Management to Control the Quality of Life Bas Bloem's aim is to allow patients to create value in their own lives. Bloem's father taught him to get the best out of himself; now, ParkinsonNet is doing the same for its patients. Affiliated practitioners in ParkinsonNet help patients to get the most out of themselves and take charge of managing their illness. The network also supports the families of Parkinson's patients as well as volunteers and care-givers in the community who work with such patients. But how does that work for patients, exactly?

Patients can use the online Parkinson's Care Search Engine to find quality specialists close to home, aided by family members, friends or healthcare practitioners. The advantage of contacting ParkinsonNet healthcare practitioners is that they will coordinate treatment in order to adapt it to the patient's wishes, so that the patient receives optimized multidisciplinary care. Together, they guarantee good quality treatment. The quality of care naturally varies from region to region. Patients can track the quality of healthcare practitioners with the online ParkinsonAtlas. The quality assessment is regional rather than individual, but the benchmarks in the ParkinsonAtlas do spur healthcare practitioners in a particular region to work on improving themselves. Patients thus benefit from the healthcare practitioners' network membership.

---

[36] See parkinsonNet.info for more background information.

The network consists solely of healthcare practitioners, so patients are not members. There are, however, ParkinsonNet initiatives that enable patients to communicate with other patients, for example by visiting a Parkinson's Café in their own regions. Patients also feel supported by the stories in Sparks Magazine, which discuss what Parkinson's patients can do. ParkinsonNet issued the magazine in 2012 in order to highlight the positive side of the disease.

Delivery: The Best Possible Care for Parkinson's Patients ParkinsonNet's core business is to maintain and grow its network of selected healthcare practitioners. The network is made up of healthcare practitioners who specialize in different fields, i.e., neurologists, physiotherapists, occupational therapists, speech therapists, and nurses. Other services include continuous professional development of members through training, a conference to help members build a community, and furnishing information directly to patients. As a pioneer with enthusiastic and mediagenic founders and an interesting story, ParkinsonNet has attracted a lot of attention and has little need to promote itself. Because the services are available online, people can retrieve information where and when they require it. Patients communicate online or get together at meetings. Healthcare practitioners and patients also communicate by means of referrals (including a large group of neurologists) and through other members.

ParkinsonNet organizes a large number of training days every year. Examples include basic ParkinsonNet training for different specialist groups, case seminars, regional coordinators' seminars, and movement dysfunction master classes. Besides training, ParkinsonNet also organizes an annual conference for network members. The conference covers the latest research results and care trends and allows members to discuss practical network matters. In ParkinsonNet's brilliant business model, the "sales activities" differ from what is customary. Patients gain access to ParkinsonNet healthcare practitioners by using the Parkinson's Care Search Engine. The healthcare practitioners are responsible for "selling" themselves to the patient, but make grateful use of the national network's growing reputation. ParkinsonNet members keep in touch in a web-based community. Here, they can set up their own patient-specific chat groups.

Operation: Outside the Operating Theater To fulfill the promise to provide the best possible healthcare for patients, the organization behind ParkinsonNet maintains advanced supporting operations that function as the backbone for ParkinsonNet. The organization focuses on the process of mutual referrals and the treatment process. Internal processes consist of selecting, registering and certifying members and measuring the quality of care and making it transparent. It uses a communication platform to achieve this, made up of an e-mail module, a library for sharing training documents, and a survey option. A maximum of 400 healthcare practitioners are admitted to ParkinsonNet each year. The number differs per region. The organization monitors the balance between that number and the treatment volume per healthcare practitioner in each region. To qualify as a basic registered member, applicants must enroll in ParkinsonNet courses and commit to upholding its policy (e.g., transparency) and agreements. Members must reregister every 2 years.

The parkinsonatlas.nl website offers transparency concerning the quality of the participating healthcare practitioners. The ParkinsonAtlas is an interactive map on the ParkinsonNet website. It was set up in 2012 and shows treatments and variations in practices. For example, it shows that:

- 30 % of Parkinson's patients are receiving physiotherapy. However, there are twice as many referrals to physiotherapists in the Limburg region as there are in the rest of the country, indicating that patients still do not have enough control over the care process;
- the care delivered to a Parkinson's patient costs an average of EUR 7000 per year in 2009/2010, but exceeded EUR 10,000 in some regions.

ParkinsonNet intends to act as a consultant for regions and to organize review discussions with the team of healthcare practitioners in regions. By broaching the subject of regional variation, ParkinsonNet works on improving the quality of care. The regions are responsible for internal collaboration, continuous learning and self-improvement. For example, one ParkinsonNet region has set up a structure that has a coordinator for each discipline and four regional knowledge-sharing meetings a year. Internal communication is via the regional community, where members can find the agenda, minutes and online discussions. ParkinsonNet has also fuelled interest in the Parkinson Café.

Who would believe that the ParkinsonNet coordination center would have only 18 staff members, most of them working part time? In addition to the two-person management team, the coordination center consists of experts (e.g., a physiotherapist), a Research & Development team, and a back office, which takes care of membership, communication and events. The coordination center helps keep the network running smoothly. The team supports the regional networks in setting up healthcare in accordance with the latest standards. It also advises the healthcare practitioners in the network and helps them work according to the standards. A simplified version of those standards is now available for patients and caregivers in the community, so that everyone can understand them. The coordination center also works to make the quality of care more transparent online through the ParkinsonAtlas. The Atlas gives referring physicians and patients an idea of the care that they can expect and motivates healthcare practitioners to work according to the standards and to measure themselves against well-performing regions. The team contracts out activities that are outside the network's core business. ParkinsonNet for instance works with IT suppliers, training organizations, and research agencies.

The organization is in the vanguard in Parkinson's-related scientific and medical research. One of its success factors is its many and varied partners. Besides the members themselves, 20 pharmacists have also joined the network. Other partners include health insurers, which are enthusiastic about the results of offering quality healthcare which reduces healthcare costs. In 2012, that enthusiasm led to ParkinsonNet and Zorgverzekeraars Nederland (the industry association of Dutch health insurers) signing a contract in which the latter undertook to provide financial support for a 3-year period. The members of ParkinsonNet and health insurers are currently sharing the costs. The aim is to finance the network under the regular healthcare costs after 3 years. Other partners provide financial and medical support. They include associations of patients, occupational groups and funding bodies.

Value for customers

Result *What do I get?*
- Referrals to experienced care providers; the best possible care

Process *How do I get it?*
- Quick access to affiliated care providers via Parkinson Care search engine

Emotion *What do I feel?*
- Empowered, I am at the steering wheel of my treatment

Price *What are the costs?*
- The Parkinson search engine is freely accessible; treatments are lower in price due to ParkinsonNet

Effort *What do I have to do for it?*
- The online search engine is easy to find and enables me to make a choice based on quality

Risk *How uncertain is it?*
- Low risk thanks to selection and transparency of quality of care providers

Market segments

Position
- Network with 2700 specialized care providers and with monopoly to offer the best possible care for Parkinson patients. ParkinsonNet has more than 40,000 patients in the national network existing of 55 regions

Competition
- Indirect competition by care providers that are not part of the national network and who independently support people with Parkinson's treatments

Target group
- Patients with Parkinson's and atypical Parkinsonism looking for the best care. Patients open to self-management. In the Netherlands there are 50,000 patients with a type of Parkinson's; projections are that this number will double by 2020

Customer insights
- Patients with Parkinson's conditions can and will be able to deal with a higher level of self-management

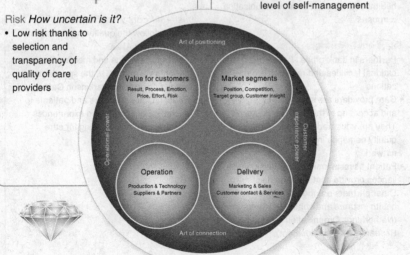

Figure 7.2.2 Value for customers and Market segments of ParkinsonNet

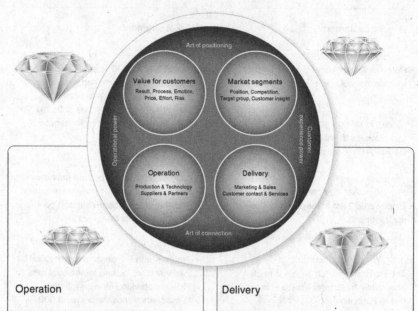

Operation

Production & Technology

- The ParkinsonNet project team has a coordinating role to support and optimize the network existing of 2700 care providers and 40,000 patients
- 1st application is the Parkinson Dossier
- 2nd application is MijnZorgnet.nl ('my-healthnet'), developed for communication purposes

Suppliers & Partners

- Partners in back-office IT systems, educational facilities and research organizations
- Care providers are selected per region and according to the quality system. They are educated and have to meet quality demands in order to access the network
- Patient associations and professional alliances provide content-related support. Other partners are the government, health insurers and subsidy partners (Netherlands Organisation for Health Research and Development)

Delivery

Marketing & Sales

- Customer communication: via guidance, partners and the website
- Yearly Parkinson's Conference
- Parkinson Care search engine for access to professionals specialized in Parkinson treatments

Customer contact & Services

- Able to follow the quality in your region via ParkinsonAtlas
- Gaining knowledge and meeting Parkinson's patients via online TV, the specialized magazine and the Parkinson Cafés
- Enabling care providers and patients to exchange questions and experiences
- Accreditation and training for care providers

Figure 7.2.3 Operation and Delivery of ParkinsonNet

7.2.3 The Result: Self-Management Key to Alleviate Pressure on the Healthcare System

Value is being created for all the stakeholders, resulting in enthusiastic ParkinsonNet healthcare practitioners, greater patient satisfaction, less pressure on the healthcare system and lower costs. ParkinsonNet's patient satisfaction rating is impressive. The network's power is its focus on individual self-management. Patients learn that they can take control of the quality of their lives by managing their illness themselves. Bloem therefore proposes giving patients a greater say in their own treatment, regardless of the disorder involved.

ParkinsonNet's results have not gone unnoticed. It has received various prestigious awards in the Netherlands and citations and recognition on an international level.

In its current financial model, 50 % of ParkinsonNet's expenses are covered by healthcare insurers. The other 50 % is covered by member healthcare practitioners, who pay an annual fee of EUR 95 per provider as well as for training and the annual conference. This model has created a certain structure to support the growth and upkeep of the digital ParkinsonNet. At the moment, ParkinsonNet still depends on funding to support innovation. Project funding was required in the start-up phase to demonstrate the network's added value. Now that that value is clear, new project funding is being applied towards innovation and upscaling. Examples of new initiatives are:

- the launch of Spark Magazine on 11 April 2012, with a circulation of 100,000 (cost: approximately EUR 250,000). By organizing distribution through its members, ParkinsonNet has been able to circulate the magazine throughout much of the Netherlands, reaching not only patients but also their families and neighbors. The magazine offers a positive view of Parkinson's, with actor Michael J. Fox serving as a role model. The underlying theme is: "This is who I am—and look at what I *can* do"
- the production of a number of informative videos
- an initial live broadcast in 2013 on ParkinsonTV online, with experts answering patient questions during the course of a 2-h time slot
- the launch of ParkinsonNet in Germany and jointly with Kaiser Permanente in the USA.

Bas Bloem firmly believes that a reward system should be introduced in healthcare based on health outcomes. ParkinsonNet wants to play a leading role in such a system and negotiates contracts with insurers on this basis. Bloem believes that doctors should be rewarded in the same manner as the Chinese emperor's doctor: he received pay only on the days when the emperor was healthy. Bloem further thinks that patients should be much more closely involved in their treatment. "Explain the medical decisions and the costs to them. That way they can help decide and doctors will have a better idea of what's truly important to the patient. This will give healthcare practitioners the right sort of incentives. It's about healing—not about generating more income," says Bloem.[37]

In terms of the ParkinsonNet staff, we can differentiate between the 18 employees who *facilitate* the ParkinsonNet network and, naturally, the healthcare practitioners who are members of the network. The staff at the central organization feel committed to helping patients who want more control over the quality of their lives, and they see ParkinsonNet as a means of guaranteeing the quality of healthcare. The value for the patient subsequently lies in the overall network of healthcare practitioners, who work to deliver the most appropriate care to the Parkinson's patient.

A study by Munneke et al. (2009) on the value of ParkinsonNet shows that the quality of care clearly improved, with a demonstrable increase in efficiency: spending on healthcare for Parkinson's patients has been reduced by no less than EUR 73 million years in the Netherlands. Beersen et al. (2011) reconfirmed these outcomes 2 year later. The benefit to society is undisputed. As the population ages there is a growing risk that there will not be enough healthcare practitioners to go around in the near future. If patients can maintain their health by managing their illness themselves to some extent, then not only will there be health benefits for them but we can take pressure off the healthcare system at the same time.

---

[37] As stated by Bas Bloem is an interview as source for this case.

Value by customers

- Number of patients connected to ParkinsonNet: 40,000
- Patient satisfaction is impressive. By letting patients define what their quality of life is and supporting them in managing their disease, people with Parkinson's feel empowered
- Academic research has shown that the increase in quality of care is striking

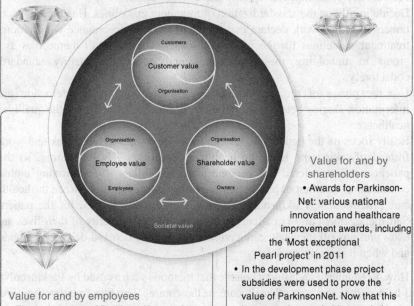

Value for and by shareholders

- Awards for ParkinsonNet: various national innovation and healthcare improvement awards, including the 'Most exceptional Pearl project' in 2011
- In the development phase project subsidies were used to prove the value of ParkinsonNet. Now that this is proven, these subsidies are being used for innovation and scaling.
- In 2014 a cooperation with Kaiser Permanente was officially announced.
- Cost reduction of EUR 73 million on a yearly base for Parkinson's care in the Netherlands

Value for and by employees

- The project team of ParkinsonNet consists of 18 motivated individuals doing their utmost to optimize the ParkinsonNet network
- Employees feel connected to the patients looking to gain greater control over the quality of their lives and work hard to continue to guarantee the best care for Parkinson's patients

Value for and by society

- ParkinsonNet patients have better control of their lives, improving the quality of life
- Academic studies show that ParkinsonNet has realized better quality of care against lower costs. These results have also been confirmed by a study commissioned by the healthcare insurers' association in the Netherlands

Figure 7.2.4   Value for and by stakeholders of ParkinsonNet

7.2.4 Brilliant Lessons to Be Learned from ParkinsonNet

What brilliant insights can we derive from the ParkinsonNet story?

- Lower costs by improving quality. By promoting the expertise of the selected healthcare practitioners through training, the annual conference and research, ParkinsonNet has improved quality and lowered costs.
- Decide jointly on the standardization of treatment guidelines. Healthcare practitioners in the network declare that they will work in accordance with national treatment guidelines for the relevant disorder. They commit themselves as a group to upholding these guidelines and adopt the quality standards collectively.
- Use the power of the network. By promoting continuous interaction and information-sharing between its members, ParkinsonNet improves the quality of healthcare.
- Really focus on the patient and let that focus steer the way you think and work. Instead of taking the lead, the healthcare practitioner is facilitating, so that patients are empowered and become more self-reliant. By improving mutual coordination, continuous interaction and information sharing between the healthcare practitioners, ParkinsonNet improves the quality of care for the patient. Self-management allows patients to take control of the quality of their lives and takes pressure off the healthcare system by providing demand-driven care where and when it is really needed.

How do Munneke and Bloem believe that methods such as used by ParkinsonNet will help reduce the cost of healthcare in the future? The two founders list three ways:

1. Replace more expensive secondary care (e.g., rehabilitation centers) with less expensive primary care, i.e., living at home independently with the assistance of caregivers in the community.
2. By concentrating diagnosis and treatment with healthcare practitioners who are especially trained in the field, there is less uncertainty and less spending on expensive diagnostic procedures.
3. Encouraging cooperation between healthcare practitioners reduces the cost of care. Such cooperation has, for example, revealed that patients do not need to embark on two simultaneous pathways, one for physiotherapy and one for speech therapy. Patients can first focus entirely on speech and later on walking, and in both cases the therapy is more effective.

7.3 Laastari Lähiklinikka

A plaster for the wound

Monique Heeren & Jennifer op't Hoog @: Jennifer.op.t.hoog@achmea.nl,
Phone: 0031 651226420

Prelude *In Finland, it's not uncommon to wait two months for an appointment with your doctor, unless your condition is life threatening.[38] What do you do if you have a painful bladder infection and you're a working mother who has to attend important meetings all day and pick up your children from childcare in the evening? You go to Laastari, where you can get immediate help, without an appointment, until 8 pm. It's very easy: you just walk into one of the clinics at a pharmacy and a nurse will see you immediately. Armed with an iPad, she will ask you a number of questions and perform an additional examination. She then sends the data to a doctor or specialist elsewhere, and the two consults by means of a video link. The doctor confirms the diagnosis and treatment and sends the nurse a prescription for you on her iPad. Fifteen minutes later, you're back on the street with the medication in hand and clear instructions and tips about your infection printed out on a sheet of paper.*

The founders of Laastari want to show that healthcare can be better: more efficient, easier to access, with more services, no waiting lists, patient-focused and cheaper. Inspired by MinuteClinics® in the USA (see the box "A brief history of retail healthcare"), they launched a similar retail concept in 2011 in Finland and Sweden.[39] But what makes Laastari special—in other words, why is it a brilliant learn-and-copy case?

Introduction What do you do if you're an enterprising individual, live in a country where access to healthcare is steadily declining, and you come across a retail healthcare concept in the USA that stands out as a brilliant business model? You set up Laastari (Finnish for "plaster"). Ville Öhman (former management consultant), Juha Lindfors (private-equity investor), Ron Liebkind (doctor specializing in neurology), and Miina Öhman (doctor and geneticist) began developing this new retail concept in Sweden and Finland in 2010.

---

[38] Wiegant (2012).

[39] Aggarwal and Chick (2013).

Brief History of Retail Healthcare Concepts[40,41]   Retail clinics had their origins in the land of unlimited opportunity—the USA. While retail clinics do not appear to be replacing traditional primary care in the neighborhood, they seem to be permanently enriching the differentiated system of healthcare.

Retail clinics have become commonplace in American towns and cities. The healthcare system in the USA is nothing like that in Scandinavia, however. It is interesting to explore whether and how a business model can be applied in an entirely different healthcare system. Laastari had to alter the model drastically for the concept to succeed in Scandinavia. For example, the US clinics work with "nurse practitioners," nurses who are capable of independently diagnosing throat, ear, and bladder infections and other non-life-threatening but frequent illnesses and who are authorized to start treatment and prescribe medication. That was impossible in the Scandinavian healthcare system, where by law such actions are the exclusive preserve of doctors. The entrepreneur-founders were forced to adapt the business model, resulting in a number of innovations. For example, they built an iPad-based IT system for triage purposes (questions designed to assess the seriousness of the patient's condition) and in order to document nurses' anamnesis, photograph the examination, and support supervision by doctors. This made it possible to share medical information online directly with a doctor located elsewhere, allowing him or her to establish a diagnosis, decide on treatment and prescribe medication. After a couple years of experience, they even skipped the nurse part. Now, it is also possible to connect directly with the doctor via an e-consult. The concept made healthcare more customer-focused, faster, and cheaper.

The medical aspect also had to be adapted to the specific region. Öhman and Lindfors had a background in economics and IT, but no knowledge of medicine. They therefore approached Liebkind, a doctor who worked in Finland in both the public and private healthcare system, to develop the medical side of the concept. He developed a triage model for a number of low-complexity disorders based on specified protocols. The team then faced the challenge of convincing regulators and government. Initially, there was resistance to the business model. Government was and still is reluctant to finance it from the public purse. Doctors were also skeptical about outsourcing medical care to non-doctors, and the interference with continuity of care even if they would only be undertaking a limited number of treatments. A further complication was Finland's strict rules about the establishment and logistics of private clinics (a room of no less than 12 m² with an examination table). Ultimately, frequent and lengthy discussion with regulators and doctors wore down their resistance. They began to understand the business model, and the barriers were dismantled, slowly but surely.

---

[40] http://en.wikipedia.org/wiki/MinuteClinic.
[41] Nale and Boston (2012).

7.3.1   The Cornerstone: Real Entrepreneurs Spy a Market

"We want to show that healthcare can change, that we can deliver the right care", according to Ron Liebkind. Laastari has its roots in the wish to improve the accessibility, service-mindedness and efficiency of healthcare. The well-organized healthcare systems of Finland and Sweden set an example for the rest of the world in the late seventies. Unfortunately, that has changed dramatically (see the boxes about healthcare in Sweden and Finland). Both countries have long waiting lists for consultations. Because their systems are largely publicly financed, the cost of care is not transparent. Inspired by the simple retail concept, Laastari's founders got to work adapting it for the healthcare system in Scandinavia. They believe that everyone's access to healthcare will improve if it is organized differently. How? By making the customer the priority when organizing treatment for common health problems. Their higher goal is to provide evidence that care can be better organized.

As described in the introduction, Laastari was founded as a partnership between international entrepreneurs and doctors. They were inspired by the MinuteClinic® retail concept in the USA and showed enormous perseverance in preparing the model for the Swedish and Finnish market. The challenge lay specifically in the legal obstacles and in the Scandinavian healthcare system. An innovative IT solution, extensive lobbying and other actions ultimately led to Laastari's launch in 2011.

The audacious goal is reasonably specific: make the treatment of common illnesses available to as many people as possible for USD 50 (EUR 45) per visit (Finland price). The brand promise that the company makes is: Laastari will provide fast, personal and economical care for common health issues. It is fast and easy because it has long opening hours. It is personal because patients see experienced nurses who listen empathetically to their complaints. And it is economical because patients pay a small, transparent fee that is always the same.

The core and brand values underlying this promise are ease, accessibility, and proximity. At Laastari, non-complex care is readily available and nearby, for example in a shopping mall or pharmacy located in busy, populated areas. Opening hours are long and the list of services is transparent. Laastari makes very clear to patients what they can expect and what price they will have to pay. The core qualities facilitating its approach are entrepreneurship, service-mindedness, and transparency. And the organization's burden of proof? It charges a fixed price for consultations (USD 50 or EUR 45 in Finland and USD 28 or EUR 25 in Sweden) and vaccinations USD 56 or EUR 50 in Finland and US 28 or EUR 25 in Sweden). It is the customer (and not the healthcare system) who pays this fee directly, and the cost price is about 30–50 % lower than in the market. The clinics are easy to reach and there are no waiting lists. Personal care is guaranteed by the experienced nurses who see the patients and check their findings with a doctor elsewhere.

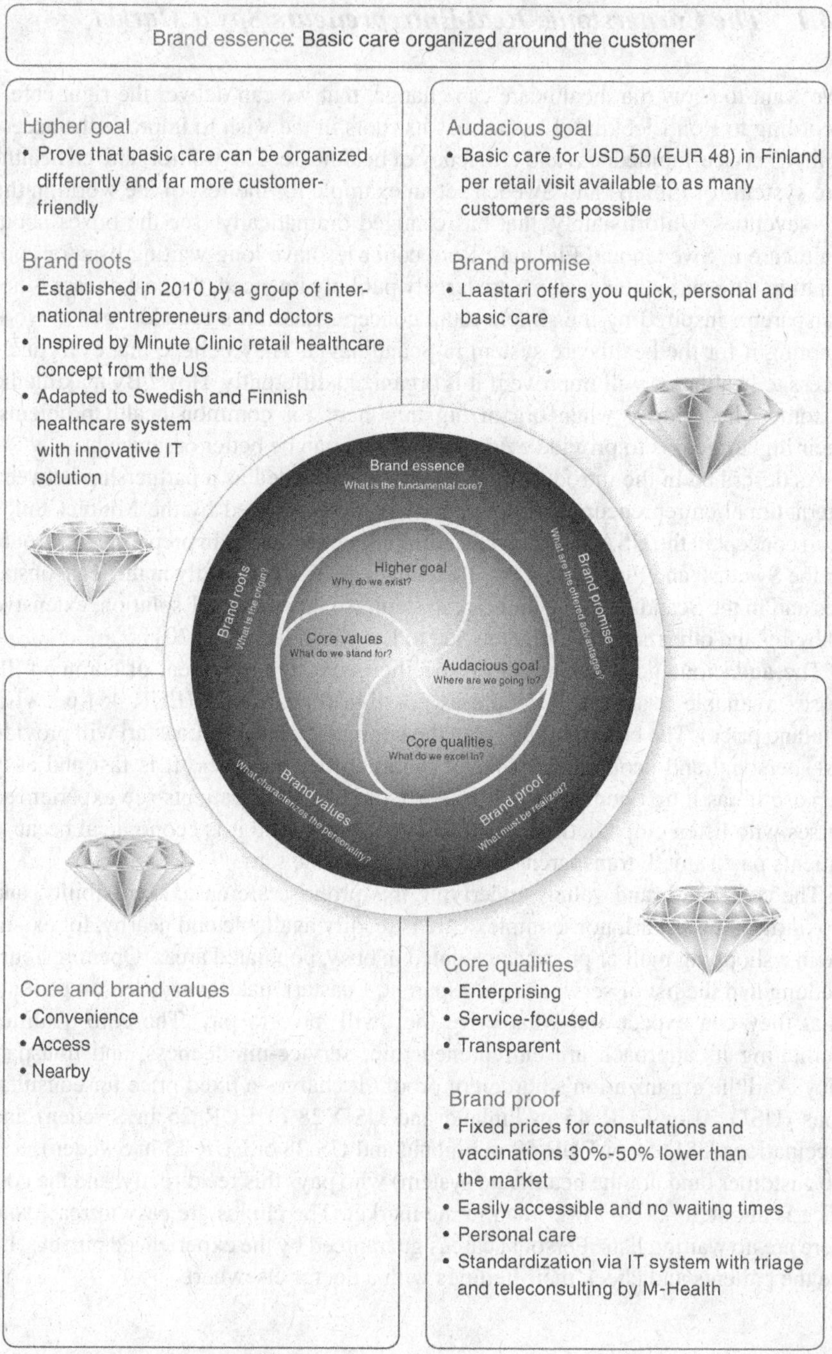
Brand essence: Basic care organized around the customer
Higher goal
• Prove that basic care can be organized differently and far more customer-friendly
Audacious goal
• Basic care for USD 50 (EUR 48) in Finland per retail visit available to as many customers as possible
Brand roots
• Established in 2010 by a group of international entrepreneurs and doctors
• Inspired by Minute Clinic retail healthcare concept from the US
• Adapted to Swedish and Finnish healthcare system with innovative IT solution
Brand promise
• Laastari offers you quick, personal and basic care
Brand essence
What is the fundamental core?
Brand promise
What are the offered advantages?
Brand roots
What is the origin?
Higher goal
Why do we exist?
Core values
What do we stand for?
Audacious goal
Where are we going to?
Core qualities
What do we excel in?
Brand values
What characterizes the personality?
Brand proof
What must be realized?
Core and brand values
• Convenience
• Access
• Nearby
Core qualities
• Enterprising
• Service-focused
• Transparent
Brand proof
• Fixed prices for consultations and vaccinations 30%-50% lower than the market
• Easily accessible and no waiting times
• Personal care
• Standardization via IT system with triage and teleconsulting by M-Health

Figure 7.3.1 Vision and Positioning of Laastari

7.3.2 The Business Model: Predictable Healthcare for a Low Fixed Price

Healthcare in Sweden Healthcare in Sweden is decentralized and operates at three levels: centrally (legislation, guidelines, and supervision of quality and accessibility), regionally (financing and organization of the curative side) and locally (approximately a 1000 healthcare centers for basic treatment and care). Ninety percent of the providers are publicly funded. The number of private healthcare practitioners has grown in recent years. Sweden gets very good marks in many areas. Everyone there has free access to healthcare (no referral necessary) and is only obliged to cover a small amount of the expense themselves (maximum of SEK 2659 (USD 311 EUR 280 a year); the rest is funded from tax revenues). The cost of care has scarcely increased in the past 10 years, while the quality has. But a shortage of healthcare practitioners and local freedom in budget spending have led to long waiting lists. Very long, in fact. For nonurgent basic care, patients may have to wait several months for an appointment. The same is true for clinical or outpatient appointments. Recently, the Swedish legislature adopted a law that is supposed to make access to a doctor possible within 7 days for primary care and 90 days for specialist care.

Healthcare in Finland Healthcare in Finland is also decentralized, with healthcare centers providing basic and preventive care. Healthcare is funded in three ways in Finland: by local government, by the private healthcare sector and by the occupational healthcare sector. Doctors are funded by local government (71 %), the private sector (16 %) and the occupational healthcare system (13 %). Hospitals are funded by the public sector (95 %); the rest is covered by the private sector. These different sources of financing mean that employees and the unemployed have nowhere near the same access to healthcare. The latter must often resort to public healthcare facilities, which have very long waiting lists. It's not uncommon to wait 2 months for an appointment with a doctor or outpatient clinic. On the other hand, eHealth (Finland is sparsely populated) and the quality of care are good compared with other countries. In terms of the cost of healthcare, Finland ranks 11th in the EU27.

Market Segments: Competing Between New and Traditional The retail care concept has spread from the USA to Canada and Australia,[42] but beyond Laastari, very few other European providers have taken it up since 2011. There are only a few countries in Europe with retail clinic. Examples are found in Ireland and the Netherlands. In Ireland,[43] a medical insurer VHI has set up a chain of walk-in SwiftCare Clinics. SwiftCare is less standardized and has less IT support than Laastari, and it therefore operates according to a somewhat different business model. In the Netherlands a small local initiative started at a big train station (CaretoGo), with big resistance from medical parties.

---

[42] http://en.wikipedia.org/wiki/Convenient_care_clinic.
[43] https://www.vhi.ie/swiftcare/index.jsp.

So Laastari's biggest competitor is not another retail chain, in fact, but the public healthcare system. Public healthcare is accessible to everyone without the need for them to pay many extra costs (patients pay a small fee between USD 17 and USD 22 (EUR 15 and EUR 20). Many people would rather not pay themselves, or do not wish to take out extra insurance. They are familiar with the public healthcare system, even if the waiting lists are very long. On top of this, one of the effects of having poor access to healthcare is that people find it perfectly normal to have to wait a long time for an appointment, and tend not to consult their doctor about minor complaints. On the one hand, this makes it all the more appealing to go to Laastari; on the other, people are having a hard time getting used to the new concept. In Sweden, Laastari now has three clinics in and around Stockholm (870,000 inhabitants).[44] In Finland, there are clinics in Helsinki (almost 500,000 inhabitants) and the towns of Lathi (95,000), Tempere (216,000), and Jyväskylä (almost 70,000).[45] People of all ages come to Laastari, but most of the customers are women aged between 30 and 45 and parents bringing in their children. The clinics are busiest at lunchtime and in the evening. The chain's insight into customers is that people want fast, straightforward help for common complaints (non-life-threatening but frequent illnesses).

Customer Value: Knowing What You Are Getting The core of the concept is that care is patient-centered, instead of being driven by organizational processes and procedures. Laastari is customer-focused, with locations and opening hours that meet patients' needs. Care is available 7 days a week, with opening hours from 10 am to 8 pm.[46] The clinics are located in shopping malls or pharmacies, making it easy for patients to get a prescription filled after their visit. The care provided is clear and patients are charged a single standard fee for ten selected complaints, ranging from the "flu" and sore throat to fungal skin infections and infected nail beds, which account for about 7 % of all the care provided by General Practitioners. Patients never find themselves paying an unexpected bill for extra tests. They know what to expect and what they are paying for. If they are referred to a specialist because the clinic cannot treat their disorder, they pay nothing. They also pay a fixed fee for vaccinations (hepatitis A and B, HPV, DTP, "flu," and tick-borne encephalitis) and for allergy tests (including dog, cat, grass and tree pollen). In Finland, about 50 % of Laastari patients pay out of pocket; the rest are reimbursed by their medical or occupational healthcare insurers. In Sweden, only one insurer reimburses patients so far, so the percentage of customers who pay themselves is higher. Patients receive personalized care from a nurse who has time for them and

---

[44] http://nl.wikipedia.org/wiki/Stockholm.
[45] http://nl.wikipedia.org/wiki/Lijst_van_grote_Finse_steden.
[46] www.laastari.com.

can consult a doctor directly. In the mainstream public healthcare system, patients often have to tell their story several times, first to a receptionist, then to the nurse and finally to the doctor. That is not necessary at a Laastari clinic. Consultation with the doctor is also very transparent. By giving them instructions and explaining the diagnoses, the clinics make everything clear and also ensure that patients take control of their own health. Recently, two extra services where introduced to the business model. Instead of going to the walk-in-clinic, people can also make an appointment directly in the agenda of the GP for an e-consult or call the phone service for a quick advise. The entrepreneurs are further improving and remodeling their business with self-service, efficiency and real contact in mind.

Delivery: Self-Service Combined with Real Contact Laastari's founders are not only innovative entrepreneurs; they are also skilled at marketing. They have attracted attention both regionally and internationally by promoting their innovative business model in the media. A case study about Laastari has been developed at INSEAD (one of the world's most prestigious business schools) and a series of YouTube videos shows patients talking about their experiences at the clinics. A low-cost approach that reaches a wide audience. The business model was introduced and promoted in Sweden and Finland through traditional, regional marketing channels (local newspapers, radio) and social media. Special care was taken to avoid the risk of medicalization (encouraging people to visit the clinic too often or too easily). For example, Laastari had considered distributing vouchers for free visits as a marketing gimmick, but eventually decided against this.

Customer contact is defined by a combination of self-service, the nurses' prominent rôle and remote supervision by the doctor. As in a shop, Laastari expects customers to help themselves more than they would in the public healthcare sector. Patients must decide in advance whether they probably have one of the 13 common illnesses, and they play an active role in treatment once the diagnosis has been established. Laastari is considering extending the self-service options even further, for example adapting the software used in the IT system so that patients can fill in their information on a mobile website before they visit. This would further improve efficiency, with appointments taking even less time and patients whom Laastari cannot treat being referred directly to other (public) healthcare institutions. The idea of shifting care to patients is in line with the trend of giving them more control over their own health and illness.

The nurses play a prominent role as the physical point of contact for patients. Personal attention, empathy and professionalism are the key drivers behind patients' loyalty and word-of-mouth advertising. Doctors take on a new role as experts working in the background and explaining things to patients if necessary.

Operation: Keeping Fixed Costs as Low as Possible Because it charges a preset low fee, it is important to Laastari to keep its operational costs low. The average Laastari clinic is as small as possible, about 10 m^2. Locations are selected because they have the right combination of accessibility, size (small) and price (inexpensive). Suitable locations are "embedded" in a shopping mall or pharmacy.

In Sweden, Laastari has begun to work with Kronans Droghandel Apotek, a pharmacy chain that agrees that cooperation will generate mutual benefits. By organizing the provision of care together, the partners can increase both Laastari's clientele and Kronans' sale of medicines.

Each clinic is open more than 70 h a week and is run by only two or three nurses who work at multiple locations. Flexibility is maximized. The nurses often work alone. The doctors work remotely and can advise on cases in Sweden and in Finland. There is no language barrier because employees speak both Swedish and Finnish, permitting highly efficient deployment. The IT system is one of the main foundations of the business model and was developed specifically for Laastari.[47] Its purpose is to support the nurses' triage system, facilitate privacy-proof telecommunications with the doctors, and offer remote prescription functionality. Laastari also wanted to maintain records on its care services so that it could report to the regulators and further provide evidence of its financial and qualitative results. Ordering a custom-made IT system made it possible to meet these specific medical and other demands. It was a one-off investment that should produce returns in the years ahead. Collaboration with partners has also led to new distribution channels. In 2012, Laastari signed a major contract with an insurance company, Pohjola. In Finland, people take out extra insurance that gives them rapid access to private healthcare. As in the public sector, insurers charge customers a fee (the deductible or excess). Because Laastari's prices are significantly lower than other healthcare institutions, the insurance may reimburse a patient's entire fee, producing a win–win–win situation for the customer (who pays nothing extra), the insurer (attractive services and lower costs), and Laastari (new patients). Negotiations with other insurers have also been successful. SMEs were willing to cooperate after seeing evidence of the model's feasibility, the rapid access to treatment and the low fixed price. Occupational healthcare occupies an important place in the basic healthcare system for employees in Sweden and Finland. A number of SMEs have made Laastari their exclusive treatment provider for certain illnesses. Their employees are guaranteed rapid access to care outside working hours, perhaps leading to lower sick leave figures at these firms.

---

[47] Lohvansuu and Laitinen (2011).

Value for customers

Result *What do I get?*
- Diagnosis & treatment of my basic symptoms

Process *How do I get it?*
- Personal care when I need it, without waiting times

Emotion *What do I feel?*
- I am relieved to receive care when I need it and feel I have been helped properly

Price *What are the costs?*
- Direct payment of USD 28 (EUR 25) in Sweden and USD 50 (EUR 45) in Finland for diagnosis and treatment

Effort *What do I have to do for it?*
- Extensive opening hours at easily accessible locations without long waiting times (Note: Public system is not easily and quickly accessible)

Risk *What are the uncertainties?*
- After the consultation I either receive help for my symptoms or am referred to a specialist

Market segments

Position
- These were the first retail clinics in Europe. Market has grown significantly in the US

Competition
- Greatest competitor of retail clinics is the public healthcare system, which is less expensive but also less accessible

Target group
- Everyone older than two with symptoms related to the 13 selected illnesses
- Largest segment up to now comprises women between 30-45 years of age and children

Customer insights
- Care is not easily accessible in Finland and Sweden; people appreciate receiving rapid assistance for simple conditions and are willing to pay a small extra fee for this service

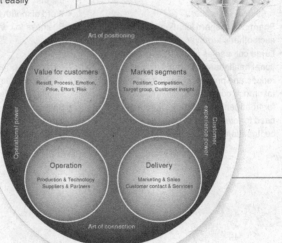

Figure 7.3.2 Value for customers and Market segments of Laastari

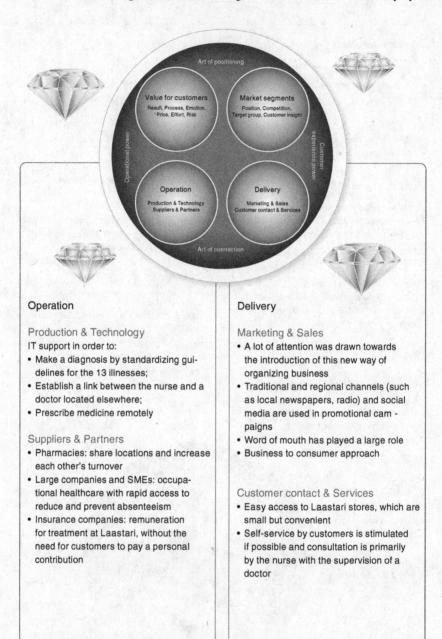

Operation

Production & Technology
IT support in order to:
- Make a diagnosis by standardizing guidelines for the 13 illnesses;
- Establish a link between the nurse and a doctor located elsewhere;
- Prescribe medicine remotely

Suppliers & Partners
- Pharmacies: share locations and increase each other's turnover
- Large companies and SMEs: occupational healthcare with rapid access to reduce and prevent absenteeism
- Insurance companies: remuneration for treatment at Laastari, without the need for customers to pay a personal contribution

Delivery

Marketing & Sales
- A lot of attention was drawn towards the introduction of this new way of organizing business
- Traditional and regional channels (such as local newspapers, radio) and social media are used in promotional campaigns
- Word of mouth has played a large role
- Business to consumer approach

Customer contact & Services
- Easy access to Laastari stores, which are small but convenient
- Self-service by customers is stimulated if possible and consultation is primarily by the nurse with the supervision of a doctor

Figure 7.3.3 Operation and Delivery of Laastari

7.3.3   The Result: Benefits for Customers and for Society

Besides repeat visits and a high level of loyalty, customers can create value in another way: by participating in a model that can lower the cost of healthcare. Comparable publicly funded care is twice as expensive on average; Laastari's own calculations show that treating the thirteen common health complaints costs an average of USD 117 (EUR 105). Primary care, which is paid for from tax revenues, can be made much cheaper. The model would therefore create many opportunities if applied in the public healthcare sector. Laastari's entrepreneurs have long been talking to regional and local government about obtaining public funding for its clinics and extending its services to monitoring chronic disorders such as diabetes and high blood·pressure. But change happens very slowly in the public healthcare system owing to resistance, complex hierarchical structures and the autonomy that individuals/doctors have. Laastari is not making as much progress in these talks as it would wish. There is also the highly relevant question of whether volumes (and thus costs) will increase in healthcare if access is improved—a question that is difficult to answer in advance. The business model for customers is simple: accessible care when the patient needs it for the fixed fee. This is in stark contrast to public healthcare, where patients have to wait about two months and still pay an excess. Laastari is also customer-focused, clear and personal. Customers have to get used to the idea that healthcare is available without delay, but once they have been treated at a clinic the advantages are clear. Their positive experience leads to loyalty and very high satisfaction scores.

96 % of Laastari's patients rate it as outstanding or good. 99 % of our customers will recommend us to their family and friends and say they would come back. Customers appreciate the accessibility and convenience most.

The business model seems simple and brilliant, but in fact it is financially very challenging. So far, four years after Laastari's launch, its entrepreneurs' biggest worry is the chain's financial situation. It has yet to reach critical mass. The start-up capital per clinic (USD 22,250 or EUR 20,000) combined with the high fixed costs (about 90 % of the total costs) mean that it takes a long time to reach the break-even point. That's why it is crucial to attract a sufficient number of patients to the clinics. Every additional patient can add value without increasing the costs. Not every clinic is financially independent yet. Convincing customers to try a totally new healthcare concept is taking more time than initially thought. In addition, local and regional governments are not easily persuaded of the brilliance of this business model. The chain's will and motivation to grow is unabated, however. It continues to be inspired by the results of the MinuteClinics, but cannot turn itself into an exact copy. There are now more than 800 clinics in 27 states in the USA. The organization handles more than 18 million patient visits a year. The concept was launched in 2000 and the chain grew rapidly in the first few years, peaking in 2005, with the number of clinics quadrupling.

Although Laastari has not grown as rapidly as expected, the entrepreneurs and partners are still convinced of its potential. That conviction has been conveyed to other partners, in part because of the results that the chain has already achieved.

Besides the original entrepreneurs and participating doctors, in 2011 Global Health Partner (GPH) became a minority shareholder.[48] GPH, an international healthcare business based in Sweden that has various independent specialist treatment centers, contributed the capital needed to achieve growth. The company is studying the possibility of expanding to other countries. The local healthcare system is crucial in this regard. What is most important is not the internal organization of the business model, but the way in which the model can be applied in the local environment. The company is considering southern and eastern Europe. The entrepreneurs want to find partners for their international venture that already have a solid network, a good reputation and loyal customers, for example pharmacy chains or chains of independent treatment centers.

The work performed by nurses has changed considerably. Instead of playing a supporting role as a link in the chain, they are now pivotal in providing care. Nurses must be able to work independently and have an enterprising attitude. The senior nurses, selected by Laastari for their ample experience (more than 8 years) and knowledge, appreciate the large measure of independence, responsibility and autonomy that they are given. They run the small clinics by themselves, and are therefore committed and loyal employees. Laastari's doctors work for the company part time. This gives them an appealing combination of predictable healthcare tasks and their work in the public system. Working for Laastari is also meaningful because it involves contributing to an innovative business model that is lowering the threshold to healthcare, improving its quality and reducing its cost.

Perhaps the business model's greatest value lies in the benefits that it offers society. While the societal context has impeded implementation, the business model also has the potential to change healthcare considerably in a number of ways. The fact that it provides better access to healthcare is hugely valuable to those who require care. It is in most western countries difficult to imagine not being able to visit your doctor when you need to. In addition, the business model has shown enormous potential when it comes to making healthcare more affordable. A few relatively simple changes (redistribution of tasks and standardization) have made it possible to halve the cost of non-complex or repeat treatment. The model helps raise patient awareness of healthcare and costs. It also encourages public healthcare practitioners to make the cost of care more transparent and to streamline their work processes. Standardization and redistribution of tasks can naturally also be applied in existing healthcare organizations.

Laastari has demonstrated that it is possible to make healthcare more affordable and accessible without compromising on quality. By adhering to standardized diagnosis and treatment procedures, it provides predictable, consistent quality in accordance with guidelines. Redistributing tasks between doctors and nurses creates more scope for giving patients personal attention, and the consultation with the doctor is extremely transparent. The patient is treated with dignity and is required to exercise a certain degree of self-management, which can lower costs in the long run.

---

[48] Global Health Partner (2011).

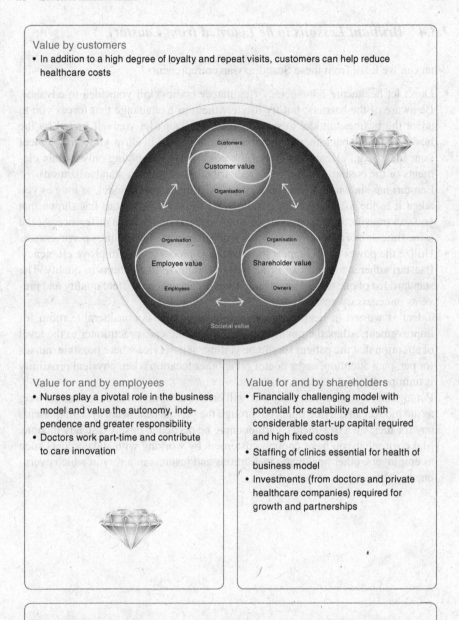

Value by customers
- In addition to a high degree of loyalty and repeat visits, customers can help reduce healthcare costs

Value for and by employees
- Nurses play a pivotal role in the business model and value the autonomy, independence and greater responsibility
- Doctors work part-time and contribute to care innovation

Value for and by shareholders
- Financially challenging model with potential for scalability and with considerable start-up capital required and high fixed costs
- Staffing of clinics essential for health of business model
- Investments (from doctors and private healthcare companies) required for growth and partnerships

Value for and by society
- Affordability of care: transparent price that is significantly lower compared to public care
- Good quality of care: standardization ensures consistent quality in accordance with guidelines and personal attention for the customer

Figure 7.3.4   Value for and by stakeholders of Laastari

7.3.4 Brilliant Lessons to be Learned from Laastari

What can we learn from these Scandinavian entrepreneurs?

- Don't let healthcare bureaucracy (regulatory bodies) kill your idea in advance. Be aware of the barriers, but try to view them as a challenge that forces you to adapt the business model to suit the situation. Don't let yourself be led by the business model, but rather by creative solutions that will allow you to implement your ideas, e.g., eHealth. Consider the possibility of applying only certain elements of the business model (e.g., redistribution of tasks or standardization).
- Laastari has shown that you *can* copy an existing business model, as long as you adapt it to the local situation, customs and legislation. Laastari has shown that you can transfer an existing idea to a new context and make a difference. At the same time, it has also shown that this is far from easy and requires perseverance.
- Utilize the power of IT support to standardize processes and improve efficiency. Laastari adheres to the Lean Principles to minimize fluctuations in quality. The standard list of questions concerning illnesses ensures consistent quality and prevents unnecessary costs.
- Talent is wasted in healthcare, an area where there is considerable room for improvement. Adapt the qualifications of the healthcare practitioner to the level of attention that the patient should be getting: self-service where possible, nurses for personal attention, and a doctor (at another location when physical proximity is unimportant) for medical treatment.
- Put together a solid partnership that will ensure a robust revenue model. As long as the model can only be financed through the private healthcare system (patients pay for their own treatment), partners may be needed to ensure a steady income. Make sure that you have enough customers by working with stakeholders such as employers, other healthcare institutions and insurers in a way in which everyone benefits.

7.4   Patrick Lund Dental Happiness

Dental Happiness

Tim Widdershoven, Rick Kasper & Jeroen Geelhoed @: J.Geelhoed@samhoud.com, Phone: 0031 622408791

Prelude *If I were to tell you about a dentist who "fired" 75% of his customers, locked the front door of his practice, took his name out of the phone book, removed any identifying signs outside his office, stopped all marketing, and accepts new customers by introduction only, you'd probably guess that he was about to retire. Or that he was crazy or about to go bankrupt ... Nothing could be further from the truth.*

This is the story of Dr. Patrick Lund. After suffering depression and even considering suicide, he decided to turn his life upside down. He made drastic changes to his dental practice. He decided to build his business in a way that would generate happiness -and he was successful. He, his employees, and his customers are all much happier now, and his practice is more efficient and profitable.[49]

Introduction   Let's go back a few steps. Dr. Patrick Lund, Paddi to his friends, is at that time a dentist like many others. He works long hours and earns a lot of money in the belief that it will bring him happiness. Despite the exotic holidays and fancy cars, however, the more Lund earns the unhappier he is. His mistake is that he thinks he can buy happiness, and he tries to do that by working harder and harder. He is spending a lot of time on paperwork, chasing down payments and dealing with unpleasant customers who ring him in the middle of the night.[50] The mood at his dental office is dreadful, his employees are often irritable and bark at him.[51] So Paddi asks himself: "If the goal of life is happiness, why am I spending the prime hours of the prime

---

[49] Basch (2002a, b, c); and the official website www.paddilund.com.
[50] Abrahams (1998a, b, c).
[51] Idem.

years of my life in a job that doesn't give me happiness?"[52] After researching the matter, he makes the shocking discovery that the suicide rate among dentists is a hundred times higher than in the average population.[53] That's when he realizes that he is not the only one with a problem. But he hasn't yet discovered a way to solve it.

He decides that he has to figure out how to derive more happiness from his work. In an attempt to create some order in his chaotic life, he begins to collect information. In his search for happiness, he resolves to ask his employees and himself two questions at the end of every working day: how happy and how stressed did they feel on that particular day? The point of these conversations is to achieve better, more efficient team communication. At first, however, they do not produce much useful information. The employees are aware that they are being probed. They consistently give high marks for happiness and low marks for stress.[54] After persisting for a few months, however, it becomes clear to Lund that his employees are exposed to a great deal of stress and that they are generally unhappy. Thanks to these conversations, he discovers the main reason: their interaction with one another and with customers. To improve matters, Lund introduces a number of workplace rules of conduct. Ultimately, this evolves into a courtesy system of eight simple rules that everyone involved in the practice has to abide by: employees, customers and Lund himself.

The rules are as follows:

1. Greet everyone by name at the start of the day: shake hands and make eye contact. The same goes when you say farewell at the end of the working day.
2. Speak politely.
3. Apologize and make restitution if you upset someone.
4. Use positive conversation, even when discussing problems (of an interpersonal nature).
5. Discuss problems openly and honestly.
6. When you talk about persons who are not present, use their names in each sentence in which you refer to them. That way you will always treat them as people.
7. If something goes wrong, blame the system, not a person.
8. Tell the truth.

But the courtesy system is only the start, the first step along a path which will lead to a happiness-centered business.

7.4.1   The Cornerstone: Dental Happiness

Making happiness a priority supports the higher goal of Dr. Lund's practice: dental happiness. This means creating a setting in which the staff, the customers and the owner are all happy. Dr. Lund achieves this by listening closely to his customers and

---

[52] Basch, *Part 1: Adventures with Dr Paddi Lund*, p. 39.
[53] Basch (2002a, b, c).
[54] Abrahams (1998a, b, c).

team. These conversations give him useful information and bring problems to the fore so that they can be tackled. Dr. Lund even changed the name of his dental office. It is now known as "Patrick Lund Dental Happiness."[55] This is the essence of Dr. Lund's brand. Dental Happiness is what it's all about.

One of Paddi's audacious goals is to build deeper, long-lasting relationships with his customers so that they will be happier with him. This also brings him more customers, allowing him to build a better business.[56] In other words, Paddi wants to show the world his philosophy, the happiness-centered business, and share it with as many people as possible. In his view, that will lead to a better world.[57] Alongside this audacious goal, he still wants to offer his customers dental happiness. Should any new problems arise, or if a new customer expresses a fear that hasn't been dealt with yet, then Dr. Lund and his team will naturally try to find a solution.

The brand promise of Dr. Lund's practice is: "dental happiness." But it goes beyond this. For example, Dr. Lund promises customers that he will never be more than a minute late for an appointment. In fact, if he is, he gives the relevant customer a bottle of champagne worth AUD 80 (around USD 65 or EUR 59). Dr. Lund's team also try to make customers feel at home. Instead of a waiting room, customers have their own personal lounge, for example, where they have time for a nice chat with the dentist or a more personal conservation with one of the assistants. The personal ties and friendships between customers and assistants are genuine, as shown by the attention lavished on customers. For example, when a customer marries, the team sends a bouquet of flowers in congratulations.[58]

The aim of dental happiness is also reflected in the core values of the practice, one of which is, of course, happiness. The highest priority is to ensure the happiness of everyone who is part of business family, i.e., Dr. Lund and his team, and the extended business family, his customers and suppliers. The other core values, courtesy and responsibility, are also crucial. The courtesy system described previously is the practical manifestation of this. The eight rules that make up this system are meant to improve relationships between the team members, the customers and Paddi himself. This allows Lund to build the positive and long-term relationships that he refers to in his audacious goal. It is of course crucial that the team and Paddi, but also customers, observe the rules. And this brings us to the third core value: responsibility. Without a sense of responsibility, people will not consistently adhere to a courtesy system such as the one described above.

---

[55] Basch, *Part 1: Adventures with Dr Paddi Lund,* p. 41.

[56] Basch transcript, p. 24.

[57] Idem.

[58] Basch transcript, p. 15/16.

To make his services truly exceptional, Lund has gone pretty far. At the time that he reinvents his practice he asks customers what their biggest anxieties are when visiting the dentist. This ultimately leads to a list of 37 "horrors" or problems. Lund then goes to work with his team to come up with solutions for each of the 37 horrors. They are quite innovative at times to arrive at an acceptable result. The most important horrors and the relevant solutions are described below:

- Customers' sense of getting value for money: Lund tackles this by improving the customer experience. Customers may have trouble judging the quality of dental work, but they can accurately assess the level of attention and service they are given. That is why Lund does everything possible to create a real service experience for customers, for example with tastefully furnished waiting rooms, personal assistants and so on. He also introduced "absolutely critical non-essentials," a topic we return to later.
- Pain: According to Dr. Lund, 95 % of dental procedures are not painful.[59] The pain that customers feel is largely a matter of perception—the expectation of pain. To solve this problem, Lund and his team introduced the pain button. Customers are told to press the button whenever they feel pain during an appointment.[60] By introducing the pain button, Lund and his team created a greater sense of trust between the dentist and his customers. Pain is no longer a reason to stay away from the dentist.
- Long waiting times: A deal is a deal. If a customer's appointment begins more than a minute late, he or she receives a bottle of champagne in compensation. Customers also bear a share of the responsibility in this regard, something that is communicated to them in the Welcome Book for new customers. A customer who is habitually late for appointments is politely asked to seek another dentist.
- Smell: Paddi found out that customers abhorred the smell of the dental office. Many of them associated it with terrible childhood visits to the dentist. The team first tried to solve this problem by putting perfume in the air-conditioning system. The effect was disappointing. They then tried grinding coffee beans. Although the association was a positive one for customers, the scent evaporated too quickly and it got too expensive. Finally, one of the team members came up with the idea of dental biscuits. Baked fresh in the office every day, these biscuits (which are good for teeth) ensure that there is always a heavenly fresh-baked smell in the office.

These examples illustrate how Paddi and his employees work. They focus on customers, really listen to them, and are able to offer an exceptional caliber of service thanks to their ingenuity and skill at structuring successful systems. This foundation has ultimately made Lund, his employees and his customers much happier, and his practice more efficient and profitable.[61]

---

[59] Basch (2002a, b, c).
[60] Idem.
[61] Idem and the official website www.paddilund.com.

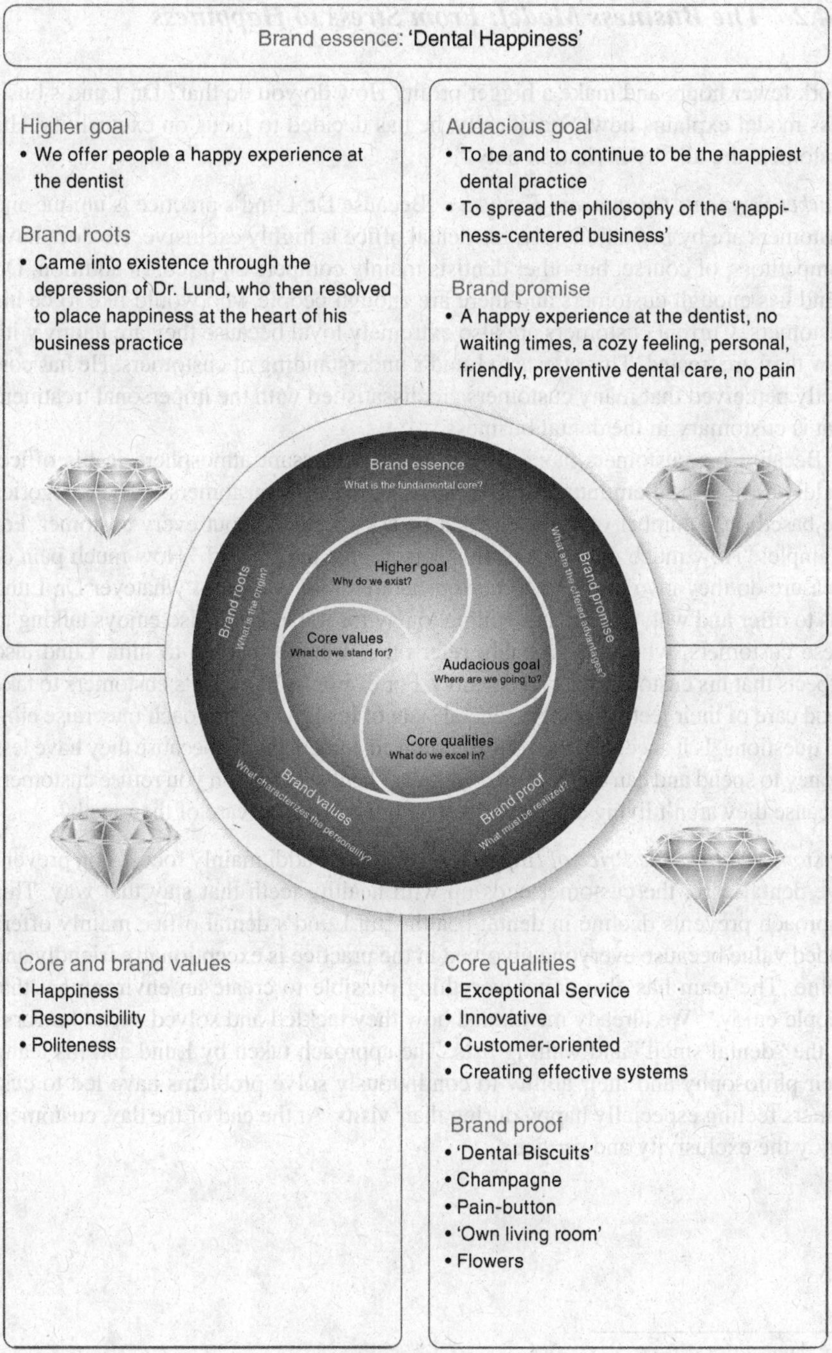

Brand essence: 'Dental Happiness'

Higher goal
- We offer people a happy experience at the dentist

Brand roots
- Came into existence through the depression of Dr. Lund, who then resolved to place happiness at the heart of his business practice

Audacious goal
- To be and to continue to be the happiest dental practice
- To spread the philosophy of the 'happiness-centered business'

Brand promise
- A happy experience at the dentist, no waiting times, a cozy feeling, personal, friendly, preventive dental care, no pain

Brand essence
What is the fundamental core?

Brand roots
What is the origin?

Higher goal
Why do we exist?

Core values
What do we stand for?

Audacious goal
Where are we going to?

Core qualities
What do we excel in?

Brand values
What characterizes the personality?

Brand proof
What must be realized?

Brand promise
What are the offered advantages?

Core and brand values
- Happiness
- Responsibility
- Politeness

Core qualities
- Exceptional Service
- Innovative
- Customer-oriented
- Creating effective systems

Brand proof
- 'Dental Biscuits'
- Champagne
- Pain-button
- 'Own living room'
- Flowers

Figure 7.4.1 Vision and Positioning of Patrick Lund

7.4.2   The Business Model: From Stress to Happiness

Work fewer hours and make a bigger profit? How do you do that? Dr. Lund's business model explains how. Specifically, he has decided to focus on exclusivity. His customers are all "by invitation only!"

Market Segment: Unique and Exclusive   Because Dr. Lund's practice is unique and customers are by invitation only, his dental office is highly exclusive. He does have competitors, of course, but other dentists mainly compete on price. In addition, Dr. Lund has enough customers and there are enough people who would like to be his customers. Current customers are also extremely loyal because they are happy with how they are treated. This attests to Lund's understanding of customers. He has correctly perceived that many customers are dissatisfied with the impersonal treatment that is customary in the dental business.

Because his customers have to help create a pleasant atmosphere in his office, Paddi has divided them into four groups: A, B, C and D customers.[62] The categories are based on a number of questions that he asks himself about every customer. For example: "How much money does this person give me?"[66] and "How much pain or pleasure do they give me?"[63] "A" customers are those who want whatever Dr. Lund has to offer and who can and are willing to pay for it. Dr. Lund also enjoys talking to these customers, who will probably refer other friendly people to him. Lund also expects that his customers act responsibly. For example, he expects customers to take good care of their teeth and their general state of health. His approach may raise ethical questions. Is it acceptable to refuse certain customers purely because they have less money to spend and can only afford a "regular" dentist? And can you refuse customers because they aren't living a healthy lifestyle or taking good care of their teeth?

Customer Value: The Price of Happiness   Because Paddi mainly focuses on preventive dental care, the customer ends up with healthy teeth that stay that way. This approach prevents decline in dental health. But Lund's dental office mainly offers added value because everyone involved in the practice is exceptionally friendly and polite. The team has also done everything possible to create an environment that people enjoy.[64] We already mentioned how they tackled and solved such "horrors" as the "dental smell" and waiting lists. The approach taken by Lund and his team, their philosophy and their ability to continuously solve problems have led to customers feeling especially happy during their visits. At the end of the day, customers enjoy the exclusivity and service.

---

[62] Basch transcript, p. 11.

[63] Idem.

[64] Idem.

The other side of the coin is that they pay somewhat more. Dr. Lund's office is located well outside Brisbane, but he charges fees comparable to dentists located in the city center. It is also quite difficult to become one of his customers. First of all, Lund himself has to decide to accept more customers. If and when he does, he gives a number of his current customers a gold card with which to invite friends to become customers. These friends naturally have to match Dr. Lund's profile of the ideal customer. Once someone has been admitted as a customer, they are expected to act responsibly and follow the rules. Finally, customers are expected to take the financial risk: they must always pay in advance or when they arrive for their appointment.

Delivery: Not Marketing, But Managing Expectations The form of delivery is special. The door to the dental office is locked and there are no signs outside indicating where it is, making it hard for new customers to find it. The map in the Welcome Book for new customers is therefore very handy because it shows precisely how to get to the office. The Welcome Book in itself is another important component in selling the "product," i.e., Lund's philosophy and vision. Ideally, current customers refer suitable new customers who fit in with the business's core value system. The Welcome Book ensures that the new customers immediately know what to expect and what is expected of them in turn.

As mentioned before, customers are generally unable to judge the quality of dental work. If it feels good, they're satisfied.[65] To offer customers quality that they can actually appreciate, the dental office has to excel in other ways. For example, the office interior is tasteful and of excellent quality, and the toilets are always spotless. The excellent service starts right at the front door, which has to be opened by the customer's personal assistant. This makes the office seem like home; after all, explains one of the assistants, when friends come over, they ring the bell and you greet them, don't you? A few seconds after customers ring the doorbell, an assistant opens the door and welcomes them by name, or however they prefer being called. What strikes visitors immediately is that there is no reception area or collective waiting room, two things that are typical of virtually every dental office. Instead, the assistants take their customers to a private lounge, where they can sip exclusive tea and coffee and have a delicious dental bun. Each customer always has the same own assistant. That makes it easy for them to build a long-term relationship, something that often happens. For example, some customers who have given birth called the office to tell her assistant, and if the assistant wasn't in she naturally rung the customer back.[66]

Because people can only become customers by invitation, Lund does not invest actively in marketing. That is an enormous cost saving. The word-of-mouth advertising is naturally excellent[67] and the virtues of the business model have been extolled in articles and business cases (such as this one). Lund does market his happiness-centered business, as he calls it, in books and lectures by himself and others.

---

[65] Idem, p. 194.

[66] Basch (2002a, b, c).

[67] Basch transcript, pp. 15–16.

Operation: Systems that Support Happiness and Personal Perception Lund has also introduced other innovations and systems to give customers the best possible experience. These are meant to remove their fears and help customers feel more relaxed and happier when visiting the dentist. The first is naturally the courtesy system, which lays down clear rules of conduct. Then there is an education system, with the Welcome Book as one of the components. This system is meant to ensure that customers also conduct themselves according to the courtesy system and know what is expected of them. The referral system described above, serves to recruit new customers. There is also a system for staff deployment, known as the care person system (assistants are referred to as "care nurses" in Lund's practice). Ensuring that customers are always welcomed by the same assistant is also more efficient, profitable and satisfactory for staff.[68] Staff and customer satisfaction are also guaranteed by a full feedback system, which evolved from the conversations that Lund has with his staff about happiness and stress. We also mentioned payment in advance. This is not the customary payment procedure in the dental business, but it is very important to Lund. The buying cycle, as Lund calls it, serves to create a payment process that is pleasant for everyone. It's pleasant for him and his staff because they have already received the money and don't have to worry about late payment or defaults. This improves the level of service, with customers feeling satisfied with the results. It also builds a relationship of trust with customers because there are no discussion and questions anymore about bills which still have to be paid. Additionally, there are the absolutely critical non-essentials.[68] They consist of a number of simple systems that provide that "wow factor" for customers. Examples include serving fresh buns and tea in fine bone china.

Dr. Lund realizes that his own happiness is tied to the happiness of his business family—his staff—and his extended business family—his customers and suppliers. His relationship with his suppliers is excellent. Fellow dentists can be regarded as Dr. Lund's business partners in this respect, because he refers customers who do not match his "A" profile to other dentists who may well be happy with that customer.

---

[68] Basch *Part 2, Adventures with Dr Paddi Lund,* p. 39.

Value for customers

Result *What do I get?*
- My teeth and mouth stay healthy and dental decay is prevented

Process *How do I get it?*
- I am treated in a friendly and polite manner and the service is excellent. There are no waiting times

Emotion *What do I feel?*
- I feel happy at the dentist. I enjoy the exclusivity

Price *What are the costs?*
- I pay more than I would for a regular dentist

Effort *What do I have to do for it?*
- First of all, I have to be invited. Moreover, I need to take good care of my teeth. I need to honor the commitments I have entered into

Risk *What are the uncertainties?*
- I pay up front, but I have faith in my dentist. The cozy feeling and the friendly people drive away my fears

Market segments

Position
- Unique in the dental market. Premium service for a premium price. Very exclusive thanks to referral system

Competition
- Competition offers lower prices. The customers that pick a different dentist for that particular reason are not suitable for Dr. Lund's practice

Target group
- Classification into customer group is based on attractiveness with focus on the so-called 'A customers' under the A, B, C and D customers
- People who want their dental health insured and take care of their teeth
- Ability and willingness to pay premium price

Customer insights
- Dr. Lund recognized that customers like to have a more personal, politer and friendlier approach.
- Fears of customers have been addressed and resolved one by one

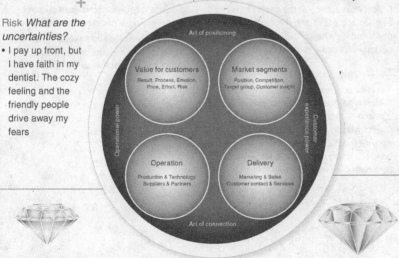

Figure 7.4.2   Value for customers and Market segments of Patrick Lund

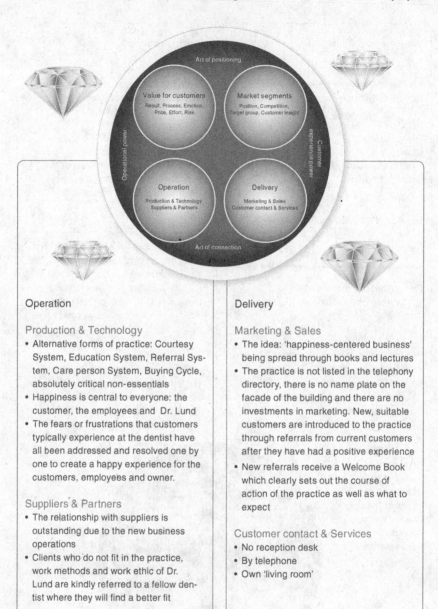

Operation

Production & Technology

- Alternative forms of practice: Courtesy System, Education System, Referral System, Care person System, Buying Cycle, absolutely critical non-essentials
- Happiness is central to everyone: the customer, the employees and Dr. Lund
- The fears or frustrations that customers typically experience at the dentist have all been addressed and resolved one by one to create a happy experience for the customers, employees and owner.

Suppliers & Partners

- The relationship with suppliers is outstanding due to the new business operations
- Clients who do not fit in the practice, work methods and work ethic of Dr. Lund are kindly referred to a fellow dentist where they will find a better fit

Delivery

Marketing & Sales

- The idea: 'happiness-centered business' being spread through books and lectures
- The practice is not listed in the telephony directory, there is no name plate on the facade of the building and there are no investments in marketing. New, suitable customers are introduced to the practice through referrals from current customers after they have had a positive experience
- New referrals receive a Welcome Book which clearly sets out the course of action of the practice as well as what to expect

Customer contact & Services

- No reception desk
- By telephone
- Own 'living room'

Figure 7.4.3 Operation and Delivery of Patrick Lund

7.4.3 The Result: A Radiant Smile for All Stakeholders

Customer value is evident in the loyalty displayed by Lund's customers. Although they pay a premium price for his service, they stay with him. For example, one customer travelled back and forth from Sydney at an expense of over AUD 800 (around USD 650 or EUR 585) to visit Lund's practice. The same person said that Lund's customers are treated with more dignity, respect and caring than at a five-star resort.[69] As stated earlier in this section, customers are generally unable to judge the quality of dental work. The willingness from Lund's customers to pay more is therefore due to the excellent caliber of service and how they are treated. The customer value is also clear when we consider what a privilege customers think it is to be allowed to refer their friends to Lund.[70] They enjoy the exclusivity of it.[71]

Because Lund's dental office is a relatively small business and no annual reports are available, we cannot provide exact financial figures. Nevertheless, there are various hints on which we can base an estimate. For example, Lund's website claims that he earns about three times more than the average dentist.[72] The average dentist in Australia earns approximately AUD 90,000 a year (USD 73,000 or EUR 66,000). Based on this information, we can estimate that Lund earns almost AUD 330,000 (USD 244,000 or EUR 220,000) in his practice.[73] That is spectacular compared to his colleagues, especially considering that he works around 22 h a week, instead of the 60 h he used to work. Other shareholder value comes in the shape of happiness, of course.

That is also the case for the employees. Indeed, employees never resign—a highly unusual situation in the dental business, where average staff turnover exceeds 60 %. When asked what she would do if her husband were transferred to another city and she had to move there with him, one of Lund's team members said that she'd divorce him first before she left the practice.[74] She was obviously joking, but she had made her point; Lund's employees are delighted with their jobs. Another employee, 19 at the time, said that she wanted to work at Lund's office for the rest of her life if possible.[75] Beyond their salaries, the employees' financial reward takes the form of a profit-sharing system, so that staff members also share in the practice's profits.[76]

---

[69] Basch (2002a, b, c).

[70] Abrahams (1998a, b, c).

[71] Basch transcript, p. 20.

[72] Basch (2002a, b, c).

[73] Average income of dentists in Australia based on information from http://www.healthcare-salaries.com/physicians/dentist-salary and http://www.payscale.com/research/AU/Job=Dentist/Salary.

[74] Basch (2002a, b, c).

[75] Idem.

[76] Idem.

Finally, Paddi Lund's story also has something valuable for society. His preventive approach to dental care boosts his customer's health. Admittedly, this is reserved for the people who have the privilege of being one of his customers. Lund also sees to it that other customers are referred to dentists who are a better fit. If someone isn't suitable for his practice, he gives them a friendly referral to a fellow dentist who is a better match. The biggest value to society, however, is Lund's philosophy—the happiness-centered business. This philosophy may also help reduce the suicide rate among dentists, which is now shockingly high. In addition, being afraid of the dentist is one reason people neglect their teeth, and better dental care is not only good for teeth but for general health. The inspiration goes beyond the dental practice. Within the world of healthcare, Lund shows how the patient journey can be improved with valuable examples on how to reduce anxiety, stimulate own responsibility in prevention, and improve the human interface in healthcare treatments. The value to society in a broader perspective also lies in Lund's audacious goal of ensuring that his philosophy will generate more prosperity and happiness in other businesses around the world. Lund certainly does not lack ambition.

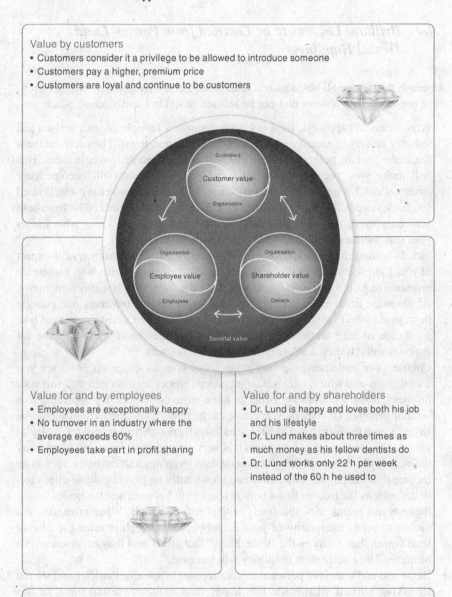

Value by customers
- Customers consider it a privilege to be allowed to introduce someone
- Customers pay a higher, premium price
- Customers are loyal and continue to be customers

Value for and by employees
- Employees are exceptionally happy
- No turnover in an industry where the average exceeds 60%
- Employees take part in profit sharing

Value for and by shareholders
- Dr. Lund is happy and loves both his job and his lifestyle
- Dr. Lund makes about three times as much money as his fellow dentists do
- Dr. Lund works only 22 h per week instead of the 60 h he used to

Value for and by society
- Preventive approach of dental care and as such fewer dental problems
- Better fit between clients and dentists, which makes both groups happier
- A brilliant business model that can be applied in other industries as well
- The suicide rate among dentists 100 times higher than the societal average. Lund's story can change this figure

Figure 7.4.4 Value for and by stakeholders of Patrick Lund

7.4.4   Brilliant Lessons to be Learned from Patrick Lund Dental Happiness

Although this is a small business in a branch not known for innovation and variety, there are many wise lessons that can be learned from Dr. Lund's dental office.

- From stress to happiness. Find out what customers hate about your service and industry and try to identify what causes them fear and stress. Then convert these fears into genuine points of service that will surprise and delight customers. This will make your organization unique and your customers will become your ambassadors. Listen and observe very carefully, make sure you have a well-oiled feedback system, and make good use of it. That feedback should come from both your employees and your customers. Do not rest until you know what makes your stakeholders happy and what makes them unhappy.
- Strictly manage mutual expectations. Make very clear what customers can expect of you. Patrick Lund does this with his courtesy system, but also with his service promises (e.g., if a customer has to wait more than a minute, he gets champagne). At the same time, make it clear what you expect from customers and educate them to play their role and be compliant as well. Dr. Lund's customers must take good care of their teeth (or be prepared to) and they must arrive on time for appointments. If they don't comply, they are sent away.
- Choose your customers. Be very clear about your target group. Who are you focusing on, and who is *not* your target group? Not every customer will suit your business, and it's not always better to have more customers. By appealing to a smaller group of customers, you create exclusivity. Your target group should be large enough to ensure your existence and small enough for exclusivity. As Paddi puts it, "Your message is best when it is very seductive to some, but turns away the majority."[77] Lund not only focuses on demographic characteristics, such as an income that can pay his bills, but more importantly on psychographic characteristics, such as the trouble that a person takes with his teeth and his health.
- Score bonus points with absolutely critical non-essentials. When customers are unable to judge the quality of your actual product (which is often the case in healthcare), then focus on the "little things" that affect how they experience your business. Their perception of quality will increase.
- Begin and end with your personal motivation and happiness. Patrick Lund started by asking himself what made him happy (and unhappy). From there, he has rebuilt his dental practice. By putting the happiness and satisfaction of the health-care practitioners first, we can create wonderful new business models! An owner and employees who are happy and enjoy their work will inspire their customers. The customers will then be more satisfied. All of this leads to greater efficiency, more profitability, and free marketing. Happiness is infectious!

---

[77] Idem.

Chapter 8
Breakthrough: Deploying Services and Instruments to Help Customers Take Control

How Can Innovation and Process Streamlining Be Used to Improve the Lives of Patients?

The focus in healthcare is on saving lives, and the adoption of new technology and services is often slow since clinical tests and medical proofs are required. Compared to service-oriented businesses with years of experience in cost-cutting, such as in recreation, telephony, logistics, and retail, the provision of healthcare is not always superior when it comes to optimum services at minimum costs. There is a lot to learn from other industries to stimulate self-service and improve accessibility.

- *Ryhov shows that patients with kidney disorder are capable to conduct their own dialysis if you are willing to open up hospitals, machines, and teaching programs to enable self management.*
- *BerylHealth has taken call-centre technology to improve non-core processes within the hospitals such as being reachable, planning appointments, and conducting market and satisfaction research at the same time.*
- *M-PESA has taken the lead in payments and financial services in Kenya by understanding and building upon the way people use their cellular phones and SIM-Cards.*
- *Jaipur Foot enabled more than one million people in India to participate fully by using mass-production technology and streamlined processes to provide durable prosthesis for less than 1 % of the costs in Western countries.*

The importance of many things in life pales in comparison to saving lives and making people healthy again. Healthcare has succeeded in making a significant contribution to increasing life expectancy and improving people's health. In comparison with the major achievements in this field, it appears that innovation in other areas such as efficiency and service-improvement has been neglected somewhat. The growth in labor productivity has not been enough to finance all new opportunities at the same percentage of GNP.[1] At the same time, there have been

---

[1] Pomp (2010).

© Springer International Publishing Switzerland 2017
J. Kemperman et al. (eds.), *Brilliant Business Models in Healthcare*,
DOI 10.1007/978-3-319-26440-0_8

developments in other sectors around the world, resulting in the improvement and renewal of customer focus and service, as well as a reduction in costs. For instance, the food sector provides more people in the world with food than ever before, all at lower costs and in the affluent countries with a fraction of the labor force compared to the past. While the food production might raise some questions in terms of sustainability and health, that is still an impressive achievement. Fixed and mobile telephony as well as IT have conquered the world and demonstrably provide exponentially more for increasingly less money. Air travel has never been so cheap. Whereas the effects on the environment can be questioned, it is nonetheless remarkable how many people can now afford to fly to all kinds of destinations around the world. The amount of technology in a small vehicle like the Tata Nano car in India is greater than what was available in an entire town a century ago. In short: progress and efficiency can go hand in hand and in disruptive innovation this is often happening. Where it concerns both the previously described mutual help in groups, prevention and self-management as well as the healthcare near and around the patient, this demands improvement close by home. This can be supported via social innovation with IT and big health data. In more specialized care, the focus is placed more on the guiding institutional principles to organize for the optimalization of processes or for the bundling of knowledge. As in many other sectors, the challenge is to make things efficient and effective, and more customer-friendly and accessible at the same time. A brief review of the developments in self-service, customer contact, mobility, and product simplification provides inspiration.

A promising manner to give people more control over their own health and care and simultaneously keep the healthcare system affordable is self-service. Aside from the mutual support, information and interventions for self-management, it also concerns practical instruments and process design to ensure people can help themselves. In other sectors, this can be seen in self-service at the petrol station, the POS terminal and online banking, for example. It also revolves around grabbing things off the shelf, taking them home and assembling furniture like at IKEA. That often demands the standardization of processes and technology, so that it can also be done by someone who has not been trained or is not being paid to do so.[2] Besides self-service in healthcare, the logistical process of planning and making appointments can also be simplified and improved. In comparison with making reservations and bookings for cinemas, airplanes and travel, making an appointment with healthcare practitioners is often a challenge. Certainly when patients have to travel a lot and/or several appointments have to be made one after the other, there is often unnecessary fuss for patients. Mobile and online applications can accelerate the logistical process for making appointments, selecting care and gaining initial information. In that regard, other sectors are revealing developments that will also have an impact on the healthcare sector. In order to obtain an impression of the possibilities, the most affluent countries would do well to consider the breakthroughs in developing

---

[2] See: Frei and Morriss (2012) and Kemperman et al. (2013).

countries which are switching straight to mobile telephony for the purpose of opening up difficult-to-reach areas.[3] In particular, the tiger economies are also an example when it comes to breakthroughs in product simplification.[4]

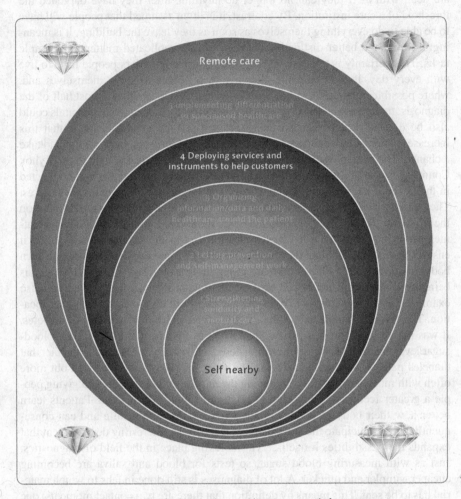

Figure 8.0.1 Breakthrough: Deploying services and instruments to help customers

---

[3] For breakthroughs in financial services and network applications of mobile telephony, see: Rhyne (2009) and Adner (2012).

[4] This is in keeping with the analyses of Christensen (1997, 2008) that demonstrate that many innovative breakthroughs do not arise from extra complexity but rather a simplification in combination with the work of Prahalad (2009) which shows that it is precisely the customer groups with the least amount of money at 'the base of the pyramid' often challenge organizations to undertake these kinds of innovations.

Brilliant Business Models Like Ryhov Self-service relates to self-management and prevention, but also simply to your own physical diagnosis, treatment and monitoring. It automatically seems to be the case in the healthcare sector that patients are dealt with as if they can no longer do anything after they have darkened the threshold of a care institution. By contrast, it is often assumed that people will have to be able to do everything themselves as soon as they leave the building. It is meaningful to make a better distinction between truly complicated matters and simple tasks. This certainly is the case if it concerns chronic disorders people have to live with every day. It is worthwhile allowing such people to serve themselves and, where possible, making them less site-dependent. It appears that almost half of the diagnosis, treatment and monitoring which is currently concucted in hospitals could also be done at home. The advantage of self-service in healthcare is that this increases patients' independence and feeling of self-worth and beckons them to take a chance. The example selected for our purposes is the dialysis clinic in the Ryhov County Hospital in Sweden. The operation of dialysis equipment is still conducted in the hospital but is already being carried out largely by the patients themselves. They simply have an access card that allows them to gain entry to the hospital on their own time. This gives the patients much more freedom to fit the dialysis treatment into their schedules, it saves working hours in the healthcare sector and it ensures that people feel like they have considerably more ownership over their own body, treatment and health. There are many more examples where self-service is being used to great effect or can be used more extensively instead. There are also examples of kidney dialysis that people can carry out at home or on another location. The classic example and future of self-service in healthcare is that of diabetes. It was not so long ago that patients had to go to the hospital to have their blood-sugar level measured and insulin administered. Now everyone is used to the fact that diabetes patients do that themselves. The work can therefore be carried out more often with much smaller doses, reducing the number of side effects and giving people a greater feeling of ownership in relation to their own disease. Patients learn better how their body responds to daily exercise, diet and insulin and can consequently better anticipate the consequences thereof. An interesting development that expands the possibilities for self-service is taking place in the field of diagnostics. Just as with measuring blood sugar, so tests for blood and saliva are becoming cheaper, simpler and quicker. A lot of diagnoses is still done in labs to which material has to be sent. This means by definition that there are two contact moments: one for measuring and one for disclosing the results. Diagnostics are now shifting more and more to hospitals, primary care and even the home of the patient. In that regard, it is increasingly about immediate results. A diagnosis can be completed in a single contact moment, which saves everyone time. A trendsetter in this regard is the i-STAT Corporation in New Jersey, USA, with its portable blood diagnostic equipment. These breakthroughs can potentially change this type of testing into self-service. It can also relate to the patient's own role in healthcare and care. As indicated by Dr. Shetty of the Narayana Hrudayalaya Cardiac Hospital in India, parents outside the healthcare sector are capable of independently caring for a baby and raising him/her to adulthood. It strikes him as strange that within the walls of a hospital the prevailing assumption is that parents cannot help. Consequently, parents are now being deployed in simple care in the hospital and are instructed via a video clip to continue the care at home.

Business Models Like BerylHealth The logistical organization and the scheduling of patients have been set up in the healthcare sector based on the scarce time of healthcare practitioners. In that regard, less attention is paid to the time and planning of patients. Even if the scheduling of healthcare practitioners must be optimized fully beforehand, it can still be done in a way that is a lot more customer-friendly. For inspiration in that regard, we will now turn our attention to BerylHealth. This is essentially a normal call center to which hospitals can outsource their scheduling services. By doing this in an excellent, intelligent and customer-friendly manner, BerylHealth makes a contribution to customer satisfaction and efficiency. In the process, the call center immediately surveys how customers selected the hospital, what they thought of it and how satisfied they were with their treatment. As a result, BerylHealth plays a key role in the marketing and improvement of the customer focus of hospitals. There are many more opportunities to improve the customer process with online and call center solutions. Simply deploying still relatively simple online reservation and booking systems is already a big improvement relative to telephones that are redirected to answering machines with information on the hours of operation. Websites and call centers could potentially also be used for simple activities in the care process. They provide options to find an alternative treatment provider that does not have a waiting list. Customer experiences can also be compiled. Based on quality data, a mentor role can be filled in the selection of and referral to secure and proper care. These are also the type of functions that are done by care intermediary services of insurers and within primary care. In that regard, call centers and online applications can act as both a link and a screen for simple diagnosis and explanation. This dovetails with the movement toward retail solutions as described in Chap. 7.3 on Laastari. Documentation can, for instance be organized in preparation for the appointment and standard communication material can be used to answer initial questions that are posed. In that regard, a short telephone consultation can serve as primary care and preselection, by which appointments are no longer necessary or can in fact be accelerated.

Business Models Like M-PESA Mobile, online technology offers new possibilities for self-management and logistics. But it does not stop just there. It can also be deployed more broadly for transactions, for identification, and as a distribution channel for all kinds of information. In the process, regions can be reached that previously were too remote for technical or practical reasons. In order to obtain a better picture of the possibilities that this offers, we would do well to look at countries where relatively large areas are difficult to reach. Then we look at breakthroughs in developing countries. This is where landlines for telephony are being skipped and mobile telephony immediately embraced, as a result of which many people and new areas are being connected to the world.[5] An example thereof from another industry is the business

---

[5] See: Rhyne (2009) and Adner (2012).

model of M-PESA, Vodafone's proposition via a joint venture in Safari.com in Kenya. M-PESA is a modern variant of the DHAN Foundation as described in Sect. 5.2. It has been expanded from mobile telephony to include micro-banking for groups with the lowest incomes. In the process, the SIM card is being used as a mobile savings account. At the time of writing, this application is being expanded even further and will soon feature a "Health Wallet" with which healthcare expenses can be paid. Furthermore, information can be disseminated via the telephone that helps patients lead healthier lives. And healthcare practitioners can, for instance, call each other for free to discuss a patient's diagnosis and exchange information. In order to obtain a better picture of the broader distribution possibilities with mobile phones, we can look, for instance, at mobile banking via G-Cash in the Philippines and at Wizzit and MTN in South Africa. In that regard, the Japanese NTT DoCoMo shows how people can identify themselves and pay by tapping their mobile wallet at the cashier's desk. The application possibilities provided by mobile telephony within healthcare are still in their infancy. It should be clear that on the one hand it helps to realize the desired breakthroughs in self-management and integrated care surrounding the patient and on the other hand to streamline the logistics and planning thereof. In that regard, many new possibilities have arisen due to the fact that the mobile phone is portable and always available. Simple points where the process can still be improved include checking in at a hospital's casualty ward, support and quicker diagnostics for victims involved in an accident, and identification and data compilation for vitality programs.

Business Models Like Jaipur Foot Innovation based on product simplification ensures more affordable products that can be operated more easily. As previously outlined with Ryhov, this offers opportunities to permit patients to do more themselves. In that regard, it also offers opportunities to make resources and instruments radically cheaper, as a result of which they become accessible to many more people and uses. The Jaipur Foot has been selected as an example of this kind of disruptive innovation. The organization behind it has equipped well over a million people in India with prostheses. Consequently, these patients have been transformed from disabled individuals into productive people in society who are able to provide for themselves once again. Whereas making and measuring a prosthesis in the West quickly amounts to some USD 8200 (EUR 7000), an artificial foot from Jaipur Foot costs a mere USD 53 or EUR 45 (i.e., less than 1 % compared to the price in Western countries). At the same time, the requirements placed on this artificial foot are greater than those in the West given the different living and working conditions in India. The need to do things not just 10 % better, but rather to find completely new solutions also creates an open mindset to search for opportunities elsewhere. We can for instance look at resources and instruments that are made based on comparable quality standards for radically lower rates. Based on the understanding that necessity is the mother of invention, this provides the inspiration to use the scarce resources in healthcare, also in the West, more economically and efficiently. As outlined for Ryhov, there is a need, for instance, for product simplification in diagnostics to bring tests closer to the patient. Examples of companies that provide diagnostic equipment for points of care are Iverness and Guidel. SonoSite is a pioneer in portable scanning devices.[6] Now GE Healthcare in India has developed a portable scanning device for less than USD 1200 (EUR 1000), which has blossomed into a company with a turnover exceeding USD 295 million (EUR 250 million) within a few years. This does not replace the more advanced MRI scans, but does allow people in primary care to make a quick diagnosis on-site.

8.1 Ryhov

Innovations in kidney dialysis by co creation

Bonny van Rest & Jennifer op't Hoog @: Jennifer.op.t.hoog@achmea.nl, Phone: 0031 651226420

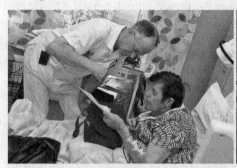 

Prelude *Patrick, aged 30, visits the hospital three times a week for kidney dialysis. Each treatment consumes between 4 and 5 h of his time. Assuming there were no queues, consultations that drag on or emergency cases, this means at least 20 h per week in the hospital. Furthermore, he is waiting for a kidney transplant, creating a cloud of uncertainty over his future. Patrick is dependent and his days are defined by his illness. This schedule makes maintaining a working and social life a major challenge. Even going on holiday creates more fuss than relaxation. Patrick lives to dialyze, but wants just the opposite: to dialyze in order to live!*

Thanks to a kidney transplant, Patrick has been able to realize this dream. Together with his wife, he has led a carefree life for the past year. He is able to play sports again, has a fulltime job and he and his spouse are expecting their second son soon. A life that only a couple of years ago seemed impossible became reality. But how much nicer could Patrick's life have been up until his kidney transplant had he done his dialysis at Ryhov?

Thanks to Ryhov, kidney patients in Sweden can once again lead much more normal lives. It is a brilliant example not only because of the enormously positive effect on the daily lives of people, but also due to the manner in which the innovation came about. This new care concept arose from an intensive and open cocreation

---

[6] See: Christensen et al. (2008) and Christensen and Dann (2001) 'SonoSite a view inside', HBR Case 9-602-056.

between a patient and a nurse and resulted directly in a significant increase in the level of quality of the life for the patient. Ryhov has shown that it has the nerve to do things differently. The idea, the vision of one patient, and the courage of an employee has turned the hospital's approach upside down. Truly listening to the patient and acting accordingly—how is that done?

Introduction The *Lanssjukhuset Ryhov* (Ryhov County Hospital), founded in 1988, is the largest of three hospitals in the Swedish region of Jönköping. Some 3300 employees are spread out over 25 specializations, including pediatrics, psychiatry and oncology. A special unit within Ryhov is the dialysis clinic, where one simple question from a patient combined with one patient-oriented, open-minded nurse resulted in a unique self-service concept in healthcare. Since 2005 the rule in the Ryhov dialysis clinic that dialysis treatment is entirely focused on the patient's personal needs, preferences and circumstances. Furthermore, patients are no longer the direct object of a treatment, but rather the person himself/herself who determines his/her own approach to treatment. In the words of initiator and patient Christian Farman: "I have a new definition of health."[7]

Of course, the innovative approach requires another setup and environment. The dialysis clinic reopened in March 2011 with 12 self-dialysis stations to allow patients to play a greater role in their treatment. Learning from one another, both fellow patients and nurses, is the focus here. But how does that work in practice? Sixty percent of the dialysis patients in Ryhov perform the dialysis treatment independently. The patients help, coach, and inspire one another and provide themselves qualitatively good care. The self-dialysis approach hinges on giving each patient his/her own key to the dialysis clinic. The result is that kidney patients are in control of their own treatment, which reduces dependence, increases flexibility and lowers healthcare costs by 33 %.[8]

8.1.1 The Cornerstone: Always the Best for You

Christian Farman had worked for many years as an engineer at SAAB Avitronics and was passionate about sports. Earlier in his life he had had a kidney transplant and received news in 2005 that he had to undergo dialysis again. His world was turned upside down. Just the thought of returning to a lifestyle where he had to go to the hospital three times per week and spend 3–5 h hooked up to dialysis equipment was oppressive to him. And that was not even taking the nausea, fatigue and thirst into account. For Christian, this was unacceptable; he wanted to regain control over his life. Something had to happen. Christian conducted research into self-dialysis and became convinced that if he could perform the treatments himself, he

---

[7] Levy (2011).

[8] Aside from the literature referred to, information on the following sites has been used: www.lj.se/ryhov, http://www.youtube.com/watch?v=VEk-A3k98QA and the presentation of Donald Berwick, Leiden 2 October 2013.

would have more control over the side effects, could reduce the risk of infections and could better schedule the dialysis treatments based on the needs of his body. With this conviction, he appealed to his nurse, Britt-Mari Banck.[9] Britt-Mari saw day in and day out the clinic's patients struggle to cope and search for opportunities to lead as normal a life as possible. But she had never received such a direct question from a patient to help him understand dialysis and to perform it independently. His nerve and resolve inspired and encouraged her to try this in practice. With the aid of the methods and techniques used to train other nurses, Britt-Mari spent several weeks giving Christian an improvised crash course in performing dialysis entirely independently. The results were better than anticipated: the side effects declined significantly and Christian began to regain control of his life.

Ryhov hopes to realize a success rate of serving 75 % of its patients via independent kidney dialysis and, consequently, making a contribution to the quality of life for kidney patients. For Ryhov this is the goal that it is actively aiming for and uses as its benchmark based on the conviction that you get what you measure. Christian never resumed his position at Saab, but now works as a nurse in the ENT unit at Ryhov, where he himself makes a contribution to a better quality of life for the hospital's patients. Patient-focused care is in his blood: "I have an advantage: I see the patient as a resource."[10] By regarding the patient as a resource, treating him/her accordingly and providing care based on that fact, Christian is giving meaning to Ryhov's mission: "Always the best for you." The origin of this innovative care concept illustrates how self-evident the importance of independence, trust and quality of life are in this hospital. In this way, the core values that underlie this approach to work in the dialysis clinic are being implemented directly. Values that are acknowledged and experienced by both employees and patients. Patients immediately experience that things are done here differently. Here they are no longer at the mercy of often unintelligible specialized care, but are the focus of the entire process. In this hospital the patients are in charge and support is given where required. Patients feel they are taken seriously and understood by the hospital's staff members, who truly listen to them. It is the evidence of successful care that is simultaneously created and experienced by both employees and patients. It is a significantly different approach to work where both employee ("I went from being the technical expert to coach") and patient ("I want to live a full life! I have more energy and feel complete") experience the benefits thereof.[11]

Britt-Mari Banck showed courage and trust to make a difference together with Christian. This is something that demands a lot of an organization, especially in terms of flexibility, empowerment and the ability to think outside the box. These core qualities have also not remained unnoticed in society. For instance, Britt-Mari Banck received the Pioneer Award[12] within the context of female leadership day in

---

[9] Bisognano (2013a, b).

[10] Idem, p. 2 annual report 2012.

[11] Idem.

[12] Aberg (2013).

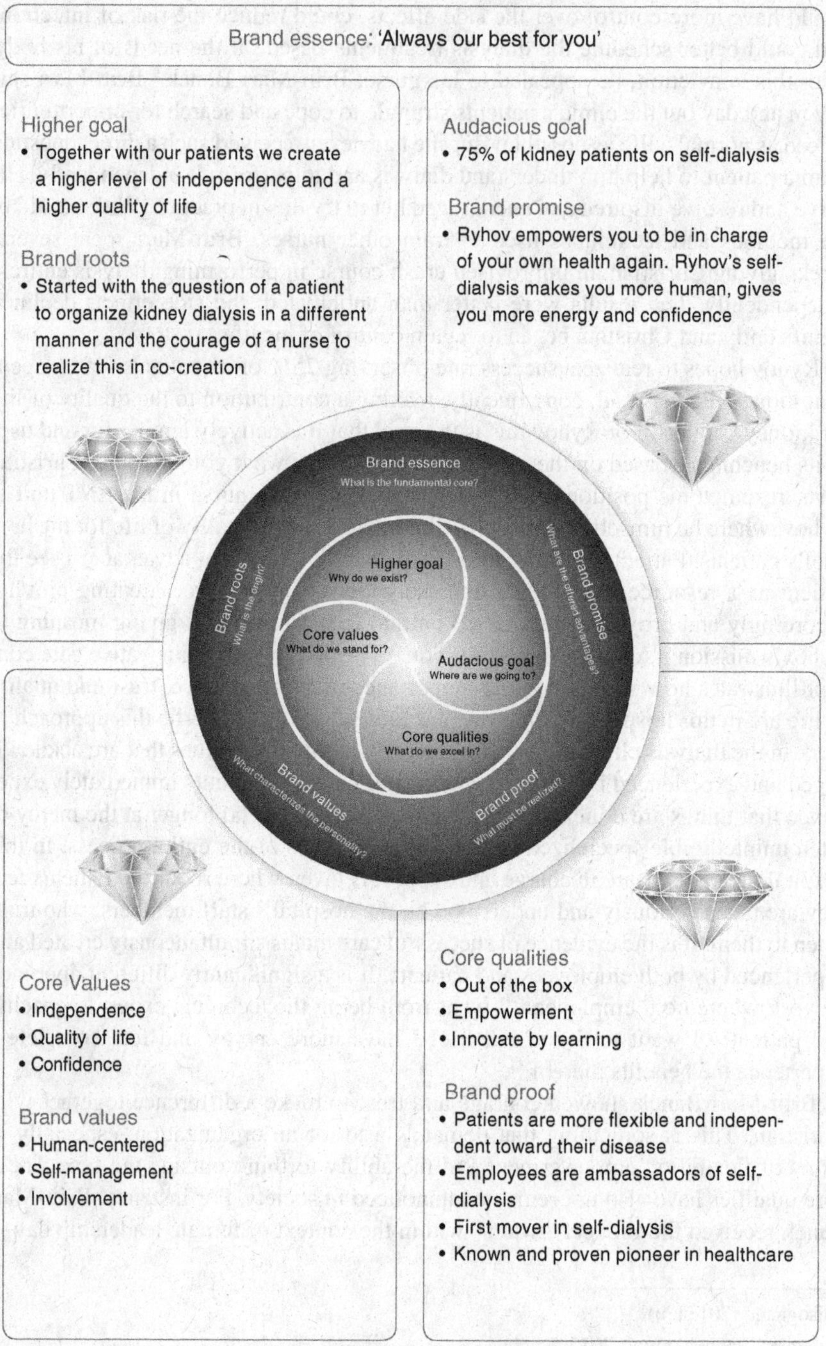

Brand essence: 'Always our best for you'

Higher goal
- Together with our patients we create a higher level of independence and a higher quality of life

Brand roots
- Started with the question of a patient to organize kidney dialysis in a different manner and the courage of a nurse to realize this in co-creation

Audacious goal
- 75% of kidney patients on self-dialysis

Brand promise
- Ryhov empowers you to be in charge of your own health again. Ryhov's self-dialysis makes you more human, gives you more energy and confidence

Brand essence
What is the fundamental core?

Brand roots
What is the origin?

Higher goal
Why do we exist?

Core values
What do we stand for?

Brand promise
What are the offered advantages?

Audacious goal
Where are we going to?

Core qualities
What do we excel in?

Brand values
What characterizes the personality?

Brand proof
What must be realized?

Core Values
- Independence
- Quality of life
- Confidence

Brand values
- Human-centered
- Self-management
- Involvement

Core qualities
- Out of the box
- Empowerment
- Innovate by learning

Brand proof
- Patients are more flexible and independent toward their disease
- Employees are ambassadors of self-dialysis
- First mover in self-dialysis
- Known and proven pioneer in healthcare

Figure 8.1.1 Vision and Positioning in kidney dialysis of Ryhov

Sweden and the dialysis clinic received an honorable mention for the 2013 Guldskalpellen for innovative care.[13] Beyond Sweden, Ryhov's dialysis clinic is regularly referred to as an inspiring example of innovation in healthcare. Maureen Bisognano, CEO of the Institute of Health Improvement (IHI), referred explicitly to the Ryhov dialysis clinic in her 2012 Annual Report.[14] In the UK, a visit to Ryhov in 2011 resulted in the launch of a program[15] based on the relevant findings. In addition, Ryhov is referred to as an inspiring example of self-care in both a research report by the American Hospital Association and presentations by Don Berwick.[16] All of this is sufficient cause to take a closer look at Ryhov's business model.

8.1.2 The Business Model: From Care Receiver to Cocreator

Market Segments: What IKEA Furniture and Self-Dialysis Have in Common IKEA has become a giant by making designer or other furniture in ready-to-assemble packages. In doing so, it literally reveals its business model by which the customer becomes part of the production process. The result is, of course, relatively good quality at a low price. It can be of little coincidence that Ryhov's self-care concept has developed in the country where IKEA originated. The patient is encouraged to play a major, active role in his/her own care process.

First of all, it is wise to place the business model within the context of the Swedish healthcare system. In Sweden, healthcare is organized per region and medical care is largely managed by the administration of the relevant province, region or municipality. They see to it that inhabitants have access to qualitatively good medical care. In addition, doctors have a private practice especially in the larger cities. Since distances in Sweden are great, inhabitants generally choose a healthcare practitioner within their own region. Following the regional setup of healthcare, the competition also remains restricted to the relevant region or province. With the exception of a maximized personal contribution of SEK 1100 (USD 136 or EUR 115), healthcare costs are financed from taxpayers' money. Taxes are relatively high, but so too is the quality of life.

Ryhov is the largest of the three hospitals in the region of Jönköping, a care area of 130,000 inhabitants (some 10,000 km^2). According to estimates, Sweden has around 7000 kidney patients, 3000 of whom are treated with dialysis. For dialysis patients, the distance to a dialysis clinic is of vital importance given that the frequency of treatments averages three to four times per week. When dialysis at home is not possible, dialysis patients often opt for the nearest hospital. There is barely any competition outside the region. Ryhov treats more than half (60 %) of the

---

[13] Toresson (2013).

[14] Idem, p. 2.

[15] NHS (2012).

[16] Chu et al. (2013).

dialysis patients in the region (104 patients). Thanks to the personalized coaching program, described later in this chapter, self-dialysis has been made suitable for every kidney patient. This is also reflected in the increase of the average age of self-dialysis patients, namely from 49.2 years of age in 2006 to 63 in 2012.

For years now, Sweden has been a textbook example due to its combination of low healthcare costs and good medical results. One of the keys to its success in healthcare has been transparency. Sweden was one of the very first countries to succeed in making differences between hospitals in terms of quality comprehensible. This insight makes it possible to shift the focus from limiting healthcare costs to increasing the "value" of the care provided (and improving the price-quality ratio of healthcare). Quality can be compared by both healthcare practitioners and patients, if best practices are recognized this makes it possible for all parties to learn more quickly from one another. The public disclosure of this quality information provides a stimulus to continue increasing the level of quality of the care provided.

The continuous quest to increase the quality of provided care, which helps reduce healthcare costs, challenges care institutions to be innovative. This dynamic is also tangible in the Ryhov County Hospital and gave it the scope to guide improvements in the quality of provided services in its own way. In Ryhov, the participants saw and recognized the differences in patients' individual needs. Patients want to play a more active role in their own care process, think along with healthcare practitioners and indicate what is important to them. This insight has reinforced the belief that the only way to truly improve the quality of provided care is by involving the patient in the process. The result of this change in approach is also that patients themselves have become the director and cocreator of the dialysis process.

Customer Value: Doing More Yourself for a Suitable Treatment and a More Flexible Life Patients play an active role in their own care process at the Ryhov dialysis clinic. This means that something else is also demanded of the patient. The path to self-dialysis requires the development of both medical and technical skills. In other words, patients must do quite a bit themselves. The experiences of patients who have undertaken the steps toward self-dialysis indicate, however, that it is worth the investment. Combining the time that patients spend in the hospital during dialysis with training and education does not demand any extra investment in time. On the contrary, the time spent on dialysis is utilized more efficiently. As a result of the tremendous involvement of nurses and other patients during the transition to self-dialysis, the trust of the patient grows. The process of regaining control of your own life and your health and, consequently, your independence, starts with the first steps toward self-dialysis. And as it turns out, self-dialysis is suitable for a broad range of kidney patients. For instance, the oldest self-dialyzing patient is 83 years old. This change is made possible by the flexibly arranged training pathway in which learning from one another plays a major role. The value for customers turns out to be rather positive. Patients make more of an effort but are properly supervised and trained in that regard, and also receive a lot for it in return. They receive care suited to their personal needs and are able to lead a more regular lifestyle with greater flexibility.

Delivery: Personalized Coaching Program The care in the Ryhov dialysis clinic is adjusted to the medical or other needs of patients, their personal circumstances and preferences. The nurses encourage a patient to take the required steps in the so-called Self-Dialysis Staircase Model, which was developed to help patients learn how to perform self-dialysis step by step. The pace and the height of the self-management level is determined by the patient. It also happens that some patients never fully convert to self-dialysis, but Ryhov considers every step in that direction as a gain for both the patient and the organization. It helps people get a grip on their own lives.

The Staircase Model is an educational model that supports patients to move from assisted dialysis to full self-dialysis step by step. This model focuses on an understanding of the disorder, medical and technical skills, the physical state and especially the individual. Learning from one another and sharing experiences are central to this model. Patients and their family members learn from the experiences of people in similar circumstances. This can be of an emotional support, but certainly also practical assistance for sharing experiences such as tips on how to adjust equipment. Those practical tips can have an enormous effect. For instance, there was one tip about increasing the frequency of dialysis from three to four times per week, simply because a patient felt better due to fewer side effects. In addition, the Pavilion, which opened in 2011, has been equipped entirely based on these learning principles. A learning café—where patients, their family members and experienced employees come together to share know-how—has been fitted out. Patients can come and go when that suits them and conditioning facilities (a home trainer and weightlifting equipment) are available for workouts both before and sometimes during dialysis.

Not only patients but also employees have a different role in this model. They are no longer the healthcare practitioners, but fulfill a coaching role. This requires the necessary retraining and refresher courses for nurses. Employees are ambassadors for the self-dialysis program, because they see what this approach means for patients. At the same time, it provides opportunities for them to flesh out their own positions. For instance, Annet, one of the nurses, has taken the initiative to help patients reintegrate into society. Annet realized that many kidney patients were confronted with unemployment and came up with a way to help them in that regard. Specifically, she coaches them in writing their CVs. Once that is done, they make contact with potential employers in the region via the employment office. Thanks to her efforts, a large number of patients have been able to find work again. The collaboration between nurses and patients provides for a continuously developing service in the Ryhov dialysis clinic. Collaborating and learning outside of Ryhov also provides direction. For instance, intense collaboration takes place with a number of external organizations, including the Swedish Kidney Foundation.

Operation: Small Changes, Major Consequences The gain in efficiency and speed are merely a result of patient-focused care; neither of them has been a goal in and of itself. The driving force behind the way of working is found in the people (the patients and nurses) and the involvement in the welfare of the patients. Still, a number of amazingly efficient ways of working can be identified. For instance, when

Value for customers

Result *What do I get?*
- In charge of my own life and health

Process *How do I get it?*
- I can do my own dialysis in my way and at the time I prefer

Emotion *What do I feel?*
- Independent

Price *What are the costs?*
- No extra costs

Effort *What do I have to do for it?*
- Within 5 weeks I am taught step by step how to organize my dialysis

Risk *What are the uncertainties?*
- I learn self-dialysis step-by-step and can count on the expertise of the nurse; this makes me feel safe

Market segments

Position
- The Ryhov hospital is situated in the region of Jonköping, and delivers care to 130,000 inhabitants
- This regional hospital was founded in 1988 with 25 departments and 3300 employees

Competition
- Ryhov differentiates itself from the two other regional hospitals by the self-dialysis it organizes

Target group
- About 7000 Swedes have a kidney disease, of whom 3000 are treated with dialysis. This concerns 104 people at Ryhof from the Jonköping region

Customer insights
- Patients want the right treatment, customized to their personal needs

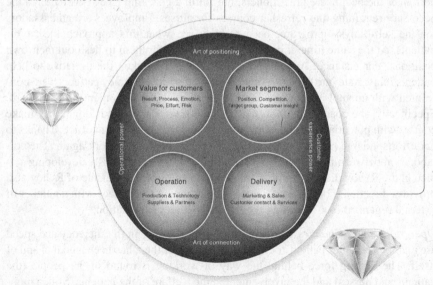

Figure 8.1.2 Value for customers and Market segments in kidney dialysis of Ryhov

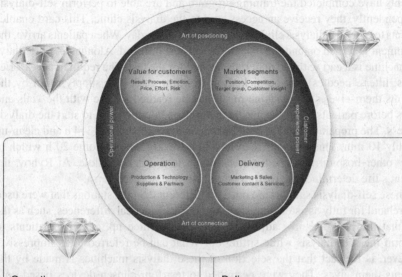

Operation

Production & Technology

- Self-dialysis takes place in cooperation with nurses and the patient and relatives
- After a 5-week training period, a patient is able to independently carry out the treatment
- 12 self-dialysis locations
- Results of the dialysis are measured and monitored in real time on "My health plan"; future appointments can also be made via this tool

Suppliers & Partners

- The largest supplier is the patient him - self via knowledge, skills and personal preferences
- Suppliers of dialysis equipment, medi - cine and other medical equipment
- Qulturum (center for innovation) and the patient association are important partners and involved in the further development of the self-management concept

Delivery

Marketing & Sales

- National and international media praise for Ryhov regarding innovative and human-centered approach to kidney patients
- Patients find and select the care easy due to the digital "My health plan", where the medical offers are easily displayed. Often,however, the choice for a hospital is made based on travel distance

Customer contact & Services

- Customer contact is personal and based on reciprocal respect and trust. Nurses act as lifestyle coaches for the patient
- A learning café, a meeting place for patients, has been set up where family and nurses can exchange knowledge

Figure 8.1.3 Operation and Delivery in kidney dialysis of Ryhov

patients have completed the training program and are able to perform self-dialysis independently, they receive an access card to the dialysis clinic. This card enables patients to enter the dialysis clinic at any moment of the day. When patients arrive, the equipment is turned on and the machine's self-test initiated. Alongside every dialysis machine is a cart with the materials needed for the test. The required accessories (vials, filters, needles) can be picked up from the self-serve supply room by the patients themselves. The machine must then be readied for use with the vials and filters before patients insert the needle themselves into their arm to start the dialysis process. The preparation phase lasts 20 min on average, dialysis 3–4 h and clean-up roughly 10 min. This amounts therefore to a weekly total of some 20 h which in every other hospital is carried out according to a strict schedule. At Ryhov, the patient's life determines the rhythm of dialysis and not vice versa.

These self-dialysis stations are not a lot different than the stations that were used beforehand for fully assisted dialysis. But there are practical differences, such as the fact that the beds are now adjustable and can be tilted up, enabling patients to perform the self-dialysis while sitting up. What can be referred to as impressive, however, is the fact that the selection of these dialysis machines is made by the patients themselves. They were permitted to test four chosen devices based on a variety of considerations, including ease of use. The equipment that came out on top is now used by all patients. Patients that perform self-dialysis completely on their own may decide at what time they come in for dialysis. Both patients and nurses can use an online platform ("My Health Plan") to monitor the results of the approach to treatment in real time. It also offers the option of schedules and reminders that can be activated. In the future, patients will also be able to use this platform to reserve dialysis equipment, review their patient records and participate in a forum to come into contact with one another.

Important in this approach is the focus on the result instead of on the treatment. Once it is clear what the most important goals are for the patient in terms of quality of life, the process can be set up with that in mind. That sounds logical, but practice often shows that the focus is on improving the process or the treatment. The approach with the focus on results also means that if it becomes evident that self-dialysis is not making a contribution to a patient's goals, he or she shall only partially continue with the steps in the model or not at all.

8.1.3   Result: Self-Care—A Value or Condition for Good Care

What is striking at Ryhov is the prevailing modesty and obviousness of it all. The way of working is internally truly a way of living, which is the cause of much surprise for outsiders. Barely any attention is paid on the organization's own website to this unique way of working. Employees talk about this brilliant concept as if it were the most natural thing in the world. And it is precisely that obviousness about it all that is one of the aspects that make this business model so successful, because it represents a natural focus placed on learning and innovation.

Firstly, the biggest result achieved in the dialysis clinic is the higher quality of life of kidney patients. Patients are in control of their own life again, with fewer side effects and greater energy levels. Ryhov is a fantastic example of cocreation in healthcare, whereby an increased level of personal responsibility is increasing the quality of services. And this result is shared with more than half of dialysis patients. Currently 60 % of patients have switched to self-dialysis; the goal is 75 %.

The value creation extends further than just value for patients and their families. The unit's more than 20 nurses have seen their job description change—one they themselves contributed to—from healthcare practitioner and technical expert to partner and coach. It is a role from which, according to employees, they derive greater satisfaction, as the impact on the patient is greater. It is a role that also goes hand in hand with more trust and variation to be able to meet the preferences and desires of the individual patient. It is also a transformation on which employees, who have already spent years in the profession, have courageously and willingly worked while it also meant that less nurses would be needed to do the job. The dialysis clinic has become a social community where doctors, employees and patients are on equal footing, as a result of which they work better together and from which they derive much more pleasure. Ideas for improvements or the resolution of individual problems are discussed in multidisciplinary teams and turned into a success on the basis of shared responsibilities.

Some may question whether the healthcare system will incur unnecessary additional costs when this freedom is introduced and the patient is put in control. Others may express their concern that renewal, innovation and experimentation will ultimately drive up overall costs. Nonetheless, the opposite turns out to be the case. Since 2011, the number of self-dialysis patients has increased to 60 %, but total costs have declined by 33 %. The biggest savings are found in the increased level of quality: fewer complications, fewer side effects and fewer infections. When compared with dialysis in other Swedish hospitals, Ryhov is no less than 50 % cheaper.

In other words, customer value, employee value and financial value have found their equilibrium at Ryhov. In the capacity of healthcare practitioner, Ryhov also plays an important role in society. The dialysis clinic contributes to a healthier society at the lowest possible price. Societal value is defined as a decline in unemployment thanks to self-dialysis. Generally speaking, the unemployment figure amongst the kidney patient population is higher than the national average, primarily due to the fact that dialysis takes so much time. Thanks to the way in which Ryhov, together with its patients, performs dialysis, patients become more flexible and their labor participation rate significantly higher then is usual for dialysis patients. In addition, the dialysis clinic, in its role of trendsetter in the field of self-care, has created an inspiring example. It is evidence that investing in self-care or patient empowerment truly is worthwhile. And this will hopefully leave a lasting legacy.

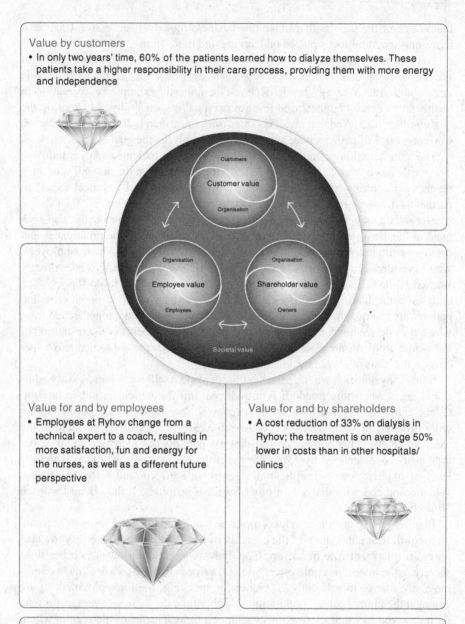

Value by customers
- In only two years' time, 60% of the patients learned how to dialyze themselves. These patients take a higher responsibility in their care process, providing them with more energy and independence

Value for and by employees
- Employees at Ryhov change from a technical expert to a coach, resulting in more satisfaction, fun and energy for the nurses, as well as a different future perspective

Value for and by shareholders
- A cost reduction of 33% on dialysis in Ryhov; the treatment is on average 50% lower in costs than in other hospitals/clinics

Value for and by society
- Self-dialysis leads to better medical results, enabling patients to participate more actively in society
- Ryhov inspires healthcare professionals and shows the importance of humancentered care

Figure 8.1.4 Value for and by stakeholders in kidney dialysis of Ryhov

8.1.4 The Brilliant Lessons of Ryhov

The quality of provided care, while maintaining or reducing costs, is an issue that is high on political agendas around the world. The approach to work at Ryhov shows that it is possible to increase the level of quality and reduce costs at the same time. The most important lessons in this regard are listed below:

- Put the focus on the patient and then review what this requires in terms of processes and the division of roles. Thinking should be based on a renewed solution instead of on the existing organization and distribution of duties. Seeing the person instead of the patient provides added value for the customer (higher quality of life) on the one hand and for both the organization and society (lower costs and higher labor participation rate) on the other. Where Ryhov shines is in the open conversation with patients regarding the personal meaning of quality of healthcare and life. It is a conversation that has moved from "What's the matter?" to "What matters to you?"[17] For Christian Farman, independence and feeling energetic were the most important results of the new approach for his kidney disorder. In conversation with a doctor and a nurse, this need resulted in him being able to perform the dialysis himself at times that suit him and in a rhythm by which he is able to feel energetic once again. It is a gain that perhaps can be realized for more patients and other disorders.
- Create transparency in healthcare. Make healthcare results transparent and use them to improve the quality of the care provided. Since the results of healthcare practitioners in Sweden are so visible and comparable, a climate is being created in which participants can learn from each other, healthy competition and innovation can take place, and what does and does not work can be revealed. Transparency in healthcare outcomes—both internal and external—results in more improvement and innovations.
- Use cocreation. Listening to both customers and patients and innovating together results in a greater chance of success. When the patient's needs are clear and in focus during the treatment process, the health gain increases. Give the patient an active role and a level of responsibility in the care process. This allows the patient to understand the care process better and to adjust it when necessary. The result of the Ryhov dialysis clinic's approach is fewer infections, fewer complications and reduced medicine use.
- Involve employees proactively in quality improvements based on trust instead of control. Give employees the space to think about how to improve the quality of care provided. Granting trust and freedom to discover and experiment within an organization for the purpose of arriving at improvements results in innovation. Britt-Mari Banck felt she had the freedom not only to train other nurses, but also to try to train patients themselves. Aside from an increase in the level of quality and a reduction in costs, this freedom has resulted in repeated recognition for the pioneering result.

---

[17]Bisognano (2013a, b).

- Move from social worker to coach. This involves transforming the role of a nurse into one of assisting and coaching people in arriving at the highest possible quality of life. This last lesson is also confirmed by the theory of Dr. Margaret A. Newman, a giant in the field of nursing theories. She is convinced that the quality of care can be improved by shifting the treatment of complaints to the search for patterns in awareness. In that regard, she defines the role of nurses as follows: "From viewing the nursing role as addressing the problems of disease to assisting people to get in touch with their own pattern of expanding consciousness."[18]

8.2   BerylHealth

A Call Center that Makes Hospitals' Customers Happy

Jeroen Geelhoed & Tim Widdershoven @: J.Geelhoed@samhoud.com, Phone: 0031 622408791

Prelude *The reception is phenomenal. We enter the building, are met in the reception hall by COO Lance Shipp on his Segway, walk through the call center that has around 500 workstations and then it happens just as we are walking around the corner to the presentation hall. Suddenly we hear loud cheering, coming from some 30 people standing in a double row. They scream, clap and give high fives. We are surprised by this warm welcome and ask one of the BerylHealth employees standing in the double row: "This is amazing. What's this? Why are you doing this?" The answer is as simple as characteristic of the culture: "Nice, isn't it? This is how we always welcome our new employees on their first day at work." We can assure you that you do not come away from this type of welcome untouched.[19]*

---

[18] Newman (1999).

[19] This case is based on multiple visits to BerylHealth from the end of 2009 to the start of 2013. A previous description of the Beryl business model (Geelhoed and Samhoud 2011, pp. 87–91) acts as the basis of this section. This description is enriched and supplemented by the experiences of the later visit.

Introduction BerylHealth is a call center that is established by Paul Spiegelman. Call centers are not the most attractive companies to work for, but BerylHealth is not your average call center. It is a unique organization with a clear vision and a sophisticated business model. It focuses on hospitals and assumes their responsibilities for customer contact. In 1985 Paul Spiegelman and his two brothers start a small business for emergency medical assistance. A combination of factors led to its incorporation. Paul's older brother, Mark, is a whiz kid. The family is running a successful alarm and security company when their grandfather starts having problems with heart failure. Paul: "When Mark saw our grandpa in such a vulnerable state, the idea emerged to develop an emergency call system that could help other people as well." And thus begins their new business under the name Emergency Response Systems (ERS).[20] But after roughly a decade, they discontinue operations because they discover it is becoming too capital-intensive for them. The brothers sell ERS and go in search of new opportunities.

8.2.1 The Cornerstone: Connecting People to Healthcare

The new opportunity arises when Columbia/HCA, the world's largest healthcare organization, requests a proposal for managing the National Physician Referral program. At first glance Paul Spiegelman has little chance against competitors who have an eye on the contract. But Paul and his team set to work quickly, pulling out all the stops to submit an attractive proposal. They spend 9 months working practically day and night on the pitch—successfully. Paul Spiegelman is awarded the contract and an unlimited budget to set up a new call center near Dallas, Texas. His dream becomes a reality—until 3 years later when Columbia pulls the plug on the project. This gives Paul a fright, but he eventually purchases the entire call center and expands it into one that strives to serve the patients of hospitals exceptionally well by providing outstanding service and sophisticated information.[21] And that is how BerylHealth came to be: a call center that is continuing to grow and attract even more customers. By 2012 the business had more than 500 employees.

The driving forces and sources of inspiration of BerylHealth are articulated in the company's vision. Its higher goal entails connecting people to healthcare. This means that patients are treated as people and that outstanding service is provided, so that people start to feel connected to healthcare. BerylHealth uses the following core values:

- passion for customer service;
- always do the right thing;
- never water down quality;
- spirit of camaraderie;
- commitment to accountability.

---

[20] Spiegelman (2007), p. 3.
[21] Idem, p. 10.

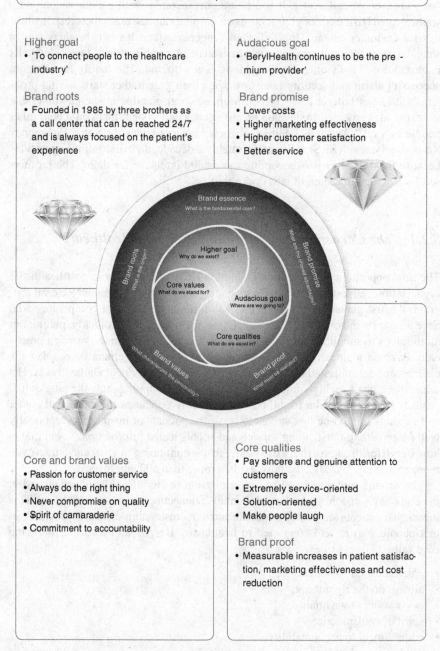

Brand essence: 'We help our clients build measurable and profitable patient relationships'

Higher goal
- 'To connect people to the healthcare industry'

Brand roots
- Founded in 1985 by three brothers as a call center that can be reached 24/7 and is always focused on the patient's experience

Audacious goal
- 'BerylHealth continues to be the premium provider'

Brand promise
- Lower costs
- Higher marketing effectiveness
- Higher customer satisfaction
- Better service

Core and brand values
- Passion for customer service
- Always do the right thing
- Never compromise on quality
- Spirit of camaraderie
- Commitment to accountability

Core qualities
- Pay sincere and genuine attention to customers
- Extremely service-oriented
- Solution-oriented
- Make people laugh

Brand proof
- Measurable increases in patient satisfaction, marketing effectiveness and cost reduction

Figure 8.2.1 Vision and Positioning of BerylHealth

These core values are deeply embedded in the organization. They are the rules of inspiration and touchstones for the daily actions of all BerylHealth employees. Later in this chapter we will see in one example how this functions in practice. You notice the core qualities of BerylHealth immediately if you spend a couple of hours within the company. The people have the competence of giving others their genuine attention. They are extremely service-oriented, think in terms of solutions and are able to make you smile. The audacious goal is to *remain* the premium provider in the market. In other words, BerylHealth is the market leader by far. And it is the task to remain at the top.

The brand essence fits seamlessly with the organization's vision. Specifically, BerylHealth desires to help customers build measurable and profitable patient relationships. The promise is crystal clear: lower costs, greater marketing effectiveness, higher customer satisfaction levels and better service. In that respect, their promise extends quite far. At the same time, however, they can simply point to the fact that it is true what they promise, because BerylHealth simply makes everything measurable. But we will leave that discussion until a later point.

8.2.2   The Business Model: Two Target Groups with One Stone

The question is now: how does this organization create value? BerylHealth realizes a profit margin of 21 %, which is exceptionally high in the call center sector. How is that possible? How are they able to achieve that year in and year out? The answer lies in the sophisticated business model.

Market Segments: Hospitals with More Than 400 Beds The target group is very specific, that is to say the larger hospitals in America which have at least 400 beds. Hospitals with fewer beds turn out not to immediately have the issues for which BerylHealth has a solution. These customers are not interested in the service of BerylHealth—something that is also not necessary, as the hospitals are queuing up for BerylHealth. The reason is that BerylHealth provides incredible value for both its customers and its customers' patients.

Customer Value: More Satisfied Patients, Higher Turnover and Lower Costs The service is unique. Firstly, the organization takes over the telephone service for the patients of the hospitals it serves. In doing so, it earns per minute and not per conversation. This means BerylHealth is also financially rewarded for taking the time for customers and not rushing through discussions. A patient who calls "his" hospital in New York, will get a BerylHealth employee in Texas on the line. The patient can then arrange a number of options through this employee, such as being referred to a doctor, scheduling a visit to an outpatient clinic or making an appointment for an operation. The employees of BerylHealth arrange for appointment reminders. Patients with health-related questions can also obtain answers from BerylHealth because the call center's staff have at least the same level of knowledge as a nurse. After an operation, for example, patients receive a phone call a week later from a

BerylHealth employee enquiring how they are doing and whether everything went as hoped. In other words, the patient contact is taken over completely and top-quality service provided in the process. One example cannot be withheld: a patient called an employee of BerylHealth to announce that his father was in a New York hospital in serious condition. He wanted to go visit his father but did not know which hospital he was in. The relevant employee did not skip a beat and proceeded to call every hospital in New York City to find out where the patient's father was. As a result, the second core value—"always do the right thing"—was properly put into practice. Whereas this is special in terms of service, the conclusion cannot yet be drawn that this is also a special business model.

However, we will be able to draw that conclusion after reviewing the second service of BerylHealth. In the USA, patients personally select the hospital they visit. Hospitals must use marketing campaigns to recruit customers. They would prefer to spend their marketing funds as effectively as possible. In order to measure the effects of these marketing campaigns, they should conduct research into the effectiveness thereof. But that, in turn, costs money—money they can no longer invest in the necessary marketing campaigns. BerylHealth capitalizes on this situation by incorporating its research immediately into the service provided. If a patient calls to make an appointment, the employee might answer: "Thank you for calling. How did you end up at our hospital?" That question makes it possible to measure the effectiveness of hospitals in one fell swoop. BerylHealth analyzes these results, reports on them, and makes recommendations to the relevant hospitals. This way hospitals are able to spend their marketing funds more effectively. The result of this dual service for hospitals is that BerylHealth does not provide a cost-saving service with a few extra activities, but rather a service that increases turnover. The services of most call centers are engaged by companies to reduce costs and effort. These kinds of services are always negotiated down to the last cent. In those situations, the margins of call centers are very narrow. However, BerylHealth's services are engaged to increase the profit margin, as a result of which the added value is much greater and, consequently, higher prices can be demanded.

But BerylHealth goes one step further by helping their customers—the hospitals—to reduce costs in other areas. BerylHealth calls patients after they have been treated in hospital. They enquire about their health, give tips for further recovery, provide information and answer questions. As a result, many readmissions are prevented, which saves patients a great deal of trouble. At the same time, it provides the relevant hospital with a considerable cost-saving. It is an example of another win-win situation!

All these services have been placed into four service packages for hospitals:

- CareConnect: marketing information to recruit new patients;
- CareAdvice: recommendations to hospitals regarding patient experiences and patient needs;
- CareMetrics: data analyses of the patient population for targeted deployment of services;
- CareTransitions: follow-up of patients after their discharge, from information to the prevention of readmissions.

Delivery: Telephone, Online and Science The hospitals have frequent contact with BerylHealth—in person, by telephone and via an online platform where they can consult all data, dialing codes and statistics online. The patients of the hospitals are in contact with the call center primarily by telephone. Incidentally, BerylHealth has only one call center, situated near Dallas, where all call center employees sit in an enormous space in a building that used to belong to Walmart. A conscious decision was made in this regard to ensure that there is one common culture. As a supplement to the "regular work" performed by BerylHealth, the Beryl Institute[22] was established to conduct research into how customer service can be improved in healthcare. In cooperation with various professors and with the aid of data compiled on a daily basis, scientific papers on this topic are published. The results are made available to everyone (at no cost). In this way a contribution is also being made to the higher goal. Furthermore, BerylHealth participates in the Small Giants Community. This is a movement for corporations with a unique culture that does a lot for the local community, have an eye for customers and perform well. In short, these are organizations that have something special about them. This is also referred to as "mojo" by Bo Burlingham, the author of the book entitled Small Giants.[23] Paul Spiegelman fulfills the pioneering role in the Small Giants Community. It is in that context that he publishes books and holds talks and workshops, by which BerylHealth is surrounded by a positive buzz, which in turn results in extra word-of-mouth advertising.

Operation: Culture, Culture, Culture and IT Needless to say, BerylHealth has converted the culture into every detail of the organization. We will single out a few examples below. Firstly, new employees are selected with extreme care and based on the core values. It is striking that the company looks specifically for people without call center experience. Instead, they prefer to attract waiters or customer service employees. Since the new employees are selected primarily on the basis of the core values, they are then forced to take demanding courses in medicine so that they are able to answer all kinds of medical questions. After all, they will act as representatives of a hospital! In addition, significant energy is spent on the development of the BerylHealth culture. Specifically, the core values must be expressed in employees' daily work. And it is for that reason that a special position has been created focusing on maintaining and promoting the culture. The title of this position—the Queen of fun and laughter—immediately gives an impression of how this is implemented.

Of course, BerylHealth keeps all kinds of indicators up to date, such as the handling time of phone calls and the extent to which a caller is assisted in a single conversation. But the most important indicator is the patient satisfaction level. Patient satisfaction is used to steer operations purposefully, but also to exuberantly facilitate them. Above we made reference to the recruitment and selection, the courses and the attention paid to the culture. But the technical side of the equation must not be forgotten! BerylHealth is immensely proud of its IT systems. These

[22] See also: www.theberylinstitute.org/.

[23] Burlingham (2005).

Value for customers

Result *What do I get?*

- BerylHealth is helping me in such a way that my patients are very satisfied, my revenues are increasing, and my costs are decreasing

✛

Process *How do I get it?*

- As a customer, I have the same service experience as my patients

✛

Emotion *What do I feel?*

- Beryl feels like a good partner. They can be trusted with providing service. The measurability offers me a handle. They really understand healthcare

---

Price *What are the costs?*

- Contact with clients is paid per spoken minute

✛

Effort *What do I have to do for it?*

- I have to transfer a large amount of knowledge and information to Beryl, which enables them to help my patients in the best possible way

✛

Risk *What are the uncertainties?*

- I experience a small amount of risk because per-formance agree-ments are made and everything is transparent

Market segments

Position

- BerylHealth offers the most compelling value proposition for customers, as it not only reduces costs, but also creates value

Competition

- Beryl distinguishes itself by being not only a cost-saving service, but also a revenue-enhancing company
- They have a market share of 90% in their target group

Target group

- Larger American hospitals with a mini-mum of 400 beds

Customer insights

- Hospitals do not only wish to outsource their service (costs), but also want to realize an increased marketing effect (value)

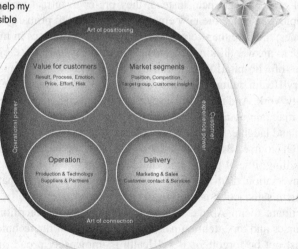

Figure 8.2.2 Value for customers and Market segments of BerylHealth

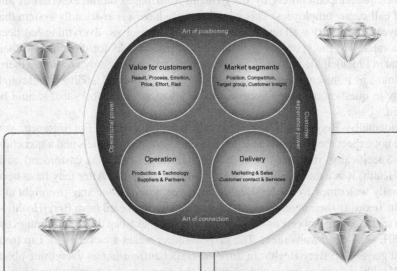

Operation

Production & Technology
- Company guided by vision and culture (Queen of fun and laughter)
- Service-oriented employees
- Call duration not the main determining indicator in operation
- Recruitment and selection based on culture
- Medical or other training of employees essential for delivering services to patients
- All technological systems, such as telephone and CRM, managed in-house
- Technology serves as enabler, yet value comes from people

Suppliers & Partners
- Hotels and taxi companies

Delivery

Marketing & Sales
- Beryl lets the results speak for themselves. They share them through their website, through the Beryl Institute, and via books, blogs and seminars
- PR as participant in a network of small corporate giants
- New customers find the company through word-of-mouth advertising

Customer contact & Services
- Customers: their website includes a client login where all available data and key indicators can be found
- Patients: through the internet, but mostly by telephone

Figure 8.2.3 Operation and Delivery of BerylHealth

have been developed entirely by BerylHealth itself based on the experiences and tips of call center employees. This way they truly have a user-friendly system that employees know very well and can even modify themselves. Everything has been incorporated into the system. For instance, if a patient asks for directions to their hospital in Philadelphia, the employee can tell the patient precisely how to get there. It is almost as if the employees are taking you by the hand and leading you through the city in question, and they even warn you about any roadworks that should be avoided.

Incidentally, BerylHealth has some striking partnerships. For instance, you would not expect them to have an extensive partnership with hotels and a taxi company. Specifically, if managers of a hospital (read: potential customers) visit BerylHealth, it is natural in the USA to fly to the company. After they have been personally welcomed by a BerylHealth employee, guests often stay overnight at a hotel in Texas. In their hotel room they find a handwritten card from BerylHealth — with a snack or some sweets as well. And if they are picked up the next morning, the "BerylHealth" taxi awaits them. The taxi chauffeur wears a jacket and a cap from … you guessed it: BerylHealth. In turn, the taxi chauffeur knows everything about BerylHealth, the person being picked up and the person with whom the guest has an appointment at the company. All of this is designed to let the customer experience that this is an organization which attaches immense importance to service. And usually part of the deal has already been secured in this way, remarks COO Lance Shipp, in passing while riding on his Segway.

In summary, it can be stated that BerylHealth has laid the foundation for a sophisticated business model. The target group is hospitals with a minimum of 400 beds. The offer is very attractive to customers, specifically not just taking over the telephone customer service, but also improving marketing effectiveness. This extra value creation is then organized in such a way that it costs little additional effort, as a result of which leverage is created which ensures that the business can generate a good profit margin. The organization subsequently invests this profit in the development of its employees and the improvement of its service, thereby creating a cycle of self-improvement: higher profit margins are invested in employees, which raises the level of customer satisfaction and causes the profit margin to rise again.

8.2.3 Result: It Starts with Happy Employees

BerylHealth scores exceptionally high in respect of customers. Its market share is 90 %. BerylHealth belongs to the top 20 outsourcing firms in the US healthcare sector. In that regard, its customers are rather loyal: 98 % actually remain a customer.[24] BerylHealth is valued immensely by the patient (or the citizen). Patient satisfaction

---

[24] See:http://www.berylhealth.com/ceo-of-the-beryl-companies-is-finalist-for-ernst-young-entrepreneur-of-the-year-award/.

levels have been persistently high. And thanks to the research and recommendations of the Beryl Institute, the service provided to patients is becoming better and better. Moreover, no one else has all this information. When looking at employee value, we see that BerylHealth has been a Great Place to Work winner several times, both in the state of Texas and at a national level in the USA. This can only be expected when you have a Queen of fun and laughter in your midst!

The results of consistently implementing the business model for the shareholder are pretty clear. As mentioned above, BerylHealth realizes a profit margin of no less than 21 %! That is exceptional for a call center business. Based on their growth figures, BerylHealth has made it onto the Inc. 5000 list—the national growth list in America—three times in a row. Further, Paul Spiegelman has won the 2010 Entrepreneur of the Year award. Creating shareholder value is therefore a strength of BerylHealth.

In the meantime, BerylHealth has been steadily working on realizing its vision. At the beginning of this chapter, we indicated that it demands a lot to stay at the top. And since recently, this will become even more difficult—at least that is our opinion! The reason is that during our last visit, it transpired that Paul Spiegelman had sold BerylHealth to Stericycle. He weighed up this decision carefully. Previous attempts by other companies to acquire BerylHealth had failed. For instance, in 2003 a competitor announced that it wanted to purchase the business. However, after a couple of months of discussions, Paul discontinued negotiations because they were not proceeding honestly. In 2009, Paul entered into discussions with a private equity company. But that deal also floundered, because the boys from the private equity firm were only after the big money instead of realizing the higher goal. In fact, this was immediately evident from the flashy cars they drove, the expensive hotels they stayed in and the exclusive bottles of wine they ordered.

In 2012, however, a deal was done. Stericycle also has operations in the healthcare sector, but not in the same field as BerylHealth. Stericycle really wanted to grow and saw the acquisition of BerylHealth as an opportunity that also matched their vision. Paul trusted these men and noticed that they were also driven by the same values that drive BerylHealth. It also became evident that Stericycle greatly valued the culture and people of BerylHealth. Thus arose the deal, with the idea being that the BerylHealth model would be scaled up to 12,000 employees in 12 countries.[25] Nonetheless, discussions are being held about adjusting the core values. At the same time, the question is whether the BerylHealth culture can simply be rolled out from that one large space in Texas and exported to so many new people in all these different countries. The next few years will reveal whether a brilliant business model with a unique culture as its foundation can continue to be successful if it is incorporated into an organization that is 12 times its current size. Time will tell whether that is possible. In the meantime, we can draw some conclusions from the past few years at BerylHealth and its current approach to work.

---

[25] http://www.inc.com/paul-spiegelman/sell-your-company-what-you-need-to-know.html.

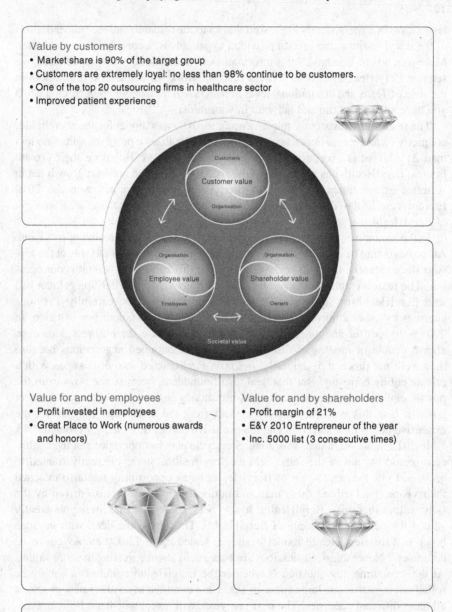

Value by customers
- Market share is 90% of the target group
- Customers are extremely loyal: no less than 98% continue to be customers.
- One of the top 20 outsourcing firms in healthcare sector
- Improved patient experience

Value for and by employees
- Profit invested in employees
- Great Place to Work (numerous awards and honors)

Value for and by shareholders
- Profit margin of 21%
- E&Y 2010 Entrepreneur of the year
- Inc. 5000 list (3 consecutive times)

Value for and by society
- Establishment of Beryl Institute that contributes to improving the service provided to healthcare patients

Figure 8.2.4 Value for and by stakeholders of BerylHealth

8.2.4 The Brilliant Lessons of BerylHealth

The following lessons can be drawn from the story of BerylHealth:

- Figure out how you can create a whole lot of extra value for your customer with just a tiny bit of extra effort. BerylHealth does just that by posing a couple of extra questions to patients who call. This makes it possible to measure marketing effectiveness and offer a lot of additional value for their direct customers, the hospitals it targets.
- Dare to select a target group. BerylHealth consciously chooses hospitals with more than 400 beds. This choice makes it immediately clear who your customers are *not* and enables you to focus better on what actually preoccupies your true target group. Consequently, you are better able to assist them, as a result of which they become more satisfied and recommend you to others, which in turn enables you to keep growing. If you do not make a choice for a particular target group, you will be everything to everyone and eventually nothing to anyone.
- Ensure that you are on the revenue side of the ledger instead of on the cost side for your customer. You can learn from BerylHealth to offer a service that generates greater turnover instead of one that is to be outsourced at the lowest possible cost.
- Hire employees first and foremost based on their attitude. If service is the most important aspect, this must be your first selection criterion, also if applicants come from different sectors. Whereas knowledge can always be brushed up on, attitude is far more difficult to change.
- Ensure that you have your IT systems under control. If your services are so dependent upon IT, you must ensure that front-line employees are able to work very well and simply with the systems you have in place. That might mean you have to develop the systems yourself, just as BerylHealth has done.
- This last lesson, however, might be the most important. BerylHealth shows that culture is a crucial part of a business model that requires a great deal of investment. The entire business model of BerylHealth would collapse if a service-oriented culture were not paired with a passion for patients. Ensure therefore that your culture is safeguarded in the management team, even if that does not per se mean via nutty titles such as the Queen of fun and laughter. Although …

8.3   M-PESA

Smart scalability

Wouter Houtman & Jennifer op't Hoog @: Jennifer.op.t.hoog@achmea.nl, Phone: 0031 651226420

Prelude *Developments in mobile telephony offer a growing number of opportunities to pay for and insure healthcare on the one hand, and to provide healthcare services on the other. The truly impactful and innovative concepts, however, are not necessarily found in cities such as Geneva, London or New York. No, they are rather to be found in Kenya, at Safaricom with its mobile financial service M-PESA, which in Swahili literally means "mobile money."[26] Prior to the introduction of M-PESA, Kenyans saved some money that they set aside for tomorrow or borrowed money to pay for today's bills. Cash funds earmarked for supporting oneself were kept at home or stashed away at the home of a good friend for rainy days. Saving for the future of children occurred, for instance, by way of purchasing jewels, which held their value. That or Kenyans collected a pile of stones, so that at some point they were able to build an extra room for their home. According to estimates, more than two billion people around the world still live in circumstances like these. The lack of a good financial infrastructure is doubtless one of the reasons why people are permanently caught in a spiral of poverty. Their incomes vary and often fluctuate daily. Without any reliable way to deposit or withdraw money in bad times, they are occasionally confronted with the difficult decision of either taking their children out of school or putting less food on the table.*

M-PESA was founded as a micro-financing initiative of Safaricom for Kenya. It has turned out to be the most successful innovation in the past few years in the world of financial services in developing countries. In spite of (or perhaps because of) the difficult times, a strong entrepreneurial spirit and sense of creativity have combined to ensure that major problems and challenges were overcome. Can you imagine a world without banks in the vicinity? In Kenya, the nearest bank is often 6 miles away while people have to walk, which means you spend 2 h just to get there and then you

---

[26]This innovation from the bottom of the welfare pyramid is, for instance, also described by Prahalad (2009).

have to come back. Add the time spent waiting at the bank and you quickly end up devoting 5 h for a simple trip. In other words, you will spend half of your working day going to the bank. Taking the bus, if you can, costs roughly 25% of the money you earn on a good day. Many people simply opt not to have a bank account. Now imagine a world without credit instruments or electronic payments, i.e., no current account, checks, bank cards, money orders, debt collection, or Internet banking. All transactions take place in cash or by way of barter; all exchanges are physical, one to one and from hand to hand. Consider as well all the fuss and the risk associated with sending money to distant relatives, business partners or banks. Could you work in a world like that? Thankfully, there is now a solution for this type of world and it is found in M-PESA! M-PESA uses the informal structures of sharing and transferring money between family and friends on the one hand and city and countryside on the other. Thanks to the possibility of banking by mobile phone, the connection has become both stronger and simpler. At the same time, people have more ways to save and pay for agriculture, education, and healthcare.

Introduction Mobile phone operator Vodafone changed the lives of Kenyans forever when in March 2007 it introduced to the market the revolutionary M-PESA via its Kenyan subsidiary Safaricom. With M-PESA, everyone is able—even with the simplest of mobile phones—to deposit money into an account, transfer money to other users (including sellers of goods and services) via a text message and convert credit balances into cash. Users are charged only a small fee to transfer and withdraw money. M-PESA is completely focused on transferring funds simply and efficiently. Via M-PESA, people in the countryside are not only connected with one another, but also with their friends and family in urban areas. In this way, it has become possible to send and receive money for essential expenses such as for paying school fees and healthcare costs. All hospitals in Kenya currently accept M-PESA for both clinic and outpatient services. But that is not all! Thanks to the mobile financial service, it becomes possible to undertake an initial step toward a new healthcare system in developing countries.

8.3.1 The Cornerstone: Simple, Efficient, and Customer-Oriented

The brand essence for M-PESA is clear and deeply rooted in the organization, a simple and efficient mobile financial service. M-PESA developed extremely quickly; it is now the most successful mobile-phone-based financial service in the Third World. In 2012, Kenya had some 17 million M-PESA accounts registered, via which roughly EUR 445 million per month circulated—an amount equivalent to 20% of Kenya's BNP.[27] The organization primarily aims to offer affordable, reliable, and customer-oriented mobile financial services to everyone.

---

[27] http://www.wamda.com/2012/11/cashless-in-kenya-a-mobile-money-experiment-using-M-PESA.

Let us first go back to the origin of this inspiring organization to see where this vision came from. In 2002, researchers at Gamos and the Commonwealth Telecommunications Organization (CTO), financed by the Department for International Development (DFID), discovered that people in Uganda, Botswana, and Ghana were using their call minutes as a way to transfer money. As it turned out, call minutes were being sent to family members and friends who then used or sold on these minutes to generate a source of income. The researchers at Gamos contacted MCel in Mozambique to share their discovery and in 2004 MCel introduced the first authorized credit exchange via calling minutes, a predecessor of M-PESA. The idea was discussed by the Commission for Africa and DFID and introduced to the researchers of Vodafone, who were thinking of supporting micro-financing and back-office banking via mobile phones. Simon Batchelor (Gamos) and Nick Hughes (Vodafone CSR) then considered how a payment system could be set up in Kenya. The pilot phase began 1 year later. In 2007, M-PESA was introduced to the market by Safaricom, the largest provider of mobile telephone services in Kenya (market share exceeding 75 %) and partly owned by Vodafone (more than 40 %).[28] The audacious goal to help create an economy whereby people no longer need be concerned about their day-to-day worries, but rather are able to make plans for their future and the future of their children was slowly becoming a reality with every improvement made along the way. M-PESA was designed first and foremost as a system by which micro-financing debts could be paid off so as to effect lower settlement fees as a result of which lower interest rates became possible. After the tests in the pilot phase, however, the system was expanded to include a general payment transaction scheme. As soon as customers have registered, they bring money into the system by depositing cash at one of the 60,000 Safaricom agents (usually a shop or outlet that sells, among other things, calling minutes) who deposit the money on the customer's M-PESA account. Customers can then withdraw money by going to another agent. This second agent checks whether the balance is sufficient before debiting the account and handing over the cash. Customers can also transfer money to other persons or organizations via a menu on their mobile phone. With this new system, money can be sent quickly, securely, and simply from one place to another. Customers no longer have to walk around with a lot of cash in their pockets or ask others to carry or transport it for them. This way mobile financial services are becoming available to everyone with a SIM card! This is the brand promise of M-PESA and it is particularly useful in a country where many employees in cities send money back to their family members in the countryside. Thanks to electronic transfers, both time and money are saved, whilst the associated risk is reduced, as a result of which people can be more productive in other areas.

---

[28] http://blog.usaid.gov/2013/04/video-of-the-week-animating-M-PESA/.

Dozens of mobile money systems have been introduced to the market, but M-PESA has become the most successful. How is that possible? Let us take another look at the organization's beginnings. The system offers a number of advantages and the correct path was taken a number of times.[29] The values and core competences of Safaricom played an essential role. When M-PESA was introduced, Safaricom already enjoyed a dominant position in the market and used it efficiently to set up a simple, accessible, and effective marketing campaign ("send money home"). After the introduction, Michael Joseph, former CEO of Safaricom, invested large sums in new SIM cards on which M-PESA software was preprogrammed. All existing customers of Safaricom received this new SIM card without having to pay a cent. In this way, all existing Safaricom customers were able to use M-PESA immediately after its introduction. Another external and enabling factor was the decision at that time of the regulatory body to continue the scheme on an experimental basis but without any formal approval. This lead to an efficient system by which cash could circulate behind the scenes. Specifically, M-PESA was not viewed as a bank and did not, therefore, fall under those regulations. M-PESA uses banks for depositing money and receives interest thereon; the organization itself is not, however, a bank. It works in such a way that M-PESA uses this interest via the M-PESA Foundation to finance three types of social programs: Agriculture, Healthcare, and Education. A further external influence originated in the violence that occurred after the elections in early 2008. This led to a distrustful society. The focus of the organization on reliability gave customers a solid basis in which they were able to trust. This played an important role in the development of M-PESA. In the first instance, M-PESA was used to transfer money to people who at that time were stuck in the slums of Nairobi. In addition, some Kenyans also considered M-PESA as a safer place to keep their money than banks which enjoyed little trust because they caught up in ethnic differences. Once a file of initial users was set up and everyone had access via a new SIM card M-PESA was able to profit from network effects and an innovative approach. As the service became relevant to people, the critical mass was achieved: the more people who made use of the service, the more logical it became for others to register as well. An important driver was affordability. The organization always had it in the back of its mind that the service had to be provided at low cost in order to remain affordable and accessible to as many people as possible. In developments in the years that followed, a customer-oriented approach also played an essential role. Core qualities of M-PESA include listening to customers in order to involve them in the development process, as a result of which the service became simple and innovative. In combination with the aforementioned factors, this has resulted in the success outlined by the executive director of the M-PESA Foundation, Les Baillie: "As the situation currently exists, 75 % of the adult Kenyan population use M-PESA on a daily basis."[30]

---

[29] http://www.cgap.org/blog/10-things-you-thought-you-knew-about-M-PESA.
[30] http://www.pharmaccess.org/RunScript.asp?page=24&Article_ID=254&NWS=NWS&ap=NewsDetail.asp&p=ASP\~Pg24.asp.

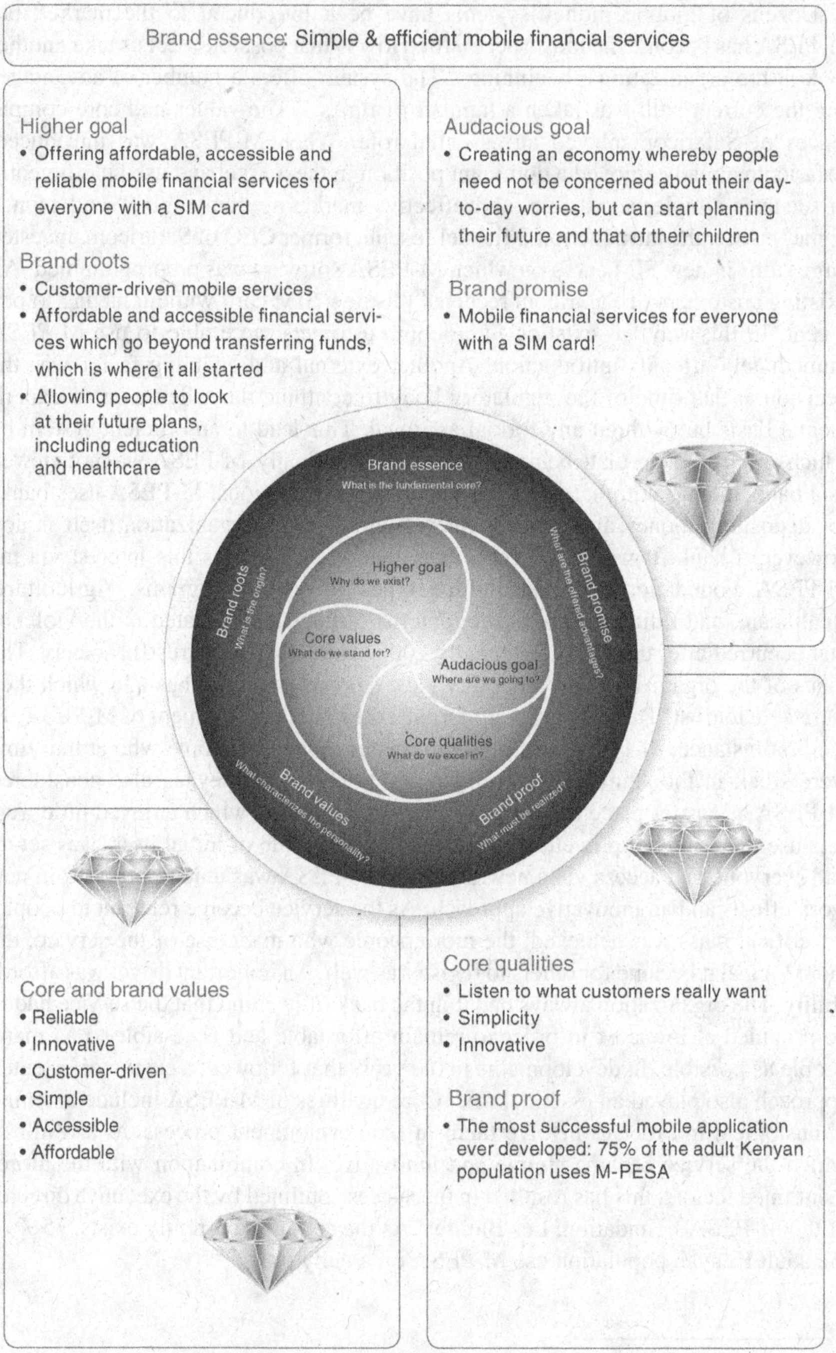

Brand essence: Simple & efficient mobile financial services

Higher goal
• Offering affordable, accessible and
  reliable mobile financial services for
  everyone with a SIM card

Brand roots
• Customer-driven mobile services
• Affordable and accessible financial services which go beyond transferring funds,
  which is where it all started
• Allowing people to look
  at their future plans,
  including education
  and healthcare

Audacious goal
• Creating an economy whereby people
  need not be concerned about their day-
  to-day worries, but can start planning
  their future and that of their children

Brand promise
• Mobile financial services for everyone
  with a SIM card!

Brand essence
What is the fundamental core?

Higher goal
Why do we exist?

Brand roots
What is the origin?

Core values
What do we stand for?

Brand promise
What are the offered advantages?

Audacious goal
Where are we going to?

Core qualities
What do we excel in?

Brand values
What characterizes the personality?

Brand proof
What must be realized?

Core and brand values
• Reliable
• Innovative
• Customer-driven
• Simple
• Accessible
• Affordable

Core qualities
• Listen to what customers really want
• Simplicity
• Innovative

Brand proof
• The most successful mobile application
  ever developed: 75% of the adult Kenyan
  population uses M-PESA

Figure 8.3.1 Vision and Positioning of M-Pesa

With the foundation of a payment system and of international money transfers in place upon which services that add value could be built, a range of various health-related mobile financial services can be established on this same infrastructure. Customers want to use the payment system services for many suppliers, such as healthcare practitioners, for which they need larger or unexpected amounts. This provides a better access to healthcare when required. From prepaid credits to health insurance, mobile platforms are attempting to ensure that affordable healthcare is not exclusively a luxury, but rather a universal right. M-PESA provides a platform by which not only products and services are sold, but also the service is used as an interaction point for providing information about healthcare.

8.3.2   The Business Model: Secure Banking and Living in Safety

Market Segments: Simply Changing the Lives of People The Kenyan market is characterized by a low per-capita income, a relatively stable political situation (at the time of introduction to the market) and a quick habituation with the use of mobile services by the population. The expectation is that in 2016 more than a billion people in Africa will make use of mobile telephony.[31] Safaricom's market share in Kenya amounted to more than 75 % when the service was introduced. Thanks to this massive basis, a network effect was able to take place, which expressed itself in the large number of consumers who started using the service. The customer base of more than 17 million Kenyans can no longer imagine life without M-PESA. In 2013, 75 % of the market was using M-PESA's services. Despite the very modest revenues per transfer, the service still manages to generate a profit thanks to scale. Since its introduction, M-PESA has a market share of roughly 65 % and Safaricom a market share of almost 80 %. Seventy percent of all financial transactions in Kenya are conducted via M-PESA.[32] The success of M-PESA follows on strongly from the success of Safaricom, which is partially owned by Vodafone. M-PESA was set up by Vodafone in cooperation with Safaricom. Safaricom is the first and largest mobile telephone company in Kenya. It was established in 1999 and already had no fewer than 11 million customers by 2008. The impressive growth of M-PESA is largely due to the decision to provide every Kenyan customer with a new SIM card programmed with M-PESA software after the introduction of the company. As a result, all Safaricom customers were instantly able to use M-PESA. And even at the time of writing, the service's growth figures were still high, with roughly 10,000 new subscribers per day. When the service was introduced, there was not a lot of competition. The biggest competition at that time came via other ways to transfer money which were more time-consuming as well as more expensive, such as trans-

---

[31] Peter Diamandis, A World of Abundance, 21 November 2013, Carré Amsterdam.

[32] http://webcolleges.uva.nl/Mediasite/Play/e4832ffc580f49cf84e59e11f776e8e11d.

fer offices (expensive and not trusted a lot), informal channels (lorry drivers who act as couriers in return for a fee), a family member (not always safe) or personal delivery (time-consuming). M-PESA's target group consists of SIM cardholders of Safaricom. It began organically with Kenyan holders of a Safaricom SIM card who wanted to make payments or transfer money. In fact this applies to all inhabitants of Kenya. In Africa—and in particular in Kenya—people have become used to having more than one SIM card from different providers. People either do not have any telephone or they have one with several SIM cards, because telephones are expensive and SIM cards cheap. In other words, the provider of SIM cards faces the challenge of ensuring that customers keep their cards activated. The solution to this challenge is to issue a provider-linked service such that people benefit so much from it that they continue to use this provider's SIM card. For Safaricom, this was the most important customer insight behind the success of their business. The introduction of this service as an add-on now means that Safaricom has profited from it, because these SIM cards are used more often and M-PESA can be used to reach a number of potential customers via the Safaricom customer database. The step that the organization will now take and will initially promote via the M-PESA Foundation is to exercise significant influence in the field of healthcare, education and agriculture. Safaricom's gigantic database could have enormous consequences for society at large. The areas in which current innovations in healthcare are taking place are: communication, for instance by ensuring that physicians in countries such as Ghana can call each other for free; information, for example by setting up a healthcare service, including a toll-free telephone consultation with a nurse; and financing, for instance by making payment for healthcare services simpler via a health wallet. These initiatives and innovations are now in the pilot phase and financed with donations. As soon as the golden egg and the enabling factor in healthcare have been discovered, it will become an add-on service and therefore part of the regular core business.

Customer Value: A Big Selling Point The brilliance of M-PESA is that it is very user-friendly and affordable and consequently very accessible. Within 10 s users can make payments or transfer money (only three clicks and a PIN code are required). In addition, all actions can be performed on a mobile phone in combination with a local shopkeeper where users can deposit or withdraw money. Thanks to the ease of use and the speed of this method of banking, people can now use their time and money more efficiently. Another attractive advantage is that customers feel safer. After all, you no longer have to walk around with your pockets full of money and be scared of having them picked. Mobile financial services like M-PESA also play an important role in security at another level. In research conducted by Georgetown University, it was concluded that "… households that have access to M-PESA and are situated close to an agency, are better able to maintain their purchasing power in times that their income suffers a hit."

Safaricom has kept the price of the product very transparent and lower than that of alternative services. The product is simple, efficient to use and very cheap, certainly if you compare it with the option of personally taking money to the other side of the country or engaging the services of someone to do so on your behalf.

And now M-PESA is expanding its scope by offering new financial services made possible thanks to further digitization. It is interesting to see that several of these services are healthcare-oriented, such as mobile savings accounts which patients can use to plan their finances and save money for their future healthcare needs. Severe injury and funerals are mentioned as the financial emergencies that occur the most. Another example is the aforementioned mobile health wallet. Patients use it to pay the costs of their medical treatment in hospital or medical centers. Each clinic has its own unique number which can be used as a reference number. This type of transaction normally costs money, but since the hospitals share these data with healthcare-oriented organizations such as AAR Healthcare, they are free of charge and boost accessibility. In return, AAR can help the hospitals set up an efficient healthcare system based on the data they receive from the hospitals. Aside from facilitating healthcare-related payments, M-PESA is used to provide relevant healthcare information to people. From a medical perspective, this does not just concern why and how people should save for medical treatments, but it also uses M-PESA for mobile care or mHealth. In this way, people who live far from a hospital receive relevant medical information and preventive education, as a result of which they become more autonomous and less dependent upon medical care provided by experts. And if users do need help, they can first consider attending a virtual consultation before undertaking the (half-day) trip to the hospital. Some 79 % of Kenyans live in remote areas; in those circumstances gaining access to healthcare is difficult. By applying mHealth therefore, M-PESA can make a real difference in the lives of people. This way of providing mHealth is the fastest-growing method of healthcare in Africa. A virtual consultation costs roughly USD 0.70 (EUR 0.60), whereas a doctor's visit quickly amounts to USD 14 (EUR 12). Healthcare is becoming more affordable and therefore increasingly accessible for many more people.

Delivery: Simple Communication and Anticipating Customer Needs M-PESA's marketing and communication are characterized by both simplicity and efficiency. In the first years after launching, it was especially important to position with the strong service brand of Safaricom as doing so offered trust and affinity. At the start of the service, the communication was simple and focused on guest workers, as was evident from the slogan "send money home". A large portion of the customer contact proceeds via clear instructions on the mobile phone; the next contact point is the local shopkeeper who is paid by M-PESA for his/her services. The presence of local agents where money can be deposited or withdrawn can, of course, be a very costly affair. However, what Safaricom does extremely well with M-PESA is to use the network that was already in existence and extended upon existing distribution. Delivery is based on contracts with existing, local shopkeepers who are well known and trusted in the neighborhood. With M-PESA, they can add something extra to their package of services as a supplementary source of income. Safaricom selects it agents with care; after all, they are the face of the company and act as co-guarantors of trust. The already existing, extensive network of sellers of Safaricom call minutes has been and is being fully exploited to set up a reliable, consistent network of shops.

Every agent must meet the requirements of M-PESA (including an assessment and training) in order to become an authorized retail agent. Safaricom guarantees consistent branding, training and continuous supervision of the shops for the purpose of effecting the right customer experience. Furthermore, it has a special call center customer service available. In Kenya, especially since not everyone is literate, the likelihood of people making a mistake and sending money to the wrong person is greater. Safaricom works with back-office support in order to help people retrieve their money where possible. M-PESA has its own dedicated call center to do that. Safaricom guarantees very high quality customer service. Thanks to the strong back-office support, the business has not only engendered trust, but also attracted users afraid of technology.

An important factor in the commercial success of Safaricom—and by extension of M-PESA—is the ability to listen. This amounts to listening attentively to what the customer wants and quickly responding to these needs. By listening to the customer, M-PESA was able to convert the payment of microloans into helping people make P2P (person-to-person) payments to friends and family. A few years after the company's launch, customers started to say that they wanted to make cross-border payments to family in other African countries or that they wanted to receive money from family residing in more developed parts of the world. This was reason enough to dig everything out of the archives to realize these demands. M-PESA properly understood the message that the customer is king. M-PESA understands that the organization can only exist if customers consider it relevant and that it can only continue to be relevant by offering customers what they want or need.

Since the organization has an extensive customer database, it understands more and more that it can play an important role in society—by informing people about healthcare-related topics or training opportunities. In this way, customers receive information, for instance, on hygiene, nutrition, and pregnancy. M-PESA makes this information available to everyone. This education is in turn required to undertake the next step in the direction of other financial services or in offering healthcare insurance.

Operation: Accessibility as a Boundary Condition Since M-PESA began as an additional service for the Safaricom SIM card, an important part of M-PESA's services is facilitated by Safaricom. Safaricom and M-PESA maintain close contact with their customers to give them access to the right information at all times and maintain a high level of trust. If the server is slow, for example, it notifies its users so that they are not unsettled. The reason that customers have a high level of trust has everything to do with the company's customer focus thanks to a very responsive back office. Safaricom always keeps a finger on the pulse of the consumer. The combination of the service with very simple communication is the key to success.

Value for customers

Result *What do I get?*
- Accessible, affordable and reliable mobile financial services

Process *How do I get it?*
- Through my mobile phone, only 3 clicks away

Emotion *What do I feel?*
- Safe and ready for the future

Price *What are the costs?*
- Only USD 0.10 (EUR 0.085) per financial transaction (25 times cheaper than transactions via the bank)

Effort *What do I have to do for it?*
1. Get a Safaricom SIM card.
2. Register as user
3. Start using M-PESA

✛

Risk *What are the uncertainties?*
- Very low risk. Biggest risk is that the mobile network fails, temporarily making the service unavailable

Market segments

Position
- M-PESA has around 18 million users
- There are over 40,000 authorized dealers
- Safaricom's market share exceeds 75%
- By offering more financial services through M-PESA, such as health insurance, the client base will grow even quicker

Competition
- The only real competition M-PESA now has might come from financial service providers, but they don't have the infrastructural advantage M-PESA has

Target group
- Everyone with a mobile phone who is looking for an affordable, accessible and reliable way for transferring and saving money – mostly adult Kenyans

Customer insights
- I want a simple and reliable way to transfer and save money

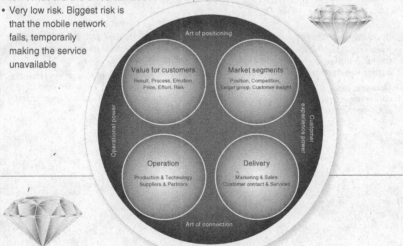

Figure 8.3.2 Value for customers and Market segments of M-Pesa

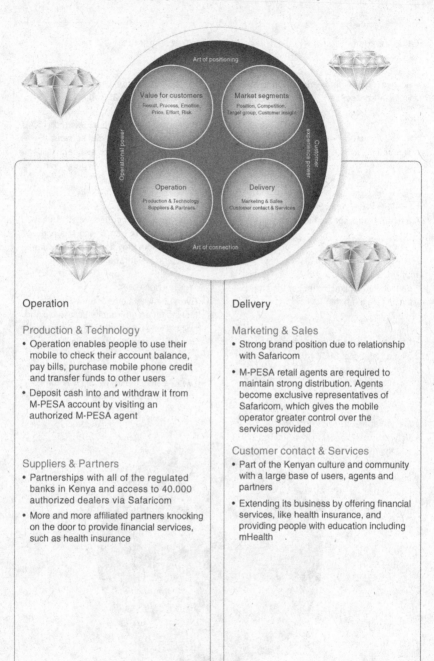

Operation

Production & Technology
- Operation enables people to use their mobile to check their account balance, pay bills, purchase mobile phone credit and transfer funds to other users
- Deposit cash into and withdraw it from M-PESA account by visiting an authorized M-PESA agent

Suppliers & Partners
- Partnerships with all of the regulated banks in Kenya and access to 40.000 authorized dealers via Safaricom
- More and more affiliated partners knocking on the door to provide financial services, such as health insurance

Delivery

Marketing & Sales
- Strong brand position due to relationship with Safaricom
- M-PESA retail agents are required to maintain strong distribution. Agents become exclusive representatives of Safaricom, which gives the mobile operator greater control over the services provided

Customer contact & Services
- Part of the Kenyan culture and community with a large base of users, agents and partners
- Extending its business by offering financial services, like health insurance, and providing people with education including mHealth

Figure 8.3.3 Operation and Delivery of M-Pesa

To gain access to the services of M-PESA, new customers sign up at an authorized retail agent. After registration, customers receive a personal electronic account managed by Safaricom. Safaricom deposits the value of the money that its customers have deposited in their M-PESA accounts in an umbrella account at a bank. Safaricom therefore issues the M-PESA accounts. The balances are situated at the commercial bank collaborating with M-PESA. Consequently, Safaricom does not take over the role and function of the bank, but rather focuses on facilitating the transaction. Given that M-PESA is not positioned as an alternative to banks, the know-your-customer regulations and requirements are not so strict. By contrast to what happens at the banks, users only need to identify themselves to gain access to the service. As a result, the service is increasingly becoming accessible. In particular to people in the countryside, where proof of where one lives and other documents usually demanded by banks are difficult to come by. The relationship with both the bank and the government is important: Safaricom has involved the Central Bank of Kenya since the launch of the organization and continues to work together with it. On 4 May 2009, the Central Bank gave the instruction to audit the M-PESA service of Safaricom. The Kenyan government was concerned that criminals could use the service to launder money. Safaricom passed the audit thanks to completely transparent activities and the proactive sharing of data. The Central Bank then declared the service secure and in compliance with the government's objectives for financial inclusion.

8.3.3 Result: "Relax, You've Got M-PESA"

M-PESA started as a corporate social responsibility initiative for micro-financing, but was soon converted into a successful enterprise. That was of primary importance, because charity is not scalable, while a money-earning company is. An investment to provide free SIM cards to all with M-PESA software would for instance never been conducted for charity alone. M-PESA has meant a lot to the people of Kenya. They are better able to make plans for the future—whether it concerns planning for their own home, their children's education or medical treatments. That is why M-PESA is more than just mobile money. It is an infrastructure that not only provides access to financial services, but also makes all kinds of other services such as healthcare-related services available to everyone with a mobile phone.

As discussed in the business model, prior to launch customers created value for M-PESA by indicating and showing through their actions what they were looking for in financial products and services. In the area of customer confidence, M-PESA scores very high according to the independent trust Financial Sector Deepening Kenya (FSD), whose objective is to support the development of inclusive financial markets in Kenya. Research conducted by FSD Kenya demonstrates that more than 90 % of M-PESA's users believe that their money is safe.[33]

---

[33] http://www.fsdkenya.org/pdf_documents/11-02-14_Mobile_payments_in_Kenya.pdf.

As a service, M-PESA plays a pivotal role in the daily lives of its customers. The Safaricom SIM card is therefore significantly less exchangeable with those of competitors. Consequently, loyal M-PESA customers are creating a large degree of brand loyalty for Safaricom. The more the customer database of M-PESA grows, the more the customer database of Safaricom grows, which ultimately contributes to customer loyalty. Its market share continues to grow and by the middle of 2013 had reached a record high. Vodafone, one of the shareholders with a 40% stake in Safaricom, profits as a result thereof. Since the introduction of M-PESA, Vodafone has continued to be a principal owner of M-PESA. In return, Vodafone receives some 10 % of the turnover of Safaricom[34], which was roughly USD 20 million (EUR 17 million) in 2013. Banks also profit from the growth and success of M-PESA, since money is deposited into their accounts via M-PESA.

M-PESA works with more than 60,000 agents, mostly local shopkeepers providing an extra service by acting as replacements for cash machines. In this way the agents are assisted in several ways. Firstly, they are helped by the extra source of income in addition to the articles sold in their shops. Secondly, shopkeepers previously were confronted with the problem that they had too much cash in their shops (which could be unsecure). This problem has been resolved since the money is deposited by the M-PESA customer. And thirdly, this extra service ensures that more customers come to shopkeepers' stores. The question is: what does M-PESA get in return for all of this? First and foremost, M-PESA acquires a close network of trusted local agents who are the face of the organization in an environment where little trust exists.

The value for society is evident in many ways: money is used more effectively (quicker and safer and at lower costs); businesses can make mobile payments instead of using cash; crime rate is lower (electronic transfers result in less crime); and the system creates employment. Furthermore, international cash transactions allow Kenyans to offer financial support to family members living abroad and to receive it. Thanks to the high degree of market penetration as well as the original corporate social responsibility intent of the organization, M-PESA has started playing a role in initiating social-welfare challenges, such as creating awareness in the field of insurance policies and launching healthcare and study (e-learning) programs. Examples of this include healthcare programs that are being implemented by various foundations—such as the Health Insurance Fund—in various fields, including pregnancy, hygiene and nutrition. In addition, the network is also being used to solicit funds. And given the high degree of solidarity among the Kenyan population, much of the money flows via M-PESA to people who have the least amount of money.

---

[34] http://www.businessdailyafrica.com/Corporate-News/Vodafone-takes-home-Sh2-3bn-of-M-PESA-revenue/-/539550/1852810/-/m9igv0/-/index.html.

Value by customers
• M-PESA has created a huge amount of brand loyalty for Safaricom as mobile operator.
  Since M-PESA is a way of living and Safaricom is the provider of M-PESA, people all want
  to be connected to Safaricom

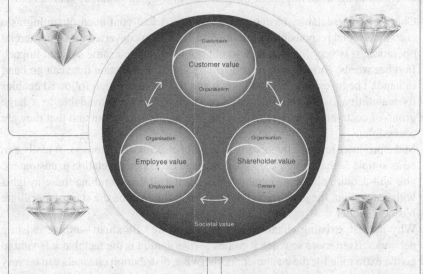

Value for and by employees
• M-PESA has over 40,000 exclusive
  agents, mostly local shop owners who
  provide an extra service while they do
  not have to keep much cash in store
  (which can be unsafe)
• Agents provide the local and entrusted
  face of the organization in a low-trust
  services environment
• Employees of Safaricom can be proud
  of their organization, its innovativeness
  and social impact

Value for and by shareholders
• The market share keeps on growing
• Vodafone profits since it has a 40%
  share in Safaricom
• Banks profit as money is being
  deposited through M-PESA on their
  bank accounts

Value for and by society
• Money is used more effectively (received sooner and safer at lower costs), with a lower
  crime rate
• The possibility of international transfers enabled Kenyans to help or receive financial help
  from their families living abroad
• M-PESA has been able to raise financial and insurance awareness and provide the
  foundation for education and eHealth.

Figure 8.3.4   Value for and by stakeholders of M-Pesa

8.3.4   The Brilliant Lessons of M-PESA

After a thorough review of M-PESA's vision and mission, its business model and its value creation, the most important insights into this organization are set out below:

- Charity is not scalable, business is. If M-PESA had continued operating as a corporate social responsibility initiative and not been converted into commercial operation, it is very likely that it would not have had the same societal impact. In other words, earning money and "doing good" at the same time can go hand in hand! The investments in the launch and the success which followed enables its scalability. If you want to make products or services available to a large group of customers, ensure that it is clear what they are about and that they are accessible.
- Make products relevant by looking at actual behavior of customers. It really can be as simple as that. If you keep your eyes and ears open in relation to customers, you will acquire all the insights to succeed. If you then combine these insights with innovation, the greater the likelihood that this will be the start of a brilliant business model.
- Why not use existing channels and infrastructure? Be smart—utilize existing networks. Even more so when it comes to distribution is the fact that it is vital to go the extra mile for the customer.[35] Otherwise, distribution channels can be very expensive, certainly in personal contact. By using existing channels, employees can be active locally and on a personal level without the associated high costs.
- Look for a way to strengthen one self-financing business model with another self-financing business model. This can be done, for instance, just as M-PESA provided an add-on service—one that is relevant to the customer but does not require any investment or only a small investment for the existing parent organization and distribution partners. It will ultimately result in lower costs and access to a broad market.

8.4   The Jaipur Foot of Bhagwan Mahaveer Viklang Sahayata Samiti (BMVSS)

Mass innovation for people without a handicap

Kristin Fransz, Ilse Hoogervorst & Jeroen Kemperman @: Jeroen.Kemperman@ achmea.nl, Phone: 0031 651222099

---

[35] Rhyne (2009).

Prelude   *As a small girl, Sudha Chandran[36] (1964) has already demonstrated her striking talent for dancing. Her father does not permit Sudha to participate in sports or play outside too often[37] as he is concerned about injuries that could hinder her career or dance training. Her future looks rosy, but in 1981 fate intervenes. Sudha is injured in a bus accident and her leg develops gangrene because her wounds are not treated properly.[38] Doctors have to amputate her right leg to save her life.*

From that moment on, Sudha's life changes dramatically. She is suddenly disabled. In India that means, generally speaking, that you are no longer able to participate fully in society. Sudha refuses to believe that she will never walk again. Her passion reinforces her mission, so she starts looking for a way to be able to dance again. In her quest, she hears about P.K. Sethi, an orthopedic surgeon, and writes him a letter. He replies that it might be possible for her to dance once again with a prosthesis, specifically with the Jaipur Foot.

After this prosthesis is measured for her, she is able to walk—but she wants more. Through sheer perseverance and will power, she is ultimately able to dance again. This achievement became known in India and Sudha's story became increasingly well known. In 1984, a film based on her life story was screened. In it, Sudha herself played the main role. Since then she has become a famous dancer, TV and film actress in India and beyond. She has also become a symbol of hope for millions of disabled individuals. Pupils in India learn about her life story.[39] Without the Jaipur Foot, she could never have reached these heights.

Introduction   Due to a special collaboration between a sculptor and a group of doctors, Jaipur Foot has permanently changed the lives of more than a million people over the years. This artificial foot may have been developed back in 1968, but the Jaipur Foot is still a work of art in the world of prostheses. The "artwork" was created by Ram Chandra, an innovative sculptor. The "footwork" was designed by S.M.S.

---

[36] Meenu (2009).

[37] Patel (2011).

[38] http://msmunited.com/uncategorized/sudha-chandran-inspiring-story-dancer-part-1.

[39] Meenu (2009).

Medical College Hospital together with a number of orthopedic surgeons (including P.K. Sethi). The Jaipur Foot is an answer to the prohibitive costs of prostheses made in the West and the limited usefulness thereof in Indian living conditions. For the purpose of promoting the prostheses, it was decided not to patent the Jaipur Foot. This is a philosophy aimed at sharing—something currently also seen in the open-source work of Linux. In 1975, the nonprofit organization Bhagwan Mahaveer Viklang Sahayata Samiti (BMVSS) was founded by Mr. Mehta, Dr. Purohit, and Dr. Bapna, among others, to ensure that the prostheses would become available to a greater portion of the populace. The technology is still freely available today.[40]

BMVSS is the world's largest nonprofit organization for the benefit of physically disabled individuals. The Jaipur Foot was developed further and other aids have been added over the years. Each year BMVSS helps approximately 65,000 people receive a prosthesis or other orthopedic aid. To date, some 1.3 million individuals have been helped. BMVSS also operates on an international level, such as in conflict areas. Typical for BMVSS is the ease with which it can be approached by patients and the quick turnaround time for helping them. They can seek assistance at any time of the day in one of the 22 clinics across India and one of the camps in 26 countries. They may stay there at no charge while their prostheses are being measured. They are helped within 1–3 days on average, upon which they may leave with their prostheses or another orthopedic aid. Patients come from throughout India for the Jaipur Foot. The prosthesis does not cost them a cent and is amazingly well suited for difficult living conditions in developing countries like India. It actually enables individuals to participate fully in society once again.

8.4.1   The Cornerstone: A Prosthesis at Hand

In India an average of 25,000 people a year lose a limb due to illness or accident. A majority of the population lives below the poverty line and is consequently unable to afford insurance, healthcare costs or a prosthesis.[41] People lose limbs quicker in poor countries than in the West. This is caused, among other things, by illness, accidents due to unsafe conditions and landmines, or the inability to effectively combat the complications thereof. This is also the case in India. Although polio has been eradicated in India, there are still some four million people who have to live with the consequences of this disease. Diabetes and wound infections are important causes of amputations.

Dr. Bapna, Dr. Purohit and Mr. Mehta see it as their duty to help underprivileged patients who are amputees. There is no organization other than BMVSS in India where patients can receive a made-to-measure prosthesis at no charge. It is no surprise then that the higher goal of BMVSS is "physical, economic and social reha-

---

[40] Menon and Kumar (2008).
[41] Mack et al. (2003).

bilitation of the disabled, so that they regain their mobility and dignity, thereby making them normal, self-respecting and productive members of society."[42] In order to achieve this, BMVSS produces a prosthesis at a fraction of the cost compared with one from the West. The unique aspect of a Jaipur Foot is that it costs USD 50 (EUR 40) to produce and measure it. By comparison, a similar prosthesis in America costs an average of USD 12,000 (EUR 9600)[43]; the costs in Europe are a bit lower, but often exceed USD 5900 (EUR 4700) as well!

Everyone who requires a prosthesis is helped free of charge at BMVSS. One of the founders, Mr. Mehta, explains why: "Once you start asking for a fee for the service, the most vulnerable section of the population is affected, whilst this population group serves society the most."[44] The higher goal of BMVSS is implemented by participants focusing on the needs of the disabled instead of on their ability to pay for a prosthesis. For the purpose of focusing on these needs and at the same time providing the prosthesis at no charge, both the production costs and overhead costs are kept as low as possible. An important strategy for monitoring the operational integrity and frugality of the organization is to focus on financial expenses from time to time.[45] At 14 %, the overhead costs of BMVSS are exceptionally low; comparable nonprofit organizations have an overhead level of 20 %. In that regard, 86 % is spent on the primary process, while the comparable figure for western producers of prostheses is closer to 50 %. Mr. Mehta explains that each dollar is spent on their core objective: "From the beginning, I have aimed for a culture where money is only spent on our goal. We even go so far as to avoid serving tea at our meetings, even though a cup of tea costs a mere two cents in India."

BMVSS excels in cost leadership and operational excellence which enables them to provide people with a physical handicap with a prosthesis at no charge. The prosthesis is of such high quality that it can even be used in difficult living conditions. The disabled can cycle, run, walk and even dance again. The most vulnerable population group is empowered. BMVSS ensures that the physically disabled regain their dignity and mobility. This desirer is also expressed by Mr. Mehta as follows: "We want to recover and enhance the dignity and self-respect of those we serve." The disabled can participate fully in society once again.

Aside from the fact that BMVSS enables the disabled to regain their self-respect and dignity, the quality of the Jaipur Foot is equal to that of prostheses produced in the West. A study conducted by Royal Liverpool Hospital into the quality of the Jaipur Foot revealed that it provides the most natural performance compared to other prostheses. The Jaipur Foot comes closest to the flexibility of a real foot or a real leg. BMVSS has become the world's largest producer of prostheses. Since 1975 it has helped over 1.3 million disabled people. In the clinics of BMVSS, an average of 20,000 disabled people receive a prosthesis every year and 45,000 crutches,

---

[42] See: http://www.jaipurfoot.org/who_we_are/vision_and_mission.html op Jaipur Foot (2013).

[43] See: http://www.jaipurfoot.org/images/JAIPUR_FOOT_KNEE-LIMB_BROCHURE.pdf op Jaipur Foot (2013).

[44] Kanani (2011).

[45] Idem.

Brand essence: The need of a disabled individual is the most important thing and not his/her ability to pay

Higher goal
- Physical, economic and social rehabilitation of all disabled individuals, so that they can regain their mobility and dignity

Brand roots
- Developed in 1968 as an answer to the western prostheses which were not affordable and usable in Indian living conditions
- From 1975 on marketed on a bigger scale via BMVSS

Audacious goal
- Enable as many people as possible with a disability to participate fully in society

Brand promise
- We offer prostheses and other orthopedic devices for free which enable customers to participate fully in society again

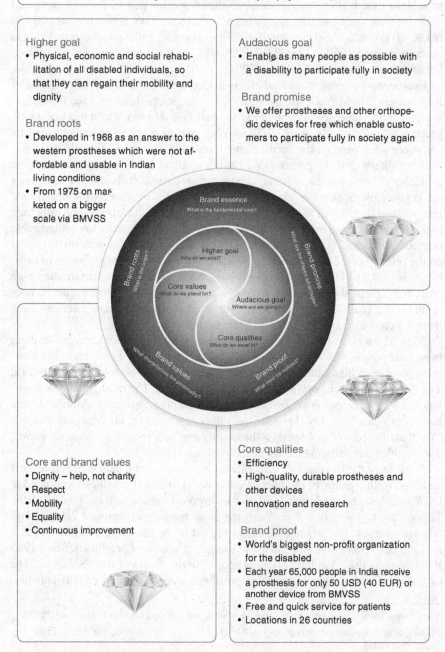

Core and brand values
- Dignity – help, not charity
- Respect
- Mobility
- Equality
- Continuous improvement

Core qualities
- Efficiency
- High-quality, durable prostheses and other devices
- Innovation and research

Brand proof
- World's biggest non-profit organization for the disabled
- Each year 65,000 people in India receive a prosthesis for only 50 USD (40 EUR) or another device from BMVSS
- Free and quick service for patients
- Locations in 26 countries

Figure 8.4.1 Vision and Positioning of Jaipur Foot

wheelchairs or another aid. BMVSS has an annual budget of USD 3.5 million (approximately EUR 2.6 million): 10 % is financed by its own revenues, 60 % comes from donors around the world and 30 % stems from government subsidies.

BMVSS has established mobile clinics in 26 countries where poverty is prevalent. Examples of such countries include the Philippines, Afghanistan, and Sudan—current or former war zones where many people are injured by landmines, for example. Doctors and technicians on location are responsible for measuring, producing, and delivering the prosthesis. "You'll find the Jaipur Footprint in countries with the most difficult conditions. These are places where people need help the most," notes Mr. Mehta.

BMVSS is completely dependent upon donations and subsidies. This is also the bottleneck that determines the total number of prostheses that are produced and delivered.[46] It is not possible for them to utilize the maximum capacity of the organization. "We have the capacity to produce 10.000 more prostheses annually, but this production is not maximized due to our dependence upon donations," says Mr. Mehta.

8.4.2 The Business Model: Participating in Society Again

A technological masterpiece within everyone's reach—that could well be an apt description of the Jaipur Foot. It is an organization that makes patients the focal point instead of letting them wade through reams of bureaucratic red tape. Everything is done to work as efficiently as possible to assist as many physically disabled individuals as possible. It is, after all, a product that literally changes people's lives!

Market Segments: Everyone Who Requires a Prosthesis BMVSS is the world's largest nonprofit organization for the benefit of physically disabled individuals. Its target group is broad: all physically disabled individuals worldwide who need a prosthesis or other orthopedic aid. Segmentation is not part of the equation; everyone in need of a prosthesis is helped. It does not matter who you are; BMVSS makes sure that you can walk and fully participate in society again. If the physically disabled individual cannot come to BMVSS, BMVSS will go to the patient by organizing an on-site treatment camp in remote areas of India. BMVSS focuses in particular on physically disabled individuals who under normal circumstances cannot afford a prosthesis. That sets BMVSS apart from other prosthetic manufacturers that focus on patients who can pay. SACH and Seattle Foot also offer prostheses, but these are considerably more expensive. Competition is not viewed as something negative given that these organizations also wish to assist as many people as possible. This philosophy is also reflected in the fact that BMVSS did not file a patent for the Jaipur Foot. The number of people that BMVSS is able to reach is limited in particular by practical limitations, such as the necessary funds to make and measure more

---

[46] To understand the meaning and the role of a bottleneck, see for instance the standard work on this topic by Goldratt and Cox (1986).

prostheses. The focus lies on where the need is greatest and people can be helped the most. The patients helped in India are primarily people who have lost a limb through illnesses such as polio, wound infections and complications from chronic disorders like diabetes. Furthermore, BMVSS focuses globally in particular on rendering assistance in conflict zones, where large groups of people lose a limb due to landmines, for example.

Customer Value: I Can Walk and Participate in Society Again! Disabled individuals in India often lead a "second-class life." If they cannot work, there is no safety net to catch them. After receiving a prosthesis, BMVSS customers can participate in society once again. Where at first they could no longer work due to the absence of a limb, a prosthesis now allows them to return to work and provide an income for themselves. This is vital, especially in developing countries where social security systems are largely absent. In that case, a prosthesis makes a world of difference and produces much joy and relief. BMVSS helps patients maintain their dignity. Customers do not have to pay, but the financial assistance provided is not emphasized. The process from the initial assessment to obtaining a prosthesis takes 1–3 days. A major difference with the Western world is that after patients have had their prosthesis measured, they only need to return one time after several weeks to have it tailored to their size and fit. Sometimes patients in the West have to visit a clinic a number of times before everything is fine. If this were to happen in India or other developing countries, it would create huge barriers given the long distances and the transport options that people have or do not have. In this way, BMVSS makes an enormous difference for people with a physical disability who otherwise would never receive the required prosthesis or aids due to their financial and social circumstances. Although putting on a prosthesis and seeing how it works continues to be a tense moment for most if not all amputees, the wealth of experience and huge numbers of people with a BMVSS prosthesis engenders considerable trust. In addition, if you are disabled in a country lacking a social safety net and can only benefit from this prosthesis, receiving one will give you hope for a future in which you can care for yourself once again.

Delivery: Care When and Where You Want It True marketing and sales relate primarily to finding and convincing donors. This often concerns major funds and governments that do receive an enormous benefit in exchange for their investments, because people will become productive in and for society again after they have been fitted with a prosthesis. Investments are achieved via networking for fundraising, which is supported by free publicity and seminars to spread the BMVSS story far and wide. Future donors are proactively invited to come and take a look behind the scenes of BMVSS. Demonstrating to donors the difference that Jaipur Foot makes in people's lives elicits larger donations and greater involvement in the organization's ambitions. The Jaipur Foot also sells itself. An example of this is the word-of-mouth advertising that occurs when someone has just received a prosthesis. People who walk around with a Jaipur Foot also provide a very visible and mobile means of advertising. Organizations are inspired to set up a treatment camp in collaboration with BMVSS, such as in the case of ArcelorMittal in Liberia.[47]

Patients are given attention and treated with empathy and care. They can seek assistance in the mobile or other clinics of BMVSS at any time on any given day. By setting up mobile clinics in addition to its regular clinics in more remote areas, BMVSS enables people below the poverty line to gain better access to a prosthesis.

They can be admitted 24 h per day. During treatment, patients along with any family members who have travelled with them may stay at BMVSS free of charge. An appointment is not necessary—in accordance with Indian culture. So if a new patient has to wait, that is all part of the process. The initial assessment is unique when compared with what normally happens in healthcare. Every patient at BMVSS is first observed and then registered (instead of vice versa). A permanent staff member is then assigned to the patient throughout his/her stay. Measuring a prosthesis takes 3 h on average. Within 1–3 days, patients can return home with a prosthesis or other orthopedic aid.

Operation: According to the Assembly Line Method   Whereas a BMVSS prosthesis might be a fraction of the cost normally associated with prostheses in the West, the requirements for its effective use in some territories is not lower but rather higher. For instance, a solution had to be found to complete the process of measuring, producing and tailoring within 1–3 days, so that individuals need travel to and from the clinic for the actual treatment only once and be assisted quickly. That is why the production process is incredibly simple with standard procedures for receiving, registering and measuring patients, producing and adjusting the prosthesis, and discharging patients. Consequently, product requirements are more extreme in terms of durability, functionality and maintenance. And production is provided in an entirely different approach than in the West, where it is all about made-to-measure prostheses instead of mass production. In Western countries, prostheses are an exception that may certainly command a price. The development and further improvement of a prosthesis at BMVSS is therefore a typical example of innovation originating in drastic simplification, cost reduction and economies of scale which occur because it is the only way to solve the problem.[48]

Each prosthesis is tailored by a specialized technician. The material costs for a prosthesis above the knee are on average USD 7.68 (EUR 5.65). The technology used is unique in the world. The Jaipur Foot is manufactured from HDPE plastic, which is flexible and light, but also strong. Furthermore, it is suitable for changing weather conditions. This is very important for use in countries like India. In many countries people walk around on bare feet or unprotected prostheses. Given the volumes, extreme requirements and social relevance, BMVSS is a challenging but attractive partner for Western companies that want to stay ahead. The lyrics "If I can make it there, I'll make it anywhere" from Frank Sinatra's signature song

---

[47] Pearson (2012).
[48] Christensen (1999, 2009).

Value for customers

Result *What do I get?*
- I can walk again and participate fully in society without limitations

Process *How do I get it?*
- Attention, empathy and personal care are given to me during my treatment

Emotion *What do I feel?*
- Happy, enabled and, relieved

Price *What are the costs?*
- I do not have to pay and the bill for the sponsor is extremely low with USD 50 (EUR 40) for a Jaipur foot

Effort *What do I have to do for it?*
- I can always come and receive a new prosthesis in 1 to 3 days

Risk *What are the uncertainties?*
- I am not certain how my life will be affected by a prosthesis, but I am guided properly and they have a lot of experience

Market segments

Position
- The largest non-profit organization in the world for the physically disabled. 65,000 people are helped each year

Competition
- The question is not the 'how' but the 'why': the primary market consists of people who do not have a prosthesis and there is no lack of demand.
- In terms of prostheses, SACH Foot and Seattle Foot (but far too expensive for the target group of BMVSS)

Target group
- All physically disabled individuals in the world who need a prosthesis or other orthopedic or medical device
- Besides India active in 26 countries in Asia, Africa and Central-America

Customer Insights
- When the physically disabled are provided with a prosthesis or device which is useable in their living conditions, they can participate fully and productively in society again

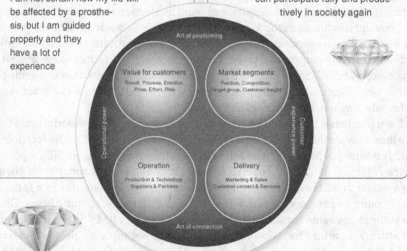

Figure 8.4.2   Value for customers and Market segments of Jaipur Foot

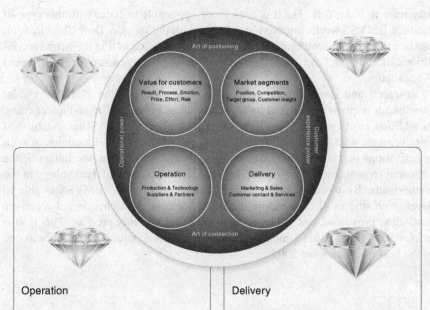

Operation

Production & Technology

- Approximately 60 patients a day receive a prosthesis which takes an average of 3 hours using an assembly line method.
- Durable high quality using HDPE plastics

Suppliers & Partners

- Dow Chemicals delivers supplies for the plastics and helps in product development.
- Innovation via intensive cooperation with a range of renowned scientific research institutes such as Stanford University and MIT in the US and Delft University of Technology in the Netherlands
- Cooperation with donors for funding of treatments and in starting up activities in new fields and areas

Delivery

Marketing & Sales

- Promotion via word-of-mouth advertising through satisfied, enabled patients who with their prosthesis are visible, tangible proof and walking examples
- Active recruitment of donors via partnerships, networks and publicity

Customer contact & Services

- Patients are central to the Jaipur Foot. They can come in 24 hours a day at no cost and without an appointment.
- Everyone is first admitted and registered only afterwards, which is unique in the medical world.
- Patients are given attention, empathy and personal care by one dedicated staff member

Figure 8.4.3 Operation and Delivery of Jaipur Foot

may refer to New York, but it is even more applicable to India with this type of product. BMVSS works intensively together with the supplier Dow Chemicals on plastics for product development. Wheelchairs that work well in the extreme conditions of India and are simultaneously affordable are procured by Whirlwind Wheelchairs.

Research and development are an important part of the BMVSS vision. Continuous improvement based on science ensures better quality and lower costs. In addition to its technologically advanced suppliers, BMVSS has established joint ventures with leading organizations in and beyond India. Examples of such organizations include Stanford University and MIT in America, the Indian Space Research Organization (ISRO) in India and Delft University of Technology in the Netherlands. By working together with leading universities, BMVSS is able to develop prostheses of outstanding quality. As a result, patients do not receive a third-class prosthesis, but rather an innovative, high-quality product. This is also evident from the fact that Time Magazine selected the Stanford-Jaipur Knee as one of the best innovations in 2009.[49]

8.4.3   Result: Participation in Society

BMVSS has helped more than 1.3 million customers. Each year, the organization assists 65,000 people, 20,000 of whom receive a prosthesis and 45,000 another aid. The value that BMVSS provides for these customers is abundantly clear: the accessible, high-quality and free prostheses and other aids ensure that physically disabled individuals, who often live below the poverty line, are able once again to participate fully in society both socially and in terms of work. The impact that this has on society is the fuel on which employees, initiators, donors and society run.

BMVSS is a nongovernmental organization with its head office in Jaipur, India, and 26 clinics throughout the country. The Executive Committee consists of public figures, such as social workers, medical experts and financial experts. The founder, Mr. Mehta, is still the incumbent CEO. Due to its NGO status, BMVSS is completely dependent upon donations. In general, BMVSS enjoys a lot of awareness with donors in India itself and abroad. Thirty percent of its budget comes from the Indian government, 60 % from donors and 10 % from other sources such as contributions by customers themselves. BMVSS has an annual budget of USD 3.5 million (approximately EUR 2.6 million).[50]

There is still more demand for prostheses than can be met with funds which are provided by the Indian government, philanthropic organizations and other donors.

---

[49] See: http://jaipurfoot.org/what_we_do/prosthesis/stanford_jaipur_knee.html at Jaipur Foot (2013).

[50] Kanani (2011).

The funds are invested for the purpose of producing as many prostheses as possible. As a nonprofit organization with the aim of helping as many disabled individuals as it can, BMVSS is focused on cost control.[51] Costs are kept low in a variety of ways, including by working with locally sourced materials. Thanks to this approach, 43 % of BMVSS costs goes towards material, 31 % on labor, 12 % on mobile clinics, and 14 % on overhead. That means that 86 % of the costs of BMVSS are related to the production process.[52] This makes BMVSS unique! For instance, Ossur, a producer in Iceland, only spends 48 % of funds on the production process.

The 200 employees of BMVSS are highly motivated. The production process is labor-intensive, and the technicians who work for BMVSS receive special training before they may begin. In addition, further specialization is encouraged. Everything is focused on helping the patient better and setting up the production process more efficiently. Aside from one permanent doctor who has been hired, local doctors donate their time on a part-time basis. The intrinsic motivation among employees is enormous, because they make a difference in the lives of patients. Technicians earn on average USD 100 dollars (EUR 80) per month—twice as much as the average wage in India, but far less then the salary they could make elsewhere.[53]

India does not have any social security or medical benefits for its citizens, which means that they are completely dependent upon family members. Many people die of easily treatable diseases, simply because the money for treatment is not available.[54] The loss of a limb is disastrous for the lives of working people. If these people are furnished with a prosthesis, they can participate in society again and the labor participation rate increases. It makes someone who is an invalid able-bodied again. Consequently, delivering "free" prostheses has a very favorable impact on the Indian economy.

BMVSS has received various humanitarian and innovation awards. The Jaipur Foot is a high-quality prosthesis comparable with Western prostheses in terms of quality, but produced at a fraction of the cost thanks to operational excellence.

8.4.4   The Brilliant Lessons of Jaipur Foot

What can we learn from BMVSS's example? And what lessons can we draw from this business model?

- BMVSS is a typical example of the type of breakthrough required to make a difference at the "bottom of the social pyramid", where most people with the least amount of money are found.[55] This is the type that is only found if that is the only

---

[51] Mack et al. (2003).

[52] Idem.

[53] Idem.

[54] https://www.solidairmetindia.nl/uploads/newsletter/128d816e04c4aa95345ba7c35564d08 c0a506087.pdf.

[55] Prahalad (2009).

Value by customers
- So far 1.3 million patients have been helped free of charge. That is the equivalent of 65,000 customers a year, 20,000 of whom receive a prosthesis and another 45,000 a different device
- Customers reveal the purpose and success of BMVSS by being the walking example of the impact the Jaipur Foot has had on them to become productive members of society again

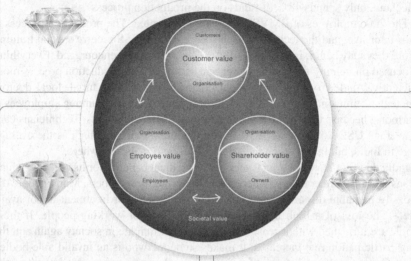

Value for and by employees
- 200 people work for BMVSS in 20 clinics.
- Patients are given attention, empathy and personal care thanks to the devotion and commitment of the care providers
- Jaipur Foot does not pay very poorly as an employer: a technical specialist who fits the prosthesis earns approximately twice the average wage in India.
- Employees are well trained and certified which contributes to their employability

Value for and by shareholders
- The donations for Jaipur Foot are provided by government (30%), charitable organizations and private donors, including existing and former patients
- The Jaipur Foot costs USD 50 (EUR 40) – in the US this is about USD 12000 (EUR 9600)! 86% of the budget is invested directly in the primary process (compared to around 50% in Western factories)

Value for and by society
- The prosthesis and devices make a huge difference: they enable people to participate fully and productively in society and take care of themselves and others
- People who are enabled need less support from public funding and conversely can make a contribution to it
- The Stanford-Jaipur Knee was selected as one of the top innovations in 2009 by Time Magazine

Figure 8.4.4 Value for and by stakeholders of Jaipur Foot

way to resolve a problem, simply because there are no more resources available. If necessity is the mother of invention, then innovation is a driving factor in the pathway to success.[56] The quality of the Jaipur Foot is comparable with that of Western prostheses and its patents are freely available. Since BMVSS gets the most out of challenging circumstances, its success could create competition for existing producers of prostheses in affluent countries. If you can make it in the type of conditions prevalent in India, then you make it anywhere in the world.

- By constantly innovating, BMVSS remains an inspiring partner that has to be regarded as a player in the global market. This attracts leading universities that are helping to strengthen the operations of BMVSS. In this way, BMVSS continues to improve its product—prostheses—in cooperation with these universities. In return, these educational institutions gladly attach their name to the mission of BMVSS.
- Operational excellence and cost leadership create the opportunity to produce prostheses at a fraction of the cost compared with those of other producers. An optimum process generates minimal waste, allowing almost all of the money to be spent on patients and more to be produced for less.

As set out above, capacity is not being maximized. The revenue model is not set up in such a way that it is able to entirely finance potential growth. BMVSS could research how it could optimize this aspect. One idea to that end is that patients pay according to their ability to do so. People who are missing a limb have no money, but a contribution could also be deferred based on their future ability to pay. If after the measurement of a prosthesis people become self-sufficient again, they could, for example, still pay for part or all of their prosthesis with the money they have earned after a year. A wonderful idea would be if someone with a new prosthesis donated money, so that two other persons as a present could receive a new prosthesis!

---

[56] Christensen (1997, 2009).

Chapter 9
Breakthrough: Implementing Differentiation in Specialized Healthcare

How Can Schedulable and Academic Healthcare Be Organized Best in the Second and Third Line?

Besides the primary care and chronical diseases where the proximity to the patient is leading there is also specialized Healthcare where concentration of treatments helps to improve health and/or lowers costs. This concerns schedulable treatments where economies of scale can be realized in terms of quality and/or price. Further, there is and always will be a need for a very select number of top academic institutes. If it involves specific diagnoses and treatments which can be provided stand-alone this can be done in specialized hospitals to avoid complexity and overhead. If it concerns integrated treatments in which different medical conditions are involved it can require broad general or academic hospitals.

- *Narayana Hrudayalaya is a brilliant example of the sort of hospitals which arise in India to provide excellent quality of care for 5 % of the costs in the west by optimal use of scarce resources.*
- *ThedaCare is a showcase of a hospital which uses the lean way of working to improve care continuously for patients in close cooperation with all its employees.*
- *Princess Margaret Cancer Centre shows the result which can be made with concentrating expertise while overcoming the challenges this poses with the large distances in Canada.*
- *Mayo Clinic shows what you can offer to the world and patients if you skip all barriers to do the right thing and simply concentrate of giving patients the best care you can envision.*

The last breakthrough to look at is specialized healthcare. The schedulable part of this can be optimized with the "process" serving as a guiding principle to optimize in the organization. In addition, this relates to highly specialized care that really should be bundled based on "knowledge". In countries where the healthcare

© Springer International Publishing Switzerland 2017   311
J. Kemperman et al. (eds.), *Brilliant Business Models in Healthcare*,
DOI 10.1007/978-3-319-26440-0_9

infrastructure has recently been built up or the population density is very low, there has often traditionally been a lot of concentration based on process and/or knowledge. In particular the challenge is how to go about reaching people in cooperation with primary healthcare supported by technology such as telemedicine. That is a whole lot different than the situation in Europe and both coasts of the continental USA. In these areas the current healthcare infrastructure can only be partially understood based on the current demand for healthcare services. Such demand has also, historically speaking, grown in a period when people had to travel long distances on foot, by horse or by carriage and certainly not everyone had a car. That limited people's range of operation. In the 1960s there was still little in the way of specialization. The lion's share of hospital work was done by the surgeon and the internist with nurses. In that regard, hospitals were very similar but this was no problem since they primarily had a regional function.[1] In other words, most patients could rightfully talk about "my" or "our" hospital in the neighborhood. Over the past years, conscious or unconscious decisions have been made regarding differentiation and focus on the specializations in which healthcare providers want to be the best. This still concerns an organic process and it is not even close to being completed. In the upcoming decade many hospitals in Western countries will make a conscious decision for the business model by which they want to stand out. This is also needed to create a clear position with added value in networks in which treatment paths are conducted in cooperation between different healthcare providers. Some of the providers will merge with another entity or disappear entirely. While the phasing out of capacity is needed, it is also a difficult and painful process during which people must subordinate their own interests and grant each other the necessary slack to that end. This goal will, for instance, often demand mergers, alliances, and acquisitions before duties are reallocated. The parties concerned will then be able to continue working in new entities that are partially or even fully independent. This development is already visible in various countries in the West.

A rough picture of the possible healthcare infrastructure of the future can be outlined for countries that are currently setting up a healthcare infrastructure or where the existing infrastructure is being adapted in order to make this secure for the future.[2] In general segmentation terms, a distinction can be made in the positioning of healthcare providers based on the extent of specialization versus breadth on the one hand and based on the guiding principle in organizing (nearby, process or expertise) on the other.

As outlined in the previous chapters, in the future part of the care will be provided at home and by people themselves. In the physical healthcare infrastructure, there is primary care and cure that can best be organized near the patient with the

---

[1] Al (1981).

[2] See for instance: Porter and Teisberg (2006), Bohmer (2009) and World Economic Forum and McKinsey (2013).

personal approach 'nearby' serving as the guiding principle to optimize in organizing healthcare. This typically plays a role in primary healthcare that is not particularly complex. This for instance concerns one or more doctors and primary caregivers that share a building. In addition, there also seems to be more space for specialized diagnosis centers near the primary care for simple tests and scans that are carried out often. In terms of organizational characteristics, these combine customer-oriented retail services for primary care with elements of more streamlined schedulable care. In addition, there remains a need for small hospitals with a more local function for acute healthcare with a maximum of traveling distances and for treatments that often occur such as for broken bones and pregnancies. All these forms of physical healthcare seem to primarily benefit from organization based on the personal approach 'nearby', otherwise the danger of overhead and bureaucracy is greater than the potential for synergy. Different types of organizations that share this basis of being organized around the customer are UCLA's Value Quotient, ParkinsonNet, Laastari, Patrick Lund, and Ryhov.

Aside from the movement to bring healthcare closer to the patient, there is also care that benefits from being bundled and concentrated in hospitals with a greater or much greater service area. In that regard there are primarily two arguments that can be made in favor of bundling. Firstly, it is possible that things can be done much more efficiently and with fewer errors thanks to economies of scale with process optimization as the guiding principles in organization. Secondly, it is also possible that things will truly become better if all expertise is bundled at one location with knowledge serving as the guiding principle in organization.[3] In both the process optimization and the bundling of knowledge, it is possible to do so with the focus on one specific treatment or with the broader scope on various treatments. On this basis, we can look for inspiration at four archetypes of business models for larger hospitals. It should be noted in that regard that some roles undermine each other if they are integrated in a single organization, but that a number can be combined or at least share the same location. In this way it seems entirely logical that a broad-based hospital with streamlined processes or rather with bundled expertise also fulfills the role of regional hospital within its own environment. Further, it is useful to imagine that a broad-based hospital with streamlined processes also has a specific treatment unit for one schedulable, standardized treatment which is organized and managed as a relatively separate entity. A top academic club will not only excel in a specific field, but generally also has an educational goal, which means that relatively easy treatments must also be carried out there. It is also possible that it has a specific field in which it is a leader both nationally and internationally.

---

[3] For a description of a possible healthcare infrastructure of the future, see for instance: Porter and Teisberg (2006), de Lugt et al. (2013) and Idenburg and Van Schaik (2013).

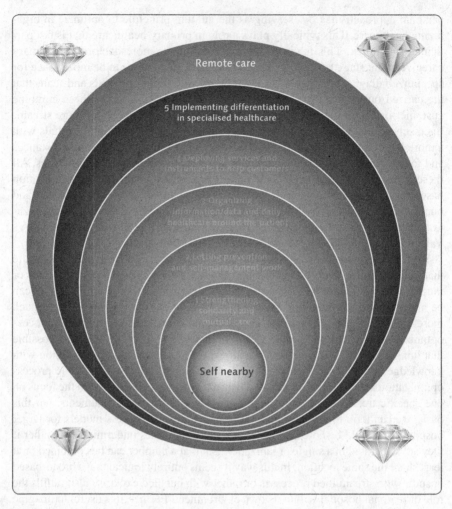

Figure 9.0.1 Breakthrough: Implementing differentiation in specialised healthcare

Business Models Like Narayana Hrudayalaya Truly specialized work within healthcare is shifting to diagnosis and more complex disorders. Where traditionally almost all healthcare treatments required broad expertise, they themselves are increasingly becoming relatively standardized processes.[4] These can be described and improved by endless repetition and refinement, i.e., by way of specialization. This applies to simple surgeries, such as laser eye procedures and hip and knee surgeries, but also to complex procedures, such as open-heart surgery. Schedulable treatments where economies of scale can be realized in terms of quality and/or

---

[4]Christensen et al. (2009).

price will become increasingly concentrated. This bundling increases the value and quality of the treatment due to the fact that expertise and experience increase, while at the same time it reduces the costs as the process and the surgery become even more streamlined.[5] Good examples of this are provided by hospitals that focus on the customer and the market to specialize in one treatment as a focused factory,[6] also known as the value-added process business.[7] The most pioneering examples of these focused factories are currently found in India. This is where hospitals can be found that realize volumes comparable with the entire number of treatments in medium-sized European countries or several states in America. Consequently, they also deliver comparably high levels of quality but for merely 5–15 % of the costs. The example under discussion here is the Narayana Hrudayalaya Cardiac Hospital. This hospital has been in existence since 2001. It has developed into a hospital that carries out most complex heart operations in the world at a fraction of the cost in Western countries. It has the capacity to carry out 50 treatments per day during peak times. It has adapted innovatively in a country where the demand for health-care services is extremely greater than the volume of healthcare services provided. It has done so by optimizing its use of available capacity in terms of funds, resources and people. Rich people pay a bit more, as a result of which poor people can also be helped. At the same time the hospital is very profitable, which is necessary to finance its further growth. Narayana Hrudayalaya is, however, no exception; another famous example is Aravind Eye Hospital.[8] The inspiration for standardiz-ing eye operations is the process for cooking hamburgers at McDonald's. The suc-cess percentages rival and beat top Western hospitals, while its costs—at USD 35–41 per treatment (EUR 31–37)—are merely around 5 %. Focused factories are, however, not a new development. The classic example is Shouldice, which special-izes in hernia operations. Since the 1980s, this hospital has been reviewed multiple times and it is in the top five of the best-sold cases of Harvard.[9] Because this is a historical landmark and example, it is described separately at the end of this sec-tion. There are many more examples of this type of focused factory. In the field of hernia operations in the Netherlands, for instance, there is a specialized ward in the Diakonessenhuis hospital and in the field of hand and wrist surgery a good example is ExpertClinic. In Finland, the Coxa Hospital performs many relatively simple operations, such as hip and knee surgery. This also holds true for more complex operations: Geisinger concentrates on cardiology, whereas Cancer Treatment Centers of America specializes in oncology, but then across the board, providing many supplemental and alternative treatments.

---

[5] For descriptions of the concentration and optimization of hospitals, see for instance: Porter and Teisberg (2006), Bohmer (2009) and Christensen et al. (2009).

[6] See for instance: Herzlinger (1994, 1996).

[7] Christensen et al. (2009).

[8] Kemperman et al. (2013).

[9] See Heskett (2003) and Heskett and Hallowell (2005), Heskett et al. (1997), Herzlinger (1994, 1996) and Khandelwal (2009).

Business Models Like ThedaCare Many patients require more care than just one specific treatment. While it is often not possible to have all the treatments in a regional hospital, this does not mean that it requires an organization with a range of academic disciplines. In that light, there also seems to be room in the long term for a number of broad-based hospitals that organize and coordinate processes efficiently and in a customer-oriented manner. This actually relates to the subgroup of "regular" patients for whom there is no very specific, defined surgery. It concerns, for instance, people with various disorders or a medical history or age for whom there is a major risk that different treatments may be required due to complications. This demands general hospitals that optimize their processes within and between units. Perhaps even more than with the solution shops that optimize their processes in treatment centers, the best hospitals in this category work extensively in accordance with the Lean philosophy, as it has become known at Toyota. The example studied to that end is ThedaCare. This is a trend-setting example of a broad-based hospital that continuously improves itself on the basis of customer focus and leadership. Examples of comparative broad-based hospitals with streamlined collaboration are Virginia Mason and the University of Pittsburgh Medical Centre.

Business Models Like Princess Margaret Cancer Centre There is integrated care and primary retail solutions organized around the patient, acute and simple care in local care institutions, and standardized, concentrated care in efficient hospitals. Further, there will always be a need for top university institutes. In that regard, knowledge is brought together for the purpose of jointly and truly expanding ideas, conducting research and carrying out new, complex treatments. This concerns in particular those areas that are truly knowledge-intensive, i.e., where the best specialists are needed. The people that work there are often very motivated and driven by the content and prepared to work and learn hard. At the same time, these are not the most efficient organizations. Top university institutes also need leeway and room to experiment and acquire in-depth information. It can concern broad-based teaching hospitals, as well as a disorder that is, relatively speaking, a stand-alone case and regarding which there is room for a specific, first-rate expertise center. This can also be called a "solution shop."[10] The example that has been studied here is that of Princess Margaret Cancer Centre, a leading clinical hospital in Canada focused on oncological disorders. Located in the middle of universities and other knowledge-intensive institutes, the organization brings science and practice under one roof. Doctors accomplish top results in both fields by coming alongside patients during their treatments and supporting them in a coaching role in order to take up the fight against cancer together. Another example is the National Jewish Medical & Research Centre in Denver, Colorado, which focuses primarily on diagnoses and is a true expertise center when it comes to asthma.

---

[10] Christensen et al. (2009).

Business Models Like Mayo Clinic Aside from the specialized and highly specialized top institutes, there is a need for a very select number of top, broad-based academic hospitals. This concerns in particular the truly knowledge-intensive areas that require a multidisciplinary approach. Above all, where it concerns complicated combinations of symptoms, a collection of academic expertise is ideal and often sorely needed. It relates to, for instance, the diagnosis of exotic disorders whereby it is unclear as to what that patient has. In that case, we can think of the patients that spend a year being cared for by various healthcare professionals and constantly trying different treatments without this resulting in a clear analysis of the disorder and the corresponding treatment. It can also concern various surgeries and unexpected complications that involve different areas of expertise. That demands that the services of the best specialists in the country or even in the world are bundled into the relevant fields of specialization. These are locations where research and practice are combined, and are producing state-of-the-art innovation. The best known example of a hospital that provides this is Mayo Clinic. Within Mayo Clinic, multidisciplinary teams work at the top level, fully focused on making the patient better. Within such broad-based top academic institutes, these are in fact solution shops where broad-based expertise is organized around a specific organ like the heart. Another example of such an approach is Cleveland Clinic, which employs solution shops for neurology and cardiology.

The Brilliant Business Model of Shouldice[11]

Experience is irreplaceable

Karlijn Korten, André Kok & Jeroen Kemperman @: Jeroen.Kemperman@achmea.nl, Phone: 0031 651222099

Shouldice is famous worldwide. It is one of the bestselling Harvard business cases of all time and currently used as case material in over 500 MBA programs. This case was described for the first time by Heskett in 1983 and has since been enriched and spread around the world. When we look at it today, the hospital is still faithful to its roots, principles and methods of the past decennia. It is still a world-class example from the perspective of customer excellence and journeys, and social design. It scores remarkably high in relation to customer satisfaction and NPS. From a purely medical perspective, the "Shouldice method" is no longer the best practice and standard in the world. Additionally, growth is limited as a private hospital with a fixed number of beds in the public system of Canada. Since Shouldice is rather well known, we chose to discuss the case of NH Cardiac Hospital as an example of a focused factory in more detail. But we naturally could not overlook the legendary and inspiring example of Shouldice which has been and is an example for so many hospitals and service providers in other industries. Why did Shouldice become so famous?

---

[11] See for the case for instance: Heskett (2003), Heskett and Hallowell (2005), Heskett et al. (1997), Herzlinger (1994, 1996), Khandelwal (2009) and Korten (2008). See for the medical status for instance the European guidelines for treatment of inguinal hernias. This case is also described as a full case following the conceptual framework of Brilliant Business models in Kemperman et al. (2014).

The roots of Shouldice can be traced back to the Second World War. At that time, Dr. Edward Earle Shouldice, an army major, notices that many volunteers cannot join the army because of their hernias. He develops a fast new treatment that enables 70 men to enlist. After the war, 200 civilians contact him seeking treatment and he opens the Shouldice hospital, which focuses exclusively on hernia treatments for people who are otherwise healthy.

The Cornerstone of Shouldice: There Is No Substitute for Experience From the outset, Shouldice has focused on providing the perfect hernia treatment: fast, efficient and excellent. This has been optimized and optimized by the experience of doctors and the experience of patients. The Shouldice treatment was unique in the way it integrated the perspective, behavior and responsibilities of the customer within the process from the very beginning. The standardization also implies that Shouldice focuses purely on healthy patients. It is all about standardization towards perfection and empowerment of the customer as a quest and not as a patient. The result for the customer is a rapid, healthy recovery in a beautiful environment that looks like a hotel, but is actually a brilliant social design focused on the recovery of hernia patients.

The Business Model: Walking Through the Shouldice Experience Shouldice focuses on customers who only have a hernia (more specifically, abdominal wall fractures such as inguinal hernia, umbilical hernia repairs and femoral hernias). Someone who is overweight is not admitted until the excess weight has been lost. In the case of multiple diseases, people are redirected to a general hospital more able to deal with any complications. Due to its extreme focus, Shouldice does not have any direct competitors and has been able to treat more than 350,000 patients since its establishment. Its value for customer is the high success rates thanks to the combination of experience and standardization, the competitive price and the unique experience of the treatment itself which gives a feeling of comfort and self-control. People take control of their treatment instead of the treatment taking control of them. The delivery process is unique and filled with small highly intelligent details that stimulate self-control and recovery. When people arrive, they eat lunch together with people who just had surgery the day before and can share their experiences. Newly admitted patients see people playing pool who had a hernia the day before. People are asked to climb off the operating table themselves directly after surgery. There are no TVs in the rooms to stimulate people to leave their rooms (a trick which was of course easier before the mobile phone). The steps of the stairs are somewhat lower to give you the impression you can climb them in no time. The garden has different heights to encourage exercise. In short, this is one major customer journey to walk through and recover!

The Results: The Customer Attraction of Customers The result of the Shouldice treatment is that people stimulate themselves and each other to work on their own recovery, which increases the success rate. The actual loyalty rate is very low since people are not supposed to require another treatment, but they do return, for the reunions which used to be organized by Shouldice. People also enjoy sharing their experiences. Shouldice has many stories to offer in this regard and therefore shares these as well, with or without social media and not only in their private networks but also in cases and books such as these. That constantly attracts many new customers. The doctors within the process focus on the hospital: they are not big innovators but specialists who enjoy optimizing one treatment and taking good care of patients in a friendly environment. Shares in the hospital are owned by two families, including the Shouldice descendants. The current turnover is CAD 20 million (EUR 13.8) and the family business has always provided a regular stream of income and profit based on the predictability of the number of treatments and costs. One of the difficulties faced by this private hospital is the fact that it exists within a public Canadian system, which limits expansion possibilities. The families are looking for international partners to operate abroad but this has proven difficult up until now due to permits. Even a Shouldice needs the support of society to flourish.

The Brilliant Lessons of Shouldice Shouldice has always been a leading example of a focused factory model. Nowadays there are also signs of the Phase 4 risks in which the challenge is to continue renewing while maintaining the core. This is an additional challenge since the business model is about polishing the details and deliberately avoiding major changes. How do you deal with the possibility of day treatments and recovery at home when your results in relation to self-management and additional fees are based on overnight stays in your recovery hotel? What always was and still is fascinating about Shouldice is the way in which it has designed the treatment as a social process. Theories on self-management and the personal responsibility of patients in treatment processes have been implemented in tangible and visible ways at Shouldice. Doing so not only required a medical understanding of the body, but also profound and practical human insights. The experience of Shouldice is not only valuable for doctors and patients, but for all people who want to help people improve their health.

9.1   Narayana Hrudayalaya

So much cardiology with scarce resources

Raymond Fafié, Jennifer op 't Hoog, and Jeroen Kemperman
@: Jennifer.op.t.hoog@achmea.nl, Phone: 0031 651226420
@: Jeroen.Kemperman@achmea.nl, Phone: 0031 651222099

Prelude *You don't expect to find cardiac care combined with a mass-market approach. The first time I heard about it I was surprised. The idea of exploiting economies of scale in the delivery of extremely complex surgery was new to me. But the Narayana Hrudayalaya Cardiac Hospital demonstrates the feasibility and advantages of this idea. It immediately made me think of my nephew, who was born with a hole in the dividing wall between the two chambers of his heart. By the time he was 16 he had undergone several heart operations. His life was one long round of trips to see the best cardiac surgeons in the Netherlands. There were always concerns for his family and the doctors who treated him, because it was possible that simply growing up would affect his heart function. These days my nephew leads a normal life, but would this be the case if he had been born into different circumstances, in India for example? What prospects would children such as my nephew face if the NH Cardiac Hospital did not exist? The hospital aims to provide high-quality care that is both affordable and accessible. Is the business model implemented by NH Cardiac Hospital capable of improving cardiac care worldwide with the quality of care required by people such as my nephew? After experiencing the social problems associated with healthcare during a stay in India, I became even more interested to find out how the business model adopted by this hospital is endeavoring to meet the high demand for care in India, starting with the demand for cardiac care. All of this led me to study the extremely inspiring business model pursued by the NH Cardiac Hospital, which is the subject of this case.*

Introduction   Imagine a hospital in a developing country—a country with extreme differences between social classes and extreme differences in income. A hospital where everyone is welcome, irrespective of their social class, status or financial situation. A hospital precisely like this was set up by the highly praised and inspiring Dr. Shetty, who is also its director. He has made cardiac care, which is usually costly, both affordable and accessible for many people in India and from other countries. Dr. Shetty wants to provide everyone in the world with affordable high-quality care and is working hard to achieve his dream. It is this dream that led to the establishment of the NH Cardiac Hospital in Bangalore in India. With 1000 beds, 24 operating theaters and an infrastructure that enables 50 major heart surgery operations daily, it is one of the world's largest cardiac hospitals.[12] Patients come here from more than 73 countries, the NH Cardiac Hospital performs the largest number of pediatric heart surgery operations worldwide and its doctors are able to implant the latest generation of artificial hearts. These impressive results are clearly underpinned by an inspiring business model.

Dr. Shetty is a cardiac surgeon who has created a revolution in cardiac care by offering high quality medical care in India at prices that are between 5 % and 10 % of those charged in America. Dr. Shetty's ultimate dream is to resolve the health problems of poor people throughout the world for just one dollar per person per day. This is a dream that many people will share with him. Yet the way that Dr. Shetty is seeking to achieve this dream is making an impression on both medical specialists and entrepreneurs. His business model enables the delivery of dangerous and high-risk surgery at progressively lower costs thanks to economies of scale. The way in which this is being accomplished is unique and the fact that it works is confirmed by the results. The nature of the business model means that large-scale operation is essential: lower costs lead to lower prices, which lead to higher volumes. These higher volumes then make it possible to keep costs low. The model seems to work extremely well in the Indian cardiac care market, where the demand for care exceeds the scarce supply. The NH Cardiac Hospital achieves better success rates (fewer complications and a lower mortality rate during the first 30 days after surgery) compared to similar hospitals in the USA.[13] In addition, the NH group has a higher after-tax profit margin (7.7 %) than American hospitals (6.9 %).[14] The results speak for themselves, but Dr. Shetty does not intend to stop here. With the help of his business model he is determined to change healthcare for the better throughout the world.

9.1.1 The Cornerstone: Why Bigger Is Better

The development of a new economic model in healthcare was prompted by cardiac care that is usually expensive. The model improves the accessibility of care for poor Indians, and ultimately enhances care throughout the world. To understand the need for new solutions it is good to take a look on the big challenges in India.

---

[12] Narayanahospitals.com and Anand (2009).

[13] Kemperman, Geelhoed & op 't Hoog (2013).

[14] Kothandaraman and Mookerjee (2007). Used more frequently in this case.

Healthcare in India is in scarce supply, especially in the countryside with cases where there is only one doctor available for around 200,000 people. On average, India has less than one doctor per 1000 people while in the USA this is 2.56 doctors per 1000 people. According to Ajay Dhankar from McKinsey Healthcare, healthcare in India appears hopeless in view of the sheer level of poverty and a government that does not fund basic care (India spent a mere 1 % of GDP in 2002/2003 on public healthcare). It is estimated that only 14 % of Indians have health insurance and can pay for treatment or borrow money to do so. More and more treatment is also being received by medical tourists: an estimated 150,000 foreign patients were treated in 2005. India has approximately 170 medical training programs, but 18,000 graduate doctors could not fill the gap of 45,000 doctors required in 2012. FICC/ Ernst & Young estimates an increase of one million beds that were required for hospital beds and surgical treatment in 2012. That is more than the Indian healthcare sector could and can cope with. Cardiovascular disease is the number one cause of deaths in India. Research shows that the Indian subcontinent accounts for 45 % of the global problem of cardiovascular disease. The average age at which a heart attack occurs there is 45, compared to 65 in the West. Of the estimated 2.4 million operations required in 2004, only 60,000 were performed that year.

India evidently needs a solution to the high demand for cardiovascular care. The business model used by NH Cardiac Hospital provides a response to this and facilitates the organization of care. The brand essence can be described as: "be the best hospital in the provision of affordable quality care for all, starting with cardiac care." The focus is on affordable quality care for everyone. Becoming the best hospital through this business model goes hand in hand with the realization of the specified goals.

Dr. Devi Prahad Shetty was born in Karnataka, India on 8 May 1953. Upon obtaining his graduate degree in medicine he went on to specialize in general surgery. After completing his studies and working in London he returned to India and cofounded the Asia Heart Foundation in Calcutta. During that period he was also involved in the construction of several large cardiac hospitals. In 1984, Dr. Shetty met Mother Theresa in Calcutta when treating her following a heart attack. Afterwards Mother Theresa accompanied Dr. Shetty on his hospital rounds for children with heart problems. She noticed the good work he did and told him that God had sent him to this world to help these children. That changed his outlook on his life and he started following her vision. To this day, he is dedicated to helping the less privileged. He opened the MHF hospital in Bangalore in 1997 and returned to this city in 2000, making it the centre of the NH Group. Narayana Hrudayalaya literally means "God's compassionate home." The NH Group comprises several healthcare institutions situated in different areas. Its flagship institution, the NH Cardiac Hospital, founded in 2001 and located in Bangalore, is the best-known example of Dr. Shetty's successful business model. Dr. Shetty's perseverance in attaining his goal to make advanced healthcare available to large groups of people must have compelled him to only take those decisions that support that higher goal. Certainly in a developing country such as India.

The moment Dr. Shetty established the NH Cardiac Hospital, he did so using a clear vision and promise to serve people and society. The hospital promised to provide affordable and accessible cardiac care for everyone, regardless of their caste, class, religion, and whether or not they were able to pay. The hospital would accept everyone in need of treatment and always uphold this promise. Today the group's staff are still inspired by Dr. Shetty's dream to ultimately heal the poor of the world for merely one dollar a day per person. And even if this dream is difficult to fulfill, it is still the audacious goal that drives the organization every day. Dr. Shetty has expressed a desire to set up "Health Cities" in all Indian states in the future, and to be represented in every emerging economy in the world without increasing healthcare costs. To get closer to the audacious goal, he strives to provide holistic and on-time care, expand knowledge and technology continuously, improve customer relations, and offer patients an enriching healthcare experience.

The NH Cardiac Hospital uses guiding values to successfully attain the specified goals. These values are: accessibility, affordability, high quality and a service-oriented approach, all of which are geared to serving society. Accessibility in India is still low due to the financial and infrastructural limitations affecting the majority of poor people. To make cardiac care accessible and affordable, it is important that people who need treatment actually also receive it. At the same time this requires a commercial solution and not a nonprofit one, according to Dr. Shetty who states that "Charity is not scalable". Expansion can only be realized by earning money which can be invested to finance the growth. The hospital devotes considerable energy to helping the less privileged, and the service-oriented approach can be described as the brand and core value. It seems logical for service to be the focal point within healthcare given the numerous contact moments with patients. The hospital also focuses on improving systems continuously in order to optimize service. Up until now, the values are clearly reflected in brand proof and core qualities.

The NH Cardiac Hospital must implement its core qualities in full to attain maximum accessibility, affordability, high quality, and excellent service. Efficiency is a key component in day-to-day work: specialization and standardization help bring the values to life. Innovation is also a core quality, in addition to specialist training and a leading position in the world of suppliers and partnerships. The economies of scale that NH achieves in the world of high-risk operations allow everyone in need of cardiac care to receive it at a lower cost compared to practically all similar hospitals. There are more factors that demonstrate the success of the business model: quality proof can be found, for example, in lower mortality rates in comparison with other hospitals, including the best in the US. Accessibility is proven by extensive NH networks throughout India and affordability because patients are always assisted, regardless of their financial position. People know beforehand exactly how much their treatment will cost. The NH Cardiac Hospital performs over 20 major operations daily and has a capacity for fifty, making it the largest pediatric heart hospital in the world. In addition, the overall approach taken by the NH Cardiac Hospital makes it a pioneer in a number of specific heart operations.

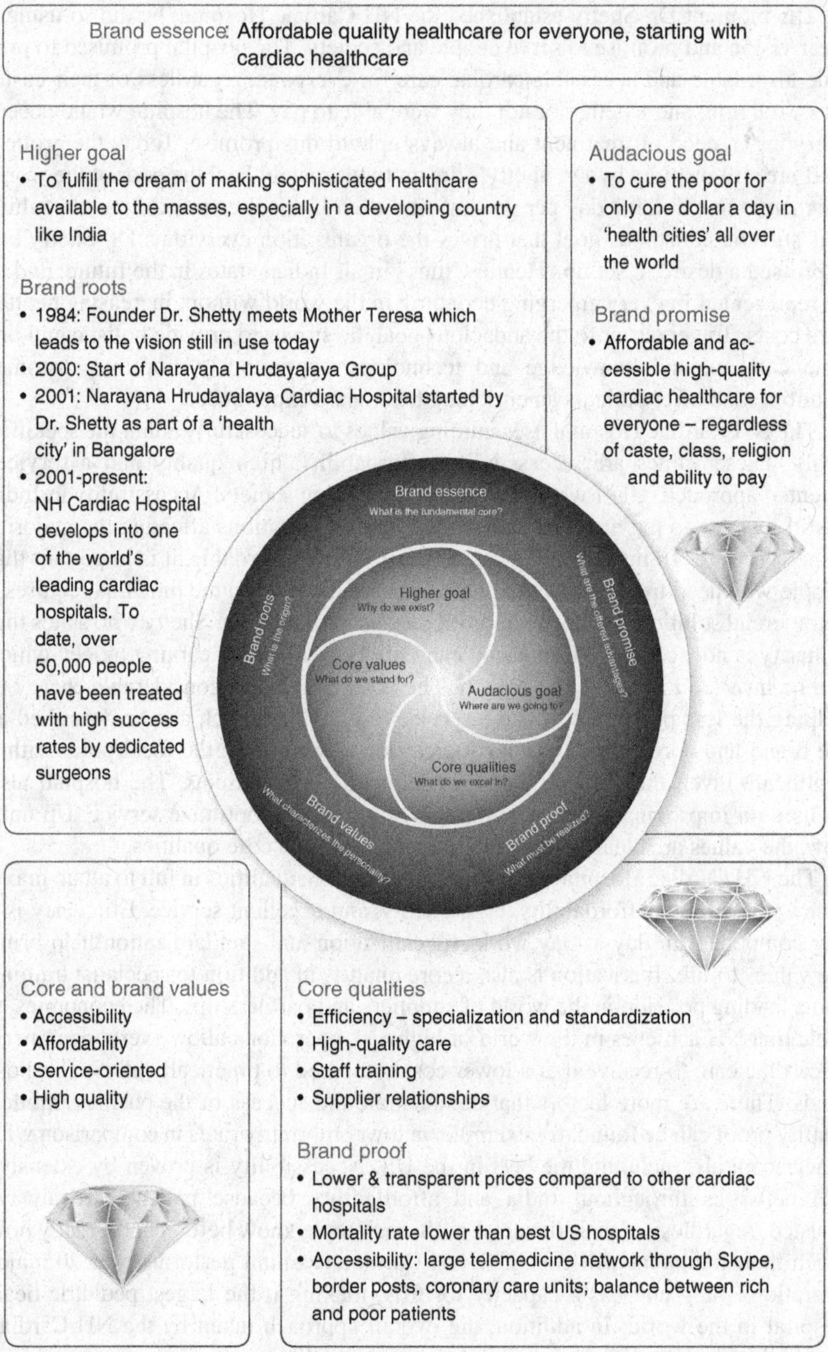
Brand essence: Affordable quality healthcare for everyone, starting with cardiac healthcare
Higher goal
• To fulfill the dream of making sophisticated healthcare available to the masses, especially in a developing country like India
Brand roots
• 1984: Founder Dr. Shetty meets Mother Teresa which leads to the vision still in use today
• 2000: Start of Narayana Hrudayalaya Group
• 2001: Narayana Hrudayalaya Cardiac Hospital started by Dr. Shetty as part of a 'health city' in Bangalore
• 2001-present: NH Cardiac Hospital develops into one of the world's leading cardiac hospitals. To date, over 50,000 people have been treated with high success rates by dedicated surgeons
Audacious goal
• To cure the poor for only one dollar a day in 'health cities' all over the world
Brand promise
• Affordable and accessible high-quality cardiac healthcare for everyone – regardless of caste, class, religion and ability to pay
Brand essence
What is the fundamental core?
Brand promise
What are the offered advantages?
Brand proof
What must be realized?
Brand values
What characterizes the personality?
Brand roots
What is the origin?
Higher goal
Why do we exist?
Core values
What do we stand for?
Audacious goal
Where are we going to?
Core qualities
What do we excel in?
Core and brand values
• Accessibility
• Affordability
• Service-oriented
• High quality
Core qualities
• Efficiency – specialization and standardization
• High-quality care
• Staff training
• Supplier relationships
Brand proof
• Lower & transparent prices compared to other cardiac hospitals
• Mortality rate lower than best US hospitals
• Accessibility: large telemedicine network through Skype, border posts, coronary care units; balance between rich and poor patients

Figure 9.1.1 Vision and Positioning of Narayana Hrudayalaya Cardiac Hospital

9.1.2 The Business Model: When Bigger Is Better—Economies of Scale in Healthcare

To understand the business model of the NH Cardiac Hospital, it is important to realize that the things which are scarce in India differ from those in the Western world. To start with, the demand for healthcare greatly exceeds the supply. Devices, medicine and operating equipment are far more expensive and resources lacking in these areas are a reason why people cannot be treated and die. The impact of this is visible in the relative number of by-pass operations compared to the placement of stents. In the Western world, a ratio of four stents to one by-pass is pretty usual since by-pass operations are considered to be more complicated and far more expensive. In India, the ratio is the other way round: stents make the operation expensive, success rates of by-pass operations are the same and reduce the number of people who have to return within a few years.

Volume and scale are the driving forces behind the business model. They are fundamental to the way in which the NH Cardiac Hospital performs. Comparisons are often made between the NH Cardiac Hospital and Henry Ford's mass-manufacturing approach in the previous century, as well as influences from "Taylorism" that can be found in the daily approach to work and the vision. The core of the business model can be visualized as a rising spiral in which low costs, low prices and high volumes reinforce one another.

The way in which NH Cardiac Hospital improves its business model in practice is more characteristic of continuous and organic learning than of a mathematical scientific design. Dr. Shetty is also a thrifty man who hates to spend too much money. He is constantly looking for new and creative ways to save money and makes this a sport. The use of standardization, economies of scale, process design and purchasing benefits creates a continuous process in which lower costs result in lower prices that in turn provide higher volumes. It is important that this always goes hand in hand with the attainment of a higher quality of care. The hospital has scarce (financial) resources for the use of high-tech equipment and medicines to meet the excessive demand for care. This demand cannot be met at the current cost level. Such a situation stimulates a pioneering spirit and innovative thinking. The business model therefore appears to be the result of the driving force and need to find new solutions to a changing environment. It would seem logical to expect an end to the upward spiral somewhere on the basis of scale, but this does not appear to have been reached yet. The model has, in the meantime, proven itself within healthcare. In the future it can also be of greater assistance in finding a solution to the increasing demand for healthcare.

Market Segments: Helping Poor and Wealthy People in Need In relation to positioning and the generated media attention, it is important that the NH Cardiac Hospital is part of the NH Group. The name attracts people and the hospital is visible in many places within society. Heart clinics (Coronary Care Units) are located throughout the country and the hospital is involved in various partnerships. The NH Group provides care on more fields, such as oncology, diagnostics and support. All organizational units and associated initiatives collectively ensure a solid market position.

The NH Cardiac Hospital does not view traditional hospitals as competitors because these others focus on the segment of the population that can afford to pay for care while NH also focuses on the poor. Within a broader context, all cardiac hospitals worldwide can be regarded as competitors because the NH Cardiac Hospital is a global leader in the provision of quality care at a low cost to people, irrespective of their caste, population group or means. Demand is never lacking in such a market. The true competitor is completely different since the demand for cardiac operations always greatly exceeds the number that can be provided. Especially in a country such as India, the real competitor is no hospital and therefore no treatment.

Over 50,000 people have been treated by the NH Cardiac Hospital since it opened. The hospital focused initially on children, who are still one of its primary patient flows. The hospital is truly open to anyone in need of treatment in order to support the vision of making healthcare accessible to all. The demand for care will remain considerable in India, where millions of people require cardiac care as heart disease is the number one cause of death.[15]

Not all patients at the NH Cardiac Hospital can pay for the treatment they receive. The balance between wealthy and poor patients is important otherwise the business model would simply not hold. When wealthy patients pay for their entire treatment and extras such as private rooms, the proceeds are used to help poorer people. The discussion in the West that wealthy people are taking the place of the poor is being turned on its head: the greater the number of places for the wealthy, the greater the number of places for the poor! NH ensures that the patient flow strikes a balance between wealthy and poor people, but life-threatening situations always take precedence. About 19 % of patients pay less than the break-even costs and in some cases patients even pay nothing. If people cannot afford their operation, the NH Cardiac Hospital pays half and the other half is provided by the related foundation where financial contributions are collected and saved from former patients, wealthy contributors and companies.

People from all over the world travel to India and the number of medical tourists increases every year (approximately 150,000 in 2005).[16] This helps strike the balance that is so important within the NH Cardiac Hospital.

Customer Value: Limiting Barriers to Cardiac Care Access Patients who visit the NH Cardiac Hospital for treatment receive high-quality cardiac surgery and efficient services at a low price. The hospital generally focuses on lowering financial, geographical and emotional barriers. That is not easy in a country where access to healthcare is limited by uncomfortable and expensive transport for the local population.[17] The quality of the service provided is also reflected in exceptional success rates and a low mortality rate. In 2010 the NH Cardiac Hospital performed around

---

[15] Kaul (2011) and Shetty (2010).
[16] Sharma (2010).
[17] RNCOS Research (2006).

30 major operations daily while other large Indian hospitals managed only half this number. With a mortality rate of 1.4 % within 30 days after a bypass operation (one of the most common heart operations) in 2009, the NH Cardiac Hospital is one of the best hospitals in the world (the hospital average in the USA was 1.9 %). Patients feel welcome and are treated with professionalism by well-educated, well-trained, and well-equipped staff. They receive attention, care, and commitment. The history of the hospitals founder, Dr. Shetty, most likely influences the positive emotions that these patients experience.

Patients are also charged prices that correspond to the treatment they require. The cost of the operation is determined beforehand and does not change if complications arise or if a patient has to stay longer in hospital. It depends on the patient's means to pay for treatment. The possibility to create personal (payment) plans means that the NH Cardiac Hospital never turns away even the poorest people. An open heart operation generally costs around INR 110,000 (approximately USD 1700 or EUR 1500). This is low, even for Indian standards (INR 250,000, approximately USD 4000 or EUR 3600).[18] The cost for a similar operation in the West is mostly 10–20 times higher. Nevertheless, the cost is often still (too) high for the Indian population. Ultimately, many people do not pay the full amount.

Although cardiac surgery often involves major operations, treatment does not entail any additional risks. Surgical treatment can always fail, but this risk is significantly lower at the NH Cardiac Hospital compared to other cardiac hospitals due to the high quality of the operations that are performed. The healthcare experience for foreign patients from Western countries in the hospital environment is different to what they are accustomed to in their own country. The risk for customers is generally low. The NH Cardiac Hospital creates customer value by building a bridge between demand and broad access to cardiac care.

Delivery: Bring People to Healthcare, and Healthcare to People The NH Cardiac Hospital realizes its vision through the care it delivers. Patients must acknowledge the accessibility and affordability of the treatment they require. The hospital uses its extensive network to bring healthcare to people and vice-versa. Patients can get into contact with the hospital in various ways, for example via access to the telemedicine network. The telemedicine network comprises three parts: (1) the Coronary Care Units: units in other hospitals where NH staff are on hand; (2) the Teleconsultation Network: connects state hospitals where basic screening can be carried out via teleconsultation and (3) the Family Doctors' Network, which consists of doctors equipped with software that allows them to send the results of ECG scans quickly. Family doctors receive a detailed advisory report from an NH consultant via the Internet within 15 min. Modern telecommunications technology has always been

---

[18] India Knowledge, Warton (2010) and Bhattacharyya et al. (2010).

important to the hospital, especially in order to increase access to healthcare in rural areas. Camps are also organized for people in rural areas (often sponsored by Rotary or Lions clubs), where diagnoses are made by doctors and a cardiologist with access to modern technology. If required, transport to cardiac hospitals is arranged for patients, which helps resolve the distance problem.

The number of hospitals is increasing. In doing this the costs are logically kept as low as possible. Several new hospitals are currently being built in rural areas, with only one floor to save costs. Air-conditioning is limited to operating rooms. This does not pose a problem since patients are not accustomed to having it at home. The overall cost per hospital with 300 beds is USD 5.5 million (EUR 5 million) and construction is completed within 6 months, which are incredible figures compared to Western countries. The new hospitals also extend beyond the borders of India. A new hospital is built in the Cayman Islands, which also helps patients from the US market. As Dr. Shetty states, it is extremely important to keep the NH spirit in this expansion. That is why key positions in the new hospitals are filled by true culture carriers—the "mother bees"—who have worked with NH Cardiac Hospital for a long time. They have to instill the culture and mission within the new hospitals. To support this, the way of working is recorded in a "NH Constitution". This details the prescribed way of working for all new hospitals and builds upon the original concept.

An insurance program called "Yeshasvini" has been developed to further stimulate accessible care for the poor. Dr. Shetty achieved this by working together with the government—which helped gain the trust of the local population—and with existing care facilities in the vicinity of Karnataka where there is a lack of available care for many patients. The insurance program is cost-effective and Dr. Shetty noted that poor people could use the concept of cooperatives (joining forces to create bargaining power) in more situations. The hospital strengthens the Indian healthcare system with this insurance model. More members visit hospitals without any additional costs.

Operation: The Pursuit of Operational Excellence Operations require good personnel and sound systems. Inspired by the Lean philosophy, the NH Cardiac Hospital has scrutinized the entire implementation process for cardiac care and imposed high quality standards in the quest for operational excellence. Doctors become super specialists by specializing in specific parts of the process for an heart operation. Costs are saved by not having to train personnel to carry out work they will not do anyway and by maximizing the leverage of key expertise. Top specialists are very scarce in India and used extremely efficiently in surgery. Experienced nurses and lower specialists receive intensive training to be able to prepare and finish an operation, such as opening and closing the patient's torso. This greatly increases the number of treatments done by top specialists. Whereas a specialist is usually fully booked with two operations a day, top specialists at NH Cardiac Hospital perform eight.

Doctors do not receive lower salaries then in other Indian hospitals. They receive fixed salaries but work longer and perform more surgery. In organizational terms, less than a fourth of organizational costs concern salaries. In the West, salaries account for over 50 %.[19]

---

[19] Khanna et al. (2005). Used more frequently in this case.

Salary costs help but do not result in treatments that 10–20 times less expensive compared to Western countries. All the systems used by the hospital facilitate the level of efficiency pursued within the organization. A distinction can be made between systems used directly in treatment (such as X-ray equipment) and supporting IT and information systems.

The manner in which the hospital works together with suppliers and partners is of immense value. High volumes ensure strong purchasing power. The NH Group enjoys a powerful position in the procurement market for medical supplies and equipment and is trend-setting given that it accounts for 12 % of all cardiac procedures carried out in India. It is abundantly clear that the NH Cardiac Hospital benefits from this. It keeps prices low by negotiating and avoiding long-term contracts. The name of the game for NH Cardiac Hospital is actually to increase the number of buying moments to every month or even week. Certified suppliers then have to give a quote on standardized products with stipulated quality levels and have to compete in an e-auction. A great deal of energy is invested in unraveling the supply chain to save costs. Sutures, for example, are no longer procured from a large pharmaceutical company, but from suppliers during an earlier phase of the production chain. This enables the procurement of thread and needles at 10 % of the cost. Another aspect of the business model is that the organization eliminates the process of distributors and lowers purchasing costs by negotiating more directly and forging important partnerships with private and public organizations. Some of these partnerships are innovation-based, such as that with Texas Instruments, which led to a reduction in the cost of X-ray plates. Overall decreases of 35 % are reported due to more aggressive purchasing.

The focus on quality and lower costs is also visible in IT procurement and partnerships. The entire infrastructure was replaced recently within a period of 33 months. Data is now shared in the "cloud" between 32 hospitals, and this includes digital patient records. NH Cardiac Hospitals now works with Linux (since this saves license costs) combined with SAP and ERP. The IT department responsible for coordinating and organizing this consists of five people. Realization and maintenance are outsourced entirely ("since we are not leading in IT ourselves"). Total IT costs are less than 1 % of overall costs!

Suppliers wish to remain connected to the hospital so that they can continue providing a high volume of products and services. There are even suppliers who deliver below the initial cost price because all their income on machines is profitable enough thanks to the high volume. Developing own material is another way to obtain cost-effective access to different supplies. The high volume and market position enable that. Greater innovation (e.g., own software development) also helps drive down costs, as well as partnerships with knowledge institutes and universities around the world. The aim of all these measures is to keep operating costs to a minimum. They all benefit the model: lower costs—lower prices—higher volume.

Value for customers

Result *What do I get?*
- I receive high-quality cardiac treatment

+

Process *How do I get it?*
- I find myself in a highly standardized hospital with well educated staff

+

Emotion *What do I feel?*
- I feel professionally cared for, welcome, equal, gratefull, save and hopefull

---

Price *What are the costs?*
- Depends on extra wishes. Surgery is the focus. I pay for the costs I can afford

+

Effort *What do I have to do for it?*
- Low effort. I get treated where possible; could be in NH but also in partner hospitals or care units

+

Risk *What are the uncertainties?*
- Low risk (high success factor, lower mortality rates, high reputation). I always get help

Market segments

Position
- One of the biggest cardiac hospitals in the world with a scale-based approach. Helping both poor and rich, with a good financial position. Part of the NH Group, extensive network in different health-care fields

Competition
- Direct: none because the business model aims for a balance between both rich and poor people and there is no lack of demand.
- Indirect: other cardiac hospitals in India and other parts of the world since people come to Bangalore especially for this hospital

Target group
- All people in need of cardiac healthcare. Currently, there are many operations on children. Firstly in India, eventually worldwide, regardless of caste, class, religion or ability to pay for the treatment

Customer insights
- Not everyone can pay for the treatment that is needed. A visit to the NH Cardiac Hospital gives hope

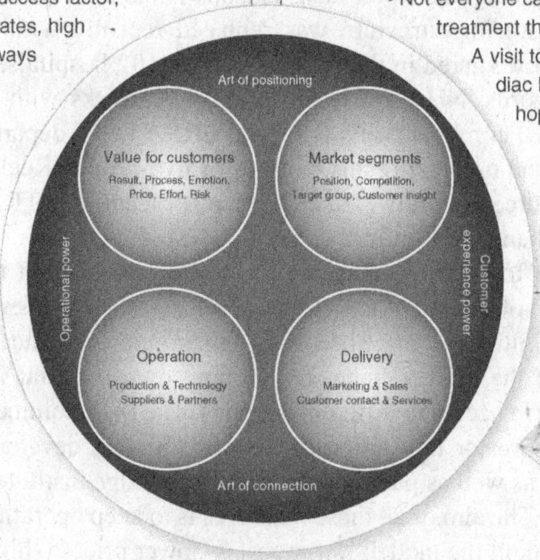

Figure 9.1.2 Value for customers and Market segments of Narayana Hrudayalaya Cardiac Hospital

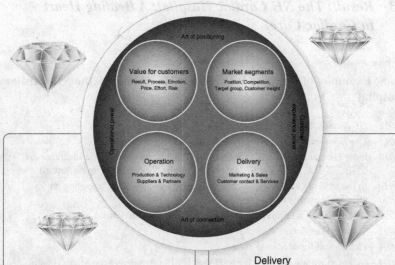

Art of positioning

Value for customers
Result, Process, Emotion,
Price, Effort, Risk

Market segments
Position, Competition,
Target group, Customer insight

Operation
Production & Technology
Suppliers & Partners

Delivery
Marketing & Sales
Customer contact & Services

Operational power

Customer experience power

Art of connection

Operation

Production & Technology

- Standardization and scale are central within the hospital. Focus is on the most efficient infrastructure, making use of the Lean philosophy. Personnel is highly trained and educated
- High-quality systems. New technology thanks to good deals with suppliers, but also efficient, self-developed technology to perform surgery and save on costs and efficiency. Systems are advanced and up to date

Suppliers & Partners

- Suppliers are cut out as much as possible so good prices can be bargained to get access to the newest techniques and products for low prices. Direct contact with producers and manufacturers in the supply chain. Strong purchasing power due to high volume and reputation
- Partnerships with private and public organizations. Good relations with NH Group, lots of sponsors and innovative knowledge-based partnerships

Delivery

Marketing & Sales

- A large part of the success reinforced via marketing. Recognition for Dr. Shetty's work is immense (TV programs, awards and media attention) and NH is used as a case study around the world. Patients are satisfied and spread awareness by word of mouth
- Balance between rich and poor to keep organization running and profitable. Different ways to get help: coronary care units, insurance schemes, etc. No lack of demand

Customer contact & Services

- High accessibility and affordability is central to customers. Contact is personal and clear, personal plans are developed for every case. While scale is central to the business model, contact is still personal – customers experience attention and care
- Making use of NH network. Extensive services in healthcare through this network and services in the field of academics and research, CSR, e-health, enterprise, medical tourism and a stem cell bank

Figure 9.1.3 Operation and Delivery of Narayana Hrudayalaya Cardiac Hospital

9.1.3   Result: The NH Cardiac Hospital: A Beating Heart in Cardiac Care!

Some Examples of the Awards Dr. Shetty Has Won with the NH Cardiac Hospital

2012	ET Awards, Entrepreneur of the Year (Dr. Shetty)
2011	*The Economist's* 2011 Award for Business Process Innovation
2010	India Healthcare Awards, organized by ICICI Lombard General Insurance and CNBC-TV18. Narayana Hrudayalaya won the "Specialty Hospital" award
2010	In the field of cardiology, Dr. Shetty received an award for "focusing on affordable quality care for everyone"
2005	Award for Social Entrepreneurship—World Economic Forum
2005	Schwab Foundation's Award
2004	Padma Shri for Medicine award
2004	India Innovation Award—By NDTV & EMPI (awarded to the Micro Health Insurance Division)
2004	The Rotary Club's Citizen Extraordinaire award
2003	Dr. B.C. Roy award
2003	Padmashree award
2003	Sir M. Visvesvaraya Memorial award
2003	Ernst & Young—Entrepreneur of the Year
2002	Rajyotsava award
2001	Karnataka Ratna award

The value that the NH Cardiac Hospital creates for patients is quite clear: the accessible and affordable care it provides can be the difference between life and death. NH Cardiac Hospital gives that to everyone, regardless of whether or not people can pay. You could say that the hospital strikes a balance by focusing on people who can easily pay and on people who would normally not be able to pay. That differs in the target group approach that traditional hospitals often seem to take. Wealthy customers contribute to the payment of the hospital's overall costs and the NH Cardiac Hospital then implements volume from all patients to strengthen the business model which is also valuable for the reputation, expertise and cost levels. In this way, the NH Cardiac Hospital makes a huge difference to people whose financial and social situation would have prevented them from ever receiving the necessary medical treatment (in 2004, 37 % of operations were at or below break-even cost). By increasing accessibility in various ways, such as via the heart clinics (Coronary Care Units), people have easier access to affordable healthcare in India from the outset. Patients of the NH Cardiac Hospital confirm their positive experience with the holistic approach to cardiac care provided by the hospital.

The NH Group is owned by Dr. Shetty and his family. JP Morgan and Pinebridge (formerly AIG) each hold a 12.5 % stake in the company, and chairman and delegated director Kiran Mazumdar-Shaw of the biotech firm Biocon holds a 2.5 % stake. The hospital has been profitable since its establishment and has a higher profit margin after tax compared to American hospitals (7.7 % compared to 6.9 %). On the whole, there is considerable attention from American investors. A foundation has also been established to enable educational programs in particular because Indian legislation does not permit such programs within private companies. The NH Cardiac Hospital is a private company and in no way affected by the restrictions imposed on nonprofit organizations in India. The combination of the various entities supports the hospital's performance in the long term.

The hospital's personnel are proud to be part of the vision of founder Dr. Shetty. Many doctors find the work they do gratifying. Training, education, facilities and the number of patients provided by the hospital promote further specialization. Everything is intended to increase the number of treatments, access and affordability for the masses. Comprehensive post-graduate training programs are provided for doctors and other medical personnel. The purpose of these is to bridge the gap between new cardiologists that are required and the decreasing number of doctors who graduate in India every year. Doctors and medical personnel become experts quickly because they only participate in training programs that relate to their specific area of work. Very few specialist personnel leave the hospital. Their salaries are good enough, the intrinsic motivation appears to be tremendous and they can dedicate themselves to helping as many patients as possible. Personnel are also grateful for the opportunities they are given to specialize. Working for the NH Cardiac Hospital also gives them a good social status. Furthermore, they gladly share the ambitions of Dr. Shetty. Besides the fixed group of personnel there is also a flexible group. Nurses are also grateful for the opportunities, training, and good work, but there is also more financial pressure to move to better-paying privatized hospitals in India or the Middle East.

The NH Cardiac Hospital is a centre of excellence created to help the global masses. Its core activity, namely treating people with heart disorders, is of immense value for society. Treatments save lives. The hospital helps to improve quality of life by working together with patients to combat the number one cause of death in India. The visible entrepreneurship within healthcare results in treatment that people need. Revenues are meant to be reinvested in the good cause of further growth and expansion. The business model of the NH Cardiac Hospital is an inspirational example for society. According to Dr. Shetty, India was in need of a new healthcare approach given the sheer size of its population. It is unique to healthcare that this mass-market approach works in this manner and yields such positive results. The business model could be used in other medical facilities or distributed globally to help more people in need.

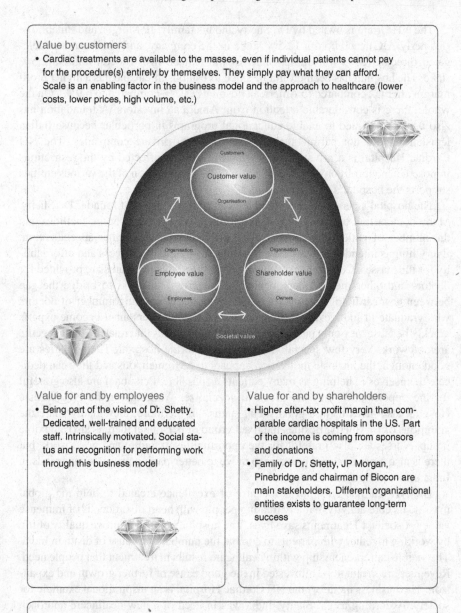

Value by customers
- Cardiac treatments are available to the masses, even if individual patients cannot pay for the procedure(s) entirely by themselves. They simply pay what they can afford. Scale is an enabling factor in the business model and the approach to healthcare (lower costs, lower prices, high volume, etc.)

Value for and by employees
- Being part of the vision of Dr. Shetty. Dedicated, well-trained and educated staff. Intrinsically motivated. Social status and recognition for performing work through this business model

Value for and by shareholders
- Higher after-tax profit margin than comparable cardiac hospitals in the US. Part of the income is coming from sponsors and donations
- Family of Dr. Shetty, JP Morgan, Pinebridge and chairman of Biocon are main stakeholders. Different organizational entities exists to guarantee long-term success

Value for and by society
- Contribution to health in India (and around the world). Entrepreneurship and profit are used to improve healthcare via the business model used

Figure 9.1.4 Value for and by stakeholders of Narayana Hrudayalaya Cardiac Hospital

9.1.4   The Brilliant Lessons of Narayana Hrudayalaya Cardiac Hospital

What can we learn from this NH Cardiac Hospital:

- The vision and mission of the NH Cardiac Hospital, namely "to make high-quality healthcare accessible and affordable for the masses throughout the world" is unique. The achievement of this vision and mission, through the exploitation of economies of scale and the adoption of a service-driven mass-market approach to cardiac care, is something that has never been done on this scale. The business model relies on standardization and economies of scale, which result in lower costs, which lead to lower prices and greater volume. This cycle repeats itself with higher volume that leads to even lower costs and lower prices. The most important lesson to be learned is that extremely complex cardiac surgery can be combined with the realization of economies of scale. The scale of the operation influences the way in which the NH Cardiac Hospital organizes care, and the development of more experienced medical personnel. This combination results in a learning organization with efficiently organized low-cost processes that deliver high success rates.
- The use of scale and reputation is cost-effective, as is the optimization of scarce resources in the effort to meet the demand for cardiac treatment. The NH Cardiac Hospital is an authority in the procurement market. Specialist procurement teams use the size of the hospital as leverage. The hospital procures machines, medicines, and other products at very low prices, and sometimes even free of charge. The volume-based approach means that the cost structure is completely different from that of other world class hospitals in western countries.
- Many people are eligible for treatment thanks to the emphasis placed on finding a balance between wealthy and poor patients. The traditional paradigm in which a decision is made to treat poor people or rich people is transcended by simultaneously increasing the volume of supply rather than simply taking the existing capacity as a given.
- When planning personnel training the emphasis is on the practical application of the training. This results in doctors who specialize in performing a single operation, or even certain parts of operations. This saves the time it would take to provide them with training in all the general aspects of the various operations, and ensures that they become even more specialized. Personnel are only employed where necessary and can progress to performing more difficult procedures on an elective basis. This ensures that they deliver the most added value in their own fields, and nurses take care of all related aspects which are less complex. This is the other way round in the Western educational model where specialists receive a broad training and then specialize in a particular area, but still perform a fairly wide range of actions (themselves).

- The business model proves that it is possible to make a profit while also contributing to social improvement. In this case the reinvestment of profit ensures that entrepreneurship serves society. The very important role that the NH Group plays in the lives of millions of people shows that doing good can really pay-off.
- Charity is not scalable. If you truly want to have an impact and change the world for many people, you have to realize that this requires a self-financing model. If you want to scale, you cannot be dependent upon donations. You need to find ways to obtain greater income if you deliver more results and provide more treatments. Use scarcity as inspiration and search for new, creative and innovative ways to overcome this.

9.2 ThedaCare

Making things a little bit better for every patient every day

Karen Willemsen, Maarten Akkerman & Jennifer op't Hoog @: Jennifer. op.t.hoog@achmea.nl, Phone: 0031 651226420

Prelude *Stanley is an expat from America who lives with his family in Amsterdam. After a bicycle accident, he ends up in a coma, lying in a hospital far removed from his relatives in Appleton, Wisconsin, USA.[20] As Stanley's family want to bring him home, he is transferred to ThedaCare on 4 September 2013. Upon arrival in the hospital in Appleton, he is admitted directly and sent for an MRI a few minutes later. By continuing to experiment and performing exercises with him, Stanley slowly emerges from his coma. Six months on, Stanley is able to do most things once again and can function fully within his family. Stanley is now living proof of the brilliant case of ThedaCare. Aside from the conspicuous desire of nurses and doctors to continue experimenting and looking for the right treatment, Stanley's relatives speak highly of the quick turnaround time for treatment and the degree of involvement in decisions surrounding his health. The experience and findings that come up for discussion in this case are also to a degree the experience of Stanley and his family. There is, of course, no scientific proof that Stanley would not have emerged from his coma in another hospital. But Stanley is convinced of this. We invite you to form your own opinion if they are able to make such a difference after reading this case.*

Introduction ThedaCare is known regionally and internationally for the highest quality care combined with relatively low costs. Its roots stretch back more than a century and find their origin in the US state of Wisconsin. Over the years the care institution has had several names and alliances, but the mission has remained unchanged. The primary focus is still accessibility to world-class care for society.

---

[20] The experiences of Stanley are personal, partially based on a true story and a fictional one.

In its current form, ThedaCare is the result of a merger between Appleton Medical Center and Theda Clark Medical Center in 1987. In 1994 the United Health of Wisconsin Insurance Company joined as a partner. Since 1999 the hospital has operated under the name ThedaCare, named after Theda Clark Peters. She was a community activist responsible for various projects within the Neenah Public Library and the hospital that now bears her name. The reasons why it was named in her honor are found in her enormous generosity and tremendous involvement to improve the health of the community.

Currently ThedaCare consists of 5 hospitals, 22 specialized clinics and more than nine affiliated care institutions. Every year, in excess of 150,000 patients are helped at the institution; in 2012 more than 6000 people were employed there.[21]

In the last decade ThedaCare has become known around the world for the application of continuous improvement in healthcare: Lean Healthcare based on the Lean concept as developed by Toyota. More than 15 million yearly incidents resulting from unnecessary medical errors in the USA, combined with continuously rising costs in healthcare, were the reason to start improving working drastically on the provision of healthcare. Curbing unnecessary errors (such as medication errors, wrong-side surgeries, infections and incidents connected to falling down) while simultaneously cutting down on the expenditures, resulted in revolutionary changes in ThedaCare's healthcare services. The results of ThedaCare's Lean-based journey over the past decade are promising: the number of errors has declined drastically, the medical results for patients have improved, the level of employee satisfaction has increased and savings of USD 27 million (EUR 24 million) have been realized.[22]

9.2.1   The Cornerstone: Patient Centered Continuous Improvement

ThedaCare desires to achieve its goals by continuous improvement—investigating what can be done better every day, for every patient and with every treatment and then simply doing it. This includes removing components or steps that do not add any value for the patient and/or employee. Continuously improving and striving for perfection in healthcare is the essence of ThedaCare. Deeply rooted in the culture is this commitment to patients and the various communities. The promise that the institution makes in that regard is: always aim at setting the highest standard and delivering accordingly. This goes hand in hand with making performances and results measurable and visible. This way customers and partners have insight into the processes and results of the organization.

---

[21] Originally from: www.thedacare.com/whoarewe, on 3 October 2013.
[22] Toussaint and Gerard (2010).

In 2002, ThedaCare starts with Lean. The CEO of ThedaCare Center for Healthcare Value Dr. John Toussaint, is also the founder of the Lean improvement culture and method in the organization., The institution goes to work, inspired by John's statement that: "I do not want ThedaCare to merely remain good. I want it to become fantastic." By studying organizations both in and outside of the healthcare industry, the doctors, internal consultants and management of ThedaCare arrived at the joint conclusion that organizations that are really focusing on continuous quality improvements can create impressive value for all stakeholders.

With the help of consultants, ThedaCare develops its own ThedaCare Inpatient System (TIS), based on the Toyota production system. "Improving the health of the community" remains, as a higher goal, the basis for ThedaCare.[23] In line with that, the audacious goal is "transforming" healthcare around three linked components:

1. improved moral of people employed in healthcare;
2. improved quality, with a focus on the reduction of unnecessary errors and the removal of waste[24];
3. improved productivity.

As the leader of ThedaCare, Dr. Toussaint desires to realize the higher and audacious goals and to create value by doing *less*. He deems this as *the* way in which to stand out amongst the increasing competition in the healthcare market. It is a flowing process in which the patient is at the center of attention and not the agenda of the doctor, the institution or other interested stakeholders. Instead of waiting for doctors and receiving the wrong medication and materials for diagnosis that are not present, the patient sees the doctor at the agreed time, full attention is given to them and consultation takes place at the right moment. This is achieved, among other ways, due to the fact that each patient has his/her own care team.

ThedaCare has determined core values and core qualities for fulfilling its goal. It is an open culture in which participants want to learn—one that demands honesty and a critical eye for yourself and your colleagues.[25] For this to work, courage is required. Within current healthcare, "shame and blame" are important cultural characteristics.[26] That is understandable due to the responsibility for people's lives, but this makes an open and transparent working culture more difficult at the same time. In order to arrive at a feedback culture in which the participants can learn from their mistakes, three elements are

---

[23] In Lean methodology, the term 'True North' is often used to indicate the direction where you want to go which results in the achievement of the higher goal. True North (*geodetic north*) refers to the direction along the earth's surface towards the geographic North Pole. A clear improvement point to be realized, so that you can check en route as to whether you are still heading towards the right place. See also: Smalley (2011).

[24] Eight forms of waste are defined on which business operations specifically focus. In that regard, it concerns: waiting, motion, talent, defects, over-production, inventory, transport and over-processing. See also: Rother and Shook (2003).

[25] Rother (2009).

[26] Toussaint and Gerard (2010).

required: courage, integrity and honesty. The demanded brand values of ThedaCare's umbrella organizations needed to fulfill their promise are: empathy, innovation, respect, and teamwork. Decisive in the creation of added value for customers, partners, and colleagues is the ability to put yourself in the shoes of the relevant stakeholder. Continuously improving by looking critically at the value stream stimulates innovative thinking *and* action. With due respect, ThedaCare strives to let everyone who is part of the value stream for the patient lead a meaningful life—both at ThedaCare and beyond. Consequently, the organization spurs its employee on to actively work on a valuable life.[27] In order to realize this and to prevent errors, communication and teamwork are crucial. ThedaCare provides demonstrable evidence for its vision and positioning. For instance, patient satisfaction levels have risen from 65 % to 85 %. In addition, the number of errors with medication adjustments between admission to the hospital, discharge and aftercare has declined to almost nil. The documentation time for nurses has also been halved, as a result of which they are able to spend more direct time with patients.[28]

---

[27] Idem.
[28] Idem.

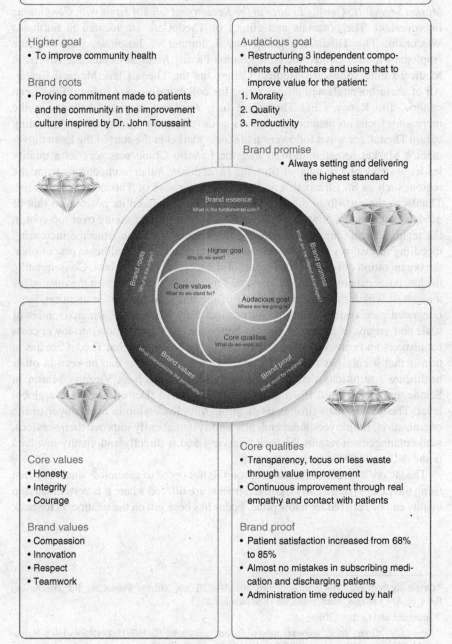

Brand essence: Continuously improving and striving for perfection in community health

Higher goal
• To improve community health

Brand roots
• Proving commitment made to patients and the community in the improvement culture inspired by Dr. John Toussaint

Audacious goal
• Restructuring 3 independent compo-nents of healthcare and using that to improve value for the patient:
1. Morality
2. Quality
3. Productivity

Brand promise
• Always setting and delivering the highest standard

Core values
• Honesty
• Integrity
• Courage

Brand values
• Compassion
• Innovation
• Respect
• Teamwork

Core qualities
• Transparency, focus on less waste through value improvement
• Continuous improvement through real empathy and contact with patients

Brand proof
• Patient satisfaction increased from 68% to 85%
• Almost no mistakes in subscribing medi-cation and discharging patients
• Administration time reduced by half

Figure 9.2.1 Vision and Positioning of Thedacare

9.2.2   The Business Model: Lean, But for People

Market Segments: Quality Leader in the Region and Global Fame with Continuous Improvement The hospitals and clinics of ThedaCare are located in northeast Wisconsin. The ThedaCare group has a number of hospitals, including the Appleton Medical Center, the New London Family Medical Center, the Riverside Medical Center, Shawano Medical Center and the Theda Clark Medical Center. All of these hospitals and clinics strive for collaborative care based on the Lean method. Jim Raney, CEO ThedaCare Inc., Appleton locations believes in the increasing focus on patient experiences as development in healthcare. According to him ThedaCare was a follower on the local market at the start of the Lean movement.[29] Market research showed that the LaSalle Clinic was seen as a quality leader instead of his own institution. In addition, other competitors from the region, such as St. Elizabeth's and Mercy, were ahead of ThedaCare on this list. Thanks to the growth in quality, ThedaCare has improved its position to that of market leader and is now financially solvable.[30] In spite of taking over top spot in the region, ThedaCare is experiencing financial competition from the increasing meddling of insurers and the resultant market forces. As a healthcare practitioner, the organization only influences a part of the total healthcare costs. Consequently, the low costs cannot be directly converted into a lower premium for the insured, as a result of which the patient sees little of the financial benefit. In addition, large integrated care systems, such as Aurora Inc. from Milwaukee, use economies of scale and groups of insured people to better convert this position into lower costs for insurers and consequently contributors.[31] The advantage that ThedaCare has in turn is that it employs its own doctors.[32] Other competitors can be seen in other healthcare institutions that are also applying lean, such as Virginia Mason in Seattle and Henry Ford Hospital in West Bloomfield (Detroit area). On a global level, ThedaCare distinguishes itself through its leadership in every layer of the organization. Employees independently and systematically improve their services, while management retains the total overview and is directly and visibly involved in the delivery of care to the customer.

ThedaCare has reduced its target group. It has opted to specialize since it started using the Lean system. Only those treatments are offered where it is certain that top quality can be realized for a low price. Focus has been put on the treatments for back

---

[29] Originally from http://article.wn.com/view/2012/04/27/Fitch_Affirms_ThedaCare_Inc_Wisconsin_Revs_at_AA_Outlook_Sta/#/video, on 19 September 2013.

[30] Toussaint and Gerard (2010).

[31] Originally from http://www.businesswire.com/news/home/20080911006086/en/Fitch-Rates-90MM-ThedaCare-Wisconsin-2008-Bond, on 19 September 2013.

[32] Originally from http://www.fiercehealthcare.com/press-releases/fitch-rates-thedacare-inc-wisconsin-2010-bonds-aa-affirms-outstanding-outlook-stable, on 19 September 2013.

and neck pain, cardiology, oncology, bariatrics and childbirth care. ThedaCare is in constant conversation with customers, integrating their feedback and the acquired customer insights into their daily process. So they are taking new steps every time in further developing their continuous improvement culture. The first step in that is to identify what customers are prepared to pay for, in other words: what they find valuable. The next step is to investigate which activities in the process add value. Based on these findings, the process of value creation can be better organized and become more streamlined. In that regard, customers are stimulated to constantly speak out on their needs, desires and suggestions.

Customer Value: Central Role Reserved for Patients ThedaCare takes a critical look at the activities in the care process and the extent to which they add value for customers. Everyone—from doctors and nurses on the front line, to insurers, employers and patients—must spend time and energy defining the actual added value in order to optimize all patient-related processes. From the patient's perspective, a loss of time is not the equivalent of a waste[33] of money but of a waste of "health."[34] In more positive terms: being helped earlier adds not only to a faster but also to a better and more complete recovery.

As a customer, you know that ThedaCare offers good treatment with regard to back and neck pain, cardiology, oncology, bariatrics, and childbirth care and that they are quick in making an appointment, whereby your schedule and care requirements as a patient receive the most attention. Thanks to the close collaboration between the many components of the hospital, care can always be offered in the vicinity of the customer. The staff has been trained to deal with customers quickly and correctly: a process characterized by the fact that you need to wait as little as possible and are decently assisted. By first listening to the customer and then jointly taking a decision concerning the care process, employees act as a partner of the customer with joint responsibility. By focusing on efficiency in the training of its employees, ThedaCare ensures that there is more time to be spent directly on patients, so that there can also be space for the emotions and experiences of the customer. This followed the latest quality benchmark in the field of customer experiences in communication from the WCHQ hospital data[35] that showed that not all components of ThedaCare already scored high in this aspect in 2013. By contrast, ThedaCare claims that since 2004 it has the lowest price increases of all hospitals in northeast Wisconsin.[36] From a risk perspective, it is valuable that the institution

---

[33] Eight forms of waste are defined on which business operations specifically focus. In that regard, it concerns: waiting, motion, talent, defects, over-production, inventory, transport and over-processing. See also: Rother and Shook (2003).

[34] Toussaint and Gerard (2010).

[35] Rother (2009).

[36] Originally from http://www.thedacare.org/Why-Thedacare/Cost-and-Quality.aspx, on 11 September 2013.

is assuming a pioneering role in making quality transparent. Based on Maslow's statement that it is better to be aware of your incompetence than unaware, this produces a lower risk profile.[37]

Delivery: Improving the DNA ThedaCare focuses on continuous improvement. This results in shorter waiting times, better collaboration between employees and the resulting experiences of customers. An interesting phenomenon amongst people who work with continuous improvement is that the greater the visibility of improvement potential, the more modest people become regarding the current situation and their performance.[38] From the perspective of marketing and sales, this is striking. The large degree of unpretentiousness of ThedaCare is also evident in the short clips to be found on the internet.

The desire to continuously improve based on what is valuable for the customer makes the role of customer contact even more important. Central to customer contact is connection and partnership. Customers are supported in all their needs and in all phases of the care process—from diagnosis to aftercare—by a dedicated team, the so-called Community Health Action Team (CHAT). The team makes sure everyone is connected where necessary and takes care of the proper coordination between the different units and institutions. It is already difficult enough for patients to find their way in one ward, let alone when they have to go to different hospitals for treatment. The CHAT team looks beyond the boundaries of its own organization to ensure that the care process proceeds optimally for the patient. An important role in making the patient central to the whole process is also fulfilled by the care team of the patient. This team consists of a doctor, nurse, pharmacist and case manager but not necessarily the same ones all the time. A care plan, setting out medication and therapies, is drawn up in consultation between the patient and the care team. These data are embedded in the electronic file, so that they are accessible and readily comprehensible for the involved healthcare practitioners. This contributes directly to the prevention of unnecessary errors and ensures that patients need to repeat themselves as little as possible thus leaving more time for relevant conversation. An important role in this embeddeding process is the servant leadership within all components and layers of the organization. This helps to get the best out of the employees and to stimulate them in their professionalism and responsibilities. The clear focus of ThedaCare on adding value to the care chain and removing waste is in the DNA of its employees and provides guidance in all its customer contact. This is what makes ThedaCare brilliant.

---

[37] This relates to the four stages of learning from Maslow's competency theory from 1954. See: http://www.ecoisonline.org/pluginfile.php/2650/mod_resource/content/0/downloads/vier_stadia_van_leren_Maslow_.pdf.

[38] Rother (2009).

Operation: Win-Win Situations The operational strength originates in the continuous focus on the total process. Focusing on customers and allowing their needs to be expressed are also central to the production process. Procedures are critically examined by discussing improvements with the customer. Many process improvements have already been applied, which reduces the time between diagnoses and treatment, curbs the chance of complications and increases the chance of survival. This has been identified and listed through the use of Value Stream Mapping. In this process, every step of a service or treatment is made comprehensible on the basis of which it can be determined if a step in the process does or does not add value. Elements that do not add any value are then removed from the process.

Of course, when optimizing the service standardization options are looked at in an effort to improve quality. The policy that ThedaCare uses for standardization consists of three different phases:

1. upstream: everything that occurs before the patient sees the doctor;
2. middle stream: the dialogue between the doctor and the patient;
3. downstream: the additional information necessary for the doctor and the patient.

In phases 1 and 3, standardization takes place to optimize the process for the patient. Phase 2 is not considered suitable for standardization.

If new technology adds value for customers, it is used at ThedaCare. The sophistication of ThedaCare is also evident from its inclusion in the list of 100 Most Wired Hospitals in the USA, a survey that measures the adoption of ICT infrastructure within healthcare.[39]

After years of internal experience with continuous improvement, the past few years have been spent optimizing its relationship with suppliers through the use of Lean. As part of the total patient experience, it is important that referrals and other deliveries take place with the same attention as paid to the patient. The aim of all of this is to flexibly adapt the process to the needs of the customer and to work error-free. Giving each other space and working on continuous improvement are paramount. The same applies for tackling bottlenecks quickly and thoroughly, and where necessary even jointly, across the boundaries of ThedaCare's own organization. Care institutions in America and abroad have become partners of ThedaCare. They share learning experiences within the network called Healthcare Value Leaders. It appears that to admit that errors are made and that the care provided is not yet perfect seems to become more debatable then ever. In various care organizations, employees are busy on a daily basis with continuous improvement. However, making this transparent, comprehensible and comparable for everyone still appears to be a constant challenge. The first steps have already been taken within the WCHQ referred to above. Since 2004, comparable quality information has been shared — unfortunately not yet nationally or in an uniform manner.

---

[39] Originally from http://www.hhnmostwired.com/winners/PDFs/2013PDFs/MostWired2013.pdf on 9 September 2013.

Value for customers

Result *What do I get?*
- Accurate and timely treatment with the patient at the centre of the process

Process *How do I get it?*
- In a way which suits me and is near my home

Emotion *What do I feel?*
- I feel that I am being taken care of

Price *What are the costs?*
- Relatively low price by insurers

Effort *What do I have to do for it?*
- Cooperation with the personal plan for my treatment

Risk *What are the uncertainties?*
- Thanks to the high level of transparency and insight, the quality is high and the risk is low

Market segments

Position
- Market leader in quality with 5 hospitals, 22 clinics and more than 9 care institutions in Northeast Wisconsin

Competition
- Regionally: Aurora in Milwaukee is a large player capable of converting financial advantage into lower premium. Virginia Maison is one of the competitors in the field of Lean management

Target group
- Patients looking for premium care for low prices

Customer insights
- Adds value for patients to be continuously involved and have a leading role in their own care path

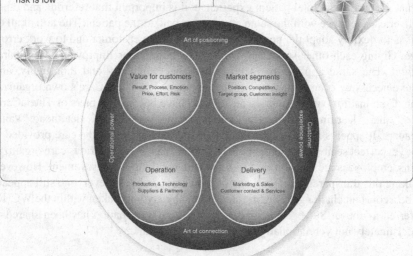

Figure 9.2.2   Value for customers and Market segments of Thedacare

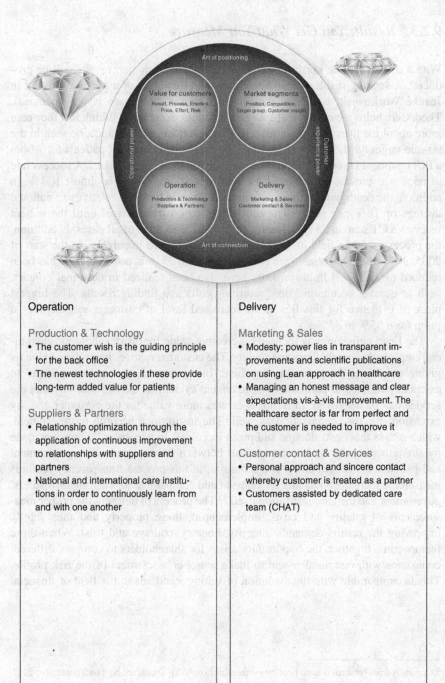

Operation

Production & Technology
- The customer wish is the guiding principle for the back office
- The newest technologies if these provide long-term added value for patients

Suppliers & Partners
- Relationship optimization through the application of continuous improvement to relationships with suppliers and partners
- National and international care institutions in order to continuously learn from and with one another

Delivery

Marketing & Sales
- Modesty: power lies in transparent improvements and scientific publications on using Lean approach in healthcare
- Managing an honest message and clear expectations vis-à-vis improvement. The healthcare sector is far from perfect and the customer is needed to improve it

Customer contact & Services
- Personal approach and sincere contact whereby customer is treated as a partner
- Customers assisted by dedicated care team (CHAT)

Figure 9.2.3 Operation and Delivery of Thedacare

9.2.3   Result: You Get What You Measure

With a course set due north for added value for the customer, results will be produced. A striking result of involvement by and treatment of a person is found in Jeanne Wachowiak, a cardiac patient. She relates: "My care is very personal. ThedaCare helps me ensure that I stay on schedule. Sometimes I think that they care more about me than I do about myself."[40] A result can, for instance, be seen in the 90-min target for the "Door to Balloon" times, the percentage of patients for whom a PCI treatment is started within 90 min of the initial medical contact. A success rate of 65 % was previously achieved for heart operations, now it is almost 100 %. In addition, the death rate for these patients was lowered to 8.8 %, relative to a national average of 18 % per year.[41] The time target to go from arrival until the patient receives a CT scan in 25 min, improved from 51 % to 89 % of all cases. In addition, the processes in the field of laboratory testing improved massively. At the start of 2005, 90 % of the analyses were completed within 33 min; now that time has been reduced to 23 min.[42] Improvements have also been realized in customer contact, such as quicker communication, returning calls and finding results. The biggest piece of evidence for this lies in the increased level of customer satisfaction—a jump from 65 % to 85 %.

The Lean philosophy is focused on creating value for all stakeholders: customers, employees, shareholders and society. The customer realizes immediate value by giving employees input for improvement. In that regard, the customer forms an essential and integral part of the improvement cycle. It is only in this way that the service can be improved. In turn this creates more value for the customer and, by extension, for the organization as well. The institutions become more efficient, which means that costs decline and profit increases. In particular, progress is made by strengthening the collaborative effort between insurers, hospitals, government and patients. As described by Dr. Toussaint, in this process transparency requires measurements in hospitals that are relevant and comparable for customers, insurers, government and the care institution itself.[43] The process of defining the proper measurements of quality and costs, implementing these properly and then jointly improving the results demands integrity, honesty, courage and trust. When these factors come together, the opportunity arises for shareholders to compare different companies with one another and to make a proper assessment of the risk profile. This is comparable with the evolution of setting standards in the field of financial

---

[40] Originally from personal note on http://www.thedacare.org/Why-Thedacare.aspx on 3 September 2013.

[41] The American Heart Association, 'Heart Disease and Stroke Statistics Update'. Originally from http://www.strokecenter.org/patients/stats.htm, on 12 September 2013.

[42] Toussaint and Gerard (2010).

[43] Toussaint (2012).

reporting. As a result major companies are using IFRS and US GAAP thanks to which shareholders can make better comparisons and proper assessments for the benefit of their investments. So the level of insight increases and the level of risk decreases simultaneously thanks to uniform methods of measurement.

In an upward spiral of more satisfied customers, the business model of ThedaCare also produces more employee value. Doctors who used to work as part of the Collaborative Care Team report that the nurses are better informed, think along better and consequently get a more important role during the treatment.[44] Nurses and junior doctors indicate that whereas the joint start to the day initially meant they had to work a bit longer, the result is that they now need to ask a lot less questions which has reduced the number of misunderstandings. Aside from these collaborative improvements, there is a higher degree of employee involvement and responsibility.[45] In contrast to these positive results, there is also negative feedback from doctors regarding the desire to standardize as much as possible. As described under Operation above, the policy is maintained here that while standardization is not applied in the dialogue between the doctor and the patient (middle stream), it is beforehand (upstream) and afterwards (downstream).

In line with the higher goal of ThedaCare to improve the health of the community, society also benefits from this. The latest WCHQ quality benchmark is indicative of this.[46] ThedaCare scores better than both the national and the state averages in preventing errors in safety targets and in mortality rates.[47]

Aside from the normal provision of care, other problems of the community are being studied by multiple disciplines in a Community Health Action Team (CHAT). In all-day sessions they experiment with possible solutions for a problem with the result being that the best solutions are tested in the community for a month. In this way value is created for the organization and process optimization takes place in various disciplines. This also yields solutions for long, drawn-out challenges for society. An example of such a solution is a project whereby poor families are introduced to a community mentor to help them become self-supporting. Another solution is a project for in uninsured farming families where information is given on prevention in order to prevent healthcare costs. In 2009, for example, ThedaCare spent a total of more than USD 30million[48] (around EUR 27 million) on services for the community. These services include research, education, and medical assistance.

---

[44] Idem, p. 27.

[45] Idem, pp. 73–74.

[46] Wisconsin Collaborative for Healthcare Quality (WCHQ) is an initiative of various care institutions from Wisconsin to uniformly measure quality information and to make it transparent for potential customers. Originally from: http://www.wchq.org/hospitals, on 11 September 2013.

[47] Originally from http://www.wicheckpoint.org/reports_detail.aspx?hospitalId=110.

[48] http://www.thedacare.org/Getting-Involved/Improving-Community-Health/Community-Benefit-Report.aspx.

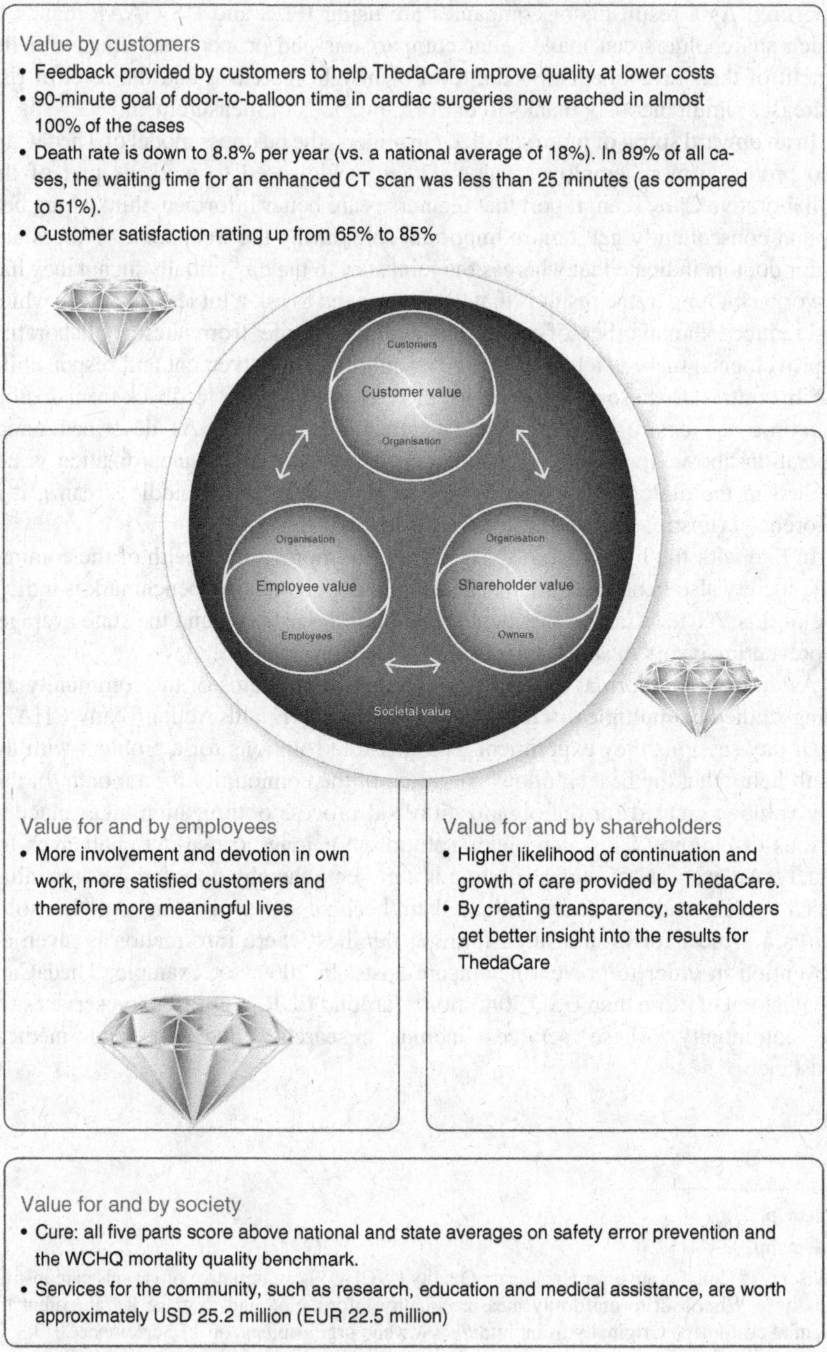

Value by customers
- Feedback provided by customers to help ThedaCare improve quality at lower costs
- 90-minute goal of door-to-balloon time in cardiac surgeries now reached in almost 100% of the cases
- Death rate is down to 8.8% per year (vs. a national average of 18%). In 89% of all cases, the waiting time for an enhanced CT scan was less than 25 minutes (as compared to 51%).
- Customer satisfaction rating up from 65% to 85%

Customers
Customer value
Organisation

Organisation
Employee value
Employees

Organisation
Shareholder value
Owners

Societal value

Value for and by employees
- More involvement and devotion in own work, more satisfied customers and therefore more meaningful lives

Value for and by shareholders
- Higher likelihood of continuation and growth of care provided by ThedaCare.
- By creating transparency, stakeholders get better insight into the results for ThedaCare

Value for and by society
- Cure: all five parts score above national and state averages on safety error prevention and the WCHQ mortality quality benchmark.
- Services for the community, such as research, education and medical assistance, are worth approximately USD 25.2 million (EUR 22.5 million)

Figure 9.2.4 Value for and by stakeholders of Thedacare

9.2.4 The Brilliant Lessons of ThedaCare

What can we learn from an organization which continuously improves itself like ThedaCare?

- Continuously carrying out short-cyclical experiments on a small scale is the key to major improvements. Since the employees themselves are improving within their sphere of influence at various locations within the organization, the process of continuous improvements takes place more quickly and the degree of involvement is higher.
- Measurements produce knowledge and stimulate employees to implement improvements in the right area. In order to guide the improvement process, it is important to properly measure the current status of operations, analyze the results of experiments, and then identify and list what it actually produced. This way successes can be celebrated and discussion is based on actual figures instead of hunches.
- Multidisciplinary teams that work properly together are necessary to continuously improve healthcare. The horizontal patient journey throughout the organization is leading and not the vertical silos of various wards, disciplines and professional hierarchy that are prevalent in healthcare. The direct result of giving the patient priority and working towards the patient goal is that the need arises to work properly together and to improve matters jointly. As a result the quality improvements experienced by the patient become enhanced and the improvements take place more quickly and are more durable.
- Dare to make a choice in the treatments available and excel therein. ThedaCare chooses to carry out only those treatments in which it can be the best based on their philosophy.
- The last major learning point from this case is the strong leadership within all components and layers of ThedaCare's organization that is visible for visitors. Servant leadership helps to get the best out of the employees and to empower them in their professionalism and responsibilities.

9.3   Princess Margaret Cancer Centre

Joining the battle against cancer together

Denise Altena, Esmée Grobbee & Jennifer op 't Hoog @: Jennifer.op.t.hoog@achmea.nl, Phone: 0031 651226420

Prelude   *This is a hospital where you are warmly welcomed. It is a place where you had never thought and hoped to arrive at, because this is where difficult times await you. At the same time it is a place where you will feel at home, where you are not only a patient, but also a human being.*

Cancer treatments often involve an intense, long-term process. It demands the utmost of patients. Cancer patients often spend a lot of time in the hospital during treatments. The Princess Margaret Cancer Centre (PMCC) in Canada proves that a hospital can be so much more than a sterile, medical environment. Needless to say, this hospital strives to provide the best treatment for the patient as well as the most personal care. The personal approach is being reintroduced to the process and the treatment which strengthens patients in their own treatment process. A stronger patient is a stronger person, which also makes the post-treatment process easier as well as reintegrating into society. Thanks to the hospitality, compassion and attention of its employees, the hospital feels like a safe haven—a place where the patient and the healthcare practitioner can fight the battle against cancer together.

Introduction   At roughly 7.6 million cases per year, cancer is one of the most important causes of death worldwide. This amounts to roughly 13 % of all deaths around the world. It is currently the most important cause of death in the Western world.[49] The expectation is that this percentage will only increase in the years to come. With an ageing society in emerging economies, it could become the same in the rest of the world.

---

[49] World Health Organization. Cancer. WHO; 2013 [30 July 2013]; Available from: http://www.who.int/mediacentre/factsheets/fs297/en/.

The Princess Margaret Cancer Centre (PMCC) in Canada provides the total care that cancer patients need. Founded as an oncological hospital in the Canadian province of Ontario, it is situated amongst other university buildings and the teaching hospital. Consequently, aside from patient care a lot of attention is paid to scientific research and the conversion thereof into the daily practice in the clinic. The focus is on the care for the patient and it is combined with carrying out science at the highest level. And by doing so, major leaps forward are made in the development of cancer treatments. The higher goal of PMCC is clear: We will conquer cancer in our lifetime! Until such time, everything is being done to treat cancer patients as well as possible. This hospital considers passion and dedication of paramount importance in the fight against cancer. This results in a combination of top-quality care at the medical level and personal attention in giving care and guidance. Physicians see a person with an illness instead of an illness with a patient. In this way a real difference is made in the life and surroundings of people. Medical science at the highest level and personal attention—all this in a country as big and vast as Canada. How can such a large province concentrate oncological care and offer personal care to people at the same time?

9.3.1 The Cornerstone: "We Will Conquer Cancer in Our Lifetime"

PMCC desires to conquer cancer by combining dedicated care and top scientific research. Recent figures have shown that one in three Canadians will develop cancer at some point.[50] This number will increase as the population ages and so that this ratio will only increase in the future. It can be concluded from this that cancer is an illness that will affect everyone, either personally or in his/her direct surroundings. Demand for oncological care is on the rise around the world.

In 1952 the institute is established as the Ontario Cancer Institute by the government of Ontario. The hospital is officially opened in 1958 and christened the Princess Margaret Hospital (PMH), named after Her Royal Highness. At that point in time, an explicit choice is made to avoid the use of the word "cancer" in the name. In those days the diagnosis of cancer feels as a death sentence since it is difficult to treat. A reference to a cancer center would have led to confusion and disquiet amongst patients instead of generating a feeling of security. In 1996 the hospital moves to its current location on University Avenue, right in the middle of the largest concentration of academic hospitals in the country.[51] Since then the combination

---

[50] http://www.cancer.ca/~/media/cancer.ca/CW/cancer%20information/cancer%20101/ Canadian%20cancer%20statistics/canadian-cancer-statistics-2013-EN.pdf.

[51] http://thepmcf.ca/Pages/AboutUs/PresidentsMessage.aspx.

of medical research and education is in the roots and genes of the PMH and still provides guidance for the hospital. In 1998 the PMH becomes a part of the University Health Network (UHN) in Ontario; the oncology wards of both Toronto General Hospital and Toronto Western Hospital also merge with the PMH.[52]

In 2012 PMCC receives its current name. Nowadays the subject of cancer is no longer taboo. The prognosis and treatment of this illness have improved drastically. PMCC is now the largest cancer center in Canada with 3000 employees serving more than 1000 patients each day in 2013. PMCC is one of the top five oncological hospitals in the world and is a leader in scientific publications. Once patients are diagnosed with cancer, they can expect to go through difficult and uncertain times. It is important that patients experience that they are not alone in this journey. Employees see themselves as innovators in oncological care, with the aim of providing optimum care and converting scientific research within oncology into daily practice. The values and qualities that guide the culture of the organization to realize the goals are: passion, dedication and providing care ("to care about care"). Not because it is your work, but because it is a calling; because good personal care for a patient is the *summum bonum* and in this manner can truly mean something in the life of someone else. In that regard, it concerns integrity and respect: every patient is unique within the hospital and has the right to respect and personalized care. When someone becomes seriously ill and his/her dependence increases, respect and self-esteem are vital. An equivalent collaboration between the patient and medical specialist based on autonomy must contribute to that end.

Scientific research must make innovation possible. An example thereof is stem cell transplantation, which originated in the laboratories of PMCC. Nowadays some 300 stem cell transplants are performed at PMCC on an annual basis. By combining care and scientific innovation, PMCC can provide its patients with the newest and most advanced therapy options. Almost one third of the patients within PMCC participate in a form of clinical research.[53] Collaboration and leadership are displayed by working together with partners and patients and by taking leadership in the field of oncological care worldwide. An example of this is the collaboration with Kenyan doctors in preventing and fighting gynecological forms of cancer, such as cervical cancer.[54]

---

[52] http://www.uhn.ca/corporate/AboutUHN/OurHospitals/Pages/pmh.aspx.

[53] http://www.research-europe.com/index.php/2013/03/dr-benjamin-neel-director-ontario-cancer-institute-princess-margaret-cancer-centre/.

[54] http://www.uhn.ca/corporate/AboutUHN/OurHospitals/Documents/PMHCP_AR_2012.pdf.

Brand essence: Fight cancer by combining top academic research with high-quality care

Higher goal
- Conquer cancer together

Brand roots
- Founded in 1952 as the Ontario Cancer Institute.
- By combining its oncological services, the organization transformed the Princess Margaret Cancer Centre into the largest hospital specialized in oncological care

Audacious goal
- We will conquer cancer in our lifetime

Brand promise
- At PMCC patients are the focus and we will try to empower you in this difficult fight

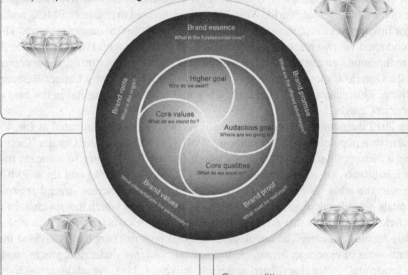

Core and brand values
- Passion and devotion
- Integrity and respect
- Academic and innovative
- Cooperation and leadership

Core qualities
- High-quality care
- Top academic research
- International cooperation

Brand proof
- World leader in stem cell research, image-guided therapeutics, lung cancer research and treatment, and patient survivorship program development

Figure 9.3.1 Vision and Positioning of PMCC

9.3.2   The Business Model: Top Research in Practice

"What we want is to give people tomorrow's care. We're not satisfied with what's done today. We're not trying to predict the future here, we're creating the future."

— Dr. Mary Gospodarowicz, CEO PMCC

Market Segments: Complex, Highly Specialized Oncological Care   Canada is provincially organized which means that the position of the health insurer and the autonomy of hospitals can vary from province to province. With 26 specialized clinics and 17 radiotherapeutic accelerators, PMCC is one of the most extensive oncological treatment centers in the world and has the largest radiation therapy treatment center in Canada. The hospital is a global leader in treatments such as stem cell therapy and cancer research. It is also one of the top five oncological research hospitals in the world. With 398,000 m^2 devoted to research, PMCC makes major investments into fundamental, translational and clinical cancer research. This is conducted via two research centers which are affiliated with PMCC and contribute to the improvement of the diagnostics and the treatment of cancer. These centers are the Ontario Cancer Institute (OCI) and the Campbell Family Cancer Research Institute. This makes PMCC the largest hospital or research hospital in the field of cancer in Canada.[55]

In 2012 the number of oncological patients in Canada was estimated at 186,400 relative to a population of 34.5 million.[56] PMCC is located in the Greater Toronto Area, a metropolitan area in the southeastern Ontario that is home to some six million inhabitants. Of all the cancer patients, 13,000 (some 27 %) end up at PMCC (see also the table "Number of new patients in 2012"). Whereas several regional hospitals provide oncological care, PMCC is the only one which has specialized in this field. The patients that arrive at PMCC are the ones who need more complex, highly specialized care. The oncological hospital provides care that is divided into several areas of expertise: breast, central nervous systems, endocrine, gastrointestinal, urogenital, gynecology, head and neck, leukemia, lung, lymphoma, myeloma, and sarcoma. PMCC has more than 210 beds for clinical admission. The 3000 employees work in 26 clinics specialized in oncology where the 12 areas of expertise are housed. In 2012, 4047 operations took place, 31,022 chemotherapy treatments and 10,150 radiation therapy treatments plus 319 stem cell transplants.[57]

---

[55] http://thepmcf.ca/Pages/AboutUs/Top5.aspx.

[56] http://www.cancer.ca/~/media/cancer.ca/CW/cancer%20information/cancer%20101/ Canadian%20cancer%20statistics/Canadian-Cancer-Statistics-2012DOUBLEHYPHEN-English. pdf.

[57] The figures and table 9.1 are based on http://www.uhn.ca/corporate/AboutUHN/OurHospitals/ Documents/PMHCP_AR_2012.pdf.

Table 9.1 Number of new patients in 2012

Disorder group		2012
Malignant	Gastrointestinal	1706
	Urogenital system	1654
	Breast	1525
	Gynecology	931
	Lung	877
	Head and neck	729
	Leukemia	666
	Lymphoma	527
	Thyroid gland	454
	Melanoma	403
	Sarcoma	321
	Central nervous system	243
	Eye (incl. melanomas and sarcomas)	145
	Other	812
Benign tumors		1825
Total tumors		12,818
Nonneoplastic		4309
Other		842
Total		17,999

Customer Value: Personalized Quality Patients come to PMCC for the combination of science and compassion in oncological healthcare. Oncological patients desire the best available care based on the latest scientific developments and personal attention in the difficult treatment process. From quick diagnosis to clinical trials, everything is used to give the patient the best personalized treatment as quickly as possible. Within this framework, patient empowerment is used so that people themselves can make choices and make their own contribution in the treatment process. Various programs exist for guiding patients in doing this. For instance, there are self-help programs and eHealth tools and patients themselves can also decide whether they want to participate in any clinical trials and, if so, which ones.

Important is that PMCC's employees truly care about providing care and consequently want to make a difference for the patient. The aim in that regard is to discover cancer earlier, to treat it more precisely with as little damage as possible to surrounding tissue and to support the patient optimally. This holds true for both the time of the treatment process and the period afterwards. An example of this is rapid diagnosis in breast cancer research. If a suspicion exists that a patient has breast cancer, radiological research is performed and the result (with a possible biopsy) is known within 1 day. If cancer is identified, the patient will immediately be offered pointers for dealing with this diagnosis. For instance, a plan is drawn up with the patient to provide insight into the illness and give hope for the future. This approach offers more than just personalized care; it increases the patient's level of self-reliance and control over the actual decisions in the treatment and the timing thereof. Patients wanting to obtain more in-depth information about the illness can find it in the library. Here they are given the opportunity to find out more about their own illness, which makes it easier for them to oversee their treatment process and take control themselves.

Quality of life is the determining factor for the setup of the process. PMCC claims that it provides good quality care, but it is difficult to measure this. Transparency in healthcare data appears not to be as developed in Canada as it is in other countries. So long-term results of treatments and provided care are not available, but might provide the opportunity for PMCC to pick this up and then really make their claims stick. For patients, the developments in scientific research and the expertise of top specialists engender trust in the care provided. Due to the many publications and PMCC's status as a leader in the field of cancer care, patients feel more confident about the treatment. So they prefer to be treated for cancer in PMCC.

> "Thankfully, my cancer was diagnosed through the Gattuso Rapid Diagnostic Centre at Princess Margaret Cancer Centre. In my opinion, they saved my life. Their willingness to push the boundaries meant that my cancer was detected at an early stage. And their vast research, knowledge and expertise have given me both direction and hope as I navigated my way to a new normal life."
>
> —Kate Mlodzik

Almost everyone is insured in the Canadian healthcare system, so patients need not be concerned as to whether they will be able to pay the bill or not. The lion's share of the population relies on the national healthcare insurer MediCare, which also pays for the care provided in PMCC. Medication is paid for via separate private health insurance that is taken out.[58,59]

Delivery: Optimizing Learning and Hospitality Scientific performances are an important foundation for the organization's reputation. In 2012 PMCC published more than 930 articles.[60] It is therefore not without reason that in 2011 the hospital was ranked third of the top five institutions in the world with the most scientific articles in the field of cancer. Scientific evidence and the application in practice are known worldwide as progressive and innovative. Consequently, PMCC is becoming well known amongst scientific societies, healthcare practitioners and patients both in Canada and abroad. PMCC makes much use of patient experiences not only to improve its internal processes through feedback loops (e.g., patient satisfaction surveys), but also to use them in its external communications. For instance, the experiential accounts of patients are shared via various communication channels, for instance online and via communications of various funds. This makes a contribution at a number of levels: it helps in society's fight against cancer and raises awareness about cancer; it creates clarity and trust for patients; and it serves as a nice spin-off for the positioning of PMCC. The delivery of personal and patient-focused care is realized by its employees. Every patient is assisted by a team consisting of a specialist, an outpatient nurse and an administrative employee. The patient is at the center of attention and every team member uses his/her own expertise to support the patient. The staff emotionally and often literally stand at the patient's side and will support him/her throughout the entire treatment process. Attention is paid to the medical aspect of the care provided, but also to the process, the emotion as well as the physical conse-

---

[58] http://www.emigratie.nl/cmsweb/canada/gezondheidszorg.html.

[59] http://thepmcf.ca/pmhonlinereport2011/?utm_source=PMCP&utm_medium=web&utm_campaign=PMCP%2BWeb.

[60] http://www.uhn.ca/corporate/AboutUHN/OurHospitals/Documents/PMHCP_AR_2012.pdf.

quences for the patient in question. Thanks to the powerful image of PMCC as a top academic center, influenced in part by the Princess Margaret Cancer Foundation and its benefit activities and campaigns, PMCC is a major attraction for motivated staff. PMCC treats only patients with cancer and employees often also consciously choose PMCC because of its involvement in fighting this illness. PMCC is truly a societal organization within the framework of realizing the goal it has set itself, which in turn results in the degree of involvement of its employees.

Aside from curative care, services are offered to stimulate current and former patients to feel better about themselves and to gain strength. For instance, there is a program called "Look Good, Feel Better," which focuses on personal care, appearance, and hair style. In addition, there are support programs and groups where the patient can receive peer support. There are also financial programs that offer help in arranging an income and healthcare or other insurance. Other services, for instance, are the health services, including dental care, mental care and dieticians. There is also help for ethical issues and spiritual care is also offered. The aim of all these programs is to provide support for current and former patients in dealing with their illness. To provide them with further support in dealing with the consequences of their treatment, there are special clinics for side-effects, such as the Cancer Pain Clinic, the Lymphedema Clinic, and the Mt. Sinai Centre for Fertility & Reproductive Health.[61]

Since Canada is a country with large thinly populated areas, the service area of hospitals like PMCC is many times greater than in densely populated countries. Distance is consequently a barrier for patients. In order to overcome the distances and to realize cooperation between hospitals, TeleHealth (or Telemedicine) is used.[62] This technology makes video conferencing within the Ontario region possible. It enables contact with patients without them having to travel great distances. Further, it offers top remote clinical care in conjunction with the doctor in the local hospital. This often occurs in cooperation with the doctor or specialized nurse, so that any physical examination can be performed immediately. If the patient has to be treated in Toronto, TeleHealth provides the opportunity to stay in touch with family members far away. Each year more than 3000 patients make use of this TeleHealth network.[63]

Operation: Knowledge and Expertise for Many People Across Great Distances The concentrated expertise and treatments at PMCC enable the use of the most advanced techniques and equipment for existing and new therapies. Examples of this include hyper-sensitive CT scans but also a robot acting as a doctor. The latter might sound somewhat futuristic, but this is a reality at PMCC. This is where the Robotic IV Automation (RIVA) is used to determine the right chemical composition for chemotherapy. Previously 2000 intravenous doses were prepared by hand each day; now this process is fully automated with RIVA, resulting in greater efficiency and improved medication safety. PMCC is the first hospital in Canada where this robotic technology is used.

Robots are deployed not only for chemotherapy, but also for surgical procedures. For instance, PMCC was the first hospital in Canada to employ robot-assisted surgery

[61] http://www.theprincessmargaret.ca/en/patientsfamilies/supportservices/pages/support-services.aspx.

[62] http://otn.ca/en/about-us.

[63] http://www.uhn.ca/PatientsFamilies/Patient_Services/Telehealth.

for lung cancer. This pioneering work also resulted in fewer complications and a quicker recovery.[64] In addition, the robot is used for minor invasive surgery in a variety of cancers, including rectal cancer. Thanks to this technology, the patient has a reduced chance of developing complications because procedures can be performed more precisely. The result is that the recovery period is shorter. In addition, PMCC has among other things 17 radiation therapy devices and is a leader in innovative research using the latest technology, such as deep brain stimulation or stem cell research.

Collaboration is of vital importance for sharing expertise. That is why PMCC is affiliated with the Cancer Care Ontario (CCO), a governmental agency with a network of 14 cancer centers in Ontario. CCO provides quality and continuous improvement in the delivery of and access to oncological care in the province. Nonetheless, the centers involved in the network still operate independently of one another. Although there is some form of consultation intensive collaboration is (still) not a reality. In other words, there is still a chance and a challenge to optimize this aspect and to increase the quality of the care provided.

PMCC is part of the University Health Network (UHN). The collaboration between hospitals in the UHN is used to help patients better in both care and services.[65] Ultimately, the aim is to optimize available equipment and specialization in the hospitals to ensure better healthcare at lower costs. For instance, the neuro-oncology unit was transferred to Toronto Western Hospital, while the surgical oncology unit moved to Toronto General Hospital.[66] As a result, specialization becomes affordable, quality increases, and costs decline.

The UHN also has an international patients program. Through this program, individuals from the entire world can take advantage of the knowledge and care in PMCC. This is possible if the care required is not available in the land of origin, in special circumstances or if a patient has friends or family who live in Toronto. For foreign patients, a quotation is drawn up based on the patient data and the estimated costs. These costs must be paid by the health insurer or by the patient himself/herself.[67,68]

At the international level, work is carried out in intensive collaboration as well. For instance, there are alliances with institutes and programs such as Yale University, OncoRay in Dresden, Liverpool Hospital, and the Cancer Control Centre. International collaboration is also aimed at bringing knowledge into practice. In Kenya, for instance, expertise is being leveraged to set up screening programs for cervical cancer in collaboration with the Moi University School of Medicine and the Moi Teaching and Referral Hospital (MTRH). As a result, women in Kenya can be treated in a timely manner, preventing deaths resulting from cervical cancer. From 2008 to 2012 alone, more than 60 women's lives were saved by this program![69] It is expected that in 2013 more than 14,000 women will be screened.

---

[64] http://www.uhn.ca/corporate/AboutUHN/OurHospitals/Documents/PMHCP_AR_2012.pdf.

[65] http://www.uhn.ca/corporate/AboutUHN/Pages/about_us.aspx.

[66] http://www.uhn.ca/corporate/AboutUHN/OurHospitals/Documents/PMHCP_AR_2012.pdf.

[67] http://www.theprincessmargaret.ca/en/PatientsFamilies/Guide/Pages/How-Do-I-Get-Referred. aspx#HowLong.

[68] http://www.uhn.ca/IHP/IPP/Pages/default.aspx.

[69] http://www.uhn.ca/corporate/AboutUHN/OurHospitals/Documents/PMHCP_AR_2012.pdf.

Value for customers

Result *What do I get?*
- I receive the best oncological care

Process *How do I get it?*
- Personal care and patient-centered approach during the process of treatment

Emotion *What do I feel?*
- I trust and feel that I am being taken good care of

Price *What are the costs?*
- The healthcare insurer decides which part is paid for from my insurance, but this is usually covered via MediCare

Effort *What do I have to do for it?*
- Having every type of care centralized increases the chance that I have to travel (far). In that case I can also opt for TeleHealth

Risk *What are the uncertainties?*
- Risk perception is low due to high quality; however, it could happen that I will have to wait for treatment

Market segments

Position
- In the top 3 of academic research organizations and in the top 5 of best oncological hospitals worldwide. Has the largest treatment center for radiotherapy in Canada

Competition
- PMCC is the largest hospital in oncological care in Canada. Competition comes from other non-specialized oncological hospitals that have the advantage of being closer to patients, which might be attractive for those with less complex types of cancer

Target group
- The incidence of cancer patients in Canada is estimated at 186,400 (2012). PMCC is primarily focused on patients from Canada, however patients worldwide can reach out for care from PMCC

Customer insights
- I want to be helped to find my own way. I want to be assisted and helped in a human approach and to be behind the steering wheel of my own treatment and be able to make my own choices in this proces

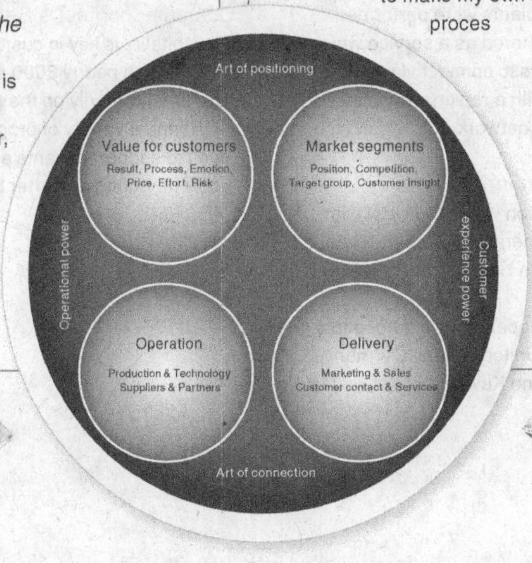

Figure 9.3.2   Value for customers and Market segments of PMCC

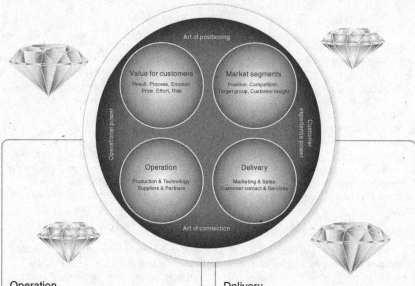

Operation

Production & Technology
- The hospital has more than 800,000m2, 210 beds and 398,000 m2 in research area. In 2012 around 18,000 new patients entered its doors, while 4047 operations, 31,022 chemotherapies, 10,155 radiotherapy treatments of which 319 stem cell transplants were performed.
- TeleHealth is offered as a service which enables patients to connect via video-conferencing with a regional hospital within the UHN network

Suppliers & Partners
- Close cooperation within the UHN with the Toronto General Hospital and the Toronto Western Hospital when delivering other care
- International cooperation with hospitals in among others United States, Germany, UK, Australia and Kuwait

Delivery

Marketing & Sales
- General free publicity and publishing academic articles in magazines that have a high impact on oncological care, immunology, molecular biology and genetics

Customer contact & Services
- Hospitality is key in customer contact. PMCC has nearly 3000 employees whose focus is primarily on the patient
- Offering a variety of programs and services to support patients and their families before, during and after treatment

Figure 9.3.3 Operation and Delivery of PMCC

9.3.3 Result: What Is the Impact of Dedication Towards Science and the Patient?

Now it is clear how the business model works, it is of course worthwhile to look at what this yields. What value is realized for and by customers, employees, and shareholders, and what result does this yield society?

In a hospital where the focus is on the patient and where the vision "conquering cancer in our lifetime" is the leitmotiv, it is not surprising that the focus is on treating the patient to the best of their ability. The scientific orientation makes it distinctive. A clear example of value for and by customers is the clinical trials, the last step in lab research before implementation in daily practice. In that regard, a new treatment, medication or improved care process is tested in real life. PMCC provides various clinical trials aimed at prevention, diagnostics, cancer treatment, and quality of life. In consultation with the attending physician, patients can choose to participate in this process. The value for patients by opting for the process is that they in every case receive the care—and perhaps even better or quicker. Through participation, they additionally help to bring the research into practice and to make a contribution in the fight against cancer.[70,71]

Patients share their experiences with PMCC to optimize processes and treatments. In this way, a greater sense of community arises, where patients come into contact with one another and exchange experiences. Qualitatively speaking, patient experiences are also made comprehensible, such as on the website of the Canadian Broadcasting Corporation (CBC). This is an independent website where patients can rate more than 132 hospitals based on a number of factors. These factors include: respect, communication, availability, hygiene and recommendations. In the spring of 2013, more than 230 patients entered their reviews, with PMCC scoring 4.5 on a scale of 1–5. That was more than a full point higher than the average of 3.5 for customer experiences at the other Canadian hospitals.[72]

The Canadian healthcare system is financed by federal and provincial taxes. Provincial governments are responsible for the set up and execution of healthcare.[73,74] This makes PMCC a semipublic care institution that is financed by the Province of Ontario and by the Princess Margaret Cancer Foundation (PMCF).[75] PMCF is the fund that financially supports PMCC in its cancer research. In 2012 that financial support amounted to CAD 84.2 million (USD 70.3 million or EUR 63 million at the time of writing). Of this amount, some 81 % was spent on research, clinical care,

---

[70] http://www.theprincessmargaret.ca/en/PatientsFamilies/library/AboutClinicalTrials/Pages/what-are-clinical-trials.aspx.

[71] http://www.uhn.ca/docs/HealthInfo/Shared%20Documents/Clinical_Trials_at_PMH.pdf.

[72] http://www.cbc.ca/news/health/features/ratemyhospital/profiles/princess-margaret-university-health-network/.

[73] http://www.justlanded.com/nederlands/Canada/Canada-Gids/Gezondheid/De-gezondheidszorg.

[74] http://www.canadian-healthcare.org/page8.html.

[75] http://www.canadian-healthcare.org/page8.html.

and training; 7 % on buildings and materials; 10 % on administration and additional fundraising; and 2 % set aside as a contribution to a financially sound continued existence of the Foundation.

In 2013 PMCF launches a new "Believe It" campaign, with the aim of generating CAD 500 million (USD 417 million or EUR 375 million) for research into personalized cancer medicine.[76] PMCF is a nonprofit organization which is dedicated to raising funds to realize its audacious goal and consequently to conquer cancer.[77] The Foundation organizes various fundraising activities. By far most of the money comes in via lotteries (41 %). Hundreds of thousands of people buy a ticket for these lotteries, hoping to win a prize (a fully furnished home or apartment).[78] In addition, sport events or sport sponsor events are organized.

In 2012 the UHN as a whole is ranked as the best of the top 40 research hospitals in Canada. UHN has also repeatedly figured in the list of Canada's Top 100 Employers, an annual survey of more than 75,000 Canadian employers. Employers are assessed based on: physical workplace, working atmosphere, family benefits, financial aspects, health, holiday opportunities, communication, trainings and courses.[79] The UHN motivates employees in their personal development, pays well and provides good employee benefits and secondary work conditions[80] In that regard, the value that it creates for the employees is returned to the organization in the form of compassion and personal attention for the patients. It is with dedication and compassion that doctors and nurses ensure that they get the most out of the situation. Employees have brought back true personal care by way of the respect and integrity that they show in their work with the patient. The dedication and contribution of the people who work at PMCC are a clear example of the UHN philosophy and show how this works in practice.

Through its societal vision "fighting and wanting to conquer cancer," PMCC makes a direct contribution to value for society. The research projects and publications contribute to the national and international sharing and consequently increasing of knowledge. Integrating research into the daily practice produces a health profit for patients and increases the quality of life through the fight against the illness. In addition, the vision makes a contribution at the societal level by raising the awareness of cancer. This happens, among other things, by fundraising via societal campaigns and by properly informing patients and parties concerned about the illness and the role that they themselves can play during and after the treatment process. The hospital is transparent in its business and its strategy. Reports, such as annual reports, but also strategy plans are accessible to the public. This ensures that the goals of PMCC are open and tangible, so that people also develop and maintain trust in the organization.

---

[76] http://www.uhn.ca/corporate/AboutUHN/OurHospitals/Documents/PMHCP_AR_2012.pdf.

[77] http://thepmcf.ca/Pages/DonorImpact/.

[78] http://www.blogpmhf.ca/Blog/PMHF-Blog/April-2011/Lotteries-and-Selling-Out-By-Early-Bird.aspx.

[79] http://www.canadastop100.com/national/.

[80] http://www.uhn.ca/corporate/Careers/Pages/who_we_are.aspx.

Value by customers
- Customers receive the best cancer care; in 2011 PMCC was high on the list in the US News & World Report's Best Hospitals.
- Participation in clinical trials makes it possible to put research into practice in treatment and to deliver value for both the patient and the organization.
- Word-of-mouth advertizing by patients scores a 4.5 out of 5

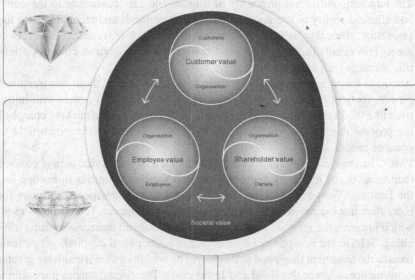

Value for and by employees
- From 2004-2009 the hospital was on the Top 100 list of Canadian employers.
- Employees are the 'face' of care for the patient
- Employees receive a learning environment and are motivated in personal development, education and health

Value for and by shareholders
- Semi-public organization and funded by provincial taxes.
- For its scientific research, PMCC often depends on the Princess Margaret Foundation and other social foundations and sponsors

Value for and by society
- Contribute to the social fight against cancer
- Transparency about figures, annual reports and strategic plans. Publications stimulate scientific and international development and learning on this topic.
- Programs and services aimed at promoting the successful return to society of former cancer patients

Figure 9.3.4 Value for and by stakeholders of PMCC

9.3.4   The Brilliant Lessons of Princess Margaret Cancer Centre

The Princess Margaret Cancer Centre is a diamond in oncological care, a hospital that provides huge volumes of oncological care in a massive area. What can we learn from PMCC's example?

- The bundling and literal proximity of science and care contribute to the quick and efficient ability to use and implement new methods and technology. At the same time, clinical trials provide science with feedback for research and accelerate it. This results in the continuous combination of innovative, complex scientific research with daily patient care.
- Attention for patients and enabling them to make choices in their own treatment process (patient empowerment) results in self-confidence. Together with initiatives like the Patient Navigation Program, this prompts patients to take charge of the process themselves and enable them to take the lead in their own fight to conquer cancer.
- PMCC has one main location from which a much larger service area is covered than usual in the generally densely populated Western countries in Europe and the East and West coasts of the USA. In order to provide specialized care for more than just the people who are physically in the hospital, TeleHealth is used, which prevents the relevant patient from having to spend unnecessary time travelling. TeleHealth is supported by a doctor in his/her local hospital, yet patients receive the treatment they need in this way. The benefits of TeleHealth are greater convenience, a lower threshold and lower costs. The circumstances have stimulated PMCC to be a frontrunner in this perspective and this now delivers best practices that are also valuable for supporting focus and cooperation in more densely populated areas.
- The financial model, with the Foundation behind the organization, contributes to both societal involvement and the stability of the organization. The mission "We will conquer cancer in our lifetime" and the campaign "Believe It!" generate a lot of publicity, while financing is arranged for further development. The mission is a major attraction for patients and employees, making the care provided societal and more personal. In addition, it attracts employees with passion and dedication.

9.4 Mayo Clinic

The highest quality care organized around you

Bas Schepman, Jennifer op 't Hoog & Jeroen Kemperman
@: Jennifer.op.t.hoog@achmea.nl, Phone: 0031 651226420
@: Jeroen.Kemperman@achmea.nl, Phone: 0031 651222099

Prelude *Imagine that you are diagnosed with a very unpleasant, serious illness. You have to be admitted to a hospital. At that point a number of questions naturally come to mind: "What am I going to have to go through in the near term? Will I go to a large hospital? If so, will I just be treated like a number? Will I see that specialist ever again after I have been admitted? Or will he send his co-assistant? And what will happen if the medication doesn't work? Do they have a fall-back option for that eventuality?" In that case, you will want to go to a hospital where they provide you with answers to those questions and where the best doctors work together with the best researchers and the best scientists. More than a century ago, in 1889, one man laid the foundation for that type of hospital: Dr. William Mayo started the Mayo Clinic.*

Mayo Clinic is the most prominent hospital in the world. Integrated care was invented here. Prior to even entering the hospital building, you have been informed about the procedures that await you. The doctor who receives you will act as your coach to guide you through the healing process in the hospital. For decades, Mayo Clinic has enjoyed the status of a leading hospital and in that regard is the place where many physicians and scientists would like to work. This demands a lot of them though. Working at Mayo Clinic is only for those who are able to place patients and their care process at the center of attention—at the expense of everything else including themselves. That patients value this approach is evident from, among other things, the impressive fact that Mayo Clinic receives an average of 750 gifts from patients every day. In 2014 that amounted to gifts worth USD 288 million (EUR 259 million)—funds that, needless to say, are reinvested in healthcare by Mayo Clinic.

Introduction Mayo Clinic is a nonprofit medical assistance and research group based in Rochester, Minnesota, USA. It employs more than 4200 doctors and researchers, 2400 fellows and residents, while some 52,900 employees work in the total network of integrated care. It specializes in the integrated diagnosis and treatment of medically specialized care for both regular care and highly complex care. In 2012 in excess of USD 923 million (EUR 831 million) was spent on research and more than 1.5 million patients were cared for worldwide.

Mayo Clinic has been ranked as one of the top hospitals in America for years; it has even topped the list for specialized fields like gynecology and diabetes care. In 2014, no fewer than 15 specializations of Mayo Clinic were ranked in the top 10 by the US News & World Report. In addition, the group has been in the list of the 100 best businesses to work for years already. These are fantastic results, but what are the roots of this success?

In order to obtain a proper understanding of the success of Mayo Clinic, it is vital to look at its origins. On 21 August 1883, a major tornado roars through the city of Rochester, leaving 40 dead and 200 injured in its wake. At that time the city does not have a hospital and the injured cannot be transported elsewhere. Dr. William Mayo, a member of a leading family of doctors in the city, takes on the task of providing care for them. Since there is no hospital in Rochester at the time, care is provided in a makeshift hospital set up in a dance hall. At the request of the local Mother Superior, Dr. Mayo takes the initiative to set up his own hospital in the city. On 30 September 1889, Saint Mary's Hospital is opened.

It is in this hospital that innovative healthcare and the pioneering spirit continues which Dr. Mayo was already pursuing in his own medical practice together with his two sons. The integration of care, the combination of care with science and research, and placing the patient at the center of attention turn this hospital into a leader in American healthcare in a short period of time. Crucial to this development is the decision in 1919 to turn Mayo Clinic into a not-for-profit organization, whereby the partner structure is terminated and the doctors and researchers become employees. The integrated approach and deeply rooted perspective, also in financial terms, that people can do more for the patient together, is still the focus of the business model of Mayo Clinic after more than 125 years. All this is reason enough to investigate this brilliant business model in further detail.

9.4.1 The Cornerstone: "The Needs of the Patient Come First"

"The sum total of medical knowledge is now so great and wide-spreading that it would be futile for any one man ... to assume that he has even a working knowledge of any part of the whole ... The best interest of the patient is the only interest to be considered, and in order that the sick may have the benefit of advancing knowledge, union of forces is necessary ... It has become necessary to develop medicine as a cooperative science; the clinician, the specialist, and the laboratory workers uniting for the good of the patient, each assisting in elucidation of the problem at hand, and each dependent upon the other for support."

—William J. Mayo, 1910

"Patients first" has become a popular saying of many healthcare practitioners. Putting the "patient first" is nonetheless a goal that in most cases has not yet been fully realized. At Mayo Clinic it has, and right from its inception. The brand essence is therefore "Patients first!" i.e., everything is done for the patient. From the very beginning in his own general medicine practice, Dr. William May sees his role as a doctor as a supporting one. Placing patients at the center of attention and making them better is what it is all about. It is with this vision and this guiding principle that Saint Mary's Hospital, the predecessor to Mayo Clinic, is established. It is a hospital that the patient enters to become better; everything is done to realize that goal. And if it is better possible to do so by integrating healthcare more effectively, then so be it. If good research and the linking of science to medical specialists produces good results, then good scientists and researchers are needed in the hospital. And in order to optimize this process, these people will have to be able to work together on the patient, and so Mayo Clinic develops an integrated patient file as early as 1907.

Just prior to that, in 1906, Mayo Clinic also sets up the Surgeons Club. There, specialists are invited to come to Rochester to share knowledge and to learn from each other. It is, in fact, one of the first open platforms for cocreation and innovation, a concept that has only really been further developed in the past few years.

Mayo Clinic desires to create hope and make a contribution to health and the welfare of people around the world. That is its higher goal. It requires not only the best care for the patient, but also the best in terms of the patient's experience and in hospital procedures. From the outset, Mayo Clinic has implemented integrated diagnoses and has organized treatments around the patient as well as being a leader in Research & Development. The goal that Mayo Clinic continuously pursues is the best care for every patient by coordinating medical research, practical experience, and learning processes. It is not uncommon for patients to be seeing one specialist after another for up to a year or more, and still not knowing what is wrong with them. At Mayo Clinic everything is done to prevent that and to make the right diagnosis immediately. Even if that demands that eight top specialists have to work together to discover what it is. That is invaluable in a world where getting the diagnosis right quickly, seems to become more difficult and requires a high degree of skill and intuition based on experience and knowledge.[81]

The promise is: everything for you as a patient and for your family. This means the best doctors—not just in terms of medical expertise, but also in the contact with you as a patient. Central to that business operation is: compassion, integrity, excellence and teamwork. Compassion is needed for and with the patient and the people directly involved with the patients. The highest possible level of professionalism, ethics and personal responsibility is pursued in all processes when it comes to integrity. And a drive for excellence is needed for the patient. The conviction is that only those that work in a team based on equality, can achieve all this.

---

[81] The importance of diagnosis and the added value of Mayo in this field is discussed, for instance, in Christensen et al. (2009).

Mayo Clinic has a number of distinctive core qualities that together with the core values create a way of working that makes it possible to organize this top-quality care for their patients. These core qualities are excellence, innovation and continuous improvement. Excellence in care is the guiding principle in all processes in the hospital: "Whatever we do, we do well." Innovation is used among other things by employing the creative ideas and unique talents of employees to maximum effect. This leads to continuous improved processes and services to heal the patient. It simultaneously contributes to keeping the organization and the spirit alive and energetic. The experience of employees and patients are sought out and shared, forming the starting point for improvement building upon stewardship to optimize the use of scarce resources. The proof that the organization has for these efforts comes in the form of satisfied patients, happy employees and top-quality care, highlighted by no less than 12 (!) top three rankings in the Best Hospitals in the USA 2014 among a total of 16 care specializations that were reviewed.[82]

Guaranteeing that the entire organization places the patient at the center of attention demands true dedication. For Mayo Clinic, it is clear that this is only possible if all employees are selected based on their ability to empathize. This is a tough selection criterion for all staff—doctors, specialists, nurses, researchers and scientists. It also plays a role in the selection of potential students of Mayo Clinic's training institute. They are also tested for their empathy levels ensuring that the organization's vision is present even before they commence their training courses.

---

[82] http://health.usnews.com/best-hospitals/rankings.

Brand essence: **The needs of the patient come first!**

Higher goal

- To inspire hope and contribute to health and well-being. Providing the best care to every patient through integrated clinical practice, education and research

Brand roots

- The needs of the customer have come first for 125 years by providing integrated care combined with innovation, research and development.
- Building upon the vision and intent of the founders, the original Mayo physicians and the Sisters of Saint Francis

Audacious goal

- Providing the best care to every patient through integrated clinical practice, education and research
- Implement the Mayo vision on patients as the standard in all healthcare institutions

Brand promise

- Through teamwork and innovation, we will give you the healthcare treatment with the best quality possible

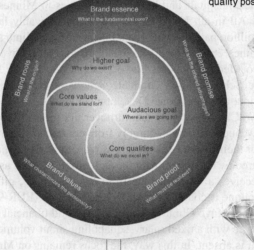

Core and brand values

- Respect
- Compassion
- Integrity

Core qualities

- Excellence
- Innovation
- Healing
- Stewardship
- Teamwork

Brand proof

- Mayo Clinic is ranked in the top 3 in 13 of 16 healthcare specialisms in the US
- Half of the patients are not privately insured, so they are not here to maximize income

Figure 9.4.1 Vision and Positioning of Mayo Clinic

9.4.2 The Business Model: "Care Should Be Available for Everyone"

Market Segments: Everyone Who Requires Care Since 1919 Mayo Clinic has developed into an enormous care business with three fully owned hospitals in America. Rochester, Minnesota is home to the largest hospital with 1132 beds, more than 62,400 annual admissions plus 51,000 operations and more than 225,000 outpatient treatments (2012). Jacksonville, Florida provides 214 beds, admits more than 12,000 people annually and performs more than 6000 operations and in excess of 45,000 outpatient treatments (2012). And finally Scottsdale/Phoenix, Arizona offers 244 beds, also has slightly more than 12,000 annual admissions, completes almost 5500 operations and carries out just under 40,000 outpatient treatments (2012).

Besides Mayo Clinic's own hospitals, Mayo Clinic Health System is a network of over 70 clinics, hospitals and healthcare facilities in Minnesota, Iowa, Georgia and Wisconsin. All in all, Mayo Clinic has an unbelievably large reach: in 2014 more than 1.3 million patients were seen. Further, Mayo Clinic also takes its role as a trainer of healthcare practitioners seriously, having set up five of its own training institutes: Mayo Medical School, Mayo Graduate School of Medical education, Mayo Graduate School, Mayo Graduate School of Health Sciences and Mayo School of Continuous Professional Development.

In 2014 Mayo Clinic had an annual turnover in excess of USD 9.7 billion (EUR 8.7 billion). Revenues are derived largely from contracts with insurers that procure care services for their insured customers. Mayo Clinic also generates income from care that is insured by the government through programs such as Medicare. Further, Mayo Clinic receives a lot of income from external funds, gifts and bequests. In 2014, bequests alone accounted for USD 103.9 million (EUR 93.5 million). From the very beginning, Mayo Clinic has been a very solid financial entity. Since everyone is an employee with a fixed salary, squabbling about volumes, bonuses or other financial stimuli is absent. In this way, the focus remains on Mayo Clinic's goal to have a patient-oriented organization that does everything in the interest of the patient and is not tempted in any way, by financial motives.

As far as integrated care is concerned, Kaiser Permanente can be seen as a large "competitor" despite the fact that they are actually not a hospital, but a health insurer using healthcare practitioners in their network. The hospital competitors of Mayo Clinic are in particular the other large private care institutions such as Cleveland Clinic, which in 2014 had a turnover of USD 6.4 billion (EUR 5.8 billion) and has 39,100 employees, MD Anderson Cancer Center which in 2012 had a turnover of USD 4.4 billion (EUR 4 billion) and more than 20,000 employees, whilst Johns Hopkins Medicine had a turnover of USD 7.7 billion (EUR 6.9 billion) and 41,000 employees. All these hospitals invest enormous sums in their facilities, training programs and knowledge, yet for the time being none of them is getting the broad acknowledgements that Mayo Clinic is receiving.

When looking at how the organization positions itself, you might get the impression that Mayo Clinic is an exclusive and expensive hospital. That perception is mainly derived from its "premium" brand image. But Mayo Clinic is in fact certainly not only available for privately insured individuals which would also not match its not-for-profit roots. In fact, Mayo Clinic delivers some 50 % of its paid medical care to patients of Medicare or similar government programs. In 2014 Mayo Clinic delivered an additional sum exceeding USD 385 million (EUR 346 million) in care that went unpaid via programs such as Medicare, Medicaid, or care-specific services for senior citizens. And people in distress who do not qualify for one of the government's programs can rely on a safety net in the Mayo support fund that paid out USD 75.9 million (EUR 68 million) in 2014.

Customer Value: Knowing What You Are Facing Patients entering Mayo Clinic know that they are in good hands. They are properly informed and know what awaits them. Right from the intake interview, all processes focus on ensuring that the patient concentrates only on one thing: getting better. This gives patients a feeling of trust: they know that everything is being done to make them better. Patients are helped by doctors and nurses who work in equal, multidisciplinary teams. The doctors and nurses are on their side and consult with the patient as equals. This plays to the strength of patients, so that they are able to take control of their own healing process. Unlike any other hospital, Mayo Clinic has really integrated care which goes beyond bringing the various elements in chronic care together (e.g., for diabetes), but includes involving scientists and researchers in the actual recovery process. That means that the latest knowledge, technology, and options are available for the patients.

Delivery: Care Literally Organized Around You The vision that is embedded in the roots of the organization forms the guiding principle in its brand management. Mayo Clinic was one of the first hospitals that hired marketers to position the hospital in the healthcare market. By now the organization is well known for its ability to integrate social media and the use of apps in their marketing strategy. This market and marketing strategy is aimed at potential patients to make sure the "patient first" approach is clear to them, but also for fundraising. Fundraising is an important part of the revenues of Mayo Clinic and this is where it cashes in on their positioning.

For customers, the entire experience is so positive that they "gladly" come back in the unfortunate event that something is again wrong with them. As previously outlined, it is clear from the moment the diagnosis is made which care procedure lays ahead. The first specialist that sees the patient will act as his/her coach throughout the whole process. At the patient's bedside are not only a co-assistant and a nurse, but also an entire team of care professionals, including a medical specialist, a scientist, and a researcher. All disciplines that are important for healing the patient join forces and together with the patient take up the fight against the illness. The specialist, the scientist and the researcher truly work together to make the patient better, whereby their knowledge is combined, and egos and/or hierarchy are left at the door. Patients never receive a "standard" form of care from their nurse, but rather the care they –with his/her particular illness at a certain phase—require. Everything—and by that we mean everything—is done for the benefit of the patient. In other words, no one is preoccupied with side issues; but everyone is focused on their job at hand. The feedback and problems of patients are taken seriously and often result in a modification of the healing process.

Operation: Striving for the Best for the Patient Delivering the best care for patients means that all processes must be continuously in order and investments in quality and reliability must be measured. If everyone in the organization is truly focused on this, things can only get better. The medical knowledge and involvement is visible everywhere in the organization. Such as the fact that the CEO is always a doctor from Mayo Clinic itself. Not a director, not a management executive, but someone who himself or herself has stood at the bedside of patients. Incidentally, that also applies to the Supervisory Board, whose members are all physicians. The fact that management is in the hands of doctors ensures that everything is reviewed through the eyes of a physician and therefore contributes to what the patient finds important. In order to keep management on their toes and to prevent any routine for arising, as well as to provide an incentive to improve care, unit heads are appointed for only 4-year terms. After this term has expired, someone else must take over.

Mayo Clinic has a multidisciplinary approach that focuses on equality. Everyone is employed by Mayo Clinic and this is underlined in the remuneration scheme. As hierarchy or financial incentives do not play a role, the mutual trust amongst employees is enhanced, teamwork proceeds more smoothly and the focus on the patient intensifies. Needless to say, Mayo Clinic disposes of the most advanced equipment, but they are also quickly modified if doing so benefits the process or the quality of the care provided. For instance, Mayo Clinic employees themselves developed the YES board—a large monitor that integrates important patient data in the accident and emergency department rooms, which is used to quickly assemble a complete picture of the situation. It is yet another innovation by which everyone can focus better on what he/she has to do for the patient and not spend precious time on boundary conditions.

Mayo Clinic is one of the few hospitals in the world with several of its own innovation departments, such as Patients Experience and Design and the Center for Innovation. The first one deals with the experience of patients during their stay in Mayo Clinic. Thanks to the use of art, furniture and upholstery, Mayo Clinic emphasizes its vision on healthcare. For instance, by using posters, they literally show the difference between a patient file from 1907 and how it is today. Which shows that healthcare changes, but the vision of Mayo Clinic does not. In the Center for Innovation physicians and process developers work continuously together in an attempt to improve the internal processes. This can be practical, such as a better setup for the examination rooms, or more treatment process-related, for instance improving the process for ears, nose, and throat examinations for children. For that matter, quality monitoring, improvement and innovation are also part of the regular training courses for new employees. In fact, Mayo Clinic is seen as an organization that can match up to well known continuous process improvement companies like Toyota with their renowned Lean program. The various employees at Mayo Clinic are given a lot of freedom to optimize their roles themselves. For instance, schedules are not based on the number of patients that must be cared for, but rather on the care that these patients actually require. Then an assessment is made every 8 h as to whether that care is still sufficient and based on these outcomes the schedule is adjusted if required. During scheduled appointments physicians are not on call, so there are no pagers that go off during doctor-patient discussions. Doctors that are not with patients are on call and can be hailed via a pager system developed internally for quick and direct contact. In this way, making a diagnosis that does not fall directly under the expertise of the doctor at the patient's bedside can be quickly realized by requesting another physician to join him. This is another good example of how the multidisciplinary teams and good communication contribute to efficiency and effective diagnosis and treatment.

Value for customers

Result *What do I get?*
- My condition is clear and I get the best possible healthcare treatment

Process *How do I get it?*
- Me and my needs to get better are central to the process

Emotion *What do I feel?*
- I feel safe, understood and treated as a human being

Price *What are the costs?*
- The insurer reimburses the costs and, if it is truly needed, I receive the care I need without insurance

Effort *What do I have to do for it?*
- Contact Mayo Clinic and go there

Risk *What are the uncertainties?*
- This is the top clinic in integrated care, so risks cannot be lower

Market segments

Position
- This is undisputedly the best hospital in the world, where the top specialists, scientist and researchers cooperate. In terms of best practices, this is the way integrated care around the patients should be organized

Competition
- Other large hospitals in the US such as Cleveland Clinic, MD Anderson Cancer Center and Johns Hopkins. As regards integrated healthcare, Kaiser Permanente is a true competitor

Target group
- Everyone who has a medical condition and wants to be healed if it concerns a serious standard condition or a complicated mix of diseases

Customer insights
- Ultimately what you want as a patient is to get the best possible healthcare treatment and if there is one place where that is provided that is Mayo Clinic

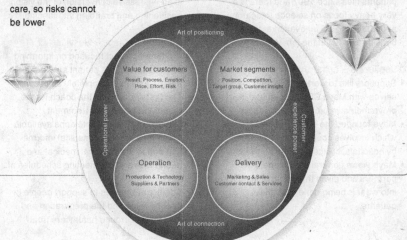

Figure 9.4.2   Value for customers and Market segments of Mayo Clinic

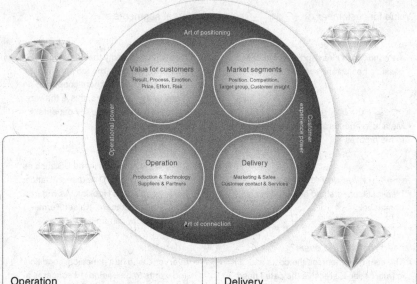

Operation

Production & Technology

- Integrated care, standardization of processes and continuous improvement of healthcare paths enable everyone to focus on curing the patient
- All technology is focused on and around the patient: there have been integrated patients files since 1907 and there is a very heavy focus on science, research and technological innovation at the bedside and not in the lab

Suppliers & Partners

- Suppliers like to work and affiliate themselves with Mayo Clinic to test and improve their own products and services.
- Mayo founded the Mayo Health System, which involves cooperation in 70 areas by hospitals, clinics and 800 specialists.
- Mayo views general practitioners as partners and gives them a lot of insight into what is being done with 'their' patients.

Delivery

Marketing & Sales

- The vision is the starting principle for the branding. Mayo Clinic was one of the first hospitals to hire marketers. It is well known for integrating traditional media, social media and apps.
- Very active in fundraising in which there is an impressive conversion of the vision, positioning and branding into funding

Customer contact & Services

- Customer contact focused on informing and supporting the patient and the family as fully and completely as possible
- The first specialist is the coach for the rest of the healthcare treatment
- Mayo Clinic has multiple apps available which give access to medical information and to the personal medical and health files and the meeting schedules of the patient
- Additional services to support people in healthy living and the preparation and revalidation around healthcare treatments

Figure 9.4.3 Operation and Delivery of Mayo Clinic

9.4.3 Result: How Does Putting the Patient First, Pay Off?

The fact that everything revolves around the patient at Mayo Clinic is clear, but at the end of the day the question is: what is the result of all these efforts?

The online reviews of Mayo Clinic are full of praise. Even in those cases where the patient deceased from the consequences of his/her illness, the responses of the surviving relatives and family regarding Mayo Clinic are still positive and heartwarming. Whereas it sounds strange in this context, the praise of patients is repaid in the form of the patient's "loyalty." He or she will certainly recommend Mayo Clinic to friends and family if they themselves need any care. This is also evident from the constant stream of revenues that Mayo Clinic receives from gifts, bequests and donations from patients. In 2012, there were 191,619 of them—no less than 750 a day! The total amount thereof in 2012 exceeded USD 361 million (EUR 325 million) Mayo Clinic devoted this entirely, of course, to research and science. Ultimately, a net operating income of USD 834 million (EUR 751 million) was posted for 2014. That is an operating margin of 8.5%, which meets the requirements of the organization's long-term vision.

For many years, Mayo Clinic is one of Fortune's *100 Best Companies to Work For*. There is, of course, a reason why Mayo Clinic is on that list. It is because all elements that play a role at the core of working within healthcare are arranged exceedingly well here. The people who come to work share the same goal: doing everything to ensure that sick people become better again and to support them in the entire process that patients have to go through to achieve that. They consciously opt for a hospital where the specialists earn a salary just like everyone else and in that sense are on equal footing with the researchers and nurses. It is a multidisciplinary team that works on the basis of mutual trust and respect and whose members strive to reach for the top, day in and day out. One where everyone makes a contribution based on integrity and professionalism in order to realize their joint goal. Important in the employee value is also directing resources based on the actual required care instead of on the number of patients in the hospital. As a result, patients receive the care they need, which contributes to an increased level of involvement on the part of the employees, who in turn also go to work with a happier feeling. That team spirit is also the reason that Mayo Clinic is an unprecedentedly strong brand as far as healthcare is concerned. Dr. Leonard Berry of Mayo Clinic took a year-long sabbatical to investigate the organization of Mayo Clinic and the experience thereof in the outside world. Together with Sandra Lampo of the London Business School, he wrote an article about the strategy of the hospital.[83] In it he explains that the success of Mayo Clinic stems from three factors: remaining faithful to your vision, building up a brand with your customers by always doing more than just the "standard" delivery of services and by having your vision radiate throughout your staff members. They are, after all, the persons who deal with patients on a daily basis.

---

[83] Berry and Lampo (2004).

Mayo Clinic delivers a significant and a unique contribution to society. Since 1919, Mayo Clinic has developed into an enormous care institute that nowadays helps more than one million patients annually. It was calculated that in 2012 Mayo Clinic contributed directly and indirectly to the maintenance or creation of 144,468 jobs. Mayo Clinic has three specific research centers whose goal is to make a contribution to better care in the world: the Center for Individualized Medicine (set up to modify medication to the genetic profile of the patient), the Center for Regenerative Medicine (focused on replacing cell material and better anticipating the total healing process of the body) and the Center for the Science of Healthcare Delivery (where evidence-based care models are further developed). As a whole, Mayo Clinic invested more than USD 885 million (EUR 796 million) in education and research programs in 2012. In that year Mayo Clinic also invested in excess of USD 2.5 billion (EUR 2.2 billion) in hundreds of local initiatives near their own hospitals to strengthen care and health, youth or other training programs, employment, and personal development.

Via its own five educational institutes, Mayo Clinic also makes a contribution to training thousands of good, motivated healthcare practitioners. It has been calculated that USD 4 million (EUR 3.6 million) in training investments now, can produce USD 40 million (EUR 36 million) in savings later. A regular part of the training courses for doctors is a residence in a medically "weak" country in order to use the vision of Mayo Clinic there and in doing so improve its care system. Upon completion of their training, the graduate healthcare practitioners (2608 in 2012) begin their careers spread around the USA. They take the vision for care of Mayo Clinic with them and disseminate it throughout the country. The continuous pursuit at Mayo Clinic to improve and to speed up the diagnosis process, contributes to a quicker recovery. This is not only in the interest of the patient, but also of others. Such as employers that incur less losses and costs in labor participation by sick employees which in turn is more advantageous for insurers, employers, and society as a whole.

Value by customers
- One million patients are treated every year throughout the entire network.
- There are countless online reviews of patients who have been cured by Mayo Clinic and even the relatives of the deceased often praise the hospital. If you listen to them, this is the place you want to go to if you have a serious disease. This high degree of loyalty and NPS is the basis for the expansion of Mayo Clinic

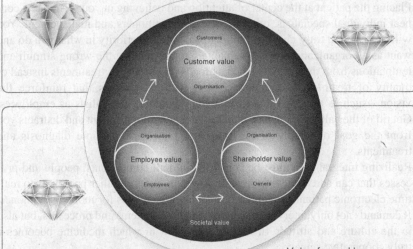

Value for and by employees
- Mayo Clinic has featured in the top 100 of best companies to work for and has been for a long time already.
- There is a lot of freedom for people who have the passion and abilities to develop and give people the best healthcare possible
- People can develop themselves not only professionally but also personally. Besides the doctors, the nurses have more influence than in other hospitals and the management of departments is often renewed with fresh blood

Value for and by shareholders
- Mayo Clinic is a non-profit organization, i.e. without commercial shareholders.
- Annual figures are nonetheless presented with the focus on the positive impact of Mayo Clinic. The annual figures are primarily used to demonstrate to donors that their contributions are making a difference in providing outstanding research and care

Value for and by society
- Mayo Clinic has developed from a local hospital to a leading healthcare institute which heals a lot of people directly and through its network
- Mayo Clinic improves healthcare as a whole via applied research and has educated thousands of medical healthcare providers in its own 5 education institutes
- Mayo Clinic also invests enormous amounts of money in hundreds of local initiatives relating to health, youth and development

Figure 9.4.4   Value for and by stakeholders of Mayo Clinic

9.4.4   The Brilliant Lessons of Mayo Clinic

This is the dream of all sick people, as the ideal place for the treatment of very complex illnesses can come true here. It is a place where everything comes together: diagnosis, science, research, integrated treatment, and teamwork involving everyone for benefit of the patient.

- Placing the patient at the center of attention and believing in your vision can connect individual specialists, other healthcare practitioners and management. You will excel if you truly give this guiding principle top priority in what you do and want as an organization. It is a valuable pursuit: remove the wrong stimuli and temptations from the system—such as focus on number of treatments instead of quality of treatments—and replace that with alternatives that reinforce the vision—such as treating all staff members including specialists as employees. Get rid of the ballast of the past that does not benefit the patient and distracts you from the goal of simply giving the patient the best possible diagnosis and treatments.
- Realizing integral care must be converted into all components, people and processes that can add value—from staff selection, work or other processes to real-time electronic patient files and now also integrated apps for mobile telephones. It demands not only interventions in information, systems and processes, but also in the culture and attitude of mutual teamwork in which medicine becomes a truly cooperative science.
- Keep on learning. Feedback loops at every level in the organization, focused on quality and attitude, are essential. Negative experiences should be enough to prompt participants to improve the process again and again. When this becomes part of your total organizational reports, not only will the quality and efficiency improve, but your employees and customers will also value it positively.

Chapter 10
Lessons for Creating Brilliant Business Models in Healthcare

The creation and construction of a brilliant business model requires years, if not decades. With the nuance that it is not about sequential steps that can be completed once and for all, three phases can be distinguished in realizing a brilliant business model. Following this there is the fourth phase with the challenge to renew yourself without losing the core. Looking upon the lessons from brilliant business models in healthcare the understanding of these phases can be deepened.

- *Phase 1: Start from a vision and bring the brand positioning in line with it. Especially in healthcare the drive to improve the health of (more) people provides the true energy to do the right thing.*
- *Phase 2: Persevere consistently in the conversion of the vision into the business model. In healthcare that requires a good mix between solidarity and responsibility, maintaining the personal scale and stimulating self-management and continuous learning from health practitioners and researchers with the patient as starting point.*
- *Phase 3: Realize breakthroughs in the value creation for all stakeholders with the business model. The triple aim to improve the health of a population and the perceived quality of treatments while lowering costs at the same time, emphasises the need for organizations which increase value for all stakeholders at the same time.*
- *Phase 4: Retain the core and stimulate progress in the business model. The challenges we face together in creating and keeping good healthcare accessible, transparent and affordable for all, makes the necessity to keep on doing the right thing even more relevant in this field!*

This book started with an explanation of the conceptual framework we use to describe brilliant business models. We described which five breakthroughs are necessary for accessible, affordable, and qualitatively good healthcare. The largest part of this book is subsequently devoted to describing each desired breakthrough and providing case studies of four organisations for each breakthrough that have realized a brilliant solution to that end. In this final chapter we want to outline the general

© Springer International Publishing Switzerland 2017   381
J. Kemperman et al. (eds.), *Brilliant Business Models in Healthcare*,
DOI 10.1007/978-3-319-26440-0_10

lessons and draw the overall conclusions from the 20 brilliant business models described above—for each and every solution is truly brilliant. The organizations described in this book excel at demonstrable value creation for all parties concerned. Apart from having implemented a breakthrough in healthcare, they have been able to "generate" very satisfied customers, very satisfied employees and good financial results plus make a positive contribution to society. How have they been able to do that? What are the overarching lessons that can be drawn from these brilliant business models?

The conceptual framework described in Part 1 was developed by integrating existing literature and studying successful companies in various sectors. The overall finding was that brilliant business models have a number of elements in common in terms of characteristics and development. This insight has been embedded in this theoretical framework. An organization with a brilliant business model (1) is driven by a vision and brand positioning, (2) perseveres in the business model with a consistent conversion of the vision and brand positioning into market segments, customer value, delivery and operation, and (3) on the basis thereof is pioneering in the value created for and by all stakeholders.[1]

The characteristics of a brilliant business model are not realized overnight. The actual creation and construction or expansion of a brilliant business model requires years, if not decades to achieve and in any case vision and perseverance. This demands leadership from the founders as well as from all other people and parties concerned. Completed phases in the step-by-step development of a company do not exist. Over the course of time, the requested focus in leadership appears to shift, however, and the challenges to alter. With the nuance that it is not about sequential steps that can be "ticked off," the following phases can be distinguished in realizing the characteristics of a brilliant business model:

Phase 1: Start from a vision and bring the brand positioning in line with it.
Phase 2: Persevere consistently in the conversion of the vision into the business model.
Phase 3: Realize breakthroughs in the value creation for all stakeholders with the business model.

This is a process of nested phasing, each time satisfying an extra characteristic of an organization with a brilliant business model. Phase 1 and 2 are not easy and can also result in failure, but organizations that successfully complete these phases receive confirmation and appreciation in phase 3. But it does not just stop there. The impression could arise that the difficult work has been done after Phase 3 and that it will only become easier from that point forward. Nothing is further from the truth! In particular, when success is achieved, a new dynamic envelops organizations. The success that is created changes the interaction with stakeholders. This is not only nice, but also makes things tense. On the one hand it can lead to reinforcement, confirmation and motivation to pursue doing it even better; on the other hand it can produce conservatism, idleness, haughtiness, an inflated ego and temptation. And as Jim Collins has shown in his book *How the Mighty Fall*, the decline starts precisely

---

[1] Kemperman et al. (2013).

where pride and a self-congratulatory air start. In old Greek terminology the risk of *hybris* arises or as the book of Proverbs in the Bible states: "*a haughty spirit goes before a fall.*" Switching to more modern parlance, the company arrives at the *next level in the game* with a corresponding set of new, as yet unknown enemies and challenges. In sum, there is also a Phase 4 to come: retain the core and stimulate progress in the business model. Every brilliant business model will end up in the storms of Phase 4. Even more, a couple of organizations described in this book are currently right in the thick of it or will soon enter this phase. But we leave that discussion until a later point in this chapter ....

When we started studying brilliant business models in healthcare, it became evident that the idea of defining and phasing brilliant business models was many times stronger in the healthcare sector than in most other sectors. It was precisely here that there was generally a strong intrinsic Phase 1 drive to do good, which in and of itself is logical given the societal and human relevance of taking good care for others and the value attached to the health of both yourself and your neighbor. It was also precisely here that the difference between the brilliant companies and the also-rans ended up being found in the specific choices in and consistent conversion into the daily actions within the organization in Phase 2. Within healthcare above all, there is a subtle game that revolves around whether all stakeholders are happy with you in Phase 3. Pure profit optimization is not accepted and creates countervailing powers that threaten continuity. Organizations who create value for one stakeholder on expensive of another, instead of realizing the triple aim as a whole, meet a lot of resistance from other parties and in society as a whole. While dividends are not always needed, unadulterated altruism is not sustainable either since it does not provide additional means to invest and pay for more treatments if you are successful. Finally, healthcare is in a state of great flux. Many care institutions in Western countries have been present for a while now. As it stands, they are currently confronted with the Phase 4 challenge of having to reinvent themselves if they do not want to become part of the problem, but rather part of the solution. Think for instance about the challenges associated with altering your role when healthcare treatments are less bound to a geographical location while your entire organization continues perceiving itself as a physical place where care and cure are provided to visiting patients who also stay over for the night.

In order to inspire people who want to set up or help set up a brilliant business model in healthcare or who want to make an existing company beautiful or even more beautiful, we ponder below the four phases on the basis of the organizations described in this book.

10.1   Phase 1: Start from a Vision and Bring the Brand Positioning in Line with It

A brilliant business model begins with a vision. In other words, it starts with a deep conviction and feeling of need that things have to be done differently. That is to say that it begins from an internal motive and not so much from an explicit market demand or customer need in the sense of "*your wish is our command.*" Every organization in this book has a major passion to start doing things differently and to truly make a contribution. This ambition is usually deployed from the actual start by the founder, but sometimes also at a later time by the successors. Often these goals, and the manner in which the company is set up, are revolutionary. Healthcare must become fundamentally better and more accessible. People must be made healthier. Patients must start to manage their own disorder. In order to treat far more people, the costs have to decline by 95 %. It is no longer accepted that a disease is chronic; it has to be cured. Or a specific disorder must be ruled out forever. The consequences of such convictions and ideas are that in any case the status quo will start to change. Incidentally, there must be many entrepreneurs who never got further than the dream phase, while a brilliant business model could have been derived from it. We will return to this topic later in Phase 2. What is worth noting at this point, however, is that the organization is not initially viewed as a means of becoming rich. The organization and earning money are in particular instruments for realizing the goal for the purpose of improving something in the world or in the company's own sector for citizens, patients or the insured. You do not look merely to find something you must do to get paid. You look for a way to get paid for what you want to do.

This lesson is quite important for entrepreneurship within healthcare. The last thing that healthcare needs is trite entrepreneurs—ones that see a commercial niche in the healthcare market and want to fill it to earn as much money as possible. The phenomenon that patients often do not pay the bill themselves in the healthcare sector provides opportunities to maximize profits and that would erode healthcare in its entirety. Pure profit-driven entrepreneurs will not help healthcare advance, but rather erode the basis of support for mutual caring and sharing. To be sure, they will probably earn money, and possibly a whole lot, too. But whether they will start to realize the desired breakthroughs necessary to make qualitatively good healthcare accessible and affordable is still very much up in the air. Brilliant business models in healthcare do not only require a feel for customers, business and finances, but also for integrity and moral standing to do the right thing. It is precisely healthcare that needs entrepreneurs, employees and managers that operate from a deep inner drive, on the basis of an authentic vision and compassion that it has to be done differently and better for patients and persons in need of care. At the same time, the war will not be won on altruistic ideals. The realization of results that extend further than 3-year terms of subsidies and temporarily innovation budgets demands visionary entrepreneurs. People whose heart is in the right place *and* have a vision for long-term growth and the financing thereof in an organization where many people want to make a contribution.

"Care" is a verb! The heart of many people who work in healthcare is in the right place: they love people and want to help and heal them. Paradoxically, the sum total of all those beautiful, vision-driven people does not add up to beautiful, vision-driven organizations. That is why just removing the barriers for healthcare practitioners to do the right thing as a professional already helps a lot. Whereas many employees have a heart for patients and work from a passion, it appears that does not nearly always go for established care institutions as organizations. Or if we were to put a positive spin on it: there are still lots of opportunities for growth in the field of vision-driven organizations. Whatever the case may be, a strong vision is a significant characteristic and strength for the brilliant business models in this book.

How Our Brilliant Business Models Provided a Framework for Phase 1   For illustrative purposes, we can ponder the objectives which get people moving and the ambitious promises at the start of the brilliant business models that have been discussed in this book:

Algemeen Ziekenfonds Amsterdam (A.Z.A.): The A.Z.A. health insurance fund was started by doctors to make good healthcare available to the average working man who was not on poor relief but was nevertheless unable to pay for heath care himself. In that regard, the doctors involved wanted to break the power of the directors of sick money boxes who abused their positions in relation to the insured and the doctors themselves.

DHAN: This foundation was based on the ambition to help people organize themselves and help themselves. The goal is to consequently arrive at greater economic self-reliance by lending funds to members and to share risks, such as healthcare costs, among members.

Courtyard houses: These houses were started from bequests by people who, by doing so, wanted to provide a home for people where they could grow old with the guarantee of living space, a monthly provision and the company of familiar people.

Liebenau Stiftung: The foundation was started on the basis of brotherly love, with the goal of creating preconditions for a dignified life for young and old. The foundation wants to help people help themselves, but also by having people help each other. Many related, very successful projects have arisen as a result thereof.

Discovery: The philosophy is that not only a health insurance business is necessary, but also a vitality company to motivate people using positive stimuli and to reward them to stay healthy, so that they require less care.

Healthways: The goal is to make people demonstrably healthier, so that they require less care and will live longer. That can also be offered as a promise to parties that have an interest therein, such as employers, insurers and authorities.

Kaiser Permanente: This started from the insight that it is costly to organize care for everyone and that prevention and health programs result in lower healthcare costs. Kaiser Permanente prompts people to lead a healthy and safe life. In that regard, it looks at more than just the individual, taking his/her environment into consideration as well. It offers care in an integrated healthcare system, employing general practitioners and owning hospitals to ensure that the care is organized as efficiently as possible.

PatientsLikeMe: This platform was started on the idea that it is possible to give people with a serious illness a better quality of life by arranging to exchange experiences with others in similar circumstances. In the process, PatientsLikeMe wants to bring about change in the way in which patients deal with their illnesses.

UCLA: The Value Quotient program was established on the philosophy that healthcare can be organized around the common motive of patients, health practitioners and researchers to create value for the patient by increasing self-reliance, quality of life and productivity.

ParkinsonNet: This was established on the conviction that patients being treated by various healthcare practitioners would benefit from coordinated support in their self-management and treatments. Healthcare is already complicated enough. This network provides tools that help to provide insight into qualitatively good healthcare that can be found nearby or elsewhere.

Laastari: This started from the best practices of MinuteClinic, the retail clinic in the USA. The founders saw the success in America, recognized the necessity thereof in their own country due to the waiting list at general practitioners and decided to start a retail clinic on Scandinavian soil to make basic healthcare more accessible.

Patrick Lund: This dentist drastically changed his practice to contribute to the happiness of people: the happiness of patients as well as that of his employees and himself. It was a unique and inspiring step. The number of suicides among dentists is 100 times higher than the average. And happiness also does not initially come to the minds of patients when they think of dentists.

Ryhov: A unique self-serve concept for kidney dialysis patients has arisen to give people control over their lives again, thanks to the open mind of a nurse, an involved patient thinking along and a philosophy of "always the best care for you."

BerylHealth: The founder Paul Spiegelman was driven by the motivation to make patients truly happy by providing excellent service, connecting people to healthcare and at the same time building a business where employees would really like to work.

M-PESA: This initiative was established simply by listening to and observing the customer. In this case, it resulted from the insight that in Kenya paid airtime was often being transferred via mobile as an alternative to banking. M-Pesa decided to make payment via mobile phone possible.

Jaipur Foot: The ambition here was to have people in India and other developing countries take full part in society once again by providing them at unprecedented high volumes and low prices with a prosthesis by which they can resume a normal place in society.

Narayana Hrudayalaya Cardiac Hospital: The heart hospital was founded to save the lives of many more children and later adults with heart conditions who could not be helped due to the lack of healthcare in India.

ThedaCare: This hospital focused on continuous improvement with the patient at the center of attention. Learning and improving are part of the organization and for everyone, thus making it possible to make good healthcare as *lean & mean* as possible.

Princess Margaret Cancer Centre (PMCC): The higher goal behind PMCC is unmistakable: together we will conquer cancer. This higher goal forges in a special way a state-of-the-art knowledge-driven process on the one hand and the personal approach on the other.

Mayo Clinic: The ambition here is to bring the best specialists from various disciplines together to make the optimum diagnosis and then do everything to give patients the best conceivable treatment possible.

10.2 Phase 2: Persevere Consistently in the Conversion of the Vision into the Business Model

Whereas an inspiring vision and a matching brand positioning are very important, we are still only talking about words and ideas. This does not mean that the actual work is done yet. It is only when they are converted into and implemented in a business model that something actually starts to happen. This means that a sound entity is made up of the customer group to be selected and the corresponding needs (market segments), the value to be offered (customer value), how the product or service arrives at the customer and how the customer contact is carried out (delivery), and the organizational processes are set up to make everything possible (operation). This requires entrepreneurship, creativity and perseverance, as it does not simply happen from 1 day to the next. It is a growth track of continuous listening, learning, experimenting and polishing.

Characteristic of the organizations described in this book is the fact that they consistently and unscrupulously convert their vision into their business models. Compromises are not tolerated. Issues keep on being reviewed as long as is required to find a way to get the job done. If ideas or proposals are in conflict with the vision and market positioning, it seems as if the truly brilliant businesses are opting to show more backbone and to stay true to the principles. In doing so, they find extremely creative ways to do justice to their vision *and* to create value for all parties concerned at the same time. Questions that arise in the process include:

- What are our biggest cost drivers? How can we reduce costs by 60 % in a way that creates much more value for customers and employees?
- How can we convert the conflicting demands we set into paradoxes and turn our weaknesses into strengths?
- What do our customers want to do and what are they capable of doing themselves, so that we do not have to do that? How do we help customers take control?
- What are our truly scarce resources and factors? And how can we deploy them optimally?
- What services are we better off discontinuing altogether, because they do not provide any added value?

In that regard, you notice that brilliant organizations are stubborn in pursuing their vision and living their brand but at the same time more inclined than less brilliant colleagues to reverse decisions that have been taken if these decisions turn out not so well based on experience and progressive insight. Even when it is difficult, "B" is not said simply because "A" has already been said. In this regard, where it concerns leadership, a dominant, charismatic leader deciding which action to take is not necessarily needed. If the vision and market positioning are broadly support and embedded, that will not only guide the decisions in the upper echelons of management, but also throughout the "capillaries" of the business. It is also clearly present in the smaller, day-to-day decisions and actions of employees where the business model must be consistently fulfilled. It is precisely in the daily practice that this results in the creation of practical examples and narratives that give the vision true substance and that people share with one another.

Tailored to this book, healthcare organizations reveal a number of striking substantive aspects that nearly all of them have implemented in their business model and that reinforce one another:

- *A healthy mix of solidarity and responsibility:* Brilliant organizations in healthcare have found a creative and intelligent mix of everyone's rights and responsibilities. Business models are realized where it is clear what everyone must do and why that is good for everyone. In this way the foundation of the A.Z.A. health insurance fund was in the interest of the doctors who were guaranteed regular income and work on the one hand and the insured who were guaranteed good healthcare for an affordable premium, whereby they could even choose from many doctors, on the other hand. In the business model of Kaiser Permanente, Discovery and Healthways, it is clear that it is in everyone's interest to keep people healthy as this demonstrably makes a difference in healthcare costs and increases productivity. The system works only on the basis of checks and balances; people are rewarded if they live up to their responsibilities, but also vice versa. The shared interests fit practically and intuitively with the common interest to keep healthcare accessible for everyone. Perhaps this is precisely the case because people have to live up to their own responsibilities!

- *A personal approach and self-management:* Connection on the personal level is always a significant part in the brilliant organizations described, irrespective of whether they are large or small. A lot of care is truly organized around people, but even if the process or the knowledge serves as the institutional principle, in the brilliant business models it continues to be all about people. Also, in large, specialized organizations such as the Princess Margaret Cancer Centre, and in massive operations such as NH Cardiac Hospital and Jaipur Foot the patient is at the center of attention. Human contact and the personal discussions with patients result in some situations even in complete innovations, as is seen at Ryhov. A large part of the care and prevention is also done by way of self-management. That is also in keeping with people living up to their own responsibilities. What can people, groups and patients do or still do themselves? To that end, stimuli and incentives are built into the system. You let people do the things they can also do themselves. That results in an upward spiral in which people are "activated," feel happier and become more pro-active, while their health is simultaneously positively impacted and the costs are reduced. This is abundantly clear at Stiftung Liebenau, where residents help each other and only a single part-time employee is necessary to serve a community. We also see it at DHAN, where self-help groups form the heart of the organization. The movement is further directed from a small office with major shared values (instead of the other way around). This spiral also works downwards. If people need healthcare and are immediately treated as if they cannot do anything by themselves anymore, they will also behave accordingly. Then they are less capable of helping themselves and the whole process has a paralyzing or even negative effect. In that case, it will become comparable to the group holiday where people can no longer find the way themselves after a tour leader has been assigned. The principle of living up to your own responsibilities and self-management does not prevent mutual caring and sharing. In fact, it belongs to the process.

- *Learning capacity and big data:* The organizations in this book are focused on facts to improve themselves and help their customers to do the same. They constantly reflect on how they are garnering and imbedding information in their organizational processes to constantly realize improvement in their daily work. They have incorporated a learning capacity based on information, customer feedback and ideas into their business model. This often demands enormous investments in big data, advanced information systems and the implementation and maintenance of digital patient dossiers. The information is used in various ways and is truly the fuel in the machine. Data and feedback loops are used at three levels.

1. It is used directly as a feedback loop on the first level for the relevant person in charge of a case or the patient who assumes personal responsibility for making choices in that specific treatment. This is ideally also the level at which the ownership is felt and information is enriched.
2. It is clustered, and often made anonymous, into mirror information and a feedback loop on the second level. This helps to learn what does and does not work and when and thus provides input for better prevention, diagnosis, intervention and choices in general.
3. It is ultimately used as a feedback loop on the third level to have evidence and information on the basis of which the relevant parties can review and assess what each individual's added value is and the joint result. In that regard, information makes it possible to clarify and tighten up the joint interests to make people healthy, be thrifty in allocating available healthcare resources and save healthcare costs.

These different levels are present in diverse business models, such as those of A.Z.A., Discovery, PatientsLikeMe, Healthways, Value Quotient of UCLA, Kaiser Permanente and the Mayo Clinic. While words like big data are new, the fundamental way of working goes further back. This is not a trend. It appears to attentive readers that there is indeed a leitmotiv here.

How Our Brilliant Business Models Provided a Framework for Phase 2 For illustrative purposes, we can ponder a number of choices of the organizations in this book to conduct to implement practises and behave in a way which is truly consistent with their business model:

Algemeen Ziekenfonds Amsterdam (A.Z.A.): When major losses were being incurred in the first year, it turned out that the doctors themselves were prepared to give up part of their salaries to make up for the shortfall, by which they immediately showed that they took the responsibility to do the right thing.

DHAN: The possibility of achieving self-reliance and being the desired change oneself is internalized and embedded in the way of working. This is done following the principles how relevant parties work together to maintain the water supply which was already being used during earlier centuries in India.

Courtyard houses: Each of these houses was designed with the front door facing the inner courtyard. As a result, the fulfillment of the desire to give people a safe and protected place for their old age was made immediately tangible and visible.

Liebenau Stiftung: Helping people to help themselves and each other has produced a very effective model, whereby the youth help the elderly in a residential community—and vice versa. As a result only one part-time employee is needed for a community of more than 100 residents to function.

Discovery: The company intelligently converts the ambition to insure people and to make them healthier by providing and marketing a sophisticated savings and reward system that prompts and tempts people to really start leading healthier lives.

Healthways: Employing a cash-on-the-barrelhead type of proposition, this organization links its own compensation to the promise and allows itself to be paid only if costs have really been saved and profit has been made for the employer, insurers and/or the authorities.

Kaiser Permanente: This company prompts people who want to lead a healthy life to do so for themselves and with people around them. In that regard, the relevant parties strive for prevention based on the conviction that this results in better health and lower costs. All this is supported by an integrated healthcare system that contributes to transparency and insight, leading to efficiency.

PatientsLikeMe: PatientsLikeMe succeeds in building a community of patients who share similar circumstances based on a revenue model with paying partners from the healthcare sector. These partners buy the data of PatientsLikeMe at an aggregated level, based on which they can improve their products and services, so that societal value is created as well. One customer group does the work for the other one!

UCLA: The Value Quotient program organizes online platforms supplemental to the normal physical interaction of patients, healthcare practitioners and researchers. These are deployed so that the relevant parties can really work together and learn for the purpose of arriving at the best treatment(s) to create value for patients.

ParkinsonNet: This network as a whole arrives at quality standardization and forms a "quality mark" in healthcare for Parkinson's disease. This creates one coordinating point for the customer and the healthcare practitioner to realize the best available healthcare for the disorder.

Laastari: This company helps patients go from a 2-month waiting period for a doctor's visit to being immediately helped in a retail clinic, at an accessible location and for a fixed price — and with the possibility to leave the clinic with a prescription and/or medication in no time.

Patrick Lund: Patrick Lund set out to really listen and discovered what made people unhappy during a visit to the dentist. He then flipped all these experiences involving accidents and fear into practises of happiness. All this has thrown the entire approach of the traditional dental practice overboard in a radical manner.

Ryhov: By letting patients do what they are able to do themselves and breaking through objectives such as perceived safety risks and loss of work, this hospital allows them to experience more self-control and improve the quality of their lives. At the same time, the costs consequently declined by one third and patients could be further assisted to learn to live with a chronic disorder, for instance by means of a personal health plan and a learning café.

BerylHealth: By focusing on a very specific target group (hospitals with more than 400 beds), Beryl was able to really listen to and deliver what that target group needed. Beryl became an unique organization not only by reducing costs for hospitals as an efficient call center, but by also expanding services that help the hospitals generate more turnover and making patients fans of the hospital concerned.

M-PESA: This telecom operator now facilitates mobile money transactions for everyone, in a country where a bank account is only for the happy few. This has resulted in the more secure and more efficient use and transfer of money and makes certain services, such as dedicated healthcare wallets, accessible as well.

Jaipur Foot: This organization provides an artificial foot for less than 1 % (!) of the cost of a similar prosthesis in the West. At the same time, it meets more extreme demands on daily use in India and is able to offer a prosthesis that can be measured in one continuous appointment, so that customers do not have to travel twice.

Narayana Hrudayalaya Cardiac Hospital: This heart hospital has to deal with more demand than it can take on. It grows rapidly to help more people and has never opted to increase the return and make the work lighter by helping fewer but wealthier people and let them pay more.

ThedaCare: This hospital stands for continuous learning and improving, keeping the patient at the center of attention. It is all about delivering patient-focused care and improving a little bit every day. Improvement dialogues, insight and transparency in quality play the leading role here.

Princess Margaret Cancer Centre (PMCC): By making a clear choice to become a top institute for treating cancer, PMCC has laid the basis for their unique business model. On the one hand, this guarantees the customization for people, the focus on hospitality and the patient-focused care processes. On the other, the focus on top research is indispensable. The combination of these factors makes PMCC unique.

Mayo Clinic: The Mayo Clinic is fulfilling its ambition to realize the best conceivable diagnosis and treatment in the world and become the hospital regarded around the world as the best place for a complicated diagnosis and treatment.

10.3   Phase 3: Use Pioneering Value Creation for All Stakeholders to Realize the Business Model

"*Charity is not scalable.*" These words of Dr. Shetty—the visionary leader behind the pioneering Narayana Hrudalayala Cardiac Hospital—came as a bombshell to us. It summarized and concluded some long-lasting discussions we faced in healthcare. At first, you think: "What in the world?" But if you consider Dr. Shetty's comment carefully, there is much more than a kernel of truth to it. You can do good things for society, but if they are not backed up by a revenue model, it is extremely difficult (if not impossible) to let it grow and to have even more people benefit from it. After all, at that point you are reliant upon the benevolence of others willing to do something without being paid or getting value in return. In other words, the creation of societal value in and of itself does not make you a brilliant. The key is to create societal value in a way that is not dependent upon charity or subsidies. A self-supporting and –reinforcing business model produces something for all stakeholders—and all this in such a way that all parties concerned are content with what the organization does for them, so that in return they also continue to do their best to make their own contribution.

Brilliant organizations identify what the joint interests of the various stakeholders are. In that regard, they certainly take financial results into consideration, but in particular also customer value, employee value and societal value. These insights are often already incorporated within the way the business model works. The resulting "value creation for all" is at the heart of Phase 3. When organizations, driven by a vision and a matching brand positioning, implement this throughout their business model, this will get results. Most "average" companies focus on optimizing a single goal such as shareholder value and are willing to do that at the expense of the other parties involved. Those with brilliant business models bear the value they are creating for all stakeholders in mind when taking really important decisions. In healthcare they look upon the impact they have on the triple aim as a whole. The realization of the vision must create balanced value for all parties concerned. In practice that does not always happen simultaneously from the start. An example of this is innovation. This often gets off the ground or going when two or more stakeholders profit from such an effort. But brilliant organizations continue to develop it into a model where balanced value is eventually realized for everyone. A good example of this is Ryhov, where an individual patient and an employee arrived at a pioneering idea for self-dialysis. Over time this was developed into a model where pioneering financial and societal value have also been created. If you fail to create value for all parties concerned, your business model will not be sustainable on the long term because there are players who wait for the moment they can step out of the equation.

Balanced value creation is an important element in the thoughts of leaders in organizations with brilliant business models. Leaders in organizations that create value for all stakeholders have a creative win-win mindset instead of a trade-off mentality. The latter requires thinking in a straightforward way in terms of "either–or". For instance, when turnover declines, costs have to be reined in and staff members therefore have to be laid off. You can also use the current free capacity in resources to innovate at the edges of the business model by investing with the people, machines, and space that are already paid for. A win-win mindset thinks creatively and can transform dilemmas and paradoxes in solutions which alter the perceived reality. Scarcity is a source of problems but this makes it also a source of new energy and creative innovation and destruction. It demands creativity to grapple with an urgent business problem and simultaneously create value for all stakeholders, but it is certainly not impossible and it is fun as well. That is at least what the examples in this book clearly reveal.

How Our Brilliant Business Models Provided a Framework for Phase 3 For instance, we can look at whether, aside from the regular value parameters, this book also contains examples of unique and surprising value exchange for and by stakeholders in the brilliant cases:

Algemeen Ziekenfonds Amsterdam (A.Z.A.): A.Z.A. created a new reality where doctors more than ever before could rely on the fact that they would receive a reasonable salary and regular work, while the insured could count on the healthcare they needed at a reasonable price.

DHAN: Thanks to the self-reliance of groups within the DHAN Foundation, people improve their own economic position. At the same time, they themselves are also the most important, unpaid employees—the heart and motor of DHAN. They are DHAN.

Courtyard houses: The deposit of a personal contribution in the form of an annuity when people took up residence in these houses ensured that they were also guaranteed of having a home and food when they became very old; yet at the same time, it improved the resources of the almshouse and paid for others when people unexpectedly died young.

Stiftung Liebenau: The strength of the foundation lies in bringing diverse parties together. For instance, the foundation works closely together with municipalities, healthcare practitioners and parties in the real estate market in a way that is valuable to everyone concerned. During our visit to one of the projects, the local burgomaster consequently wanted to join in to express his appreciation for everything that Liebenau had meant for the town.

Discovery: If people start working on their health, this leads to lower healthcare costs and people will simultaneously benefit from it themselves: they become healthier, more attractive and even earn some extra privileges, such as a visit to the cinema or an airfare reduction.

Healthways: If the parties concerned succeed in making people healthier, the resulting benefits impact everyone. The patients themselves become better, literally, the insurer has fewer healthcare costs, the employer has more productive employees and the collective resources of society are relied on less. Healthways succeeds also in specifying this generally accepted shared interest on an abstract level and in implementing it in the revenue model based on the evidence in practice.

Kaiser Permanente: Kaiser offers prevention and safety measures for both individuals and their surroundings. By doing so, healthcare costs are reduced and the health of the customers is increased. Employees, including doctors and nurses, are proud to work for these renowned hospitals.

PatientsLikeMe: Patients feel that they are no longer on their own and are also more compliant in respect of their therapy as they are part of a community with experienced people in similar circumstances. At the same time, they get this for free by paying in kind with the valuable health data only they can provide and the medical world is enriched by the new experiential knowledge of the patients.

UCLA: Learning together about the disorder and improving the treatment thereof is good for everyone involved in the Value Quotient program. Patients get a better handle on their disorder, improve the quality of their lives and are more productive. Healthcare practitioners need to do less administration (as patients do more themselves) and receive greater appreciation based on the health profit derived. Researchers have unique study materials and UCLA is strengthening its position in relation to all previously mentioned parties and sponsors.

ParkinsonNet: Customers can find their specific quality care more easily. Healthcare practitioners improve cooperation and form a network that contributes to efficiency and insight. As a whole this results in savings on healthcare costs, support for patients in self-management and the ability of healthcare practitioners to connect and complement each other better while increasing the number of Parkinson patients as member of the network.

Laastari: The organization assists people with straightforward symptoms and disorders in getting direct consultation for a fixed and low fee. Patients are assisted with compassion by a nurse with years of experience; if necessary, consultations with doctors take place remotely, so that more people can be helped. At the societal level, this has various effects, including the fact that people with latent conditions are not kept waiting too long, because healthcare is made more accessible.

Patrick Lund: Customers do pay a bit more to Lund than at other dental practices. More extreme: they are prepared to travel 800 km to get there. Lund has set the standard as regards happy dental service and is consequently a source of inspiration for many other organizations within healthcare and beyond.

Ryhov: By basing the business model on self-management, healthcare costs have declined by 33 %, the demand on the time of persons treating patients is less, the level of patients' control, ability to plan and the overall happiness in life has increased, and the number of complications has dropped.

BerylHealth: It is a massive achievement for a call center to be crowned a "Great Place to Work" winner. The combination of the vision and their business model was the basis for this. In addition, for the hospitals that are customers (98 % of whom are, incidentally, loyal) and the patients that call there, the services provided by Beryl are priceless.

M-PESA: This organization has made financial transactions and healthcare applications available to everyone via mobile services, resulting in a customer database that is growing exponentially, increased turnover for its agents, and more efficient and safer use of money. And last but not least: increased loyalty to the telecom provider by a service you do not want to miss.

Jaipur Foot: More than one million people have been helped so far. Individuals who can walk again are more productive for themselves, their neighbor and society. Consequently, sponsors receive an unprecedented *do good* return on their investment of a mere USD 50 (EUR 40).

Narayana Hrudayalaya Cardiac Hospital: The heart hospital saves many lives on a daily basis. It performs surgery on people who otherwise could not have afforded an operation. This is valuable for society, but also for employees: in addition to earning a reasonable salary and gaining a lot of experience, they perform truly meaningful work that they can be proud of.

Thedacare: More improvements and less waste means higher satisfaction levels amongst patients and employees and lowers costs — and, of course, a higher level of quality care for everyone.

Princess Margaret Cancer Centre (PMCC): The organization is *the* cancer institute in the world when it comes down to both science and patients. Despite the scale of the hospital, patients boast about the personal hospitality and the customization for people. It is also a "Great Place to Work" winner.

Mayo Clinic: The strong reputation of the Mayo Clinic acts as a magnet, enabling growth. It attracts all stakeholders: new patients that are also prepared to pay for the best treatment, the best specialists that go for the best results and desire to learn (instead of earn) a lot, and donors who gift money to strengthen the Clinic.

10.4   Phase 4: Retain the Core and Stimulate Progress in the Business Model

And then we have a vision that is consistently embedded in a business model that has developed into a platform for interaction where the parties concerned exchange value in a fundamentally new manner! The mountain peak has been reached and brilliance has become reality. This produces the type of examples that we can learn from now and in the future no matter what happens. But what should your organization do once it has reached the top? The challenge is to define and conquer new peaks based on your organization's roots and vision. But that is not necessarily easy; even more, it is a treacherous endeavor. The success that has been achieved results in a new dynamic where pride, obstinacy, inertia, haughtiness, laziness and such vices can take root. It is the phase in which precisely the giants who are revered by everyone can also fall.[2] In essence and logically, there are two dangers that must be avoided by brilliant organizations:

- *Too much conservation.* There is a tendency to start believing entirely or too much in your own success and becoming the captive of that belief by becoming stagnant, resting on your laurels, discontinuing the improvement processes and leaving everything the way it is. After all, success has been achieved by the way in which we approached the matter; hence, we should not change a thing, or so goes the thinking. Given the achievements that have successfully been made in the past and the position reached, this way of thinking can certainly last quite a while. The parties concerned will carry on for years, producing value for the company, also if they themselves derive a bit less from it. This conservation can arise due to laziness or from an attitude of *"we're untouchable"* but also by listening carefully to existing customers and missing potential new markets and technologies that appear inferior at the start.[3] It is also the risk of organizations that have conquered much and especially now are driven by the fear of losing what they have. That is one of the most important reasons for market leaders that have achieved their position by changing the rules of the game to ultimately lose it when a competitor does the same thing.

- *Too much progression.* The other tendency is to start believing in your own success and becoming the captive of that belief but in an entirely different way. In that regard, haughtiness and too much self-confidence form the basis for looking endlessly for even higher goals and ambitions, which only ends when the company starts to falter. There are a great many well-known examples of this outside healthcare. It falls rather into the category of the decline and fall experienced by both Enron and Lehman Brothers. The problem here is that the organization loses sight of its own roots and the human dimension. It starts to make growth promises about revenues, market share and profit that are excessive and thereby orchestrate its own failure in the future. Once these promises are out in the open the company is considered a failure when targets are not realized. In connection with this, decisions come to mind that appear commercially interesting in the short term, but ultimately do not quite match the vision or the brand positioning. It smells like Harley Davidson venturing into aftershave. A small but clear example of this sort of smell was when Starbucks suddenly started selling hot cheese rolls, because that was commercially interesting. The wonderful aroma of coffee (the core of Starbucks) was masked by the penetrating odour of grilled cheese. And so it went from bad to worse. Thankfully, Starbucks retraced its footsteps and is now fully back on track.[4]

The challenge in Phase 4 is to find the right balance between retaining the core and renewing for the future in the continued development of the vision, the business

---

[2] Collins (1999).

[3] Christensen (1997).

[4] Schultz and Gordon (2011).

model and value creation. It concerns discovering the renewed business model based on the inspiration of the roots of yesterday and the technology and challenges of tomorrow. This places a tremendous demand on intellectual capacity and creativity as well as on the ability to persist and to connect. In that regard, it relies on the integrity and ethics of leadership. The opportunity and challenge is now to exploit the acquired position and to use that responsibility to make the business model even more brilliant in an honest and bold way.

How Our Brilliant Business Models Provided a Framework for Phase 4 By way of illustration, we will look at whether the companies from the cases are being or could be confronted with new challenges as successful brilliant business models and how they are dealing or could deal with them.

Algemeen Ziekenfonds Amsterdam (A.Z.A.): At the end of the 19th century, A.Z.A. saw new competitors that stated that A.Z.A. was not doing enough for the lower middle class workers they were serving, whereas that was in fact the initial raison d'être for its creation. Ultimately A.Z.A. remained the leading health insurance fund of Amsterdam and now is the biggest European health insurer via Zilveren Kruis with Achmea in the twenty-first century.

DHAN: This foundation has found a unique way to provide for continuous innovation due to the fact that new groups are set up when the old ones become too large. The pitfall is, however, that it could become difficult to transition to a more modern, professional organization if that were desirable.

Courtyard houses: Most of these houses still have residents, but after a couple of successful centuries most are no longer operating in their original form. The primary reason appears to be that the living demands of seniors have increased over time, but also that they do not comply with pretty bureaucratic legislation on own apartments versus shared houses in the twenty-first century in The Netherlands.

Stiftung Liebenau: Liebenau is still growing thanks to the scalability and replicability of the initiatives. This has made it possible for them to fan out quickly throughout Germany and the surrounding countries. But the growth is also due to new projects, by which the foundation repeatedly reinvents itself, while at the same time honoring its vision.

Discovery: Discovery Health and Discovery Vitality are very successful in South Africa and the formula of insurance policies *plus* prevention has turned out to be effective in other areas as well, such as non-life and life insurance. At the same time, some 80 % of all South Africans are not privately insured and international expansion is not taking place as quickly as within the country's borders. In other words, there are still large parts of the market to be tapped into and conquered.

Healthways: After a successful period of growth, Healthways has stabilized the last few years and is now faced with the challenge of reinventing itself and going global. The formula of being paid based on a demonstrable health benefits and fulfilling the role of a front runner in that regard is and continues to be an on-going challenge. Additionally new competitors such as technology providers are entering the (e) health market with large budgets and consumer technology and low prices.

Kaiser Permanente: In regions where Kaiser Permanente has not traditionally been established via its own hospitals, as along the east coast of the USA, a new formula had to be found to start with managed care. Kaiser Permanente appears to have solved that puzzle by working intensively with dedicated general practitioners and is currently also succeeding in areas where it does not own any hospitals.

PatientsLikeMe: PatientsLikeMe can be characterized as the LinkedIn of the medical world. This model is replicable and could—for instance on another continent—be set up by a new arrival on the market. Consequently, it is essential to continually connect patient groups and partners from the medical world to PatientsLikeMe, so that they do not leave when a competitor arrives, and at the same time to keep the patient first and not to sell out.

UCLA: The Value Quotient program has actually only just begun. The results of Phases 2 and 3 are promising, but additional hard evidence is just being produced. Following that its service is currently expanded to include other disorders and care institutions.

ParkinsonNet: Based on the vision of and conversion into the business model, ParkinsonNet is creating balanced value for the parties concerned. The next step to be taken is to be structurally rewarded for the health outcome of patients. The new ambition is to grow internationally. A big promising step is now being taken via a partnership with the established brilliant business model of Kaiser Permanente.

Laastari: For this relatively young organization, the first successes have already been achieved, but it continues to struggle to set up a commercial healthcare practitioner within a public system. In order to continue growing and to create value in the same way as MinuteClinic they will have to expand step by step, tenaciously holding onto their vision.

Patrick Lund: The fact that the prices at Patrick Lund are markedly higher than at other dentists' can be explained: the level of service is also significantly higher. In the context of solidarity and accessibility, however, questions can be raised about this approach. The next nut that Lund may have to crack is: how can we make a happy dental experience accessible for everyone?

Ryhov: The challenge for Ryhov could be described as: how can we expand the legacy of ideas and the practice of self-service kidney dialysis further within the regionally organized Swedish healthcare sector and in the rest of the world?

BerylHealth: Beryl has already reinvented itself, for instance, as the Beryl Institute that performs research into how to give patients optimum service. In the meantime, that institute has already become a business unit that generates its own turnover. Time will tell whether Beryl will also remain brilliant and unique after its acquisition by Stericycle.

M-PESA: The fourth phase has been used by M-PESA to not just play a role in making financial transactions possible, but more precisely to utilize its existing knowledge and network to quickly and efficiently share information on healthcare and to increase and insure accessibility to it.

Jaipur Foot: There is still more capacity and need for Jaipur "feet". It is limited by the number of people that want to contribute to this charity. What would happen if everyone who becomes productive after a treathment and starts earning money again is encouraged to give 2 prothesis as present to following patients?

Narayana Hrudayalaya Cardiac Hospital: The heart hospital is just barely originated in comparison with hospitals in the West. The challenge is to build up a business that is not dependent upon its founder. In that regard, the challenge remains to ensure that scale continues to reduce costs and simultaneously increases the quality while retaining the culture. Logically, this becomes more difficult with several large hospitals in various countries and on different continents.

ThedaCare: If you are truly involved in continuous learning as an organization, you will not quickly arrive in the fourth phase. ThedaCare has now started to share the learning beyond the walls of its own organization, for instance by way of knowledge exchange via national and international networks to jointly achieve a higher level of quality.

Princess Margaret Cancer Centre (PMCC): Although the Princess Margaret Cancer Center operates only from one site, it has succeeded in finding a solution for the problem of remoteness via TeleHealth and partnerships with other hospitals and physicians. This has taken place in a manner that does not detract from quality and simultaneously makes it easier and more accessible for the patient. It is a clever example of "stimulating progress" and "retaining the core".

Mayo Clinic: Given the success that has been achieved, the Mayo Clinic has every reason to become smug. For the time being, it does not appear to be entering Phase 4 and continues to act as a magnet, attracting new patients, specialists and sponsors who in turn effect innovation. The ambition to deliver the best conceivable healthcare to patients apparently keeps stakeholders young at heart as well, and continues to inspire them!

In Which Phase Are We? And in Which One Are You?   In this last section we discussed which lessons can be drawn from the brilliant business models that make an appearance in this book. We described which four phases occur in realizing a brilliant business model. This book is finished, but our quest for inspiring business models is far from over. Together with others—and perhaps with you—we will continue to discover and learn from brilliant business models. More books with brilliant business models will follow. In this way we can be inspired by organizations that follow their vision, do something completely different than others have done before, turn the world upside down and make an impact for all parties concerned— businesses that we can learn from for our own organizations. This is necessary, for we are living in a time when many brilliant business models are needed.

About the Editors

Jeroen Kemperman is Senior Manager Strategy & Business Development at Zilveren Kruis, the health division of Achmea. His responsibilities and experiences involve change programs, integrations, mergers, vision and strategy processes, reorganizations, brand portfolio issues, brand positioning, investments, business model development, and innovation. He is a frequent speaker at congresses and guest lecturer in educational programs. His previous books include *De merkrolmethode* and *Briljante Businessmodellen, Briljante Businessmodellen in de Zorg, Briljante Businessmodellen in Finance and Briljante Businessmodellen in Food (Dutch)*. @: Jeroen.Kemperman@achmea.nl, Phone: 0031 651222099.

Jeroen Geelhoed is a partner at &samhoud. He advises large organizations in various sectors and has experience with change programs, vision and strategy processes, business model innovation, leadership and fun management. He is also responsible for knowledge development within &samhoud. Jeroen has spoken, amongst others, at TEDx Sheffield and published various books, including *Plezier & Prestatie, Kus de visie wakker, Creating Lasting Value* and *Briljante Businessmodellen, Briljante Businessmodellen in de Zorg, Briljante Businessmodellen in Finance and Briljante Businessmodellen in Food (Dutch)*. @: J.Geelhoed@samhoud.com, Phone: 0031 622408791.

Jennifer op't Hoog is manager Productmanagement at Achmea Bank. She has experience with change programs, vision and strategy processes, and the Business Transformation Model. In her current role she is responsible for product policies, development and innovations at Achmea Bank, for bankproducts such as mortgages and savings accounts. She often speaks at congresses and previously published the books *Briljante Businessmodellen, Briljante Businessmodellen in de Zorg, Briljante Businessmodellen in Finance and Briljante Businessmodellen in Food (Dutch)*. @: Jennifer.op.t.Hoog@achmea.nl, Phone: 0031 651226420.

© Springer International Publishing Switzerland 2017
J. Kemperman et al. (eds.), *Brilliant Business Models in Healthcare*,
DOI 10.1007/978-3-319-26440-0

About the Case Authors

Maarten Akkerman, Former Senior Manager Purchasing Medical Specialized Care at Achmea, Zilveren Kruis, was constantly on the lookout for improvements within healthcare. Thanks to his background as a pharmacist, in sales within the pharmaceutical industry and within the health services procurement, Maarten is well versed in many aspects of healthcare. Several years ago he became inspired by the application of Lean in healthcare during the start of the Dutch healthcare network and wrote the ThedaCare case.

Denise Altena is project manager in the Quality and Innovation division at Achmea, Zilveren Kruis. With her practical and scientific insights based on her background as a nurse and health scientist, she desires to stimulate innovations within healthcare in such a way as to organize it more efficiently and more effectively with a view to create better quality care for everyone.

Thomas Bachet is a strategic advisor working on realizing a life style platform for Zilveren Kruis and Achmea. He is specialized in business model innovation, value network analysis and innovation management. In his work, he develops and advises on various topics, including business models for new products and services.

Mirthe van de Belt is a healthcare services purchaser at Achmea, Zilveren Kruis. Her background is in business administration with a focus on service management. Based on this focus, she is interested in healthcare organizations that are successful in applying a business model based on the principles of service management.

Sanne Boevé is an advisor at &samhoud. The visit to the Liebenau foundation inspired her massively and confirmed her belief that community spirit and mutual connection can indeed result in significant value creation for all parties concerned.

Heleen Borleffs is the owner of tangible-result.com in Digital Health Solutions. Results driven and passionate with a proven record in formulating and leading the execution of innovative digital solutions, Heleen delivers powerful strategies while laying the foundation for creative solutions in revenue growth and market product

© Springer International Publishing Switzerland 2017
J. Kemperman et al. (eds.), *Brilliant Business Models in Healthcare*,
DOI 10.1007/978-3-319-26440-0

acceptance. "Thrive with creativity during uncertainty" her mission is to enable people to enjoy their lives while overcoming (chronic) health issues by delivering excellent personalized health services.

Tom Buijtendorp is publicist in the area of strategy and history, and is member of the provincial parliament of North-Holland (D66). He has conducted considerable historical and archeological research and received his Ph.D. in this area from VU University Amsterdam in 2010. As a strategist, he always searches for subjects from the past and present that can be applied in practice to create a better society in the future. In his former job as Senior Manager at the Group Strategy of Achmea, he was involved in a variety of projects, including the micro-insurance activities of Achmea, and has had contact with DHAN in that capacity with regard to strategy and insurance activities.

Kristin Fransz is Manager Company Office at Achmea HR. Previously she worked at Achmea Zilveren Kruis, where she developed various courses for employees with customer contact. The aim of these courses was to increase the level of both customer value and employee value. Continuous improvement is an important motive for her. The fact that this can and must be the case in healthcare has become all the more clear to her thanks to her literary contribution to this book.

Esmée Grobbee is a physician-researcher at the stomach-intestine-liver illness department at Erasmus University Medical Center in Rotterdam. She studied medical science at Leiden University and is currently pursuing her doctorate in colorectal cancer screening at Erasmus University Medical Center. Thanks to her background as a physician, she is very familiar with the challenges facing oncological care in hospitals.

Koen Harms is entrepreneur in healthcare and former Project Manager Innovation at Achmea, Zilveren Kruis. Supported by his background as a healthcare researcher, Koen believes that an integral approach to health and welfare and the use of technology are the keys to a healthcare system that produces high quality healthcare at affordable prices.

Kerwin Hartman is a manager at Achmea. As management trainee, he has gained experience within the organization with *Lean*, healthcare investments and the development of online distribution in Russia. As a manager, he believes in team performance through mutual inspiration and complementary collaboration. His interests are aroused by the optimization of organizational processes aimed at providing customer-oriented service.

Monique Heeren is a manager at Achmea, Zilveren Kruis. After her medical studies, she started at Achmea, where she discovered her real passion: improving business operations in healthcare to be able to even better support patients and reduce costs. She is driven to let people in healthcare take charge themselves—to not complain but make a contribution themselves to a brilliant business model.

Wouter Houtman is responsible for content marketing, social media and partly for community building at Achmea, Zilveren Kruis. He recently took a Business Studies courses part-time at the University of Amsterdam. For his thesis, he conducted research into the impact that a context of regulated competition has for the business operations of Dutch healthcare insurers. He also writes on healthcare in combination with online marketing, innovation and mobile for various blogs and papers, including *Zorgmarketeers*, *Zorgvisie*, *Zorgmarkt*, and *Mobile Marketing*. In addition, Wouter is a big fan of Africa!

Daniel Hommes is a director of the UCLA Health System, Center for Inflammatory Bowel Diseases. He is a medical specialist who focuses on improving the quality of life of patients that suffer from Inflammatory Bowel Diseases (IBD) through fundamental science, applicable research, and innovations in healthcare.

Ilse Hoogervorst works as a project manager at Achmea, Zilveren Kruis. During her courses in business studies, she researched innovative business models in South Korea. Her interest is aroused by organizations that are vision-driven—innovative or not—to change the world and consequently to create customer value in a unique way. This reinforces her motivation to continue to be in motion and to inspire individuals to innovate.

Rick Kasper is a student. After completing his studies in Groningen, the Netherlands, and in Denmark, he worked as a student trainee at &samhoud. He helped write two business cases for this book: Patrick Lund Dental Happiness and Stiftung Liebenau. He is currently studying Knowledge Based Entrepreneurship at the University of Gothenburg in Sweden.

André Kok is a manager at Health Group Manna. Previously he worked at &samhoud as Senior Advisor. The last few years he has preoccupied himself primarily with care in general and care for the elderly specifically. He is captivated by topics such as leadership, change management, and healthcare. He is a strong believer in the power of individuals. His daily challenge is to elicit the passion and energy in individuals for such goals.

Karlijn Korten is working for the Achmea Foundation and was formerly a health procurement policy advisor at Achmea, Zilveren Kruis. She visited Shouldice for her dissertation in healthcare science and is intrigued by the brilliant business model of this private hospital in the public healthcare system of Canada. She deepens her knowledge in challenging fields such as this by conducting the Private & Public MBA program at Nyenrode Business University.

Annemijn Kuenen is a student trainee at &samhoud. She has gained experience in this organization in the field of knowledge development. She is inspired by companies that dare to make a major impact with their unique business model and know how to create value in several fields.

Wim Niesing is Advisor Strategy at Achmea, Zilveren Kruis. After his studies in econometrics, he began his career as a life actuary at Nationale Nederlanden, but left soon after for Erasmus University Rotterdam for doctoral research into labor market economy. Since 1993 he has worked in the health insurance business of Achmea successively as a researcher, (certifying) actuary, actuary division manager and strategy advisor. His attention is focused on historical developments in the healthcare insurance systems, the development of risk equalization, the design of solidarity, and the behavioral change of the parties in the healthcare system.

Rosanne Preyde-de Koning works at &samhoud as Senior Consultant for the healthcare market. In addition, she is responsible for &samhoud people. Rosanne has specialized in change management and the creation of sustainable value for organizations. In that regard she is working based on the philosophy of Harvard on the Value Profit Chain: investments in employee value result in customer value, which in turn leads to financial value. Her audacious goal is to create Great Places To Work in healthcare.

Raheel Raisi is Senior Manager Productmanagement at Achmea, Zilveren Kruis. She has experience in Continuous Improvement (lean) methods with the aim of balanced value creation for all stakeholders. She has experience with change processes, including integrations, identity development, and Lean implementation.

Bonny van Rest works as Chain Manager at Achmea, Zilveren Kruis. In her work, she is driven by adding value for the customer by connecting individuals, each with their own unique talents and intrinsic motivation. She is inspired by organizations or initiatives whereby the delivered value is a result of genuine collaboration between an organization and its customer or patient. She is convinced that this is the way to effect improvements in healthcare.

Bastiaan Schepman is an advisor at Achmea Corporate Relations and was formerly Product Manager at Achmea Health. It is impossible to develop health insurance propositions, products and services if you do not know what is going on in the field of healthcare. Due in part to his international MBA, he enjoys in that regard looking beyond borders to gain knowledge and inspiration.

Tim Widdershoven was an advisor at &samhoud, specializing in healthcare. Thanks to his medical background, he knows from experience the challenges facing healthcare. In his work, he is driven by the idea that healthcare can and must function so much better for all parties concerned.

Karen Willemsen works within Achmea, Zilveren Kruis as a strategic and financial projectmanager. The knowledge gained in her previous position as Program Manager "Lean in Health" has not been lost. The applications of Lean at national and global levels have resulted in a complete mind shift within healthcare and beyond—as well as at a personal level. She has a preference for figures, but decided upon contributing in describing this brilliant case as a step in the continuous improvement of healthcare.

Sytze de With was Marketeer at Achmea, Zilveren Kruis. Given his background in business administration, he is interested in how other parties involved in healthcare are able to create added value or added customer value and market it effectively. He enjoys drawing inspiration and ideas from this interest that can be used in his everyday work.

Acknowledgment

We would like to thank a considerable number of people who have played a role in the creation of this book. Many thanks to everyone who has helped in this and previous research into brilliant business models. Thank you for deepening and disseminating this beautiful legacy of ideas. At the same time, we would also like to apologize to all colleagues, friends, and neighbors whom we bombarded (and still bombard) repeatedly with stories about—in our opinion—unique companies. There are definitely a lot of you, but some we would like to thank in particular.

Besides the members of the editorial team and each case author, a number of individuals in particular lent a hand by bringing information to the table and critically co-reading and thinking along with us. We want to thank Nicky van der Heijden for conducting many organizational, support and selection tasks. We would like to extend our gratitude to both Bernard Dries and Sander Asma for sharing the experiences of their visit to BerylHealth, as well as Lance Shipp and Paul Spiegelman of BerylHealth for their time and flexibility. Thanks should also go to Cees Hesp, Pieter Walhof, and Onno Schellekens of Pharmaccess for their contribution to the M-PESA case. A big thank you to Else van Harten for much sparring, thinking along and organizing around various cases from the book, in particular those concerning ParkinsonNet, Stiftung Liebenau, BerylHealth, PatientsLikeMe, and Patrick Lund Dental Happiness. Dr. Urquhart, Maarten Simons, Geertjan Clever, and Peter Dunki Jacobs deserve our gratitude for their in-depth insights regarding the Shouldice case. We would like to thank both Ernst J. Kuipers, stomach-intestine-liver specialist and Board Chairperson of the Erasmus University Medical Center, and Theo Hiemstra, Program Manager Oncology at Achmea Care & Health, for their time and effort in the creation of the chapter on the Princess Margaret Cancer Centre (PMCC). Special thanks also go to Mary Gospodarowicz, Medical Director of PMCC, for her inspiring insights into oncological care at PMCC. As regards the case of ParkinsonNet, we are very grateful to Marten Munneke, Managing Director of ParkinsonNet, and Lonneke Rompen, Process Coordinator at ParkinsonNet. We are indebted to Bas Geerdes for his part in the section on Thedacare. And in respect of the contributions for the Laastari case, we would like to take this time to thank

Ron Liebkind, Toni Haapanen, Ken Liebkind (of Laastari), and Alinda de Wit (McKinsey). We are very grateful to Brett Tromp, CFO of Discovery Health, who deepened our understanding further raised our enthusiasm on Discovery. A big thank you is also due to those employees of Stiftung Liebenau and those residents of the *Lebensräume* projects that we spoke with for sharing their stories and checking the texts. We are also indebted to Vera Hoynck van Papendrecht and Erik van der Maat (both of &samhoud) for their assistance with the section on Liebenau. Additionally, we would like to thank Dr. Shetty, Dr. Raghuwanshi, and Sunil Kumar for the inspirational insights and for sharing their experience at NH Cardiac Hospital. We would also like to thank Sophie Hulshoff for collecting information on this case and Kees Isendoorn and Ansju Gupta (both Gupta Strategists) for their in-depth work to acquire a true understanding of the business model of NH Cardiac Hospital.

Needless to say, we would also like to especially thank Willem van Duin (Chairman Achmea) Roelof Konterman (Vice Chairman Achmea), Norbert Hoogers (Chairman, Zilveren Kruis, Achmea), and Salem Samhoud (Founder of &samhoud and Organizational Advisor), who externally underline the importance of conceptual consistency and inspiration and give the space for this to be honed to a fine edge. The conceptual building blocks from &samhoud have been integrated, further developed and applied within Achmea. This framework forms the basis for the case descriptions in this book. Since this was a joint effort with dozens of colleagues, we are not going to exclude any individuals by restricting our list. Elke Vergoossen, Wieke Oosthoek, and Rinus Vermeulen helped us to convert all our thinking into book form for the Dutch edition. And now we would like to thank the full team of Springer headed by Janet Kim from the US and with Savariraj Dhivya Geno as projectmanager in India. They helped us tremendously to transform our formerly Dutch book into the current new international edition. Then there is, of course, Vida Falkeisen with her creative insights and design and Anke Werkman-Kramer for bringing together the collective ideas in our community on wikibusinessmodels. com. Thank you to each and every one of you!

In practice our daily agendas were already full, so writing always took place close to home. Jeroen Kemperman would like to thank Francien Al as the touchstone where it concerns integrity in organizations and leadership; and Job and Pip because they are there. Jeroen Geelhoed would like to thank Evelien Geelhoed as well as Bram, Daniël, and Thomas, who now also know what a writer's evening is. Jennifer op't Hoog would like to thank Jaap van den Berg for both his support and for listening to every brilliant amazement regarding care institutions.

Key Terms and Definitions[1]

Brand This is a name (and/or a logo) with a reputation that has the capacity to give energy and direction to customers and employees to act in a certain way. It is a communicative conversion of the vision. Strong brands are credible and true. They have a personality to which customers feel attracted, in which they trust, to which customers want to belong and with which they gladly enter into a relationship of trust.

Brilliant business models A description of a business that (1) is driven by a vision and brand positioning, (2) perseveres in the business model with a consistent conversion of the vision and brand positioning into market segments, customer value, delivery and operation, and (3) on the basis thereof creates high value created for and by all stakeholders.

Customer value Customers are a party involved in the value creation of an organization. Customer value comprises the value of the organization for the customer on the one hand and the value of the customer for the organization on the other. Aside from the organization's value for the customer (which is part of the business model), the customer also has value for the organization which can be measured in terms of loyalty, cocreation, referral behavior, and portfolio share (which is part of the value creation for all stakeholders).

Delivery Delivery is part of the business model, comprising the marketing, sales, customer contact and services by which the offering is provided to the customer. Since the customer is most directly involved with the delivery, this interface has the most brand touch points by which the brand can differentiate itself and stand out in the market.

Employee value An employee is a party involved in the value creation of an organization. Employee value comprises the value of the organization for the employee on the one hand and the value of the employee for the organization on the other. The

---

[1] Kemperman et al. (2013), Winter and Van der Weijden (2008), Kemperman and Trampe (2012), and Geelhoed et al. (2014).

© Springer International Publishing Switzerland 2017
J. Kemperman et al. (eds.), *Brilliant Business Models in Healthcare*,
DOI 10.1007/978-3-319-26440-0

organization's value for the employees relates to the pleasure derived from challenges, inspirational working environment, reward, appreciation and confirmation, openness, degrees of freedom, celebration moments, and balance. Conversely, the employee has value for the customer via performances in customer bonding, ideas, motivation, loyalty, attracting other employees, production and turnover, and transferring knowledge and culture.

Market segments Market segments are part of the business model. Segmentation is the process of dividing a heterogeneous group of customers into subgroups that are relatively more homogeneous. Customers can be segmented in various ways. The potential of a segment can be tested and described on the position of the organization, the competition, the target group itself, and the unique customer insight to which the organization can respond.

Operation The operation is part of the business model, comprising production and technology plus the suppliers and partners with which the organization works together. This interface contains customer touch points where the organization can make the difference, the enabling technology in people and systems, but it also concerns the basic operation. In respect of the delivery processes, the emphasis in the basic operation lies more on error-free, generally automated processes where synergy and efficiency must be achieved.

Positioning This concerns the position that the organization chooses for the brand or has in respect of other brands on the market and stakeholders. Positioning can be defined based on the brand promise, brand values, brand roots, brand proof, and brand essence.

Shareholder value Shareholders are parties involved in the value creation of an organization. Shareholder value comprises the value of the organization for the shareholder on the one hand and the value of the shareholder for the organization on the other. The organization's value for the shareholders and other lenders relates to yield, the organization's market value, profitability, growth, and for some investors societal impact. Conversely, the shareholder has value for the organization via loyalty, co-entrepreneurship, investments, referrals, and portfolio share.

Societal value Society is, as a party, involved in the value creation of an organization. Societal value comprises the value of the organization for society on the one hand and the value of society for the organization on the other. The organization's value for society relates to the creation of employment, welfare, health, happiness and prosperity. Additionally the products themselves and the way they are made can be helpful or harmful for goals in society. Conversely, society has value for the organization via the acquisition of goodwill, a positive image, the confirmation and appreciation of the societal contribution made by the organization, and via government policy and legislation.

Vision Vision is both the picture of the future and the basic philosophy of an organization and forms the guideline for all its actions. The vision of an organization lays down in a clear, concise, and orderly manner its core values and core qualities, as well as the higher goal and audacious goal that is strives to realize.

Value for the customer The value for the customer is part of the business model. This is where the organization can define which value it wants customers to expect and experience based on the brand promises and brand essence. It connects the vision and the strategy with the market segment and determines what you want to be with this brand in relation to the customer. Customer value can be defined as follows: Customer value = (What does the customer receive in terms of result + process + emotion)/(What does the customer give in terms of price + effort + risk).

Sources

Aaker, D. A. A. (1991). *Managing brand equity—Capitalizing on the value of a brand name*. New York: Free Press.

Aaker, D. A. A. (1996). *Building strong brands*. New York: Free Press.

Aaker, D. A. A., & Joachimsthaler, E. (2000). *Brand leadership*. New York: Free Press.

Aberg, E. (2013). *Britt Marie Banck blev Arets banbrytare*. Retrieved September 13, 2013, from http://www.jnytt.se/britt-marie-banck-blev-arets-banbrytare/.

Abrahams, J. (1998a). *Part 1: Jay Abrahams interview transcript—Paddi's management model*. Wauwatosa: Solution Press.

Abrahams, J. (1998b). *Part 2: Jay Abrahams interview transcript—Paddi's management model*. Wauwatosa: Solution Press.

Abrahams, J. (1998c). *What does it mean: Happiness in business? Mixing happiness and profit*. Wauwatosa: Solution Press.

Adner, R. (2012). *The wide lens—A new strategy for innovation*. London: Penguin Business.

Aggarwal, R., & Chick, S. E. (2013). *Laastari: Building a Retail Health Clinic Chain*. Fontainebleau: INSEAD.

Al, C. J. (1981). *Het Ziekenhuis: Een plan voor verandering* (2nd rev. ed.). Deventer: Van Loghum Slaterus.

Altron Medical Aid. (2013), *Benefit information. Enhanced option*. Retrieved September 2, 2013, from http://www.altronmedicalaid.co.za/schemes/altron/benefit-information.

Altron Medical Aid. (2013). *Medical schemes*. Retrieved September 2, 2013, from http://www.altronmedicalaid.co.za/medicalschemes_za/altron/web/pdfs/benefit_schedule.pdf.

An, R., Patel, D., Segal, D., & Sturm, R. (2013). Eating better for less: A national discount program for healthy food purchases in South Africa. *American Journal of Health Behavior, 37*(1), 56–61.

Anand, G. (2009, November 25). The Henry Ford of heart surgery. In India, a factory model for hospitals is cutting costs and yielding profits. *Wall Street Journal*.

Ananthakrishnan, A. N., McGinley, E. L., Binion, D. G., & Saeian, K. (2011). A nationwide analysis of changes in severity and outcomes of inflammatory bowel disease hospitalizations. *Journal of Gastrointestinal Surgery, 15*(2), 267–276.

Archimedes. (2013). Quantifying health. Retrieved August 23, 2013, from www.archimedesmodel.com.

Arets, M. (2011). *Brand expedition: Een reis langs Europa's meest inspirerende Merken*. Delft: Eburon Business.

Arts in Zweden. (2014). Retrieved January 20, 2014, from http://www.artsinzweden.nl/Default.aspx?pg=5.

© Springer International Publishing Switzerland 2017
J. Kemperman et al. (eds.), *Brilliant Business Models in Healthcare*,
DOI 10.1007/978-3-319-26440-0

Ataguba, J., & Akazili, J. (2010). Health care financing in South Africa: Moving toward universal Coverage. *Continuing Medical Education, 28*(2), 74.

Axelrod, R. (1984). *The evolution of cooperation*. New York: Basic Books.

Barron, C. (2013). *Discovery Health chief executive Adrian Gore on profits vs people*. Retrieved September 2, 2013, from http://www.bdlive.co.za/business/healthcare/2013/03/10/discovery-health-chief-executive-adrian-gore-on-profits-vs-people.

Basch, M. (2002a). *Customer culture: How FedEx® and other great companies put the customer first every day*. NJ: Prentice Hall.

Basch, M. (2002b). *Adventures with Dr. Paddi Lund*. Wauwatosa: Solution Press.

Basch, M. (2002c). *Paddi & Mike transcript*. Wauwatosa: Solution Press.

Beersen, N., Berg, M., van Galen, M., Huijsmans, K., & Hoeksema, N. (2011). *Onderzoek naar de meerwaarde van ParkinsonNet. Plexus & Vektis on the instructions of Zorgverzekeraars Nederland*. Zeist: Zorgverzekeraars Nederland.

Bekkum, T. (2013). *Bouwen aan organisatie identiteit—Sturen op waardecreatie, reputatie en verandering met het corporate merk*. Amsterdam: Adfo Groep.

Berry, L., & Lampo, S. (2004, Spring). Branding labour-intensive services. *London Business School's Business Strategy Review, 15*, 1.

Berwich, D. M., Nolan T. W., & Whittington, J. (2012). The triple aim: Care, health, and cost, May 2008. *Health Affairs, 27*(3), 759–769.

Berwick, D. M. (2004). *Escape fire—Designs for the future of health care, collected speeches, 1992–2002—The institute of healthcare improvement's national forum on quality improvement in health care*. San Francisco: Jossey-Bass—A Wiley Imprint.

Bhattacharyya, O., et al. (2010). Innovative health service delivery models in low and middle income countries—What can we learn from the private sector? *Health Research Policy and Systems, 8*, 24.

Billing Views. (2012). *M-Pesa—A Kenyan success story in perspective*. Retrieved October 18, 2013, from www.billingviews.com/m-pesa-kenyan-success-story-perspective/.

Bisognano, M. (2013). *A patient directs his own care—2012 IHI annual report*. Retrieved July 7, 2013, from http://www.ihi.org/about/Documents/IHI_AnnualReport_2012.pdf.

Bisognano, M. (2013). *Lessons from yesterday, plans for tomorrow—Fifth annual South Carolina patient safety symposium (IHI)*. Retrieved September 16, 2013, from http://www.scha.org/files/mbisognano_lessons_from_yesterday.pdf.

Björnberg, A. (2012). *Euro health consumer index, 2012-05-15—Health consumer powerhouse*. Retrieved January 19, 2014, from http://www.healthpowerhouse.com.

Blackwell, T. (2012, May 8). State is stifling innovation at hospitals: Health-care executive. In *National Post*, Toronto.

Blackwell, T. (2012, September 7). Pioneering for-profit Shouldice hernia clinic sold for $14-million. In *National Post*, Toronto.

Bohmer, R. M. J. (2009). *Designing care—Aligning the nature and management of health care*. Boston: Harvard Business Press.

Broomberg, J. (2013). Discovery Health presentation to DHMS 2013 AGM. Retrieved September 2, 2013, from https://www.discovery.co.za/discovery_coza/web/linked_content/pdfs/health/dhms/agm_administrator_presentation.pdf.

Brouwer, J. J., van der Zwan, G., & Van Marrewijk, M. (2013). *Koplopers in de zorg—50 formules voor succes*. The Hague: Content to Image.

Burlingham, B. (2005). *Small giants*. London: Penguin.

Business Daily Africa. (2012). *Vodafone takes home Sh2-3bn of M-Pesa revenue*. Retrieved October 8, 2013, from http://www.businessdailyafrica.com/Corporate-News/Vodafone-takes-home-Sh2-3bn-of-M-Pesa-revenue/-/539550/1852810/-/m9igv0/-/index.html.

Canadian Cancer Society. (2013). *Canadian cancer statistics 2012*. Retrieved January 19, 2014, from http://www.cancer.ca/~/media/cancer.ca/CW/cancer%20information/cancer%20101/Canadian%20cancer%20statistics/Canadian-Cancer-Statistics-2012---English.pdf.

Canadian Cancer Society. (2013). *Canadian cancer statistics 2013*. Retrieved January 19, 2014, from http://www.cancer.ca/~/media/cancer.ca/CW/cancer%20information/cancer%20101/ Canadian%20cancer%20statistics/canadian-cancer-statistics-2013-EN.pdf.

CGAP. (2010). *10 things you thought you knew about M-PESA*. Retrieved October 11, 2013, from http://www.cgap.org/blog/10-things-you-thought-you-knew-about-m-pesa.

Chilingerian, J. (2004). *Clinical focus in health care: Some international lessons*. Waltham: Heller School for Social Policy and Management.

Christensen, C. M., & Dann, J. (2001). *SonoSite a view inside, HBR Case 9-602-056*. Boston: Harvard Business School Press.

Christensen, C. M. (1997). *The innovator's solution: Creating and sustaining successful growth*. Boston: Harvard Business School Press.

Christensen, C. M., Grossman, J. H., & Hwang, J. (2009). *The innovator's prescription—A disruptive solution for health care*. New York: McGraw-Hill.

Chu, B. K., O'Brien, J.G., Anderson, R., Bell, T.L., Blank, A., Blunt, M., Brier, P.S., et. al. (2013). *Engaging health care users: A framework for healthy individuals and communities, a report of the AHA committee*. Retrieved September 13, 2013, from http://www.aha.org/research/cor/ content/engaging_health_care_users.pdf.

Chuma, J., Thiede, M., & Molyneux, C. (2006). Rethinking the economic costs of malaria at the household level: Evidence from applying a new analytical framework in rural Kenya. *Malaria Journal, 5*.

Collins, D., Morduch, J., Rutherford, S., & Ruthven, O. (2009). *Portfolios of the poor – How the world's poor live on $2 a day*. Princeton: Princeton University Press.

Collins, J. C. (1999). *How the mighty fall: And why some companies never give in*. New York: Harper Collins Publishers.

Collins, J. C. (2001). *Good to great*. New York: Harper Business.

Collins, J. C., & Porras, J. I. (1994). *Built to last: Successful habits of visionary companies*. New York: Harper Collins.

Companje, K. P. (1994). *Ziekenzorg—De geschiedenis van een ziekenfonds en zijn eigen instellingen*. Zeist: Stichting Historie Ziekenfondswezen.

David Geffen School of Medicine at UCLA. (2012, Spring). *Beyond the scope, a report of the UCLA Division of Digestive Diseases*. Los Angeles, CA; School of Medicine at UCLA.

Davis, R. (2013). SA healthcare: Some are still more equal than others. Retrieved September 2, 2013, from http://www.dailymaverick.co.za/article/2013-07-17-sahealthcare-some-are-still-more-equal-than-others/.

Debarati, R. *Narayana Hrudayalaya, prescribed cloud to deliver better healthcare services: A case study on cloud computing in Pharma & Healthcare*. Retrieved January 15, 2015, from www.cio.in.

Dercksen, M. (2012). *Dialysecafé in Zweden inspireert Britse zorg*. Retrieved January 19, 2014, from http://www.niernieuws.nl/?action=showcomments&id=5607#.

DHAN Foundation. (2013). *Annual report 2012, Madurai*. Retrieved January 19, 2014, from http://www.dhan.org/.

Canadian Cancer Society. (2012). *Canadian cancer statistics 2011*. Retrieved January 19, 2014, from https://www.discovery.co.za/discovery_za/web/pdfs/health/annual_financial_statements_2011.pdf.

Discovery. (2013). *Healthy food benefit*. Retrieved September 2, 2013, from http://www.discovery. co.za/vi-rsa/genericTCB.do?type=TCB_PnP_HEALTHY_FOOD.

Discovery. (2013). *Key facts*. Retrieved September 2, 2013, from http://www.discovery.co.za/discovery_za/web/logged_out/investor_relations/our_business/key_facts.html.

Discovery. (2013). *Keyfit benefit rules*. Retrieved September 2, 2013, from https://www.discovery. co.za/discovery_coza/web/linked_content/pdfs/keyfit/keyfit_benefit_rules.pdf.

Discovery. (2013). *Performance reviews for 2012*. Retrieved September 2, 2013, from https:// www.discovery.co.za/discovery_coza/web/linked_content/pdfs/about_us/performance_ reviews_1_2012.pdf.

Discovery. (2013). *Plan comparison*. Retrieved September 2, 2013, from http://www.hr.uct.ac.za/usr/hr/remuneration/healthcare/discovery_health_2013_plan_comparison.pdf.

Discovery. (2013). *User agreement living vitality*. Retrieved September 2, 2013, from https://www.livingvitality.discovery.co.za/lv/terms_and_conditions.

Discovery. (2013). *What happens when you run out of funds in your medical savings account?* Retrieved September 2, 2013, from https://www.discovery.co.za/portal/individual/health-faqs.

Donga, H. (2008). *Christoffel van Brants en zijn hofje—De geschiedenis van het Van Brants Rus Hofje vanaf 1733*. Hilversum: Verloren.

Driessen, G. L. (1948). De Leidse Hofjes. In *Jaarboekje voor Geschiedenis en Oudheidkunde van Leiden en omstreken* (pp. 47–74). Leiden: Vereniging Oud-Leiden.

Korsten, J., & Vonk, R. (2011). In T. Duffhues (Ed.), *Van Achlum naar Achmea—De historische route naar een coöperatieve verzekeringsgroep*. Zutphen: Walburg Pers.

Duncan, T. R., & Moriarty, S. (1997). *Driving brand value. Using integrated marketing to manage profitable stakeholder relationships*. New York: McGraw-Hill.

Economist. (2013). *The world's fastest-growing continent—Aspiring Africa*. Retrieved September 2, 2013, from http://www.economist.com/news/leaders/21572773-pride-africasachievements-should-be-coupled-determination-make-even-faster.

Economist. (2013). *Why does Kenya lead the world in mobile money?* Retrieved October 10, 2013, from http://www.economist.com/blogs/economist-explains/2013/05/economist-explains-18.

van Eeghen, I. H. (1967). *Brieven van het Deutzenhofje—Madame de Nerhad en Mirabeau*. Haarlem: Tjeenk Willink & Zoon.

Elster, J. (Ed.). (1984). *Ulysses and the Sirens: Studies in rationality and irrationality*. Cambridge: Cambridge University Press.

Epping-Jordan, J., Pruitt, S., Bengoa, R., & Wagner, E. (2004), Improving the quality of health care for chronic conditions. In *Quality and safety in health care*, May 2004 (p. 299). London: BMJ Pub.

Erdman, S. (2013). *Healthcaretechnology.com; Patient experience and design at Mayo Clinic: Case study*. Retrieved January 19, 2014, from http://www.healthcaretechnologyonline.com/doc/patient-experienceand-design-at-mayo-clinic-case-study-0001.

van Essen, J. P. (2012). *De Provenier tussen Theorie en Praktijk*, Bachelor thesis, Utrecht University, Utrecht.

Floor, J. (2012). *Discovery demonstrates vitality*. Retrieved September 2, 2013, from http://www.cover.co.za/investment/discovery-demonstrates-vitality.

Forsakringskassan. (2014). Retrieved January 20, 2014, from http://www.forsakringskassan.se/privatpers/.

Franzen, G., & van den Berg, M. (2003). *Strategisch management van merken* (2nd ed.). Alphen aan den Rijn: Kluwer.

Frei, F., & Morriss, A. (2012). *Uncommon service – How to win by putting customers at the core of your business*. Boston: Harvard Business Review Press.

FSD Kenya. (2011). *Mobile payments in Kenya*. Retrieved October 8, 2013, from http://www.fsdkenya.org/pdf_documents/11-02-14_Mobile_payments_in_Kenya.pdf.

Gawande, A. (2002). *Complicaties, notities van een chirurg*. Amsterdam: de Arbeiderspers.

Geelhoed, J., Samhoud, S., & Hamurcu, N. (2014). *Creating lasting value—How to lead, manage and market your stakeholder value*. London: Kogan Page.

Geelhoed, J., & Samhoud, S. (2011). *Be useful*. The Hague: Academic Service.

Global Health Partner AB. (2011). *Global health partner invests in Finnish Laastar Lahiklinikka*. Retrieved January 19, 2014, from http://news.cision.com/global-health-partner-ab/r/global-health-partnerinvests-in-finnish-laastari-lahiklinikka,c9170287.

Goldratt, E. M., & Cox, J. (1986), *The goal—A process of ongoing improvement* (rev edn.). Croton-on-Hudson, NY: North River Press.

Goudge, J., Akazili, J., Ataguba, J., Kuwawenaruwa, A., Borghi, J., Harris, B., et al. (2012). Social solidarity and willingness to tolerate risk-and income-related cross-subsidies within health insurance: Experiences from Ghana, Tanzania and South Africa. *Health Policy & Planning, 27*(1), 55–63.

Grönroos, C. (2000). *Service management & marketing—A customer relationship management approach* (2nd ed.). Chichester: John Wiley & Sons.

de Groot, H., van Hout, J., Teeuwen, B., & Nauta, F. (2010). *ParkinsonNet—Regionaal netwerk voor mensen met de ziekte van Parkinson*. Arnhem: Prima Praktijken.

Gruijters, T. M. D. (Ed.). (2013). *Financierbaarheid van de Zorg*. Amsterdam: Coincide.

Gupta, S., & Riis, J. (2012). *PatientsLikeMe: An online community of patients*. Boston: Harvard Business School.

GSMA. (2012). *Keys to M-PESA's success*. Retrieved October 8, 2013, from http://www.gsma. com/mobilefordevelopment/wp-content/uploads/2012/03/keystompesassuccess4jan69.pdf.

Halley, E. (1693, January). An estimate of the degrees of the mortality of mankind, drawn from the curious tables of the birth and funerals at the City of Breslaw with an attempt to ascertain the price of annuities upon lives. *Philosophical Transactions,* (3), no. 196.

Hardin, G. (1968). The tragedy of the commons. *Science, 162,* 1243–1248.

Harvard Business School. (2011). *Mobile banking for the unbanked*. Retrieved October 11, 2013, from http://hbswk.hbs.edu/item/6729.html.

Health News. (2013). *Best hospitals in the USA*. Retrieved January 19, 2014, from http://health. usnews.com/besthospitals/rankings.

Healthways. (2013). *Annual report 2012*. Retrieved October 10, 2013, from www.healthways. com.

Henley Business School. (2012). *Up close and personal with Adrian Gore*. Retrieved September 2, 2013, from http://www.henleysa.ac.za/perspectives/up-close-and-personalwith-adrian-gore. html.

Herzlinger, R. E. (1994). *Consumer-driven health care: Implications for providers, payers and policymakers*. San Francisco, CA: Jossey Bass.

Herzlinger, R. E. (1996). *Market-driven health care*. Reading, MA: Addison-Wesley Publishing Company.

Heskett, J. L., Sasser, E., & Schlesinger, L. A. (1997). *The service profit chain*. New York: Free Press.

Heskett, J. L. (2003). Shouldice Hospital Limited. *Harvard Business School*, June 9, case 683-068.

Heskett, J. L. & Hallowell, R. (2005). Shouldice Hospital Abridged. *Harvard Business School*, January 9, case 805-002.

Heskett, J. L., Sasser, W. E., Jr., & Schlesinger, L. (2003). *The value profit chain—Treat employees like customers and customers like employees*. New York: Free Press.

Heskett, J. L., Sasser, W. E., Jr., & Wheeler, J. (2008). *The ownership quotient—Putting the service profit chain to work for unbeatable competitive advantage*. Boston, MA: Harvard Business Press.

Homan, M. (2011, March 26). Zara zegeviert met omgekeerd bedrijfsmodel. In *Het Financiële Dagblad* (pp. 20–22).

Hommes, D. (2013). Chronic disease management in the Triple Aim Era of U.S. Health Care System Reform: Accountable care transformation and innovation within the UCLA Health System. In *UCLA IBD Center white paper series*, No. 1 October 2013 (p. 3).

Hsiao, W. C., Medina, A., Ly, C., & Dukhan, Y. (2013). Orient express in south, east and Pacific Asia. In A. S. Preker, M. E. Lindner, D. Chernichovsky, & O. P. Schellekens (Eds.), *Scaling up affordable health insurance—Staying the course*. Washington: The World Bank.

Huber, M. (2014), *Towards a new dynamic concept of health—Its operationalisation and use in public health and healthcare and in evaluating health effects of food*. Dissertation at the School for Public Health and Primary Care CAPHRI, Maastricht University.

Idenburg, P., & van Schaik, M. (2013). *Diagnose Zorginnovatie—Over technologie en Ondernemerschap*. Scriptum: Scriptumx.

India Knowledge @ Warton. (2010). Narayana Hrudayalaya: A model for accessible, affordable health care?, July 2001.

Institute for Healthcare Improvement. (2012). Retrieved January 15, 2015, from http://www.ihi. org/Engage/Initiatives/TripleAim/pages/default.aspx.

International Federation of Health Plans. (2012). *Comparative price report. Variation in medical and hospital prices by Country*. Retrieved September 2, 2013, from http://static.squarespace. com/static/518a3cfee4b0a77d03a62c98t/51dfd9f9e4b0d1d8067dcde2/1373624825901/ 2012%20iFHP%20Price%2Report%20FINAL%20April%203.pdf.

InVentiv Health, Inc. (2013). *PatientsLikeMe And inVentive Health partner to accelerate clinical trial research*. Retrieved January 19, 2014, from http://www.prnewswire.com/newsreleases/ patientslikeme-and-inventiv-health-partner-to-accelerate-clinical-trialresearch-211806441. html.

Ismail, S., Malone, M., & van Geest, Y. (2014). *Exponential organizations (Engels)—Why new organizations are ten times better, faster, and cheaper than yours (and what to do about it)*. New York: Diversion Books.

Jaipur Foot. (2013). *Plan comparison*. Retrieved September 2, 2013, from www.jaipurfoot.org.

de Jong, M. (2012). *Gezondheidszorg in Zweden*. Retrieved January 19, 2014, from http://www. emigreren-naarzweden.com/gezondheidszorg-in-zweden.html.

Kalan, J. (2012). *Cashless in Kenya: A mobile money experiment using M-PESA*. Retrieved January 19, 2014, from http://www.wamda.com/2012/11/cashless-inkenya-a-mobile-money-experiment-using-m-pesa.

de Kam, R. (1998). *Voor de armen alhier—De geschiedenis van vijf Utrechtse fundatiën en hun vrijwoningen*. Utrecht: Matrijs.

Kanani, R. (2011). Jaipur Foot: One of the most technological advanced social enterprises of the world. Retrieved January 19, 2014, from http://www.forbes.com/sites/rahimkanani/2011/08/08/ jaipur-foot-one-of-the-most-technologically-advanced-social-enterprises-in-the-world/.

Kania, J., & Kramer, M. (2011, Winter). Collective impact. *Stanford Social Innovation Review*.

Kaul, R. (2011, February 23). *Learning from Narayana's 'Lean' model to scale services*. NextBillion, development through enterprise.

Kemperman, J. E. B., & van Engelen, J. M. L. (1999). Operationalizing the customer value concept. In L. Hildebrand, D. Annacker, & D. Klapper (Eds.), *Marketing and Competition in the Information Age—Proceedings of the Annual Conference of the European Marketing Academy*, 14 May 2011. Berlin: European Marketing Academy.

Kemperman, J. (2013). VOC, De handelspartner voor Azië'. In J. Kemperman, J. Geelhoed, & J. op't Hoog (Eds.), *Briljante businessmodellen—Een bijzondere benadering voor betere business*. The Hague: Academic Service.

Kemperman, J., Geelhoed, J., & op't Hoog, J. (2013). *Briljante businessmodellen—Een bijzondere benadering voor betere business*. The Hague: Academic Service.

Kemperman, J., Geelhoed, J., & op't Hoog, J. (2014). *Briljante businessmodellen in de Zorg— Baanbrekende benaderingen voor betere betaalbare zorg*. The Hague: Academic Service.

Kemperman, J., Geelhoed, J., & op't Hoog, J. (2015). *Briljante businessmodellen in Finance— Baanbrekers voor betrouwbaar bankieren en verzekeren*. The Hague: Academic Service.

Kemperman, J. E. B., Edelman, T., & van der Pool, H. (2000, May). Strategisch ketenmanagement. In *Holland Management Review*, no. 71.

Kemperman, J. E. B., & Trampe, L. (2012). *De Merkrolmethode—Over merkportfolio's, kalkoenen en grindbakken*. Schiedam: Scriptum.

Kernkamp, G. W. (1910). Bengt Ferrners dagboek van zijnen reise door Nederland in 1759. *Bijdragen en mededeelingen van het Historisch Genootschap, 31*, 314–509.

Keus, S. H. J., Oude Nijhuis, L. B., Nijkrake, M. J., Bloem, B. R., & Munneke, M. (2012). Improving community healthcare for patients with Parkinson's disease: The Dutch model. *Parkinson's Disease, 2012*. Article ID 543426.

Khanna, T., Rangan, V. K., & Manocaran, M. (2005, June). Narayana Hrudayalaya Heart Hospital: Cardiac care for the poor. *Harvard Business School*, N9-505-078.

Khandelwal, T. (2009). *Case study Shouldice Hospital*. Retrieved November 25, 2013, from www. slideshare.net/tarunkdl/shouldice-hospital.

van der Klauw, D., Munneke, M., & Bloem, B. R. (2011). Beter samenwerken vanuit specialisme. *Medisch Contact, 66*, nr. 13.

Kothandaraman, P., & Mookerjee, S. (2007). *Healthcare for all: Narayana Hrudayalaya, Bangalore. Growing inclusive markets, UNDP, case study.*

Korten, K. (2008). *Focused factories in healthcare.* Maastricht: Maastricht University.

Kotler, P. (2000). *Marketing management* (The millennium ed.). NJ: Prentice-Hall.

Kotter, J. P., & Cohen, D. S. (2002). *The heart of change: Real-life stories of how people change their organizations.* Boston: Harvard Business Press.

KPMG Advisory. (2013). *Wie doet het met wie in de zorg.* Amstelveen: KPMG.

Kuenen, J. W., et al. (2011). *Zorg voor waarde. Meer kwaliteit voor minder geld: wat de Nederlandse gezondheidszorg kan leren van Zweden.* Amsterdam: Boston Consulting Group.

Kumar, A. A., Shanta, G. P. S., Kahan, S., et al. (2012, February). Intentional weight loss and dose reductions of anti-diabetic medications—A retrospective cohort study. *PLoS One, 7*(2), e32395. www.plosone.org.

Leclerq, W. L. (1947). *Geschiedenis van het Algemeen Ziekenfonds voor Amsterdam 1847–1947.* Amsterdam: Drukkerij en Uitgeverij J.H. de Bussy.

Lee, F. (2004). *If Disney ran your hospital: 9 1/2 things you would do differently.* Bozeman: Second River Healthcare Press.

Leene, G. J. F. (1997). Over hofjes, voor en van ouderen. *Medische Antropologie, 9*(1).

Levy, P. (2011). *Self dialysis in Sweden—Not running a hospital.* Retrieved June 7, 2013, from http://runningahospital.blogspot.nl/2011/08/self-dialysis-in-sweden.html.

LIdZ. (2014). Retrieved January 20, 2014, from www.lidz.nl.

Lindström, J., Ilanne-Parikka, P., Peltonen, M., et al. (2006, November 11). Sustained reduction in the incidence of type 2 diabetes by lifestyle intervention: Follow-up of the Finnish Diabetes Prevention Study. *Lancet, 368*, 1673–1679. www.TheLancet.com.

Link, H. (1983). *Die Stiftung Liebenau und ihr Gründer Adolf Aich.* Meckenbeurer: Stiftung Liebenau.

Lohvansuu, J., & Laitinen, V.-P. (2011). *iPad app healthcare innovator.* Retrieved January 19, 2014, from http://www.userintelligence.com/portfolio/case-studies/ipad-app-healthcare-innovator.

van der Loo, H., Geelhoed, J., & Samhoud, S. (2007). *Kus de visie wakker: Organisaties energiek en effectief maken.* The Hague: Sdu Uitgevers.

de Lugt, P., Cerfontaine, I., & Jonk, G. (2013). *Het stormt in de polder—Een anticiperende kijk op het zorglandschap.* Oosterhout: Pharmapartners, Pinkroccade en Benthurst & Co.

Mack, S., Misra, R., & Sharma, A. (2003). *Case study series Jaipur Foot: Challenging convention.* Michigan: Michigan Business School.

Mastenbroek, W. F. G. (1993). *Macht, Organisatie en Communicatie.* Heemstede: Holland Business Publications.

Matthew. (1st century A.D.). The Gospel according to St. Matthew. *New Testament, 25*, 31–46.

Mayo. (2013). *Annual report Mayo 2012*: via www.mayoclinic.com.

Medema, G. H. (2010). 'Om van een grote overlast en van leeggangers bevrijd te zijn—De bouw van stedelijke armen- en werkhuizen in de 18e eeuw. *Holland, 42*(3), 206–221.

Meenu, K. (2009). The Jaipur foot. *Cornelia Street Café, Central Coast California, Entertaining Science Blogspot.*

Menon, S., & Kumar, A. (2008). Who invented the Jaipur Foot? Retrieved January 19, 2014, from http://www.business-standard.com/article/economy-policy/whoinvented-the-jaipur-foot-108011501095_1.html.

Mondloch, M. V., Cole, D. C., & Frank, J. W. (2013). *Does How You Do Depend on How You Think You'll Do? A Systematic Review of the Evidence of a Relation Between Patients' Recovery Expectations and Health Outcomes.* Ottawa, ON: Canadian Medical Association.

Montessori, M. (1967). *The absorbent mind.* New York: Delta.

Munneke, M., Nijkrake, M. J., Keus, S. H., Kwakkel, G., Berendse, H. W., Roos, R. A., et al. (2009, December). Trial Study Group, Effectiveness of community-based networks for physiotherapy, in Parkinson's disease: a cluster-randomised trial. *The Lancet Neurology*, 46–54.

Nale, A., & Boston, D. (2012). *Retail medical clinics: From Foe to friend?* Retrieved January 19, 2014, from www.accenture.com.

National Geographic. (2012). *The invisible bank: How Kenya has beaten the world in mobile money*. Retrieved October 11, 2013, from http://newswatch.nationalgeographic.com/2012/07/04/the-invisible-bank-how-kenya-has-beaten-the-world-in-mobilemoney/.

Narayana Hospitals. (2014). Retrieved January 20, 2014, from Narayanahospitals.com.

Neren, U. (2010). Why innovation thrives at Mayo Clinic. Retrieved September 1, 2014, from http://blogs.hbr.org/2010/08/why-innovation-thrives-at-the/.

Newman, M. A. (1999). *Health as expanding consciousness*. Lincoln, NE: iUniverse.

NHS. (2012). *Developing shared self-management for hospital haemodialysis patients*. Retrieved September 13, 2013, from http://www.yhscg.nhs.uk/Networks/sharing-haemodialysis-care.htm.

Nooteboom, B. (1994). *Management van partnerships in toeleveren en uitbesteden*. Schoonhoven: Academic Service.

Nossel, C. (2011). *The vitality wellness program experience from South Africa*. Retrieved September 2, 2013, from http://www.c3health.org/wp-content/uploads/2011/08/Craig-Nossel-C3-slides-20110721.pdf.

Ohno, T. (2012). *Taiichi Ohnos workplace management* (special 100th birthday ed.). New York: McGraw-Hill.

Osterwalder, A., & Pigneur, Y. (2010). *Business model generation*. Hoboken: John Wiley and Sons. (Dutch edition), Deventer: Kluwer.

ParkinsonNet. (2013, May). *Patiënt neemt regie over eigen ziekte*. Het Brein—Telegraaf Special (p. 8).

Eimers, M., Boots, S., Munneke, M., Bloem, B., van Galen, M., & Huijsmans, K. (2013). *ParkinsonNet in cijfers*. Nijmegen: Zorgverzekeraars Nederland, ParkinsonNet & Vektis.

Patel, P. J. (2011), I choose to fight in my live: Sudha Chandran. *The Times of India*, at: http://articles.timesofindia.indiatimes.com/2011-12-09/tv/30491022_1_film-industry-hema-malini-roles.

PatientsLikeMe. (2011). *Let patients help: The undying mission of E-Patient Dave*. Retrieved January 19, 2014, from http://blog.patientslikeme.com/2011/07/18/let-patients-help-the-undying-missionof-e-patient-dave/#sthash.NSvL3i2D.dpuf.

PatientsLikeMe. (2012). *A day in the life of health data and patient safety clinical specialist Christine Caligtan*. Retrieved January 19, 2014, from http://blog.patientslikeme.com/tag/patientslikeme-yoga-class/.

Pearson, H. (2012). Liberia, ArcelorMittal Liberia transforms life for amputees. Retrieved January 19, 2014, from http://www.gnnliberia.com/index.php?option=com_content&view=article&id=3519:liberia-arcelormittal-liberia-transforms-life-for-amputees&catid=34:politics&Itemid=54.

Peckham, H. (1772). The tour of Holland, Dutch Brabant, the Austrian Netherlands and Part of France, in which is included a description of Paris and its environments. London, 1772. In Medema, G. H. (2010). Om van een grote overlast en van leeggangers bevrijd te zijn—De bouw van stedelijke armen—en werkhuizen in de 18e eeuw. In Crisis!. Speciaal nr. van: *Holland, 42*(3), 206–221.

PharmAccess. (2013). *Les Baillie tells "M-PESA Story" in Amsterdam*. Retrieved October 8, 2013, from http://www.pharmaccess.org/RunScript.asp?page=24&Article_ID=254&NWS=NWS&ap=NewsDetail.asp&p=ASP\~Pg24.asp.

Polard, A. (2008). *Discovery Vitality Journal. Reducing the cost of healthcare through lifestyle intervention*. Johannesburg: Ultra Litho.

Pomp, M. (2010). *Een beter Nederland—De gouden eieren van de gezondheidszorg*. Amsterdam: Uitgeverij Balans.

Porter, M. E. (1980). *Competitive strategy*. New York: Free Press.

Porter, M. E. (1985). *Competitive advantage*. New York: Free Press.

Porter, M. E., & Teisberg, E. O. (2006). *Redefining health care—Creating value-based competition on results*. Boston, MA: Harvard Business Press.

Prahalad, C. K. (2009). *The fortune at the bottom of the pyramid: Eradicating poverty through profits* (revised and updated 5th anniversary ed.). Boston, MA: Pearson Prentice Hall.

Preez, L. (2013). Are wellness programs worth it? Retrieved September 2, 2013, from http://www.iol.co.za/business/personal-finance/are-wellness-programs-worthit-1.1508115.

Preker, A. S., Lindner, M. E., Chernichovsky, D., & Schellekens, O. P. (2013). *Scaling up affordable health insurance—Staying the course*. Washington: The World Bank.

Princess Margaret Cancer Centre. (2012). *Annual report PMCC 2011*. Retrieved January 19, 2014, from http://thepmcf.ca/pmhonlinereport2011/?utm_source=PMCP&utm_medium=web&utm_campaign=PMCP%2BWeb.

Princess Margaret Cancer Centre. (2012). *Annual report PMCC, 2012*. http://www.uhn.ca/corporate/AboutUHN/OurHospitals/Documents/PMHCP_AR_2012.pdf.

Reddy, A. C., Buskirk, B. D., & Kaicker, A. (1993). Tangibilizing the intangibles: Some strategies for services marketing. *Journal of Service Marketing, 7*(3), 13–17.

RATN. (2013). *PharmAccess Group partners with Safaricom and the M-PESA Foundation*. Retrieved October 8, 2013, from http://www.ratn.org/index.php?option=com_content&view=article&id=452:pharmaccess-group-is-partnering-with-safaricom-and-them-pesa-foundation&catid=111&Itemid=813.

Redmon, J. B., Bertone, A. G., Connelly, S., et al. (2010). *Effect of the look AHEAD study intervention on medication use and related cost to treat cardiovascular disease risk factors in individuals with type 2 diabetes*.

Regenesys Business School. (2012). *Leadership conversations: Adrian Gore*. Retrieved September 2, 2013, from http://www.youtube.com/watch?v=hubqgTevrTM.

Reichheld, F. F. (1996). *The loyalty effect: The hidden force behind growth, profits and lasting value*. Boston, MA: Harvard Business School Press.

Research Infosource Inc. (2012). *Canada's hospital innovation leaders*. Retrieved January 19, 2014, from http://www.researchinfosource.com/pdf/Top%2040%20LR-2012.pdf.

Reuters. (2013). *Africa's emerging middle class drives growth and democracy*. Retrieved September 2, 2013, from http://www.reuters.com/article/2013/05/10/usafrica-investment-idUSBRE9490DV20130510.

Rhyne, E. (2009). *Microfinance for bankers and investors—Understanding the opportunities and challenges of the market at the bottom of the pyramid*. New York: McGraw-Hill.

Ries, A., & Trout, J. (1981). *Positioning: The battle for your mind*. New York: McGraw-Hill.

Rijksinstituut voor Volksgezondheid en Milieu. (2013). *Volksgezondheid Toekomst Verkenning*. Bilthoven: Nationaal Kompas Volksgezondheid.

RNCOC Research. (2006, June 15). RNCOS research: Medical tourism: The next awaiting avenue for Indian Tourism Industry. 24-7 Press release.

Rother, M. (2009). *Toyota Kata: Managing people for improvement, adaptiveness and superior results* (1st ed.). New York: McGraw-Hill.

Rother, M., & Shook, J. (2003). *Learning to see* (1st ed., 1.4). Cambridge: Lean Enterprise Institute.

Russel, S., & Abdella, K. (2002). *Too poor to be sick: coping with the costs of illness in East Hararghe, Ethiopia*. London: Save the Children.

Safaricom. (2013). *Website Safaricom*. Retrieved October 10, 2013, from http://www.safaricom.co.ke.

Schmitz, H. (1965). *Het proveniershuys te Schiedam—Vijf eeuwen instelling van weldadigheid*. Schiedam: Stichting De Schiedamse gemeenschap.

Schultz, H., & Gordon, J. (2011). *Onward*. Chichester: John Wiley & Sons.

Schumpeter, J. A. (1934). *The theory of economic development*. Boston: Harvard Business School Press.

Sharma, D. C. (2010, April 12). India's No.1 killer: Heart disease. *India Today*.

Shetty Dr., D. (2010, August 26). How Mother Teresa touched my heart. *DNA India Column*.

Simons, M. P., de Lange, D. H., Aufenacker, T. J., Simmermacher, R. K. J., & Miserez, M. (2013). *Europese richtlijn voor behandeling van liesbreuken*. Amsterdam: Nederlands Tijdschrift Voor Geneeskunde. Retrieved January 19, 2014, from http://www.ntvg.nl/publicatie/671323/volledig.

Sisodia, R., Wolfe, D. B., & Sheth, J. H. (2007). *Firms of endearment*. NJ: Wharton School Publishing.

Smalley, A. (2011). Toyota's true north concept. Retrieved January 19, 2014, from http://the-leanedge.org/?p=3343.

Smith, A. N. (2010). Mayo Clinic: Design thinking in health care—case study synopsis. Retrieved January 19, 2014, from http://changeobserver.designobserver.com/feature/mayo-clinicdesign-thinking-in-health-care--case-study-synopsis--teaching-objectives/23128/.

Smith, M., Halvorson, G., & Kaplan, G. (2012). What's needed is a Health Care System that learns—recommendations from an IOM Report, Chicago. *Journal of American Medical Association, 308*(16), 1637.

South African Medical Research Council. (2002). *What are the top causes of death in South Africa?* Retrieved September 2, 2013, from http://www.mrc.ac.za/bod/faqdeath.htm.

Spaans, J. (2002). Weduwen, Wezen en Vreemdelingen. Sociale Zorg en Tolerantie. In T. de Nijs, & E. Beukers (Eds.), *Geschiedenis van Holland 1572 tot 1795* (pp. 255–286).

Spence, R. M., Jr., & Rushing, H. (2009). *It's not what you sell, it's what you stand for—Why every extraordinary business is driven by purpose*. New York: Penguin Group.

Spiegelman, P. (2007). *Why is everyone smiling?* Texas: Brown.

Spiegelman, P. (2013). 6 reasons to choose a strategic buyer over private equity. Retrieved January 19, 2014, from http://www.inc.com/paul-spiegelman/sell-your-company-what-you-need-toknow.html.

Spijkerman, C. (2013, March 1). Als ik ren, voel ik me zeker. In *de Verdieping—Trouw* (pp. 6–7).

Stassen, W. (2012). *Many too poor to access free health services*. Retrieved September 2, 2013, from http://www.health-e.org.za/2012/09/06/many-too-poor-to-accessfree-health-services/.

Statistics South Africa. (2012). *General household survey*. Retrieved September 2, 2013, from http://www.statssa.gov.za/publications/P0318/P0318April2012.pdf.

Statistics South Africa. (2012). *Income and expenditure survey 2010/2011*. Retrieved September 2, 2013, from http://www.statssa.gov.za/news_archive/press_statements/IES_%202010_2011_Press%20Statement_6_November_2012.pdf.

Stiftung Liebenau. (2010). *Befragung der 'Lebensräume für Jung und Alt' zur Weiterentwicklung des Qualitätsmanagementsystems*. Meckenbeurer: Stiftung Liebenau.

Taylor, D. J. (2007). *Never mind the sizzle... Where's the sausage?—Branding based on substance not spin*. Chichester: John Wiley & Sons.

ThedaCare. (2013). *Company benefit report*. Retrieved September 11, 2013, from http://www.thedacare.org/Getting-Involved/Improving-Community-Health/Community-Benefit-Report.aspx.

Thomashuizen. (2013, October). www.thomashuizen.nl.

Toresson, M. (2013). Patienterna fixar dialysen själva. In *Dagensmedicin*. Retrieved September 13, 2013, from http://www.dagensmedicin.se/nyheter/patienterna-fixar-dialysensjalva/.

Toussaint, J. (2012). *Potent medicine* (2nd ed.). Appleton, WI: ThedaCare Center for Healthcare Value.

Toussaint, J., & Gerard, R. A. (2010). *On the mend: Revolutionizing healthcare to save lives and transform the industry* (1st ed.). Cambridge: Lean Enterprise Institute.

Treacy, M., & Wiersema, F. (1997). *The discipline of market leaders—Choose your customers, narrow your focus, dominate your market*. New York: The Perseus Books Group.

UCLA Center for Inflammatory Bowel Diseases. (2013). *Value-based healthcare at UCLAIBD*. Retrieved October 23, 2013, from http://www.youtube.com/watch?v=da7dRLSQPEI.

UCLA Center for Inflammatory Bowel Diseases. (2012). *Key performance report 2012*. Los Angeles: The Regents of University of California.

UCLA Health System Center for Inflammatory Bowel Diseases. (2013). Retrieved October 23, 2013, from http://www.uclaibd.com.

University Health Network. (2007). *Clinical trials at PMH*. Retrieved January 19, 2014, from http://www.uhn.ca/docs/HealthInfo/Shared%20Documents/Clinical_Trials_at_PMH.pdf.

US AID. (2013). *The M-PESA story.* Retrieved October 18, 2013, from http://blog.usaid. gov/2013/04/video-of-the-week-animating-m-pesa/.

van der Velde, H. (2010). *Gezondheidszorg en Volksgezondheid.* Retrieved January 19, 2014, from http://www.culturescope.nl/index.php?option=com_content&view=article&id=86:gezondheid szorgenvolksgezondheid&catid=33&Itemid=44&lang=nl.

Veltman, C. (1995). *De woonsituatie van ouderen in hofjes. Een onderzoek naar de mogelijkheden en beperkingen van het wonen en samenleven in hofjes.* Final dissertation on Social Gerontology, Amsterdam, VU.

Vitality Group. (2013). *Our company background.* Retrieved September 2, 2013, from http://www. thevitalitygroup.com/content/our-company-background.

Vitality Institute. (2013). *Vitality Institute: We're sharing research.* Retrieved September 2, 2013, from http://www.thevitalityinstitute.org/#research.

Vitality Summit. (2013). *Speakers.* Retrieved September 2, 2013, from http://www.vitalitysummit. com/#speakers.

Vivium. (2013). Retrieved January 15, 2015, from www.vivium.nl/hogewey_media_pers.nl.

van der Voort, M. R., & Menders, J. (2012). *Lean in de zorg—De praktijk van continu verbeteren.* Den Haag: Boom Lemma uitgevers.

Wennberg, J. E. (2010). *Tracking medicine—A researcher's quest to understand health care.* New York: Oxford University Press.

Wiegant, E. (2012). Huisartsenzorg in Finland: Ooit rolmodel, nu "een zooitje"'. *De dokter—LHV magazine*, nr. 12, pp. 36–37.

van Wijngaarden, A. (2012). *Zeven vette jaren in de zorg—Zelfverrijking, miljoenenfraude en medische missers.* Groningen: Uitgeverij Passage.

Wikipedia. (2013). *M-PESA.* Retrieved October 8, 2013, from http://en.wikipedia.org/ wiki/M-Pesa.

Williams, D. E. (2008). *Interview with Ben Heywood, CEO of PatientsLikeMe (transcript).* Retrieved September 15, 2013, from http://healthbusinessblog.com/2008/01/23/interview-with-ben-heywoodceo-of-patientslikeme-transcript/.

Winter, E., & van der Weijden, W. (2008). *Authentieke organisaties. Echte merken. Hoe internal branding wel werkt.* Culemborg: Van Duuren Management.

World Economic Forum & McKinsey. (2013). *Sustainable health systems—Visions, strategies, critical uncertainties and scenarios.* Cologny/Switzerland: World Economic Forum/Geneva.

World Health Organization. (2010). Bridging the gap in South Africa. *Bulletin of the World Health Organization, 88*(11), 797–876.

World Health Organization. (2013). Cancer. WHO; 2013 [30-07-2013]. Available from: http:// www.who.int/mediacentre/factsheets/fs297/en/.

Zeithaml, V. A., Parasuraman, A., & Berry, L. L. (1985). Problems and strategies in services marketing. *Journal of Marketing, 49*(4), 33–46.

Zeithaml, V. A., Parasuraman, A., & Berry, L. L. (1990). *Delivering quality service—Balancing customer perception and expectations.* New York: Free Press.

Zimmerman, R. (2011). *DIY dialysis, and other stories about improving patients' lives.* Retrieved January 19, 2014, from http://commonhealth.wbur.org/2011/12/improving-patients-lives.

Zuithof, M. (2007). *Lebensräume für Jung und Alt: Burenhulp als toekomst voor de vergrijzing.* Retrieved January 19, 2014, from http://www.zorgwelzijn.nl/Welzijnswerk/Nieuws/2007/5/ Lebensraume-fur-Jungund-Alt-Burenhulp-als-uitkomst-voor-de-vergrijzing-ZWZ011433W/.

Index

A

Achmea, 3, 56, 61, 64, 71, 89, 124
Aetna & Aetna's Smartsource, 193
Aging population, 36
Alcoholic Anonymous (AA), 127
America's Health Insurance Plan's (AHIP's), 56
Apple, 122, 192
Aravind, 8, 194, 315
Argoz, 59
Audacious goals, 3, 5–7, 10, 19, 64, 78, 108,
      130, 162, 176, 185, 187, 188, 212, 225,
      239, 248, 273, 284, 323, 339, 364
AXA, 56

B

Bank Rakyat in Indonesia (BRI), 57
BerylHealth, ix, 251, 255, 270–285, 287–290,
      293, 294, 296, 386, 391, 395, 398
Bhagwan Mahaveer Viklang Sahayata Samiti
      (BMVSS), x, 296–309
Big data, 119, 121, 389
Blue Cross/Blue Shield, 126
Brands, vii, xiv, xvii, xviii, 3, 4, 8–13, 15–20,
      26, 30, 136, 137, 273, 283, 284, 289,
      290, 294, 322, 323, 340, 369, 372, 373,
      377, 381–387, 392, 396
   essence, 3, 9, 19, 77, 107, 108, 175, 273,
      283, 322, 369
   promise, 3, 9, 10, 19, 78, 108, 176,
      225, 239
   proof, 3, 9, 10, 19, 78, 108, 323
   roots, 3, 9, 19
   values, 3, 9, 10, 19, 108, 225, 323, 340

Brilliant business model, xiii–xv, xvii, xviii
   phases and characteristics, 382
BUPA, 56
Business drivers, 43
Business model, xiv, xviii

C

Call centers, 255, 270, 271, 273–275, 278,
      279, 281, 290, 391, 395
Canadian Broadcasting Company (CBC), 363
Cancer Treatment Centers of America, 315
Caser, 56
Charity, 45, 91, 93, 98, 120, 293, 296, 323,
      336, 392, 399
Christi Health Systems, 126
Chronic disorders, 13, 36–38, 41, 47, 196,
      200, 233, 254, 301, 391
Cleveland Clinic, 317, 372
Competition, 5, 11, 12, 14, 16, 17, 66, 91, 95,
      151, 157, 165, 179, 261, 269, 287, 301,
      309, 339, 342
Concordia, 127
Core qualities, 3, 5, 6, 8, 10, 19, 31, 78, 93,
      108, 130, 162, 177, 225, 259, 273, 285,
      323, 339, 370
Core values, 3, 5, 6, 8, 10, 19, 78, 108, 142,
      162, 177, 212, 239, 243, 259, 271,
      273–275, 279, 323, 339, 370
Courtyard houses, 58, 385, 390, 393, 397
Covea, 56
Coxa Hospital, 315
Creative destruction, 39, 393
CSS, 124, 127

© Springer International Publishing Switzerland 2017
J. Kemperman et al. (eds.), *Brilliant Business Models in Healthcare*,
DOI 10.1007/978-3-319-26440-0

Customer, v, xiv, xvii
  contact, xviii–xx, 22, 49, 166, 229, 252,
      271, 289, 344, 348, 387
  insight, 11, 12, 14, 15, 80, 214, 288, 343
  value, 11, 15–19, 28, 30, 66, 67, 80, 81, 96,
      111, 134, 165, 166, 180, 214, 228, 229,
      242, 243, 247, 262, 268, 273, 274, 288,
      289, 302, 326, 327, 343, 357, 358, 373,
      382, 387, 392

D
Dashboards, 144
Delivery, vii, 10, 11, 18–21, 30, 67, 68, 81,
      82, 96, 97, 111, 112, 135–137, 142,
      150, 152, 153, 162, 166, 167, 170,
      171, 181, 201, 215, 229, 243, 263,
      275, 289, 290, 301–303, 307, 315,
      318, 320, 321, 327–329, 335, 336,
      338, 342, 344, 345, 358–360, 366,
      373, 377, 378, 382, 387, 391
Dental care, 189, 194, 242, 248, 359
Desired breakthroughs in healthcare, 381, 384
DHAN, viii, 57, 75–78, 80–82, 85, 86, 88,
      256, 385, 389, 390, 393, 397
Dialysis, 251, 254, 257–269, 386, 392, 398
Discovery, viii, 7, 9, 56, 119, 123–125,
      128–144, 176, 238, 269, 271, 284, 357,
      369, 385, 388–390, 393, 397
Disruptive innovations, 38–41, 252
dLife.com, 127
Docvia, 192
Do the right thing, 43, 45, 130, 271, 274, 311,
      381, 384, 390
Dr. Shetty, 44, 254, 321–323, 325, 327, 328,
      332, 333, 392

E
Efforts, xvi, xvii, 7, 16, 17, 20, 40, 41, 49, 76,
      81, 151, 156, 187, 202, 208, 212, 262,
      263, 274, 278, 281, 335, 345, 348, 370,
      377, 392
eHealth, 43
Emotions, 16, 17, 20, 43, 69, 80, 83, 99, 107,
      113, 139, 154, 168, 182, 184, 201,
      203, 217, 231, 245, 263, 264, 276,
      291, 304, 326, 327, 330, 343, 346,
      358, 361, 375
Employee, xiii, xiv, xvii
Employee programs, 263
Employee value, 29, 185, 187, 279,
      349, 392
Eurapco, 56
ExpertClinic, 315

F
Focused factories, 315, 317, 319
Ford Clinics, 194

G
G-Cash, 58, 256
GE Healthcare, 257
Geisinger, 315
General Healthcare fund Amsterdam (A.Z.A.),
      56, 57
General hospitals, 316, 318, 354, 360
General practitioners, 189, 190, 228, 385,
      386, 398
Google, 122, 192
Gothaer, 56
Grameen Bank, 57
Guidel, 256

H
Happiness, 29, 386, 391, 394
Healthcare infrastructure, 49, 171, 311–313
Healthcare challenges, xiii, 35–41,
      43–50
Healthcare costs, v, xv
Healthcare organizations, vi
Health care system, 252, 261, 268, 283, 289,
      328, 358, 363, 385, 390
Health definition, 258
Health insurance, 56, 57, 62–64, 67, 68, 71,
      73, 81, 85, 124, 129, 130, 136, 147,
      164–166, 287, 294, 322, 358, 385,
      388, 397
Health Maintenance Organization (HMO),
      126, 164
Healthways, viii, 15, 56, 119, 124, 125,
      144–159, 385, 388–390, 394, 397
Healthy food, 131, 138
Healthy lifestyle, 119–122, 125, 134, 166,
      170, 242
Healthy mix of solidarity and
      responsibility, 388
Heart surgery, 145, 314, 321
Helsana, 124, 127
Hernias, 315, 317, 318
Higher goals, 3, 5–7, 9, 19, 63, 73, 77, 78,
      91, 107, 111, 118, 162, 176, 225, 238,
      271, 275, 279, 298, 339, 349, 353, 369,
      386, 396

I
IBM, 192
IKEA, 5, 8, 252, 261

Inflammatory bowel diseases (IBD), 189, 192, 196–198, 200–202, 205, 208
Intermountain Healthcare, 126
International Federation Health Plans (IFHP), 57, 141
i-STAT Corporation, 254
Iverness, 256

J
Jaipur Foot, x, 251, 256, 257, 296–309, 386, 388, 391, 395, 399

K
Kaiser Permanente, viii, 119, 124–126, 160–173, 212, 219, 372, 385, 388–390, 394, 398
Kidney disorder, 251, 269
Kinzigtal, 126

L
Laastari Lähiklinikka, viii, 223–236
Länsförsäkringar, 56
Learning capacity and big data, 389
Lean philosophy and continuous improvement, 316, 328, 348
Liebenau, 385, 389, 390, 393, 397

M
Managed care, 56, 62, 74, 124, 126, 127, 161, 165, 398
Marketing, 4, 19, 20, 26, 85, 119, 121, 133, 136, 146, 152, 181, 188, 229, 243, 250, 255, 273, 274, 281, 285, 289, 302, 344, 373, 390
Market segments, xiv, 11–15, 30, 66, 80, 95, 96, 110, 133, 150, 151, 164, 179, 200, 214, 227, 228, 242, 261, 262, 273, 287, 288, 301, 325, 326, 342, 343, 356, 357, 372, 382, 387
Mayo Clinic, x, 311, 317, 367–380, 387, 389, 392, 395, 399
MedCo, 194
Medibank, 56
mHealth, 289
Micro finance and micro insurance, 57, 58
Microsoft, 122, 192
Minute Clinic & CVS, 189
M-PESA, x, 58, 251, 255, 256, 282–296, 386, 391, 395, 398
Mutual care, 46, 53, 59, 61, 90

N
Narayana Hrudayalaya, ix, x, 45, 254, 311, 314, 315, 320–336, 386, 391, 395, 399
Nationaal Verbond van Socialistische Mutualiteiten, 56
National Jewish Medical & Research Centre, 316
NTT DoCoMo, 256
Nursing, 54, 90, 106, 110, 111, 171, 270

O
Onafhankelijke Ziekenfondsen, 56
Oncology, 258, 315, 316, 325, 343, 354, 356, 357, 360, 366
Operations, vii, 10, 11, 13, 16, 18, 19, 21–23, 30, 44, 54, 68, 81, 82, 85, 97, 98, 108, 112, 130, 137, 152, 156, 167, 215, 216, 229, 230, 254, 255, 263, 266, 273, 275, 278, 290, 293, 296, 303, 306, 312, 315, 320–323, 325–329, 332, 335, 339, 343, 345, 348, 349, 351, 356, 359, 360, 369, 372–374, 382, 387, 388, 395
Organizing principles healthcare providers, 48
Oscar, 124
Overvecht, 126

P
ParkinsonNet, ix, 189, 192, 193, 209–223, 313, 386
Parkinson's disease, 390
Partners, xiv, xv, 13, 20–22, 30, 50, 82, 98, 110, 111, 115, 118, 122, 136, 138, 146, 150, 156, 166, 167, 177, 181, 185, 187, 202, 206, 211, 216, 230, 233, 234, 236, 244, 268, 283, 296, 303, 309, 319, 329, 338, 340, 345, 354, 368, 390, 398
Patient-centered organizations, 35, 48, 49, 189–198, 200–202, 205, 206, 208–212, 214–216, 219, 220, 222–225, 227–230, 233, 234, 236–240, 242–244, 247, 248, 250
PatientsLikeMe, viii, 119, 127, 174–188, 192, 202, 385, 389, 390, 394, 398
Patrick Lund Dental Happiness, ix, 15, 194, 237–250
Permanente, 163, 169
Personal approach and self-management, 388
Personal, medical, patient and health files, 376
Point of service (POS), 126, 252
Position, xiv, 3, 4, 8, 9, 11–14, 30, 31, 41, 131, 152, 153, 179, 259, 263, 275, 285, 289, 293, 312, 323, 325, 328, 329, 340, 342, 356, 358, 372, 373, 381–388, 392–394, 396, 397

Positioning, vii, 3, 4, 8–10, 16, 18–20, 22, 25,
    26, 30, 67, 137, 142, 145
Precision medicine, 122, 192
Preferred Provider Organization (PPO), 126
Prevention, viii, 35, 44, 45, 47, 48, 54, 56, 60,
    68, 81, 82, 119–122, 124–131,
    133–138, 141, 142, 144–148, 150–157,
    159–162, 164–167, 170, 171, 173–177,
    179–181, 184, 185, 187, 188, 194, 202,
    248, 252, 254, 274, 332, 344, 349, 354,
    360, 363, 366, 369, 374, 385, 388–390,
    394, 397
Prices, ix, 15–17, 50, 57, 62, 111, 126, 137,
    152, 161, 162, 164, 166, 194, 225,
    227–233, 242, 247, 256, 274, 311, 315,
    318, 321, 325–327, 329, 335, 342, 343,
    386, 391, 393, 397, 398
Princess Margaret Cancer Centre (PMCC),
    viii, x, 311, 316, 351–366, 386, 388,
    391, 395, 399
Process, xv, 4, 7, 12, 13, 16, 17, 19, 20, 22,
    30, 35, 39, 42, 44, 48–50, 80, 82, 97,
    104, 112, 123, 125, 127, 152, 160,
    191, 211, 215, 216, 244, 251, 252,
    255, 256, 259, 261, 262, 266, 269,
    274, 285, 299, 302, 303, 307, 309,
    311–313, 315, 316, 318, 319, 325,
    328, 329, 335, 338, 339, 343–345,
    348, 349, 351, 352, 357–359, 363,
    364, 366, 367, 369, 370, 373, 374,
    377, 378, 380, 382, 385, 387–389,
    392, 396
Production, 21, 22, 81, 152, 219, 251, 252,
    261, 299, 303, 307, 329, 339, 345
Prosthesis, 251, 256, 297–299, 301–303, 306,
    307, 309, 386, 391
Prudential, 124, 131

Q
Quantified self, 122

R
Rediclinic, 194
Reimbursement systems, 43, 56
Restless Legs Syndrome Foundation
    (RLSF), 192
Results, viii–x, xiii, xiv, xvii, 4, 7–9, 11, 13,
    16, 17, 22, 25–31, 36, 37, 45, 46, 48,
    50, 61, 62, 64, 68, 71–73, 77, 80,
    85–88, 96, 101–105, 115–118, 120,
    121, 125, 126, 128, 129, 131, 134, 137,
    141–142, 146, 148, 150–153, 156, 159,

    165, 167, 170–173, 175, 177, 180, 181,
    184–187, 190, 192, 194, 196–198, 201,
    202, 205–208, 215, 216, 219–222, 230,
    233–236, 240, 244, 247–250, 252,
    254–256, 258, 259, 261–263, 266–269,
    274, 275, 278–281, 284, 285, 287, 289,
    293–296, 306–307, 311, 315, 316, 318,
    319, 321, 325, 327, 329, 332–336,
    338–340, 342, 344, 348, 349, 351, 353,
    357–360, 363–366, 368, 369, 373,
    377–380, 382, 384, 385, 388–390, 392,
    394–396, 398
Retail solutions, 189, 191, 255, 316
Risks, xiv, 13, 16, 17, 29, 31, 37–42, 47, 50,
    53, 54, 57, 62, 66, 75, 81, 82, 86, 88,
    96, 98, 120, 123, 124, 127, 129–131,
    137, 142, 144, 148, 151–153, 156, 166,
    167, 180, 187, 190, 220, 229, 243, 259,
    283, 284, 316, 319, 321, 323, 327, 343,
    344, 348, 383, 385, 391, 396
Ryhov, ix, 251, 254, 256–270, 313, 386, 388,
    391, 392, 394, 398

S
Safaricom, 282–285, 287–290, 293, 294
Sales, 13, 19, 20, 92, 112, 145, 152, 167, 185,
    215, 302, 344
Samsung, 122, 192
Scarcity, 39–41, 164, 393
SERMO.com, 193
Services, 11, 13, 16, 17, 19, 20, 22, 26, 27, 35,
    42, 43, 46, 49, 56, 58, 66, 68, 81, 112,
    129, 130, 136, 146, 150–153, 156, 161,
    162, 164, 165, 173, 176, 197, 198, 200,
    206, 210, 215, 223, 225, 229, 230, 233,
    240, 251–259, 261–263, 266, 268–271,
    273–275, 278, 279, 281–285, 287–290,
    293, 294, 296–299, 301–303, 306, 307,
    309, 312, 313, 315, 317, 323, 326, 329,
    335, 338, 342, 345, 348, 349, 359, 360,
    366, 370, 372, 373, 377, 386, 387, 390,
    391, 394, 395, 398
Shareholder value, 28, 247, 279, 392
Sharing economy, 54
Shouldice, 194, 315, 317–319
SilverSneakers, 145, 152
SimulConsul, 193
Social design, 44, 97, 101, 317, 318
Societal value, 28, 29, 268, 390, 392
Solution shops, 316, 317
Stakeholder, v, xiii–xv, xviii
Stiftung Liebenau, viii, 59, 106–118, 385, 389,
    390, 393, 397

Suppliers, 14, 20–22, 68, 82, 85, 98, 124, 126, 156, 181, 202, 216, 239, 244, 287, 306, 323, 329, 345

Swica, 127

T

Takecare Clinics, 194

Target Clinic, 194

Target groups, ix, 3, 11, 12, 14, 15, 66, 80, 81, 95, 159, 165, 170, 179, 180, 200, 250, 273–278, 281, 288, 301, 332, 342, 391

Technology, 7, 10, 20–22, 38, 39, 43, 50, 82, 115, 121, 122, 152, 153, 157, 167, 181, 190, 208, 251, 252, 255, 290, 298, 301, 303, 312, 323, 327, 328, 345, 359, 360, 366, 373, 396, 397

Telemedicine, 312, 327, 359

Thedacare, x, 311, 316, 337–351, 386, 391, 395, 399

Top academic institutes, 50, 311, 317

Triple aim, 35, 38, 43, 119, 125, 192, 197, 198, 206, 381, 383, 392

U

UCLA, ix, 189, 192, 195–208, 313, 386, 389, 390, 394, 398

University Health Network (UHN), 354, 360, 364

University of Pittsburgh Medical Centre, 316

V

Value-added process business, 315

Value creation, viii, xi, 4, 13, 25–32, 48, 101, 156, 184–188, 201, 268, 278, 296, 343, 381, 382, 392–395, 397

Value for the customer, 11, 15–17, 20, 28, 115, 151, 152, 200, 201, 269, 348

Value profit chain, 26, 27

Value quotient (VQ), 196, 198, 313, 386, 389, 390, 394, 398

VHI, 56

Virginia Mason, 316, 342

Vision, xi, xiv, xvii, xviii, 3–9, 11, 12, 18, 22, 25, 26, 30–32, 38–40, 75–77, 110, 130, 142, 156, 171, 177, 243, 258, 271, 273, 279, 284, 296, 299, 306, 322, 323, 325–327, 333, 335, 340, 363, 364, 369, 370, 373, 374, 377, 378, 380–392, 395, 396, 398, 399

W

Walmart, 194, 275

Waterfront Media, 192

Watson, 192

Web MD, 192

Weight Watchers, 127

World Health Organization (WHO), 36, 37, 133, 147

Z

Zilveren Kruis & samhoud, 3, 56, 71, 397